The Deluge: An Historical Novel of Poland, Sweden, and Russia. Vol. 1

CONTENT

CHAPTER I.

There was in Jmud a powerful family, the Billeviches, descended from Mendog, connected with many, and respected, beyond all, in the district of Rossyeni. The Billeviches had never risen to great offices, the highest they had filled were provincial; but in war they had rendered the country unsurpassed services, for which they were richly rewarded at various times. Their native nest, existing to this day, was called Billeviche; but they possessed many other estates, both in the neighborhood of Rossyeni and farther on toward Krakin, near Lauda, Shoi, Nyevyaja, and beyond Ponyevyej. In later times they branched out into a number of houses, the members of which lost sight of one another. They all assembled only when there was a census at Rossyeni of the general militia of Jmud on the plain of the invited Estates. They met also in part under the banners of the Lithuanian cavalry and at provincial diets; and because they were wealthy and influential, even the Radzivills, all powerful in Lithuania and Jmud, had to reckon with them.

In the reign of Yan Kazimir, the patriarch of all the Billeviches, was Heraclius, colonel of light-horse and under-chamberlain of Upita. He did not dwell in the ancestral nest, which was rented at that time by Tomash, the sword-bearer of Rossyeni; Heraclius Billevich owned also Vodokty, Lyubich, and Mitruny, situated near Lauda, surrounded, as if with a sea, by agriculturists of the petty nobility.

Besides the Billeviches there were only a few of the more considerable families in the neighborhood, such as the Sollohubs, the Montvills, the Schyllings, the Koryznis, the Sitsinskis,—though there was no lack of smaller nobility of these names; finally, the whole river region of Lauda was thickly studded with so-called "neighborhoods," or, in common parlance, *zastsianki*, occupied by the nobility of Lauda, renowned and celebrated in the history of Jmud.

In other neighborhoods of the region the families took their names from the places, or the places from the families, as was customary in Podlyasye; but along the river region of Lauda it was different. In Morezi dwelt the Stakyans, whom Batory in his time settled there for bravery at Pskoff; in Volmontovichi, on good land, swarmed the Butryms, the bulkiest fellows in all Lauda, noted for few words and heavy hands,—men who in time of provincial diets, raids on property, or wars were wont to go in close rank and in silence. The lands in Drojeykani and Mozgi were managed by the numerous Domasheviches, famed hunters; these men tramped through the wilderness of Zyelonka as far as Wilkomir on bear-trails. The Gashtovts occupied Patsuneli; their women were famous for beauty, so that finally all pretty girls around Krakin, Ponyevyej, and Upita were known as Patsuneli girls. The Sollohubs Mali were rich in horses and excellent cattle, bred in forest pastures. The Gostsyeviches in Goshchuni made tar in the woods, from which occupation they were called Gostsyevichi Charni (Black) or Dymni (Smoky),—the Black or Smoky Gostsyeviches.

There were other villages and families also. The names of many of them are still extant; but these villages are not situated as before, and men call them by other names. Wars came too with misfortunes and fires, villages were not always rebuilt on the ruins; in a word, much has changed. But in that time old Lauda was still flourishing in its primeval estate; and the nobles had reached their highest repute a few years before, when, fighting at Loyovo against the uprisen Cossacks, they covered themselves with great glory under the lead of Yanush Radzivill.

All the Lauda men served in the regiment of old Heraclius Billevich,—the richer with two horses, the poorer with one, and the poorest as attendants. In general, these nobles were warlike, and especially enamoured of a knightly career; but in questions which formed the ordinary subjects of discussion at a provincial diet they were less skilled. They knew that there was a king in Warsaw; that Radzivill and Pan Hlebovich were starostas in Jmud, and Pan Billevich at Vodokty in Lauda. That was sufficient for them; and they voted as Pan Billevich instructed them, convinced that he wanted the same as Pan Hlebovich, and that the latter went hand in hand with Radzivill. Radzivill was the king's arm in Lithuania and Jmud; the king was the consort of the Commonwealth, the father of the legion of nobles.

Pan Billevich was, in fact, a friend rather than a client of the powerful oligarchs in Birji, and a greatly esteemed one at that; for at every call he had a thousand voices and a thousand Lauda sabres,—and sabres in the hands of the Stakyans, the Butryms, the Domasheviches, or the Gashtovts were despised at that period by no man on earth. It was only later that everything changed, just at the time when Pan Heraclius Billevich was no more.

This father and benefactor of the nobles of Lauda died in 1654. In that year a terrible war flamed forth along the whole eastern line of the Commonwealth; Pan Billevich did not go to it, for his age and his deafness did not permit; but the Lauda men went. When tidings came that Radzivill was defeated at Shklov, and the Lauda regiment in an attack on the hired infantry of France was cut almost to pieces, the old colonel, stricken by apoplexy, yielded his soul.

These tidings were brought by a certain Pan Michael Volodyovski, a young but very famous warrior, who instead of Heraclius had led the Lauda regiment by appointment of Radzivill. The survivors came with him to their inherited fields, wearied, weighed down, and famished; in common with the whole army, they complained that the grand hetman, trusting in

6

the terror of his name and the spell of victory, had rushed with small forces on a power ten times greater than his own, and thus had overwhelmed the army and the whole country.

But amid the universal complaining not one voice was raised against Volodyovski. On the contrary, those who had escaped lauded him to the skies, relating wonders of his skill and his deeds. And the only solace left the survivors was the memory of the exploits performed under the young colonel's leadership,— how in the attack they had burst through the first line of reserves as through smoke; how later they fell on the French mercenaries and cut to pieces with their sabres the foremost regiment, on which occasion Pan Volodyovski with his own hand killed the colonel; how at last, surrounded and under fire from four sides, they saved themselves from the chaos by desperate fighting, falling in masses, but breaking the enemy.

Those of the Lauda men who, not serving in the Lithuanian quota, were obliged to form a part of the general militia, listened in sorrow but with pride to these narratives. It was hoped on all sides that the general militia, the final defence of the country, would soon be called. It was agreed already that Volodyovski would be chosen captain of Lauda in that event; for though not of the local residents, there was no man among them more celebrated than he. The survivors said, besides, that he had rescued the hetman himself from death. Indeed, all Lauda almost bore him in its arms, and one neighborhood seized him from another. The Butryms, the Domasheviches, and the Gashtovts disputed as to whose guest he should be for the longest period. He pleased that valiant nobility so much that when the remnant of Radzivill's troops marched to Birji so as to be brought to some order after the defeat, he did not go with others, but passing from village to village took up his abode at last in Patsuneli with the

Gashtovts, at the house of Pakosh Gashtovt, who had authority over all in that place.

In fact, Pan Volodyovski could not have gone to Birji in any event, for he was so ill as to be confined to the bed. First an acute fever came on him; then from the contusion which he had received at Tsybihovo he lost the use of his right arm. The three daughters of his host, who were noted for beauty, took him into their tender care, and vowed to bring back to his original health such a celebrated cavalier. The nobility to the last man were occupied with the funeral of their former chief, Heraclius Billevich.

After the funeral the will of the deceased was opened, from which it transpired that the old colonel had made his granddaughter, Aleksandra Billevich, daughter of the chief hunter of Upita, the heiress of all his property with the exception of the village of Lyubich. Guardianship over her till her marriage he confided to the entire nobility of Lauda—

"who, as they were well wishing to me," continued he in the will, "and returned kindness for kindness, let them do the same too for the orphan in these times of corruption and wickedness, when no one is safe from the license of men or free of fear; let them guard the orphan from mischance, through memory of me.

"They are also to see that she has safe use of her property with the exception of the village of Lyubich, which I give, present, and convey to the young banneret of Orsha, so that he may meet no obstacle in entering into possession of it. Should any man wonder at this my affection for Andrei Kmita, or see in it injustice to my own granddaughter Aleksandra, he must and should know that I held in friendship and true brotherly love from youthful years till the day of his death the father of Andrei Kmita. I was with him in war, he saved my life many times; and when

8

the malice and envy of the Sitsinskis strove to wrest from me my fortune, he lent me his aid to defend it. Therefore I, Heraclius Billevich, under-chamberlain of Upita, and also an unworthy sinner standing now before the stern judgment of God, went four years ago, while alive and walking upon the earthly vale, to Pan Kmita, the father, the sword-bearer of Orsha, to vow gratitude and steady friendship. On that occasion we made mutual agreement, according to ancient noble and Christian custom, that our children—namely his son Andrei and my granddaughter Aleksandra—were to be married, so that from them posterity might rise to the praise of God and the good of the State, which I wish most earnestly; and by the will here written I bind my granddaughter to obedience unless the banneret of Orsha (which God forbid) stain his reputation with evil deeds and be despoiled of honor. Should he lose his inheritance near Orsha, which may easily happen, she is to take him as husband with blessing; and even should he lose Lyubich, to pay no heed to the loss.

"However, if by the special favor of God, my granddaughter should wish in praise of Him to make an offering of her virginity and put on the habit of a nun, it is permitted her to do so, for I know that the praise of God is to precede that of man."

In such fashion did Pan Heraclius Billevich dispose of his fortune and his granddaughter, at which no one wondered much. Panna Aleksandra had been long aware of what awaited her, and the nobles had heard from of old of the friendship between Billevich and the Kmitas; besides, in time of defeat the thoughts of men were occupied with other things, so that soon they ceased to talk of the will.

But they talked of the Kmitas continually in the house at Vodokty, or rather of Pan Andrei, for the old sword-bearer also was dead. The younger Kmita had fought at Shklov with his own banner and with volunteers from Orsha. Then he vanished from the eye; but it was not admitted that he had perished, since the death of so noted a cavalier would surely not have escaped notice. The Kmitas were people of birth in Orsha, and lords of considerable fortune; but the flame of war had ruined those regions. Districts and entire lands were turned into deserts, fortunes were devoured, and people perished. After the crushing of Radzivill no one offered firm resistance. Gosyevski, full hetman, had no troops; the hetmans of the Crown with their armies in the Ukraine were struggling with what strength they had left and could not help him, exhausted as well as the Commonwealth by the Cossack wars. The deluge covered the land more and more, only breaking here and there against fortified walls; but the walls fell one after another, as had fallen Smolensk. The province of Smolensk, in which lay the fortune of the Kmitas, was looked on as lost. In the universal chaos, in the general terror, people were scattered like leaves in a tempest, and no man knew what had become of the banneret of Orsha.

But war had not reached Jmud yet. The nobles of Lauda returned to their senses by degrees. "The neighborhoods" began to assemble, and discuss both public and private affairs. The Butryms, readiest for battle, muttered that it would be necessary to go to Rossyeni to the muster of the general militia, and then to Gosyevski, to avenge the defeat of Shklov; the Domasheviches, the hunters, had gone through the wilderness of Rogovo by the forests till they found parties of the enemy and brought back news; the Smoky Gostsyeviches smoked meat in their huts for a future expedition. In private affairs it was decided to send tried and experienced men to find Pan Andrei Kmita.

The old men of Lauda held these deliberations under the presidency of Pakosh Gashtovt and Kassyan Butrym, two neighborhood patriarchs. All the nobility, greatly flattered by the confidence which the late Pan Billevich had placed in them, swore to stand faithfully by the letter of the will, and to surround Panna Aleksandra with well-nigh fatherly care. This was in time of war, when even in places to which war had not come disturbance and suffering were felt. On the banks of the Lauda all remained quiet, there were no disputes, there was no breaking through boundaries on the estates of the young heiress, landmarks were not shifted, no ditches were filled, no branded pine-trees were felled on forest borders, no pastures were invaded. On the contrary, the heiress was aided with provisions,—whatever the neighborhood had; for instance, the Stakjans on the river sent salt-fish, wheat came from the surly Butryms at Voimontovichi, hay from the Gashtovts, game from the Domasheviches (the hunters), tar and pitch from the Gostsyeviches. Of Panna Aleksandra no one in the villages spoke otherwise than as "our lady," and the pretty girls of Patsuneli waited for Pan Kmita perhaps as impatiently as she.

Meanwhile came the summons calling the nobility. The Lauda men began to move. He who from being a youth had grown to be a man, he whom age had not bent, had to mount his horse. Yan Kazimir arrived at Grodno, and fixed that as the place of general muster. There, then, they mustered. The Butryms in silence went forth; after them others, and the Gashtovts last,—as they always did, for they hated to leave the Patsuneli girls. The nobles from other districts appeared in scant numbers only, and the country was left undefended; but God-fearing Lauda had appeared in full quota.

Pan Volodyovski did not march, for he was not able yet to use his arm; he remained therefore as if district commander among the women. The neighborhoods were deserted, and only old men and women sat around the fires in the evening. It was quiet in Ponyevyej and Upita; they were waiting on all sides for news.

Panna Aleksandra in like manner shut herself in at Vodokty, seeing no one but servants and her guardians of Lauda.

CHAPTER II.

The new year 1655 came. January was frosty, but dry; a stern winter covered sacred Jmud with a white coat three feet thick, the forests were bending and breaking under a wealth of snow bunches, snow dazzled the eyes during days of sunshine, and in the night by the moon there glittered as it were sparks vanishing on a surface stiffened by frost; wild beasts approached the dwellings of men, and the poor gray birds hammered with their beaks the windows covered with hoar frost and snow-flowers.

On a certain evening Panna Aleksandra was sitting in the servants' hall with her work-maidens. It was an old custom of the Billeviches, when there were no guests, to spend evenings with the servants singing hymns and edifying simple minds by their example. In this wise did Panna Aleksandra; and the more easily since among her house-maidens were some really noble, very poor orphans. These performed every kind of work, even the rudest, and were servants for ladies; in return they were trained in good manners, and received better treatment than simple girls. But among them were peasants too, differing mainly in speech, for many did not know Polish.

Panna Aleksandra, with her relative Panna Kulvyets, sat in the centre, and the girls around on benches; all were spinning. In a great chimney with sloping sides pine-logs were burning, now dying down and now flaming freshly with a great bright blaze or with sparks, as the youth standing near the chimney threw on small pieces of birch or pitch-pine. When the flame shot upward brightly, the dark wooden walls of the great hall were to be seen, with an unusually low ceiling resting on cross-beams. From the beams hung, on threads, many-colored stars, made of wafers, trembling in the warm air; behind, from both sides of the beams, were bunches of combed flax, hanging like captured Turkish horse-tail standards. Almost the whole ceiling was covered with them. On the dark walls glittered, like stars, tin plates, large and small, standing straight or leaning on long oaken shelves.

In the distance, near the door, a shaggy-haired man of Jmud was making a great noise with a hand-mill, and muttering a song with nasal monotone. Panna Aleksandra slipped her beads through her fingers in silence; the spinners spun on, saying nothing the one to the other.

The light of the flame fell on their youthful, ruddy faces. They, with both hands raised,—with the left feeding the soft flax, with the right turning the wheel,—spun eagerly, as if vying with one another, urged on by the stern glances of Panna Kulvyets. Sometimes, too, they looked at one another with quick eye, and sometimes at Panna Aleksandra, as if in expectation that she would tell the man to stop grinding, and would begin the hymn; but they did not cease working. They spun and spun on; the threads were winding, the wheel was buzzing, the distaff played in the hand of Panna Kulvyets, the shaggy-haired man of Jmud rattled on with his mill.

But at times he stopped his work. Evidently something was wrong with the mill, for at those times was heard his angry voice: "It's down!"

Panna Aleksandra raised her head, as if roused by the silence which followed the exclamations of the man; then the blaze lighted up her face and her serious blue eyes looking from beneath black brows. She was a comely lady, with flaxen hair, pale complexion, and delicate features. She had the beauty of a white flower. The mourning robes added to her dignity. Sitting before the chimney, she seemed buried in thought, as in a dream; doubtless she was meditating over her own lot, for her fates were in the balance. The will predestined her to be the wife of a man whom she had not seen for ten years; and as she was now almost twenty, there remained to her but unclear childhood reminiscences of a certain boisterous boy, who at the time when he with his father had come to Vodokty, was more occupied with racing through the swamps with a gun than in looking at her. "Where is he, and what manner of man is he now?" These were the questions which thrust themselves on the mind of the dignified lady. She knew him also, it is true, from the narratives of the late under-chamberlain, who four years before had undertaken the long journey to Orsha. According to those narratives, he was a cavalier "of great courage, though very quick-tempered." By the contract of marriage for their descendants concluded between old Billevich and Kmita the father, Kmita the son was to go at once to Vodokty and be accepted by the lady; but a great war broke out just then, and the cavalier, instead of going to the lady, went to the fields of Berestechko. Wounded at Berestechko, he recovered at home; then he nursed his sick father, who was near death; after that another war broke out, and thus four years passed. Since the death of the old colonel considerable time had elapsed, but no tidings of Kmita.

Panna Aleksandra therefore had something to meditate upon, and perhaps she was pining for the unknown. In her pure heart, especially because it knew not love as yet, she bore a great readiness for that feeling. A spark only was needed to kindle on that hearth a flame quiet but bright, and as steady as the undying sacred fire of Lithuania.

14

Disquiet then seized her,—at times pleasant, at times bitter; and her soul was ever putting questions to which there was no answer, or rather the answer must come from distant fields. The first question was whether he would marry her with good-will and respond with readiness to her readiness. In those days contracts by parents for the marriage of their children were usual; and if the parents died the children, held by the blessing, observed in most cases the contract. In the engagement itself the young lady saw nothing uncommon; but good pleasure does not always go hand in hand with duty; hence the anxiety that weighed down the blond head of the maiden. "Will he love me?" And then a flock of thoughts surrounded her, as a flock of birds surround a tree standing alone in spacious fields: "Who art thou? What manner of person? Art walking alive in the world, or perhaps thou hast fallen? Art thou distant or near?" The open heart of the lady, like a door open to a precious guest, called involuntarily to distant regions, to forests and snow-fields covered with night: "Come hither, young hero; for there is naught in the world more bitter than waiting."

That moment, as if in answer to the call, from outside, from those snowy distances covered with night, came the sound of a bell.

The lady trembled, but regaining her presence of mind, remembered that almost every evening some one came to Vodokty to get medicine for the young colonel.

Panna Kulvyets confirmed that idea by saying, "Some one from the Gashtovts for herbs."

The irregular sound of the bell shaken by the shaft rang more distinctly each moment; at last it stopped on a sudden. Evidently the sleigh had halted before the door.

"See who has come," said Panna Kulvyets to the man of Jmud who was turning the mill.

The man went out of the servants' hall, but soon returned, and taking again the handle of the mill, said phlegmatically, "Panas Kmitas."

"The word is made flesh!" cried Panna Kulvyets.

The spinners sprang to their feet; the flax and the distaffs fell to the floor.

Panna Aleksandra rose also. Her heart beat like a hammer; a flush came forth on her face, and then pallor; but she turned from the chimney, lest her emotion might be seen.

Then in the door appeared a certain lofty figure in a fur mantle and fur-bound cap. A young man advanced to the middle of the room, and seeing that he was in the servants' hall, inquired in a resonant voice, without removing his cap, "Hei! but where is your mistress?"

"I am the mistress," said Panna Billevich, in tones sufficiently clear.

Hearing this, the newly arrived removed his cap, cast it on the floor, and inclining said, "I am Andrei Kmita."

The eyes of Panna Aleksandra rested with lightning-like swiftness on the face of Kmita, and then dropped again to the floor; still during that time the lady was able to see the tuft shaven high, yellow as wheat, an embrowned complexion, blue eyes, looking quickly to the front, dark mustache, a face youthful, eagle-like, but joyous and gallant.

He rested his left hand on his hip, raised his right to his mustache, and said: "I have not been in Lyubich yet, for I hastened here like a bird to bow down at the feet of the lady, the chief hunter's daughter. The wind—God grant it was a happy one!—brought me straight from the camp."

"Did you know of the death of my grandfather?" asked the lady.

"I did not; but I bewailed with hot tears my benefactor when I learned of his death from those rustics who came from this region to me. He was a sincere friend, almost a brother, of my late father. Of course it is well known to you that four years ago he came to us at Orsha. Then he promised me your ladyship, and showed a portrait about which I sighed in the night-time. I wished to come sooner, but war is not a mother: she makes matches for men with death only."

This bold speech confused the lady somewhat. Wishing to change the subject, she said, "Then you have not seen Lyubich yet?"

"There will be time for that. My first service is here; and here the dearest inheritance, which I wish to receive first. But you turned from the hearth, so that to this moment I have not been able to look you in the eye—that's the way! Turn, and I will stand next the hearth; that's the way!"

Thus speaking, the daring soldier seized by the hand Olenka, who did not expect such an act, and brought her face toward the fire, turning her like a top. She was still more confused, and covering her eyes with her long lashes, stood abashed by the light and her own beauty. Kmita released her at last, and struck himself on the doublet.

"As God is dear to me, a beauty! I'll have a hundred Masses said for my benefactor because he left you to me. When the betrothal?"

"Not yet awhile; I am not yours yet," said Olenka.

"But you will be, even if I have to burn this house! As God lives, I thought the portrait flattered. I see that the painter aimed high, but missed. A thousand lashes to such an artist, and stoves to paint, not beauties, with which eyes are feasted! Oh, 'tis a delight to be the heir to such an inheritance, may the bullets strike me!"

"My late grandfather told me that you were very hot-headed."

"All are that way with us in Smolensk; not like your Jmud people. One, two! and it must be as we want; if not, then death."

Olenka laughed, and said with a voice now more confident, raising her eyes to the cavalier, "Then it must be that Tartars dwell among you?"

"All one! but you are mine by the will of parents and by your heart."

"By my heart? That I know not yet."

"Should you not be, I would thrust myself with a knife!"

"You say that laughing. But we are still in the servants' hall; I beg you to the reception-room. After a long road doubtless supper will be acceptable. I beg you to follow me."

Here Olenka turned to Panna Kulvyets. "Auntie, dear, come with us."

The young banneret glanced quickly. "Aunt?" he inquired,—"whose aunt?"

"Mine,—Panna Kulvyets."

"Then she is mine!" answered he, going to kiss her hand. "I have in my company an officer named Kulvyets-Hippocentaurus. Is he not a relative?"

"He is of the same family," replied the old maid, with a courtesy.

"A good fellow, but a whirlwind like myself," added Kmita.

Meanwhile a boy appeared with a light. They went to the antechamber, where Pan Andrei removed his shuba; then they passed to the reception-room.

Immediately after their departure the spinners gathered in a close circle, and one interrupted another, talking and making remarks. The stately young man pleased them greatly; therefore they did not spare words on him, vying with one another in praises.

"Light shines from him," said one; "when he came I thought he was a king's son."

"And he has lynx eyes, so that he cuts with them," said another; "do not cross such a man."

"That is worst of all," said a third.

"He met the lady as a betrothed. It is easily seen that she pleased him greatly, for whom has she not pleased?"

"But he is not worse than she, never fear! Could you get his equal, you would go even to Orsha, though likely that is at the end of the world."

"Ah, lucky lady!"

"It is always best for the rich in the world. Ei, ei, that's gold, not a knight."

"The Patsuneli girls say that that cavalry captain who is stopping with old Pakosh is a handsome cavalier."

"I have not seen him; but how compare him with Pan Kmita! Such another as Pan Kmita surely there is not in the world!"

"It's down!" cried the man of Jmud on a sudden, when something broke again in the mill.

"Go out, shaggy head, with thy freaks! Give us peace, for we cannot hear.—True, true; hard to find better than Pan Kmita in the whole world; surely in Kyedani there is none such."

"Dream of one like him!"

"May his like come in a dream!"

In such fashion did the girls talk among themselves in the servants' hall. Meanwhile in the dining-room the table was laid in all haste, while in the drawing-room Panna Aleksandra conversed face to face with Kmita, for Aunt Kulvyets had gone to bustle about the supper.

19

Pan Andrei did not remove his gaze from Olenka, and his eyes shot sparks more and more every moment; at last he said,—

"There are men to whom land is dearer than all things else; there are others who chase after plunder in war, others love horses; but I would not give you for any treasure. As God lives, the more I look the more I wish to marry; so that even if it were to-morrow— Oh, that brow,—just as if painted with burned cork!"

"I hear that some use such strange things, but I am not of that kind."

"And eyes as from heaven! From confusion, words fail me."

"You are not greatly confused, if in my presence you can be so urgent that I am wonder-stricken."

"That is our way in Smolensk,—to go boldly at women as we do into battle. You must, my queen, grow accustomed to this, for thus will it ever be."

"You must put it aside, for thus it cannot be."

"Perhaps I may yield, may I be slain! Believe, believe me not, but with gladness would I bend the skies for you. For you, my queen, I am ready to learn other manners; for I know myself that I am a simple soldier, I have lived more in camps than in chambers of castles."

"Oh, that harms nothing, for my grandfather was a soldier; but I give thanks for the good-will," said Olenka; and her eyes looked with such sweetness on Pan Andrei that his heart melted like wax in a moment, and he answered,—

"You will lead me on a thread."

"Ah, you are not like those who are led on threads; to do that is most difficult with men who are unsteady."

Kmita showed in a smile teeth as white as a wolf's teeth, "How is that?" asked he. "Are the rods few that the fathers broke on me in the monastery to bring me to steadiness and make me remember various fair maxims for guidance in life—"

"And which one do you remember best?"

"'When in love, fall at the feet,'—in this fashion."

When he had spoken, Kmita was already on his knees. The lady screamed, putting her feet under the table.

"For God's sake! they did not teach that in the monastery. Leave off, or I shall be angry—my aunt will come this minute—"

Still on his knees, he raised his head and looked into her eyes. "Let a whole squadron of aunts come; I shall not forbid their pleasure."

"But stand up!"

"I am standing."

"Sit down!"

"I am sitting."

"You are a traitor, a Judas!"

"Not true, for when I kiss 'tis with sincerity,—will you be convinced?"

"You are a serpent!"

Panna Aleksandra laughed, however, and a halo of youth and gladness came from her. His nostrils quivered like the nostrils of a young steed of noble blood.

"Ai! ai!" said he. "What eyes, what a face! Save me, all ye saints, for I cannot keep away!"

"There is no reason to summon the saints. You were absent four years without once looking in here; sit still now!"

"But I knew only the counterfeit. I will have that painter put in tar and then in feathers, and scourge him through the square of Upita. I will tell all in sincerity,—forgive, if it please you; if not, take my head. I thought to myself when looking at that portrait: 'A pretty little rogue, pretty; but there is no lack of pretty ones in the world. I have time.' My late father urged me hither, but I had always one answer: 'I have time! The little wife will not vanish; maidens go not to war and do not perish.' I was not opposed at all to the will of my father, God is my witness; but I wanted first to know war and feel it on my own body. This moment I see my folly. I might have married and gone to war afterward; and here every delight was waiting for me. Praise be to God that they did not hack me to death! Permit me to kiss your hand."

"Better, I'll not permit."

"Then I will not ask. In Orsha we say, 'Ask; but if they don't give, take it thyself.'"

Here Pan Andrei clung to the hand of the lady and began to kiss it; and the lady did not resist too greatly, lest she might exhibit ill-will.

Just then Panna Kulvyets came in. When she saw what was going on, she raised her eyes. That intimacy did not please her, but she dared not scold. She gave invitation to supper.

Both went to the supper-room, holding each the other's hand as if they were related. In the room stood a table covered, and on it an abundance of all kinds of food, especially choice smoked meats and a mouldy thick bottle of strength-giving wine. It was pleasant for the young people with each other, gladsome, vivacious. The lady had supped already; therefore Kmita sat alone, and began to eat with animation equal to that with which he had just been conversing.

Olenka looked at him with sidelong glance, glad that he was eating and drinking. When he had appeased his first hunger, she began again to inquire,—

"Then you are not direct from Orsha?"

"Scarcely do I know whence I come,—here to-day, tomorrow in another place. I prowled near the enemy as a wolf around sheep, and what was possible to seize I seized."

"And how had you daring to meet such a power, before which the grand hetman himself had to yield?"

"How had I daring? I am ready for all things, such is the nature within me."

"That is what my grandfather said. Great luck that you were not killed!"

"Ai, they covered me with cap and with hand as a bird is covered on the nest; but I, whom they covered, sprang out and bit them in another place. I made it so bitter for them that there is a price on my head— A splendid half-goose!"

"In the name of the Father and the Son!" cried Olenka, with unfeigned wonder, gazing with homage on that young man who in the same moment mentions the price on his head and the half-goose. "Had you many troops for defence?"

"I had, of course, my poor dragoons,—very excellent men, but in a month they were all kicked to bits. Then I went with volunteers whom I gathered wherever I could without question. Good fellows for battle, but knave upon knave! Those who have not perished already will sooner or later be meat for the crows."

Pan Andrei laughed, emptied his goblet of wine, and added: "Such plunderers you have not seen yet. May the hangman light them! Officers,—all nobles from our parts, men of family, worthy people, but against almost every one of them is a sentence of outlawry. They are now in Lyubich, for where else could I send them?"

"So you have come to us with the whole squadron?"

"I have. The enemy took refuge in towns, for the winter is bitter. My men too are as ragged as brooms after long sweeping.

23

The prince voevoda assigned me winter quarters in Ponyevyej. God knows the breathing-spell is well earned!"

"Eat, I beg you."

"I would eat poison for your sake! I left a part of my ragged fellows in Ponyevyej, a part in Upita, and the most worthy officers I invited to Lyubich as guests. These men will come to beat to you with the forehead."

"But where did the Lauda men find you?"

"They found me on the way to winter quarters in Ponyevyej. Had I not met them I should have come here."

"But drink."

"I would drink even poison for you!"

"Were the Lauda men the first to tell you of my grandfather's death and the will?"

"They told of the death.—Lord, give light to the soul of my benefactor!—Did you send those men to me?"

"Think not such a thing! I had nothing but mourning and prayer on my mind."

"They too said the same. They are an arrogant set of homespuns. I wanted to give them a reward for their toil; instead of accepting it, they rose against me and said that the nobility of Orsha might take drink-money, but the Lauda men never. They spoke very foully to me; while listening, I thought to myself: 'If you don't want money, then I'll command to give you a hundred lashes.'"

Panna Aleksandra seized her head. "Jesus Mary! and did you do that?"

Kmita looked at her in astonishment. "Have no fears! I did not, though my soul revolts within me at such trashy nobility, who pretend to be the equal of us. But I thought to myself, 'They will cry me down without cause in those parts, call me tyrant, and calumniate me before you!'"

"Great is your luck," said Olenka, drawing a deep breath of relief, "for I should not have been able to look you in the eyes."

"But how so?"

"That is a petty nobility, but ancient and renowned. My dear grandfather always loved them, and went with them to war. He served all his life with them. In time of peace he received them in his house. That is an old friendship of our family which you must respect. You have moreover a heart, and will not break that sacred harmony in which thus far we have lived."

"I knew nothing of them at that moment,—may I be slain if I did!—but yet I confess that this barefooted nobledom somehow cannot find place in my head. With us a peasant is a peasant, and nobles are all men of good family, who do not sit two on one mare. God knows that such scurvy fellows have nothing to do with the Kmitas nor with the Billeviches, just as a mudfish has nothing to do with a pike, though this is a fish and that also."

"My grandfather used to say that blood and honor, not wealth, make a man; and these are honorable people, or grandfather would not have made them my guardians."

Pan Andrei was astonished and opened wide his eyes, "Did your grandfather make all the petty nobility of Lauda guardians over you?"

"He did. Do not frown, for the will of the dead is sacred. It is a wonder to me that the messengers did not mention this."

"I should have— But that cannot be. There is a number of villages. Will they all discuss about you? Will they discuss me,— whether I am to their thinking or not? But jest not, for the blood is storming up in me."

"Pan Andrei, I am not jesting; I speak the sacred and sincere truth. They will not debate about you; but if you will not repulse them nor show haughtiness, you will capture not only them, but my heart. I, together with them, will thank you all my life,—all my life, Pan Andrei."

Her voice trembled as if in a beseeching request; but he did not let the frown go from his brow, and was gloomy. He did not burst into anger, it is true, though at moments there flew over his face as it were lightnings; but he answered with haughtiness and pride,—

"I did not look for this! I respect the will of the dead, and I think the under-chamberlain might have made those petty nobles your guardians till the time of my coming; but when once I have put foot here, no other, save me, will be guardian. Not only those gray coats, but the Radzivills of Birji themselves have nothing in this place to do with guardianship."

Panna Aleksandra grew serious, and answered after a short silence: "You do ill to be carried away by pride. The conditions laid down by my late grandfather must be either all accepted or all rejected. I see no other way. The men of Lauda will give neither trouble nor annoyance, for they are worthy people and peaceful. Do not suppose that they will be disagreeable. Should any trouble arise, they might say a word; but it is my opinion that all will pass in harmony and peace, and then the guardianship will be as if it had not been."

Kmita held silence a moment, then waved his hand and said: "It is true that the marriage will end everything. There is nothing to quarrel about. Let them only sit quietly and not force themselves on me; for God knows I will not let my mustache be blown upon. But no more of them. Permit an early wedding; that will be best."

"It is not becoming to mention that now, in time of mourning."

"Ai, but shall I be forced to wait long?"

"Grandfather himself stated that no longer than half a year."

"I shall be as dried up as a chip before that time. But let us not be angry. You have begun to look on me as sternly as on an offender. God be good to you, my golden queen! In what am I to blame if the nature within me is such that when anger against a man takes me I would tear him to pieces, and when it passes I would sew him together again."

"'Tis a terror to live with such a man," answered Olenka, more joyously.

"Well, to your health! This is good wine; for me the sabre and wine are the basis. What kind of terror to live with me? You will hold me ensnared with your eyes, and make a slave of me,— a man who hitherto would endure no superior. At the present time I chose to go with my own little company in independence rather than bow to the hetman. My golden queen, if anything in me does not please you, overlook it; for I learned manners near cannon and not among ladies, in the tumult of soldiers and not at the lute. Our region is restless, the sabre is never let go from the hand. There, though some outlawry rests on a man, though he be pursued by sentences, 'tis nothing! People respect him if he has the daring of a warrior. For example, my companions who in some other place would have long been in prison are in their fashion worthy persons. Even women among us go in boots, and with sabres lead parties,—like Pani Kokosinski, the aunt of my lieutenant. She died a hero's death; and her nephew in my command has avenged her, though in life he did not love her. Where should we, even of the greatest families, learn politeness? But we know when there is war how to fight, when there is a diet how to talk; and if the tongue is not enough, then the sabre. That's the position; as a man of such action did the late chamberlain know me, and as such did he choose me for you."

"I have always followed the will of my grandfather willingly," answered the lady, dropping her eyes.

"Let me kiss your hand once again, my dear girl! God knows you have come close to my heart. Feeling has so taken hold of me that I know not how I can find that Lyubich which I have not yet seen."

"I will give you a guide."

"Oh, I shall find the way. I am used to much pounding around by night. I have an attendant from Ponyevyej who must know the road. And there Kokosinski and his comrades are waiting for me. With us the Kokosinskis are a great family, who use the seal of Pypka. This one was outlawed without reason because he burned the house of Pan Orpishevski, carried off a maiden, and cut down some servants. A good comrade!— Give me your hand once more. I see it is time to go."

Midnight began to beat slowly on the great Dantzig clock standing in the hall.

"For God's sake! 'tis time, 'tis time!" cried Kmita. "I may not stay longer. Do you love me, even as much as would go around your finger?"

"I will answer another time. You will visit me, of course?"

"Every day, even if the ground should open under me! May I be slain!"

Kmita rose, and both went to the antechamber. The sleigh was already waiting before the porch; so he enrobed himself in the shuba, and began to take farewell, begging her to return to the chamber, for the cold was flying in from the porch.

"Good-night, my dear queen," said he, "sleep sweetly, for surely I shall not close an eye thinking of your beauty."

"May you see nothing bad! But better, I'll give you a man with a light, for there is no lack of wolves near Volmontovichi."

"And am I a lamb to fear wolves? A wolf is a friend to a soldier, for often has he profit from his hand. We have also firearms in the sleigh. Good-night, dearest, good-night."

"With God."

Olenka withdrew, and Pan Kmita went to the porch. But on the way, through the slightly open door of the servants' hall he saw a number of pairs of eyes of maidens who waiting to see him once more had not yet lain down to sleep. To them Pan Andrei sent, soldier-fashion, kisses from his mouth with his hand, and went out. After a while the bell began to jingle, at first loudly, then with a continually decreasing sound, ever fainter and fainter, till at last it was silent.

It grew still in Vodokty, till the stillness amazed Panna Aleksandra. The words of Pan Andrei were sounding in her ears; she heard his laughter yet, heartfelt, joyous; in her eyes stood the rich form of the young man; and now after that storm of words, mirth, and joyousness, such marvellous silence succeeded. The lady bent her ear,—could she not hear even one sound more from the sleigh? But no! it was sounding somewhere off in the forest, near Volmontovichi. Therefore a mighty sadness seized the maiden, and never had she felt so much alone in the world.

Taking the light, slowly she went to her chamber, and knelt down to say the Lord's Prayer. She began five times before she could finish with proper attention; and when she had finished, her thoughts, as if on wings, chased after that sleigh and that figure sitting within. On one side were pine-woods, pine-woods on the other, in the middle a broad road, and he driving on,—Pan Andrei! Here it seemed to Olenka that she saw as before her the blond foretop, the blue eyes, the laughing mouth in which are gleaming teeth as white as the teeth of a young dog. For this dignified lady could hardly deny before her own face that this wild cavalier had greatly pleased her. He alarmed her a little, he frightened her a little, but he attracted her also with that daring, that joyous freedom and sincerity, till she was ashamed that he pleased her, especially with his haughtiness when at mention of the guardians he reared his head like a Turkish war-horse and said, "Even the Radzivills of Birji themselves have nothing to do here with guardianship."

"That is no dangler around women; that is a true man," said the lady to herself. "He is a soldier of the kind that my grandfather loved most of all,—and he deserved it!"

So meditated the lady; and a happiness undimmed by anything embraced her. It was an unquiet; but that unquiet was something dear. Then she began to undress; the door creaked, and in came Panna Kulvyets, with a candle in her hand.

"You sat terribly long," said she. "I did not wish to interfere with young people, so that you might talk your fill the first time. He seems a courteous cavalier. But how did he please you?"

Panna Aleksandra gave no answer at first, but barefooted ran up to her aunt, threw herself on her neck, and placing her bright head on her bosom, said with a fondling voice, "Auntie, oh, Auntie!"

"Oho!" muttered the old maid, raising her eyes and the candle toward heaven.

CHAPTER III.

When Pan Andrei drove up to the mansion at Lyubich, the windows were gleaming, and bustle reached the front yard. The servants, hearing the bell, rushed out through the entrance to greet their lord, for they had learned from his comrades that he would come. They greeted him with submission, kissing his hands and seizing his feet. The old land-steward, Znikis, stood in the entrance holding bread and salt, and beating worship with the forehead; all gazed with uneasiness and curiosity,—how would their future lord look? Kmita threw a purse full of thalers on the tray, and asked for his comrades, astonished that no one of them had come forth to meet his proprietary mightiness.

But they could not come forth, for they were then the third hour at the table, entertaining themselves at the cup, and perhaps in fact they had not taken note of the sounding of the bell outside. But when he entered the room, from all breasts a loud shout burst forth: "The heir, the heir has come!" and all his comrades, springing from their places, started toward him with their cups. But he placed his hands on his hips, and laughed at the manner in which they had helped themselves in his house, and had gone to drinking before his arrival. He laughed with increasing heartiness when he saw them advance with tipsy solemnity.

Before the others went the gigantic Pan Yaromir Kokosinski, with the seal of Pypka, a famous soldier and swaggerer, with a terrible scar across his forehead, his eye, and his cheek, with one mustache short, the other long, the lieutenant and friend of Kmita, the "worthy comrade," condemned to loss of life and honor in Smolensk for stealing a maiden, for murder and arson. At that time war saved him, and the protection of Kmita, who was of the same age; and their lands were adjoining in Orsha till Pan Yaromir had squandered his away. He came up holding in both hands a great-eared bowl filled with dembniak.

Next came Ranitski, whose family had arms,—Dry Chambers (Suche Komnaty). He was born in the province of Mstislavsk, from which he was an outlaw for killing two noblemen, landowners. One he slew in a duel, the other he shot without an encounter. He had no estate, though he inherited his step-mother's land on the death of his father. War saved him, too, from the executioner. He was an incomparable hand-to-hand sword-slasher.

The third in order was Rekuts-Leliva, on whom blood did not weigh, save the blood of the enemy. But he had played away, drunk away his substance. For the past three years he had clung to Kmita.

With him came the fourth, also from Smolensk, Pan Uhlik, under sentence of death and dishonor for breaking up a court. Kmita protected him because he played beautifully on the flageolet.

Besides them was Pan Kulvyets-Hippocentaurus, in stature the equal of Kokosinski, in strength even his superior; and Zend, a horse-trainer, who knew how to imitate wild beasts and all kinds of birds,—a man of uncertain descent, though claiming to be a noble of Courland; being without fortune he trained Kmita's horses, for which he received an allowance.

These then surrounded the laughing Pan Andrei. Kokosinski raised the eared bowl and intoned:—

"Drink with us, dear host of ours,
Dear host of ours!
With us thou mightst drink to the grave,
Drink to the grave!"

Others repeated the chorus; then Kokosinski gave Kmita the eared bowl, and Zend gave Kokosinski a goblet.

Kmita raised high the eared bowl and shouted, "Health to my maiden!"

"Vivat! vivat!" cried all voices, till the window-panes began to rattle in their leaden fittings. "Vivat! the mourning will pass, the wedding will come!"

They began to pour forth questions: "But how does she look? Hei! Yendrus, is she very pretty, or such as you pictured her? Is there another like her in Orsha?"

"In Orsha?" cried Kmita. "In comparison with her you might stop chimneys with our Orsha girls! A hundred thunders! there's not another such in the world."

"That's the kind we wanted for you," answered Ranitski. "Well, when is the wedding to be?"

"The minute the mourning is over."

"Oh, fie on the mourning! Children are not born black, but white."

"When the wedding comes, there will be no mourning. Hurry, Yendrus!"

"Hurry, Yendrus!" all began to exclaim at once.

"The little bannerets of Orsha are crying in heaven for the earth," said Kokosinski.

"Don't make the poor little things wait!"

"Mighty lords," added Rekuts-Leliva, with a thin voice, "at the wedding we'll drink ourselves drunk as fools."

"My dear lambs," said Kmita, "pardon me, or, speaking more correctly, go to a hundred devils, let me look around in my own house."

"Nonsense!" answered Uhlik. "To-morrow the inspection, but now all to the table; there is a pair of demijohns there yet with big bellies."

"We have already made inspection for you. This Lyubich is a golden apple," said Ranitski.

"A good stable!" cried Zend; "there are two ponies, two splendid hussar horses, a pair of Jmud horses, and a pair of Kalmuks,—all in pairs, like eyes in the head. We will look at the mares and colts to-morrow."

Here Zend neighed like a horse; they wondered at his perfect imitation, and laughed.

"Is there such good order here?" asked Kmita, rejoiced.

"And how the cellar looks!" piped Rekuts; "resinous kegs and mouldy jugs stand like squadrons in ranks."

"Praise be to God for that! let us sit down at the table."

"To the table! to the table!"

They had barely taken their places and filled their cups when Ranitski sprang up again: "To the health of the Under-chamberlain Billevich!"

"Stupid!" answered Kmita, "how is that? You are drinking the health of a dead man."

"Stupid!" repeated the others. "The health of the master!"

"Your health!"

"May we get good in these chambers!"

Kmita cast his eyes involuntarily along the dining-hall, and he saw on the larch wood walls, blackened by age, a row of stern eyes fixed on him. Those eyes were gazing out of the old portraits of the Billeviches, hanging low, within two ells of the floor, for the wall was low. Above the portraits in a long unbroken row were fixed skulls of the aurochs, of stags, of elks, crowned with their antlers: some, blackened, were evidently very old; others were shining with whiteness. All four walls were ornamented with them.

"The hunting must be splendid, for I see abundance of wild beasts," said Kmita.

"We will go to-morrow or the day after. We must learn the neighborhood," answered Kokosinski. "Happy are you, Yendrus, to have a place to shelter your head!"

"Not like us," groaned Ranitski.

"Let us drink for our solace," said Rekuts.

"No, not for our solace," answered Kulvyets-Hippocentaurus, "but once more to the health of Yendrus, our beloved captain. It is he, my mighty lords, who has given here in

Lyubich an asylum to us poor exiles without a roof above our heads."

"He speaks justly," cried a number of voices; "Kulvyets is not so stupid as he seems."

"Hard is our lot," piped Rekuts. "Our whole hope is that you will not drive us poor orphans out through your gates."

"Give us peace," said Kmita; "what is mine is yours."

With that all rose from their places and began to take him by the shoulders. Tears of tenderness flowed over those stern drunken faces.

"In you is all our hope, Yendrus," cried Kokosinski, "Let us sleep even on pea straw; drive us not forth."

"Give us peace," repeated Kmita.

"Drive us not forth; as it is, we have been driven,—we nobles and men of family," said Uhlik, plaintively.

"To a hundred fiends with you, who is driving you out? Eat, drink! What the devil do you want?"

"Do not deny us," said Ranitski, on whose face spots came out as on the skin of a leopard. "Do not deny us, Andrei, or we are lost altogether."

Here he began to stammer, put his finger to his forehead as if straining his wit, and suddenly said, looking with sheepish eyes on those present, "Unless fortune changes."

And all blurted out at once in chorus, "Of course it will change."

"And we will yet pay for our wrongs."

"And come to fortune."

"And to office."

"God bless the innocent! Our prosperity!"

"Your health!" cried Pan Andrei.

"Your words are holy, Yendrus," said Kokosinski, placing his chubby face before Kmita. "God grant us improvement of fortune!"

Healths began to go around, and tufts to steam. All were talking, one interrupting the other; and each heard only himself, with the exception of Rekuts, who dropped his head on his breast and slumbered. Kokosinski began to sing, "She bound the flax in bundles," noting which Uhlik took a flageolet from his bosom and accompanied him.

Ranitski, a great fencer, fenced with his naked hand against an unseen opponent, repeating in an undertone, "You thus, I thus; you cut, I strike,—one, two, three, check!"

The gigantic Kulvyets-Hippocentaurus stared fixedly for some time at Ranitski; at last he waved his hand and said: "You're a fool! Strike your best, but still you can't hold your own before Kmita with a sabre."

"For no one can stand before him; but try yourself."

"You will not win against me with a pistol."

"For a ducat a shot."

"A ducat! But where and at what?"

Ranitski cast his eyes around; at last he cried out, pointing at the skulls, "Between the antlers, for a ducat!"

"For what?" asked Kmita.

"Between the antlers, for two ducats, for three! Bring the pistols!"

"Agreed!" cried Kmita. "Let it be three. Zend, get the pistols!"

All began to shout louder and louder, and bargain among themselves; meanwhile Zend went to the antechamber, and soon returned with pistols, a pouch of bullets, and a horn with powder.

Ranitski grasped for a pistol. "Is it loaded?" asked he.

"Loaded."

"For three, four, five ducats!" blustered Kmita, drunk.

"Quiet! you will miss, you will miss."

"I shall hit at that skull between the antlers—one! two!"

All eyes were turned to the strong elk-skull fixed in front of Ranitski. He straightened his arm; the pistol turned in his palm.

"Three!" cried Kmita.

The shot sounded; the room was filled with powder smoke.

"He has missed, he has missed! See where the hole is!" cried Kmita, pointing with his hand at the dark wall from which the bullet had torn out a brighter chip.

"Two shots each time!"

"No; give it to me," cried Kulvyets.

At that moment the astonished servants ran in at the sound of the shot.

"Away! away!" called Kmita. "One! two! three!"

Again the roar of a shot; this time the pieces fell from the bone.

"But give us pistols too!" shouted all at the same time.

And springing up, they began to pound on the shoulders of their attendants, urging them to hurry. Before a quarter of an hour had passed, the whole room was thundering with shots. The smoke hid the light of the candles and the forms of the men shooting. The report of discharges was accompanied by the voice of Zend, who croaked like a raven, screamed like a falcon, howled like a wolf, bellowed like an aurochs. The whistle of bullets interrupted him; bits flew from the skulls, chips from the wall, and portraits from their frames; in the disorder the Billeviches were shot, and Ranitski, falling into fury, slashed them with his sabre.

The servants, astonished and terrified, stood as if bereft of their senses, gazing with startled eyes on that sport which resembled a Tartar invasion. The dogs began to howl and bark. All in the house were on their feet; in the yard groups of people assembled. The girls of the house ran to the windows, and putting their faces to the panes, flattening their noses, gazed at what was passing within.

Zend saw them at last; he whistled so piercingly that it rang in the ears of all, and then shouted, "Mighty lords! titmice are under the window,—titmice!"

"Titmice! titmice!"

"Now for a dance!" roared dissonant voices.

The drunken crowd sprang through the anteroom to the porch. The frost did not sober their steaming heads. The girls, screaming in voices that rose to the sky, ran in every direction through the yard; but the men chased them, and brought each one they seized to the room. After a while they began dancing in the midst of smoke, bits of bone, and chips around the table on which spilled wine lay in pools.

In such fashion did Pan Kmita and his wild company revel in Lyubich.

CHAPTER IV.

For a number of subsequent days Pan Andrei was at Vodokty daily; and each time he returned more in love, and admired more and more his Olenka. He lauded her to the skies, too, before his companions, till on a certain day he said to them,—

"My dear lambs, you will go to-day to beat with the forehead; then, as we have stipulated with the maiden, we will go to Mitruny to have a sleigh-ride through the forests and look at the third estate. She will entertain us there, and do you bear yourselves decently; for I would cut into hash the man who offended her in anything."

The cavaliers hurried willingly to prepare, and soon four sleighs were bearing the eager young men to Vodokty. Kmita sat in the first sleigh, which was highly ornamented and had the form of a silvery bear. This sleigh was drawn by three captured Kalmuk horses in variegated harness, in ribbons and peacock feathers, according to the Smolensk fashion, borrowed from more distant neighbors. A young fellow sitting in the neck of the bear drove the horses. Pan Andrei was dressed in a green velvet coat buttoned on golden cords and trimmed with sable, and wore a sable cap with a heron's feather. He was gladsome, joyous, and spoke to Kokosinski sitting at his side,—

"Listen, Kokoshko! I suppose we played tricks wild beyond measure on two evenings, and especially the first, when the skulls and the portraits suffered. But the case of the girls was still worse. The Devil always pushes forward that Zend, and then on whom does he pound out the punishment? On me. I am afraid that people will talk, for in this place my reputation is at stake."

"Hang yourself on your reputation; it is good for nothing else, just like ours."

"And who is to blame for that, if not you men? Remember, Kokoshko, they held me for a disturbing spirit in Orsha, and tongues were sharpened on me like knives on a whetstone."

"But who dragged Pan Tumgrat out in the frost with a horse; who cut up that official, who asked whether men walked on two feet in Orsha or on four? Who hacked the Vyzinskis, father and son? Who broke up the last provincial Diet?"

"I broke up the Diet in Orsha, not somewhere else; that was a home affair. Pan Tumgrat forgave me when he was dying; and as to the others, speak not, for a duel may happen to the most innocent."

"I have not told all yet; I have not spoken of the trials in the army, of which two are still waiting for you."

"Not for me, but for you men; for I am to blame only for letting you rob the people. But no more of this! Shut your mouth, Kokoshko, and say nothing to Olenka about the duels, and especially nothing of that shooting at the portraits and of the girls. If it is told, I shall lay the blame on you. I have informed the servants and the girls that if a word is said, I will order belts taken out of their skins."

"Have yourself shod like a horse, Yendrus, if you are in such dread of your maiden. You were another man in Orsha. I see already that you will go in leading-strings, and there is no good in that. Some ancient philosopher says, 'If you will not manage Kahna, Kahna will manage you.' You have given yourself to be tied up in all things."

"You are a fool, Kokoshko! But as to Olenka you will stand on one foot and then on the other when you put eyes on her, for another woman with such proper intent is not to be found. What is good she will praise in a moment, but the bad she will blame without waiting; for she judges according to virtue, and has in herself a ready measure. The late under-chamberlain reared her in that way. Should you wish to boast of warlike daring before her, and say that you trampled on justice, you will soon be ashamed; for at once she will say, 'An honorable citizen should not do that; it is against the country.' She will speak so to you that it will be as if some one had slapped you on the face, and you'll wonder that you did not know these things yourself. Tfu! shame! We have raised fearful disorder, and now must stand open-eyed before virtue and innocence. The worst was those girls—"

"By no means the worst. I have heard that in the villages there are girls of the petty nobility like blood and milk, and probably not stubborn at all."

"Who told you?" asked Kmita, quickly.

"Who told me? Who, if not Zend? Yesterday while trying the roan steed he rode to Volmontovichi; he merely rode along the highway, but he saw many titmice, for they were coming from vespers. 'I thought,' said he, 'that I should fly off the horse, they were so handsome and pretty.' And whenever he looked at any one of them she showed her teeth directly. And no wonder! for all the grown men of the nobles have gone to Rossyeni, and it is dreary for the titmice alone."

Kmita punched his companion in the side with his fist. "Let us go, Kokoshko, some time in the evening,—pretend we are astray,—shall we?"

"But your reputation?"

"Oh, to the Devil! Shut your mouth! Go alone, if that is the way; but better drop the matter. It would not pass without talk, and I want to live in peace with the nobles here, for the late under-chamberlain made them Olenka's guardians."

"You have spoken of that, but I would not believe it. How did he have such intimacy with homespuns?"

"Because he went with them to war, and I heard of this in Orsha, when he said that there was honorable blood in those Lauda men. But to tell the truth, Kokoshko, it was an immediate wonder to me, for it is as if he had made them guards over me."

"You will yield to them and bow to your boots before dish-cloths."

"First may the pestilence choke them! Be quiet, for I am angry! They will bow to me and serve me. Their quota is ready at every call."

"Some one else will command this quota. Zend says that there is a colonel here among them—I forget his name—Volodyovski or something? He led them at Shklov. They fought well, it appears, but were combed out there."

"I have heard of a Volodyovski, a famous warrior—But here is Vodokty in sight."

"Hei, it is well for people in Jmud; for there is stern order. The old man must have been a born manager. And the house,—I see how it looks. The enemy brought fire here seldom, and the people could build."

"I think that she cannot have heard yet of that outburst in Lyubich," said Kmita, as if to himself. Then he turned to his comrade: "My Kokoshko, I tell you, and do you repeat it to the others, that you must bear yourselves decently here; and if any man permits himself anything, as God is dear to me, I will cut him up like chopped straw."

"Well, they have saddled you!"

"Saddled, saddled not, I will cut you up!"

"Don't look at my Kasia or I'll cut you to pieces," said Kokosinski, phlegmatically.

"Fire out thy whip!" shouted Kmita to the driver.

The youth standing in the neck of the silvery bear whirled his whip, and cracked it very adroitly; other drivers followed his example, and they drove with a rattling, quick motion, joyous as at a carnival.

Stepping out of the sleighs, they came first to an antechamber as large as a granary, an unpainted room; thence Kmita conducted them to the dining-hall, ornamented as in Lyubich with skulls and antlers of slain beasts. Here they halted, looking carefully and with curiosity at the door of the adjoining room, by which Panna Aleksandra was to enter. Meanwhile, evidently keeping in mind Kmita's warning, they spoke with one another in subdued tones, as in a church.

"You are a fellow of speech," whispered Uhlik to Kokosinski, "you will greet her for us all."

"I was arranging something to say on the road," answered Kokosinski, "but I know not whether it will be smooth enough, for Yendrus interrupted my ideas."

"Let it be as it comes, if with spirit. But here she is!"

Panna Aleksandra entered, halting a little on the threshold, as if in wonder at such a large company. Kmita himself stood for a while as if fixed to the floor in admiration of her beauty; for hitherto he had seen her only in the evening, and in the day she seemed still more beautiful. Her eyes had the color of star-thistles; the dark brows above them were in contrast to the forehead as ebony with white, and her yellow hair shone like a crown on the head of a queen. Not dropping her eyes, she had the self-possessed mien of a lady receiving guests in her own house, with clear face seeming still clearer from the black dress trimmed with ermine. Such a dignified and exalted lady the warriors had not seen; they were accustomed to women of another type. So they stood in a rank as if for the enrolling of a company, and shuffling their feet they also bowed together in a row; but Kmita pushed forward, and kissing the hand of the lady a number of times, said,—

"See, my jewel, I have brought you fellow soldiers with whom I fought in the last war."

"It is for me no small honor," answered Panna Billevich, "to receive in my house such worthy cavaliers, of whose virtue and excellent qualities I have heard from their commander, Pan Kmita."

When she had said this she took her skirt with the tips of her fingers, and raising it slightly, courtesied with unusual dignity. Kmita bit his lips, but at the same time he was flushed, since his maiden had spoken with such spirit.

The worthy cavaliers continuing to shuffle their feet, all nudged at the same moment Pan Kokosinski: "Well, begin!"

Kokosinski moved forward one step, cleared his throat, and began as follows: "Serene great mighty lady, under-chamberlain's daughter—"

"Chief-hunter's daughter," corrected Kmita.

"Serene great mighty lady, chief-hunter's daughter, but to us right merciful benefactress," repeated Kokosinski,—"pardon, your ladyship, if I have erred in the title—"

"A harmless mistake," replied Panna Aleksandra, "and it lessens in no wise such an eloquent cavalier—"

"Serene great mighty lady, chief-hunter's daughter, benefactress, and our right merciful lady, I know not what becomes me in the name of all Orsha to celebrate more,—the extraordinary beauty and virtue of your ladyship, our benefactress, or the unspeakable happiness of the captain and our fellow-soldier, Pan Kmita; for though I were to approach the clouds, though I were to reach the clouds themselves—I say, the clouds—"

"But come down out of those clouds!" cried Kmita.

With that the cavaliers burst into one enormous laugh; but all at once remembering the command of Kmita, they seized their mustaches with their hands.

Kokosinski was confused in the highest degree. He grew purple, and said, "Do the greeting yourselves, pagans, since you confuse me."

Panna Aleksandra took again, with the tips of her fingers, her skirt. "I could not follow you gentlemen in eloquence," said she, "but I know that I am unworthy of those homages which you give me in the name of all Orsha."

And again she made a courtesy with exceeding dignity, and it was somehow out of place for the Orsha roisterers in the presence of that courtly maiden. They strove to exhibit themselves as men of politeness, but it did not become them.

Therefore they began to pull their mustaches, to mutter and handle their sabres, till Kmita said,—

"We have come here as if in a carnival, with the thought to take you with us and drive to Mitruny through the forest, as was the arrangement yesterday. The snow-road is firm, and God has given frosty weather."

"I have already sent Aunt Kulvyets to Mitruny to prepare dinner. But now, gentlemen, wait just a little till I put on something warm."

Then she turned and went out.

Kmita sprang to his comrades. "Well, my dear lambs, isn't she a princess? Now, Kokosinski, you said that she had saddled me, and why were you as a little boy before her? Where have you seen her like?"

"There was no call to interrupt me; though I do not deny that I did not expect to address such a person."

"The late under-chamberlain," said Kmita, "lived with her most of the time in Kyedani, at the court of the prince voevoda, or lived with the Hleboviches; and there she acquired those high manners. But her beauty,—what of that? You cannot let your breath go yet."

"We have appeared as fools," said Ranitski, in anger; "but the biggest fool was Kokosinski."

"Traitor! why punch me with your elbow? You should have appeared yourself, with your spotted mouth."

"Harmony, lambs, harmony!" said Kmita; "I will let you admire, but not wrangle."

"I would spring into the fire for her," said Rekuts. "Hew me down, Yendrus, but I'll not deny that."

Kmita did not think of cutting down; he was satisfied, twisted his mustache, and gazed on his comrades with triumph. Now Panna Aleksandra entered, wearing a marten-skin cap, under which her bright face appeared still brighter. They went out on the porch.

"Then shall we ride in this sleigh?" asked the lady, pointing to the silvery bear. "I have not seen a more beautiful sleigh in my life."

"I know not who has used it hitherto, for it was captured. It suits me very well, for on my shield is a lady on a bear. There are other Kmitas who have banners on their shield, but they are descended from Filon Kmita of Charnobil; he was not of the same house from which the great Kmitas are descended."

"And when did you capture this bear sleigh?"

"Lately, in this war. We poor exiles who have fallen away from fortune have only what war gives us in plunder. But as I serve that lady faithfully, she has rewarded me."

"May God grant a better; for war rewards one, but presses tears from the whole dear fatherland."

"God and the hetmans will change that."

Meanwhile Kmita wrapped Panna Aleksandra in the beautiful sleigh robe of white cloth lined with white wolfskin; then taking his own seat, he cried to the driver, "Move on!" and the horses sprang forward at a run.

The cold wind struck their faces with its rush; they were silent, therefore, and nothing was heard save the wheezing of frozen snow under the runners, the snorting of the horses, their tramp, and the cry of the driver.

At last Pan Andrei bent toward Olenka. "Is it pleasant for you?"

"Pleasant," answered she, raising her sleeve and holding it to her mouth to ward off the rush of air.

The sleigh dashed on like a whirlwind. The day was bright, frosty; the snow sparkled as if some one were scattering sparks on it. From the white roofs of the cottages, which were like piles of snow, rosy smoke curled in high columns. Flocks of crows from among the leafless trees by the roadside flew before the sleighs with shrill cawing.

About eighty rods from Vodokty they came out on a broad road into dark pine-woods which stood gloomy, hoary, and silent as if sleeping under the thick snow-bunches. The trees flitted before the eye, appeared to be fleeing to some place in the rear of the sleigh; but the sleigh flew on, every moment swiftly, more swiftly, as if the horses had wings. From such driving the head turns, and ecstasy seizes one; it seized Panna Aleksandra. She leaned back, closed her eyes, and yielded completely to the impetus. She felt a sweet powerlessness, and it seemed to her that that boyar of Orsha had taken her by violence: that he is rushing away like a whirlwind, and she growing weak has no strength to oppose or to cry,—and they are flying, flying each moment more swiftly. Olenka feels that arms are embracing her; then on her cheek as it were a hot burning stamp. Her eyes will not open, as if in a dream; and they fly, fly.

An inquiring voice first roused the sleeping lady: "Do you love me?"

She opened her eyes. "As my own soul."

"And I for life and death."

Again the sable cap of Kmita bent over the marten-skin cap of Olenka. She knew not herself which gave her more delight,—the kisses or the magic ride.

And they flew farther, but always through pine-woods, through pine-woods. Trees fled to the rear in whole regiments. The snow was wheezing, the horses snorting; but the man and the maiden were happy.

"I would ride to the end of the world in this way," cried Kmita.

"What are we doing? This is a sin!" whispered Olenka.

"What sin? Let us commit it again."

"Impossible! Mitruny is not far."

"Far or near, 'tis all one!"

And Kmita rose in the sleigh, stretched his arms upward, and began to shout as if in a full breast he could not find place for his joy: "Hei-ha! hei-ha!"

"Hei-hop! hoop-ha!" answered the comrades from the sleighs behind.

"Why do you shout so?" asked the lady.

"Oh, so, from delight! And shout you as well!"

"Hei-ha!" was heard the resonant, thin alto voice.

"O thou, my queen! I fall at thy feet."

"The company will laugh."

After the ecstasy a noisy joyousness seized them, as wild as the driving was wild. Kmita began to sing,—

"Look thou, my girl! look through the door,
To the rich fields!
Oh, knights from the pine-woods are coming, my mother,
Oh, that's my fate!
Look not, my daughter! cover thy eyes,
With thy white hands,
For thy heart will spring out of thy bosom
With them to the war."

"Who taught you such lovely songs?" asked Panna Aleksandra.

"War, Olenka. In the camp we sang them to one another to drive away sadness."

Further conversation was interrupted by a loud calling from the rear sleighs: "Stop! stop! Hei there—stop!"

Pan Andrei turned around in anger, wondering how it came to the heads of his comrades to call and stop him. He saw a few tens of steps from the sleigh a horseman approaching at full speed of the horse.

"As God lives, that is my sergeant Soroka; what can have happened?" said Pan Andrei.

That moment the sergeant coming up, reined his horse on his haunches, and began to speak with a panting voice: "Captain!—"

"What is the matter, Soroka?"

"Upita is on fire; they are fighting!"

"Jesus Mary!" screamed Olenka.

"Have no fear!—Who is fighting?"

"The soldiers with the townspeople. There is a fire on the square! The townspeople are enraged, and they have sent to Ponyevyej for a garrison. But I galloped here to your grace. I can barely draw breath."

During this conversation the sleighs behind caught up; Kokosinski, Ranitski, Kulvyets-Hippocentaurus, Uhlik, Rekuts, and Zend, springing out on the snow, surrounded the speakers with a circle.

"What is the matter?" asked Kmita.

"The townspeople would not give supplies for horses or men, because there was no order for it; the soldiers began to take by force. We besieged the mayor and those who barricaded themselves in the square. Firing was begun, and we burned two houses; at present there is terrible violence, and ringing of bells—"

Kmita's eyes gleamed with wrath.

"We must go to the rescue!" shouted Kokosinski.

"The rabble are oppressing the army!" cried Ranitski, whose whole face was covered at once with red, white, and dark spots. "Check, check! mighty lords!"

Zend laughed exactly as a screech-owl hoots, till the horses were frightened; and Rekuts raised his eyes and piped, "Strike, whoso believes in God! smoke out the ruffians!"

"Be silent!" roared Kmita, till the woods echoed, and Zend, who stood nearest, staggered like a drunken man. "There is no need of you there, no need of slashing! Sit all of you in two sleighs, leave me the third. Drive back to Lyubich; wait there unless I send for succor."

"How is that?" asked Ranitski, opposing.

But Pan Andrei laid a hand on his throat, and his eyes gleamed more terribly. "Not a breath out of you!" said he, threateningly.

They were silent; evidently they feared him, though usually on such familiar footing.

"Go back, Olenka, to Vodokty," said Kmita, "or go for your Aunt Kulvyets to Mitruny. Well, our party was not a success. But it will be quieter there soon; only a few heads will fly off. Be in good health and at rest; I shall be quick to return."

Having said this, he kissed her hand, and wrapped her in the wolf-skin; then he took his seat in the other sleigh, and cried to the driver, "To Upita!"

CHAPTER V.

A number of days passed, and Kmita did not return; but three men of Lauda came to Vodokty with complaints to the lady. Pakosh Gashtovt from Patsuneli came,—the same who was entertaining at his house Pan Volodyovski. He was the patriarch of the village, famed for wealth and six daughters, of whom three had married Butryms, and received each one hundred coined dollars as dowry, besides clothing and cattle. The second who came was Kassyan Butrym, who remembered Batory well, and with him the son-in-law of Pakosh, Yuzva Butrym; the latter, though in the prime of life,—he was not more than fifty years old,—did not go to Rossyeni to the registry of the general militia, for in the Cossack wars a cannon-ball had torn off his foot. He was called on this account Ankle-foot, or Yuzva Footless. He was a terrible man, with the strength of a bear, and great sense, but harsh, surly, judging men severely. For this reason he was feared somewhat in the capitals, for he could not pardon either himself or others. He was dangerous also when in liquor; but that happened rarely.

These men came, then, to the lady, who received them graciously, though she divined at once that they had come to make complaints, and wanted to hear something from her regarding Pan Kmita.

"We wish to pay our respects to Pan Kmita, but perhaps he has not come back yet from Upita," said Pakosh; "so we have come to inquire, our dear darling, when it will be possible to see him."

"I think the only hindrance is that he is not here," answered the lady. "He will be glad with his whole soul to see you, my guardians, for he has heard much good concerning you,—in old times from my grandfather, and lately from me."

"If only he does not receive us as he received the Domasheviches when they went to him with tidings of the colonel's death," muttered Yuzva, sullenly.

The lady listened to the end, and answered at once with animation: "Be not unjust about that. Perhaps he did not receive them politely enough, but he has confessed his fault in this house. It should be remembered too that he was returning from a war in which he endured much toil and suffering. We must not wonder at a soldier, even if he snaps at his own, for warriors have tempers like sharp swords."

Pakosh Gashtovt, who wished always to be in accord with the whole world, waved his hand and said: "We did not wonder, either. A beast snaps at a beast when it sees one suddenly; why should not a man snap at a man? We will go to old Lyubich to greet Pan Kmita, so that he may live with us, go to war and to the wilderness, as the late under-chamberlain used to do."

"Well, tell us, dear darling, did he please you or did he not please you?" asked Kassyan Butrym. "It is our duty to ask this."

"God reward you for your care. Pan Kmita is an honorable cavalier, and even if I had found something against him it would not be proper to speak of it."

"But have you not seen something, our dearest soul?"

"Nothing! Besides, no one has the right to judge him here, and God save us from showing distrust. Let us rather thank God."

"Why thank too early? When there will be something to thank for, then thank; if not, then not thank," answered the sullen Yuzva, who, like a genuine man of Jmud, was very cautious and foreseeing.

"Have you spoken about the marriage?" inquired Kassyan.

Olenka dropped her eyes: "Pan Kmita wishes it as early as possible."

"That's it! and why shouldn't he wish it?" muttered Yuzva; "he is not a fool! What bear is it that does not want honey from a tree? But why hurry? Is it not better to see what kind of man he is? Father Kassyan, tell what you have on your tongue; do not doze like a hare at midday under a ridge."

"I am not dozing, I am only turning in my head what to say," answered the old man. "The Lord Jesus has said, 'As Kuba [Jacob] is to God, so will God be to Kuba.' We wish no ill to Pan Kmita, if he wishes no ill to us,—which God grant, amen."

"If he will be to our thinking," said Yuzva.

Panna Billevich frowned with her falcon brows, and said with a certain haughtiness: "Remember that we are not receiving a servant. He will be master here; and his will must have force, not ours. He will succeed you in the guardianship."

"Does that mean that we must not interfere?" asked Yuzva.

"It means that you are to be friends with him, as he wishes to be a friend of yours. Moreover he is taking care of his own property here, which each man manages according to his wish. Is not this true, Father Pakosh?"

"The sacred truth," answered the old man of Patsuneli.

Yuzva turned again to old Butrym. "Do not doze, Father Kassyan!"

"I am not dozing, I am only looking into my mind."

"Then tell what you see there."

"What do I see? This is what I see: Pan Kmita is a man of great family, of high blood, and we are small people. Moreover he is a soldier of fame; he alone opposed the enemy when all had dropped their hands,—God give as many as possible of such men! But he has a company that is worthless. Pan Pakosh, my neighbor, what have you heard about them from the Domasheviches? That they are all dishonored men, against whom outlawry has been declared, infamous and condemned, with declarations and trials hanging over them, children of the hangman. They were grievous to the enemy, but more grievous to their own people. They burned, they plundered, they rioted; that is what they did. They may have slain people in duels or carried out executions,—that happens to honest men; but they have lived in pure Tartar fashion, and long ago would have been rotting in prison but for the protection of Pan Kmita, who is a powerful lord. He favors and protects them, and they cling to him just as flies do in summer to a horse. Now they have come hither, and it is known to all what they are doing. The first day at Lyubich they fired out of pistols,—and at what?—at the portraits of the dead Billeviches, which Pan Kmita should not have permitted, for the Billeviches are his benefactors."

Olenka covered her eyes with her hands. "It cannot be! it cannot be!"

"It can, for it has been. He let them shoot at his benefactors, with whom he was to enter into relationship; and then they dragged the girls of the house into the room for debauchery. Tfu! an offence against God! That has never been among us! The first day they began shooting and dissoluteness,—the first day!"

Here old Kassyan grew angry, and fell to striking the floor with his staff. On Olenka's face were dark blushes, and Yuzva said,—

"And Pan Kmita's troops in Upita, are they better? Like officers, like men. Some people stole Pan Sollohub's cattle; it is said they were Pan Kmita's men. Some persons struck down on the road peasants of Meizagol who were drawing pitch. Who did this? They, the same soldiers. Pan Sollohub went to Pan Hlebovich for satisfaction, and now there is violence in Upita again. All this is in opposition to God. It used to be quiet here as in no other place, and now one must load a gun for the night and stand guard; but why? Because Pan Kmita and his company have come."

"Father Yuzva, do not talk so," cried Olenka.

"But how must I talk? If Pan Kmita is not to blame, why does he keep such men, why does he live with such men? Great mighty lady, tell him to dismiss them or give them up to the hangman, for otherwise there will be no peace. Is it a thing heard of to shoot at portraits and commit open debauchery? Why, the whole neighborhood is talking of nothing else."

"What have I to do?" asked Olenka. "They may be evil men, but he fought the war with them. If he will dismiss them at my request?"

"If he does not dismiss them," muttered Yuzva, in a low voice, "he is the same as they."

With this the lady's blood began to boil against those men, murderers and profligates.

"Let it be so. He must dismiss them. Let him choose me or them. If what you say is true,—and I shall know to-day if it is true,—I shall not forgive them either the shooting or the debauchery. I am alone and a weak orphan, they are an armed crowd; but I do not fear them."

"We will help you," said Yuzva.

"In God's name," continued Olenka, more and more excited, "let them do what they like, but not here in Lyubich. Let them be as they like,—that is their affair, their necks' answer; but let them not lead away Pan Kmita to debauchery. Shame and disgrace! I thought they were awkward soldiers, but now I see that they are vile traitors, who stain both themselves and him. That's the truth! Wickedness was looking out of their eyes; but I, foolish woman, did not recognize it. Well, I thank you, fathers, for opening my eyes on these Judases. I know what it beseems me to do."

"That's it!" said old Kassyan. "Virtue speaks through you, and we will help you."

"Do not blame Pan Kmita, for though he has offended against good conduct he is young; and they tempt him, they lead him away, they urge him to license with example, and bring disgrace to his name. This is the condition; as I live, it will not last long."

Wrath roused Olenka's heart more and more, and indignation at the comrades of Pan Kmita increased as pain increases in a wound freshly given; for terribly wounded in her were the love special to woman and that trust with which she had given her whole unmixed feeling to Pan Andrei. She was ashamed, for his sake and for her own, and anger and internal shame sought above all guilty parties.

The nobles were glad when they saw their colonel's granddaughter so terrible and ready for unyielding war against the disturbers from Orsha.

She spoke on with sparkling eyes: "True, they are to blame; and they must leave not only Lyubich, but the whole country-side."

"Our heart, we do not blame Pan Kmita," said old Kassyan. "We know that they tempt him. Not through bitterness nor venom against him have we come, but through regret that he keeps near his person revellers. It is evident, of course, that being young he is foolish. Even Pan Hlebovich the starosta was foolish when he was young, but now he keeps us all in order."

"And a dog," said the mild old man from Patsuneli, with a voice of emotion,—"if you go with a young one to the field, won't the fool instead of running after the game fall about your feet, begin to play, and tug you by the skirts?"

Olenka wanted to say something, but suddenly she burst into tears.

"Do not cry," said Yuzva Butrym.

"Do not cry, do not cry," repeated the two old men.

They tried to comfort her, but could not. After they had gone, care, anxiety, and as it were an offended feeling against them and against Pan Andrei remained. It pained the proud lady more and more deeply that she had to defend, justify, and explain him. But the men of that company! The delicate hands of the lady clinched at thought of them. Before her eyes appeared as if present the faces of Pan Kokosinski, Uhlik, Zend, Kulvyets-

Hippocentaurus, and the others; and she discovered what she had not seen at first, that they were shameless faces, on which folly, licentiousness, and crime had all fixed their stamps in common. A feeling of hatred foreign to Olenka began to seize her as a rattling fire seizes fuel; but together with this outburst offence against Pan Kmita increased every minute.

"Shame, disgrace," whispered the maiden, with pallid lips, "that yesterday he went from me to house-wenches!" and she felt herself overborne. A crushing burden stopped the breath in her breast.

It was growing raw out of doors. Panna Aleksandra walked in the room with hurried step, but anger was seething in her soul without ceasing. Hers was not the nature to endure the persecutions of fate without defending herself against them. There was knightly blood in the girl. She wanted straightway to begin a struggle with that band of evil spirits,—straightway. But what remained to her? Nothing, save tears and the prayer that Pan Andrei would send to the four winds those shame-bringing comrades. But if he will not do that—And she did not dare to think more of the question.

The meditations of the lady were interrupted by a youth who brought an armful of juniper sticks to the chimney, and throwing them down at the side of the hearth, began to pull out the coals from under the smouldering ashes. Suddenly a decision came to Olenka's mind.

"Kostek!" said she, "sit on horseback for me at once, and ride to Lyubich. If the master has returned, ask him to come here; but if he is not there, let the manager, old Znikis, mount with thee and come straight to me, and quickly."

The youth threw some bits of pitch on the coals and covered them with clumps of dry juniper. Bright flames began to crackle and snap in the chimney. It grew somewhat lighter in Olenka's mind.

"Perhaps the Lord God will change this yet," thought she to herself, "and maybe it is not so bad as the guardians have said."

After a while she went to the servants' room to sit, according to the immemorial custom of the Billeviches, with the maidens to oversee the spinning and sing hymns.

In two hours Kostek entered, chilled from cold. "Znikis is in the antechamber," said he. "The master is not in Lyubich."

The lady rose quickly. The manager in the antechamber bowed to her feet. "But how is your health, serene heiress? God give you the best."

They passed into the dining-hall; Znikis halted at the door.

"What is to be heard among you people?" asked the lady.

The peasant waved his hand. "Well, the master is not there."

"I know that, because he is in Upita. But what is going on in the house?"

"Well!—"

"Listen, Znikis, speak boldly; not a hair will fall from thy head. People say that the master is good, but his companions wild?"

"If they were only wild, serene lady!—"

"Speak candidly."

"But, lady, if it is not permitted me—I am afraid—they have forbidden me."

"Who has forbidden?"

"My master."

"Has he?" asked the lady.

A moment of silence ensued. She walked quickly in the room, with compressed lips and frowning brow. He followed her with his eyes. Suddenly she stopped before him.

"To whom dost thou belong?"

"To the Billeviches. I am from Vodokty, not from Lyubich."

"Thou wilt return no more to Lyubich; stay here. Now I command thee to tell all thou knowest."

The peasant cast himself on his knees at the threshold where he was standing. "Serene lady, I do not want to go back; the day of judgment is there. They are bandits and cut-throats; in that place a man is not sure of the day nor the hour."

Panna Billevich staggered as if stricken by an arrow. She grew very pale, but inquired calmly, "Is it true that they fired in the room, at the portraits?"

"Of course they fired! And they dragged girls into their rooms, and every day the same debauchery. In the village is weeping, at the house Sodom and Gomorrah. Oxen are killed for the table, sheep for the table. The people are oppressed. Yesterday they killed the stable man without cause."

"Did they kill the stable-man?"

"Of course. And worst of all, they abused the girls. Those at the house are not enough for them; they chase others through the village."

A second interval of silence followed. Hot blushes came out on the lady's face, and did not leave it.

"When do they look for the master's return?"

"They do not know, my lady. But I heard, as they were talking to one another, that they would have to start to-morrow for Upita with their whole company. They gave command to have horses ready. They will come here and beg my lady for attendants and powder, because they need both there."

"They are to come here? That is well. Go now, Znikis, to the kitchen. Thou wilt return to Lyubich no more."

"May God give you health and happiness!"

Panna Aleksandra had learned what she wanted, and she knew how it behooved her to act.

The following day was Sunday. In the morning, before the ladies had gone to church, Kokosinski, Uhlik, Kulvyets-Hippocentaurus, Ranitski, Rekuts, and Zend arrived, followed by the servants at Lyubich, armed and on horseback, for the cavaliers had decided to march to Upita with succor for Kmita.

The lady went out to meet them calmly and haughtily, altogether different from the woman who had greeted them for the first time a few days before. She barely motioned with her head in answer to their humble bows; but they thought that the absence of Pan Kmita made her cautious, and took no note of the real situation.

Kokosinski stepped forward more confidently than the first time, and said,—

"Serene great mighty lady, chief-hunter's daughter, benefactress; we have come in here on our way to Upita to fall at the feet of our lady benefactress and beg for assistance, such as powder, and that you would permit your servants to mount their horses and go with us. We will take Upita by storm, and let out a little blood for the basswood-barks."

"It is a wonder to me," answered Panna Billevich, "that you are going to Upita, when I heard myself how Pan Kmita commanded you to remain quietly in Lyubich, and I think that it beseems him to command and you to obey, as subordinates."

The cavaliers hearing these words looked at one another in astonishment. Zend pursed out his lips as if about to whistle in bird fashion. Kokosinski began to draw his broad palm over his head.

"As true as life," said he, "a man would think that you were speaking to Pan Kmita's baggage-boys. It is true that we were to sit at home; but since the fourth day is passing and

Yendrus has not come, we have reached the conviction that some serious tumult may have risen, in which our sabres, too, would be of service."

"Pan Kmita did not go to a battle, but to punish turbulent soldiers, and punishment may meet you also if you go against orders. Besides, a tumult and slashing might come to pass more quickly if you were there."

"It is hard to deliberate with your ladyship. We ask only for powder and men."

"Men and powder I will not give. Do you hear me, sirs!"

"Do I hear correctly?" asked Kokosinski. "How is this? You will not give? You will spare in the rescue of Kmita, of Yendrus? Do you prefer that some evil should meet him?"

"The greatest evil that can meet him is your company."

Here the maiden's eyes began to flash lightning, and raising her head she advanced some steps toward the cutthroats, and they pushed back before her in astonishment.

"Traitors!" said she, "you, like evil spirits, tempt him to sin; you persuade him on. But I know you,—your profligacy, your lawless deeds. Justice is hunting you; people turn away from you, and on whom does the shame fall? On him, through you who are outlaws, and infamous."

"Hei, by God's wounds, comrades, do you hear?" cried Kokosinski. "Hei, what is this? Are we not sleeping, comrades?"

Panna Billevich advanced another step, and pointing with her hand to the door, said, "Be off out of here!"

The ruffians grew as pale as corpses, and no one of them found a word in answer. But their teeth began to gnash, their hands to quiver toward their sword-hilts, and their eyes to shoot forth malign gleams. After a moment, however, their spirits fell through alarm. That house too was under the protection of the powerful Kmita; that insolent lady was his betrothed. In view of

61

this they gnawed their rage in silence, and she stood unflinchingly with flashing eyes pointing to the door with her finger.

At last Kokosinski spoke in a voice broken with rage: "Since we are received here so courteously, nothing remains to us but to bow to the polished lady and go—with thanks for the entertainment."

Then he bowed, touching the floor with his cap in purposed humility; after him all the others bowed, and went out in order. When the door closed after the last man, Olenka fell exhausted into the armchair, panting heavily, for she had not so much strength as daring.

They assembled in counsel in front of the entrance near their horses, but no man wanted to speak first. At last Kokosinski said, "Well, dear lambs, what's that?"

"Do you feel well?"

"Do you?"

"Ei! but for Kmita," said Ranitski, rubbing his hands convulsively, "we would revel with this lady here in our own fashion."

"Go meet Kmita," piped Rekuts.

Ranitski's face was covered completely with spots, like the skin of a leopard. "I'll meet him and you too, you reveller, wherever it may please you!"

"That's well!" cried Rekuts.

Both rushed to their sabres, but the gigantic Kulvyets-Hippocentaurus thrust himself between. "See this fist!" said he, shaking as it were a loaf of bread; "see this fist!" repeated he. "I'll smash the head of the first man who draws his sabre." And he looked now at one and now at the other, as if asking in silence who wished to try first; but they, addressed in such fashion, were quiet at once.

"Kulvyets is right," said Kokosinski. "My dear lambs, we need agreement now more than ever. I would advise to go with all speed to Kmita, so that she may not see him first, for she would describe us as devils. It is well that none of us snarled at her, though my own hands and tongue were itching. If she is going to rouse him against us, it is better for us to rouse him first. God keep him from leaving us! Straightway the people here would surround us, hunt us down like wolves."

"Nonsense!" said Ranitski. "They will do nothing to us. There is war now; are there few men straggling through the world without a roof, without bread? Let us collect a party for ourselves, dear comrades, and let all the tribunals pursue us. Give your hand, Rekuts, I forgive you."

"I should have cut off your ears," piped Rekuts; "but let us be friends, a common insult has met us."

"To order out cavaliers like us!" said Kokosinski.

"And me, in whom is senatorial blood!" added Ranitski.

"Honorable people, men of good birth!"

"Soldiers of merit!"

"And exiles!"

"Innocent orphans!"

"I have boots lined with wool, but my feet are freezing," said Kulvyets. "Shall we stand like minstrels in front of this house? They will not bring us out heated beer. We are of no use here; let us mount and ride away. Better send the servants home, for what good are they without guns and weapons? We will go on alone."

"To Upita!"

"To Yendrus, our worthy friend! We will make complaint before him."

"If only we do not miss him."

"To horse, comrades, to horse!"

They mounted, and moved on at a walk, chewing their anger and shame. Outside the gate Ranitski, whom rage still held as it were by the throat, turned and threatened the house with his fist. "Ei! I want blood! I want blood!"

"If we can only raise a quarrel between her and Kmita," said Kokosinski, "we shall go through this place yet with fire."

"That may happen."

"God aid us!" added Uhlik.

"Oh, pagan's daughter, mad heath-hen!"

Railing thus, and enraged at the lady, snarling sometimes too at themselves, they reached the forest. They had barely passed the first trees when an enormous flock of crows whirled above their heads. Zend began at once to croak in a shrill voice; thousands of voices answered him from above. The flock came down so low that the horses began to be frightened at the sound of their wings.

"Shut your mouth!" cried Ranitski to Zend. "You'll croak out misfortune on us yet. Those crows are circling over us as over carrion."

The others laughed. Zend croaked continually. The crows came down more and more, and the party rode as if in the midst of a storm. Fools! they could not see the ill omen.

Beyond the forest appeared Volmontovichi, toward which the cavaliers moved at a trot, for the frost was severe; they were very cold, and it was still a long way to Upita, but they had to lessen their speed in the village itself. In the broad road of the village the space was full of people, as is usual on Sundays. The Butryms, men and women, were returning on foot and in sleighs from Mitruny after receiving indulgence. The nobles looked on these unknown horsemen, half guessing who they were. The young women, who had heard of their license in Lyubich and of the notorious public sinners whom Pan Kmita had brought, looked at them with still greater curiosity. But they rode proudly in imposing military posture, with velvet coats which they had captured, in panther-skin caps, and on sturdy horses. It was to be seen that they were soldiers by profession,—their gestures frequent and haughty, their right hands resting on their hips, their heads erect. They gave the way to no man, advancing in a line and shouting from time to time, "Out of the road!" One or another of the Butryms looked at them with a frown, but yielded; the party chatted among themselves about the village.

"See, gentlemen," said Kokosinski, "what sturdy fellows there are here; one after another like an aurochs, and each with the look of a wolf."

"If it were not for their stature and swords, they might be taken for common trash."

"Just look at those sabres,—regular tearers, as God is dear to me!" remarked Ranitski. "I would like to make a trial with some of those fellows." Here he began to fence with his hand: "He thus, I thus! He thus, I thus—and check!"

"You can easily have that delight for yourself," said Rekuts. "Not much is needed with them for a quarrel."

"I would rather engage with those girls over there," said Zend, all at once.

"They are candles, not girls!" cried Rekuts, with enthusiasm.

"What do you say,—candles? Pine-trees! And each one has a face as if painted with crocus."

"It is hard to sit on a horse at such a sight."

Talking in this style, they rode out of the village and moved on again at a trot. After half an hour's ride they came to a public house called Dola, which was half-way between Volmontovichi and Mitruny. The Butryms, men and women, generally stopped there going to and returning from church, in order to rest and warm themselves in frosty weather. So the cavaliers saw before the door a number of sleighs with pea-straw spread in them, and about the same number of saddle-horses.

"Let us drink some gorailka, for it is cold," said Kokosinski.

"It wouldn't hurt," answered the others, in a chorus.

They dismounted, left their horses at the posts, and entered the drinking-hall, which was enormous and dark. They found there a crowd of people,—nobles sitting on benches or standing in groups before the water-pail, drinking warmed beer, and some of them a punch made of mead, butter, vudka, and spice. Those were the Butryms themselves, stalwart and gloomy; so sparing of speech that in the room scarcely any conversation was heard. All were dressed in gray overcoats of home-made or coarse cloth from Rossyeni, lined with sheepskin; they had leather belts, with sabres in black iron scabbards. By reason of that uniformity of dress they had the appearance of soldiers. But they were old men of sixty or youths under twenty. These had remained at home for the winter threshing; the others, men in the prime of life, had gone to Rossyeni.

When they saw the cavaliers of Orsha, they drew back from the water-bucket and began to examine them. Their handsome soldierly appearance pleased that warlike nobility; after a while, too, some one dropped the word,—

"Are they from Lyubich?"

"Yes, that is Pan Kmita's company!"

"Are these they?"

"Of course."

The cavaliers drank gorailka, but the punch had a stronger odor. Kokosinski caught it first, and ordered some. They sat around a table then; and when the steaming kettle was brought they began to drink, looking around the room at the men and blinking, for the place was rather dark. The snow had blocked the windows; and the broad, low opening of the chimney in which the fire was burning was hidden completely by certain figures with their backs to the crowd.

When the punch had begun to circulate in the veins of the cavaliers, bearing through their bodies an agreeable warmth, their cheerfulness, depressed by the reception at Vodokty, sprang up again; and all at once Zend fell to cawing like a crow, so perfectly that all faces were turned toward him.

The cavaliers laughed, and the nobles, enlivened, began to approach, especially the young men,—powerful fellows with broad shoulders and plump cheeks. The figures sitting at the chimney turned their faces to the room, and Rekuts was the first to see that they were women.

Zend closed his eyes and cawed, cawed. Suddenly he stopped, and in a moment those present heard the cry of a hare choked by a dog; the hare cried in the last agony, weaker and lower, then screamed in despair, and was silent for the ages; in place of it was heard the deep bellow of a furious stag as loud as in spring-time.

The Butryms were astonished. Though Zend had stopped, they expected to hear something again; but they heard only the piping voice of Rekuts,—

"Those are titmice sitting near the chimney!"

"That is true!" replied Kokosinski, shading his eyes with his hand.

"As true as I live!" added Uhlik, "but it is so dark in the room that I could not see them."

"I am curious. What are they doing?"

"Maybe they have come to dance."

"But wait; I will ask," said Kokosinski. And raising his voice, he asked, "My dear women, what are you doing there at the chimney?"

"We are warming our feet," answered thin voices.

Then the cavaliers rose and approached the hearth. There were sitting at it, on a long bench, about ten women, old and young, holding their bare feet on a log lying by the fire. On the other side of the log their shoes wet from the snow were drying.

"So you are warming your feet?" asked Kokosinski.

"Yes, for they are cold."

"Very pretty feet," piped Rekuts, inclining toward the log.

"But keep at a distance," said one of the women.

"I prefer to come near. I have a sure method, better than fire, for cold feet; which is,—only dance with a will, and the cold flies away."

"If to dance, then dance," said Uhlik. "We want neither fiddles nor bass-viols. I will play for you on the flageolet."

Taking from its leather case which hung near his sabre the ever-present flageolet, he began to play; and the cavaliers, pushing forward with dancing movement to the maidens, sought to draw them from the benches. The maidens appeared to defend themselves, but more with their voices than their hands, for in truth they were not greatly opposed. Maybe the men, too, would have been willing in their turn; for against dancing on Sunday after Mass and during the carnival no one would protest greatly. But the reputation of the "company" was already too well known in Volmontovichi; therefore first the gigantic Yuzva Butrym, he who had but one foot, rose from the bench, and approaching Kulvyets-Hippocentaurus, caught him by the breast, held him, and said with sullen voice,—

"If your grace wants dancing, then dance with me."

Kulvyets-Hippocentaurus blinked, and began to move his mustaches convulsively. "I prefer a girl," said he; "I can attend to you afterward."

Meanwhile Ranitski ran up with face already spotted, for he sniffed a quarrel. "Who are you, road-blocker?" asked he, grasping his sabre.

Uhlik stopped playing, and Kokosinski shouted, "Hei, comrades! together, together!"

But the Butryms were already behind Yuzva; sturdy old men and great youths began to assemble, growling like bears.

"What do you want? Are you looking for bruises?" asked Kokosinski.

"No talk! Be off out of here!" said Yuzva, stolidly.

Then Ranitski, whose interest it was that an hour should not pass without a fight, struck Yuzva with the hilt of his sword in the breast, so that it was heard in the whole room, and cried, "Strike!"

Rapiers glittered; the scream of women was heard, the clatter of sabres, uproar and disturbance. Then the gigantic Yuzva pushed out of the crowd, took a roughly hewn bench from beside a table, and raising it as though it were a light strip of wood, shouted, "Make way! make way!"

Dust rose from the floor and hid the combatants; but in the confusion groans were soon heard.

CHAPTER VI.

In the evening of that same day Pan Kmita came to Vodokty, at the head of a hundred and some tens of men whom he had brought from Upita so as to send them to Kyedani; for he saw himself that there were no quarters in such a small place for a large number of soldiers, and when the townspeople had been brought to hunger the soldiers would resort to violence, especially soldiers who could be held in discipline only by fear of a leader. A glance at Kmita's volunteers was enough to convince one that it would be difficult to find men of worse character in the whole Commonwealth. Kmita could not have others. After the defeat of the grand hetman, the enemy deluged the whole country. The remnants of the regular troops of the Lithuanian quota withdrew for a certain time to Birji and Kyedani, in order to rally there. The nobility of Smolensk, Vityebsk, Polotsk, Mstislavsk, and Minsk either followed the army or took refuge in the provinces still unoccupied. Men of superior courage among the nobility assembled at Grodno around the under-treasurer, Pan Gosyevski; for the royal proclamation summoning the general militia appointed that as the place of muster. Unfortunately few obeyed the proclamation, and those who followed the voice of duty assembled so negligently that for the time being no one offered real resistance save Kmita, who fought on his own account, animated more by knightly daring than patriotism. It is easy to understand that in the absence of regular troops and nobility he took such men as he could find, consequently men who were not drawn by duty to the hetmans and who had nothing to lose. Therefore there gathered around him vagrants without a roof and without a home, men of low rank, runaway servants from the army, foresters grown wild, serving-men from towns, or scoundrels pursued by the law. These expected to find protection under a flag and win profit from plunder. In the iron hands of Kmita they were turned into daring soldiers, daring even to madness; and if Kmita had been prudent he might have rendered high service to the Commonwealth. But Kmita was insubordinate himself, his spirit was always seething; besides, whence could he take provisions and arms and horses, since being a partisan he did not hold even a commission, and could not look for any aid from the treasury of the Commonwealth? He took therefore with violence,—often from the enemy, often from his own,—could suffer no opposition, and punished severely for the least cause.

In continual raids, struggles, and attacks he had grown wild, accustomed to bloodshed in such a degree that no common thing could move the heart within him, which however was good by nature. He was in love with people of unbridled temper who were ready for anything. Soon his name had an ominous sound. Smaller divisions of the enemy did not dare to leave the towns and the camps in those regions where the terrible partisan was raging. But the townspeople ruined by war feared his men little less than they did the enemy, especially when the eye of Kmita in person was not resting on them. When command was taken by his officers, Kokosinski, Uhlik, Kulvyets, Zend, and particularly by Ranitski,—the wildest and most cruel of them all, though a man of high lineage,—it might always be asked, Are those defenders or ravagers? Kmita at times punished his own men without mercy when something happened not according to his humor; but more frequently he took their part, regardless of the rights, tears, and lives of people. His companions with the exception of Rekuts, on whom innocent blood was not weighing, persuaded the young leader to give the reins more and more to his turbulent nature. Such was Kmita's army. Just then he had taken his rabble from Upita to send it to Kyedani.

When they stopped in front of the house at Vodokty, Panna Aleksandra was frightened as she saw them through the window, they were so much like robbers. Each one had a different outfit: some were in helmets taken from the enemy; others in Cossack caps, in hoods and Polish caps; some in faded overcoats, others in sheep-skin coats; their arms were guns, spears, bows, battle-axes; their horses, poor and worn, were covered with trappings, Polish, Russian, or Turkish.

Olenka was set at rest only when Pan Andrei, gladsome and lively as ever, entered the room and rushed straight to her hands with incredible quickness.

And she, though resolved in advance to receive him with dignity and coldness, was still unable to master the joy which his coming had caused her. Feminine cunning too may have played a certain part, for it was necessary to tell Pan Andrei about turning his comrades out of doors; therefore the clever girl wished to incline him first to her side. And in addition he greeted her so sincerely, so lovingly that the remnant of her offended feeling melted like snow before a blaze.

"He loves me! there is no doubt about that," thought she.

And he said: "I so longed for you that I was ready to burn all Upita if I could only fly to you the sooner. May the frost pinch them, the basswood barks!"

"I too was uneasy lest it might come to a battle there. Praise be to God that you have returned!"

"And such a battle! The soldiers had begun to pull around the basswood barks a little—"

"But you quieted them?"

"This minute I will tell you how it all happened, my jewel; only let me rest a little, for I am wearied. Ei! it is warm here. It is delightful in this Vodokty, just as in paradise. A man would be glad to sit here all his life, look in those beautiful eyes, and never go away—But it would do no harm, either, to drink something warm, for there is terrible frost outside."

"Right away I will have wine heated, with eggs, and bring it myself."

"And give my gallows' birds some little keg of gorailka, and give command to let them into the stable, so that they may warm themselves a little even from the breath of the cattle. They have coats lined with wind, and are terribly chilled."

"I will spare nothing on them, for they are your soldiers."

While speaking she smiled, so that it grew bright in Kmita's eyes, and she slipped out as quietly as a cat to have everything prepared in the servants' hall.

Kmita walked up and down in the room, rubbing the top of his head, then twirling his young mustache, thinking how to tell her of what had been done in Upita.

"The pure truth must be told," muttered he; "there is no help for it, though the company may laugh because I am here in leading-strings." And again he walked, and again he pushed the foretop on his forehead; at last he grew impatient that the maiden was so long in returning.

Meanwhile a boy brought in a light, bowed to the girdle, and went out. Directly after the charming lady of the house entered, bringing with both hands a shining tin tray, and on it a small pot, from which rose the fragrant steam of heated Hungarian, and a goblet of cut glass with the escutcheon of the Kmitas. Old Billevich got this goblet in his time from Andrei's father, when at his house as a guest.

Pan Andrei when he saw the lady sprang toward her. "Hei!" cried he, "both hands are full, you will not escape me."

He bent over the tray, and she drew back her head, which was defended only by the steam which rose from the pot. "Traitor! desist, or I will drop the drink."

But he feared not the threat; afterward he cried, "As God is in heaven, from such delight a man might lose his wits!"

"Then you lost your wit long ago. Sit down."

He sat down obediently; she poured the drink into the goblet.

"Tell me how you sentenced the guilty in Upita."

"In Upita? Like Solomon!"

"Praise to God for that! It is on my heart that all in this region should esteem you as a steady and just man. How was it then?"

Kmita took a good draught of the drink, drew breath, and began,—

"I must tell from the beginning. It was thus: The townspeople with the mayor spoke of an order for provisions from the grand hetman or the under-treasurer. 'You gentlemen,' said they to the soldiers, 'are volunteers, and you cannot levy contributions. We will give you quarters for nothing, and provisions we will give when it is shown that we shall be paid.'"

"Were they right, or were they not?"

"They were right according to law; but the soldiers had sabres, and in old fashion whoever has a sabre has the best argument. They said then to the basswood barks, 'We will write orders on your skins immediately.' And straightway there rose a tumult. The mayor and the people barricaded themselves in the street, and my men attacked them; it did not pass without firing. The soldiers, poor fellows, burned a couple of barns to frighten the people, and quieted a few of them also."

"How did they quiet them?"

"Whoso gets a sabre on his skull is as quiet as a coward."

"As God lives, that is murder!"

"That is just why I went there. The soldiers ran to me at once with complaints and outcries against the oppression in which they were living, being persecuted without cause. 'Our stomachs are empty,' said they, 'what are we to do?' I commanded the mayor to appear. He hesitated long, but at last came with three other men. They began: 'Even if the soldiers had not orders, why did they beat us, why burn the place? We should have given them to eat and to drink for a kind word; but they wanted ham, mead, dainties, and we are poor people, we have not these things for ourselves. We will seek defence at law, and you will answer before a court for your soldiers.'"

"God will bless you," cried Olenka, "if you have rendered justice as was proper."

"If I have." Here Pan Andrei wriggled like a student who has to confess his fault, and began to collect the forelock on his forehead with his hand. "My queen!" cried he at last, in an imploring voice, "my jewel, be not angry with me!"

"What did you do then?" asked Olenka, uneasily.

"I commanded to give one hundred blows apiece to the mayor and the councillors," said Kmita, at one breath.

Olenka made no answer; she merely rested her hands on her knees, dropped her head on her bosom, and sank into silence.

"Cut off my head!" cried Kmita, "but do not be angry! I have not told all yet!"

"Is there more?" groaned the lady.

"There is, for they sent then to Ponyevyej for aid. One hundred stupid fellows came with officers. These men I frightened away, but the officers—for God's sake be not angry!—I ordered to be chased and flogged with braided whips, naked over the snow, as I once did to Pan Tumgrat in Orsha."

Panna Billevich raised her head; her stern eyes were flashing with indignation, and purple came out on her cheeks. "You have neither shame nor conscience!" said she.

Kmita looked at her in astonishment, he was silent for a moment, then asked with changed voice, "Are you speaking seriously or pretending?"

"I speak seriously; that deed is becoming a bandit and not a cavalier. I speak seriously, since your reputation is near my heart; for it is a shame to me that you have barely come here, when all the people look on you as a man of violence and point at you with their fingers."

"What care I for the people? One dog watches ten of their cabins, and then has not much to do."

"There is no infamy on those modest people, there is no disgrace on the name of one of them. Justice will pursue no man here except you."

"Oh, let not your head ache for that. Every man is lord for himself in our Commonwealth, if he has only a sabre in his hand and can gather any kind of party. What can they do to me? Whom fear I here?"

"If you fear not man, then know that I fear God's anger, and the tears of people; I fear wrongs also. And moreover I am not willing to share disgrace with any one; though I am a weak woman, still the honor of my name is dearer to me than it is to a certain one who calls himself a cavalier."

"In God's name, do not threaten me with refusal, for you do not know me yet."

"I think that my grandfather too did not know you."

Kmita's eyes shot sparks; but the Billevich blood began to play in her.

"Oh, gesticulate and grit your teeth," continued she, boldly; "but I fear not, though I am alone and you have a whole party of robbers,—my innocence defends me. You think that I know not how you fired at the portraits in Lyubich and dragged in the girls for debauchery. You do not know me if you suppose that I shall humbly be silent. I want honesty from you, and no will can prevent me from exacting it. Nay, it was the will of my grandfather that I should be the wife of only an honest man."

Kmita was evidently ashamed of what had happened at Lyubich; for dropping his head, he asked in a voice now calmer, "Who told you of this shooting?"

"All the nobles in the district speak of it."

"I will pay those homespuns, the traitors, for their good will," answered Kmita, sullenly. "But that happened in drink,—in company,—for soldiers are not able to restrain themselves. As for the girls I had nothing to do with them."

"I know that those brazen ruffians, those murderers, persuade you to everything."

"They are not murderers, they are my officers."

"I commanded those officers of yours to leave my house."

Olenka looked for an outburst; but she saw with greatest astonishment that the news of turning his comrades out of the house made no impression on Kmita; on the contrary, it seemed to improve his humor.

"You ordered them to go out?" asked be.

"I did."

"And they went?"

"They did."

"As God lives, you have the courage of a cavalier. That pleases me greatly, for it is dangerous to quarrel with such people. More than one man has paid dearly for doing so. But they observe manners before Kmita! You saw they bore themselves obediently as lambs; you saw that,—but why? Because they are afraid of me."

Here Kmita looked boastfully at Olenka, and began to twirl his mustache. This fickleness of humor and inopportune boastfulness enraged her to the last degree; therefore she said haughtily and with emphasis, "You must choose between me and them; there is no other way."

Kmita seemed not to note the decision with which she spoke, and answered carelessly, almost gayly: "But why choose when I have you and I have them? You may do what you like in Vodokty; but if my comrades have committed no wrong, no license here, why should I drive them away? You do not understand what it is to serve under one flag and carry on war in company. No relationship binds like service in common. Know that they have saved my life a thousand times at least. I must protect them all the more because they are pursued by justice. They are almost all nobles and of good family, except Zend, who is of uncertain origin; but such a horse-trainer as he there is not in the whole Commonwealth. And if you could hear how he imitates wild beasts and every kind of bird, you would fall in love with him yourself."

Here Kmita laughed as if no anger, no misunderstanding, had ever found place between them; and she was ready to wring her hands, seeing how that whirlwind of a nature was slipping away from her grasp. All that she had said of the opinions of men, of the need of sedateness, of disgrace, slipped along on him like a dart on steel armor. The unroused conscience of this soldier could give no response to her indignation at every injustice and every dishonorable deed of license. How was he to be touched, how addressed?

"Let the will of God be done," said she at last; "since you will resign me, then go your way. God will remain with the orphan."

"I resign you?" asked Kmita, with supreme astonishment.

"That is it!—if not in words, then in deeds; if not you me, then I you. For I will not marry a man weighted by the tears and blood of people, whom men point at with their fingers, whom they call an outlaw, a robber, and whom they consider a traitor."

"What, traitor! Do not bring me to madness, lest I do something for which I should be sorry hereafter. May the thunderbolts strike me this minute, may the devils flay me, if I am a traitor,—I, who stood by the country when all hands had dropped!"

"You stand by the country and act like an enemy, for you trample on it. You are an executioner of the people, regarding the laws neither of God nor man. No! though my heart should be rent, I will not marry you; being such a man, I will not!"

"Do not speak to me of refusal, for I shall grow furious. Save me, ye angels! If you will not have me in good-will, then I'll take you without it, though all the rabble from the villages were here, though the Radzivills themselves were here, the very king himself and all the devils with their horns stood in the way, even if I had to sell my soul to the Devil!"

"Do not summon evil spirits, for they will hear you," cried Olenka, stretching forth her hands.

"What do you wish of me?"

"Be honest!"

Both ceased speaking, and silence followed; only the panting of Pan Andrei was heard. The last words of Olenka had penetrated, however, the armor covering his conscience. He felt himself conquered; he knew not what to answer, how to defend himself. Then he began to go with swift steps through the room. She sat there motionless. Above them hung disagreement, dissension, and regret. They were oppressive to each other, and the long silence became every instant more unendurable.

"Farewell!" said Kmita, suddenly.

"Go, and may God give you a different inspiration!" answered Olenka.

"I will go! Bitter was your drink, bitter your bread. I have been treated here to gall and vinegar."

"And do you think you have treated me to sweetness?" answered she, in a voice in which tears were trembling.

"Be well."

"Be well."

Kmita, advancing toward the door, turned suddenly, and springing to her, seized both her hands and said, "By the wounds of Christ! do you wish me to drop from the horse a corpse on the road?"

That moment Olenka burst into tears; he embraced her and held her in his arms, all quivering, repeating through her set teeth, "Whoso believes in God, kill me! kill, do not spare!"

At last he burst out: "Weep not, Olenka; for God's sake, do not weep! In what am I guilty before you? I will do all to please you. I'll send those men away, I'll come to terms in Upita, I will live differently,—for I love you. As God lives, my heart will burst! I will do everything; only do not cry, and love me still."

And so he continued to pacify and pet her; and she, when she had cried to the end, said: "Go now. God will make peace between us. I am not offended, only sore at heart."

The moon had risen high over the white fields when Pan Andrei pushed out on his way to Lyubich, and after him clattered his men, stretching along the broad road like a serpent. They went through Volmontovichi, but by the shortest road, for frost had bound up the swamps, which might therefore be crossed without danger.

The sergeant Soroka approached Pan Andrei. "Captain," inquired he, "where are we to find lodgings in Lyubich?"

"Go away!" answered Kmita.

And he rode on ahead, speaking to no man. In his heart rose regret, at moments anger, but above all, vexation at himself. That was the first night in his life in which he made a reckoning with conscience, and that reckoning weighed him down more than the heaviest armor. Behold, he had come into this region with a damaged reputation, and what had he done to repair it? The first day he had permitted shooting and excess in Lyubich, and thought that he did not belong to it, but he did; then he permitted it every

80

day. Further, his soldiers wronged the townspeople, and he increased those wrongs. Worse, he attacked the Ponyevyej garrison, killed men, sent naked officers on the snow. They will bring an action against him; he will lose it. They will punish him with loss of property, honor, perhaps life. But why can he not, after he has collected an armed party of the rabble, scoff at the law as before? Because he intends to marry, settle in Vodokty, serve not on his own account, but in the contingent; there the law will find him and take him. Besides, even though these deeds should pass unpunished, there is something vile in them, something unworthy of a knight. Maybe this violence can be atoned for; but the memory of it will remain in the hearts of men, in his own conscience, and in the heart of Olenka.

When he remembered that she had not rejected him yet, that when he was going away he read in her eyes forgiveness, she seemed to him as kind as the angels of heaven. And behold the desire was seizing him to go, not to-morrow, but straightway, as fast as the horse could spring, fall at her feet, beg forgetfulness, and kiss those sweet eyes which today had moistened his face with tears. Then he wished to roar with weeping, and felt that he loved that girl as he had never in his life loved any one. "By the Most Holy Lady!" thought he, in his soul, "I will do what she wishes; I will provide for my comrades bountifully, and send them to the end of the world; for it is true that they urge me to evil."

Then it entered his head that on coming to Lyubich he would find them most surely drunk or with girls; and such rage seized him that he wanted to slash somebody with a sabre, even those soldiers whom he was leading, and cut them up without mercy.

"I'll give it to them!" muttered he, twirling his mustache. "They have not yet seen me as they will see me."

Then from madness he began to prick the horse with his spurs, to pull and drag at the reins till the steed grew wild. Soroka, seeing this, muttered to the soldiers,—

"The captain is mad. God save us from falling under his hand!"

Pan Andrei had become mad in earnest. Round about there was great calm. The moon shone mildly, the heavens were glittering with thousands of stars, not the slightest breeze was moving the limbs on the trees; but in the heart of the knight a tempest was raging. The road to Lyubich seemed to him longer than ever before. A certain hitherto unknown alarm began to play upon him from the gloom of the forest depths, and from the fields flooded with a greenish light of the moon. Finally weariness seized Pan Andrei,—for, to tell the truth, the whole night before he had passed in drinking and frolicking in Upita; but he wished to overcome toil with toil, and rouse himself from unquiet by swift riding; he turned therefore to the soldiers and commanded,—

"Forward!"

He shot ahead like an arrow, and after him the whole party. And in those woods and along those empty fields they flew on like that hellish band of knights of the cross of whom people tell in Jmud,—how at times in the middle of bright moonlight nights they appear and rush through the air, announcing war and uncommon calamities. The clatter flew before them and followed behind, from the horses came steam, and only when at the turn of the road the roofs of Lyubich appeared did they slacken their speed.

The swinging gate stood open. It astonished Kmita that when the yard was crowded with his men and horses no one came out to see or inquire who they were. He expected to find the windows gleaming with lights, to hear the sound of Uhlik's flageolet, of fiddles, or the joyful shouts of conversation. At that time in two windows of the dining-hall quivered an uncertain light; all the rest of the house was dark, quiet, silent. The sergeant Soroka sprang first from his horse to hold the stirrup for the captain.

"Go to sleep," said Kmita; "whoever can find room in the servants' hall, let him sleep there, and others in the stable. Put the horses in the cattle-houses and in the barns, and bring them hay from the shed."

"I hear," answered the sergeant.

Kmita came down from the horse. The door of the entrance was wide open, and the entrance cold.

"Hei! Is there any one here?" cried Kmita.

No one answered.

"Hei there!" repeated he, more loudly.

Silence.

"They are drunk!" muttered Pan Andrei.

And such rage took possession of him that he began to grit his teeth. While riding he was agitated with anger at the thought that he should find drinking and debauchery; now this silence irritated him still more.

He entered the dining-hall. On an enormous table was burning a tallow lamp-pot with a reddish smoking light. The force of the wind which came in from the antechamber deflected the flame so that for a time Pan Andrei could not see anything. Only when the quivering had ceased did he distinguish a row of forms lying just at the wall.

"Have they made themselves dead drunk or what?" muttered he, unquietly.

Then he drew near with impatience to the side of the first figure. He could not see the face, for it was hidden in the shadow; but by the white leather belt and the white sheath of the flageolet he recognized Pan Uhlik, and began to shake him unceremoniously with his foot.

"Get up, such kind of sons! get up!"

But Pan Uhlik lay motionless, with his hands fallen without control at the side of his body, and beyond him were lying others. No one yawned, no one quivered, no one woke, no one muttered. At the same moment Kmita noticed that all were lying on their backs in the same position, and a certain fearful presentiment seized him by the heart. Springing to the table, he took with trembling hand the light and thrust it toward the faces of the prostrate men.

The hair stood on his head, such a dreadful sight met his eyes. Uhlik he was able to recognize only by his white belt, for his face and his head presented one formless, foul, bloody mass, without eyes, without nose or mouth,—only the enormous mustaches were sticking out of the dreadful pool. Kmita pushed the light farther. Next in order lay Zend, with grinning teeth and eyes protruding, in which in glassy fixedness was terror before death. The third in the row, Ranitski, had his eyes closed, and over his whole face were spots, white, bloody, and dark. Kmita took the light farther. Fourth lay Kokosinski,—the dearest to Kmita of all his officers, being his former near neighbor. He seemed to sleep quietly, but in the side of his neck was to be seen a large wound surely given with a thrust. Fifth in the row lay the gigantic Kulvyets-Hippocentaurus, with the vest torn on his bosom and his face slashed many times. Kmita brought the light near each face; and when at last he brought it to the sixth, Rekuts, it seemed that the lids of the unfortunate victim quivered a little from the gleam.

Kmita put the light on the floor and began to shake the wounded man gently. After the eyelids the face began to move, the eyes and mouth opened and closed in turn.

"Rekuts, Rekuts, it is I!" said Kmita.

The eyes of Rekuts opened for a moment; he recognized the face of his friend, and groaned in a low voice, "Yendrus—a priest—"

"Who killed you?" cried Kmita, seizing himself by the hair.

"Bu-try-my-" (The Butryms), answered he, in a voice so low that it was barely audible. Then he stretched himself, grew stiff, his open eyes became fixed, and he died.

Kmita went in silence to the table, put the tallow lamp upon it, sat down in an armchair, and began to pass his hands over his face like a man who waking from sleep does not know yet whether he is awake or still sees dream figures before his eyes. Then he looked again on the bodies lying in the darkness. Cold sweat came out on his forehead, the hair rose on his head, and suddenly he shouted so terribly that the panes rattled in the windows,—

"Come hither, every living man! come hither!"

The soldiers, who had disposed themselves in the servants' hall, heard that cry and fell into the room with a rush. Kmita showed them with his hand the corpses at the wall.

"Murdered! murdered!" repeated he, with hoarse voice.

They ran to look; some came with a taper, and held it before the eyes of the dead men. After the first moment of astonishment came noise and confusion. Those hurried in who had found places in the stables and barns. The whole house was bright with light, swarming with men; and in the midst of all that whirl, shouting, and questioning, the dead lay at the wall unmoved and quiet, indifferent to everything, and, in contradiction to their own nature, calm. The souls had gone out of them, and their bodies could not be raised by the trumpet to battle, or the sound of the goblets to feasting.

Meanwhile in the din of the soldiers shouts of threatening and rage rose higher and higher each instant. Kmita, who till that moment had been as it were unconscious, sprang up suddenly and shouted, "To horse!"

Everything living moved toward the door. Half an hour had not passed when more than one hundred horsemen were rushing with breakneck speed over the broad snowy road, and at the head of them flew Pan Andrei, as if possessed of a demon, bareheaded and with a naked sabre in his hand. In the still night was heard on every side the wild shouts: "Slay! kill!"

The moon had reached just the highest point on its road through the sky, when suddenly its beams began to be mingled and mixed with a rosy light, rising as it were from under the ground; gradually the heavens grew red and still redder as if from the rising dawn, till at last a bloody glare filled the whole neighborhood. One sea of fire raged over the gigantic village of the Butryms; and the wild soldiers of Kmita, in the midst of smoke, burning, and sparks bursting in columns to the sky, cut down the population, terrified and blinded from fright.

The inhabitants of the nearer villages sprang from their sleep. The greater and smaller companies of the Smoky Gostsyeviches and Stakyans, Gashtovts and Domasheviches, collected on the road before their houses, and looking in the direction of the fire, gave alarm from mouth to mouth: "It must be that an enemy has broken in and is burning the Butryms,—that is an unusual fire!"

The report of muskets coming at intervals from the distance confirmed this supposition.

"Let us go to assist them!" cried the bolder; "let us not leave our brothers to perish!"

And when the older ones spoke thus, the younger, who on account of the winter threshing had not gone to Rossyeni, mounted their horses. In Krakin and in Upita they had begun to ring the church bells.

In Vodokty a quiet knocking at the door roused Panna Aleksandra.

"Olenka, get up!" cried Panna Kulvyets.

"Come in, Aunt, what is the matter?"

"They are burning Volmontovichi!"

"In the name of the Father, Son, and Holy Ghost!"

"Shots are heard, there is a battle! God have mercy on us!"

Olenka screamed terribly; then she sprang out of bed and began to throw on her clothes hurriedly. Her body trembled as in a fever. She alone guessed in a moment what manner of enemy had attacked the ill-fated Butryms.

After a while the awakened women of the whole house rushed into the room with crying and sobbing. Olenka threw herself on her knees before an image; they followed her example, and all began to repeat aloud the litany for the dying.

They had scarcely gone through half of it when a violent pounding shook the door of the antechamber. The women sprang to their feet; a cry of alarm was rent from their breasts.

"Do not open! do not open!"

The pounding was heard with redoubled force; it seemed that the door would spring from its hinges. That moment the youth Kostek rushed into the midst of the assembled women.

"Panna!" cried he, "some man is knocking; shall I open or not?"

"Is he alone?"

"Alone."

"Go open."

The youth hurried away. She, taking a light, passed into the dining-room; after her, Panna Kulvyets and all the spinning-women.

She had barely put the light on the table when in the antechamber was heard the rattle of iron bolts, the creak of the opening door; and before the eyes of the women appeared Pan Kmita, terrible, black from smoke, bloody, panting, with madness in his eyes.

"My horse has fallen at the forest," cried he; "they are pursuing me!"

Panna Aleksandra fixed her eyes on him: "Did you burn Volmontovichi?"

"I—I—"

He wanted to say something more, when from the side of the road and the woods came the sound of voices and the tramp of horses approaching with uncommon rapidity.

"The devils are after my soul; let them have it!" cried Kmita, as if in a fever.

Panna Aleksandra that moment turned to the women. "If they ask, say there is no one here; and now go to the servants' hall and come here at daylight!" Then to Kmita: "Go in there," said she, pointing to an adjoining room; and almost by force she pushed him through the open door, which she shut immediately.

Meanwhile armed men filled the front yard; and in the twinkle of an eye the Butryms, Gostsyeviches, Domasheviches, with others, burst into the house. Seeing the lady, they halted in the dining-room; but she, standing with a light in her hand, stopped with her person the passage to doors beyond.

"Men, what has happened? What do you want?" asked she, without blinking an eye before the terrible looks and the ominous gleam of drawn sabres.

"Kmita has burned Volmontovichi!" cried the nobles, in a chorus. "He has slaughtered men, women, children,—Kmita did this."

"We have killed his men," said Yuzva Butrym; "now we are seeking his own head."

"His head, his blood! Cut down the murderer!"

"Pursue him!" cried the lady. "Why do you stand here? Pursue him!"

"Is he not hidden here? We found his horse at the woods."

"He is not here! The house was closed. Look for him in the stables and barns."

"He has gone off to the woods!" cried some noble. "Come, brothers."

"Be silent!" roared with powerful voice Yuzva Butrym. "My lady," said he, "do not conceal him! That is a cursed man!"

Olenka raised both hands above her head: "I join you in cursing him!"

"Amen!" shouted the nobles. "To the buildings, to the woods! We will find him! After the murderer!"

"Come on! come on!"

The clatter of sabres and tramp of feet was heard again. The nobles hurried out through the porch, and mounted with all speed. A part of them searched still for a time in the stables, the cow-houses, and hay-shed; then their voices began to retreat toward the woods.

Panna Aleksandra listened till they had ceased altogether; then she tapped feverishly at the door of the room in which she had hidden Kmita. "There is no one here now, come out."

Pan Andrei pushed himself forth from the room as if drunk. "Olenka!" he began.

She shook her loosened tresses, which then covered her face like a veil. "I wish not to see you or know you. Take a horse and flee hence!"

"Olenka!" groaned Kmita, stretching forth his hands.

"There is blood on your hands, as on Cain's!" screamed she, springing back as if at the sight of a serpent. "Be gone, for the ages!"

CHAPTER VII.

The day rose gray, and lighted a group of ruins in Volmontovichi,—the burned remnants of houses, out-buildings, bodies of people and horses burned or slain with swords. In the ashes amidst dying embers crowds of pale people were seeking for the bodies of the dead or the remains of their property. It was a day of mourning and misfortune for all Lauda. The numerous nobility had obtained, it is true, a victory over Kmita's men, but a grievous and bloody one. Besides the Butryms, who had fallen in greater numbers than the others, there was not a village in which widows were not bewailing husbands, parents sons, or children their fathers. It was the more difficult for the Lauda people to finish the invaders, since the strongest were not at home; only old men or youths of early years took part in the battle. But of Kmita's soldiers not one escaped. Some yielded their lives in Volmontovichi, defending themselves with such rage that they fought after they were wounded; others were caught next day in the woods and killed without mercy. Kmita himself was as if he had dropped into water. The people were lost in surmising what had become of him. Some insisted that he had reached the wilderness of Zyelonka and gone thence to Rogovsk, where the Domasheviches alone might find him. Many too asserted that he had gone over to Hovanski and was bringing the enemy; but these were the fewest, their fears were untimely.

Meanwhile the surviving Butryms marched to Vodokty, and disposed themselves as in a camp. The house was full of women and children. Those who could not find a place there went to Mitruny, which Panna Aleksandra gave up to those whose homes had been burned. There were, besides, in Vodokty for defence about a hundred armed men in parties which relieved one another regularly, thinking that Kmita did not consider the affair ended, but might any day make an attempt on the lady with armed hand. The most important houses in the neighborhood, such as the Schyllings, the Sollohubs, and others, sent their attendant Cossacks and haiduks. Vodokty looked like a place awaiting a siege. And Panna Aleksandra went among the armed men, the nobles, the crowds of women, mournful, pale, suffering, hearing the weeping of people, and the curses of men against Pan Kmita,—which pierced her heart like swords, for she was the mediate cause of all the misfortune. For her it was that that frenzied man had come to the neighborhood, disturbed the peace, and left the memory of blood behind, trampled on laws, killed people, visited villages with fire and sword like an infidel, till it was a wonder that one man could commit so much evil in such a short time, and he a man neither entirely wicked nor entirely corrupt. If there was any one who knew this best, it was Panna Aleksandra, who had become acquainted with him most intimately. There was a precipice between Pan Kmita himself and his deeds. But it was for this reason precisely that so much pain was caused Panna Aleksandra by the thought that that man whom she had loved with the whole first impulse of a young heart might be different, that he possessed qualities to make him the model of a knight, of a cavalier, of a neighbor, worthy to receive the admiration and love of men instead of their contempt, and blessings instead of curses.

At times, therefore, it seemed to the lady that some species of misfortune, some kind of power, great and unclean, impelled him to all those deeds of violence; and then a sorrow really measureless possessed her for that unfortunate man, and unextinguished love rose anew in her heart, nourished by the fresh remembrance of his knightly form, his words, his imploring, his loving.

Meanwhile a hundred complaints were entered against him in the town, a hundred actions threatened, and the starosta, Pan Hlebovich, sent men to seize the criminal. The law was bound to condemn him.

Still, from sentences to their execution the distance was great, for disorder increased every hour in the Commonwealth. A terrible war was hanging over the land, and approaching Jmud with bloody steps. The powerful Radzivill of Birji, who was able alone to support the law with arms, was too much occupied with public affairs and still more immersed in great projects touching his own house, which he wished to elevate above all others in the country, even at the cost of the common weal. Other magnates too were thinking more of themselves than of the State. All the bonds in the strong edifice of the Commonwealth had burst from the time of the Cossack war.

A country populous, rich, filled with a valiant knighthood, had become the prey of neighbors; and straightway arbitrariness and license raised their heads more and more, and insulted the law, so great was the power which they felt behind them. The oppressed could find the best and almost the only defence against the oppressor in their own sabres; therefore all Lauda, while protesting in the courts against Kmita, did not dismount for a long time, ready to resist force with force.

But a month passed, and no tidings of Kmita. People began to breathe with greater freedom. The more powerful nobility withdrew the armed servants whom they had sent to Vodokty as a guard. The lesser nobles were yearning for their labors and occupations at home, and they too dispersed by degrees. But when warlike excitement calmed down, as time passed, an increased desire came to that indigent nobility to overcome the absent man with law and to redress their wrongs before the tribunals. For although decisions could not reach Kmita himself, Lyubich remained a large and handsome estate, a ready reward and a payment for losses endured. Meanwhile Panna Aleksandra restrained with great zeal the desire for lawsuits in the Lauda people. Twice did the elders of Lauda meet at her house for counsel; and she not only took part in these deliberations but presided over them, astonishing all with her woman's wit and keen judgment, so that more than one lawyer might envy her. The elders of Lauda wanted to occupy Lyubich with armed hand and give it to the Butryms, but "the lady" advised against this firmly.

"Do not return violence for violence," said she; "if you do, your case will be injured. Let all the innocence be on your side. He is a powerful man and has connections, he will find too in the courts adherents, and if you give the least pretext you may suffer new wrongs. Let your case be so clear that any court, even if made up of his brothers, could not decide otherwise than in your favor. Tell the Butryms to take neither tools nor cattle, and to leave Lyubich completely in peace. Whatever they need I will give them from Mitruny, where there is more than all the property that was at any time in Volmontovichi. And if Pan Kmita should appear here again, leave him in peace till there is a decision, let them make no attempt on his person. Remember that only while he is alive have you some one from whom to recover for your wrongs."

Thus spoke the wise lady with prudent intent, and they applauded her wisdom, not seeing that delay might benefit also Pan Andrei, and especially in this that it secured his life. Perhaps too Olenka wished to guard that unfortunate life against sudden attack. But the nobility obeyed her, for they were accustomed from very remote times to esteem as gospel every word that came from the mouth of a Billevich. Lyubich remained intact, and had Pan Andrei appeared he might have settled there quietly for a time. He did not appear, but a month and a half later a messenger came to the lady with a letter. He was some strange man, known to no one. The letter was from Kmita, written in the following words:—

"Beloved of my heart, most precious, unrelinquished Olenka! It is natural for all creatures and especially for men, even the lowest, to avenge wrongs done them, and when a man has suffered evil he will pay it back gladly in kind to the one who inflicted it. If I cut down those insolent nobles, God sees that I did so not through cruelty, but because they murdered my officers in defiance of laws human and divine, without regard to their youth and high birth, with a death so pitiless that the like could not be found among Cossacks or Tartars. I will not deny that wrath more than human possessed me; but who will wonder at wrath which had its origin in the blood of one's friends? The spirits of Kokosinski, Ranitski, Uhlik, Rekuts, Kulvyets, and Zend, of sacred memory; slain in the flower of their age and repute, slain without reason, put arms in my hands when I was just thinking,— and I call God to witness,—just thinking of peace and friendship with the nobles of Lauda, wishing to change my life altogether according to your pleasant counsels. While listening to complaints against me, do not forget my defence, and judge justly. I am sorry now for those people in the village. The innocent may have suffered; but a soldier avenging the blood of his brothers cannot distinguish the innocent from the guilty, and respects no one. God grant that nothing has happened to injure me in your eyes. Atonement for other men's sins and faults and my own just wrath is most bitter to me, for since I have lost you I sleep in despair and I wake in despair, without power to forget either you or my love. Let the tribunals pass sentence on me, unhappy man;

let the diets confirm the sentences, let them trumpet me forth to infamy, let the ground open under my feet, I will endure everything, suffer everything, only, for God's sake, cast me not out of your heart! I will do all that they ask, give up Lyubich, give up my property in Orsha,—I have captured rubles buried in the woods, let them take those,—if you will promise to keep faith with me as your late grandfather commands from the other world. You have saved my life, save also my soul; let me repair wrongs, let me change my life for the better; for I see that if you will desert me God will desert me, and despair will impel me to still worse deeds."

How many voices of pity rose in the soul of Olenka in defence of Pan Andrei, who can tell! Love flies swiftly, like the seed of a tree borne on by the wind; but when it grows up in the heart like a tree in the ground, you can pluck it out only with the heart. Panna Billevich was of those who love strongly with an honest heart, therefore she covered that letter of Kmita's with tears. But still she could not forget everything, forgive everything after the first word. Kmita's compunction was certainly sincere, but his soul remained wild and his nature untamed; surely it had not changed so much through those events that the future might be thought of without alarm. Not words, but deeds were needed for the future on the part of Pan Andrei. Finally, how could she say to a man who had made the whole neighborhood bloody, whose name no one on either bank of the Lauda mentioned without curses, "Come! in return for the corpses, the burning, the blood, and the tears, I will give you my love and my hand"? Therefore she answered him otherwise:—

"Since I have told you that I do not wish to know you or see you, I remain in that resolve, even though my heart be rent. Wrongs such as you have inflicted on people here are not righted either with property or money, for it is impossible to raise the dead. You have not lost property only, but reputation. Let these nobles whose houses you have burned and whom you have killed forgive you, then I will forgive you; let them receive you, and I will receive you; let them rise up for you first, then I will listen to their intercession. But as this can never be, seek happiness elsewhere; and seek the forgiveness of God before that of man, for you need it more."

Panna Aleksandra poured tears on every word of the letter; then she sealed it with the Billevich seal and took it herself to the messenger.

"Whence art thou?" asked she, measuring with her glance that strange figure, half peasant, half servant.

"From the woods, my lady."

"And where is thy master?"

"That is not permitted me to say. But he is far from here; I rode five days, and wore out my horse."

"Here is a thaler!" said Olenka. "And thy master is well?"

"He is as well, the young hero, as an aurochs."

"And he is not in hunger or poverty?"

"He is a rich lord."

"Go with God."

"I bow to my lady's feet."

"Tell thy master—wait—tell thy master—may God aid him!"

The peasant went away; and again began to pass days, weeks, without tidings of Kmita, but tidings of public affairs came worse and worse. The armies of Moscow under Hovanski spread more and more widely over the Commonwealth. Without counting the lands of the Ukraine, in the Grand Duchy of Lithuania alone, the provinces of Polotsk, Smolensk, Vitebsk, Mstislavsk, Minsk, and Novgorodek were occupied; only a part of Vilna, Brest-Litovsk, Trotsk, and the starostaship of Jmud breathed yet with free breast, but even these expected guests from day to day.

The Commonwealth had descended to the last degree of helplessness, since it was unable to offer resistance to just those forces which hitherto had been despised and which had always been beaten. It is true that those forces were assisted by the unextinguished and re-arisen rebellion of Hmelnitski, a genuine hundred-headed hydra; but in spite of the rebellion, in spite of the exhaustion of forces in preceding wars, both statesmen and warriors gave assurance that the Grand Duchy alone might be and was in a condition not only to hurl back attack, but to carry its banners victoriously beyond its own borders. Unfortunately internal dissension stood in the way of that strength, paralyzing the efforts even of those citizens who were willing to sacrifice their lives and fortunes.

Meanwhile thousands of fugitives had taken refuge in the lands still unoccupied,—both nobles and common people. Towns, villages, and hamlets in Jmud were filled with men brought by the misfortunes of war to want and despair. The inhabitants of the towns were unable either to give lodgings to all or to give them sufficient food; therefore people died not infrequently of hunger,—namely, those of low degree. Not seldom they took by force what was refused them; hence tumults, battles, and robbery became more and more common.

The winter was excessive in its severity. At last April came, and deep snow was lying not only in the forests but on the fields. When the supplies of the preceding year were exhausted and there were no new ones yet, Famine, the brother of War, began to rage, and extended its rule more and more widely. It was not difficult for the wayfarer to find corpses of men lying in the field, at the roadside, emaciated, gnawed by wolves, which having multiplied beyond example approached the villages and hamlets in whole packs. Their howling was mingled with the cries of people for charity; for in the woods, in the fields, and around the many villages as well, there gleamed in the night-time fires at which needy wretches warmed their chilled limbs; and when any man rode past they rushed after him, begging for a copper coin, for bread, for alms, groaning, cursing, threatening all at the same time. Superstitious dread seized the minds of men. Many said that those wars so disastrous, and those misfortunes till then unexampled, were coupled with the name of the king; they explained readily that the letters "J. C. K." stamped on the coins signified not only "Joannes Casimirus Rex," but also "Initium Calamitatis Regni" (beginning of calamity for the kingdom). And if in the provinces, which were not yet occupied by war, such terror rose with disorder, it is easy to understand what happened in those which were trampled by the fiery foot of war. The whole Commonwealth was distracted, torn by parties, sick and in a fever, like a man before death. New wars were foretold, both foreign and domestic. In fact, motives were not wanting. Various powerful houses in the Commonwealth, seized by the storm of dissension, considered one another as hostile States, and with them entire lands and districts formed hostile camps. Precisely such was the case in Lithuania, where the fierce quarrel between Yanush Radzivill, the grand hetman, and Gosyevski, full hetman, and also under-treasurer of Lithuania, became almost open war. On the side of the under-treasurer stood the powerful Sapyeha, to whom the greatness of the house of Radzivill had long been as salt in the eye. These partisans loaded the grand hetman with heavy reproaches indeed,—that wishing glory for himself alone, he had destroyed the army at Shklov and delivered the country to plunder; that he desired more than the fortune of the Commonwealth, the right for his house of sitting in the diets of the German Empire; that he even imagined for himself an independent crown, and that he persecuted the Catholics.

It came more than once to battles between the partisans of both sides, as if without the knowledge of their patrons; and the patrons made complaints against one another in Warsaw. Their quarrels were fought out in the diets; at home license was let loose and disobedience established. Such a man as Kmita might be sure of the protection of one of those magnates the moment he stood on his side against his opponent.

Meanwhile the enemy were stopped only here and there by a castle; everywhere else the advance was free and without opposition. Under such circumstances all in the Lauda region had to be on the alert and under arms, especially since there were no hetmans near by, for both hetmans were struggling with the troops of the enemy without being able to effect much, it is true, but at least worrying them with attacks and hindering approach to the provinces still unoccupied. Especially did Pavel Sapyeha show resistance and win glory. Yanush Radzivill, a famous warrior, whose name up to the defeat at Shklov had been a terror to the enemy, gained however a number of important advantages. Gosyevski now fought, now endeavored to restrain the advance of the enemy by negotiations; both leaders assembled troops from winter quarters and whencesoever they could, knowing that with spring war would blaze up afresh. But troops were few, and the treasury empty; the general militia in the provinces already occupied could not assemble, for the enemy prevented them. "It was necessary to think of that before the affair at Shklov," said the partisans of Grosyevski; "now it is too late." And in truth it was too late. The troops of the kingdom could not give aid, for they were all in the Ukraine and had grievous work against Hmelnitski, Sheremetyeff, and Buturlin.

Tidings from the Ukraine of heroic battles, of captured towns, of campaigns without parallel, strengthened failing hearts somewhat, and gave courage for defence. The names of the hetmans of the kingdom thundered with a loud glory, and with them the name of Stefan Charnetski was heard more and more frequently in the mouths of men; but glory could not take the place of troops nor serve as an auxiliary. The hetmans of Lithuania therefore retreated slowly, without ceasing to fight among themselves.

At last Radzivill was in Jmud. With him came momentary peace in Lauda. But the Calvinists, emboldened by the vicinity of their chief, raised their heads in the towns, inflicting wrongs and attacking Catholic churches. As an offset, the leaders of various volunteer bands and parties—it is unknown whose—who under the colors of Radzivill, Grosyevski, and Sapyeha had been ruining the country, vanished in the forests, discharged their ruffians, and let people breathe more freely.

Since it is easy to pass from despair to hope, a better feeling sprang up at once in Lauda. Panna Aleksandra lived quietly in Vodokty. Pan Volodyovski, who dwelt continually in Patsuneli, and just now had begun to return gradually to health, gave out the tidings that the king with newly levied troops would come in the spring, when the war would take another turn. The encouraged nobles began to go out to the fields with their ploughs. The snows too had melted, and on the birch-trees the first buds were opening. Lauda River overflowed widely. A milder sky shone over that region, and a better spirit entered the people.

Meanwhile an event took place which disturbed anew the quiet of Lauda, tore away hands from the plough, and let not the sabres be stained with red rust.

CHAPTER VIII.

Pan Volodyovski—a famous and seasoned soldier, though a young man—was living, as we have said, in Patsuneli with the patriarch of the place, Pakosh Gashtovt, who had the reputation of being the wealthiest noble among all the small brotherhood of Lauda. In fact, he had dowered richly with good silver his three daughters who had married Butryms, for he gave to each one a hundred thalers, besides cattle, and an outfit so handsome that not one noble woman or family had a better. The other three daughters were at home unmarried; and they nursed Volodyovski, whose arm was well at one time and sore at another, when wet weather appeared in the world. All the Lauda people were occupied greatly with that arm, for Lauda men had seen it working at Shklov and Sepyel, and in general they were of the opinion that it would be difficult to find a better in all Lithuania. The young colonel, therefore, was surrounded with exceeding honor in all the neighborhoods. The Gashtovts, the Domasheviches, the Gostsyeviches, the Stakyans, and with them others, sent faithfully to Patsuneli fish, mushrooms, and game for Volodyovski, and hay for his horses, so that the knight and his servants might want for nothing. Whenever he felt worse they vied with one another in going to Ponyevyej for a barber; in a word, all strove to be first in serving him.

Pan Volodyovski was so much at ease that though he might have had more comforts in Kyedani and a noted physician at his call, still he remained in Patsuneli. Old Gashtovt was glad to be his host, and almost blew away the dust from before him, for it increased his importance extremely in Lauda that he had a guest so famous that he might have added to the importance of Radzivill himself.

After the defeat and expulsion of Kmita, the nobility, in love with Volodyovski, searched in their own heads for counsel,

101

and formed the project of marrying him to Panna Aleksandra. "Why seek a husband for her through the world?" said the old men at a special meeting at which they discussed this question. "Since that traitor has so befouled himself with infamous deeds that if he is now alive he should be delivered to the hangman, the lady must cast him out of her heart, for thus was provision made in the will by a special clause. Let Pan Volodyovski marry her. As guardians we can permit that, and she will thus find an honorable cavalier, and we a neighbor and leader."

When this proposition was adopted unanimously, the old men went first to Volodyovski, who, without thinking long, agreed to everything, and then to "the lady," who with still less hesitation opposed it decisively. "My grandfather alone had the right to dispose of Lyubich," said she, "and the property cannot be taken from Pan Kmita until the courts punish him with loss of life; and as to my marrying, do not even mention it. I have too great sorrow on my mind to be able to think of such a thing. I have cast that man out of my heart; but this one, even though the most worthy, bring not hither, for I will not receive him."

There was no answer to such a resolute refusal, and the nobles returned home greatly disturbed. Less disturbed was Pan Volodyovski, and least of all the young daughters of Gashtovt,— Terka, Maryska, and Zonia. They were well-grown, blooming maidens, with hair like flax, eyes like violets, and broad shoulders. In general the Patsuneli girls were famed for beauty; when they went in a flock to church, they were like flowers of the field. Besides, old Gashtovt spared no expense on the education of his daughters. The organist from Mitruny had taught them reading and church hymns, and the eldest, Terka, to play on the lute. Having kind hearts, they nursed Volodyovski sedulously, each striving to surpass the others in watchfulness and care. People said that Maryska was in love with the young knight; but the whole truth was not in that talk, for all three of them, not she alone, were desperately in love with Pan Michael. He loved them too beyond measure, especially Maryska and Zonia, for Terka had the habit of complaining too much of the faithlessness of men.

It happened often in the long winter evenings that old Gashtovt, after drinking his punch, went to bed, and the maidens with Pan Michael sat by the chimney; the charming Terka spinning flax, mild Maryska amusing herself with picking down, and Zonia reeling thread from the spindle into skeins. But when Volodyovski began to tell of the wars or of wonders which he had seen in the great houses of magnates, work ceased, the girls gazed at him as at a rainbow, and one would cry out in astonishment, "Oh! I do not live in the world! Oh, my dears!" and another would say, "I shall not close an eye the whole night!"

Volodyovski, as he returned to health and began at times to use his sword with perfect freedom, was more joyous and told stories more willingly. A certain evening they were sitting as usual, after supper, in front of the chimney, from beneath which the light fell sharply on the entire dark room. They began to chat; the girls wanted stories, and Volodyovski begged Terka to sing something with the lute.

"Sing something yourself," answered she, pushing away the instrument which Volodyovski was handing her; "I have work. Having been in the world, you must have learned many songs."

"True, I have learned some. Let it be so to-day; I will sing first, and you afterward. Your work will not run away. If a woman had asked, you would not have refused; you are always opposed to men."

"For they deserve it."

"And do you disdain me too?"

"Oh, why should I? But sing something."

Volodyovski touched the lute; he assumed a comic air, and began to sing in falsetto,—

"I   have   come   to   such   places
Where no girl will have me!—"

"Oh, that is untrue for you," interrupted Maryska, blushing as red as a raspberry.

"That's a soldier's song," said Volodyovski, "which we used to sing in winter quarters, wishing some good soul to take pity on us."

"I would be the first to take pity on you."

"Thanks to you. If that is true, then I have no reason to sing longer, and I will give the lute into worthier hands."

Terka did not reject the instrument this time, for she was moved by Volodyovski's song, in which there was more cunning indeed than truth. She struck the strings at once, and with a simpering mien began,—

"For berries of elder go not to the green wood. Trust   not   a   mad   dog,   believe   not   a   young   man. Each   man   in   his   heart   bears   rank   poison; If he says that he loves thee, say No."

Volodyovski grew so mirthful that he held his sides from laughter, and cried out: "All the men are traitors? But the military, my benefactress!"

Panna Terka opened her mouth wider and sang with redoubled energy,—

"Far worse than mad dogs are they, far worse, oh, far worse!"

"Do not mind Terka; she is always that way," said Marysia.

"Why not mind," asked Volodyovski, "when she speaks so ill of the whole military order that from shame I know not whither to turn my eyes?"

"You want me to sing, and then make sport of me and laugh at me," said Terka, pouting.

"I do not attack the singing, but the cruel meaning of it for the military," answered the knight. "As to the singing I must confess that in Warsaw I have not heard such remarkable trills. All that would be needed is to dress you in trousers. You might sing at St. Yan's, which is the cathedral church, and in which the king and queen have their box."

"Why dress her in trousers?" asked Zonia, the youngest, made curious by mention of Warsaw, the king, and the queen.

"For in Warsaw women do not sing in the choir, but men and young boys,—the men with voices so deep that no aurochs could bellow like them, and the boys with voices so thin that on a violin no sound could be thinner. I heard them many a time when we came, with our great and lamented voevoda of Rus, to the election of our present gracious lord. It is a real wonder, so that the soul goes out of a man. There is a host of musicians there: Forster, famous for his subtle trills, and Kapula, and Gian Battista, and Elert, a master at the lute, and Marek, and Myelchevski,— beautiful composers. When all these are performing together in the church, it is as if you were listening to choirs of seraphim in the flesh."

"Oh, that is as true as if living!" said Marysia, placing her hands together.

"And the king,—have you seen him often?" asked Zonia.

"I have spoken with him as with you. After the battle of Berestechko he pressed my head. He is a valiant lord, and so kind that whoso has once seen him must love him."

"We love him without having seen him. Has he the crown always on his head?"

"If he were to go around every day in the crown, his head would need to be iron. The crown rests in the church, from which its importance increases; but his Grace the King wears a black cap studded with diamonds from which light flashes through the whole castle."

"They say that the castle of the king is even grander than that at Kyedani?"

"That at Kyedani! The Kyedani castle is a mere plaything in comparison. The king's castle is a tremendous building, all walled in so that you cannot see a stick of wood. Around are two rows of chambers, one more splendid than the other. In them you can see different wars and victories painted with brushes on the wall,—such as the battles of Sigismund III. and Vladislav; a man could not satisfy himself with looking at them, for everything is as if living. The wonder is that they do not move, and that those who are fighting do not shout. But not even the best artist can paint men to shout. Some chambers are all gold; chairs and benches covered with brocade or cloth of gold, tables of marble and alabaster, and the caskets, bottle-cases, clocks showing the hour of day and night, could not be described on an ox-hide. The king and queen walk through those chambers and delight themselves in plenty; in the evening they have a theatre for their still greater amusement—"

"What is a theatre?"

"How can I tell you? It is a place where they play comedies and exhibit Italian dances in a masterly manner. It is a room so large that no church is the equal of it, all with beautiful columns. On one side sit those who wish to see, and on the other the arts are exhibited. Curtains are raised and let down; some are turned with screws to different sides. Darkness and clouds are shown at one moment; at another pleasant light. Above is the sky with the sun or the stars; below you may see at times hell dreadful—"

"Oh, God save us!" cried the girls.

"—with devils. Sometimes the boundless sea; on it ships and sirens. Some persons come down from the skies; others rise out of the earth."

"But I should not like to see hell," cried Zonia, "and it is a wonder to me that people do not run away from such a terrible sight."

"Not only do they not run away, but they applaud from pleasure," said Volodyovski; "for it is all pretended, not real, and those who take farewell do not go away. There is no evil spirit in the affair, only the invention of men. Even bishops come with his Grace the King, and various dignitaries who go with the king afterward and sit down to a feast before sleeping."

"And what do they do in the morning and during the day?"

"That depends on their wishes. When they rise in the morning they take a bath. There is a room in which there is no floor, only a tin tank shining like silver, and in the tank water."

"Water, in a room—have you heard?"

"It is true; and it comes and goes as they wish. It can be warm or altogether cold; for there are pipes with spigots, running here and there. Turn a spigot and the water runs till it is possible to swim in the room as in a lake. No king has such a castle as our gracious lord, that is known, and foreign proverbs tell the same. Also no king reigns over such a worthy people; for though there are various polite nations on earth, still God in his mercy has adorned ours beyond others."

"Our king is happy!" sighed Terka.

"It is sure that he would be happy were it not for unfortunate wars which press down the Commonwealth in return for our discords and sins. All this rests on the shoulders of the king, and besides at the diets they reproach him for our faults. And why is he to blame because people will not obey him? Grievous times have come on the country,—such grievous times as have not been hitherto. Our most despicable enemy now despises us,—us who till recently carried on victorious wars against the Emperor of Turkey. This is the way that God punishes pride. Praise be to Him that my arm works well in its joints,—for it is high time to remember the country and move to the field. 'Tis a sin to be idle in time of such troubles."

"Do not mention going away."

"It is difficult to do otherwise. It is pleasant for me here among you; but the better it is, the worse it is. Let men in the Diet give wise reasons, but a soldier longs for the field. While there is life there is service. After death God, who looks into the heart, will reward best those who serve not for advancement, but through love of the country; and indeed the number of such is decreasing continually, and that is why the black hour has come."

Marysia's eyes began to grow moist; at last they were filled with tears which flowed down her rosy cheeks. "You will go and forget us, and we shall pine away here. Who in this place will defend us from attack?"

"I go, but I shall preserve my gratitude. It is rare to find such honest people as in Patsuneli. Are you always afraid of this Kmita?"

"Of course. Mothers frighten their children with him as with a werewolf."

"He will not come back, and even if he should he will not have with him those wild fellows, who, judging from what people say, were worse than he. It is a pity indeed that such a good soldier stained his reputation and lost his property."

"And the lady."

"And the lady. They say much good in her favor."

"Poor thing! for whole days she just cries and cries."

"H'm!" said Volodyovski; "but is she not crying for Kmita?"

"Who knows?" replied Marysia.

"So much the worse for her, for he will not come back. The hetman sent home a part of the Lauda men, and those forces are here now. We wanted to cut him down at once without the court. He must know that the Lauda men have returned, and he will not show even his nose."

"Likely our men must march again," said Terka, "for they received only leave to come home for a short time."

"Eh!" said Volodyovski, "the hetman let them come, for there is no money in the treasury. It is pure despair! When people are most needed they have to be sent away. But good-night! it is time to sleep, and let none of you dream of Pan Kmita with a fiery sword."

Volodyovski rose from the bench and prepared to leave the room, but had barely made a step toward the closet when suddenly there was a noise in the entrance and a shrill voice began to cry outside the door—

"Hei there! For God's mercy! open quickly, quickly!"

The girls were terribly frightened. Volodyovski sprang for his sabre to the closet, but had not been able to get it when Terka opened the door. An unknown man burst into the room and threw himself at the feet of the knight.

"Rescue, serene Colonel!—The lady is carried away!"

"What lady?"

"In Vodokty."

"Kmita!" cried Volodyovski.

"Kmita!" screamed the girls.

"Kmita!" repeated the messenger.

"Who art thou?" asked Volodyovski.

"The manager in Vodokty."

"We know him," said Terka; "he brought herbs for you."

Meanwhile the drowsy old Gashtovt came forth from behind the stove, and in the door appeared two attendants of Pan Volodyovski whom the uproar had drawn to the room.

"Saddle the horses!" cried Volodyovski. "Let one of you hurry to the Butryms, the other give a horse to me!"

"I have been already at the Butryms," said the manager, "for they are nearer to us; they sent me to your grace."

"When was the lady carried away?" asked Volodyovski.

"Just now—the servants are fighting yet—I rushed for a horse."

Old Gashtovt rubbed his eyes. "What's that? The lady carried off?"

"Yes; Kmita carried her off," answered Volodyovski. "Let us go to the rescue!" Then he turned to the messenger: "Hurry to the Domasheviches; let them come with muskets."

"Now, my kids," cried the old man suddenly to his daughters, "hurry to the village, wake up the nobles, let them take their sabres! Kmita has carried off the lady—is it possible—God forgive him, the murderer, the ruffian! Is it possible?"

"Let us go to rouse them," said Volodyovski; "that will be quicker! Come; the horses are ready, I hear them."

In a moment they mounted, as did also the two attendants, Ogarek and Syruts. All pushed on their way between the cottages of the village, striking the doors and windows, and crying with sky-piercing voices: "To your sabres, to your sabres! The lady of Vodokty is carried away! Kmita is in the neighborhood!"

Hearing these cries, this or that man rushed forth from his cottage, looked to see what was happening, and when he had learned what the matter was, fell to shouting himself, "Kmita is in the neighborhood; the lady is carried away!" And shouting in this fashion, he rushed headlong to the out-buildings to saddle his horse, or to his cottage to feel in the dark for his sabre on the wall.

Every moment more voices cried, "Kmita is in the neighborhood!" There was a stir in the village, lights began to shine, the cry of women was heard, the barking of dogs. At last the nobles came out on the road,—some mounted, some on foot. Above the multitude of heads glittered in the night sabres, pikes, darts, and even iron forks.

Volodyovski surveyed the company, sent some of them immediately in different directions, and moved forward himself with the rest.

The mounted men rode in front, those on foot followed, and they marched toward Volmontovichi to join the Butryms. The hour was ten in the evening, and the night clear, though the moon had not risen. Those of the nobles whom the grand hetman had sent recently from the war dropped into ranks at once; the others, namely the infantry, advanced with less regularity, making a clatter with their weapons, talking and yawning aloud, at times cursing that devil of a Kmita who had robbed them of pleasant rest. In this fashion they reached Volmontovichi, at the edge of which an armed band pushed out to meet them.

"Halt! who goes?" called voices from that band.

"The Gashtovts!"

"We are the Butryms. The Domasheviches have come already."

"Who is leading you?" asked Volodyovski.

"Yuzva the Footless at the service of the colonel."

"Have you news?"

"He took her to Lyubich. They went through the swamp to avoid Volmontovichi."

"To Lyubich?" asked Volodyovski, in wonder. "Can he think of defending himself there? Lyubich is not a fortress, is it?"

"It seems he trusts in his strength. There are two hundred with him. No doubt he wants to take the property from Lyubich;

they have wagons and a band of led horses. It must be that he did not know of our return from the army, for he acts very boldly."

"That is good for us!" said Volodyovski. "He will not escape this time. How many guns have you?"

"We, the Butryms, have thirty; the Domasheviches twice as many."

"Very good. Let fifty men with muskets go with you to defend the passage in the swamps, quickly; the rest will come with me. Remember the axes."

"According to command."

There was a movement; the little division under Yuzva the Footless went forward at a trot to the swamp. A number of tens of Butryms who had been sent for other nobles now came up.

"Are the Gostsyeviches to be seen?" asked Volodyovski.

"Yes, Colonel. Praise be to God!" cried the newly arrived. "The Gostsyeviches are coming; they can be heard through the woods. You know that they carried her to Lyubich?"

"I know. He will not go far with her."

There was indeed one danger to his insolent venture on which Kmita had not reckoned; he knew not that a considerable force of the nobles had just returned home. He judged that the villages were as empty as at the time of his first stay in Lyubich; while on the present occasion counting the Gostsyeviches, without the Stakyans, who could not come up in season, Volodyovski was able to lead against him about three hundred sabres held by men accustomed to battle and trained.

In fact, more and more nobles joined Volodyovski as he advanced. At last came the Gostsyeviches, who had been expected till that moment. Volodyovski drew up the division, and his heart expanded at sight of the order and ease with which the men stood in ranks. At the first glance it was clear that they were soldiers, not ordinary untrained nobles. Volodyovski rejoiced for another reason; he thought to himself that soon he would lead them to more distant places.

They moved then on a swift march toward Lyubich by the pine-woods through which Kmita had rushed the winter before. It was well after midnight. The moon sailed out at last in the sky, and lighting the woods, the road, and the marching warriors, broke its pale rays on the points of the pikes, and was reflected on the gleaming sabres. The nobles talked in a low voice of the unusual event which had dragged them from their beds.

"Various people have been going around here," said one of the Domasheviches; "we thought they were deserters, but they were surely his spies."

"Of course. Every day strange minstrels used to visit Vodokty as if for alms," said others.

"And what kind of soldiers has Kmita?"

"The servants in Vodokty say they are Cossacks. It is certain that Kmita has made friends with Hovanski or Zolotarenko. Hitherto he was a murderer, now he is an evident traitor."

"How could he bring Cossacks thus far?"

"With such a great band it is not easy to pass. Our first good company would have stopped him on the road."

"Well, they might go through the forests. Besides, are there few lords travelling with domestic Cossacks? Who can tell them from the enemy? If these men are asked they will say that they are domestic Cossacks."

"He will defend himself," said one of the Gostsyeviches, "for he is a brave and resolute man; but our colonel will be a match for him."

"The Butryms too have vowed that even if they have to fall one on the other, he will not leave there alive. They are the most bitter against him."

"But if we kill him, from whom will they recover their losses? Better take him alive and give him to justice."

"What is the use in thinking of courts now when all have lost their heads? Do you know that people say war may come from the Swedes?"

"May God preserve us from that! The Moscow power and Hmelnitski at present; only the Swedes are wanting, and then the last day of the Commonwealth."

At this moment Volodyovski riding in advance turned and said, "Quiet there, gentlemen!"

The nobles grew silent, for Lyubich was in sight. In a quarter of an hour they had come within less than forty rods of the building. All the windows were illuminated; the light shone into the yard, which was full of armed men and horses. Nowhere sentries, no precautions,—it was evident that Kmita trusted too much in his strength. When he had drawn still nearer, Pan Volodyovski with one glance recognized the Cossacks against whom he had warred so much during the life of the great Yeremi, and later under Radzivill.

"If those are strange Cossacks, then that ruffian has passed the limit."

He looked farther; brought his whole party to a halt. There was a terrible bustle in the court. Some Cossacks were giving light with torches; others were running in every direction, coming out of the house and going in again, bringing out things, packing bags into the wagons; others were leading horses from the stable, driving cattle from the stalls. Cries, shouts, commands, crossed one another in every direction. The gleam of torches lighted as it were the moving of a tenant to a new estate on St. John's Eve.

Kryshtof, the oldest among the Domasheviches, pushed up to Volodyovski and said, "They want to pack all Lyubich into wagons."

"They will take away," answered Volodyovski, "neither Lyubich nor their own skins. I do not recognize Kmita, who is an experienced soldier. There is not a single sentry."

"Because he has great force,—it seems to me more than three hundred strong. If we had not returned he might have passed with the wagons through all the villages."

"Is this the only road to the house?" asked Volodyovski.

"The only one, for in the rear are ponds and swamps."

"That is well. Dismount!"

Obedient to this command, the nobles sprang from their saddles. The rear ranks of infantry deployed in a long line, and began to surround the house and the buildings. Volodyovski with the main division advanced directly on the gate.

"Wait the command!" said he, in a low voice. "Fire not before the order."

A few tens of steps only separated the nobles from the gate when they were seen at last from the yard. Men sprang at once to the fence, bent forward, and peering carefully into the darkness, called threateningly, "Hei! Who are there?"

"Halt!" cried Volodyovski; "fire!"

Shots from all the guns which the nobles carried thundered together; but the echo had not come back from the building when the voice of Volodyovski was heard again: "On the run!"

"Kill! slay!" cried the Lauda men, rushing forward like a torrent.

The Cossacks answered with shots, but they had not time to reload. The throng of nobles rushed against the gate, which soon fell before the pressure of armed men. A struggle began to rage in the yard, among the wagons, horses, and bags. The powerful Butryms, the fiercest in hand-to-hand conflict and the most envenomed against Kmita, advanced in line. They went like a herd of stags bursting through a growth of young trees, breaking, trampling, destroying, and cutting wildly. Alter them rolled the Domasheviches and the Gostsyeviches.

Kmita's Cossacks defended themselves manfully from behind the wagons and packs; they began to fire too from all the windows of the house and from the roof,—but rarely, for the trampled torches were quenched, and it was difficult to distinguish their own from the enemy. After a while the Cossacks were pushed from the yard and the house to the stables; cries for quarter were heard. The nobles had triumphed.

But when they were alone in the yard, fire from the house increased at once. All the windows were bristling with muskets, and a storm of bullets began to fall on the yard. The greater part of the Cossacks had taken refuge in the house.

"To the doors!" cried Volodyovski.

In fact, the discharges from the windows and from the roof could not injure those at the very walls. The position, however, of the besiegers was difficult. They could not think of storming the windows, for fire would greet them straight in the face. Volodyovski therefore commanded to hew down the doors. But that was not easy, for they were bolts rather than doors, made of oak pieces fixed crosswise and fastened with many gigantic nails, on the strong heads of which axes were dented without breaking the doors. The most powerful men pushed then from time to time with their shoulders, but in vain. Behind the doors wore iron bars, and besides they were supported inside by props. But the Butryms hewed with rage. At the doors of the kitchen leading also to the storehouse the Domasheviches and Gashtovts were storming.

After vain efforts of an hour the men at the axes were relieved. Some cross-pieces had fallen, but in place of them appeared gun-barrels. Shots sounded again. Two Butryms fell to the ground with pierced breasts. The others, instead of being put to disorder, hewed still more savagely.

By command of Volodyovski the openings were stopped with bundles of coats. Now in the direction of the road new shouts were heard from the Stakyans, who had come to the aid of their brethren; and following them were armed peasants from Vodokty.

The arrival of these reinforcements had evidently disturbed the besieged, for straightway a voice behind the door called loudly: "Stop there! do not hew! listen! Stop, a hundred devils take you! let us talk."

Volodyovski gave orders to stop the work and asked; "Who is speaking?"

"The banneret of Orsha, Kmita; and with whom am I speaking?"

"Col. Michael Volodyovski."

"With the forehead!" answered the voice from behind the door.

"There is no time for greetings. What is your wish?"

"It would be more proper for me to ask what you want. You do not know me, nor I you; why attack me?"

"Traitor!" cried Volodyovski. "With me are the men of Lauda who have returned from the war, and they have accounts with you for robbery, for blood shed without cause and for the lady whom you have carried away. But do you know what *raptus puellæ* means? You must yield your life."

A moment of silence followed.

"You would not call me traitor a second time," said Kmita, "were it not for the door between us."

"Open it, then! I do not hinder."

"More than one dog from Lauda will cover himself with his legs before it is open. You will not take me alive."

"Then we will drag you out dead, by the hair. All one to us!"

"Listen with care, note what I tell you! If you do not let us go, I have a barrel of powder here, and the match is burning already. I'll blow up the house and all who are in it with myself, so help me God! Come now and take me!"

This time a still longer silence followed. Volodyovski sought an answer in vain. The nobles began to look at one another in fear. There was so much wild energy in the words of Kmita that all believed his threat. The whole victory might be turned into dust by one spark, and Panna Billevich lost forever.

"For God's sake!" muttered one of the Butryms, "he is a madman. He is ready to do what he says."

Suddenly a happy thought came to Volodyovski, as it seemed to him. "There is another way!" cried he. "Meet me, traitor, with a sabre. If you put me down, you will go away in freedom."

For a time there was no answer. The hearts of the Lauda men beat unquietly.

"With a sabre?" asked Kmita, at length. "Can that be?"

"If you are not afraid, it will be."

"The word of a cavalier that I shall go away in freedom?"

"The word—"

"Impossible!" cried a number of voices among the Butryms.

"Quiet, a hundred devils!" roared Volodyovski; "if not, then let him blow you up with himself."

The Butryms were silent; after a while one of them said, "Let it be as you wish."

"Well, what is the matter there?" asked Kmita, derisively. "Do the gray coats agree?"

"Yes, and they will take oath on their swords, if you wish."

"Let them take oath."

"Come together, gentlemen, come together!" cried Volodyovski to the nobles who were standing under the walls and surrounding the whole house.

After a while all collected at the main door, and soon the news that Kmita wanted to blow himself up with powder spread on every side. They were as if petrified with terror. Meanwhile Volodyovski raised his voice and said amid silence like that of the grave,—

"I take you all present here to witness that I have challenged Pan Kmita, the banneret of Orsha, to a duel, and I have promised that if he puts me down he shall go hence in freedom, without obstacle from you; to this you must swear on your sword-hilts, in the name of God and the holy cross—"

"But wait!" cried Kmita,—"in freedom with all my men, and I take the lady with me."

"The lady will remain here," answered Volodyovski, "and the men will go as prisoners to the nobles."

"That cannot be."

"Then blow yourself up with powder! We have already mourned for her; as to the men, ask them what they prefer."

Silence followed.

"Let it be so," said Kmita, after a time. "If I do not take her to-day, I will in a month. You will not hide her under the ground! Take the oath!"

"Take the oath!" repeated Volodyovski.

"We swear by the Most High God and the Holy Cross. Amen!"

"Well, come out, come out!" cried Volodyovski.

"You are in a hurry to the other world?"

"No matter, no matter, only come out quickly."

The iron bars holding the door on the inside began to groan.

Volodyovski pushed back, and with him the nobles, to make room. Soon the door opened, and in it appeared Pan Andrei, tall, straight as a poplar. The dawn was already coming, and the first pale light of day fell on his daring, knightly, and youthful face. He stopped in the door, looked boldly on the crowd of nobles, and said,—

"I have trusted in you. God knows whether I have done well, but let that go. Who here is Pan Volodyovski?"

The little colonel stepped forward. "I am!" answered he.

"Oh! you are not like a giant," said Kmita, with sarcastic reference to Volodyovski's stature, "I expected to find a more considerable figure, though I must confess you are evidently a soldier of experience."

"I cannot say the same of you, for you have neglected sentries. If you are the same at the sabre as at command, I shall not have work."

"Where shall we fight?" asked Kmita, quickly.

"Here,—the yard is as level as a table."

"Agreed! Prepare for death."

"Are you so sure?"

"It is clear that you have never been in Orsha, since you doubt. Not only am I sure, but I am sorry, for I have heard of you as a splendid soldier. Therefore I say for the last time, let me go! We do not know each other; why should we stand the one in the way of the other? Why attack me? The maiden is mine by the will, as well as this property; and God knows I am only seeking my own. It is true that I cut down the nobles in Volmontovichi, but let God decide who committed the first wrong. Whether my officers were men of violence or not, we need not discuss; it is enough that they did no harm to any one here, and they were slaughtered to the last man because they wanted to dance with girls in a public house. Well, let blood answer blood! After that my soldiers were cut to pieces. I swear by the wounds of God that I came to these parts without evil intent, and how was I received? But let wrong balance wrong, I will still add from my own and make losses good in neighbor fashion. I prefer that to another way."

"And what kind of people have you here? Where did you get these assistants?" asked Volodyovski.

"Where I got them I got them. I did not bring them against the country, but to obtain my own rights."

"Is that the kind of man you are? So for private affairs you have joined the enemy. And with what have you paid him for this service, if not with treason? No, brother, I should not hinder you from coming to terms with the nobles, but to call in the enemy is another thing. You will not creep out. Stand up now, stand up, or I shall say that you are a coward, though you give yourself out as a master from Orsha."

"You would have it," said Kmita, taking position.

But Volodyovski did not hurry, and not taking his sabre out yet, he looked around on the sky. Day was already coming in the east. The first golden and azure stripes were extended in a belt of light, but in the yard it was still gloomy enough, and just in front of the house complete darkness reigned.

"The day begins well," said Volodyovski, "but the sun will not rise soon. Perhaps you would wish to have light?"

"It is all one to me."

"Gentlemen!" cried Volodyovski, turning to the nobles, "go for some straw and for torches; it will be clearer for us in this Orsha dance."

The nobles, to whom this humorous tone of the young colonel gave wonderful consolation, rushed quickly to the kitchen. Some of them fell to collecting the torches trampled at

121

the time of the battle, and in a little while nearly fifty red flames were gleaming in the semi-darkness of the early morning.

Volodyovski showed them with his sabre to Kmita. "Look, a regular funeral procession!"

And Kmita answered at once: "They are burying a colonel, so there must be parade."

"You are a dragon!"

Meanwhile the nobles formed in silence a circle around the knights, and raised the burning torches aloft; behind them others took their places, curious and disquieted; in the centre the opponents measured each other with their eyes. A grim silence began; only burned coals fell with a crackle to the ground. Volodyovski was as lively as a goldfinch on a bright morning.

"Begin!" said Kmita.

The first clash raised an echo in the heart of every onlooker. Volodyovski struck as if unwillingly; Kmita warded and struck in his turn; Volodyovski warded. The dry clash grew more rapid. All held breath. Kmita attacked with fury. Volodyovski put his left hand behind his back and stood quietly, making very careless, slight, almost imperceptible movements; it seemed that he wished merely to defend himself, and at the same time spare his opponent. Sometimes he pushed a short step backward, again he advanced; apparently he was studying the skill of Kmita. Kmita was growing heated; Volodyovski was cool as a master testing his pupil, and all the time calmer and calmer. At last, to the great surprise of the nobles, he said,—

"Now let us talk; it will not last long. Ah, ha! is that the Orsha method? 'Tis clear that you must have threshed peas there, for you strike like a man with a flail. Terrible blows! Are they really the best in Orsha? That thrust is in fashion only among tribunal police. This is from Courland, good to chase dogs with.

Look to the end of your sabre! Don't bend your hand so, for see what will happen! Raise your sabre!"

Volodyovski pronounced the last words with emphasis; at the same time he described a half-circle, drew the hand and sabre toward him, and before the spectators understood what "raise" meant, Kmita's sabre, like a needle pulled from a thread, flew above Volodyovski's head and fell behind his shoulders; then he said,—

"That is called shelling a sabre."

Kmita stood pale, wild-eyed, staggering, astonished no less than the nobles of Lauda; the little colonel pushed to one side, and repeated again,—

"Take your sabre!"

For a time it seemed as if Kmita would rush at him with naked hands. He was just ready for the spring, when Volodyovski put his hilt to his own breast, presenting the point. Kmita rushed to take his own sabre, and fell with it again on his terrible opponent.

A loud murmur rose from the circle of spectators, and the ring grew closer and closer. Kmita's Cossacks thrust their heads between the shoulders of the nobles, as if they had lived all their lives in the best understanding with them. Involuntarily shouts were wrested from the mouths of the onlookers; at times an outburst of unrestrained, nervous laughter was heard; all acknowledged a master of masters.

Volodyovski amused himself cruelly like a cat with a mouse, and seemed to work more and more carelessly with the sabre. He took his left hand from behind his back and thrust it into his trousers' pocket. Kmita was foaming at the mouth, panting heavily; at last hoarse words came from his throat through his set lips,—

"Finish—spare the shame!"

"Very well!" replied Volodyovski.

A short terrible whistle was heard, then a smothered cry. At the same moment Kmita threw open his arms, his sabre dropped to the ground, and he fell on his face at the feet of the colonel.

"He lives!" said Volodyovski; "he has not fallen on his back!" And doubling the skirt of Kmita's coat, he began to wipe his sabre.

The nobles shouted with one voice, and in those shouts thundered with increasing clearness: "Finish the traitor! finish him! cut him to pieces!"

A number of Butryms ran up with drawn sabres. Suddenly something wonderful happened,—and one would have said that little Volodyovski had grown tall before their eyes: the sabre of the nearest Butrym flew out of his hand after Kmita's, as if a whirlwind had caught it, and Volodyovski shouted with flashing eyes,—

"Stand back, stand back! He is mine now, not yours! Be off!"

All were silent, fearing the anger of that man; and he said: "I want no shambles here! As nobles you should understand knightly customs, and not slaughter the wounded. Enemies do not do that, and how could a man in a duel kill his prostrate opponent?"

"He is a traitor!" muttered one of the Butryms. "It is right to kill such a man."

"If he is a traitor he should be given to the hetman to suffer punishment and serve as an example to others. But as I have said, he is mine now, not yours. If he recovers you will be free to get your rights before a court, and it will be easier to obtain satisfaction from a living than a dead man. Who here knows how to dress wounds?"

"Krysh Domashevich. He has attended to all in Lauda for years."

"Let him dress the man at once, then take him to bed, and I will go to console the ill-fated lady."

So saying, Volodyovski put his sabre into the scabbard. The nobles began to seize and bind Kmita's men, who henceforth were to plough land in the villages. They surrendered without resistance; only a few who had escaped through the rear windows of the house ran toward the ponds, but they fell into the hands of the Stakyans who were stationed there. At the same time the nobles fell to plundering the wagons, in which they found quite a plentiful booty; some of them gave advice to sack the house, but they feared Pan Volodyovski, and perhaps the presence of Panna Billevich restrained the most daring. Their own killed, among whom were three Butryms and two Domasheviches, the nobles put into wagons, so as to bury them according to Christian rites. They ordered the peasants to dig a ditch for Kmita's dead behind the garden.

Volodyovski in seeking the lady burst through the whole house, and found her at last in the treasure-chamber situated in a corner to which a low and narrow door led from the sleeping-room. It was a small chamber, with narrow, strongly barred windows, built in a square and with such mighty walls, that Volodyovski saw at once that even if Kmita had blown up the house with powder that room would have surely remained unharmed. This gave him a better opinion of Kmita. The lady was sitting on a chest not far from the door, with her head drooping, and her face almost hidden by her hair. She did not raise it when she heard the knight coming. She thought beyond doubt that it was Kmita himself or some one of his people. Pan Volodyovski stood in the door, coughed once, a second time, and seeing no result from that, said,—

125

"My lady, you are free!"

"From under the drooping hair blue eyes looked at the knight, and then a comely face appeared, though pale and as it were not conscious. Volodyovski was hoping for thanks, an outburst of gladness; but the lady sat motionless, distraught, and merely looked at him. Therefore the knight spoke again,—

"Come to yourself, my lady! God has regarded innocence,—you are free, and can return to Vodokty."

This time there was more consciousness in the look of Panna Billevich. She rose from the chest, shook back her hair, and asked, "Who are you?"

"Michael Volodyovski, colonel of dragoons with the voevoda of Vilna."

"Did I hear a battle—shots? Tell me."

"Yes. We came to save you."

She regained her senses completely. "I thank you," said she hurriedly, with a low voice, through which a mortal disquiet was breaking. "But what happened to him?"

"To Kmita? Fear not, my lady! He is lying lifeless in the yard; and without praising myself I did it."

Volodyovski uttered this with a certain boastfulness; but if he expected admiration he deceived himself terribly. She said not a word, but tottered and began to seek support behind with her hands. At last she sat heavily on the same chest from which she had risen a moment before.

The knight sprang to her quickly: "What is the matter, my lady?"

"Nothing, nothing—wait, permit me. Then is Pan Kmita killed?"

"What is Pan Kmita to me?" interrupted Volodyovski; "it is a question here of you."

126

That moment her strength came back; for she rose again, and looking him straight in the eyes, screamed with anger, impatience, and despair: "By the living God, answer! Is he killed?"

"Pan Kmita is wounded," answered the astonished Volodyovski.

"Is he alive?"

"He is alive."

"It is well! I thank you."

And with step still tottering she moved toward the door. Volodyovski stood for a while moving his mustaches violently and shaking his head; then he muttered to himself, "Does she thank me because Kmita is wounded, or because he is alive?"

He followed Olenka, and found her in the adjoining bed room standing in the middle of it as if turned to stone. Four nobles were bearing in at that moment Pan Kmita; the first two advancing sidewise appeared in the door, and between them hung toward the floor the pale head of Pan Andrei, with closed eyes, and clots of black blood in his hair.

"Slowly," said Krysh Domashevich, walking behind, "slowly across the threshold. Let some one hold his head. Slowly!"

"With what can we hold it when our hands are full?" answered those in front.

At that moment Panna Aleksandra approached them, pale as was Kmita himself, and placed both hands under his lifeless head.

"This is the lady," said Krysh Domashevich.

"It is I. Be careful!" answered she, in a low voice.

Volodyovski looked on, and his mustaches quivered fearfully.

Meanwhile they placed Kmita on the bed. Krysh Domashevich began to wash his head with water; then he fixed a plaster previously prepared to the wound, and said,—

"Now let him lie quietly. Oh, that's an iron head not to burst from such a blow! He may recover, for he is young. But he got it hard."

Then he turned to Olenka: "Let me wash your hands,— here is water. A kind heart is in you that you were not afraid to put blood on yourself for that man."

Speaking thus, he wiped her palms with a cloth; but she grew pale and changed in the eyes.

Volodyovski sprang to her again: "There is nothing here for you, my lady. You have shown Christian charity to an enemy; return home." And he offered her his arm.

She however, did not look at him, but turning to Krysh Domashevich, said, "Pan Kryshtof, conduct me."

Both went out, and Volodyovski followed them. In the yard the nobles began to shout at sight of her, and cry, "Vivat!" But she went forward, pale, staggering, with compressed lips, and with fire in her eyes.

"Long life to our lady! Long life to our colonel!" cried powerful voices.

An hour later Volodyovski returned at the head of the Lauda men toward the villages. The sun had risen already; the early morning in the world was gladsome, a real spring morning. The Lauda men clattered forward in a formless crowd along the highway, discussing the events of the night and praising Volodyovski to the skies; but he rode on thoughtful and silent. Those eyes looking from behind the dishevelled hair did not leave his mind, nor that slender form, imposing though bent by grief and pain.

128

"It is a marvel what a wonder she is," said he to himself,—
"a real princess! I have saved her honor and surely her life, for
though the powder would not have blown up the treasure-room
she would have died of pure fright. She ought to be grateful. But
who can understand a fair head? She looked on me as on some
serving-lad, I know not whether from haughtiness or perplexity."

CHAPTER IX.

These thoughts did not let Volodyovski sleep on the night
following. For a number of days he was thinking continually of
Panna Aleksandra, and saw that she had dropped deeply into his
heart. Besides, the Lauda nobles wished to bring about a marriage
between them. It is true that she had refused him without
hesitation, but at that time she neither knew him nor had seen him.
Now it was something quite different. He had wrested her in
knightly fashion from the hands of a man of violence, had
exposed himself to bullets and sabres, had captured her like a
fortress. Whose is she, if not his? Can she refuse him anything,
even her hand? Well, shall he not try? Perhaps affection has begun
in her from gratitude, since it happens often in the world that the
rescued lady gives straightway her hand to her rescuer. If she has
not conceived an affection for him as yet, it behooves him all the
more to exert himself in the matter.

"But if she remembers and loves the other man still?"

"It cannot be," repeated Volodyovski to himself; "if she
had not rejected him, he would not have taken her by force. She
showed, it is true, uncommon kindness to him; but it is a woman's
work to take pity on the wounded, even if they are enemies. She
is young, without guardianship; it is time for her to marry. It is
clear that she has no vocation for the cloister, or she would have
entered one already. There has been time enough. Men will annoy
such a comely lady continually,—some for her fortune, others for

her beauty, and still others for her high blood. Oh, a defence the reality of which she can see with her own eyes will be dear to her. It is time too for thee to settle down, my dear Michael!" said Volodyovski to himself. "Thou art young yet, but the years hurry swiftly. Thou wilt win not fortune in service, but rather more wounds in thy skin, and to thy giddy life will come an end."

Here through the memory of Pan Volodyovski passed a whole line of young ladies after whom he had sighed in his life. Among them were some very beautiful and of high blood, but one more charming and distinguished there was not. Besides, the people of these parts exalted that family and that lady, and from her eyes there looked such honesty that may God give no worse wife to the best man.

Pan Volodyovski felt that a prize was meeting him which might not come a second time, and this the more since he had rendered the lady such uncommon service. "Why delay?" said he to himself. "What better can I wait for? I must try."

Pshaw! but war is at hand. His arm was well. It was a shame for a knight to go courting when his country was stretching forth its hands imploring deliverance. Pan Michael had the heart of an honest soldier; and though he had served almost from boyhood, though he had taken part in nearly all the wars of his time, he knew what he owed his country, and he dreamed not of rest.

Precisely because he had served his country not for gain, reward, or praise, but from his soul, had he in that regard a clean conscience, he felt his worth, and that gave him solace. "Others were frolicking, but I was fighting," thought he. "The Lord God will reward the little soldier, and will help him this time."

But he saw that soon there would be no time for courting; there was need to act promptly, and put everything on the hazard at once,—to make a proposal on the spot, and either marry after short bans or eat a watermelon. "I have eaten more than one; I'll eat another this time," muttered Volodyovski, moving his yellow mustaches. "What harm will it do?"

But there was one side to this sudden decision which did not please him. He put the question to himself if going with a visit so soon after saving the lady he would not be like an importunate creditor who wishes a debt to be paid with usury and as quickly as possible. Perhaps it will not be in knightly fashion? Nonsense! for what can gratitude be asked, if not for service? And if this haste does not please the heart of the lady, if she looks askance at him, why, he can say to her, "Gracious lady, I would have come courting one year, and gazed at you as if I were near-sighted; but I am a soldier, and the trumpets are sounding for battle!"

"So I'll go," said Pan Volodyovski.

But after a while another thought entered his head: if she says, "Go to war, noble soldier, and after the war you will visit me during one year and look at me like a nearsighted man, for I will not give in a moment my soul and my body to one whom I know not!"

Then all will be lost! That it would be lost Pan Volodyovski felt perfectly; for leaving aside the lady whom in the interval some other man might marry, Volodyovski was not sure of his own constancy. Conscience declared that in him love was kindled like straw, but quenched as quickly.

Then all will be lost! And then wander on farther, thou soldier, a vagrant from one camp to another, from battle to battle, with no roof in the world, with no living soul of thy kindred! Search the four corners of earth when the war will be over, not knowing a place for thy heart save the barracks!

At last Volodyovski knew not what to do. It had become in a certain fashion narrow and stifling for him in the Patsuneli house; he took his cap therefore to go out on the road and enjoy the May sun. On the threshold he came upon one of Kmita's men taken prisoner, who in the division of spoils had come to old Pakosh. The Cossack was warming himself in the sun and playing on a bandura.

"What art thou doing here?" asked Volodyovski.

"I am playing," answered the Cossack, raising his thin face,

"Whence art thou?" asked Volodyovski, glad to have some interruption to his thoughts.

"From afar, from the Viahla."

"Why not run away like the rest of thy comrades? Oh, such kind of sons! The nobles spared your lives in Lyubich so as to have laborers, and your comrades all ran away as soon as the ropes were removed."

"I will not run away. I'll die here like a dog."

"So it has pleased thee here?"

"He runs away who feels better in the field; it is better for me here. I had my leg shot through, and the old man's daughter here dressed it, and she spoke a kind word. Such a beauty I have not seen before with my eyes. Why should I go away?"

"Which one pleased thee so?"

"Maryska."

"And so thou wilt remain?"

"If I die, they will carry me out; if not, I will remain."

"Dost thou think to earn Pakosh's daughter?"

"I know not."

"He would give death to such a poor fellow before he would his daughter."

"I have gold pieces buried in the woods," said the Cossack,—"two purses."

"From robbery?"

"From robbery."

"Even if thou hadst a pot of gold, thou art a peasant and Pakosh is a noble."

"I am an attendant boyar."

"If thou art an attendant boyar, thou art worse than a peasant, for thou'rt a traitor. How couldst thou serve the enemy?"

"I did not serve the enemy."

"And where did Pan Kmita find thee and thy comrades?"

"On the road. I served with the full hetman; but the squadron went to pieces, for we had nothing to eat. I had no reason to go home, for my house was burned. Others went to rob on the road, and I went with them."

Volodyovski wondered greatly, for hitherto he had thought that Kmita had attacked Olenka with forces obtained from the enemy.

"So Pan Kmita did not get thee from Trubetskoi?"

"Most of the other men had served before with Trubetskoi and Hovanski, but they had run away too and taken to the road."

"Why did you go with Pan Kmita?"

"Because he is a splendid ataman. We were told that when he called on any one to go with him, thalers as it were flowed out of a bag, to that man. That's why we went. Well, God did not give us good luck!"

Volodyovski began to rack his head, and to think that they had blackened Kmita too much; then he looked at the pale attendant boyar and again racked his head.

"And so thou art in love with her?"

"Oi, so much!"

Volodyovski walked away, and while going he thought: "That is a resolute man. He did not break his head; he fell in love and remained. Such men are best. If he is really an attendant boyar, he is of the same rank as the village nobles. When he digs up his gold pieces, perhaps the old man will give him Maryska.

133

And why? Because he did not go to drumming with his fingers, but made up his mind that he would get her. I'll make up my mind too."

Thus meditating, Volodyovski walked along the road in the sunshine. Sometimes he would stop, fix his eyes on the ground or raise them to the sky, then again go farther, till all at once he saw a flock of wild ducks flying through the air. He began to soothsay whether he should go or not. It came out that he was to go.

"I will go; it cannot be otherwise."

When he had said this he turned toward the house; but on the way he went once more to the stable, before which his two servants were playing dice.

"Syruts, is Basior's mane plaited?"

"Plaited, Colonel!"

Volodyovski went into the stable. Basior neighed at him from the manger; the knight approached the horse, patted him on the side, and then began to count the braids on his neck. "Go— not go—go." Again the soothsaying came out favorably.

"Saddle the horse and dress decently," commanded Volodyovski.

Then he went to the house quickly, and began to dress. He put on high cavalry boots, yellow, with gilded spurs, and a new red uniform, besides a rapier with steel scabbard, the hilt ornamented with gold; in addition a half breastplate of bright steel covering only the upper part of the breast near the neck. He had also a lynxskin cap with a beautiful heron feather; but since that was worn only with a Polish dress, he left it in the trunk, put on a Swedish helmet with a vizor, and went out before the porch.

"Where is your grace going?" asked old Pakosh, who was sitting on the railing.

"Where am I going? It is proper for me to go and inquire after the health of your lady; if not, she might think me rude."

"From your grace there is a blaze like fire. Every bulfinch is a fool in comparison! Unless the lady is without eyes, she will fall in love in a minute."

Just then the two youngest daughters of Pakosh hurried up on their way home from the forenoon milking, each with a pail of milk. When they saw Volodyovski they stood as if fixed to the earth from wonder.

"Is it a king or not?" asked Zonia.

"Your grace is like one going to a wedding," added Marysia.

"Maybe there will be a wedding," laughed old Pakosh, "for he is going to see our lady."

Before the old man had stopped speaking the full pail dropped from the hand of Marysia, and a stream of milk flowed along till it reached the feet of Volodyovski.

"Pay attention to what you are holding!" said Pakosh, angrily. "Giddy thing!"

Marysia said nothing; she raised the pail and walked off in silence.

Volodyovski mounted his horse; his two servants followed him, riding abreast, and the three moved on toward Vodokty. The day was beautiful. The May sun played on the breastplate and helmet of the colonel, so that when at a distance he was gleaming among the willows it seemed that another sun was pushing along the road.

"I am curious to know whether I shall come back with a ring or a melon?" said the knight to himself.

"What is your grace saying?" asked Syruts.

"Thou art a blockhead!"

Syruts reined in his horse, and Volodyovski continued: "The whole luck of the matter is that it is not the first time!"

This idea gave him uncommon comfort.

When he arrived at Vodokty, Panna Aleksandra did not recognize him at the first moment, and he had to repeat his name. She greeted him heartily, but ceremoniously and with a certain constraint; but he presented himself befittingly,—for though a soldier, not a courtier, he had still lived long at great houses, had been among people. He bowed to her therefore with great respect, and placing his hand on his heart spoke as follows:—

"I have come to inquire about the health of my lady benefactress, whether some pain has not come from the fright. I ought to have done this the day after, but I did not wish to give annoyance."

"It is very kind of you to keep me in mind after having saved me from such straits. Sit down, for you are a welcome guest."

"My lady," replied Volodyovski, "had I forgotten you I should not have deserved the favor which God sent when he permitted me to give aid to so worthy a person."

"No, I ought to thank first God, and then you."

"Then let us both thank; for I implore nothing else than this,—that he grant me to defend you as often as need comes."

Pan Michael now moved his waxed mustaches, which curled up higher than his nose, for he was satisfied with himself for having gone straight in *medias res* and placed his sentiments, so to speak, on the table. She sat embarrassed and silent, but beautiful as a spring day. A slight flush came on her cheeks, and she covered her eyes with the long lashes from which shadows fell on the pupils.

"That confusion is a good sign," thought Volodyovski; and coughing he proceeded: "You know, I suppose, that I led the Lauda men after your grandfather?"

"I know," answered Olenka. "My late grandfather was unable to make the last campaign, but he was wonderfully glad when he heard whom the voevoda of Vilna had appointed to the command, and said that he knew you by reputation as a splendid soldier."

"Did he say that?"

"I myself heard how he praised you to the skies, and how the Lauda men did the same after the campaign."

"I am a simple soldier, not worthy of being exalted to the skies, nor above other men. Still I rejoice that I am not quite a stranger, for you do not think now that an unknown and uncertain guest has fallen with the last rain from the clouds. Many people are wandering about who call themselves persons of high family and say they are in office, and God knows who they are; perhaps often they are not even nobles."

Pan Volodyovski gave the conversation this turn with the intent to speak of himself and of what manner of man he was. Olenka answered at once,—

"No one would think that of you, for there are nobles of the same name in Lithuania."

"But they have the seal Ossorya, while I am a Korchak Volodyovski and we take our origin from Hungary from a certain noble, Atylla, who while pursued by his enemies made a vow to the Most Holy Lady that he would turn from Paganism to the Catholic faith if he should escape with his life. He kept this vow after he had crossed three rivers in safety,—the same rivers that we bear on our shield."

"Then your family is not from those parts?"

"No, my lady, I am from the Ukraine of the Russian Volodyovskis, and to this time I own villages there which the enemy have occupied; but I serve in the army from youth, thinking less of land than of the harm inflicted on our country by strangers. I have served from the earliest years with the voevoda of Rus, our not sufficiently lamented Prince Yeremi, with whom I have been in all his wars. I was at Mahnovka and at Konstantinoff; I endured the hunger of Zbaraj, and after Berestechko our gracious lord the king pressed my head. God is my witness that I have not come here to praise myself, but desire that you might know, my lady, that I am no hanger-on, whose work is in shouting and who spares his own blood, but that my life has been passed in honorable service in which some little fame was won, and my conscience stained in nothing, so God be my aid! And to this worthy people can give testimony."

"Would that all were like you!" sighed Olenka.

"Surely you have now in mind that man of violence who dared to raise his godless hand against you."

Panna Aleksandra fixed her eyes on the floor, and said not a word.

"He has received pay for his deeds," continued Volodyovski, "though it is said that he will recover, still he will not escape punishment. All honorable people condemn him, and even too much; for they say that he had relations with the enemy so as to obtain reinforcements,—which is untrue, for those men with whom he attacked you did not come from the enemy, but were collected on the highway."

"How do you know that?" asked the lady, raising her blue eyes to Volodyovski.

"From the Cossacks themselves. He is a wonderful man, that Kmita; for when I accused him of treason before the duel he made no denial, though I accused him unjustly. It is clear that there is a devilish pride in him."

"And have you said everywhere that he is not a traitor?"

"I have not, for I did not know that he was not a traitor; but now I will say so. It is wrong to cast such a calumny even on our own greatest enemy."

Panna Aleksandra's eyes rested a second time on the little knight with an expression of sympathy and gratitude. "You are so honorable a man that your equal is rare."

Volodyovski fell to twitching his mustaches time after time with contentment. "To business, Michael dear!" said he, mentally. Then aloud to the lady: "I will say more: I blame Pan Kmita's method, but I do not wonder that he tried to obtain you, my lady, in whose service Venus herself might act as a maid. Despair urged him on to an evil deed, and will surely urge him a second time, should opportunity offer. How will you remain alone, with such beauty and without protection? There are more men like Kmita in the world; you will rouse more such ardors, and will expose your honor to fresh perils. God sent me favor that I was able to free you, but now the trumpets of Gradivus call me. Who will watch over you? My gracious lady, they accuse soldiers of fickleness, but unjustly. Neither is my heart of rock, and it cannot remain indifferent to so many excellent charms."

Here Volodyovski fell on both knees before Olenka. "My gracious lady," said he, while kneeling, "I inherited the command after your grandfather; let me inherit the granddaughter too. Give me guardianship over you; let me enjoy the bliss of mutual affection. Take me as a perpetual protection, and you will be at rest and free from care, for though I go to the war my name itself will defend you."

The lady sprang from the chair and heard Pan Volodyovski with astonishment; but he still spoke on:—

"I am a poor soldier, but a noble, and a man of honor. I swear to you that on my shield and on my conscience not the slightest stain can be found. I am at fault perhaps in this haste; but understand too that I am called by the country, which will not yield even for you. Will you not comfort me,—will you not give me solace, will you not say a kind word?"

"You ask the impossible. As God lives, that cannot be!" answered Olenka, with fright.

"It depends on your will."

"For that reason I say no to you promptly." Here she frowned. "Worthy sir, I am indebted to you much, I do not deny it. Ask what you like, I am ready to give everything except my hand."

Pan Volodyovski rose. "Then you do not wish me, my lady? Is that true?"

"I cannot."

"And that is your last word?"

"The last and irrevocable word."

"Perhaps the haste only has displeased you. Give me some hope."

"I cannot, I cannot."

"Then there is no success for me here, as elsewhere there was none. My worthy lady, offer not pay for services, I have not come for that; and if I ask your hand it is not as pay, but from your own good-will. Were you to say that you give it because you must, I would not take it. Where there is no freedom there is no happiness. You have disdained me. God grant that a worse do not meet you. I go from this house as I entered, save this that I shall not come here again. I am accounted here as nobody. Well, let it be so. Be happy even with that very Kmita, for perhaps you are angry because I placed a sabre between you. If he seems better to you, then in truth you are not for me."

Olenka seized her temples with her hands, and repeated a number of times: "O God! O God! O God!"

But that pain of hers made no impression on Volodyovski, who, when he had bowed, went out angry and wrathful; then he mounted at once and rode off.

"A foot of mine shall never stand there again!" said he, aloud.

His attendant Syruts riding behind pushed up at once. "What does your grace say?"

"Blockhead!" answered Volodyovski.

"You told me that when we were coming hither."

Silence followed; then Volodyovski began to mutter again: "Ah, I was entertained there with ingratitude, paid for affection with contempt. It will come to me surely to serve in the cavalry till death; that is fated. Such a devil of a lot fell to me,— every move a refusal! There is no justice on earth. What did she find against me?"

Here Pan Michael frowned, and began to work mightily with his brain; all at once he slapped his leg with his hand. "I know now," shouted he; "she loves that fellow yet,—it cannot be otherwise."

But this idea did not clear his face. "So much the worse for me," thought he, after a while; "for if she loves him yet, she will not stop loving him. He has already done his worst. He may go to war, win glory, repair his reputation. And it is not right to hinder him; he should rather be aided, for that is a service to the country. He is a good soldier, 'tis true. But how did he fascinate her so? Who can tell? Some have such fortune that if one of them looks on a woman she is ready to follow him into fire. If a man only knew how this is done or could get some captive spirit, perhaps he might effect something. Merit has no weight with a fair head. Pan Zagloba said wisely that a fox and a woman are the most treacherous creatures alive. But I grieve that all is lost. Oh, she is a terribly beautiful woman, and honorable and virtuous, as they say; ambitious as the devil,—that's evident. Who knows that she will marry him though she loves him, for he has offended and disappointed her sorely. He might have won her in peace, but he chose to be lawless. She is willing to resign everything,— marriage and children. It is grievous for me, but maybe it is worse for her, poor thing!"

Here Volodyovski fell into a fit of tenderness over the fate of Olenka, and began to rack his brain and smack his lips. At last he said,—

"May God aid her! I have no ill feeling against her! It is not the first refusal for me, but for her it is the first suffering. The poor woman can scarcely recover now from sorrows. I have put out her eyes with this Kmita, and besides have given her gall to drink. It was not right to do that, and I must repair the wrong. I wish bullets had struck me, for I have acted rudely. I will write a letter asking forgiveness, and then help her in what way I can."

Further thoughts concerning Pan Kmita were interrupted by the attendant Syruts, who riding forward again said: "Pardon, but over there on the hill is Pan Kharlamp riding with some one else."

"Where?"

"Over there!"

"It is true that two horsemen are visible, but Pan Kharlamp remained with the prince voevoda of Vilna. How dost thou know him so far away?"

"By his cream-colored horse. The whole array knows that horse anywhere."

"As true as I live, there is a cream-colored horse in view, but it may be some other man's horse."

"When I recognize the gait, it is surely Pan Kharlamp."

They spurred on; the other horsemen did the same, and soon Volodyovski saw that Pan Kharlamp was in fact approaching.

Pan Kharlamp was the lieutenant of a light-horse squadron in the Lithuanian quota. Pan Volodyovski's acquaintance of long standing, an old soldier and a good one. Once he and the little knight had quarrelled fiercely, but afterward while serving together and campaigning they acquired a love for each other. Volodyovski sprang forward quickly, and opening his arms cried,—

"How do you prosper, O Great-nose? Whence do you come?"

The officer—who in truth deserved the nickname of Great-nose, for he had a mighty nose—fell into the embraces of the colonel, and greeted him joyously; then after he had recovered his breath, he said, "I have come to you with a commission and money."

"But from whom?"

"From the prince voevoda of Vilna, our hetman. He sends you a commission to begin a levy at once, and another commission to Pan Kmita, who must be in this neighborhood."

"To Pan Kmita also? How shall we both make a levy in one neighborhood?"

"He is to go to Troki, and you to remain in these parts."

"How did you know where to look for me?"

"The hetman himself inquired carefully till the people from this place who have remained near him told where to find you. I came with sure information. You are in great and continual favor there. I have heard the prince himself say that he had not hoped to inherit anything from Prince Yeremi, but still he did inherit the greatest of knights."

"May God grant him to inherit the military success of Yeremi! It is a great honor for me to conduct a levy. I will set about it at once. There is no lack of warlike people here, if there was only something with which to give them an outfit. Have you brought much money?"

"You will count it at Patsuneli."

"So you have been there already? But be careful; for there are shapely girls in Patsuneli, like poppies in a garden."

"Ah, that is why stopping there pleased you! But wait, I have a private letter from the hetman to you."

"Then give it."

Kharlamp drew forth a letter with the small seal of the Radzivills. Volodyovski opened it and began to read:—

Worthy Colonel Pan Volodyovski,—Knowing your sincere wish to serve the country, I send you a commission to make a levy, and not as is usually done, but with great haste, for *periculum in mora* (there is danger in delay). If you wish to give us joy, then let the squadron be mustered and ready for the campaign by the end of July, or the middle of August at the latest. We are anxious to know how you can find good horses, especially since we send money sparingly, for more we could not hammer from the under-treasurer, who after his old fashion is unfriendly to us. Give one half of this money to Pan Kmita, for whom Pan Kharlamp has also a commission. We hope that he will serve us zealously. But tidings have come to our ears of his violence in Upita, therefore it is better for you to take the letter directed to him from Kharlamp, and discover yourself whether to deliver it to him or not. Should you consider the accusations against him too great, and creating infamy, then do not give it, for we are afraid lest our enemies—such as the under-treasurer, and the voevoda of Vityebsk—might raise outcries against us because we commit such functions to unworthy persons. But if you give the letter after having found that there is nothing important, let Pan Kmita endeavor to wipe away his faults by the greatest exertion in service, and in no case to appear in the courts, for he belongs to our hetman's jurisdiction,—we and no one else will judge him. Pay attention to our charge at once, in view of the confidence which we have in your judgment and faithful service.

Yanush Radzivill,

Prince in Birji and Dubinki, Voevoda of Vilna.

"The hetman is terribly anxious about horses for you," said Kharlamp, when the little knight had finished reading.

"It will surely be difficult in the matter of horses," answered Volodyovski. "A great number of the small nobility here will rally at the first summons, but they have only wretched little Jmud ponies, not very capable of service. For a good campaign it would be needful to give them all fresh horses."

"Those are good horses; I know them of old, wonderfully enduring and active."

"Bah!" responded Volodyovski, "but small, and the men here are large. If they should form in line on such horses, you would think them a squadron mounted on dogs. There is where the rub is. I will work with zeal, for I am in haste myself. Leave Kmita's commission with me, as the hetman commands; I will give it to him. It has come just in season."

"But why?"

"For he has acted here in Tartar fashion and taken a lady captive. There are as many lawsuits and questions hanging over him as he has hairs on his head. It is not a week since I had a sabre-duel with him."

"Ai!" cried Kharlamp. "If you had a sabre-duel with him, he is in bed at this moment."

"But he is better already. In a week or two he will be well. What is to be heard *de publicis*?"

145

"Evil in the old fashion. The under-treasurer, Pan Gosyevski, the full hetman, is ever quarrelling with the prince; and as the hetmans do not agree, affairs do not move in harmony. Still we have improved a little, and I think that if we had concord we might manage the enemy. God will permit us yet to ride on their necks to their own land. Gosyevski is to blame for all."

"But others say it is specially the grand hetman, Prince Radzivill."

"They are traitors. The voevoda of Vityebsk talks that way, for he and the under-treasurer are cronies this long time."

"The voevoda of Vityebsk is a worthy citizen."

"Are you on the side of Sapyeha against the Radzivills?"

"I am on the side of the country, on whose side all should be. In this is the evil,—that even soldiers are divided into parties, instead of fighting. That Sapyeha is a worthy citizen, I would say in the presence of the prince himself, even though I serve under him."

"Good people have striven to bring about harmony, but with no result," said Kharlamp. "There is a terrible movement of messengers from the king to our prince. They say that something is hatching. We expected with the visit of the king a call of the general militia; it has not come! They say that it may be necessary in some places."

"In the Ukraine, for instance."

"I know. But once Lieutenant Brohvich told what he heard with his own ears. Tyzenhauz came from the king to our hetman, and when they had shut themselves in they talked a long time about something which Brohvich could not overhear; but when they came out, with his own ears he heard the hetman say, 'From this a new war may come.' We racked our heads greatly to find what this could mean."

"Surely he was mistaken. With whom could there be a new war? The emperor is more friendly to us now than to our enemies, since it is proper for him to take the side of a civilized people. With the Swedes the truce is not yet at an end, and will not be for six years; the Tartars are helping us in the Ukraine, which they would not do without the will of Turkey."

"Well, we could not get at anything."

"For there was nothing. But, praise God, I have fresh work; I began to yearn for war."

"Do you wish to carry the commission yourself to Kmita?"

"I do, because, as I have told you, the hetman has so ordered. It is proper for me to visit Kmita now according to knightly custom, and having the commission I shall have a still better chance to talk with him. Whether I give the commission is another thing; I think that I shall, for it is left to my discretion."

"That suits me; I am in such haste for the road. I have a third commission to Pan Stankyevich. Next I am commanded to go to Kyedani, to remove the cannon which are there; then to inspect Birji and see if everything is ready for defence."

"And to Birji too?"

"Yes."

"That is a wonder to me. The enemy have won no new victories, and it is far for them to go to Birji on the boundary of Courland. And since, as I see, new squadrons are being formed, there will be men to defend even those parts which have fallen under the power of the enemy. The Courlanders do not think of war with us. They are good soldiers, but few; and Radzivill might put the breath out of them with one hand."

"I wonder too," answered Kharlamp, "all the more that haste is enjoined on me, and instructions given that if I find anything out of order I am to inform quickly Prince Boguslav Radzivill, who is to send Peterson the engineer."

"What can this mean? I hope 'tis no question of domestic war. May God preserve us from that! But when Prince Boguslav touches an affair the devil will come of the amusement."

"Say nothing against him; he is a valiant man."

"I say nothing against his valor, but there is more of the German or Frenchman in him than the Pole. And of the Commonwealth he never thinks; his only thought is how to raise the house of Radzivill to the highest point and lower all others. He is the man who rouses pride in the voevoda of Vilna, our hetman, who of himself has no lack of it; and those quarrels with Sapyeha and Gosyevski are the tree and the fruit of Prince Boguslav's planting."

"I see that you are a great statesman. You should marry, Michael dear, as soon as possible, so that such wisdom is not lost."

Volodyovski looked very attentively at his comrade. "Marry,—why is that?"

"Maybe you are going courting, for I see that you are dressed as on parade."

"Give us peace!"

"Oh, own up!"

"Let each man eat his own melons, not inquire about those of other men. You too have eaten more than one. It is just the time now to think of marriage when we have a levy on our hands!"

"Will you be ready in July?"

"At the end of July, even if I have to dig horses out of the ground. Thank God that this task has come, or melancholy would have devoured me."

So tidings from the hetman and the prospect of heavy work gave great consolation to Pan Michael; and before he reached Patsuneli, he had scarcely a thought of the rebuff which had met him an hour before. News of the commission flew quickly through the whole village. The nobles came straightway to inquire if the news was true; and when Volodyovski confirmed it, his words made a great impression. The readiness was universal, though some were troubled because they would have to march at the end of July before harvest. Volodyovski sent messengers to other neighborhoods,—to Upita, and to the most considerable noble houses. In the evening a number of Butryms, Stakyans, and Domasheviches came.

They began to incite one another, show greater readiness, threaten the enemy, and promise victory to themselves. The Butryms alone were silent; but that was not taken ill, for it was known that they would rise as one man. Next day it was as noisy in all the villages as in bee-hives. People talked no more of Pan Kmita and Panna Aleksandra, but of the future campaign. Volodyovski also forgave Olenka sincerely the refusal, comforting himself meanwhile in his heart that that was not the last one, as the love was not the last. At the same time he pondered somewhat on what he had to do with the letter to Kmita.

CHAPTER X.

A time of serious labor began now for Volodyovski,—of letter-writing and journeying. The week following he transferred his head-quarters to Upita, where he began the levy. The nobles flocked to him willingly, both great and small, for he had a wide reputation. But especially came the Lauda men, for whom horses had to be provided. Volodyovski hurried around as if in boiling water; but since he was active and spared no pains, everything went on successfully enough. Meanwhile he visited in Lyubich Pan Kmita, who had advanced considerably toward health; and though he had not risen yet from his bed, it was known that he would recover.

Kmita recognized the knight at once, and turned a little pale at sight of him. Even his hand moved involuntarily toward the sabre above his head; but he checked himself when he saw a smile on the face of his guest, put forth his thin hand, and said,—

"I thank you for the visit. This is courtesy worthy of such a cavalier."

"I have come to inquire if you cherish ill feeling against me," said Pan Michael.

"I have no ill feeling; for no common man overcame me, but a swordsman of the first degree. Hardly have I escaped."

"And how is your health?"

"It is surely a wonder to you that I have come out alive. I confess myself that it is no small exploit." Here Kmita laughed. "Well, the affair is not lost. You may finish me at your pleasure."

"I have not come with such intent—"

"You must be the devil," interrupted Kmita, "or must have a captive spirit. God knows I am far from self-praise at this moment, for I am returning from the other world; but before meeting you I thought, 'If I am not the best sabre in the Commonwealth, I am the second.' But I could not have warded off the first blow if you had not wished it. Tell me where did you learn so much?"

"I had some little innate capacity, and my father taught me from boyhood. He said many a time, 'God has given you insignificant stature; if men do not fear you, they will laugh at you.' Later on, while serving with the voevoda of Rus, I finished my course. With him were a few men who could stand boldly before me."

"But could there be such?"

150

"There could, for there were. There was Pan Podbipienta, a Lithuanian of high birth, who fell at Zbaraj,—the Lord light his soul!—a man of such strength that there were no means to stop him, for he could cut through opponent and weapons. Then there was Skshetuski, my heartfelt friend and confidant, of whom you must have heard."

"Of course! He came out of Zbaraj, and burst through the Cossacks. So you are of such a brace, and a man of Zbaraj! With the forehead! with the forehead! Wait a moment; I have heard of you at the castle of Radzivill, voevoda of Vilna. Your name is Michael?"

"Exactly; I am Michael. My first name is Yerzi; but since Saint Michael leads the whole host of heaven, and has gamed so many victories over the banners of hell, I prefer him as a patron."

"It is sure that Yerzi is not equal to Michael. Then you are that same Volodyovski of whom it is said that he cut up Bogun?"

"I am he."

"Well, to receive a slash on the head from such a man is not a misfortune. If God would grant us to be friends! You called me a traitor, 'tis true, but you were mistaken." When he said this, Kmita frowned as if his wound caused him pain again.

"I confess my mistake," answered Volodyovski. "I do not learn that from you; your men told me. And know that if I had not learned it I should not have come here."

"Tongues have cut me and cut me," said Kmita, with bitterness. "Let come what may, I confess more than one mark is against me; but in this neighborhood men have received me ungraciously."

"You injured yourself most by burning Volmontovichi, and by the last seizure."

"Now they are crushing me with lawsuits. I am summoned to courts. They will not give a sick man time to recover. I burned

151

Volmontovichi, 'tis true, and cut down some people; but let God judge me if I did that from caprice. The same night, before the burning I made a vow to live with all men in peace, to attract to myself these homespuns around here, to satisfy the basswood barks in Upita, for there I really played the tyrant. I returned to my house, and what did I find? I found my comrades cut up like cattle, lying at the wall. When I learned that the Butryms had done this, the devil entered me, and I took stern vengeance. Would you believe why they were cut up, why they were slaughtered? I learned myself later from one of the Butryms, whom I found in the woods. Behold, it was for this,—that they wanted to dance with the women of the nobles in a public house! Who would not have taken vengeance?"

"My worthy sir," answered Volodyovski, "it is true that they acted severely with your comrades; but was it the nobles who killed them? No; their previous reputation killed them,—that which they brought with them; for if orderly soldiers had wished to dance, surely they would not have slain them."

"Poor fellows!" said Kmita, following his own thoughts, "while I was lying here now in a fever, they came in every evening through that door from the room outside. I saw them around this bed as if living, blue, hacked up, and groaning continually, 'Yendrus! give money to have a Mass for our souls; we are in torments!' Then I tell you the hair stood on my head, for the smell of sulphur from them was in the room. I gave money for a Mass. Oh, may it help them!"

A moment of silence then followed.

"As to the carrying off," continued Kmita, "no one could have told you about that; for in truth she saved my life when the nobles were hunting me, but afterward she ordered me to depart and not show myself before her eyes. What was there left for me after that?"

"Still it was a Tartar method."

"You know not what love is, and to what despair it may bring a man when he loses that which he prizes most dearly."

"I know not what love is?" cried Volodyovski, with excitement. "From the time that I began to carry a sabre I was in love. It is true that the object changed, for I was never rewarded with a return. Were it not for that, there could have been no Troilus more faithful than I."

"What kind of love can that be when the object is changing?" said Kmita.

"I will tell you something else which I saw with my own eyes. In the first period of the Hmelnitski affair, Bogun, the same who next to Hmelnitski has now the highest respect of the Cossacks, carried off Princess Kurtsevich, a maiden loved by Skshetuski above all things. That was a love! The whole army was weeping in view of Skshetuski's despair; for his beard at some years beyond twenty grew gray, and can you guess what he did?"

"I have no means of knowing."

"Well, because the country was in need, in humiliation, because the terrible Hmelnitski was triumphing, he did not go to seek the girl. He offered his suffering to God, and fought under Prince Yeremi in all the battles, including Zbaraj, and covered himself with such glory that to-day all repeat his name with respect. Compare his action with your own and see the difference."

Kmita was silent, gnawed his mustache. Volodyovski continued,—

"Then God rewarded and gave him the maiden. They married immediately after Zbaraj, and now have three children, though he has not ceased to serve. But you by making disturbance have given aid to the enemy and almost lost your own life, not to mention that a few days ago you might have lost the lady forever."

"How is that?" asked Kmita, sitting up in the bed; "what happened to her?"

"Nothing; but there was found a man who asked for her hand and wanted to marry her."

Kmita grew very pale; his hollow eyes began to shoot flames. He wanted to rise, even struggled for a moment; then cried, "Who was this devil's son? By the living God, tell me!"

"I," said Pan Volodyovski.

"You,—you?" asked Kmita, with astonishment, "Is it possible?"

"It is."

"Traitor! that will not go with you! But she—what—tell me everything. Did she accept?"

"She refused me on the spot, without thinking."

A moment of silence followed. Kmita breathed heavily, and fixed his eyes on Volodyovski, who said,—

"Why call me traitor? Am I your brother or your best man? Have I broken faith with you? I conquered you in battle, and could have done what I liked."

"In old fashion one of us would seal this with his blood,— if not with a sabre, with a gun. I would shoot you; then let the devils take me."

"Then you would have shot me, for if she had not refused I should not have accepted a second duel. What had I to fight for? Do you know why she refused me?"

"Why?" repeated Kmita, like an echo.

"Because she loves you."

That was more than the exhausted strength of the sick man could bear. His head fell on the pillows, a copious sweat came out on his forehead, and he lay there in silence.

"I am terribly weak," said he, after a while. "How do you know that she loves me?"

"Because I have eyes and see, because I have reason and observe; just after I had received the refusal my head became clear. To begin with, when after the duel I came to tell her that she was free, for I had slain you, she was dazed, and instead of showing gratitude she ignored me entirely; second, when the Domasheviches were bringing you in, she carried your head like a mother; and third, because when I visited her, she received me as if some one were giving me a slap in the face. If these explanations are not sufficient, it is because your reason is shaken and your mind impaired."

"If that is true," said Kmita, with a feeble voice, "many plasters are put on my wounds; better balsam than your words there could not be."

"But a traitor applies this balsam."

"Oh, forgive me! Such happiness cannot find place in my mind, that she has a wish for me still."

"I said that she loves you; I did not say that she has a wish for you,—that is altogether different."

"If she has no wish for me, I will break my head against the wall; I cannot help it."

"You might if you had a sincere desire of effacing your faults. There is war now; you may go, you may render important services to our dear country, you may win glory with bravery, and mend your reputation. Who is without fault? Who has no sin on his conscience? Every one has. But the road to penance and correction is open to all. You sinned through violence, then avoid it henceforth; you offended against the country by raising disturbance in time of war, save the country now; you committed wrongs against men, make reparation for them. This is a better and a surer way for you than breaking your head."

155

Kmita looked attentively at Volodyovski; then said, "You speak like a sincere friend of mine."

"I am not your friend, but in truth I am not your enemy; and I am sorry for that lady, though she refused me and I said a sharp word to her in parting. I shall not hang myself by reason of the refusal; it is not the first for me, and I am not accustomed to treasure up offences. If I persuade you to the right road, that will be to the country a service on my part, for you are a good and experienced soldier."

"Is there time for me to return to this road? How many summonses are waiting for me? I shall have to go from the bed to the court—unless I flee hence, and I do not wish to do that. How many summonses, and every case a sure sentence of condemnation!"

"Look, here is a remedy!" said Volodyovski, taking out the commission.

"A commission!" cried Kmita; "for whom?"

"For you! You need not appear at any court, for you are in the hetman's jurisdiction. Hear what the prince voevoda writes me."

Volodyovski read to Kmita the private letter of Radzivill, drew breath, moved his mustaches, and said, "Here, as you see, it depends on me either to give you the commission or to retain it."

Uncertainty, alarm, and hope were reflected on Kmita's face. "What will you do?" asked he, in a low voice.

"I will give the commission," said Volodyovski.

Kmita said nothing at first; he dropped his head on the pillow, and looked some time at the ceiling. Suddenly his eyes began to grow moist; and tears, unknown guests in those eyes, were hanging on the lashes.

"May I be torn with horses," said he at last, "may I be pulled out of my skin, if I have seen a more honorable man! If through me you have received a refusal,—if Olenka, as you say, loves me,—another would have taken vengeance all the more, would have pushed me down deeper; but you give your hand and draw me forth as it were from the grave."

"Because I will not sacrifice to personal interests the country, to which you may render notable service. But I say that if you had obtained those Cossacks from Trubetskoi or Hovanski, I should have kept the commission. It is your whole fortune that you did not do that."

"It is for others to take an example from you," said Kmita. "Give me your hand. God permit me to repay you with some good, for you have bound me in life and in death."

"Well, we will speak of that later. Now listen! There is no need of appearing before any court, but go to work. If you will render service to the Commonwealth, these nobles will forgive you, for they are very sensitive to the honor of the State. You may blot out your offences yet, win reputation, walk in glory as in sunlight, and I know of one lady who will give you a lifelong reward."

"Hei!" cried Kmita, in ecstasy, "why should I rot here in bed when the enemy is trampling the country? Hei! is there any one there? Come, boy, give me my boots; come hither! May the thunderbolts strike me in this bed if I stay here longer in uselessness!"

Volodyovski smiled with satisfaction and said, "Your spirit is stronger than your body, for the body is not able to serve you yet."

When he had said this he began to take farewell; but Kmita would not let him go, thanked him, and wished to treat him with wine. In fact, it was well toward evening when the little knight left Lyubich and directed his course to Vodokty.

"I will reward her in the best fashion for her sharp word," said he to himself, "when I tell her that Kmita will rise, not only from his bed, but from evil fame. He is not ruined yet, only very passionate. I shall comfort her wonderfully too, and I think she will meet me better this time than when I offered myself to her."

Here our honest Pan Michael sighed and muttered: "Could it be known that there is one in the world predestined to me?"

In the midst of such meditations he came to Vodokty. The tow-headed man of Jmud ran out to the gate, but made no hurry to open; he only said,—

"The heiress is not at home."

"Has she gone away?"

"She has gone away."

"Whither?"

"Who knows?"

"When will she come back?"

"Who knows?"

"Speak in human fashion. Did she not say when she would return?"

"Maybe she will not return at all, for she went away with wagons and bags. From that I think she has gone far for a long time."

"Is that true?" muttered Pan Michael. "See what I have done!"

CHAPTER XI.

Usually when the warm rays of the sun begin to break through the wintry veil of clouds, and when the first buds appear on the trees and the green fleece spreads over the damp fields, a better hope enters the hearts of men. But the spring of 1655 brought not the usual comfort to the afflicted inhabitants of the Commonwealth. The entire eastern boundary, from the north to

158

the wilderness on the south, was bound as it were by a border of flame; and the spring torrents could not quench the conflagration, but that border grew wider continually and occupied broader regions. And besides there appeared in the sky signs of evil omen, announcing still greater defeats and misfortunes. Time after time from the clouds which swept over the heavens were formed as it were lofty towers like the flanks of fortresses, which afterward rolled down with a crash. Thunderbolts struck the earth while it was still covered with snow, pine-woods became yellow, and the limbs of trees crossed one another in strange sickly figures; wild beasts and birds fell down and died from unknown diseases. Finally, strange spots were seen on the sun, having the form of a hand holding an apple, of a heart pierced through, and a cross. The minds of men were disturbed more and more; monks were lost in calculating what these signs might mean. A wonderful kind of disquiet seized all hearts.

New and sudden wars were foretold, God knows from what source. An ominous report began to circulate from mouth to mouth in villages and towns that a tempest was coming from the side of the Swedes. Apparently nothing seemed to confirm this report, for the truce concluded with Sweden had six years yet to run; and still people spoke of the danger of war, even at the Diet, which Yan Kazimir the king had called on May 19 in Warsaw.

Anxious eyes were turned more and more to Great Poland, on which the storm would come first. Leshchynski, the voevoda of Lenchytsk, and Narushevich, chief secretary of Lithuania, went on an embassy to Sweden; but their departure, instead of quieting the alarmed, increased still more the disquiet.

"That embassy smells of war," wrote Yanush Radzivill.

"If a storm were not threatening from that direction, why were they sent?" asked others.

Kanazyl, the first ambassador, had barely returned from Stockholm; but it was to be seen clearly that he had done nothing, since immediately after him important senators were sent.

However people of more judgment did not believe yet in the possibility of war. "The Commonwealth," said they, "has given no cause, and the truce endures in full validity. How could oaths be broken, the most sacred agreements violated, and a harmless neighbor attacked in robber fashion? Besides, Sweden remembers the wounds inflicted by the Polish sabre at Kirchholm and Putsk; and Gustavus Adolphus, who in western Europe found not his equal, yielded a number of times to Pan Konyetspolski. The Swedes will not expose such great military glory won in the world to uncertain hazard before an opponent against whom they have never been able to stand in the field. It is true that the Commonwealth is exhausted and weakened by war; but Prussia and Great Poland, which in the last wars did not suffer at all, will of themselves be able to drive that hungry people beyond the sea to their barren rocks. There will be no war."

To this alarmists answered again that even before the Diet at Warsaw counsel was taken by advice of the king at the provincial diet in Grodno concerning the defence of the boundary of Great Poland, and taxes and soldiers assigned, which would not have been done unless danger was near.

And so minds were wavering between fear and hope; a grievous uncertainty weighed down the spirits of people, when suddenly an end was put to it by the proclamation of Boguslav Leshchynski, commander in Great Poland, summoning the general militia of the provinces of Poznan and Kalisk for the defence of the boundaries against the impending Swedish storm.

Every doubt vanished. The shout, "War!" was heard throughout Great Poland and all the lands of the Commonwealth.

That was not only a war, but a new war. Hmelnitski, reinforced by Buturlin, was raging in the south and the east; Hovanski and Trubetskoi on the north and east; the Swede was approaching from the west! The fiery border had become a fiery wheel.

The country was like a besieged camp; and in the camp evil was happening. One traitor, Radzeyovski, had fled from it, and was in the tent of the invaders. He was guiding them to ready spoil, he was pointing out the weak sides; it was his work to tempt the garrisons. And in addition there was no lack of ill will and envy,—no lack of magnates quarrelling among themselves or angry with the king by reason of offices refused, and ready at any moment to sacrifice the cause of the nation to their own private profit; there was no lack of dissidents wishing to celebrate their own triumph even on the grave of the fatherland; and a still greater number was there of the disorderly, the heedless, the slothful, and of those who were in love with themselves, their own ease and well being.

Still Great Poland, a country wealthy and hitherto untouched by war, did not spare at least money for defence. Towns and villages of nobles furnished as many infantry as were assigned to them; and before the nobles moved in their own persons to the camp many-colored regiments of land infantry had moved thither under the leadership of captains appointed by the provincial diet from among men experienced in the art of war.

Tan Stanislav Dembinski led the land troops of Poznan, Pan Vladyslav Vlostovski those of Kostsian, and Pan Golts, a famous soldier and engineer, those of Valets. The peasants of Kalisk were commanded by Pan Stanislav Skshetuski, from a stock of valiant warriors, a cousin of the famous Yan from Zbaraj. Pan Katsper Jyhlinski led the millers and bailiffs of Konin. From Pyzdri marched Pan Stanislav Yarachevski, who had spent his

161

youth in foreign wars; from Ktsyna, Pan Pyotr Skorashevski, and from Naklo, Pan Kosletski. But in military experience no one was equal to Pan Vladyslav Skorashevski, whose voice was listened to even by the commander in Great Poland himself and the voevodas.

In three places—at Pila, Uistsie, Vyelunie—had the captains fixed the lines on the Notets, waiting for the arrival of the nobles summoned to the general militia. The infantry dug trenches from morning till evening, looking continually toward the rear to see if the wished for cavalry were coming.

The first dignitary who came was Pan Andrei Grudzinski, voevoda of Kalisk. He lodged in the house of the mayor, with a numerous retinue of servants arrayed in white and blue colors. He expected that the nobles of Kalisk would gather round him straightway; but when no one appeared he sent for Captain Stanislav Skshetuski, who was occupied in digging trenches at the river.

"Where are my men?" asked he, after the first greetings of the captain, whom he had known from childhood.

"What men?" asked Pan Stanislav.

"The general militia of Kalisk."

A smile of pain mingled with contempt appeared on the swarthy face of the soldier.

"Serene great mighty voevoda," said he, "this is the time for shearing sheep, and in Dantzig they will not pay for badly washed wool. Every noble is now at a pond washing or weighing, thinking correctly that the Swedes will not run away."

"How is that?" asked the troubled voevoda; "is there no one here yet?"

"Not a living soul, except the land infantry. And, besides, the harvest is near. A good manager will not leave home at such a season."

162

"What do you tell me?"

"But the Swedes will not run away, they will only come nearer," repeated the captain.

The pock-pitted face of the voevoda grew suddenly purple. "What are the Swedes to me? But this will be a shame for me in the presence of the other lords if I am here alone like a finger."

Pan Stanislav laughed again: "Your grace will permit me to remark," said he, "that the Swedes are the main thing here, and shame afterward. Besides, there will be no shame; for not only the nobles of Kalisk, but all other nobles, are absent."

"They have run mad!" exclaimed Grudzinski.

"No; but they are sure of this,—if they will not go to the Swedes, the Swedes will not fail to come to them."

"Wait!" said the voevoda. And clapping his hands for an attendant, he gave command to bring ink, pen, and paper; then he sat down and began to write. In half an hour he had covered the paper; he struck it with his hand, and said,—

"I will send another call for them to be here at the latest *pro die 27 praesentis* (on the 27th of the present month), and I think that surely they will wish at this last date *non deesse patriæ* (not to fail the country). And now tell me have you any news of the enemy?"

"We have. Wittemberg is mustering his troops on the fields at Dama."

"Are there many?"

"Some say seventeen thousand, others more."

"H'm! then there will not be so many of ours. What is your opinion? Shall we be able to oppose them?"

"If the nobles do not appear, there is nothing to talk about."

"They will come; why should they not come? It is a known fact that the general militia always delay. But shall we be able to succeed with the aid of the nobles?"

"No," replied Pan Stanislav, coolly. "Serene great mighty voevoda, we have no soldiers."

"How no soldiers?"

"Your grace knows as well as I that all the regular troops are in the Ukraine. Not even two squadrons were sent here, though at this moment God alone knows which storm is greater."

"But the infantry, and the general militia?"

"Of twenty peasants scarcely one has seen war; of ten, one knows how to hold a gun. After the first war they will be good soldiers, but they are not soldiers now. And as to the general militia let your grace ask any man who knows even a little about war whether the general militia can stand before regulars, and besides such soldiers as the Swedes, veterans of the whole Lutheran war, and accustomed to victory."

"Do you exalt the Swedes, then, so highly above your own?"

"I do not exalt them above my own; for if there were fifteen thousand such men here as were at Zbaraj, quarter soldiers and cavalry, I should have no fear. But with such as we have God knows whether we can do anything worth mention."

The voevoda placed his hands on his knees, and looked quickly into the eyes of Pan Stanislav, as if wishing to read some hidden thought in them. "What have we come here for, then? Do you not think it better to yield?"

Pan Stanislav spat in answer, and said: "If such a thought as that has risen in my head, let your grace give command to impale me on a stake. To the question do I believe in victory I answer, as a soldier, that I do not. But why we have come here,— that is another question, to which as a citizen I will answer. To

164

offer the enemy the first resistance, so that by detaining them we shall enable the rest of the country to make ready and march, to restrain the invasion with our bodies until we fall one on the other."

"Your intention is praiseworthy," answered the voevoda, coldly; "but it is easier for you soldiers to talk about death than for us, on whom will fall all the responsibility for so much noble blood shed in vain."

"What is noble blood for unless to be shed?"

"That is true, of course. We are ready to die, for that is the easiest thing of all. But duty commands us, the men whom providence has made leaders, not to seek our own glory merely, but also to look for results. War is as good as begun, it is true; but still Carolus Gustavus is a relative of our king, and must remember this fact. Therefore it is necessary to try negotiations, for sometimes more can be effected by speech than by arms."

"That does not pertain to me," said Pan Stanislav, dryly.

Evidently the same thought occurred to the voevoda at that moment, for he nodded and dismissed the captain.

Pan Stanislav, however, was only half right in what he said concerning the delay of the nobles summoned to the general militia. It was true that before sheep-shearing was over few came to the camp between Pila and Uistsie; but toward the 27th of June,—that is, the date mentioned in the second summons—they began to assemble in numbers considerable enough.

Every day clouds of dust, rising by reason of the dry and settled weather, announced the approach of fresh reinforcements one after another. And the nobles travelled noisily on horses, on wheels, and with crowds of servants, with provisions, with wagons, and abundance on them of every kind of thing, and so loaded with weapons that many a man carried arms of every description for three lances, muskets, pistols, sabres, double-handed swords and hussar hammers, out of use even in that time, for smashing armor. Old soldiers recognized at once by these weapons men unaccustomed to war and devoid of experience.

Of all the nobles inhabiting the Commonwealth just those of Great Poland were the least warlike. Tartars, Turks, and Cossacks had never trampled those regions which from the time of the Knights of the Cross had almost forgotten how war looked in the country. Whenever a noble of Great Poland felt the desire for war he joined the armies of the kingdom, and fought there as well as the best; but those who preferred to stay at home became real householders, in love with wealth and with ease,—real agriculturists, filling with their wool and especially with their wheat the markets of Prussian towns. But now when the Swedish storm swept them away from their peaceful pursuits, they thought it impossible to pile up too many arms, provide too great supplies, or take too many servants to protect the persons and goods of the master.

They were marvellous soldiers, whom the captains could not easily bring to obedience. For example, one would present himself with a lance nineteen feet long, with a breastplate on his breast, but with a straw hat on his head "for coolness;" another in time of drill would complain of the heat; a third would yawn, eat, or drink; a fourth would call his attendant; and all who were in the ranks thought it nothing out of the way to talk so loudly that no man could hear the command of an officer. And it was difficult to introduce discipline, for it offended the brotherhood terribly, as being opposed to the dignity of a citizen. It is true that "articles" were proclaimed, but no one would obey them.

An iron ball on the feet of this army was the innumerable legion of wagons, of reserve and draft horses, of cattle intended for food, and especially of the multitude of servants guarding the tents, utensils, millet, grits, hash, and causing on the least occasion quarrels and disturbance.

Against such an army as this was advancing from the side of Stettin and the plains on the Oder, Arwid Wittemberg, an old leader, whose youth had been passed in the thirty years' war; he came at the head of seventeen thousand veterans bound together by iron discipline.

On one side stood the disordered Polish camp, resembling a crowd at a country fair, vociferous, full of disputes, discussions about the commands of leaders, and of dissatisfaction; composed of worthy villagers turned into prospective infantry, and nobles taken straight from sheep-shearing. From the other side marched terrible, silent quadrangles, which at one beck of their leaders turned, with the precision of machines, into lines and half-circles, unfolding into wedges and triangles as regularly as a sword moves in the hands of a fencer, bristling with musket-barrels and darts: genuine men of war, cool, calm; real masters who had attained perfection in their art. Who among men of experience could doubt the outcome of the meeting and on whose side the victory must fall?

The nobles, however, were assembling in greater and greater numbers; and still earlier the dignitaries of Great Poland and other provinces began to meet, bringing bodies of attendant troops and servants. Soon after the arrival of Pan Grudzinski at Pila came Pan Kryshtof Opalinski, the powerful voevoda of Poznan. Three hundred haiduks in red and yellow uniforms and armed with muskets went before the carriage of the voevoda; a crowd of attendant nobles surrounded his worthy person; following them in order of battle came a division of horsemen with uniforms similar to those of the haiduks; the voevoda himself was in a carriage attended by a jester, Staha Ostrojka, whose duty it was to cheer his gloomy master on the road.

The entrance of such a great dignitary gave courage and consolation to all; for those who looked on the almost kingly majesty of the voevoda, on that lordly face in which under the lofty vaulting of the forehead there gleamed eyes wise and severe, and on the senatorial dignity of his whole posture, could hardly believe that any evil fate could come to such power.

To those accustomed to give honor to office and to person it seemed that even the Swedes themselves would not dare to raise a sacrilegious hand against such a magnate. Even those whose hearts were beating in their breasts with alarm felt safer at once under his wing. He was greeted therefore joyfully and warmly; shouts thundered along the street through which the retinue pushed slowly toward the house of the mayor, and all heads inclined before the voevoda, who was as visible as on the palm of the hand through the windows of the gilded carriage. To these bows Ostrojka answered, as well as the voevoda, with the same importance and gravity as if they had been given exclusively to him.

Barely had the dust settled after the passage of Opalinski when couriers rushed in with the announcement that his cousin was coming, the voevoda of Podlyasye, Pyotr Opalinski, with his brother-in-law Yakob Rozdrajevski, the voevoda of Inovratslav. These brought each a hundred and fifty armed men, besides nobles and servants. Then not a day passed without the arrival of dignitaries such as Sendzivoi Charnkovski, the brother-in-law of Krishtof Opalinski, and himself castellan of Kalisk; Maksymilian Myaskovski, the castellan of Kryvinsk; and Pavel Gembitski, the lord of Myendzyrechka. The town was so filled with people that houses failed for the lodging even of nobles. The neighboring meadows were many-colored with the tents of the general militia. One might say that all the various colored birds had flown to Pila from the entire Commonwealth. Red, green, blue, azure, white were gleaming on the various coats and garments; for leaving aside the general militia, in which each noble wore a dress different from his neighbor, leaving aside the servants of the magnates, even the infantry of each district were dressed in their own colors.

Shop-keepers came too, who, unable to find places in the market-square, built a row of booths by the side of the town, on these they sold military supplies, from clothing to arms and food. Field-kitchens were steaming day and night, bearing away in the steam the odor of hash, roast meat, millet; in some liquors were sold. Nobles swarmed in front of the booths, armed not only with swords but with spoons, eating, drinking, and discussing, now the enemy not yet to be seen, and now the incoming dignitaries, on whom nicknames were not spared.

Among the groups of nobles walked Ostrojka, in a dress made of party-colored rags, carrying a sceptre ornamented with bells, and with the mien of a simple rogue. Wherever he showed himself men came around in a circle, and he poured oil on the fire, helped them to backbite the dignitaries, and gave riddles over which the nobles held their sides from laughter, the more firmly the more biting the riddles.

On a certain midday the voevoda of Poznan himself came to the bazaar, speaking courteously with this one and that, or blaming the king somewhat because in the face of the approaching enemy he had not sent a single squadron of soldiers.

"They are not thinking of us, worthy gentlemen," said he, "and leave us without assistance. They say in Warsaw that even now there are too few troops in the Ukraine, and that the hetmans are not able to make head against Hmelnitski. Ah, it is difficult! It is pleasanter to see the Ukraine than Great Poland. We are in disfavor, worthy gentlemen, in disfavor! They have delivered us here as it were to be slaughtered."

"And who is to blame?" asked Pan Shlihtyng, the judge of Vskov.

"Who is to blame for all the misfortunes of the Commonwealth," asked the voevoda,—"who, unless we brother nobles who shield it with our breasts?"

The nobles, hearing this, were greatly flattered that the "Count in Bnino and Opalenitsa" put himself on an equality with them, and recognized himself in brotherhood; hence Pan Koshutski answered,—

"Serene great mighty voevoda, if there were more such counsellors as your grace near his Majesty, of a certainty we should not be delivered to slaughter here; but probably those give counsel who bow lower."

"I thank you, brothers, for the good word. The fault is his who listens to evil counsellors. Our liberties are as salt in the eye to those people. The more nobles fall, the easier will it be to introduce *absolutum dominium* (absolute rule)."

"Must we die, then, that our children may groan in slavery?"

The voevoda said nothing, and the nobles began to look at one another and wonder.

"Is that true then?" cried many. "Is that the reason why they sent us here under the knife? And we believe! This is not the first day that they are talking about *absolutum dominium*. But if it comes to that, we shall be able to think of our own heads."

"And of our children."

"And of our fortunes, which the enemy will destroy *igne et ferro* (with fire and sword)."

The voevoda was silent. In a marvellous manner did this leader add to the courage of his soldiers.

"The king is to blame for all!" was shouted more and more frequently.

"But do you remember, gentlemen, the history of Yan Olbracht?" asked the voevoda.

"The nobles perished for King Olbracht. Treason, brothers!"

"The king is a traitor!" cried some bold voices.

The voevoda was silent.

Now Ostrojka, standing by the side of the voevoda, struck himself a number of times on the legs, and crowed like a cock with such shrillness that all eyes were turned to him. Then he shouted, "Gracious lords! brothers, dear hearts! listen to my riddle."

With the genuine fickleness of March weather, the stormy militia changed in one moment to curiosity and desire to hear some new stroke of wit from the jester.

"We hear! we hear!" cried a number of voices.

The jester began to wink like a monkey and to recite in a squeaking voice,—

"After his brother he solaced himself with a crown and a wife,
But let glory go down to the grave with his brother.
He drove out the vice-chancellor; hence now has the fame
Of being vice-chancellor to—the vice-chancellor's wife."

"The king! the king! As alive! Yan Kazimir!" they began to cry from every side; and laughter, mighty as thunder, was heard in the crowd.

"May the bullets strike him, what a masterly explanation!" cried the nobles.

The voevoda laughed with the others, and when it had grown somewhat calm he said, with increased dignity: "And for this affair we must pay now with our blood and our heads. See what it has come to! Here, jester, is a ducat for thy good verse."

"Kryshtofek! Krysh dearest!" said Ostrojka, "why attack others because they keep jesters, when thou not only keepest me, but payest separately for riddles? Give me another ducat and I'll tell thee another riddle."

"Just as good?"

"As good, only longer. Give me the ducat first."

"Here it is!"

The jester slapped his sides with his hands, as a cock with his wings, crowed again, and cried out, "Gracious gentlemen, listen! Who is this?"

"He complains of self-seeking, stands forth as a Cato;
Instead of a sabre he took a goose's tail-feather
He wanted the legacy of a traitor, and not getting that
He lashed the whole Commonwealth with a biting rhyme.

"God grant him love for the sabre! less woe would it bring.
Of his satire the Swedes have no fear.
But he has barely tasted the hardships of war
When following a traitor he is ready to betray his king."

All present guessed that riddle as well as the first. Two or three laughs, smothered at the same instant, were heard in the assembly; then a deep silence fell.

The voevoda grew purple, and he was the more confused in that all eyes were fixed on him at that moment. But the jester looked on one noble and then on another; at last he said, "None of you gentlemen can guess who that is?"

When silence was the only answer, he turned with the most insolent mien to the voevoda: "And thou, dost thou too not know of what rascal the speech is? Dost thou not know? Then pay me a ducat."

"Here!" said the voevoda.

"God reward thee. But tell me, Krysh, hast thou not perchance tried to get the vice-chancellorship after Radzeyovski?"

"No time for jests," replied Opalinski; and removing his cap to all present: "With the forehead, gentlemen! I must go to the council of war."

"To the family council thou didst wish to say, Krysh," added Ostrojka; "for there all thy relatives will hold council how to be off." Then he turned to the nobles and imitating the voevoda in his bows, he added, "And to you, gentlemen, that's the play."

Both withdrew; but they had barely gone a few steps when an immense outburst of laughter struck the ears of the voevoda, and thundered long before it was drowned in the general noise of the camp.

The council of war was held in fact, and the voevoda of Poznan presided. That was a strange council! Those very dignitaries took part in it who knew nothing of war; for the magnates of Great Poland did not and could not follow the example of those "kinglets" of Lithuania or the Ukraine who lived in continual fire like salamanders.

In Lithuania or the Ukraine whoever was a voevoda or a chancellor was a leader whose armor pressed out on his body red stripes which never left it, whose youth was spent in the steppes or the forests on the eastern border, in ambushes, battles, struggles, pursuits, in camp or in tabors. In Great Poland at this time dignitaries were in office who, though they had marched in times of necessity with the general militia, had never held positions of command in time of war. Profound peace had put to sleep the military courage of the descendants of those warriors, before whom in former days the iron legions of the Knights of the Cross were unable to stand, and turned them into civilians,

173

scholars, and writers. Now the stern school of Sweden was teaching them what they had forgotten.

The dignitaries assembled in council looked at one another with uncertain eyes, and each feared to speak first, waiting for what "Agamemnon," voevoda of Poznan, would say.

But "Agamemnon" himself knew simply nothing, and began his speech again with complaints of the ingratitude and sloth of the king, of the frivolity with which all Great Poland and they were delivered to the sword. But how eloquent was he; what a majestic figure did he present, worthy in truth of a Roman senator! He held his head erect while speaking; his dark eyes shot lightnings, his mouth thunderbolts; his iron-gray beard trembled with excitement when he described the future misfortunes of the land.

"For in what does the fatherland suffer," said he, "if not in its sons? and we here suffer, first of all. Through our private lands, through our private fortunes won by the services and blood of our ancestors, will advance the feet of those enemies who now like a storm are approaching from the sea. And why do we suffer? For what will they take our herds, trample our harvests, burn our villages built by our labor? Have we wronged Radzeyovski, who, condemned unjustly, hunted like a criminal, had to seek the protection of strangers? No! Do we insist that that empty title 'King of Sweden,' which has cost so much blood already, should remain with the signature of our Yan Kazimir? No! Two wars are blazing on two boundaries; was it needful to call forth a third? Who was to blame, may God, may the country judge him! We wash our hands, for we are innocent of the blood which will be shed."

And thus the voevoda thundered on further; but when it came to the question in hand he was not able to give the desired advice.

They sent then for the captains leading the land infantry, and specially for Vladyslav Skorashevski, who was not only a famous and incomparable knight, but an old, practised soldier, knowing war as he did the Lord's Prayer. In fact, genuine leaders listened frequently to his advice; all the more eagerly was it sought for now.

Pan Skorashevski advised then to establish three camps,—at Pila, Vyelunie, and Uistsie,—so near one another that in time of attack they might give mutual aid, and besides this to cover with trenches the whole extent of the river-bank occupied by a half-circle of camps which were to command the passage.

"When we know," said Skorashevski, "the place where the enemy will attempt the crossing, we shall unite from all three camps and give him proper resistance. But I with the permission of your great mighty lordships, will go with a small party to Chaplinko. That is a lost position, and in time I shall withdraw from it; but there I shall first get knowledge of the enemy, and then will inform your great mighty lordships."

All accepted this counsel, and men began to move around somewhat more briskly in the camp. At last the nobles assembled to the number of fifteen thousand. The land infantry dug trenches over an extent of six miles. Uistsie, the chief position, was occupied by the voevoda of Poznan and his men. A part of the knights remained in Vyelunie, a part in Pila, and Vladyslav Skorashevski went to Chaplinko to observe the enemy.

July began; all the days were clear and hot. The sun burned on the plains so violently that the nobles hid in the woods between the trees, under the shade of which some of them gave orders to set up their tents. There also they had noisy and boisterous feasts; and still more of an uproar was made by the servants, especially at the time of washing and watering the horses which, to the number of several thousand at once, were driven thrice each day to the Notets and Berda, quarrelling and fighting for the best approach to the bank. But in the beginning there was a good spirit in the camp; only the voevoda of Poznan himself acted rather to weaken it.

If Wittemberg had come in the first days of July, it is likely that he would have met a mighty resistance, which in proportion as the men warmed to battle might have been turned into an invincible rage, of which there were often examples. For still there flowed knightly blood in the veins of these people, though they had grown unaccustomed to war.

Who knows if another Yeremi Vishnyevetski might not have changed Uistsie into another Zbaraj, and described in those trenches a new illustrious career of knighthood? Unfortunately the voevoda of Poznan was a man who could only write; he knew nothing of war.

Wittemberg, a leader knowing not merely war but men, did not hasten, perhaps on purpose. Experience of long years had taught him that a newly enrolled soldier is most dangerous in the first moments of enthusiasm, and that often not bravery is lacking to him, but soldierly endurance, which practice alone can develop. More than once have new soldiers struck like a storm on the oldest regiments, and passed over their corpses. They are iron which while it is hot quivers, lives, scatters sparks, burns, destroys, but which when it grows cold is a mere lifeless lump.

In fact, when a week had passed, a second, and the third had come, long inactivity began to weigh upon the general militia. The heat became greater each day. The nobles would not go to drill, and gave as excuse that their horses tormented by flies would not stand in line, and as to marshy places they could not live from mosquitoes. Servants raised greater and greater quarrels about shady places, concerning which it came to sabres among their masters. This or that one coming home in the evening from the water rode off to one side from the camp not to return.

Evil example from above was also not wanting. Pan Skorashevski had given notice from Chaplinko that the Swedes were not distant, when at the military council Zygmunt Grudzinski got leave to go home; on this leave his uncle Andrei Grudzinski, voevoda of Kalisk, had greatly insisted. "I have to lay down my head and my life here," said he; "let my nephew inherit after me my memory and glory, so that my services may not be lost." Then he grew tender over the youth and innocence of his nephew, praising the liberality with which he had furnished one hundred very choice soldiers; and the military council granted the prayer of the uncle.

On the morning of July 16, Zygmunt with a few servants left the camp openly for home, on the eve almost of a siege and a battle. Crowds of nobles conducted him amid jeering cries to a distance beyond the camp. Ostrojka led the party, and shouted from afar after the departing,—

"Worthy Pan Zygmunt, I give thee a shield, and as third name Deest!"

"Vivat Deest-Grudzinski!"

"But weep not for thy uncle," continued Ostrojka. "He despises the Swedes as much as thou; and let them only show themselves, he will surely turn his back on them."

The blood of the young magnate rushed to his face, but he pretended not to hear the insults. He put spurs to his horse, however, and pushed aside the crowds, so as to be away from the camp and his persecutors as soon as possible, who at last, without consideration for the birth and dignity of the departing, began to throw clods of earth at him and to cry,—

"Here is a gruda, Grudzinski! You hare, you coward!"

177

They made such an uproar that the voevoda of Poznan hastened up with a number of captains to quiet them, and explain that Grudzinski had taken leave only for a week on very urgent affairs.

Still the evil example had its effect; and that same day there were several hundred nobles who did not wish to be worse than Grudzinski, though they slipped away with less aid and more quietly. Stanislav Skshetuski, a captain from Kalisk and cousin of the famous Yan of Zbaraj, tore the hair on his head; for his land infantry, following the example of "officers," began to desert from the camp. A new council of war was held in which crowds of nobles refused absolutely to take part. A stormy night followed, full of shouts and quarrels. They suspected one another of the intention to desert. Cries of "Either all or none!" flew from mouth to mouth.

Every moment reports were given out that the voevodas were departing, and such an uproar prevailed that the voevodas had to show themselves several times to the excited multitude. A number of thousands of men were on their horses before daybreak. But the voevoda of Poznan rode between the ranks with uncovered head like a Roman senator, and repeated from moment to moment the great words,—

"Worthy gentlemen, I am with you to live and die."

He was received in some places with vivats; in others shouts of derision were thundering. The moment he had pacified the crowd he returned to the council, tired, hoarse, carried away by the grandeur of his own words, and convinced that he had rendered inestimable service to his country that night. But at the council he had fewer words in his mouth, twisted his beard, and pulled his foretop from despair, repeating,—

"Give counsel if you can; I wash my hands of the future, for it is impossible to make a defence with such soldiers."

"Serene great mighty voevoda," answered Stanislav Skshetuski, "the enemy will drive away that turbulence and uproar. Only let the cannon play, only let it come to defence, to a siege, these very nobles in defence of their own lives must serve on the ramparts and not be disorderly in camp. So it has happened more than once."

"With what can we defend ourselves? We have no cannon, nothing but saluting pieces good to fire off in time of a feast."

"At Zbaraj Hmelnitski had seventy cannon, and Prince Yeremi only a few eight-pounders and mortars."

"But he had an army, not militia,—his own squadrons famed in the world, not country nobles fresh from sheep-shearing."

"Send for Pan Skorashevski," said the castellan of Poznan. "Make him commander of the camp. He is at peace with the nobles, and will be able to keep them in order."

"Send for Skorashevski. Why should he be in Drahim or Chaplinko?" repeated Yendrei Grudzinski, the voevoda of Kalisk.

"Yes, that is the best counsel!" cried other voices.

A courier was despatched for Skorashevski. No other decisions were taken at the council; but they talked much, and complained of the king, the queen, the lack of troops, and negligence.

The following morning brought neither relief nor calm spirits. The disorder had become still greater. Some gave out reports that the dissidents, namely the Calvinists, were favorable to the Swedes, and ready on the first occasion to go over to the enemy. What was more, this news was not contradicted by Pan Shlihtyng nor by Edmund and Yatsck Kurnatovski, also Calvinists, but sincerely devoted to the country. Besides they gave final proof that the dissidents formed a separate circle and consulted with one another under the lead of a noted disturber and cruel man. Pan Rei, who serving in Germany during his youth as a volunteer on the Lutheran side, was a great friend of the Swedes. Scarcely had this suspicion gone out among the nobles when several thousand sabres were gleaming, and a real tempest rose in the camp.

"Let us punish the traitors, punish the serpents, ready to bite the bosom of their mother!" cried the nobles.

"Give them this way!"

"Cut them to pieces! Treason is most infectious, worthy gentlemen. Tear out the cockle or we shall all perish!"

The voevodas and captains had to pacify them again, but this time it was more difficult than the day before. Besides, they were themselves convinced that Rei was ready to betray his country in the most open manner; for he was a man completely foreignized, and except his language had nothing Polish in him. It was decided therefore to send him out of the camp, which at once pacified somewhat the angry multitude. Still shouts continued to burst forth for a long time,—

"Give them here! Treason, treason!"

Wonderful conditions of mind reigned finally in the camp. Some fell in courage and were sunk in grief; others walked in silence, with uncertain steps, along the ramparts, casting timid and gloomy glances along the plains over which the enemy had to approach, or communicated in whispers worse and worse news. Others were possessed of a sort of desperate, mad joy and readiness for death. In consequence of this readiness they arranged feasts and drinking-bouts so as to pass the last days of life in rejoicing. Some thought of saving their souls, and spent the nights in prayer. But in that whole throng of men no one thought of victory, as if it were altogether beyond reach. Still the enemy had not superior forces; they had more cannon, better trained troops, and a leader who understood war.

180

And while in this wise on one side the Polish camp was seething, shouting, and feasting, rising up with a roar, dropping down to quiet, like a sea lashed by a whirlwind, while the general militia were holding diets as in time of electing a king, on the other side, along the broad green meadows of the Oder, pushed forward in calmness the legions of Sweden.

In front marched a brigade of the royal guard, led by Benedykt Horn, a terrible soldier, whose name was repeated in Germany with fear. The soldiers were chosen men, large, wearing lofty helmets with rims covering their ears, in yellow leather doublets, armed with rapiers and muskets; cool and constant in battle, ready at every beck of the leader.

Karl Schedding, a German, led the West Gothland brigade, formed of two regiments of infantry and one of heavy cavalry, dressed in armor without shoulder-pieces. Half of the infantry had muskets; the others spears. At the beginning of a battle the musketeers stood in front, but in case of attack by cavalry they stood behind the spearmen, who, placing each the butt of his spear in the ground, held the point against the onrushing horses. At a battle in the time of Sigismund III. one squadron of hussars cut to pieces with their sabres and with hoofs this same West Gothland brigade, in which at present Germans served mainly.

The two Smaland brigades were led by Irwin, surnamed Handless, for he had lost his right hand on a time while defending his flag; but to make up for this loss he had in his left such strength that with one blow he could hew off the head of a horse. He was a gloomy warrior, loving battles and bloodshed alone, stern to himself and to soldiers. While other captains trained themselves in continual wars into followers of a craft, and loved war for its own sake, he remained the same fanatic, and while slaying men he sang psalms to the Lord.

181

The brigade of Westrmanland marched under Drakenborg; and that of Helsingor, formed of sharpshooters famed through the world, under Gustav Oxenstiern, a relative of the renowned chancellor,—a young soldier who roused great hopes. Fersen commanded the East Gothland brigade; the Nerik and Werland brigades were directed by Wittemberg himself, who at the same time was supreme chief of the whole army.

Seventy-two cannon pounded out furrows in the moist meadows; of soldiers there were seventeen thousand, the fierce plunderers of all Germany, and in battle they were so accurate, especially the infantry, that the French royal guard could hardly compare with them. After the regiments followed the wagons and tents. The regiments marched in line, ready each moment for battle. A forest of lances was bristling above the mass of heads, helmets, and hats; and in the midst of that forest flowed on toward the frontier of Poland the great blue banners with white crosses in the centre. With each day the distance decreased between the two armies.

At last on July 27, in the forest at the village of Heinrichsdorf, the Swedish legions beheld for the first time the boundary pillar of Poland. At sight of this the whole army gave forth a mighty shout; trumpets and drums thundered, and all the flags were unfurled. Wittemberg rode to the front attended by a brilliant staff, and all the regiments passed before him, presenting arms,—the cavalry with drawn rapiers, the cannon with lighted matches. The time was midday; the weather glorious. The forest breeze brought the odor of resin.

The gray road, covered with the rays of the sun,—the road over which the Swedish regiments had passed,—bending out of the Heinrichsdorf forest, was lost on the horizon. When the troops marching by it had finally passed the forest, their glances discovered a gladsome land, smiling, shining with yellow fields of every kind of grain, dotted in places with oak groves, in places green from meadows. Here and there out of groups of trees, behind oak groves and far away rose bits of smoke to the sky; on the grass herds were seen grazing. Where on the meadows the water gleamed widely spread, walked storks at their leisure.

A certain calm and sweetness was spread everywhere over that land flowing with milk and honey, and it seemed to open its arms ever wider and wider before the army, as if it greeted not invaders but guests coming with God.

At this sight a new shout was wrested from the bosoms of all the soldiers, especially the Swedes by blood, who were accustomed to the bare, poor, wild nature of their native land. The hearts of a plundering and needy people rose with desire to gather those treasures and riches which appeared before their eyes. Enthusiasm seized the ranks.

But the soldiers, tempered in the fire of the Thirty Years' War, expected that this would not come to them easily; for that grainland was inhabited by a numerous and a knightly people, who knew how to defend it. The memory was still living in Sweden of the terrible defeat of Kirchholm, where three thousand cavalry under Hodkyevich ground into dust eighteen thousand of the best troops of Sweden. In the cottages of West Gothland, Smaland, or Delakarlia they told tales of those winged knights, as of giants from a saga. Fresher still was the memory of the struggles in the time of Gustavus Adolphus, for the warriors were not yet extinct who had taken part in them. But that eagle of Scandinavia, ere he had flown twice through all Germany, broke his talons on the legions of Konyetspolski.

Therefore with the gladness there was joined in the hearts of the Swedes a certain fear, of which the supreme chief, Wittemberg himself, was not free. He looked on the passing regiments of infantry and cavalry with the eye with which a shepherd looks on his flock; then he turned to the rear man, who wore a hat with a feather, and a light-colored wig falling to his shoulders.

"Your grace assures me," said he, "that with these forces it is possible to break the army occupying Uistsie?"

The man with the light wig smiled and answered: "Your grace may rely completely on my words, for which I am ready to pledge my head. If at Uistsie there were regular troops and some one of the hetmans, I first would give counsel not to hasten, but to wait till his royal Grace should come with the whole army; but against the general militia and those gentlemen of Great Poland our forces will be more than sufficient."

"But have not reinforcements come to them?"

"Reinforcements have not come for two reasons,—first, because all the regular troops, of which there are not many, are occupied in Lithuania and the Ukraine; second, because in Warsaw neither the King Yan Kazimir, the chancellor, nor the senate will believe to this moment that his royal Grace Karl Gustav has really begun war in spite of the truce, and notwithstanding the last embassies and his readiness to compromise. They are confident that peace will be made at the last hour,—ha, ha!"

Here the rear man removed his hat, wiped the sweat from his red face, and added: "Trubetskoi and Dolgoruki in Lithuania, Hmelnitski in the Ukraine, and we entering Great Poland,— behold what the government of Yan Kazimir has led to."

Wittemberg gazed on him with a look of astonishment, and asked, "But, your grace, do you rejoice at the thought?"

"I rejoice at the thought, for my wrong and my innocence will be avenged; and besides I see, as on the palm of my hand, that the sabre of your grace and my counsels will place that new and most beautiful crown in the world on the head of Karl Gustav."

Wittemberg turned his glance to the distance, embraced with it the oak-groves, the meadows, the grain-fields, and after a while said: "True, it is a beautiful country and fertile. Your grace may be sure that after the war the king will give the chancellorship to no one else but you."

The man in the rear removed his cap a second time. "And I, for my part, wish to have no other lord," added he, raising his eyes to heaven.

The heavens were clear and fair; no thunderbolt fell and crashed to the dust the traitor who delivered his country, groaning under two wars already and exhausted, to the power of the enemy on that boundary.

The man conversing with Wittemberg was Hieronim Kailzeyovski, late under-chancellor of the Crown, now sold to Sweden in hostility to his country.

They stood a time in silence. Meanwhile the last two brigades, those of Nerik and Wermland, passed the boundary; after them others began to draw in the cannon; the trumpets still played unceasingly; the roar and rattle of drums outsounded the tramp of the soldiers, and filled the forest with ominous echoes. At last the staff moved also. Radzeyovski rode at the side of Wittemberg.

"Oxenstiern is not to be seen," said Wittemberg. "I am afraid that something may have happened to him. I do not know whether it was wise to send him as a trumpeter with letters to Uistsie."

"It was wise," answered Radzeyovski, "for he will look at the camp, will see the leaders, and learn what they think there; and this any kind of camp-follower could not do."

"But if they recognize him?"

"Rei alone knows him, and he is ours. Besides, even if they should recognize him, they will do him no harm, but will give him supplies for the road and reward him. I know the Poles, and I know they are ready for anything, merely to show themselves polite people before strangers. Our whole effort is to win the praise of strangers. Your grace may be at rest concerning Oxenstiern, for a hair will not fall from his head. He has not come because it is too soon for his return."

"And does your grace think our letters will have any effect?"

Radzeyovski laughed. "If your grace permits, I will foretell what will happen. The voevoda of Poznan is a polished and learned man, therefore he will answer us very courteously and very graciously; but because he loves to pass for a Roman, his answer will be terribly Roman. He will say, to begin with, that he would rather shed the last drop of his blood than surrender, that death is better than dishonor, and the love which he bears his country directs him to fall for her on the boundary."

Radzeyovski laughed still louder. The stern face of Wittemberg brightened also.

"Your grace does not think that he will be ready to act as he writes?" asked Wittemberg.

"He?" answered Radzeyovski. "It is true that he nourishes a love for his country, but with ink; and that is not over-strong food. His love is in fact more scant than that of his jester who helps him to put rhymes together. I am certain that after that Roman answer will come good wishes for health, success, offers of service, and at last a request to spare his property and that of his relatives, for which again he with all his relatives will be thankful."

"And what at last will be the result of our letters?"

"The courage of the other side will weaken to the last degree, senators will begin to negotiate with us, and we shall occupy all Great Poland after perhaps a few shots in the air."

"Would that your grace be a true prophet!"

"I am certain that it will be as I say, for I know these people. I have friends and adherents in the whole country, and I know how to begin. And that I shall neglect nothing is made sure by the wrong which I endure from Yan Kazimir, and my love for Karl Gustav. People with us are more tender at present about their own fortunes than the integrity of the Commonwealth. All those lands upon which we shall now march are the estates of the Opalinskis, the Charnkovskis, the Grudzinskis; and because they are at Uistsie in person they will be milder in negotiating. As to the nobles, if only their freedom of disputing at the diets is guaranteed, they will follow the voevodas."

"By knowledge of the country and the people your grace renders the king unexampled service, which cannot remain without an equally noteworthy reward. Therefore from what you say I conclude that I may look on this land as ours."

"You may, your grace, you may, you may," repeated Radzeyovski hurriedly, a number of times.

"Therefore I occupy it in the name of his Royal Grace Karl Gustav," answered Wittemberg, solemnly.

While the Swedish troops were thus beginning beyond Heinrichsdorf to walk on the land of Great Poland, and even earlier, for it was on July 18, a Swedish trumpeter arrived at the Polish camp with letters from Radzeyovski and Wittemberg to the voevodas.

Vladyslav Skorashevski himself conducted the trumpeter to the voevoda of Poznan, and the nobles of the general militia gazed with curiosity on the "first Swede," wondering at his valiant bearing, his manly face, his blond mustaches, the ends combed upward in a broad brush, and his really lordlike mien. Crowds followed him to the voevoda; acquaintances called to one another, pointing him out with their fingers, laughed somewhat at his boots with enormous round legs, and at the long straight rapier, which they called a spit, hanging from a belt richly worked with silver. The Swede also cast curious glances from under his broad hat, as if wishing to examine the camp and estimate the forces, and then looked repeatedly at the crowd of nobles whose oriental costumes were apparently novel to him. At last he was brought to the voevoda, around whom were grouped all the dignitaries in the camp.

The letters were read immediately, and a council held. The voevoda committed the trumpeter to his attendants to be entertained in soldier fashion; the nobles took him from the attendants, and wondering at the man as a curiosity, began to drink for life and death with him.

Pan Skorashevski looked at the Swede with equal scrutiny; but because he suspected him to be some officer in disguise, he went in fact to convey that idea in the evening to the voevoda. The latter, however, said it was all one, and did not permit his arrest.

"Though he were Wittemberg himself, he has come hither as an envoy and should go away unmolested. In addition I command you to give him ten ducats for the road."

The trumpeter meanwhile was talking in broken German with those nobles who, through intercourse with Prussian towns, understood that language. He told them of victories won by Wittemberg in various lands, of the forces marching against Uistsie, and especially of the cannon of a range hitherto unknown and which could not be resisted. The nobles were troubled at this, and no small number of exaggerated accounts began to circulate through the camp.

That night scarcely any one slept in Uistsie. About midnight those men came in who had stood hitherto in separate camps, at Pila and Vyelunie. The dignitaries deliberated over their answer to the letters till daylight, and the nobles passed the time in stories about the power of the Swedes.

With a certain feverish curiosity they asked the trumpeter about the leaders of the army, the weapons, the method of fighting; and every answer of his was given from mouth to mouth. The nearness of the Swedish legions lent unusual interest to all the details, which were not of a character to give consolation.

About daylight Stanislav Skshetuski came with tidings that the Swedes had arrived at Valch, one day's march from the Polish camp. There rose at once a terrible hubbub; most of the horses with the servants were at pasture on the meadows. They were sent for then with all haste. Districts mounted and formed squadrons. The moment before battle was for the untrained soldier the most terrible; therefore before the captains were able to introduce any kind of system there reigned for a long time desperate disorder.

Neither commands nor trumpets could be heard; nothing but voices crying on every side: "Yan! Pyotr! Onufri! This way! I wish thou wert killed! Bring the horses! Where are my men? Yan! Pyotr!" If at that moment one cannon-shot had been heard, the disorder might easily have been turned to a panic.

Gradually, however, the districts were ranged in order. The inborn capacity of the nobles for war made up for the want of experience, and about midday the camp presented an appearance imposing enough. The infantry stood on the ramparts looking like flowers in their many-colored coats, smoke was borne away from the lighted matches, and outside the ramparts under cover of the guns the meadows and plain were swarming with the district squadrons of cavalry standing in line on sturdy

189

horses, whose neighing roused an echo in the neighboring forests and filled all hearts with military ardor.

Meanwhile the voevoda of Poznan sent away the trumpeter with an answer to the letter reading more or less as Radzeyovski had foretold, therefore both courteous and Roman; then he determined to send a party to the northern bank of the Notets to seize an informant from the enemy.

Pyotr Opalinski, voevoda of Podlyasye, a cousin of the voevoda Poznan, was to go in person with a party together with his own dragoons, a hundred and fifty of whom he had brought to Uistsie; and besides this it was given to Captains Skorashevski and Skshetuski to call out volunteers from the nobles of the general militia, so that they might also look in the eyes of the enemy.

Both rode before the ranks, delighting the eye by manner and posture,—Pan Stanislav black as a beetle, like all the Skshetuskis, with a manly face, stern and adorned with a long sloping scar which remained from a sword-blow, with raven black beard blown aside by the wind; Pan Vladyslav portly, with long blond mustaches, open under lip, and eyes with red lids, mild and honest, reminding one less of Mars,—but none the less a genuine soldier spirit, as glad to be in fire as a salamander,—a knight knowing war as his ten fingers, and of incomparable daring. Both, riding before the ranks extended in a long line, repeated from moment to moment,—

"Now, gracious gentlemen, who is the volunteer against the Swedes? Who wants to smell powder? Well, gracious gentlemen, volunteer!"

And so they continued for a good while without result, for no man pushed forward from the ranks. One looked at another. There were those who desired to go and had no fear of the Swedes, but indecision restrained them. More than one nudged his neighbor and said, "Go you, and then I'll go." The captains were growing impatient, till all at once, when they had ridden up to the district of Gnyezno, a certain man dressed in many colors sprang forth on a hoop, not from the line but from behind the line, and cried,—

"Gracious gentlemen of the militia, I'll be the volunteer and ye will be jesters!"

"Ostrojka! Ostrojka!" cried the nobles.

"I am just as good a noble as any of you!" answered the jester.

"Tfu! to a hundred devils!" cried Pan Rosinski; under-judge, "a truce to jesting! I will go."

"And I! and I!" cried numerous voices.

"Once my mother bore me, once for me is death!"

"As good as thou will be found!"

"Freedom to each. Let no man here exalt himself above others."

And as no one had come forth before, so now nobles began to rush out from every district, spurring forward their horses, disputing with one another and fighting to advance. In the twinkle of an eye there were five hundred horsemen, and still they were riding forth from the ranks. Pan Skorashevski began to laugh with his honest, open laugh.

"Enough, worthy gentlemen, enough! We cannot all go."

Then the two captains put the men in order and marched.

The voevoda of Podlyasye joined the horsemen as they were riding out of camp. They were seen as on the palm of the hand crossing the Notets; after that they glittered some time on the windings of the road, then vanished from sight.

At the expiration of half an hour the voevoda of Poznan ordered the troops to their tents, for he saw that it was impossible to keep them in the ranks when the enemy were still a day's march distant. Numerous pickets were thrown out, however; it was not permitted to drive horses to pasture, and the order was given that at the first low sound of the trumpet through the mouthpiece all were to mount and be ready.

Expectation and uncertainty had come to an end, quarrels and disputes were finished at once, for the nearness of the enemy had raised their courage as Pan Skshetuski had predicted. The first successful battle might raise it indeed very high; and in the evening an event took place which seemed of happy omen.

The sun was just setting,—lighting with enormous glitter, dazzling the eyes, the Notets, and the pine-woods beyond,—when on the other side of the river was seen first a cloud of dust, and then men moving in the cloud. All that was living went out on the ramparts to see what manner of guests these were. At that moment a dragoon of the guards rushed in from the squadron of Pan Grudzinski with intelligence that the horsemen were returning.

"The horsemen are returning with success! The Swedes have not eaten them!" was repeated from mouth to mouth.

Meanwhile they in bright rolls of dust approached nearer and nearer, coming slowly; then they crossed the Notets.

The nobles with their hands over their eyes gazed at them; for the glitter became each moment greater, and the whole air was filled with gold and purple light.

"Hei! the party is somewhat larger than when it went out," said Shlihtyng.

"They must be bringing prisoners, as God is dear to me!" cried a noble, apparently without confidence and not believing his eyes.

"They are bringing prisoners! They are bringing prisoners!"

They had now come so near that their faces could be recognized. In front rode Skorashevski, nodding his head as usual

192

and talking joyously with Skshetuski; after them the strong detachment of horse surrounded a few tens of infantry wearing round hats. They were really Swedish prisoners.

At this sight the nobles could not contain themselves; and ran forward with shouts: "Vivat Skorashevski! Vivat Skshetuski!"

A dense crowd surrounded the party at once. Some looked at the prisoners; some asked, "How was the affair?" others threatened the Swedes.

"Ah-hu! Well now, good for you, ye dogs! Ye wanted to war with the Poles? Ye have the Poles now!"

"Give them here! Sabre them, make mince-meat of them!"

"Ha, broad-breeches! ye have tried the Polish sabres?"

"Gracious gentlemen, don't shout like little boys, for the prisoners will think that this is your first war," said Skorashevski; "it is a common thing to take prisoners in time of war."

The volunteers who belonged to the party looked with pride on the nobles who overwhelmed them with questions: "How was it? Did they surrender easily? Had you to sweat over them? Do they fight well?"

"They are good fellows," said Rosinski, "they defended themselves well; but they are not iron,—a sabre cuts them."

"So they couldn't resist you, could they?"

"They could not resist the impetus."

"Gracious gentlemen, do you hear what is said,—they could not resist the impetus. Well, what does that mean? Impetus is the main thing."

"Remember if only there is impetus!—that is the best method against the Swedes."

If at that moment those nobles had been commanded to rush at the enemy, surely impetus would not have been lacking; but it was well into the night when the sound of a trumpet was heard before the forepost. A trumpeter arrived with a letter from

Wittemberg summoning the nobles to surrender. The crowds hearing of this wanted to cut the messenger to pieces; but the voevodas took the letter into consideration, though the substance of it was insolent.

The Swedish general announced that Karl Gustav sent his troops to his relative Yan Kazimir, as reinforcements against the Cossacks, that therefore the people of Great Poland should yield without resistance. Pan Grudzinski on reading this letter could not restrain his indignation, and struck the table with his fist; but the voevoda of Poznan quieted him at once with the question,—

"Do you believe in victory? How many days can we defend ourselves? Do you wish to take the responsibility for so much noble blood which may be shed to-morrow?"

After a long deliberation it was decided not to answer, and to wait for what would happen. They did not wait long. On Saturday, July 24, the pickets announced that the whole Swedish army had appeared before Pila. There was as much bustle in camp as in a beehive on the eve of swarming.

The nobles mounted their horses; the voevodas hurried along the ranks, giving contradictory commands till Vladyslav Skorashevski took everything in hand; and when he had established order he rode out at the head of a few hundred volunteers to try skirmishing beyond the river and accustom the men to look at the enemy.

The cavalry went with him willingly enough, for skirmishing consisted generally of struggles carried on by small groups or singly, and such struggles the nobles trained to sword exercise did not fear at all. They went out therefore beyond the river, and stood before the enemy, who approached nearer and nearer, and blackened with a long line the horizon, as if a grove had grown freshly from the ground. Regiments of cavalry and infantry deployed, occupying more and more space.

The nobles expected that skirmishers on horseback might rush against them at any moment. So far they were not to be seen; but on the low hills a few hundred yards distant small groups halted, in which were to be seen men and horses, and they began to turn around on the place. Seeing this, Skorashevski commanded without delay, "To the left! to the rear!"

But the voice of command had not yet ceased to sound when on the hills long white curls of smoke bloomed forth, and as it were birds of some kind flew past with a whistle among the nobles; then a report shook the air, and at the same moment were heard cries and groans of a few wounded.

"Halt!" cried Skorashevski.

The birds flew past a second and a third time; again groans accompanied the whistle. The nobles did not listen to the command of the chief, but retreated at increased speed, shouting, and calling for the aid of heaven. Then the division scattered, in the twinkle of an eye, over the plain, and rushed on a gallop to the camp. Skorashevski was cursing, but that did no good.

Wittemberg, having dispersed the skirmishers so easily, pushed on farther, till at last he stood in front of Uistsie, straight before the trenches defended by the nobles of Kalish. The Polish guns began to play, but at first no answer was made from the Swedish side. The smoke fell away quietly in the clear air in long streaks stretching between the armies, and in the spaces between them the nobles saw the Swedish regiments, infantry and cavalry, deploying with terrible coolness as if certain of victory.

On the hills the cannon were fixed, trenches raised; in a word, the enemy came into order without paying the least attention to the balls which, without reaching them, merely scattered sand and earth on the men working in the trenches.

Pan Skshetuski led out once more two squadrons of the men of Kalish, wishing by a bold attack to confuse the Swedes.

But they did not go willingly; the division fell at once into a disorderly crowd, for when the most daring urged their horses forward the most cowardly held theirs back on purpose. Two regiments of cavalry sent by Wittemberg drove the nobles from the field after a short struggle, and pursued them to the camp. Now dusk came, and put an end to the bloodless strife.

There was firing from cannon till night, when firing ceased; but such a tumult rose in the Polish camp that it was heard on the other bank of the Notets. It rose first for the reason that a few hundred of the general militia tried to slip away in the darkness. Others, seeing this, began to threaten and detain them. Sabres were drawn. The words "Either all or none" flew again from mouth to mouth. At every moment it seemed most likely that all would go. Great dissatisfaction burst out against the leaders: "They sent us with naked breasts against cannon," cried the militia.

They were enraged in like degree against Wittemberg, because without regard to the customs of war he had not sent skirmishers against skirmishers, but had ordered to fire on them unexpectedly from cannon. "Every one will do for himself what is best," said they; "but it is the custom of a swinish people not to meet face to face." Others were in open despair. "They will smoke us out of this place like badgers out of a hole," said they. "The camp is badly planned, the trenches are badly made, the place is not fitted for defence." From time to time voices were heard: "Save yourselves, brothers!" Still others cried: "Treason! treason!"

That was a terrible night: confusion and relaxation increased every moment; no one listened to commands. The voevodas lost their heads, and did not even try to restore order; and the imbecility of the general militia appeared as clearly as on the palm of the hand. Wittemberg might have taken the camp by assault on that night with the greatest ease.

Dawn came. The day broke pale, cloudy, and lighted a chaotic gathering of people fallen in courage, lamenting, and the greater number drunk, more ready for shame than for battle. To complete the misfortune, the Swedes had crossed the Notets at Dzyembovo and surrounded the Polish camp.

At that side there were scarcely any trenches, and there was nothing from behind which they could defend themselves. They should have raised breastworks without delay. Skorashevski and Skshetuski had implored to have this done, but no one would listen to anything.

The leaders and the nobles had one word on their lips, "Negotiate!" Men were sent out to parley. In answer there came from the Swedish camp a brilliant party, at the head of which rode Radzeyovski and General Wirtz, both with green branches.

They rode to the house in which the voevoda of Poznan was living; but on the way Radzeyovski stopped amid the crowd of nobles, bowed with the branch, with his hat, laughed, greeted his acquaintances, and said in a piercing voice,—

"Gracious gentlemen, dearest brothers, be not alarmed! Not as enemies do we come. On you it depends whether a drop of blood more will be shed. If you wish instead of a tyrant who is encroaching on your liberties, who is planning for absolute power, who has brought the country to final destruction,—if you wish, I repeat, a good ruler, a noble one, a warrior of such boundless glory that at bare mention of his name all the enemies of the Commonwealth will flee,—give yourselves under the protection of the most serene Karl Gustav. Gracious gentlemen, dearest brothers, behold, I bring to you the guarantee of all your liberties, of your freedom, of your religion. On yourselves your salvation depends. Gracious gentlemen, the most serene Swedish king undertakes to quell the Cossack rebellion, to finish the war in Lithuania; and only he can do that. Take pity on the unfortunate country if you have no pity on yourselves."

Here the voice of the traitor quivered as if stopped by tears. The nobles listened with astonishment; here and there scattered voices cried, "Vivat Radzeyovski, our vice-chancellor!" He rode farther, and again bowed to new throngs, and again was heard his trumpet-like voice: "Gracious gentlemen, dearest brothers!" And at last he and Wirtz with the whole retinue vanished in the house of the voevoda of Poznan.

The nobles crowded so closely before the house that it would have been possible to ride on their heads, for they felt and understood that there in that house men were deciding the question not only of them but of the whole country. The servants of the voevodas, in scarlet colors, came out and began to invite the more important personages to the council. They entered quickly, and after them burst in a few of the smaller; but the rest remained at the door, they pressed to the windows, put their ears even to the walls.

A deep silence reigned in the throng. Those standing nearest the windows heard from time to time the sound of shrill voices from within the chamber, as it were the echo of quarrels, disputes, and fights. Hour followed hour, and no end to the council.

Suddenly the doors wore thrown open with a crash, and out burst Vladyslav Skorashevski. Those present pushed back in astonishment. That man, usually so calm and mild, of whom it was said that wounds might be healed under his hand, had that moment a terrible face. His eyes were red, his look wild, his clothing torn open on his breast; both hands were grasping his hair, and he rushed out like a thunderbolt among the nobles, and cried with a piercing voice,—

"Treason! murder! shame! We are Sweden now, and Poland no longer!"

He began to roar with an awful voice, with a spasmodic cry, and to tear his hair like a man who is losing his reason. A silence of the grave reigned all around. A certain fearful foreboding seized all hearts.

Skorashevski sprang away quickly, began to run among the nobles and cry with a voice of the greatest despair: "To arms, to arms, whoso believes in God! To arms, to arms!"

Then certain murmurs began to fly through the throngs,— certain momentary whispers, sudden and broken, like the first beatings of the wind before a storm. Hearts hesitated, minds hesitated, and in that universal distraction of feelings the tragic voice was calling continually, "To arms, to arms!"

Soon two other voices joined his,—those of Pyotr Skorashevski and Stanislav Shshetuski. After them ran up Klodzinski, the gallant captain of the district of Pozpan. An increasing circle of nobles began to surround them. A threatening murmur was heard round about; flames ran over the faces and shot out of the eyes; sabres rattled. Vladyslav Skorashevski mastered the first transport, and began to speak, pointing to the house in which the council was being held,—

"Do you hear, gracious gentlemen? They are selling the country there like Judases, and disgracing it. Do you know that we belong to Poland no longer? It was not enough for them to give into the hands of the enemy all of you,—camp, army, cannon. Would they were killed! They have affirmed with their own signatures and in your names that we abjure our ties with the country, that we abjure our king; that the whole land—towns, towers, and we all—shall belong forever to Sweden. That an army surrenders happens, but who has the right to renounce his country and his king? Who has the right to tear away a province, to join strangers, to go over to another people, to renounce his own blood? Gracious gentlemen, this is disgrace, treason, murder, parricide! Save the fatherland, brothers! In God's name, whoever is a noble, whoever has virtue, let him save our mother. Let us give our lives, let us shed our blood! We do not want to be Swedes; we do not, we do not! Would that he had never been born who will spare his blood now! Let us rescue our mother!"

"Treason!" cried several hundred voices, "treason! Let us cut them to pieces."

"Join us, whoever has virtue!" cried Skshetuski.

"Against the Swedes till death!" added Klodzinski.

And they went along farther in the camp, shouting: "Join us! Assemble! There is treason!" and after them moved now several hundred nobles with drawn sabres.

But an immense majority remained in their places; and of those who followed some, seeing that they were not many, began to look around and stand still.

Now the door of the council-house was thrown open, and in it appeared the voevoda of Poznan, Pan Opalinski, having on his right side General Wirtz, and on the left Radzeyovski. After them came Andrei Grudzinski, voevoda of Kalisk; Myaskovski, castellan of Kryvinsk; Gembitski, castellan of Myendzyrechka, and Andrei Slupski.

Pan Opalinski had in his hand a parchment with seals appended; he held his head erect, but his face was pale and his look uncertain, though evidently he was trying to be joyful. He took in with his glance the crowds, and in the midst of a deathlike silence began to speak with a piercing though somewhat hoarse voice,—

"Gracious gentlemen, this day we have put ourselves under the protection of the most serene King of Sweden. Vivat Carolus Gustavus Rex!"

Silence gave answer to the voevoda; suddenly some loud voice thundered, "Veto!"

The voevoda turned his eyes in the direction of the voice and said: "This is not a provincial diet, therefore a veto is not in place. And whoever wishes to veto let him go against the Swedish cannon turned upon us, which in one hour could make of this camp a pile of ruins."

Then he was silent, and after a while inquired, "Who said Veto?"

No one answered.

The voevoda again raised his voice, and began still more emphatically: "All the liberties of the nobles and the clergy will be maintained; taxes will not be increased, and will be collected in the same manner as hitherto; no man will suffer wrongs or robbery. The armies of his royal Majesty have not the right to quarter on the property of nobles nor to other exactions, unless to such as the quota of the Polish squadrons enjoy."

Here he was silent, and heard an anxious murmur of the nobles, as if they wished to understand his meaning; then he beckoned with his hand.

"Besides this, we have the word and promise of General Wirtz, given in the name of his royal Majesty, that if the whole country will follow our saving example, the Swedish armies will move promptly into Lithuania and the Ukraine, and will not cease to war until all the lands and all the fortresses of the Commonwealth are won back. Vivat Carolus Gustavus Rex!"

"Vivat Carolus Gustavus Rex!" cried hundreds of voices. "Vivat Carolus Gustavus Rex!" thundered still more loudly in the whole camp.

Here, before the eyes of all, the voevoda of Poznan turned to Radzeyovski and embraced him heartily; then he embraced Wirtz; then all began to embrace one another. The nobles followed the example of the dignitaries, and joy became universal. They gave vivats so loud that the echoes thundered throughout the whole region. But the voevoda of Poznan begged yet the beloved brotherhood for a moment of quiet, and said in a tone of cordiality,—

"Gracious gentlemen! General Wittemberg invites us today to a feast in his camp, so that at the goblets a brotherly alliance may be concluded with a manful people."

"Vivat Wittemberg! vivat! vivat! vivat!"

"And after that, gracious gentlemen," added the voevoda, "let us go to our homes, and with the assistance of God let us begin the harvest with the thought that on this day we have saved the fatherland."

"Coming ages will render us justice," said Radzeyovski.

"Amen!" finished the voevoda of Poznan.

Meanwhile he saw that the eyes of many nobles were gazing at and scanning something above his head. He turned and saw his own jester, who, holding with one hand to the frame above the door, was writing with a coal on the wall of the council-house over the door: "Mene Tekel-Peres."

In the world the heavens were covered with clouds, and a tempest was coming.

CHAPTER XII.

In the district of Lukovo, on the edge of Podlyasye, stood the village of Bujets, owned by the Skshetuskis. In a garden between the mansion and a pond an old man was sitting on a bench; and at his feet were two little boys,—one five, the other four years old,—dark and sunburned as gypsies, but rosy and healthy. The old man, still fresh, seemed as sturdy as an aurochs. Age had not bent his broad shoulders; from his eyes—or rather from his eye, for he had one covered with a cataract—beamed health and good-humor; he had a white beard, but a look of strength and a ruddy face, ornamented on the forehead with a broad scar, through which his skull-bone was visible.

The little boys, holding the straps of his boot-leg, were pulling in opposite directions; but he was gazing at the pond, which gleamed with the rays of the sun,—at the pond, in which fish were springing up frequently, breaking the smooth surface of the water.

"The fish are dancing," muttered he to himself. "Never fear, ye will dance still better when the floodgate is open, or when the cook is scratching you with a knife." Then he turned to the little boys: "Get away from my boot-leg, for when I catch one of your ears, I'll pull it off. Just like mad horse-flies! Go and roll balls there on the grass and let me alone! I do not wonder at Longinek, for he is young; but Yaremka ought to have sense by this time. Ah, torments! I'll take one of you and throw him into the pond."

But it was clear that the old man was in terrible subjection to the boys, for neither had the least fear of his threats; on the contrary, Yaremka, the elder, began to pull the boot-leg still harder, bracing his feet and repeating,—

"Oh, Grandfather, be Bogun and steal away Longinek."

"Be off, thou beetle, I say, thou rogue, thou cheese-roll!"

"Oh, Grandfather, be Bogun!"

"I'll give thee Bogun; wait till I call thy mother!"

Yaremka looked toward the door leading from the house to the garden, but finding it closed, and seeing no sign of his mother, he repeated the third time, pouting, "Grandfather, be Bogun!"

"Ah, they will kill me, the rogues; it cannot be otherwise. Well, I'll be Bogun, but only once. Oh, it is a punishment of God! Mind ye do not plague me again!"

When he had said this, the old man groaned a little, raised himself from the bench, then suddenly grabbed little Longinek, and giving out loud shouts, began to carry him off in the direction of the pond.

Longinek, however, had a valiant defender in his brother, who on such occasions did not call himself Yaremka, but Pan Michael Volodyovski, captain of dragoons.

Pan Michael, then, armed with a basswood club, which took the place of a sabre in this sudden emergency, ran swiftly after the bulky Bogun, soon caught up with him, and began to beat him on the legs without mercy.

Longinek, playing the rôle of his mamma, made an uproar, Bogun made an uproar, Yaremka-Volodyovski made an uproar; but valor at last overcame even Bogun, who, dropping his victim, began to make his way back to the linden-tree. At last he reached the bench, fell upon it, panting terribly and repeating,—

"Ah, ye little stumps! It will be a wonder if I do not suffocate."

But the end of his torment had not come yet, for a moment later Yaremka stood before him with a ruddy face, floating hair, and distended nostrils, like a brisk young falcon, and began to repeat with greater energy,—

"Grandfather, be Bogun!"

After much teasing and a solemn promise given to the two boys that this would surely be the last time, the story was repeated in all its details; then they sat three in a row on the bench and Yaremka began,—

"Oh, Grandfather, tell who was the bravest."

"Thou, thou!" said the old man.

"And shall I grow up to be a knight?"

"Surely thou wilt, for there is good soldier blood in thee. God grant thee to be like thy father; for if brave thou wilt not tease so much—understand me?"

"Tell how many men has Papa killed?"

"It's little if I have told thee a hundred times! Easier for thee to count the leaves on this linden-tree than all the enemies which thy father and I have destroyed. If I had as many hairs on my head as I myself have put down, the barbers in Lukovsk would make fortunes just in shaving my temples. I am a rogue if I li—"

Here Pan Zagloba—for it was he—saw that it did not become him to adjure or swear before little boys, though in the absence of other listeners he loved to tell even the children of his former triumphs; he grew silent this time especially because the fish had begun to spring up in the pond with redoubled activity.

"We must tell the gardener," said he, "to set the net for the night; a great many fine fish are crowding right up to the bank."

Now that door of the house which led into the garden opened, and in it appeared a woman beautiful as the midday sun, tall, firm, black-haired, with bloom on her brunette face, and eyes like velvet. A third boy, three years old, dark as an agate ball, hung to her skirt. She, shading her eyes with her hand, looked in the direction of the linden-tree. This was Pani Helena Skshetuski, of the princely house of Bulyga-Kurtsevich.

Seeing Pan Zagloba with Yaremka and Longinek under the tree, she went forward a few steps toward the ditch, full of water, and called: "Come here, boys! Surely you are plaguing Grandfather?"

"How plague me! They have acted nicely all the time," said the old man.

The boys ran to their mother; but she asked Zagloba, "What will Father drink to-day,—dembniak or mead?"

"We had pork for dinner; mead will be best."

"I'll send it this minute; but Father must not fall asleep in the air, for fever is sure to come."

"It is warm to-day, and there is no wind. But where is Yan, Daughter?"

"He has gone to the barns."

Pani Skshetuski called Zagloba father, and he called her daughter, though they were in no way related. Her family dwelt beyond the Dnieper, in the former domains of Vishnyevetski; and as to him God alone knew his origin, for he told various tales about it himself. But Zagloba had rendered famous services to Pani Skshetuski when she was still a maiden, and he had rescued her from terrible dangers; therefore she and her husband treated him as a father, and in the whole region about he was honored beyond measure by all, as well for his inventive mind as for the uncommon bravery of which he had given many proofs in various wars, especially in those against the Cossacks. His name was known in the whole Commonwealth. The king himself was enamored of his stories and wit; and in general he was more spoken of than even Pan Skshetuski, though the latter in his time had burst through besieged Zbaraj and all the Cossack armies.

Soon after Pani Skshetuski had gone into the house a boy brought a decanter and glass to the linden-tree. Zagloba poured out some mead, then closed his eyes and began to try it diligently.

"The Lord God knew why he created bees," said he, with a nasal mutter. And he fell to drinking slowly, drawing deep breaths at the same time, while gazing at the pond and beyond the pond, away to the dark and blue pine-woods stretching as far as the eye could reach on the other side. The time was past one in the afternoon, and the heavens were cloudless. The blossoms of the linden were falling noiselessly to the earth, and on the tree among the leaves were buzzing a whole choir of bees, which soon began to settle on the edge of the glass and gather the sweet fluid on their shaggy legs.

Above the great pond, from the far-off reeds obscured by the haze of distance, rose from time to time flocks of ducks, teal, or wild geese, and moved away swiftly in the blue ether like black crosses; sometimes a row of cranes looked dark high in the air, and gave out a shrill cry. With these exceptions all around was quiet, calm, sunny, and gladsome, as is usual in the first days of August, when the grain has ripened, and the sun is scattering as it were gold upon the earth.

The eyes of the old man were raised now to the sky, following the flocks of birds, and now they were lost in the distance, growing more and more drowsy, as the mead in the decanter decreased; his lids became heavier and heavier,—the bees buzzed their song in various tones as if on purpose for his after-dinner slumber.

"True, true, the Lord God has given beautiful weather for the harvest," muttered Zagloba. "The hay is well gathered in, the harvest will be finished in a breath. Yes, yes—"

Here he closed his eyes, then opened them again for a moment, muttered once more, "The boys have tormented me," and fell asleep in earnest.

He slept rather long, but after a certain time he was roused by a light breath of cooler air, together with the conversation and steps of two men drawing near the tree rapidly. One of them was Yan Skshetuski, the hero of Zbaraj, who about a month before had returned from the hetmans in the Ukraine to cure a stubborn fever; Pan Zagloba did not know the other, though in stature and form and even in features he resembled Yan greatly.

"I present to you, dear father," said Yan, "my cousin Pan Stanislav Skshetuski, the captain of Kalish."

207

"You are so much like Yan," answered Zagloba, blinking and shaking the remnants of sleep from his eyelids, "that had I met you anywhere I should have said at once, 'Skshetuski!' Hei, what a guest in the house!"

"It is dear to me to make your acquaintance, my benefactor," answered Stanislav, "the more since the name is well known to me, for the knighthood of the whole Commonwealth repeat it with respect and mention it as an example."

"Without praising myself, I did what I could, while I felt strength in my bones. And even now one would like to taste of war, for *consuetudo altera natura* (habit is a second nature). But why, gentlemen, are you so anxious, so that Yan's face is pale?"

"Stanislav has brought dreadful news," answered Yan. "The Swedes have entered Great Poland, and occupied it entirely."

Zagloba sprang from the bench as if forty years had dropped from him, opened wide his eyes, and began involuntarily to feel at his side, as if he were looking for a sabre.

"How is that?" asked he, "how is that? Have they occupied all of it?"

"Yes, for the voevoda of Poznan and others at Uistsie have given it into the hands of the enemy," answered Stanislav.

"For God's sake! What do I hear? Have they surrendered?"

"Not only have they surrendered, but they have signed a compact renouncing the King and the Commonwealth. Henceforth Sweden, not Poland, is to be there."

"By the mercy of God, by the wounds of the Crucified! Is the world coming to an end? What do I hear! Yesterday Yan and I were speaking of this danger from Sweden, for news had come that they were marching; but we were both confident that it would end in nothing, or at most in the renunciation of the title of King of Sweden by our lord, Yan Kazimir."

"But it has begun with the loss of a province, and will end with God knows what."

"Stop, for the blood will boil over in me! How was it? And you were at Uistsie and saw all this with your own eyes? That was simply treason the most villanous, unheard of in history."

"I was there and looked on, and whether it was treason you will decide when you hear all. We were at Uistsie, the general militia and the land infantry, fifteen thousand men in all, and we formed our lines on the Notets *ab incursione hostili* (against hostile invasion). True the army was small, and as an experienced soldier you know best whether the place of regular troops can be filled by general militia, especially that of Great Poland, where the nobles have grown notably unused to war. Still, if a leader had been found, they might have shown opposition to the enemy in old fashion, and at least detained them till the Commonwealth could find reinforcements. But hardly had Wittemberg shown himself when negotiations were begun before a drop of blood had been shed. Then Radzeyovski came up, and with his persuasions brought about what I have said,—that is, misfortune and disgrace, the like of which has not been hitherto."

"How was that? Did no one resist, did no one protest? Did no one hurl treason in the eyes of those scoundrels? Did all agree to betray the country and the king?"

"Virtue is perishing, and with it the Commonwealth, for nearly all agreed. I, the two Skorashevskis, Pan Tsisvitski, and Pan Klodzinski did what we could to rouse a spirit of resistance among the nobles. Pan Vladyslav Skorashevski went almost frantic. We flew through the camp from the men of one district to those of another, and God knows there was no beseeching that we did not use. But what good was it when the majority chose to go

209

in bonds to the banquet which Wittemberg promised, rather than with sabres to battle? Seeing that the best went in every direction,—some to their homes, others to Warsaw,—the Skorashevskis went to Warsaw, and will bring the first news to the king; but I, having neither wife nor children, came here to my cousin, with the idea that we might go together against the enemy. It was fortunate that I found you at home."

"Then you are directly from Uistsie?"

"Directly. I rested on the road only as much as my horses needed, and as it was I drove one of them to death. The Swedes must be in Poznan at present, and thence they will quickly spread over the whole country."

Here all grew silent. Yan sat with his palms on his knees, his eyes fixed on the ground, and he was thinking gloomily. Pan Stanislav sighed; and Zagloba, not having recovered, looked with a staring glance, now on one, now on the other.

"Those are evil signs," said Yan at last, gloomily. "Formerly for ten victories there came one defeat, and we astonished the world with our valor. Now not only defeats come, but treason,—not merely of single persons, but of whole provinces. May God pity the country!"

"For God's sake," said Zagloba, "I have seen much in the world. I can hear, I can reason, but still belief fails me."

"What do you think of doing, Yan?" asked Stanislav.

"It is certain that I shall not stay at home, though fever is shaking me yet. It will be necessary to place my wife and children somewhere in safety. Pan Stabrovski, my relative, is huntsman of the king in the wilderness of Byalovyej, and lives in Byalovyej. Even if the whole Commonwealth should fall into the power of the enemy, they would not touch that region. To-morrow I will take my wife and children straight there."

210

"And that will not be a needless precaution," said Stanislav; "for though 'tis far from Great Poland to this place, who knows whether the flame may not soon seize these regions also?"

"The nobles must be notified," said Yan, "to assemble and think of defence, for here no one has heard anything yet." Here he turned to Zagloba: "And, Father, will you go with us, or do you wish to accompany Helena to the wilderness?"

"I?" answered Zagloba, "will I go? If my feet had taken root in the earth, I might not go; but even then I should ask some one to dig me out. I want to try Swedish flesh again, as a wolf does mutton. Ha! the rascals, trunk-breeches, long-stockings! The fleas make raids on their calves, their legs are itching, and they can't sit at home, but crawl into foreign lands. I know them, the sons of such a kind, for when I was under Konyetspolski I worked against them; and, gentlemen, if you want to know who took Gustavus Adolphus captive, ask the late Konyetspolski. I'll say no more! I know them, but they know me too. It must be that the rogues have heard that Zagloba has grown old. Isn't that true? Wait! you'll see him yet! O Lord! O Lord, all-Powerful! why hast thou unfenced this unfortunate Commonwealth, so that all the neighboring swine are running into it now, and they have rooted up three of the best provinces? What is the condition? Ba! but who is to blame, if not traitors? The plague did not know whom to take; it took honest men, but left the traitors. O Lord, send thy pest once more on the voevoda of Poznan and on him of Kalish, but especially on Radzeyovski and his whole family. But if 'tis thy will to favor hell with more inhabitants, send thither all those who signed the pact at Uistsie. Has Zagloba grown old? has he grown old? You will find out! Yan, let us consider quickly what to do, for I want to be on horseback."

"Of course we must know whither to go. It is difficult to reach the hetmans in the Ukraine, for the enemy has cut them off from the Commonwealth and the road is open only to the Crimea. It is lucky that the Tartars are on our side this time. According to my head it will be necessary for us to go to Warsaw to the king, to defend our dear lord."

"If there is time," remarked Stanislav. "The king must collect squadrons there in haste, and will march on the enemy before we can come, and perhaps the engagement is already taking place."

"And that may be."

"Let us go then to Warsaw, if we can go quickly," said Zagloba. "Listen, gentlemen! It is true that our names are terrible to the enemy, but still three of us cannot do much, therefore I should give this advice: Let us summon the nobles to volunteer; they will come in such numbers that we may lead even a small squadron to the king. We shall persuade them easily, for they must go anyhow when the call comes for the general militia,—it will be all one to them—and we shall tell them that whoever volunteers before the call will do an act dear to the king. With greater power we can do more, and they will receive us (in Warsaw) with open arms."

"Wonder not at my words," said Pan Stanislav, "but from what I have seen I feel such a dislike to the general militia that I choose to go alone rather than with a crowd of men who know nothing of war."

"You have no acquaintance with the nobles of this place. Here a man cannot be found who has not served in the army; all have experience and are good soldiers."

"That may be."

"How could it be otherwise? But wait! Yan knows that when once I begin to work with my head I have no lack of resources. For that reason I lived in great intimacy with the voevoda of Rus, Prince Yeremi. Let Yan tell how many times that greatest of warriors followed my advice, and thereby was each time victorious."

"But tell us, Father, what you wish to say, for time is precious."

"What I wish to say? This is it: not he defends the country and the king who holds to the king's skirts, but he who beats the enemy; and he beats the enemy best who serves under a great warrior. Why go on uncertainties to Warsaw, when the king himself may have gone to Cracow, to Lvoff or Lithuania? My advice is to put ourselves at once under the banners of the grand hetman of Lithuania, Prince Yanush Radzivill. He is an honest man and a soldier. Though they accuse him of pride, he of a certainty will not surrender to Swedes. He at least is a chief and a hetman of the right kind. It will be close there, 'tis true, for he is working against two enemies; but as a recompense we shall see Pan Michael Volodyovski, who is serving in the Lithuanian quota, and again we shall be together as in old times. If I do not counsel well, then let the first Swede take me captive by the sword-strap."

"Who knows, who knows?" answered Yan, with animation. "Maybe that will be the best course."

"And besides we shall take Halshka with the children, for we must go right through the wilderness."

"And we shall serve among soldiers, not among militia," added Stanislav.

"And we shall fight, not debate, nor eat chickens and cheese in the villages."

"I see that not only in war, but in council you can hold the first place," said Stanislav.

"Well, are you satisfied?"

"In truth, in truth," said Yan, "that is the best advice. We shall be with Michael as before; you will know, Stanislav, the greatest soldier in the Commonwealth, my true friend, my brother. We will go now to Halshka, and tell her so that she too may be ready for the road."

"Does she know of the war already?" asked Zagloba.

"She knows, she knows, for in her presence Stanislav told about it first. She is in tears, poor woman! But if I say to her that it is necessary to go, she will say straightway. Go!"

"I would start in the morning," cried Zagloba.

"We will start in the morning and before daybreak," said Yan. "You must be terribly tired after the road, Stanislav, but you will rest before morning as best you can. I will send horses this evening with trusty men to Byala, to Lostsi, to Drohichyn and Byelsk, so as to have relays everywhere. And just beyond Byelsk is the wilderness. Wagons will start to-day also with supplies. It is too bad to go into the world from the dear corner, but 'tis God's will! This is my comfort: I am safe as to my wife and children, for the wilderness is the best fortress in the world. Come to the house, gentlemen; it is time for me to prepare for the journey."

They went in. Pan Stanislav, greatly road-weary, had barely taken food and drink when he went to sleep straightway; but Pan Yan and Zagloba were busied in preparations. And as there was great order in Pan Yan's household the wagons and men started that evening for an all-night journey, and next morning at daybreak the carriage followed in which sat Helena with the children and an old maid, a companion. Pan Stanislav and Pan Yan with five attendants rode on horseback near the carriage. The whole party pushed forward briskly, for fresh horses were awaiting them.

Travelling in this manner and without resting even at night, they reached Byelsk on the fifth day, and on the sixth they sank in the wilderness from the side of Hainovshyna.

They were surrounded at once by the gloom of the gigantic pine-forest, which at that period occupied a number of tens of square leagues, joining on one side with an unbroken line the wilderness of Zyelonka and Rogovsk, and on the other the forests of Prussia.

No invader had ever trampled with a hoof those dark depths in which a man who knew them not might go astray and wander till he dropped from exhaustion or fell a prey to ravenous beasts. In the night were heard the bellowing of the aurochs, the growling of bears, with the howling of wolves and the hoarse screams of panthers. Uncertain roads led through thickets or clean-trunked trees, along fallen timber, swamps, and terrible stagnant lakes to the scattered villages of guards, pitch-burners, and hunters, who in many cases did not leave the wilderness all their lives. To Byalovyej itself a broader way led, continued by the Suha road, over which the kings went to hunt. By that road also the Skshetuskis came from the direction of Byelsk and Hainovshyna.

Pan Stabrovski, chief-hunter of the king, was an old hermit and bachelor, who like an aurochs stayed always in the wilderness. He received the visitors with open arms, and almost smothered the children with kisses. He lived with beaters-in, never seeing the face of a noble unless when the king went to hunt. He had the management of all hunting matters and all the pitch-making of the wilderness. He was greatly disturbed by news of the war, of which he heard first from Pan Yan.

Often did it happen in the Commonwealth that war broke out or the king died and no news came to the wilderness; the chief-hunter alone brought news when he returned from the treasurer of Lithuania, to whom he was obliged to render account of his management of the wilderness each year.

"It will be dreary here, dreary," said Stabrovski to Helena, "but safe as nowhere else in the world. No enemy will break through these walls, and even if he should try the beaters-in would shoot down all his men. It would be easier to conquer the whole Commonwealth—which may God not permit!—than the wilderness. I have been living here twenty years, and even I do not know it all, for there are places where it is impossible to go, where only wild beasts live and perhaps evil spirits have their dwelling, from whom men are preserved by the sound of church-bells. But we live according to God's law, for in the village there is a chapel to which a priest from Byelsk comes once a year. You will be here as if in heaven, if tedium does not weary you. As a recompense there is no lack of firewood."

Pan Yan was glad in his whole soul that he had found for his wife such a refuge; but Pan Stabrovski tried in vain to delay him awhile and entertain him.

Halting only one night, the cavaliers resumed at daybreak their journey across the wilderness. They were led through the forest labyrinths by guides whom the hunter sent with them.

CHAPTER XIII.

When Pan Skshetuski with his cousin Stanislav and Zagloba, after a toilsome journey from the wilderness, came at last to Upita, Pan Volodyovski went almost wild from delight, especially since he had long had no news of them; he thought that Yan was with a squadron of the king which he commanded under the hetmans in the Ukraine.

Pan Michael took them in turn by the shoulders, and after he had pressed them once he pressed them again and rubbed his hands. When they told him of their wish to serve under Radzivill, he rejoiced still more at the thought that they would not separate soon.

"Praise God that we shall be together, old comrades of Zbaraj!" said he. "A man has greater desire for war when he feels friends near him."

"That was my idea," said Zagloba; "for they wanted to fly to the king. But I said, 'Why not remember old times with Pan Michael? If God will give us such fortune as he did with Cossacks and the Tartars, we shall soon have more than one Swede on our conscience.'"

"God inspired you with that thought," said Pan Michael.

"But it is a wonder to me," added Yan, "how you know already of the war. Stanislav came to me with the last breath of his horse, and we in that same fashion rode hither, thinking that we should be first to announce the misfortune."

"The tidings must have come through the Jews," said Zagloba; "for they are first to know everything, and there is such communication between them that if one sneezes in Great Poland in the morning, others will call to him in the evening from Lithuania and the Ukraine, 'To thy health!'"

"I know not how it was, but we heard of it two days ago," said Pan Michael, "and there is a fearful panic here. The first day we did not credit the news greatly, but on the second no one denied it. I will say more; before the war came, you would have said that the birds were singing about it in the air, for suddenly and without cause all began to speak of war. Our prince voevoda must also have looked for it and have known something before others, for he was rushing about like a fly in hot water, and during these last hours he has hastened to Kyedani. Levies were made at his order two months ago. I assembled men, as did also Stankyevich and a certain Kmita, the banneret of Orsha, who, as

217

I hear, has already sent a squadron to Kyedani. Kmita was ready before the rest of us."

"Michael, do you know Prince Radzivill well?" asked Yan.

"Why should I not know him, when I have passed the whole present war under his command?"

"What do you know of his plans? Is he an honest man?"

"He is a finished warrior; who knows if after the death of Prince Yeremi he is not the greatest in the Commonwealth? He was defeated in the last battle, it is true; but against eighteen thousand he had six thousand men. The treasurer and the voevoda of Vityebsk blame him terribly for this, saying that with small forces he rushed against such a disproportionate power to avoid sharing victory with them. God knows how it was! But he stood up manfully and did not spare his own life. And I who saw it all, say only this, that if we had had troops and money enough, not a foot of the enemy would have left the country. So I think that he will begin at the Swedes more sharply, and will not wait for them here, but march on Livonia."

"Why do you think that?"

"For two reasons,—first, because he will wish to improve his reputation, shattered a little after the battle of Tsybihova; and second, because he loves war."

"That is true," said Zagloba. "I know him, for we were at school together and I worked out his tasks for him. He was always in love with war, and therefore liked to keep company with me rather than others, for I too preferred a horse and a lance to Latin."

"It is certain that he is not like the voevoda of Poznan; he is surely a different kind of man altogether," said Pan Stanislav.

Volodyovski inquired about everything that had taken place at Uistsie, and tore his hair as he listened to the story. At last, when Pan Stanislav had finished, he said,—

"You are right! Our Radzivill is incapable of such deeds. He is as proud as the devil, and it seems to him that in the whole world there is not a greater family than the Radzivills. He will not endure opposition, that is true; and at the treasurer, Pan Gosyevski, an honest man, he is angry because the latter will not dance when Radzivill plays. He is displeased also with his Grace the king, because he did not give him the grand baton of Lithuania soon enough. All true, as well as this,—that he prefers to live in the dishonorable error of Calvinism rather than turn to the true faith, that he persecutes Catholics where he can, that he founds societies of heretics. But as recompense for this, I will swear that he would rather shed the last drop of his proud blood than sign a surrender like that at Uistsie. We shall have war to wade in; for not a scribe, but a warrior, will lead us."

"That's my play," said Zagloba, "I want nothing more. Pan Opalinski is a scribe, and he showed soon what he was good for. They are the meanest of men! Let but one of them pull a quill out of a goose's tail and he thinks straightway that he has swallowed all wisdom. He will say to others, 'Son of a such kind,' and when it comes to the sabre you cannot find him. When I was young myself, I put rhymes together to captivate the hearts of fair heads, and I might have made a goat's horn of Pan Kohanovski with his silly verses, but later on the soldier nature got the upper hand."

"I will add, too," continued Volodyovski, "that the nobles will soon move hither. A crowd of people will come, if only money is not lacking, for that is most important."

"In God's name I want no general militia!" shouted Pan Stanislav. "Yan and Pan Zagloba know my sentiments already, and to you I say now that I would rather be a camp-servant in a regular squadron than hetman over the entire general militia."

"The people here are brave," answered Volodyovski, "and very skilful. I have an example from my own levy. I could not receive all who came, and among those whom I accepted there is not a man who has not served before. I will show you this squadron, gentlemen, and if you had not learned from me you would not know that they are not old soldiers. Every one is tempered and hammered in fire, like an old horseshoe, and stands in order like a Roman legionary. It will not be so easy for the Swedes with them, as with the men of Great Poland at Uistsie."

"I have hope that God will change everything," said Pan Yan. "They say that the Swedes are good soldiers, but still they have never been able to stand before our regular troops. We have beaten them always,—that is a matter of trial; we have beaten them even when they were led by the greatest warrior they have ever had."

"In truth I am very curious to know what they can do," answered Volodyovski; "and were it not that two other wars are now weighing on the country, I should not be angry a whit about the Swedes. We have tried the Turks, the Tartars, the Cossacks, and God knows whom we have not tried; it is well now to try the Swedes. The only trouble in the kingdom is that all the troops are occupied with the hetmans in the Ukraine. But I see already what will happen here. Prince Radzivill will leave the existing war to the treasurer and full hetman Pan Gosyevski, and will go himself at the Swedes in earnest. It will be heavy work, it is true. But we have hope that God will assist us."

"Let us go, then, without delay to Kyedani," said Pan Stanislav.

"I received an order to have the squadron ready and to appear in Kyedani myself in three days," answered Pan Michael. "But I must show you, gentlemen this last order, for it is clear from it that the prince is thinking of the Swedes."

When he had said this, Volodyovski unlocked a box standing on a bench under the window, took out a paper folded once, and opening it began to read:—

Colonel Volodyovski:

Gracious Sir,—We have read with great delight your report that the squadron is ready and can move to the campaign at any moment. Keep it ready and alert, for such difficult times are coming as have not been yet; therefore come yourself as quickly as possible to Kyedani, where we shall await you with impatience. If any reports come to you, believe them not till you have heard everything from our lips. We act as God himself and our conscience command, without reference to what malice and the ill will of man may invent against us. But at the same time we console ourselves with this,—that times are coming in which it will be shown definitely who is a true and real friend of the house of Radzivill and who even *in rebus adversis* is willing to serve it. Kmita, Nyevyarovski, and Stankyevich have brought their squadrons here already; let yours remain in Upita, for it may be needed there, and it may have to march to Podlyasye under command of my cousin Prince Boguslav, who has considerable bodies of our troops under his command there. Of all this you will learn in detail from our lips; meanwhile we confide to your loyalty the careful execution of orders, and await you in Kyedani.

Yanush Radzivill,

Prince in Birji and Dubinki, voevoda of Vilna, grand hetman of Lithuania.

"Yes, a new war is evident from this letter," said Zagloba.

"And the prince's statement that he will act as God commands him, means that he will fight the Swedes," added Stanislav.

"Still it is a wonder to me," said Pan Yan, "that he writes about loyalty to the house of Radzivill, and not to the country, which means more than the Radzivills, and demands prompter rescue."

"That is their lordly manner," answered Volodyovski; "though that did not please me either at first, for I too serve the country and not the Radzivills."

"When did you receive this letter?" asked Pan Yan.

"This morning, and I wanted to start this afternoon. You will rest to-night after the journey; to-morrow I shall surely return, and then we will move with the squadron wherever they command."

"Perhaps to Podlyasye?" said Zagloba.

"To Prince Boguslav," added Pan Stanislav.

"Prince Boguslav is now in Kyedani," said Volodyovski. "He is a strange person, and do you look at him carefully. He is a great warrior and a still greater knight, but he is not a Pole to the value of a copper. He wears a foreign dress, and talks German or French altogether; you might think he was cracking nuts, might listen to him a whole hour, and not understand a thing."

"Prince Boguslav at Berestechko bore himself well," said Zagloba, "and brought a good number of German infantry."

"Those who know him more intimately do not praise him very highly," continued Volodyovski, "for he loves only the Germans and French. It cannot be otherwise, since he was born of a German mother, the daughter of the elector of Brandenburg, with whom his late father not only received no dowry, but, since those small princes (the electors) as may be seen have poor housekeeping, he had to pay something. But with the Radzivills it is important to have a vote in the German Empire, of which they are princes, and therefore they make alliances with the Germans. Pan Sakovich, an old client of Prince Boguslav, who made him starosta of Oshmiani, told me about this. He and Pan

Nyevyarovski, a colonel, were abroad with Prince Boguslav in various foreign lands, and acted always as seconds in his duels."

"How many has he fought?" asked Zagloba.

"As many as he has hairs on his head! He cut up various princes greatly and foreign counts, French and German, for they say that he is very fiery, brave, and daring, and calls a man out for the least word."

Pan Stanislav was roused from his thoughtfulness and said: "I too have heard of this Prince Boguslav, for it is not far from us to the elector, with whom he lives continually. I have still in mind how my father said that when Prince Boguslav's father married the elector's daughter, people complained that such a great house as that of the Radzivills made an alliance with strangers. But perhaps it happened for the best; the elector as a relative of the Radzivills ought to be very friendly now to the Commonwealth, and on him much depends at present. What you say about their poor housekeeping is not true. It is certain, however, that if any one were to sell all the possessions of the Radzivills, he could buy with the price of them the elector and his whole principality; but the present kurfürst, Friedrich Wilhelm, has saved no small amount of money, and has twenty thousand very good troops with whom he might boldly meet the Swedes,— which as a vassal of the Commonwealth he ought to do if he has God in his heart, and remembers all the kindness which the Commonwealth has shown his house."

"Will he do that?" asked Pan Yan.

"It would be black ingratitude and faith-breaking on his part if he did otherwise," answered Pan Stanislav.

"It is hard to count on the gratitude of strangers, and especially of heretics," said Zagloba. "I remember this kurfürst of yours when he was still a stripling. He was always sullen; one would have said that he was listening to what the devil was whispering in his ear. When I was in Prussia with the late Konyetspolski, I told the kurfürst that to his eyes,—for he is a Lutheran, the same as the King of Sweden. God grant that they make no alliance against the Commonwealth!"

"Do you know, Michael," said Pan Yan, suddenly, "I will not rest here; I will go with you to Kyedani. It is better at this season to travel in the night, for it is hot in the daytime, and I am eager to escape from uncertainty. There is resting-time ahead, for surely the prince will not march to-morrow."

"Especially as he has given orders to keep the squadron in Upita," answered Pan Michael.

"You speak well!" cried Zagloba; "I will go too."

"Then we will all go together," said Pan Stanislav.

"We shall be in Kyedani in the morning," said Pan Michael, "and on the road we can sleep sweetly in our saddles."

Two hours later, after they had eaten and drunk somewhat, the knights started on their journey, and before sundown reached Krakin.

On the road Pan Michael told them about the neighborhood, and the famous nobles of Lauda, of Kmita, and of all that had happened during a certain time. He confessed also his love for Panna Billevich, unrequited as usual.

"It is well that war is near," said he, "otherwise I should have suffered greatly, when I think at times that such is my misfortune, and that probably I shall die in the single state."

"No harm will come to you from that," said Zagloba, "for it is an honorable state and pleasing to God. I have resolved to remain in it to the end of my life. Sometimes I regret that there will be no one to leave my fame and name to; for though I love Yan's children as if they were my own, still the Skshetuskis are not the Zaglobas."

"Ah, evil man! You have made this choice with a feeling like that of the wolf when he vowed not to kill sheep after all his teeth were gone."

"But that is not true," said Zagloba. "It is not so long, Michael, since you and I were in Warsaw at the election. At whom were all the women looking if not at me? Do you not remember how you used to complain that not one of them was looking at you? But if you have such a desire for the married state, then be not troubled; your turn will come too. This seeking is of no use; you will find just when you are not seeking. This is a time of war, and many good cavaliers perish every year. Only let this Swedish war continue, the girls will be alone, and we shall find them in market by the dozen."

"Perhaps I shall perish too," said Pan Michael. "I have had enough of this battering through the world. Never shall I be able to tell you, gentlemen, what a worthy and beautiful lady Panna Billevich is. And if it were a man who had loved and petted her in the tenderest way—No! the devils had to bring this Kmita. It must be that he gave her something, it cannot be otherwise; for if he had not, surely she would not have let me go. There, look! Just beyond the hills Vodokty is visible; but there is no one in the house. She has gone God knows whither. The bear has his den, the pig his nest, but I have only this crowbait and this saddle on which I sit."

"I see that she has pierced you like a thorn," said Zagloba.

"True, so that when I think of myself or when riding by I see Vodokty, I grieve still. I wanted to strike out the wedge with a wedge, and went to Pan Schilling, who has a very comely daughter. Once I saw her on the road at a distance, and she took my fancy greatly. I went to his house, and what shall I say, gentlemen? I did not find the father at home, but the daughter Panna Kahna thought that I was not Pan Volodyovski, but only

225

Pan Volodyovski's attendant. I took the affront so to heart that I have never shown myself there again."

Zagloba began to laugh. "God help you, Michael! The whole matter is this,—you must find a wife of such stature as you are yourself. But where did that little rogue go to who was in attendance on Princess Vishnyevetski, and whom the late Pan Podbipienta—God light his soul!—was to marry? She was just your size, a regular peach-stone, though her eyes did shine terribly."

"That was Anusia Borzabogati," said Pan Yan. "We were all in love with her in our time,—Michael too. God knows where she is now!"

"I might seek her out and comfort her," said Pan Michael. "When you mention her it grows warm around my heart. She was a most respectable girl. Ah, those old days of Lubni were pleasant, but never will they return. They will not, for never will there be such a chief as our Prince Yeremi. A man knew that every battle would be followed by victory. Radzivill was a great warrior, but not such, and men do not serve him with such heart, for he has not that fatherly love for soldiers, and does not admit them to confidence, having something about him of the monarch, though the Vishnyevetskis were not inferior to the Radzivills."

"No matter," said Pan Yan. "The salvation of the country is in his hands now, and because he is ready to give his life for it, God bless him!"

Thus conversed the old friends, riding along in the night. They called up old questions at one time; at another they spoke of the grievous days of the present, in which three wars at once had rolled on the Commonwealth. Later they repeated "Our Father" and the litany; and when they had finished, sleep wearied them, and they began to doze and nod on the saddles.

The night was clear and warm; the stars twinkled by thousands in the sky. Dragging on at a walk, they slept sweetly till, when day began to break. Pan Michael woke.

"Gentlemen, open your eyes; Kyedani is in sight!" cried he.

"What, where?" asked Zagloba. "Kyedani, where?"

"Off there! The towers are visible."

"A respectable sort of place," said Pan Stanislav.

"Very considerable," answered Volodyovski; "and of this you will be able to convince yourselves better in the daytime."

"But is this the inheritance of the prince?"

"Yes. Formerly it belonged to the Kishkis, from whom the father of the present prince received it as dowry with Panna Anna Kishki, daughter of the voevoda of Vityebsk. In all Jmud there is not such a well-ordered place, for the Radzivills do not admit Jews, save by permission to each one. The meads here are celebrated."

Zagloba opened his eyes.

"But do people of some politeness live here? What is that immensely great building on the eminence?"

"That is the castle just built during the rule of Yanush."

"Is it fortified?"

"No, but it is a lordly residence. It is not fortified, for no enemy has ever entered these regions since the time of the Knights of the Cross. That pointed steeple in the middle of the town belongs to the parish church built by the Knights of the Cross in pagan times; later it was given to the Calvinists, but the priest Kobylinski won it back for the Catholics through a lawsuit with Prince Krishtof."

"Praise be to God for that!"

Thus conversing they arrived near the first cottages of the suburbs. Meanwhile it grew brighter and brighter in the world, and the sun began to rise. The knights looked with curiosity at the new place, and Pan Volodyovski continued to speak,—

"This is Jew street, in which dwell those of the Jews who have permission to be here. Following this street, one comes to the market. Oho! people are up already, and beginning to come out of the houses. See, a crowd of horses before the forges, and attendants not in the Radzivill colors! There must be some meeting in Kyedani. It is always full of nobles and high personages here, and sometimes they come from foreign countries, for this is the capital for heretics from all Jmud, who under the protection of the Radzivills carry on their sorcery and superstitious practices. That is the market-square. See what a clock is on the town-house! There is no better one to this day in Dantzig. And that which looks like a church with four towers is a Helvetic (Calvinistic) meeting-house, in which every Sunday they blaspheme God; and farther on the Lutheran church. You think that the townspeople are Poles or Lithuanians,—not at all. Real Germans and Scots, but more Scots. The Scots are splendid infantry, and cut terribly with battle-axes. The prince has also one Scottish regiment of volunteers of Kyedani. Ei, how many wagons with packs on the market-square! Surely there is some meeting. There are no inns in the town; acquaintances stop with acquaintances, and nobles go to the castle, in which there are rooms tens of ells long, intended for guests only. There they entertain, at the prince's expense, every one honorably, even if for a year; there are people who stay there all their lives."

"It is a wonder to me that lightning has not burned that Calvinistic meeting-house," said Zagloba.

"But do you not know that that has happened? In the centre between the four towers was a cap-shaped cupola; on a time such a lightning-flash struck this cupola that nothing remained of it. In the vault underneath lies the father of Prince

Boguslav, Yanush,—he who joined the mutiny against Sigismund III. His own haiduk laid open his skull, so that he died in vain, as he had lived in sin."

"But what is that broad building which looks like a walled tent?" asked Pan Yan.

"That is the paper-mill founded by the prince; and at the side of it is a printing-office, in which heretical books are printed."

"Tfu!" said Zagloba; "a pestilence on this place, where a man draws no air into his stomach but what is heretical! Lucifer might rule here as well as Radzivill."

"Gracious sir," answered Volodyovski, "abuse not Radzivill, for perhaps the country will soon owe its salvation to him."

They rode farther in silence, gazing at the town and wondering at its good order; for the streets were all paved with stone, which was at that period a novelty.

After they had ridden through the market-square and the street of the castle, they saw on an eminence the lordly residence recently built by Prince Yanush,—not fortified, it is true, but surpassing in size not only palaces but castles. The great pile was on a height, and looked on the town lying, as it were, at its feet. From both sides of the main building extended at right angles two lower wings, which formed a gigantic courtyard, closed in front with an iron railing fastened with long links. In the middle of the railing towered a strong walled gate; on it the arms of the Radzivills and the arms of the town of Kyedani, representing an eagle's foot with a black wing on a golden field, and at the foot a horseshoe with three red crosses. In front of the gate were sentries and Scottish soldiers keeping guard for show, not for defence.

The hour was early, but there was movement already in the yard; for before the main building a regiment of dragoons in blue jackets and Swedish helmets was exercising. Just then the long line of men was motionless, with drawn rapiers; an officer riding in front said something to the soldiers. Around the line and farther on near the walls, a number of attendants in various colors gazed at the dragoons, making remarks and giving opinions to one another.

"As God is dear to me," said Pan Michael, "that is Kharlamp drilling the regiment!"

"How!" cried Zagloba; "is he the same with whom you were going to fight a duel at Lipkovo?"

"The very same; but since that time we have lived in close friendship."

"'Tis he," said Zagloba; "I know him by his nose, which sticks out from under his helmet. It is well that visors have gone out of fashion, for that knight could not close any visor; he would need a special invention for his nose."

That moment Pan Kharlamp, seeing Volodyovski, came to him at a trot. "How are you, Michael?" cried he. "It is well that you have come."

"It is better that I meet you first. See, here is Pan Zagloba, whom you met in Lipkovo—no, before that in Syennitsy; and these are the Skshetuskis,—Yan, captain of the king's hussars, the hero of Zbaraj—"

"I see, then, as God is true, the greatest knight in Poland!" cried Kharlamp. "With the forehead, with the forehead!"

"And this is Stanislav Skshetuski, captain of Kalisk, who comes straight from Uistsie."

"From Uistsie? So you saw a terrible disgrace. We know already what has happened."

"It is just because such a thing happened that I have come, hoping that nothing like it will happen in this place."

"You may be certain of that; Radzivill is not Opalinski."

"We said the same at Upita yesterday."

"I greet you, gentlemen, most joyfully in my own name and that of the prince. The prince will be glad to see such knights, for he needs them much. Come with me to the barracks, where my quarters are. You will need, of course, to change clothes and eat breakfast. I will go with you, for I have finished the drill."

Pan Kharlamp hurried again to the line, and commanded in a quick, clear voice: "To the left! face—to the rear!"

Hoofs sounded on the pavement. The line broke into two; the halves broke again till there were four parts, which began to recede with slow step in the direction of the barracks.

"Good soldiers," said Skshetuski, looking with skilled eye at the regular movements of the dragoons.

"Those are petty nobles and attendant boyars who serve in that arm," answered Volodyovski.

"Oh, you could tell in a moment that they are not militia," cried Pan Stanislav.

"But does Kharlamp command them," asked Zagloba, "or am I mistaken? I remember that he served in the light-horse squadron and wore silver loops."

"True," answered Volodyovski; "but it is a couple of years since he took the dragoon regiment. He is an old soldier, and trained."

Meanwhile Kharlamp, having dismissed the dragoons, returned to the knights. "I beg you, gentlemen, to follow me. Over there are the barracks, beyond the castle."

Half an hour later the five were sitting over a bowl of heated beer, well whitened with cream, and were talking about the impending war.

"And what is to be heard here?" asked Pan Michael.

"With us something new may be heard every day, for people are lost in surmises and give out new reports all the time," said Kharlamp. "But in truth the prince alone knows what is coming. He has something on his mind, for though he simulates gladness and is kind to people as never before, he is terribly thoughtful. In the night, they say, he does not sleep, but walks with heavy tread through all the chambers, talking audibly to himself, and in the daytime takes counsel for whole hours with Harasimovich."

"Who is Harasimovich?" asked Volodyovski.

"The manager from Zabludovo in Podlyasye,—a man of small stature, who looks as though he kept the devil under his arm; but he is a confidential agent of the prince, and probably knows all his secrets. According to my thinking, from these counsellings a terrible and vengeful war with Sweden will come, for which war we are all sighing. Meanwhile letters are flying hither from the Prince of Courland, from Hovanski, and from the Elector of Brandenburg. Some say that the prince is negotiating with Moscow to join the league against Sweden; others say the contrary; but it seems there will be a league with no one, but a war, as I have said, with these and those. Fresh troops are coming continually; letters are sent to nobles most faithful to the Radzivills, asking them to assemble. Every place is full of armed men. Ei, gentlemen, on whomsoever they put the grain, on him will it be ground; but we shall have our hands red to the elbows, for when Radzivill moves to the field, he will not negotiate."

"That's it, that's it!" said Zagloba, rubbing his palms. "No small amount of Swedish blood has dried on my hands, and there will be more of it in future. Not many of those old soldiers are alive yet who remember me at Putsk and Tjtsianna; but those who are living will never forget me."

"Is Prince Boguslav here?" asked Volodyovski.

"Of course. Besides him we expect to-day some great guests, for the upper chambers are made ready, and there is to be a banquet in the evening. I have my doubts, Michael, whether you will reach the prince to-day."

"He sent for me himself yesterday."

"That's nothing; he is terribly occupied. Besides, I don't know whether I can speak of it to you—but in an hour everybody will know of it, therefore I will tell you—something or another very strange is going on."

"What is it, what is it?" asked Zagloba.

"It must be known to you, gentlemen, that two days ago Pan Yudytski came, a knight of Malta, of whom you must have heard."

"Of course," said Yan; "he is a great knight."

"Immediately after him came the full hetman and treasurer. We were greatly astonished, for it is known in what rivalry and enmity Pan Gosyevski is with our prince. Some persons were rejoiced therefore that harmony had come between the lords, and said that the Swedish invasion was the real cause of this. I thought so myself; then yesterday the three shut themselves up in counsel, fastened all the doors, no one could hear what they were talking about; but Pan Krepshtul, who guarded the door, told us that their talk was terribly loud, especially the talk of Pan Gosyevski. Later the prince himself conducted them to their sleeping-chambers, and in the night— imagine to yourselves" (here Kharlamp lowered his voice)— "guards were placed at the door of each chamber."

Volodyovski sprang up from his seat. "In God's name! impossible!"

"But it is true. At the doors of each Scots are standing with muskets, and they have the order to let no one in or out under pain of death."

The knights looked at one another with astonishment; and Kharlamp was no less astonished at his own words, and looked at his companions with staring eyes, as if awaiting the explanation of the riddle from them.

"Does this mean that Pan Gosyevski is arrested? Has the grand hetman arrested the full hetman?" asked Zagloba; "what does this mean?"

"As if I know, and Yudytski such a knight!"

"But the officers of the prince must speak with one another about it and guess at causes. Have you heard nothing?"

"I asked Harasimovich last night."

"What did he say?" asked Zagloba.

"He would explain nothing, but he put his finger on his mouth and said, 'They are traitors!'"

"How traitors?" cried Volodyovski, seizing his head. "Neither the treasurer nor Pan Yudytski is a traitor. The whole Commonwealth knows them as honorable men and patriots."

"At present 'tis impossible to have faith in any man," answered Pan Stanislav, gloomily. "Did not Pan Opalinski pass for a Cato? Did he not reproach others with defects, with offences, with selfishness? But when it came to do something, he was the first to betray, and brought not only himself, but a whole province to treason."

"I will give my head for the treasurer and Pan Yudytski!" cried Volodyovski.

"Do not give your head for any man, Michael dear," said Zagloba. "They were not arrested without reason. There must have been some conspiracy; it cannot be otherwise,—how could it be? The prince is preparing for a terrible war, and every aid is precious to him. Whom, then, at such a time can he put under arrest, if not those who stand in the way of war? If this is so, if these two men have really stood in the way, then praise be to God that Radzivill has anticipated them. They deserve to sit under ground. Ah, the scoundrels!—at such a time to practise tricks,

234

communicate with the enemy, rise against the country, hinder a great warrior in his undertaking! By the Most Holy Mother, what has met them is too little, the rascals!"

"These are wonders,—such wonders that I cannot put them in my head," said Kharlamp; "for letting alone that they are such dignitaries, they are arrested without judgment, without a diet, without the will of the whole Commonwealth,—a thing which the king himself has not the right to do."

"As true as I live," cried Pan Michael.

"It is evident that the prince wants to introduce Roman customs among us," said Pan Stanislav, "and become dictator in time of war."

"Let him be dictator if he will only beat the Swedes," said Zagloba; "I will be the first to vote for his dictatorship."

Pan Yan fell to thinking, and after a while said, "Unless he should wish to become protector, like that English Cromwell who did not hesitate to raise his sacrilegious hand on his own king."

"Nonsense! Cromwell? Cromwell was a heretic!" cried Zagloba.

"But what is the prince voevoda?" asked Pan Yan, seriously.

At this question all were silent, and considered the dark future for a time with fear; but Kharlamp looked angry and said,—

"I have served under the prince from early years, though I am little younger than he; for in the beginning, when I was still a stripling, he was my captain, later on he was full hetman, and now he is grand hetman. I know him better than any one here; I both love and honor him; therefore I ask you not to compare him with Cromwell, so that I may not be forced to say something which would not become me as host in this room."

Here Kharlamp began to twitch his mustaches terribly, and to frown a little at Pan Yan; seeing which, Volodyovski fixed on Kharlamp a cool and sharp look, as if he wished to say, "Only growl, only growl!"

Great Mustache took note at once, for he held Volodyovski in unusual esteem, and besides it was dangerous to get angry with him; therefore he continued in a far milder tone,—

"The prince is a Calvinist; but he did not reject the true faith for errors, for he was born in them. He will never become either a Cromwell, a Radzeyovski, or an Opalinski, though Kyedani had to sink through the earth. Not such is his blood, not such his stock."

"If he is the devil and has horns on his head," said Zagloba, "so much the better, for he will have something to gore the Swedes with."

"But that Pan Gosyevski and Pan Yudytski are arrested, well, well!" said Volodyovski, shaking his head. "The prince is not very amiable to guests who have confided in him."

"What do you say, Michael?" answered Kharlamp. "He is amiable as he has never been in his life. He is now a real father to the knights. Think how some time ago he had always a frown on his forehead, and on his lips one word, 'Service.' A man was more afraid to go near his majesty than he was to stand before the king; and now he goes every day among the lieutenants and the officers, converses, asks each one about his family, his children, his property, calls each man by name, and inquires if injustice has been done to any one in service. He who among the highest lords will not own an equal, walked yesterday arm-in-arm with young Kmita. We could not believe our eyes; for though the family of Kmita is a great one, he is quite young, and likely many accusations are weighing on him. Of this you know best."

"I know, I know," replied Volodyovski. "Has Kmita been here long?"

"He is not here now, for he went yesterday to Cheykishki for a regiment of infantry stationed there. No one is now in such favor with the prince as Kmita. When he was going away the prince looked after him awhile and said, 'That man is equal to anything, and is ready to seize the devil himself by the tail if I tell him!' We heard this with our own ears. It is true that Kmita brought a squadron that has not an equal in the whole army,— men and horses like dragons!"

"There is no use in talking, he is a valiant soldier, and in truth ready for everything," said Pan Michael. "He performed wonders in the last campaign, till a price was set on his head, for he led volunteers and carried on war himself."

Further conversation was interrupted by the entrance of a new figure. This was a noble about forty years of age, small, dry, alert, wriggling like a mud-fish, with a small face, very thin lips, a scant mustache, and very crooked eyes. He was dressed in a ticking-coat, with such long sleeves that they covered his hands completely. When he had entered he bent double, then he straightened himself as suddenly as if moved by a spring, again he inclined with a low bow, turned his head as if he were taking it out of his own armpits, and began to speak hurriedly in a voice which recalled the squeaking of a rusty weather-cock,—

"With the forehead, Pan Kharlamp, with the forehead. Ah! with the forehead, Pan Colonel, most abject servant!"

"With the forehead, Pan Harasimovich," answered Kharlamp; "and what is your wish?"

"God gave guests, distinguished guests. I came to offer my services and to inquire their rank."

"Did they come to you, Pan Harasimovich?"

"Certainly not to me, for I am not worthy of that; but because I take the place of the absent marshal. I have come to greet them profoundly."

"It is far from you to the marshal," said Kharlamp; "for he is a personage with inherited land, while you with permission are under-starosta of Zabludovo."

"A servant of the servants of Radzivill. That is true, Pan Kharlamp, I make no denial; God preserve me therefrom. But since the prince has heard of the guests, he has sent me to inquire who they are; therefore you will answer, Pan Kharlamp, if I were even a haiduk and not the under-starosta of Zabludovo."

"Oh, I would answer even a monkey if he were to come with an order," said Big Nose. "Listen now, and calk these names into yourself if your head is not able to hold them. This is Pan Skshetuski, that hero of Zbaraj; and this is his cousin Stanislav."

"Great God! what do I hear?" cried Harasimovich.

"This is Pan Zagloba."

"Great God! what do I hear?"

"If you are so confused at hearing my name," said Zagloba, "think of the confusion of the enemy in the field."

"And this is Colonel Volodyovski," finished Kharlamp.

"And he has a famous sabre, and besides is a Radzivill man," said Harasimovich, with a bow. "The prince's head is splitting from labor; but still he will find time for such knights, surely he will find it. Meanwhile with what can you be served? The whole castle is at the service of such welcome guests, and the cellars as well."

"We have heard of the famous meads of Kyedani," said Zagloba, hurriedly.

"Indeed!" answered Harasimovich, "there are glorious meads in Kyedani, glorious. I will send some hither for you to choose from right away. I hope that my benefactors will stay here long."

"We have come hither," said Pan Stanislav, "not to leave the side of the prince."

"Praiseworthy is your intention, the more so that trying times are at hand."

When he had said this, Harasimovich wriggled and became as small as if an ell had been taken from his stature.

"What is to be heard?" asked Kharlamp. "Is there any news?"

"The prince has not closed an eye all night, for two envoys have come. Evil are the tidings, increasingly evil. Karl Gustav has already entered the Commonwealth after Wittemberg; Poznan is now occupied, all Great Poland is occupied, Mazovia will be occupied soon; the Swedes are in Lovich, right at Warsaw. Our king has fled from Warsaw, which he left undefended. To-day or to-morrow the Swedes will enter. They say that the king has lost a considerable battle, that he thinks of escaping to Cracow, and thence to foreign lands to ask aid. Evil, gracious gentlemen, my benefactors! Though there are some who say that it is well; for the Swedes commit no violence, observe agreements sacredly, collect no imposts, respect liberties, do not hinder the faith. Therefore all accept the protection of Karl Gustav willingly. For our king, Yan Kazimir, is at fault, greatly at fault. All is lost, lost for him! One would like to weep, but all is lost, lost!"

"Why the devil do you wriggle like a mudfish going to the pot," howled Zagloba, "and speak of a misfortune as if you were glad of it?"

Harasimovich pretended not to hear, and raising his eyes to heaven he repeated yet a number of times: "All is lost, lost for the ages! The Commonwealth cannot stand against three wars.

Lost! The will of God, the will of God! Our prince alone can save Lithuania."

The ill-omened words had not yet ceased to sound when Harasimovich vanished behind the door as quickly as if he had sunk through the earth, and the knights sat in gloom bent by the weight of terrible thoughts.

"We shall go mad!" cried Volodyovski at last.

"You are right," said Stanislav. "God give war, war at the earliest,—war in which a man does not ruin himself in thinking, nor yield his soul to despair, but fights."

"We shall regret the first period of Hmelnitski's war," said Zagloba; "for though there were defeats then, there were no traitors."

"Three such terrible wars, when in fact there is a lack of forces for one," said Stanislav.

"Not a lack of forces, but of spirit. The country is perishing through viciousness. God grant us to live to something better!" said Pan Yan, gloomily.

"We shall not rest till we are in the field," said Stanislav.

"If we can only see this prince soon!" cried Zagloba.

Their wishes were accomplished directly; for after an hour's time Harasimovich came again, with still lower bows, and with the announcement that the prince was waiting anxiously to see them.

They sprang up at once, for they had already changed uniforms, and went. Harasimovich, in conducting them from the barracks, passed through the courtyard, which was full of soldiers and nobles. In some places they were conversing in crowds, evidently over the same news which the under-starosta of Zabludovo had brought the knights. On all faces were depicted lively alarm and a certain feverish expectation. Isolated groups of officers and nobles were listening to the speakers, who standing in the midst of them gesticulated violently. On the way were heard the words: "Vilna is burning, Vilna is burned!—No trace of it, nor the ashes! Warsaw is taken!—Untrue, not taken yet!—The Swedes are in Little Poland! The people of Syeradz will resist!—They will not resist, they will follow the example of Great Poland!—Treason! misfortune! O God, God! It is unknown where to put sabre or hand!"

Such words as these, more and more terrible, struck the ears of the knights; but they went on pushing after Harasimovich through the soldiers and nobles with difficulty. In places acquaintances greeted Volodyovski: "How is your health, Michael? 'Tis evil with us; we are perishing! With the forehead, brave Colonel! And what guests are these whom you are taking to the prince?" Pan Michael answered not, wishing to escape delay; and in this fashion they went to the main body of the castle, in which the janissaries of the prince, in chain-mail and gigantic white caps, were on guard.

In the antechamber and on the main staircase, set around with orange-trees, the throng was still greater than in the courtyard. They were discussing there the arrest of Gosyevski and Yudytski; for the affair had become known, and roused the minds of men to the utmost. They were astonished and lost in surmises, they were indignant or praised the foresight of the prince; but all hoped to hear the explanation of the riddle from Radzivill himself, therefore a river of heads was flowing along the broad staircase up to the hall of audience, in which at that time the prince was to receive colonels and the most intimate nobility. Soldiers disposed along the stone banisters to see that the throng was not too dense, repeated, from moment to moment, "Slowly, gracious gentlemen, slowly!" And the crowd pushed forward or halted for a moment, when a soldier stopped the way with a halbert so that those in front might have time to enter the hall.

At last the blue vaultings of the hall gleamed before the open door, and our acquaintances entered. Their glances fell first on an elevation, placed in the depth of the hall, occupied by a brilliant retinue of knights and lords in rich, many-colored dresses. In front stood an empty arm-chair, pushed forward beyond the others. This chair had a lofty back, ending with the gilded coronet of the prince, from beneath which flowed downward orange-colored velvet trimmed with ermine.

The prince was not in the hall yet; but Harasimovich, conducting the knights without interruption, pushed through the nobility till he reached a small door concealed in the wall at the side of the elevation. There he directed them to remain, and disappeared through the door.

After a while he returned with the announcement that the prince asked them to enter.

The two Skshetuskis, with Zagloba and Volodyovski, entered a small but very well-lighted room, having walls covered with leather stamped in flowers, which were gilded. The officers halted on seeing in the depth of the room, at a table covered with papers, two men conversing intently. One of them, still young, dressed in foreign fashion, wearing a wig with long locks falling to his shoulders, whispered something in the ear of his elder companion; the latter heard him with frowning brow, and nodded from time to time. So much was he occupied with the subject of the conversation that he did not turn attention at once to those who had entered.

He was a man somewhat beyond forty years, of gigantic stature and great shoulders. He wore a scarlet Polish coat, fastened at the neck with costly brooches. He had an enormous face, with features expressing pride, importance, and power. It was at once the face of an angry lion, of a warrior, and a ruler. Long pendent mustaches lent it a stern expression, and altogether in its strength and size it was as if struck out of marble with great blows of a hammer. The brows were at that moment frowning from intense thought; but it could easily be seen that when they were frowning from anger, woe to those men and those armies on whom the thunders of that anger should fall.

There was something so great in the form that it seemed to those knights that not only the room, but the whole castle was too narrow for it; in fact, their first impression had not deceived them, for sitting in their presence was Yanush Radzivill, prince at Birji and Dubinki, voevoda of Vilna and grand hetman of Lithuania,—a man so powerful and proud that in all his immense estates, in all his dignities, nay, in Jmud and in Lithuania itself, it was too narrow for him.

The younger man in the long wig and foreign dress was Prince Boguslav, the cousin of Yanush. After a while he whispered something more in the ear of the hetman, and at last said audibly,—

"I will leave, then, my signature on the document and go."

"Since it cannot be otherwise, go," said Yanush, "though I would that you remained, for it is unknown what may happen."

"You have planned everything properly; henceforth it is needful to look carefully to the cause, and now I commit you to God."

"May the Lord have in care our whole house and bring it praise."

"Adieu, mon frère."

"Adieu."

The two princes shook hands; then Boguslav went out hurriedly, and the grand hetman turned to the visitors.

"Pardon me, gentlemen, that I let you wait," said he, with a low, deliberate voice; "but now time and attention are snatched from us on every side. I have heard your names, and rejoice in my

243

soul that God sent me such knights in this crisis. Be seated, dear guests. Who of you is Pan Yan Skshetuski?"

"I am, at the service of your highness."

"Then you are a starosta—pardon me, I forgot."

"I am not a starosta," answered Yan.

"How is that?" asked the prince, frowning with his two mighty brows; "they have not made you a starosta for what you did at Zbaraj?"

"I have never asked for the office."

"But they should have made you starosta without the asking. How is this? What do you tell me? You rewarded with nothing, forgotten entirely? This is a wonder to me. But I am talking at random. It should astonish no man; for in these days only he is rewarded who has the back of a willow, light-bending. You are not a starosta, upon my word! Thanks be to God that you have come hither, for here we have not such short memories, and no service remains unrewarded. How is it with you, worthy Colonel Volodyovski?"

"I have earned nothing yet."

"Leave that to me, and now take this document, drawn up in Rossyeni, by which I give you Dydkyemie for life. It is not a bad piece of land, and a hundred ploughs go out to work there every spring. Take even that, for I cannot give more, and tell Pan Skshetuski that Radzivill does not forget his friends, nor those who give their service to the country under his leadership."

"Your princely highness!" stammered Pan Michael, in confusion.

"Say nothing, and pardon that it is so small; but tell these gentlemen that he who joins his fortune for good and ill with that of Radzivill will not perish. I am not king; but if I were, God is my witness that I would never forget such a Yan Skshetuski or such a Zagloba."

"That is I!" said Zagloba, pushing himself forward sharply, for he had begun to be impatient that there was no mention of him.

"I thought it was you, for I have been told that you were a man of advanced years."

"I went to school in company with your highness's worthy father; and there was such knightly impulse in him from childhood that he took me to his confidence, for I loved the lance before Latin."

To Pan Stanislav, who knew Zagloba less, it was strange to hear this, since only the day before, Zagloba said in Upita that he had gone to school, not with the late Prince Kryshtof, but with Yanush himself,—which was unlikely, for Prince Yanush was notably younger.

"Indeed," said the prince; "so then you are from Lithuania by family?"

"From Lithuania!" answered Zagloba, without hesitation.

"Then I know that you need no reward, for we Lithuanians are used to be fed with ingratitude. As God is true, if I should give you your deserts, gentlemen, there would be nothing left for myself. But such is fate! We give our blood, lives, fortunes, and no one nods a head to us. Ah! 'tis hard; but as they sow will they reap. That is what God and justice command. It is you who slew the famous Burlai and cut off three heads at a blow in Zbaraj?"

"I slew Burlai, your highness," answered Zagloba, "for it was said that no man could stand before him. I wished therefore to show younger warriors that manhood was not extinct in the Commonwealth. But as to cutting off the three heads, it may be that I did that in the thick of battle; but in Zbaraj some one else did it."

The prince was silent awhile, then continued: "Does not that contempt pain you, gentlemen, with which they pay you?"

"What is to be done, your highness, even if it is disagreeable to a man?" said Zagloba.

"Well, comfort yourselves, for that must change. I am already your debtor, since you have come here; and though I am not king, still with me it will not end with promises."

"Your princely highness," said Pan Yan, quickly and somewhat proudly, "we have come hither not for rewards and estates, but because the enemy has invaded the country, and we wish to go with our strength to assist it under the leadership of a famous warrior. My cousin Stanislav saw at Uistsie fear, disorder, shame, treason, and finally the enemy's triumph. Here under a great leader and a faithful defender of our country and king we will serve. Here not victories, not triumphs, but defeats and death await the enemy. This is why we have come to offer our service to your highness. We are soldiers; we want to fight, and are impatient for battle."

"If such is your desire, you will be satisfied," answered the prince, with importance. "You will not wait long, though at first we shall march on another enemy, for the ashes of Vilna demand vengeance. To-day or to-morrow we shall march in that direction, and God grant will redeem the wrongs with interest. I will not detain you longer, gentlemen; you need rest, and work is burning me. But come in the evening to the hall; maybe some proper entertainment will take place before the march, for a great number of fair heads have assembled under our protection at Kyedani before the war. Worthy Colonel Volodyovski, entertain these welcome guests as if in your own house, and remember that what is mine is yours. Pan Harasimovich, tell my brother nobles assembled in the hall, that I will not go out, for I have not the time, and this evening they will learn everything that they wish to know. Be in good health, gentlemen, and be friends of Radzivill, for that is greatly important for him now."

When he had said this, that mighty and proud lord gave his hand in turn to Zagloba, the two Skshetuskis, Volodyovski, and Kharlamp, as if to equals. His stern face grew radiant with a cordial and friendly smile, and that inaccessibleness usually surrounding him as with a dark cloud vanished completely.

"That is a leader, that is a warrior!" said Stanislav, when on the return they had pushed themselves through the throng of nobles assembled in the audience-hall.

"I would go into fire after him!" cried Zagloba. "Did you notice how he had all my exploits in his memory? It will be hot for the Swedes when that lion roars, and I second him. There is not another such man in the Commonwealth; and of the former men only Prince Yeremi first, and second Konyetspolski, the father, might be compared with him. That is not some mere castellan, the first of his family to sit in a senator's chair, on which he has not yet smoothed out the wrinkles of his trousers, and still turns up his nose and calls the nobles younger brothers, and gives orders right away to paint his portrait, so that while dining he may have his senatorship before him, since he has nothing to look at behind. Pan Michael, you have come to fortune. It is evident now that if a man rubs against Radzivill he will gild at once his threadbare coat. It is easier to get promotion here, I see, than a quart of rotten pears with us. Stick your hands into the water in this place, and with closed eyes you will catch a pike. For me he is the magnate of magnates! God give you luck, Pan Michael! You are as confused as a young woman just married; but that is nothing! What is the name of your life estate? Dudkovo, or something? Heathen names in this country! Throw nuts against the wall, and you will have in the rattling the proper name of a village or noble. But names are nothing if the income is only good."

"I am terribly confused, I confess," said Pan Michael, "because what you say about easy promotion is not true. More than once have I heard old soldiers charge the prince with avarice, but now unexpected favors are showered one after the other."

"Stick that document behind your belt,—do that for me,—and if any one in future complains of the thanklessness of the prince, draw it out and give it to him on the nose. You will not find a better argument."

"One thing I see clearly: the prince is attracting people to his person, and is forming plans for which he needs help." said Pan Yan.

"But have you not heard of those plans?" asked Zagloba. "Has he not said that we have to go to avenge the ashes of Vilna? They complained that he had robbed Vilna, but he wants to show that he not only does not need other people's property, but is ready to give of his own. That is a beautiful ambition, Yan, God give us more of such senators."

Conversing thus, they found themselves in the courtyard, to which every moment rode in now divisions of mounted troops, now crowds of armed nobles, and now carriages rolled in, bringing persons from the country around, with their wives and children.

Seeing this, Pan Michael drew all with him to the gate to look at those entering.

"Who knows, Michael, this is your fortunate day? Maybe there is a wife for you among these nobles' daughters," said Zagloba. "Look! see, there an open carriage is approaching, and in it something white is sitting."

"That is not a lady, but a man who may marry me to one," answered the swift-eyed Volodyovski; for from a distance he recognized the bishop Parchevski, coming with Father Byalozor, archdeacon of Vilna.

"If they are priests, how are they visiting a Calvinist?"

"What is to be done? When it's necessary for public affairs, they must be polite."

"Oh, it is crowded here! Oh, it is noisy!" cried Zagloba, with delight. "A man grows rusty in the country, like an old key in a lock; here I think of better times. I'm a rascal if I don't make love to some pretty girl to-day."

Zagloba's words were interrupted by the soldiers keeping guard at the gate, who rushing out from their booths stood in two ranks to salute the bishop; and he rode past, making the sign of the cross with his hand on each side, blessing the soldiers and the nobles assembled near by.

"The prince is a polite man," said Zagloba, "since he honors the bishop, though he does not recognize the supremacy of the Church. God grant this to be the first step toward conversion!"

"Oh, nothing will come of it! Not few were the efforts of his first wife, and she accomplished nothing, only died from vexation. But why do the Scots not leave the line? It is evident that another dignitary will pass."

In fact, a whole retinue of armed soldiers appeared in the distance.

"Those are Ganhoff's dragoons,—I know them," said Volodyovski; "but some carriages are in the middle!"

At that moment the drums began to rattle.

"Oh, it is evident that some one greater than the bishop of Jmud is there!" cried Zagloba.

"Wait, they are here already."

"There are two carriages in the middle."

"True. In the first sits Pan Korf, the voevoda of Venden."

"Of course!" cried Pan Yan; "that is an acquaintance from Zbaraj."

249

The voevoda recognized them, and first Volodyovski, whom he had evidently seen oftener; in passing he leaned from the carriage and cried,—

"I greet you, gentlemen, old comrades! See, I bring guests!"

In the second carriage, with the arms of Prince Yanush, drawn by four white horses, sat two gentlemen of lordly mien, dressed in foreign fashion, in broad-brimmed hats, from under which the blond curls of wigs flowed to their shoulders over wide lace collars. One was very portly, wore a pointed light-blond beard, and mustaches bushy and turned up at the ends; the other was younger, dressed wholly in black. He had a less knightly form, but perhaps a higher office, for a gold chain glittered on his neck, with some order at the end. Apparently both were foreigners, for they looked with curiosity at the castle, the people, and the dresses.

"What sort of devils?" asked Zagloba.

"I do not know them, I have never seen them," answered Volodyovski.

Meanwhile the carriages passed, and began to turn in the yard so as to reach the main entrance of the castle, but the dragoons remained outside the gate. Volodyovski knew the officer leading them.

"Tokarzevich!" called he, "come to us, please."

"With the forehead, worthy Colonel."

"And what kind of hedgehogs are you bringing?"

"Those are Swedes."

"Swedes!"

"Yes, and men of distinction. The portly one is Count Löwenhaupt, and the slender man is Benedikt Schitte, Baron von Duderhoff."

"Duderhoff?" asked Zagloba.

"What do they want here?" inquired Volodyovski.

"God knows!" answered the officer. "We escorted them from Birji. Undoubtedly they have come to negotiate with our prince, for we heard in Birji that he is assembling a great army and is going to move on Livonia."

"Ah, rascals! you are growing timid," cried Zagloba. "Now you are invading Great Poland, now you are deposing the king, and now you are paying court to Radzivill, so that he should not tickle you in Livonia. Wait! you will run away to your Dunderhoff till your stockings are down. We'll soon dunder with you. Long life to Radzivill!"

"Long life!" repeated the nobles, standing near the gate.

"Defender of the country! Our shield! Against the Swedes, worthy gentlemen, against the Swedes!"

A circle was formed. Every moment nobles collected from the yard; seeing which, Zagloba sprang on the low guard-post of the gate, and began to cry,—

"Worthy gentlemen, listen! Whoso does not know me, to him I will say that I am that defender of Zbaraj who with this old hand slew Burlai, the greatest hetman after Hmelnitski; whoso has not heard of Zagloba was shelling peas, it is clear, in the first period of the Cossack war, or feeling hens (for eggs), or herding calves,—labors which I do not connect with such honorable cavaliers as you."

"He is a great knight!" called numerous voices. "There is no greater in the Commonwealth! Hear!"

"Listen, honorable gentlemen. My old bones craved repose; better for me to rest in the bakehouse, to eat cheese and cream, to walk in the gardens and gather apples, or putting my hands behind my back to stand over harvesters or pat a girl on the shoulder. And it is certain that for the enemy it would have been better to leave me at rest; for the Swedes and the Cossacks know

251

that I have a very heavy hand, and God grant that my name is as well known to you, gentlemen, as to the enemy."

"What kind of rooster is that crowing so loud?" asked some voice in the crowd, suddenly.

"Don't interrupt! Would you were dead!" cried others.

But Zagloba heard him. "Forgive that cockerel, gentlemen," said he; "for he knows not yet on which end of him is his tail, nor on which his head."

The nobles burst into mighty laughter, and the confused disturber pushed quickly behind the crowd, to escape the sneers which came raining on his head.

"I return to the subject," said Zagloba. "I repeat, rest would be proper for me; but because the country is in a paroxysm, because the enemy is trampling our land, I am here, worthy gentlemen, with you to resist the enemy in the name of that mother who nourished us all. Whoso will not stand by her to-day, whoso will not run to save her, is not a son, but a step-son; he is unworthy of her love. I, an old man, am going, let the will of God be done; and if it comes to me to die, with my last breath will I cry, 'Against the Swedes! brothers, against the Swedes!' Let us swear that we will not drop the sabre from our hands till we drive them out of the country."

"We are ready to do that without oaths!" cried numbers of voices. "We will go where our hetman the prince leads us; we will go where 'tis needful."

"Worthy brothers, you have seen how two stocking-wearers came here in a gilded carriage. They know that there is no trifling with Radzivill. They will follow him from chamber to chamber, and kiss him on the elbows to give them peace. But the prince, worthy gentlemen, with whom I have been advising and from whom I have just returned, has assured me, in the name of

252

all Lithuania, that there will be no negotiations, no parchments, nothing but war and war!"

"War! war!" repeated, as an echo, the voices of the hearers.

"But because the leader," continued Zagloba, "will begin the more boldly, the surer he is of his soldiers, let us show him, worthy gentlemen, our sentiments. And now let us go under the windows of the prince and shout, 'Down with the Swedes!' After me, worthy gentlemen!"

Then he sprang from the post and moved forward, and after him the crowd. They came under the very windows with an uproar increasing each moment, till at last it was mingled in one gigantic shout,—"Down with the Swedes! down with the Swedes!"

Immediately Pan Korf, the voevoda of Venden, ran out of the antechamber greatly confused; after him Ganhoff; and both began to restrain the nobles, quieting them, begging them to disperse.

"For God's sake!" said Korf, "in the upper hall the window-panes are rattling. You gentlemen do not think what an awkward time you have chosen for your shouting. How can you treat envoys with disrespect, and give an example of insubordination? Who roused you to this?"

"I," said Zagloba. "Your grace, tell the prince, in the name of us all, that we beg him to be firm, that we are ready to remain with him to the last drop of our blood."

"I thank you, gentlemen, in the name of the hetman, I thank you; but I beg you to disperse. Consider, worthy gentlemen. By the living God, consider that you are sinking the country! Whoso insults an envoy to-day, renders a bear's service to the Commonwealth."

"What do we care for envoys! We want to fight, not to negotiate!"

"Your courage comforts me. The time for fighting will come before long, God grant very soon. Rest now before the expedition. It is time for a drink of spirits and lunch. It is bad to fight on an empty stomach."

"That is as true as I live!" cried Zagloba, first.

"True, he struck the right spot. Since the prince knows our sentiments, we have nothing to do here!"

And the crowd began to disperse. The greater part flowed on to rooms in which many tables were already spread. Zagloba sat at the head of one of them. Pan Korf and Colonel Ganhoff returned then to the prince, who was sitting at counsel with the Swedish envoys, Bishop Parchevski, Father Byalozor, Pan Adam Komorovski, and Pan Alexander Myerzeyevski, a courtier of Yan Kazimir, who was stopping for the time in Kyedani.

"Who incited that tumult?" asked the prince, from whose lion-like face anger had not yet disappeared.

"It was that noble who has just come here, that famous Zagloba," answered Pan Korf.

"That is a brave knight," said the prince, "but he is beginning to manage me too soon."

Having said this, he beckoned to Colonel Ganhoff and whispered something in his ear.

Zagloba meanwhile, delighted with himself, went to the lower halls with solemn tread, having with him Volodyovski, with Yan and Stanislav Skshetuski.

"Well, friends, I have barely appeared and have roused love for the country in those nobles. It will be easier now for the prince to send off the envoys with nothing, for all he has to do is to call upon us. That will not be, I think, without reward, though it is more a question of honor with me. Why have you halted,

254

Michael, as if turned to stone, with eyes fixed on that carriage at the gate?"

"That is she!" said Volodyovski, with twitching mustaches. "By the living God, that is she herself!"

"Who?"

"Panna Billevich."

"She who refused you?"

"The same. Look, gentlemen, look! Might not a man wither away from regret?"

"Wait a minute!" said Zagloba, "we must have a closer look."

Meanwhile the carriage, describing a half-circle, approached the speakers. Sitting in it was a stately noble with gray mustaches, and at his side Panna Aleksandra; beautiful as ever, calm, and full of dignity.

Pan Michael fixed on her a complaining look and bowed low, but she did not see him in the crowd.

"That is some lordly child," said Zagloba, gazing at her fine, noble features, "too delicate for a soldier. I confess that she is a beauty, but I prefer one of such kind that for the moment you would ask, 'Is that a cannon or a woman?'"

"Do you know who that is who has just passed?" asked Pan Michael of a noble standing near.

"Of course," answered the noble; "that is Pan Tomash Billevich, sword-bearer of Rossyeni. All here know him, for he is an old servant and friend of the Radzivills."

CHAPTER XIV.

The prince did not show himself to the nobles that day till evening, for he dined with the envoys and some dignitaries with whom he had held previous counsel. But orders had come to the colonels to have the regiments of Radzivill's guard ready, and especially the infantry under foreign officers. It smelt of powder in the air. The castle, though not fortified, was surrounded with troops as if a battle was to be fought at its walls. Men expected that the campaign would begin on the following morning at latest; of this there were visible signs, for the countless servants of the prince were busied with packing into wagons arms, valuable implements, and the treasury of the prince.

Harasimovich told the nobles that the wagons would go to Tykotsin in Podlyasye, for it was dangerous to leave the treasury in the undefended castle of Kyedani. Military stores were also prepared to be sent after the army. Reports went out that Gosyevski was arrested because he would not join his squadrons stationed at Troki with those of Radzivill, thus exposing the whole expedition to evident destruction. Moreover preparations for the march, the movement of troops, the rattle of cannon drawn out of the castle arsenal, and all that turmoil which ever accompanies the first movements of military expeditions, turned attention in another direction, and caused the knights to forget the arrest of Pan Gosyevski and cavalier Yudytski.

The nobles dining in the immense lower halls attached to the castle spoke only of the war, of the fire at Vilna, now burning ten days and burning with ever-growing fury, of news from Warsaw, of the advance of the Swedes, and of the Swedes themselves, against whom, as against faith-breakers attacking a neighbor in spite of treaties still valid for six years, hearts and minds were indignant and souls filled with rancor. News of swift advances, of the capitulation of Uistsie, of the occupation of Great Poland and the large towns, of the threatened invasion of Mazovia and the inevitable capture of Warsaw, not only did not cause alarm, but on the contrary roused daring and a desire for battle. This took place since the causes of Swedish success were evident to all. Hitherto the Swedes had not met a real army once, or a real leader. Radzivill was the first warrior by profession with whom they had to measure strength, and who at the same time roused in the nobility absolute confidence in his military gifts, especially as his colonels gave assurance that they would conquer the Swedes in the open field.

"Their defeat is inevitable!" said Pan Stankyevich, an old and experienced soldier. "I remember former wars, and I know that they always defended themselves in castles, in fortified camps, and in trenches. They never dared to come to the open field, for they feared cavalry greatly, and when trusting in their numbers they did come out, they received a proper drilling. It was not victory that gave Great Poland into their hands, but treason and the imbecility of general militia."

"True," said Zagloba. "The Swedish people are weak, for their land is terribly barren, and they have no bread; they grind pine cones, and of that sort of flour make ash-cakes which smell of resin. Others go to the seashore and devour whatever the waves throw up, besides fighting about it as a tidbit. Terrible destitution! so there are no people more greedy for their neighbors' goods. Even the Tartars have horse-flesh in plenty, but these Swedes do not see meat once a year, and are pinched with hunger unless when a good haul of fish comes."

Here Zagloba turned to Stankyevich: "Have you ever made the acquaintance of the Swedes?"

"Under Prince Krishtof, the father of the present hetman."

"And I under Konyetspolski, the father. We gave Gustavus Adolphus many crushing defeats in Prussia, and took no small number of prisoners; there I became acquainted with them through and through, and learned all their methods. Our men wondered at them not a little, for you must know that the Swedes as a people always wading in water and having their greatest income from the sea, are divers *exquisitissimi*. What would you, gentlemen, say to what we made them do? We would throw one of the rascals into a hole in the ice, and he would swim out through another hole with a live herring in his mouth."

"In God's name, what do you tell us?"

"May I fall down a corpse on this spot if with my own eyes I have not seen this done at least a hundred times, as well as other wonderful customs of theirs! I remember also that as soon as they fed on Prussian bread, they did not want to go home. Pan Stankyevich says truly that they are not sturdy soldiers. They have infantry which is so-so; but the cavalry—God pity us! for there are no horses in their country, and they cannot train themselves to riding from childhood."

"Probably we shall not attack them first, but march on Vilna," said Pan Shchyt.

"True, I gave that advice to the prince myself, when he asked what I thought of this matter," answered Zagloba. "But when we have finished with the others, we will go against the Swedes. The envoys upstairs must be sweating!"

"They are received politely," said Pan Zalenski, "but they will not effect the least thing; the best proof of that is that orders are issued to the army."

"Dear God, dear God!" said Pan Tvarkovski, judge of Rossyeni, "how alacrity comes with danger! We were well-nigh despairing when we had to do with one enemy, but now we have two."

"Of course," answered Stankyevich. "It happens not infrequently, that we let ourselves be beaten till patience is lost, and then in a moment vigor and daring appear. Is it little that we have suffered, little endured? We relied on the king and the general militia of the kingdom, not counting on our own force, till we are in a dilemma; now we must either defeat both enemies or perish completely."

"God will assist us! We have had enough of this delay."

"They have put the dagger to our throats."

"We too will put it to theirs; we'll show the kingdom fellows what sort of soldiers we are! There will be no Uistsie with us, as God is in heaven!"

In the measure of the cups, heads became heated, and warlike ardor increased. At the brink of a precipice the last effort often brings safety; this was understood by those crowds of soldiers and that nobility whom so recently Yan Kazimir had called to Grodno with despairing universals to form the general militia. Now all hearts, all minds were turned to Radzivill; all lips repeated that terrible name, which till recently had ever been coupled with victory. In fact, he had but to collect and move the scattered and drowsy strength of the country, to stand at the head of a power sufficient to end both wars with victory.

After dinner the colonels were summoned to the prince in the following order: Mirski, lieutenant of the armored squadron of the hetman; and after him Stankyevich, Ganhoff, Kharlamp, Volodyovski, and Sollohub. Old soldiers wondered a little that they were asked singly, and not collectively to counsel; but it was a pleasant surprise, for each came out with some reward, with some evident proof of the prince's favor; in return the prince asked only loyalty and confidence, which all offered from heart and soul. The hetman asked anxiously also if Kmita had returned, and ordered that Pan Andrei's arrival be reported to him.

Kmita came, but late in the evening, when the hall was lighted and the guests had begun to assemble. He went first to the barracks to change his uniform; there he found Volodyovski, and made the acquaintance of the rest of the company.

"I am uncommonly glad to see you and your famous friends," said he, shaking the hand of the little knight, "as glad as to see a brother! You may be sure of this, for I am unable to pretend. It is true that you went through my forehead in evil fashion, but you put me on my feet afterward, which I shall not forget till death. In presence of all, I say that had it not been for you I should be at this moment behind the grating. Would more such men were born! Who thinks differently is a fool, and may the devil carry me off if I will not clip his ears."

"Say no more!"

"I will follow you into fire, even should I perish. Let any man come forward who does not believe me!"

Here Pan Andrei cast a challenging look on the officers. But no one contradicted him, for all loved and respected Pan Michael; but Zagloba said,—

"This is a sulphurous sort of soldier; give him to the hangman! It seems to me that I shall have a great liking to you for the love you bear Pan Michael, for I am the man to ask first how worthy he is."

"Worthier than any of us!" said Kmita, with his usual abruptness. Then he looked at the Skshetuskis, at Zagloba, and added: "Pardon me, gentlemen, I have no wish to offend any one, for I know that you are honorable men and great knights; be not angry, for I wish to deserve your friendship."

"There is no harm done," said Pan Yan; "what's in the heart may come to the lip."

"Let us embrace!" cried Zagloba.

"No need to say such a thing twice to me!"

They fell into each other's arms. Then Kmita said, "To-day we must drink, it cannot be avoided!"

"No need to say such a thing twice to me!" said Zagloba, like an echo.

"We'll slip away early to the barracks, and I'll make provision."

Pan Michael began to twitch his mustaches greatly. "You will have no great wish to slip out," thought he, looking at Kmita, "when you see who is in the hall tonight." And he opened his mouth to tell Kmita that the sword-bearer of Rossyeni and Olenka had come; but he grew as it were faint at heart, and turned the conversation. "Where is your squadron?" asked he.

"Here, ready for service. Harasimovich was with me, and brought an order from the prince to have the men on horseback at midnight. I asked him if we were all to march; he said not. I know not what it means. Of other officers some have the same order, others have not. But all the foreign infantry have received it."

"Perhaps a part of the army will march to-night and a part in the morning," said Pan Yan.

"In every case I will have a drink here with you, gentlemen. Let the squadron go on by itself; I can come up with it afterward in an hour."

At that moment Harasimovich rushed in. "Serene great mighty banneret of Orsha!" cried he, bowing in the doorway.

"What? Is there a fire? I am here!" said Kmita.

"To the prince! to the prince!"

"Straightway, only let me put on my uniform. Boy, my coat and belt, or I'll kill thee!"

The boy brought the rest of the uniform in a twinkle; and a few minutes later Pan Kmita, arrayed as for a wedding, was hurrying to the prince. He was radiant, he seemed so splendid. He had a vest of silver brocade with star-shaped buttons, from which there was a gleam over his whole figure; the vest was fastened at the neck with a great sapphire. Over that a coat of blue velvet; a white belt of inestimable value, so thin that it might be drawn through a finger-ring. A silver-mounted sword set with sapphires hung from the belt by silk pendants; behind the belt was thrust the baton, which indicated his office. This dress became the young knight wonderfully, and it would have been difficult in that countless throng gathered at Kyedani to find a more shapely man.

Pan Michael sighed while looking at him; and when Kmita had vanished beyond the door of the barracks he said to Zagloba, "With a fair head there is no opposing a man like that."

"But take thirty years from me," answered Zagloba.

When Kmita entered, the prince also was dressed, attended by two negroes; he was about to leave the room. The prince and Pan Andrei remained face to face.

"God give you health for hurrying!" said the hetman.

"At the service of your highness."

"But the squadron?"

"According to order."

"The men are reliable?"

"They will go into fire, to hell."

"That is good! I need such men,—and such as you, equal to anything. I repeat continually that on no one more than you do I count."

"Your highness, my services cannot equal those of old soldiers; but if we have to march against the enemy of the country, God sees that I shall not be in the rear."

"I do not diminish the services of the old," said the prince, "though there may come such perils, such grievous junctures, that the most faithful will totter."

"May he perish for nothing who deserts the person of your highness in danger!"

The prince looked quickly into the face of Kmita. "And you will not draw back?"

The young knight flushed. "What do you wish to say, your princely highness? I have confessed to you all my sins, and the sum of them is such that I thank only the fatherly heart of your

262

highness for forgiveness. But in all these sins one is not to be found,—ingratitude."

"Nor disloyalty. You confessed to me as to a father; I not only forgave you as a father, but I came to love you as that son—whom God has not given me, for which reason it is often oppressive for me in the world. Be then a friend to me."

When he had said this, the prince stretched out his hand. The young knight seized it, and without hesitation pressed it to his lips.

They were both silent for a long time; suddenly the prince fixed his eyes on the eyes of Kmita and said, "Panna Billevich is here!"

Kmita grew pale, and began to mutter something unintelligible.

"I sent for her on purpose so that the misunderstanding between you might be at an end. You will see her at once, as the mourning for her grandfather is over. To-day, too, though God sees that my head is bursting from labor, I have spoken with the sword-bearer of Rossyeni."

Kmita seized his head. "With what can I repay your highness, with what can I repay?"

"I told him emphatically that it is my will that you and she should be married, and he will not be hostile. I commanded him also to prepare the maiden for it gradually. We have time. All depends upon you, and I shall be happy if a reward from my hand goes to you; and God grant you to await many others, for you must rise high. You have offended because you are young; but you have won glory not the last in the field, and all young men are ready to follow you everywhere. As God lives, you must rise high! Small offices are not for such a family as yours. If you know, you are a relative of the Kishkis, and my mother was a Kishki. But you need sedateness; for that, marriage is the best thing. Take that maiden if she has pleased your heart, and remember who gives her to you."

"Your highness, I shall go wild, I believe! My life, my blood belongs to your highness. What must I do to thank you,— what? Tell me, command me!"

"Return good for good. Have faith in me, have confidence that what I do I do for the public good. Do not fall away from me when you see the treason and desertion of others, when malice increases, when—" Here the prince stopped suddenly.

"I swear," said Kmita, with ardor, "and give my word of honor to remain by the person of your highness, my leader, father, and benefactor, to my last breath."

Then Kmita looked with eyes full of fire at the prince, and was alarmed at the change which had suddenly come over him. His face was purple, the veins swollen, drops of sweat were hanging thickly on his lofty forehead, and his eyes cast an unusual gleam.

"What is the matter, your highness?" asked the knight, unquietly.

"Nothing! nothing!"

Radzivill rose, moved with hurried step to a kneeling desk, and taking from it a crucifix, said with powerful, smothered voice, "Swear on this cross that you will not leave me till death."

In spite of all his readiness and ardor, Kmita looked for a while at him with astonishment.

"On this passion of Christ, swear!" insisted the hetman.

"On this passion of Christ, I swear!" said Kmita, placing his finger on the crucifix.

"Amen!" said the prince, with solemn voice.

An echo in the lofty chamber repeated somewhere under the arch, "Amen," and a long silence followed. There was to be heard only the breathing of the powerful breast of Radzivill. Kmita did not remove from the hetman his astonished eyes.

"Now you are mine," said the prince, at last.

"I have always belonged to your highness," answered the young knight, hastily; "but be pleased to explain to me what is passing. Why does your highness doubt? Or does anything threaten your person? Has any treason, have any machinations been discovered?"

"The time of trial is approaching," said the prince, gloomily, "and as to enemies do you not know that Pan Gosyevski, Pan Yudytski, and the voevoda of Vityebsk would be glad to bury me in the bottom of the pit? This is the case! The enemies of my house increase, treason spreads, and public defeats threaten. Therefore, I say, the hour of trial draws near."

Kmita was silent; but the last words of the prince did not disperse the darkness which had settled around his mind, and he asked himself in vain what could threaten at that moment the powerful Radzivill. For he stood at the head of greater forces than ever. In Kyedani itself and in the neighborhood there were so many troops that if the prince had such power before he marched to Shklov the fortune of the whole war would have come out differently beyond doubt.

Gosyevski and Yudytski were, it is true, ill-wishers, but he had both in his hands and under guard, and as to the voevoda of Vityebsk he was too virtuous a man, too good a citizen to give cause for fear of any opposition or machinations from his side on the eve of a new expedition against enemies.

"God knows I understand nothing!" cried Kmita, being unable in general to restrain his thoughts.

"You will understand all to-day," said Radzivill, calmly. "Now let us go to the hall."

And taking the young colonel by the arm, he turned with him toward the door. They passed through a number of rooms. From a distance out of the immense hall came the sound of the orchestra, which was directed by a Frenchman brought on purpose by Prince Boguslav. They were playing a minuet which at that time was danced at the French court. The mild tones were blended with the sound of many voices. Prince Radzivill halted and listened.

"God grant," said he, after a moment, "that all these guests whom I have received under my roof will not pass to my enemies to-morrow."

"Your highness," said Kmita, "I hope that there are no Swedish adherents among them."

Radzivill quivered and halted suddenly.

"What do you wish to say?"

"Nothing, worthy prince, but that honorable soldiers are rejoicing there."

"Let us go on. Time will show, and God will decide who is honorable. Let us go!"

At the door itself stood twenty pages,—splendid lads, dressed in feathers and satin. Seeing the hetman, they formed in two lines. When the prince came near, he asked, "Has her princely highness entered the hall?"

"She has, your highness."

"And the envoys?"

"They are here also."

"Open!"

Both halves of the door opened in the twinkle of an eye; a flood of light poured in and illuminated the gigantic form of the hetman, who having behind him Kmita and the pages, went toward the elevation on which were placed chairs for the most distinguished guests.

A movement began in the hall; at once all eyes were turned to the prince, and one shout was wrested from hundreds of breasts: "Long live Radzivill! long live! Long live the hetman! long live!"

The prince bowed with head and hand, then began to greet the guests assembled on the elevation, who rose the moment he entered. Among the best known, besides the princess herself, were the two Swedish envoys, the envoy of Moscow, the voevoda of Venden, Bishop Parchevski, the priest Byalozor, Pan Komorovski, Pan Myerzeyevski, Pan Hlebovich, starosta of Jmud, brother-in-law of the hetman, a young Pats, Colonel Ganhoff, Colonel Mirski, Weisenhoff, the envoy of the Prince of Courland, and ladies in the suite of the princess.

The hetman, as was proper for a welcoming host, began by greeting the envoys, with whom he exchanged a few friendly words; then he greeted others, and when he had finished he sat on the chair with a canopy of ermine, and gazed at the hall in which shouts were still sounding: "May he live! May he be our hetman! May he live!"

Kmita, hidden behind the canopy, looked also at the throng. His glance darted from face to face, seeking among them the beloved features of her who at that moment held all the soul and heart of the knight. His heart beat like a hammer.

"She is here! After a while I shall see her, I shall speak to her," said he in thought. And he sought and sought with more and more eagerness, with increasing disquiet. "There! beyond the feathers of a fan some dark brows are visible, a white forehead and blond hair. That is she!" Kmita held his breath, as if fearing to frighten away the picture; then the feathers moved and the face was disclosed. "No! that is not Olenka, that is not that dear one, the dearest." His glance flies farther, embraces charming forms, slips over feathers and satin, faces blooming like flowers, and is

267

mistaken each moment. That is she, not she! Till at last, see! in the depth, near the drapery of the window, something white is moving, and it grew dark in the eyes of the knight; that was Olenka, the dear one, the dearest.

The orchestra begins to play; again throngs pass. Ladies are moving around, shapely cavaliers are glittering; but he, like one blind and deaf, sees nothing, only looks at her as eagerly as if beholding her for the first time. She seems the same Olenka from Vodokty, but also another. In that great hall and in that throng she seems, as it were, smaller, and her face more delicate, one would say childlike. You might take her all in your arms and caress her! And then again she is the same, though different,—the very same features, the same sweet lips, the same lashes casting shade on her cheeks, the same forehead, clear, calm, beloved. Here memory, like lightning-flashes, began to bring before the eyes of Pan Andrei that servants' hall in Vodokty where he saw her the first time, and those quiet rooms in which they had sat together. What delight only just to remember! And the sleigh-ride to Mitruny, the time that he kissed her! After that, people began to estrange them, and to rouse her against him.

"Thunderbolts crush it!" cried Kmita, in his mind. "What have I had and what have I lost? How near she has been and how far is she now!"

She sits there far off, like a stranger; she does not even know that he is here. Wrath, but at the same time immeasurable sorrow seized Pan Andrei,—sorrow for which he had no expression save a scream from his soul, but a scream that passed not his lips: "O thou Olenka!"

More than once Kmita was so enraged at himself for his previous deeds that he wished to tell his own men to stretch him out and give him a hundred blows, but never had he fallen into such a rage as that time when after long absence he saw her again, still more wonderful than ever, more wonderful indeed than he had imagined. At that moment he wished to torture himself; but because he was among people, in a worthy company, he only ground his teeth, and as if wishing to give himself still greater pain, he repeated in mind: "It is good for thee thus, thou fool! good for thee!"

Then the sounds of the orchestra were silent again, and Pan Andrei heard the voice of the hetman: "Come with me."

Kmita woke as from a dream.

The prince descended from the elevation, and went among the guests. On his face was a mild and kindly smile, which seemed still more to enhance the majesty of his figure. That was the same lordly man who in his time, while receiving Queen Marya Ludwika in Nyeporente, astonished, amazed, and eclipsed the French courtiers, not only by his luxury, but by the polish of his manners,—the same of whom Jean La Boureur wrote with such homage in the account of his journey. This time he halted every moment before the most important matrons, the most respectable nobles and colonels, having for each of the guests some kindly word, astonishing those present by his memory and winning in a twinkle all hearts. The eyes of the guests followed him wherever he moved. Gradually he approached the sword-bearer of Rossyeni, Pan Billevich, and said,—

"I thank you, old friend, for having come, though I had the right to be angry. Billeviche is not a hundred miles from Kyedani, but you are a *rara avis* (rare bird) under my roof."

"Your highness," answered Pan Billevich, bowing low, "he wrongs the country who occupies your time."

"But I was thinking to take vengeance on you by going myself to Billeviche, and I think still you would have received with hospitality an old comrade of the camp."

Hearing this, Pan Billevich flushed with delight, and the prince continued,—

"Time, time is ever lacking! But when you give in marriage your relative, the granddaughter of the late Pan Heraclius, of course I shall come to the wedding, for I owe it to you and to her."

"God grant that as early as possible," answered the sword-bearer.

"Meanwhile I present to you Pan Kmita, the banneret of Orsha, of those Kmitas who are related to the Kishkis and through the Kishkis to the Radzivills. You must have heard his name from Heraclius, for he loved the Kmitas as brothers."

"With the forehead, with the forehead!" repeated the sword-bearer, who was awed somewhat by the greatness of the young cavalier's family, heralded by Radzivill himself.

"I greet the sword-bearer, my benefactor, and offer him my services," said Pan Andrei, boldly and not without a certain loftiness. "Pan Heraclius was a father and a benefactor to me, and though his work was spoiled later on, still I have not ceased to love all the Billeviches as if my own blood were flowing in them."

"Especially," said the prince, placing his hand confidentially on the young man's shoulder, "since he has not ceased to love a certain Panna Billevich, of which fact he has long since informed us."

"And I will repeat it before every one's face," said Kmita, with vehemence.

"Quietly, quietly!" said the prince. "This you see, worthy sword-bearer, is a cavalier of sulphur and fire, therefore he has made some trouble; but because he is young and under my special protection, I hope that when we petition together we shall obtain a reversal of the sentence from that charming tribunal."

"Your highness will accomplish what you like," answered Pan Billevich. "The maiden must exclaim, as that pagan priestess did to Alexander the Great, 'Who can oppose thee?'"

"And we, like that Macedonian, will stop with that prophecy," replied the prince, smiling. "But enough of this! Conduct us now to your relative, for I shall be glad to see her. Let that work of Pan Heraclius which was spoiled be mended."

"I serve your highness— There is the maiden; she is under the protection of Pani Voynillovich, our relative. But I beg pardon if she is confused, for I have not had time to forewarn her."

The foresight of Pan Billevich was just. Luckily that was not the first moment in which Olenka saw Pan Andrei at the side of the hetman; she was able therefore to collect herself somewhat, but for an instant presence of mind almost left her, and she looked at the young knight as if she were looking at a spirit from the other world. And for a long time she could not believe her eyes. She had really imagined that that unfortunate was either wandering somewhere through forests, without a roof above his head, deserted by all, hunted by the law, as a wild beast is hunted by man, or enclosed in a tower, gazing with despair through the iron grating on the glad world of God. The Lord alone knew what terrible pity sometimes gnawed her heart and her eyes for that lost man; God alone could count the tears which in her solitude she had poured out over his fate, so terrible, so cruel, though so deserved; but now he is in Kyedani, free, at the side of the hetman, proud, splendid, in silver brocade and in velvet, with the baton of a colonel at his belt, with head erect, with commanding, haughty, heroic face, and the grand hetman Radzivill himself places his hand confidentially on his shoulder. Marvellous and contradictory feelings interwove themselves at once in the heart of the maiden; therefore a certain great relief, as if some one had taken a weight from her shoulders, and a certain sorrow as well that so much pity

271

and grief had gone for naught; also the disappointment which every honest soul feels at sight of perfect impunity for grievous offences and sins; also joy, with a feeling of personal weakness, with admiration bordering on terror, before that young hero who was able to swim out of such a whirlpool.

Meanwhile the prince, the sword-bearer, and Kmita had finished conversation and were drawing near. The maiden covered her eyes with her lids and raised her shoulders, as a bird does its wings when wishing to hide its head. She was certain that they were coming to her. Without looking she saw them, felt that they were nearer and nearer, that they were before her. She was so sure of this that without raising her lids, she rose suddenly and made a deep courtesy to the prince.

He was really before her, and said: "By the passion of the Lord! Now I do not wonder at this young man, for a marvellous flower has bloomed here. I greet you, my lady, I greet you with my whole heart and soul, beloved granddaughter of my Billevich. Do you know me?"

"I know your highness," answered the maiden.

"I should not have known you; you were still a young, unblossomed thing when I saw you last, not in this ornament in which I see you now. But raise those lashes from your eyes. As God lives! fortunate is the diver who gets such a pearl, ill-fated he who had it and lost it. Here he stands before you, so despairing, in the person of this cavalier. Do you know him?"

"I know," whispered Olenka, without raising her eyes.

"He is a great sinner, and I have brought him to you for confession. Impose on him what penance you like, but refuse not absolution, for despair may bring him to still greater sins."

Here the prince turned to the sword-bearer and Pani Voynillovich: "Let us leave the young people, for it is not proper to be present at a confession, and also my faith forbids me."

272

After a moment Pan Andrei and Olenka were alone. The heart beat in Olenka's bosom as the heart of a dove over which a falcon is hovering, and he too was moved. His usual boldness, impulsiveness, and self-confidence had vanished. For a long time both were silent. At last he spoke in a low, stifled voice,—

"You did not expect to see me, Olenka?"

"I did not," whispered the maiden.

"As God is true! you would be less alarmed if a Tartar were standing here near you. Fear not! See how many people are present. No harm will meet you from me. And though we were alone you would have nothing to fear, for I have given myself an oath to respect you. Have confidence in me."

For a moment she raised her eyes and looked at him, "How can I have confidence?"

"It is true that I sinned, but that is past and will not be repeated. When on the bed and near death, after that duel with Volodyovski, I said to myself: 'Thou wilt not take her by force, by the sabre, by fire, but by honorable deeds wilt thou deserve her and work out thy forgiveness. The heart in her is not of stone, and her anger will pass; she will see thy reformation and will forgive.' Therefore I swore to reform, and I will hold to my oath. God blessed me at once, for Volodyovski came and brought me a commission. He had the power not to give it; but he gave it,—he is an honorable man! Now I need not appear before the courts, for I am under the hetman's jurisdiction. I confessed all my offences to the prince, as to a father; he not only forgave me, but promised to settle everything and to defend me against the malice of men. May God bless him! I shall not be an outlaw, I shall come to harmony with people, win glory, serve the country, repair the wrongs I have committed. What will you answer? Will you not say a good word to me?" He gazed at Olenka and put his hands together as if praying to her.

"Can I believe?"

"You can, as God is dear to me; it is your duty to believe. The hetman believed, and Pan Volodyovski too. All my acts are known to them, and they believed me. You see they did. Why should you alone have no trust in me?"

"Because I have seen the result of your deeds,—people's tears, and graves not yet grown over with grass."

"They will be grown over, and I will moisten them with tears."

"Do that first."

"Give me only the hope that when I do that I shall win you. It is easy for you to say, 'Do that first.' Well, I do it; meanwhile you have married another. May God not permit such a thing, for I should go wild. In God's name I implore you, Olenka, to give me assurance that I shall not lose you before I come to terms with your nobles. Do you remember? You have written me of this yourself. I keep the letter, and when my soul is deeply downcast I read it. I ask you only to tell me again that you will wait, that you will not marry another."

"You know that by the will I am not free to marry another. I can only take refuge in a cloister."

"Oh, that would be a treat for me! By the living God, mention not the cloister, for the very thought of it makes me shudder. Mention it not, Olenka, or I will fall down here at your feet in the presence of all, and implore you not to do so. You refused Volodyovski, I know, for he told me himself. He urged me to win you by good deeds. But what use in them if you are to take the veil? If you tell me that virtue should be practised for its own sake, I will answer that I love you to distraction, and I will hear of nothing else. When you left Vodokty, I had barely risen from the bed but I began to search for you. When I was enlisting my squadron every moment was occupied; I had not time to eat food, to sleep at night, but I ceased not to seek you. I was so affected that without you there was neither life for me nor rest. I was so deeply in the toils that I lived only on sighs. At last I learned that you were in Billeviche with the sword-bearer. Then I tell you I wrestled with my thoughts as with a bear. 'To go or not to go?' I dared not go, lest I should be treated to gall. I said to myself at last: 'I have done nothing good yet, I will not go.' Finally the prince, my dear father, took pity on me, and sent to invite you and your uncle to Kyedani, so that I might fill even my eyes with my love. Since we are going to the war, I do not ask you to marry me to-morrow; but if with God's favor I hear a good word from you, I shall feel easier,—you, my only soul! I have no wish to die; but in battle death may strike any man, and I shall not hide behind others; therefore 'tis your duty to forgive me as a man before death."

"May God preserve you and guide you," responded the maiden, in a mild voice, by which Pan Andrei knew at once that his words had produced their effect.

"You, my true gold! I thank you even for that. But you will not go to the cloister?"

"I will not go yet."

"God bless you!"

And as snow melts in spring-time, their mutual distrust was now melting, and they felt nearer to each other than a moment before. Their hearts were easier, and in their eyes it grew clear. But still she had promised nothing, and he had the wit to ask for nothing that time. But she felt herself that it was not right for her to close the road to the reform of which he had spoken so sincerely. Of his sincerity she had no doubt for a moment, for he was not a man who could pretend. But the great reason why she did not repulse him again, why she left him hope, was this,—that in the depth of her heart she loved yet that young hero. Love had brought her a mountain of bitterness, disillusion, and pain; but love survived ever ready to believe and forgive without end.

"He is better than his acts," thought the maiden, "and those are living no longer who urged him to sin; he might from despair permit himself to do something a second time; he must never despair." And her honest heart was rejoiced at the forgiveness which it had given. On Olenka's cheeks a flush came forth as fresh as a rose under the morning dew; her eyes had a gleam sweet and lively, and it might be said that brightness issued from them to the hall. People passed and admired the wonderful pair; for in truth such a noble couple it would have been difficult to find in that hall, in which, however, were collected the flower of the nobility.

Besides both, as if by agreement, were dressed in like colors, for she wore silver brocade fastened with sapphire and a sacque of blue Venetian velvet. "Like a brother and sister," said persons who did not know them; but others said straightway, "Impossible, for his eyes are too ardent toward her."

Meanwhile in the hall the marshal announced that it was time to be seated at table, and at once there was unusual movement. Count Löwenhaupt, all in lace, went in advance, with the princess on his arm; her train was borne by two very beautiful pages. Next after them Baron Schitte escorted Pani Hlebovich; next followed Bishop Parchevski with Father Byalozor, both looking troubled and gloomy.

Prince Yanush, who in the procession yielded to the guests, but at the table took the highest place next to the princess, escorted Pani Korf, wife of the voevoda of Venden, who had been visiting about a week at Kyedani. And so the whole line of couples moved forward, like a hundred-colored serpent, unwinding and changing. Kmita escorted Olenka, who rested her arm very lightly on his; but he glanced sidewise at the delicate

276

face, was happy, gleaming like a torch,—the greatest magnate among those magnates, since he was near the greatest treasure.

Thus moving to the sound of the orchestra, they entered the banqueting-hall, which looked like a whole edifice by itself. The table was set in the form of a horseshoe, for three hundred persons, and was bending under silver and gold. Prince Yanush, as having in himself a portion of kingly majesty and being the blood relative of so many kings, took the highest place, at the side of the princess; and all when passing him, bowed low and took their places according to rank.

But evidently, as it seemed to those present, the hetman remembered that this was the last feast before an awful war in which the destiny of great states would be decided, for his face was not calm. He simulated a smile and joyousness, but he looked as if a fever were burning him. At times a visible cloud settled on his menacing forehead, and those sitting near him could see that that forehead was thickly covered with drops of sweat; at times his glance ran quickly over the assembled faces, and halted questioningly on the features of various colonels; then again those lion brows frowned on a sudden, as if pain had pierced them, or as if this or that face had roused in him wrath. And, a wonderful thing! the dignitaries sitting near the prince, such as the envoys, Bishop Parchevski, Father Byalozor, Pan Komorovski, Pan Myerzeyevski, Pan Hlebovich, the voevoda of Venden, and others, were equally distraught and disturbed. The two sides of the immense horseshoe sounded with a lively conversation, and the bustle usual at feasts; but the centre of it was gloomy and silent, whispered rare words, or exchanged wandering and as it were alarmed glances.

But there was nothing wonderful in that, for lower down sat colonels and knights whom the approaching war threatened at most with death. It is easier to fall in a war than to bear the responsibility for it. The mind of the soldier is not troubled, for when he has redeemed his sins with his blood, he flies from the battlefield to heaven; he alone bends his head heavily who in his soul must satisfy God and his own conscience, and who on the eve of the decisive day knows not what chalice the country will give him to drink on the morrow.

This was the explanation which men gave themselves at the lower parts of the table.

"Always before each war he talks thus with his own soul," said the old Colonel Stankyevich to Zagloba; "but the gloomier he is the worse for the enemy, for on the day of battle he will be joyful to a certainty."

"The lion too growls before battle," said Zagloba, "so as to rouse in himself fierce hatred for the enemy. As to great warriors, each has his custom. Hannibal used to play dice; Scipio Africanus declaimed verses; Pan Konyetspolski the father always conversed about fair heads; and I like to sleep an hour or so before battle, though I am not averse to a glass with good friends."

"See, gentlemen, Bishop Parchevski is as pale as a sheet of paper!" said Stanislav Skshetuski.

"For he is sitting at a Calvinist table, and may swallow easily something unclean in the food," explained Zagloba, in a low voice. "To drinks, the old people say, the devil has no approach, and those can be taken everywhere; but food, and especially soups, one should avoid. So it was in the Crimea, when I was there in captivity. The Tartar mullahs or priests knew how to cook mutton with garlic in such a way that whoever tasted it was willing that moment to desert his faith and accept their scoundrel of a prophet." Here Zagloba lowered his voice still more: "Not through contempt for the prince do I say this, but I advise you, gentlemen, to let the food pass, for God protects the guarded."

278

"What do you say? Whoso commends himself to God before eating is safe; with us in Great Poland there is no end of Lutherans and Calvinists, but I have not heard that they bewitched food."

"With you in Great Poland there is no end of Lutherans, and so they sniffed around at once with the Swedes," said Zagloba, "and are in friendship with them now. In the prince's place, I would hunt those envoys away with dogs, instead of filling their stomachs with dainties. But look at that Löwenhaupt; he is eating just as if he were to be driven to the fair with a rope around his leg before the month's end. Besides, he will stuff his pockets with dried fruit for his wife and children. I have forgotten how that other fellow from over the sea is called. Oh, may thou—"

"Father, ask Michael," said Yan.

Pan Michael was sitting not far away; but he heard nothing, he saw nothing, for he was between two ladies. On his left sat Panna Syelavski, a worthy maiden about forty years old, and on his right Olenka, beyond whom sat Kmita. Panna Syelavski shook her feather-decked head above the little knight, and narrated something with great rapidity. He looked at her from time to time with a vacant stare, and answered continually, "As true as life, gracious lady!" but understood not a word she said, for all his attention was turned to the other side. He was seizing with his ear the sound of Olenka's words, the flutter of her silver dress, and from sorrow moving his mustaches in such fashion as if he wished to frighten away Panna Syelavski with them.

"Ah, that is a wonderful maiden! Ah, but she is beautiful!" said he, in his mind. "O God, look down on my misery, for there is no lonelier orphan than I. My soul is piping within me to have my own beloved, and on whomsoever I look another soldier stands quartered there. Where shall I go, ill-fated wanderer?"

"And after the war, what do you think of doing?" inquired Panna Syelavski, all at once pursing up her mouth and fanning herself violently.

"I shall go to a monastery!" said the little knight, testily.

"Who mentions monastery here at the banquet?" cried Kmita, joyously, bending in front of Olenka. "Oh, that is Pan Volodyovski."

"There is nothing like that in your head," retorted Pan Michael; "but I think I shall go."

Then the sweet voice of Olenka sounded in his ear: "Oh, no need to think of that! God will give you a wife beloved of your heart, and honest as you are."

The good Pan Michael melted at once: "If any one were to play on a flute to me, it would not be sweeter to my ear."

The increasing bustle stopped further conversation, for it had come now to the glasses. Excitement increased. Colonels disputed about the coming war, frowning and casting fiery glances.

Pan Zagloba was describing to the whole table the siege of Zbaraj; and the ardor and daring of the hearers rose till the blood went to their faces and hearts. It might seem that the spirit of the immortal "Yarema" was flying above that hall, and had filled the souls of the soldiers with heroic inspiration.

"That was a leader!" said the famous Mirski, who led all Radzivill's hussars. "I saw him only once, but to the moment of my death I shall remember it."

"Jove with thunderbolts in his grasp!" cried old Stankyevich. "It would not have come to this were he alive now!"

"Yes; think of it! Beyond Romni he had forests cut down to open a way for himself to the enemy."

"The victory at Berestechko was due to him."

"And in the most serious moment God took him."

"God took him," repeated Pan Yan, in a loud voice; "but he left a testament behind him for all coming leaders and dignitaries and for the whole Commonwealth. This is it: to negotiate with no enemy, but to fight them all."

"Not to negotiate; to fight!" repeated a number of powerful voices, "fight! fight!"

The heat became great in the hall, and the blood was boiling in the warriors; therefore glances began to fall like lightning-flashes, and the heads shaven on the temples and lower forehead began to steam.

"Our prince, our hetman, will be the executioner of that will!" said Mirski.

Just at that moment an enormous clock in the upper part of the hall began to strike midnight, and at the same time, the walls trembled, the window-panes rattled plaintively, and the thunder of cannon was heard saluting in the courtyard.

Conversation was stopped, silence followed. Suddenly at the head of the table they began to cry: "Bishop Parchevski has fainted! Water!"

There was confusion. Some sprang from their seats to see more clearly what had happened. The bishop had not fainted, but had grown very weak, so that the marshal supported him in his chair by the shoulders, while the wife of the voevoda of Venden sprinkled his face with water.

At that moment the second discharge of cannon shook the window-panes; after it came a third, and a fourth.

"Live the Commonwealth! May its enemies perish!" shouted Zagloba.

But the following discharges drowned his speech. The nobles began to count: "Ten, eleven, twelve!"

Each time the window-panes answered with a mournful groan. The candles quivered from the shaking.

"Thirteen, fourteen! The bishop is not used to the thunder. With his timidity he has spoiled the entertainment; the prince too is uneasy. See, gentlemen, how swollen he is! Fifteen, sixteen!— Hei, they are firing as if in battle! Nineteen, twenty!"

"Quiet there! the prince wants to speak!" called the guests at once, from various parts of the table. "The prince wishes to speak!"

There was perfect silence; and all eyes were turned to Radzivill, who stood, like a giant, with a cup in his hand. But what a sight struck the eyes of those feasting! The face of the prince was simply terrible at that moment, for it was not pale, but blue and twisted, as if in a convulsion, by a smile which he strove to call to his lips. His breathing, usually short, became still shorter; his broad breast welled up under the gold brocade, his eyes were half covered with their lids, and there was a species of terror and an iciness on that powerful face such as are usual on features stiffening in the moments before death.

"What troubles the prince? what is taking place here?" was whispered unquietly around; and an ominous foreboding straitened all hearts, startled expectation was on every face.

He began to speak, with a short voice broken by asthma: "Gracious gentlemen! this toast will astonish many among you,— or simply it will terrify them,—but whoso trusts and believes in me, whoso really wishes the good of the country, whoso is a faithful friend of my house, will drink it with a will, and repeat after me, 'Vivat Carolus Gustavus Rex, from this day forth ruling over us graciously!'"

"Vivat!" repeated the two envoys, Löwenhaupt and Schitte; then some tens of officers of the foreign command.

But in the hall there reigned deep silence. The colonels and the nobles gazed at one another with astonishment, as if asking whether the prince had not lost his senses. A number of voices were heard at last at various parts of the table: "Do we hear aright? What is it?" Then there was silence again.

Unspeakable horror coupled with amazement was reflected on faces, and the eyes of all were turned again to Radzivill; but he continued to stand, and was breathing deeply, as if he had cast off some immense weight from his breast. The color came back by degrees to his face; then he turned to Pan Komorovski, and said,—

"It is time to make public the compact which we have signed this day, so that those present may know what course to take. Read, your grace!"

Komorovski rose, unwound the parchment lying before him, and began to read the terrible compact, beginning with these words:—

"Not being able to act in a better and more proper way in this most stormy condition of affairs, after the loss of all hope of assistance from the Most Serene King, we the lords and estates of the Grand Principality of Lithuania, forced by extremity, yield ourselves to the protection of the Most Serene King of Sweden on these conditions:—

"1. To make war together against mutual enemies, excepting the king and the kingdom of Poland.

"2. The Grand Principality of Lithuania will not be incorporated with Sweden, but will be joined to it in such manner as hitherto with the kingdom of Poland; that is, people shall be equal to people, senate to senate, and knighthood to knighthood in all things.

"3. Freedom of speech at the diets shall not be prohibited to any man.

"4. Freedom of religion is to be inviolable—"

And so Pan Komorovski read on further, amid silence and terror, till he came to the paragraph: "This act we confirm with

283

our signature for ourselves and our descendants, we promise and stipulate—" when a murmur rose in the hall, like the first breath of a storm shaking the pine-woods. But before the storm burst, Pan Stankyevich, gray as a pigeon, raised his voice and began to implore,—

"Your highness, we are unwilling to believe our own ears! By the wounds of Christ! must the labor of Vladislav and Sigismund Augustus come to nothing? Is it possible, is it honorable, to desert brothers, to desert the country, and unite with the enemy? Remember the name which you bear, the services which you have rendered the country, the fame of your house, hitherto unspotted; tear and trample on that document of shame. I know that I ask not in my own name alone, but in the names of all soldiers here present and nobles. It pertains to us also to consider our own fate. Gracious prince, do not do this; there is still time! Spare yourself, spare us, spare the Commonwealth!"

"Do it not! Have pity, have pity!" called hundreds of voices.

All the colonels sprang from their places and went toward him; and the gray Stankyevich knelt down in the middle of the hall between the two arms of the table, and then was heard more loudly: "Do that not! spare us!"

Radzivill raised his powerful head, and lightnings of wrath began to fly over his forehead; suddenly he burst out,—

"Does it become you, gentlemen, first of all to give an example of insubordination? Does it become soldiers to desert their leader, their hetman, and bring forward protests? Do you wish to be my conscience? Do you wish to teach me how to act for the good of the country? This is not a diet, and you are not called here to vote; but before God I take the responsibility!"

And he struck his broad breast with his fist, and looking with flashing glance on the officers, after a while he shouted again: "Whoso is not with me is against me! I knew you, I knew what would happen! But know ye that the sword is hanging over your heads!"

"Gracious prince! our hetman!" implored old Stankyevich, "spare yourself and spare us!"

But his speech was interrupted by Stanislav Skshetuski, who seizing his own hair with both hands, began to cry with despairing voice: "Do not implore him; that is vain. He has long cherished this dragon in his heart! Woe to thee, O Commonwealth! woe to us all!"

"Two dignitaries at the two ends of the Commonwealth have sold the country!" cried Yan Skshetuski. "A curse on this house, shame and God's anger!"

Hearing this, Zagloba shook himself free from amazement and burst out: "Ask him how great was the bribe he took from the Swedes? How much have they paid him? How much have they promised him yet? Oh, gentlemen, here is a Judas Iscariot. May you die in despair, may your race perish, may the devil tear out your soul, O traitor, traitor, thrice traitor!"

With this Stankyevich, in an ecstasy of despair, drew the colonel's baton from his belt, and threw it with a rattle at the feet of the prince. Mirski threw his next; the third was Yuzefovich; the fourth, Hoshchyts; the fifth, pale as a corpse, Volodyovski; the sixth, Oskyerko,—and the batons rolled on the floor. Meanwhile in that den of the lion these terrible words were repeated before the eyes of the lion from more and more mouths every moment: "Traitor! traitor!"

All the blood rushed to the head of the haughty magnate. He grew blue; it seemed that he would tumble next moment a corpse under the table.

"Ganhoff and Kmita, to me!" bellowed he, with a terrible voice.

At that moment four double doors leading to the hall opened with a crash, and in marched divisions of Scottish infantry, terrible, silent, musket in hand. Ganhoff led them from the main door.

"Halt!" cried the prince. Then he turned to the colonels: "Whoso is with me, let him go to the right side of the hall!"

"I am a soldier, I serve the hetman; let God be my judge!" said Kharlamp, passing to the right side.

"And I!" added Myeleshko. "Not mine will be the sin!"

"I protested as a citizen; as a soldier I must obey," added a third, Nyevyarovski, who, though he had thrown down his baton before, was evidently afraid of Radzivill now.

After them passed over a number of others, and quite a large group of nobles; but Mirski, the highest in office, and Stankyevich, the oldest in years, Hoshchyts, Volodyovski, and Oskyerko remained where they were, and with them the two Skshetuskis, Zagloba, and a great majority as well of the officers of various heavy and light squadrons as of nobles. The Scottish infantry surrounded them like a wall.

Kmita, the moment the prince proposed the toast in honor of Karl Gustav, sprang up from his seat with all the guests, stared fixedly and stood as if turned to stone, repeating with pallid lips, "God! God! God! what have I done?"

At the same time a low voice, but for his ear distinct, whispered near by, "Pan Andrei!"

He seized suddenly his hair with his hands. "I am cursed for the ages! May the earth swallow me!"

A flame flashed out on Olenka's face; her eyes bright as stars were fixed on Kmita. "Shame to those who remain with the hetman! Choose! O God, All Powerful!—What are you doing? Choose!"

"Jesus! O Jesus!" cried Kmita.

Meanwhile the hall was filled with cries. Others had thrown their batons at the feet of the prince, but Kmita did not join them; he did not move even when the prince shouted, "Ganhoff and Kmita, to me!" nor when the Scottish infantry entered the hall; and he stood torn with suffering and despair, with wild look, with blue lips.

Suddenly he turned to Panna Billevich and stretched his hands to her. "Olenka! Olenka!" repeated he, with a sorrowful groan, like a child whom some wrong is confronting.

But she drew back with aversion and fear in her face. "Away, traitor!" she answered with force.

At that moment Ganhoff commanded, "Forward!" and the division of Scots surrounding the prisoners moved toward the door.

Kmita began to follow them like one out of his mind, not knowing where he was going or why he was going.

The banquet was ended.

CHAPTER XV.

That same night the prince held a long consultation with the voevoda of Venden and with the Swedish envoys. The result of the treaty had disappointed his expectations, and disclosed to him a threatening future. It was the prince's plan to make the announcement in time of feasting, when minds are excited and inclined to agreement. He expected opposition in every event, but he counted on adherents also; meanwhile the energy of the protest had exceeded his reckoning. Save a few tens of Calvinist nobles and a handful of officers of foreign origin, who as strangers could have no voice in the question, all declared against the treaty concluded with Karl Gustav, or rather with his field-marshal and brother-in-law, Pontus de la Gardie.

The prince had given orders, it is true, to arrest the stubborn officers of the army, but what of that? What will the squadrons say? Will they not think of their colonels? Will they not rise in mutiny to rescue their officers by force? If they do, what will remain to the proud prince beyond a few dragoon regiments and foreign infantry? Then the whole country, all the armed nobles, and Sapyeha, voevoda of Vityebsk,—a terrible opponent of the house of Radzivill, ready to fight with the whole world in the name of the unity of the Commonwealth? Other colonels whose heads he cannot cut off, and Polish squadrons will go to Sapyeha, who will stand at the head of all the forces of the country, and Prince Radzivill will see himself without an army, without adherents, without significance. What will happen then?

These were terrible questions, for the position was terrible. The prince knew well that if he were deserted the treaty on which he had toiled so much in secret would by the force of events lose all meaning and the Swedes would despise him, or take revenge for the discovered deceit. But he had given them his Birji as a guaranty of his loyalty; by that he had weakened himself the more.

Karl Gustav was ready to scatter rewards and honors with both hands for a powerful Radzivill, but Radzivill weak and deserted by all he would despise; and if the changing wheel of fortune should send victory to Yan Kazimir, final destruction would come to that lord who this day in the morning had no equal in the Commonwealth.

When the envoys and the voevoda of Venden had gone, the prince seized with both hands his head weighed down with care, and began to walk with swift steps through the room. From without came the voices of the Scottish guards and the rattle of the departing carriages of the nobles. They drove away quickly and hurriedly, as if a pest had fallen on the lordly castle of

288

Kyedani. A terrible disquiet rent the soul of Radzivill. At times it seemed to him that besides himself there was some other person who walked behind him and whispered in his ear, "Abandonment, poverty, and infamy as well!" But he, the voevoda of Vilna and grand hetman, was already trampled upon and humiliated! Who would have admitted yesterday that in all Kyedani, in Lithuania, nay, in the whole world, there could be found a man who would dare to shout before his eyes, "Traitor!" Nevertheless he had heard it, and he lives yet, and they who spoke that word are living too. Perhaps if he were to re-enter that hall of the banquet he would still hear as an echo among the cornices and under the vaults, "Traitor! traitor!"

And wild, mad rage seized at moments the breast of the oligarch. His nostrils dilated, his eyes shot lightnings, veins came out on his forehead. Who here dares to oppose his will? His enraged mind brought before his eyes the picture of punishments and torments for rebels who had the daring not to follow his feet like a dog. And he saw their blood flowing from the axes of executioners, he heard the crunching of their bones broken by the wheel, and he took delight in and sated himself with visions of blood.

But when more sober judgment reminded him that behind those rebels is an army, that he cannot take their heads with impunity, an unendurable and hellish unquiet came back and filled his soul, and some one whispered anew in his ear, "Abandonment, poverty, judgment, and infamy!"

How is that? Is it not permitted to Radzivill to decide the fate of the country,—to retain it for Yan Kazimir or give it to Karl Gustav,—to give, to convey, to present, to whom it may please him?

The magnate looked before himself with amazement.

Who then are the Radzivills? Who were they yesterday? What was said everywhere in Lithuania? Was that all deception? Will not Prince Boguslav join the grand hetman with his regiments, after him his uncle the Elector of Brandenberg, and after all three Karl Gustav, the Swedish king, with all his victorious power, before which recently all Germany trembled through the length and the breadth of it? Did not the Polish Commonwealth itself extend its arms to the new master, and yield at the mere report of the approach of the lion of the North? Who will offer resistance to that unrestrained power?

On one side the King of Sweden, the Elector of Brandenberg, the Radzivills, in case of necessity Hmelnitski too, with all his power, and the hospodar of Wallachia, and Rakotsy of Transylvania,—almost half Europe; on the other side the voevoda of Vityebsk with Mirski, Pan Stankyevich, and those three nobles who had just come from Lukovo, and also a few rebellious squadrons! What is that?—a jest, an amusement.

Then suddenly the prince began to laugh loudly. "By Lucifer and all the Diet of hell, it must be that I have gone mad! Let them all go to the voevoda of Vityebsk!"

But after a while his face had grown gloomy again: "The powerful admit only powerful to alliance. Radzivill casting Lithuania at the feet of the Swedes will be sought for; Radzivill asking aid against Lithuania will be despised. What is to be done?"

The foreign officers will stay with him, but their power is not enough; and if the Polish squadrons go over to the voevoda of Vityebsk, he will have the fate of the country in his hands. Each foreign officer will carry out commands, it is true; but he will not devote his whole soul to the cause of Radzivill, he will not give himself to it with ardor, not merely as a soldier, but as an adherent. For devotion there is absolute need, not of foreigners, but of men of his own people to attract others by their names, by their bravery, by their reputation, by their daring example and readiness to do everything. He must have adherents in the country, even for show.

Who of his own men responded to the prince? Kharlamp, an old, worn-out soldier, good for service and nothing more; Nyevyarovski, not loved in the army and without influence; besides these a few others of still less distinction; no man of another kind, no man whom an army would follow, no man to be the apostle of a cause.

There remained Kmita, young, enterprising, bold, covered with great knightly glory, bearing a famous name, standing at the head of a powerful squadron, partly fitted out at his own expense,—a man as it were created to be the leader of all the bold and restless spirits in Lithuania, and withal full of ardor. If he should take up the cause of Radzivill, he would take it up with the faith which youth gives, he would follow his hetman blindly, and spread the faith in his name; and such an apostle means more than whole regiments, whole divisions of foreigners. He would be able to pour his faith into the heart of the young knighthood, to attract it and fill the camp of Radzivill with men.

But he too had hesitated evidently. He did not cast his baton, it is true, at the feet of the hetman, but he did not stand at his side in the first moment.

"It is impossible to reckon on any one, impossible to be sure of any man," thought the prince, gloomily. "They will all go to the voevoda of Vityebsk, and no man will wish to share with me."

"Infamy!" whispered his conscience.

"Lithuania!" answered, on the other hand, pride.

It had grown dim in the room, for the wicks had burned long on the candles, but through the windows flowed in the silver light of the moon. Radzivill gazed at those rays and fell into deep thought. Gradually something began to grow dark in those rays; certain figures rose up each moment, increasing in number, till at last the prince saw as it were an army coming toward him from the upper trails of the sky on the broad road of the moonbeams. Regiments are marching, armored hussars and light horse; a forest of banners are waving; in front rides some man without a helmet, apparently a victor returning from war. Around is quiet, and the prince hears clearly the voice of the army and people, "Vivat defensor patriae! vivat defensor patriae! (Live the defender of the country!)" The army approaches, each moment increasing in number; now he can see the face of the leader. He holds the baton in his hand; and by the number of bunchuks (horse-tails on his standard). Radzivill can see that he is the grand hetman.

"In the name of the Father and the Son!" cries the prince, "that is Sapyeha, that is the voevoda of Vityebsk! And where am I, and what is predestined to me?"

"Infamy!" whispers his conscience.

"Lithuania!" answers his pride.

The prince clapped his hands; Harasimovich, watching in the adjoining room, appeared at once in the door and bent double.

"Lights!" said the prince.

Harasimovich snuffed the candles, then went out and returned with a candlestick in his hand.

"Your Highness," said he, "it is time to repose; the cocks have crowed a second time."

"I have no wish to sleep," replied the prince. "I dozed, and the nightmare was suffocating me. What is there new?"

"Some noblemen brought a letter from Nyesvyej from the Prince Michael, but I did not venture to enter unsummoned."

"Give me the letter at once!"

Harasimovich gave the sealed letter; the prince opened it, and began to read as follows:—

May God guard and restrain your highness from such plans as might bring eternal infamy and destruction to our house! Set your mind on a hair-shirt rather than on dominion. The greatness of our house lies at my heart also, and the best proof of this is in the efforts which I made in Vienna that we should have a vote in the diets of the Empire. But I will not betray the country nor my king for any reward or earthly power, so as not to gather after such a sowing a harvest of infamy during life and damnation after death. Consider, your highness, the services of your ancestors and their unspotted fame; think of the mercy of God while the time is fitting. The enemy have surrounded me in Nyesvyej, and I know not whether this letter will reach your hands; but though destruction threatens me every moment, I do not ask God to rescue me, but to restrain your highness from those plans and bring you to the path of virtue. Even if something evil is done already, it is possible yet to draw back, and it is necessary to blot out the offences with a swift hand. But do not expect aid from me, for I say in advance that without regard to bonds of blood, I will join my forces with those of Pan Gosyevski and the voevoda of Vityebsk; and a hundred times rather would I turn my arms against your highness than put my hands voluntarily to that infamous treason. I commend your highness to God.

Michael Kazimir,

Prince in Nyesvyej and Olyta, Chamberlain of the Grand Principality of Lithuania.

When the hetman had finished the letter he dropped it on his knee, and began to shake his head with a painful smile on his face.

"And he leaves me, my own blood rejects me, because I wished to adorn our house with a glory hitherto unknown! Ah! it is difficult! Boguslav remains, and he will not leave me. With us is the Elector and Karl Gustav; and who will not sow will not reap."

"Infamy!" whispered his conscience.

"Is your highness pleased to give an answer?" asked Harasimovich.

"There will be no answer."

"May I go and send the attendants?"

"Wait! Are the guards stationed carefully?"

"They are."

"Are orders sent to the squadrons?"

"They are."

"What is Kmita doing?"

"He was knocking his head against the wall and crying about disgrace. He was wriggling like a mudfish. He wanted to run after the Billeviches, but the guards would not let him. He drew his sabre; they had to tie him. He is lying quietly now."

"Has the sword-bearer of Rossyeni gone?"

"There was no order to stop him."

"I forgot!" said the prince. "Open the windows, for it is stifling and asthma is choking me. Tell Kharlamp to go to Upita for the squadron and bring it here at once. Give him money, let him pay the men for the first quarter and let them get merry. Tell him that he will receive Dydkyemie for life instead of Volodyovski. The asthma is choking me. Wait!"

"According to order."

"What is Kmita doing?"

"As I said, your highness, he is lying quietly."

"True, you told me. Give the order to send him here. I want to speak with him. Have his fetters taken off."

"Your highness, he is a madman."

"Have no fear, go!"

Harasimovich went out. The prince took from a Venetian cabinet a case with pistols, opened it, and placed it near at hand on the table by which he sat.

In a quarter of an hour Kmita entered, attended by four Scottish soldiers. The prince ordered the men to withdraw, and remained face to face with Kmita.

There did not seem to be one drop of blood in the visage of the young man, so pale was it, but his eyes were gleaming feverishly; for the rest he was calm, resigned, though apparently sunk in endless despair.

Both were silent for a while. The prince spoke first.

"You took oath on the crucifix not to desert me."

"I shall be damned if I keep that oath, damned if I break it. It is all one to me!"

"Even if I had brought you to evil, you would not be responsible."

"A month ago judgments and punishments threatened me for killing; to-day it seems to me that then I was as innocent as a child."

"Before you leave this room, you will feel absolved from all your previous sins," said the prince.

Suddenly, changing his tone, he inquired with a certain confidential kindness, "What do you think it was my duty to do in the face of two enemies, a hundred-fold stronger than I, enemies against whom I could not defend this country?"

"To die!" answered Kmita, rudely.

"You soldiers, who can throw off so easily the pressing burden are to be envied. To die! For him who has looked death in the eyes and is not afraid, there is nothing in the world simpler. Your head does not ache over this, and it will occur to the mind of none that if I had roused an envenomed war and had died without making a treaty, not a stone would be left on a stone in this country. May God not permit this, for even in heaven my soul could not rest. *O, terque, quaterque beati* (O thrice and four times blessed) are ye who can die! Do you think that life does not oppress me, that I am not hungry for everlasting sleep and rest? But I must drain the chalice of gall and vinegar to the bottom. It is needful to save this unhappy land, and for its salvation to bend under a new burden. Let the envious condemn me for pride, let them say that I betrayed the country to exalt myself. God has seen me, God is the judge whether I desire this elevation, and whether I would not resign it could matters be otherwise. Find you who desert me means of salvation; point out the road, ye who call me a traitor, and this night I will tear that document and rouse all the squadrons from slumber to move on the enemy."

Kmita was silent.

"Well, why are you silent?" exclaimed Radzivill, in a loud voice. "I will make you grand hetman in my place and voevoda of Vilna. You must not die, for that is no achievement, but save the country. Defend the occupied provinces, avenge the ashes of Vilna, defend Jmud against Swedish invasion, nay, defend the whole Commonwealth, drive beyond the boundaries every enemy! Rush three on a thousand; die not,—for that is not permitted,—but save the country."

"I am not hetman and voevoda of Vilna," answered Kmita, "and what does not belong to me is not on my head. But if it is a question of rushing the third against thousands I will go."

"Listen, then, soldier! Since your head has not to save the country, leave it to mine."

"I cannot!" said Kmita, with set teeth.

Radzivill shook his head. "I did not count on the others, I looked for what happened; but in you I was deceived. Interrupt not, but listen. I placed you on your feet, I freed you from judgment and punishment, I gathered you to my heart as my own son. Know you why? Because I thought that in you was a daring soul, ready for grand undertakings. I needed such men, I hide it not. Around me was no man who would dare to look at the sun with unflinching eye. There were men of small soul and petty courage. To such never show a path other than that on which they and their fathers have travelled, for they will halt saying that you have sent them on a devious way. And still, where, if not to the precipice, have we all come by these old roads? What is happening to the Commonwealth which formerly could threaten the world?"

Here the prince seized his head in his hands and repeated thrice: "O God! God! God!"

After a while he continued: "The time of God's anger has come,—a time of such misfortunes and of such a fall that with the usual methods we cannot rise from this sickness; and if I wish to use new ones, which alone can bring us salvation, even those desert me on whose readiness I counted, whose duty it was to have confidence, who took oath on the cross to trust me. By the blood and wounds of Christ! Did you think that I submitted to the protection of Karl Gustav forever, that in truth I think to join this country to Sweden, that the treaty, for which I am called a traitor, will last beyond a year? Why do you look with astonished eyes? You will be still more astonished when you hear all. You will be more astonished, for something will happen which no one will think of, no one admit, which the mind of a common man has not power to grasp. But I say to you, Tremble not, for in this is the country's salvation; do not draw back, for if I find no one to help me, possibly I may perish, but with me will perish the Commonwealth and ye all for the ages. I alone can save, but I must bend and trample all obstacles. Woe to him who opposes me; for God himself will crush him through me, whether he be the voevoda of Vityebsk or Pan Gosyevski or the army, or a

297

refractory nobility. I wish to save the Commonwealth; and to me all ways, all methods are good for that end. Rome in times of disaster named dictators,—such power, nay, greater and more lasting, is needful to me. Not pride draws me to it,—whoso feels equal to this power let him take it instead of me. But if no one does I will take the power, though these walls should fall first on my head!"

Then the prince stretched both his hands upward, as if in fact he wished to support the arches falling upon his head, and there was in him something so gigantic that Kmita opened his eyes and gazed as if he had never seen him before; and at last he asked with changed voice: "Whither art thou striving, your highness? What do you wish?"

"A crown!" cried Radzivill.

"Jesus, Mary!"

A moment of deep silence followed; but an owl on the tower of the castle began to hoot shrilly.

"Listen," said the prince, "it is time to tell you all. The Commonwealth is perishing, and must perish. There is no salvation on earth for it. The question is to save first from the ruin this country (Lithuania), this our immediate fatherland, and then—then make the whole Commonwealth rise from its own ashes, as the phœnix rises. I will do this; and the crown, which I desire, I will place as a burden on my head, so as to bring out from this great tomb a new life. Do not tremble! The ground will not open, everything stands on its own place; but new times are coming. I give this country to the Swedes so as to stop with Swedish arms another enemy, to drive him beyond the boundaries, to win back what is lost, and force with the sword a treaty from that enemy in his own capital. Do you hear me? But in rocky, hungry Sweden there are not men enough, not forces enough, not sabres enough to take possession of this immense

Commonwealth. They may defeat our army once and a second time; but to hold us in obedience they cannot. If one Swede were given as a guard to every ten men in this land, there would still be many tens of them without guards. Karl Gustav knows this well, and neither does he wish nor is he able to take the whole Commonwealth. He will occupy Royal Prussia, most of Great Poland, and will be content with that. But to hold in coming time these acquisitions securely, he must break the union of the kingdom with us; otherwise he could not remain in those provinces. What will happen then to this country? To whom will it be given? Well, if I refuse the crown which God and fortune places on my head, it will be given to him who at this moment is in possession. But Karl Gustav is not willing to consent to this act, which would increase a neighboring power too greatly, and create for himself a formidable enemy. But if I refuse the crown, he will be forced to consent. Have I the right, then, to refuse? Can I allow that to take place which would threaten us with final ruin? For the tenth and the hundredth time I ask, Where are there other means of salvation? Let the will of God, then, be done! I take this burden on my shoulders. The Swedes are on my aide; the elector, our relative, promises aid. I will free the country from war! With victories and extension of boundaries will begin the rule of my house. Peace and prosperity will flourish; fire will not burn towns and villages. Thus it will be, thus it must be. So help me God and the holy cross! I feel within me power and strength from heaven, I desire the happiness of this land, and that is not yet the end of my plans. And by those heavenly lights I swear, by those trembling stars, that if only strength and health remain to me, I will build anew all this edifice, now tumbling to ruins; I will make it stronger than ever."

Fire was flashing from the pupils and eyes of the prince; his whole form shed an uncommon halo.

"Your highness," cried Kmita, "I cannot grasp that thought; my head is bursting, my eyes fear to look ahead."

"Besides," said Radzivill, as if pursuing the further course of his own thoughts, "the Swedes will not deprive Yan Kazimir of the kingdom nor of rule, but will leave him in Mazovia and Little Poland. God has not given him posterity. An election will come in time. Whom will they choose to the throne if they wish a further union with Lithuania? When did the kingdom grow strong and crush the Knights of the Cross? After Vladyslav Yagyello had mounted the throne. It will be the same this time. The Poles can call to the throne only him who will be reigning here. They cannot and will not call another, for they would perish, because the breath would not remain in their breasts between the Germans and the Turks, and as it is, the Cossack cancer is gnawing the kingdom. They can call no one else! Blind is he who does not see this; foolish who does not understand it. Both countries will unite again and become one power in my house. Then I shall see if those kinglets of Scandinavia will remain in their Prussia and Great Poland acquired to-day. Then I will say to them, *Quos ego!* and with this foot will crush their lean ribs, and create a power such as the world has not seen, such as history has not described; perhaps I may carry the cross with fire and sword to Constantinople, and in peace at home terrify the enemy. Thou great God, who orderest the circuits of the stars, grant me to save this ill-fated land, for thy glory and that of all Christendom; give me men to understand my thought, men to put their hands to salvation. There is where I stand!" Here the prince opened his arms, and raised his eyes aloft: "Thou seest me, thou judgest me!"

"Mighty prince, mighty prince!" cried Kmita.

"Go, desert me, cast the baton at my feet, break your oath, call me traitor! Let no thorn be lacking in that prickly crown which they have put on my head. Destroy ye the country, thrust it

300

over the precipice, drag away the hand that could save it, and go to the judgment of God! Let him decide between us."

Kmita cast himself on his knees before Radzivill. "Mighty prince, I am with you to the death! Father of the country, savior!"

Radzivill put both hands on his head, and again followed a moment of silence. Only the owl hooted unceasingly on the tower.

"You will receive all that you have yearned for and wished," said the prince, with solemnity. "Nothing will miss you, and more will meet you than your father and mother desired. Rise, future grand hetman and voevoda of Vilna!"

It had begun to dawn in the sky.

CHAPTER XVI.

Pan Zagloba had his head mightily full when he hurled the word "traitor" thrice at the eyes of the terrible hetman. At an hour nearer morning, when the wine had evaporated from his bald head, and he found himself with the two Skshetuskis and Pan Michael in a dungeon of Kyedani Castle, he saw, when too late, the danger to which he had exposed his own neck and the necks of his comrades, and was greatly cast down.

"But what will happen now?" asked he, gazing with dazed look on the little knight, in whom he had special trust in great peril.

"May the devil take life! it is all one to me!" answered Volodyovski.

"We shall live to such times and such infamy as the world and this kingdom have not seen hitherto!" said Pan Yan.

"Would that we might live to them!" answered Zagloba; "we could restore virtue in others by our good example. But shall we live? That is the great question."

"This is a terrible event, passing belief!" said Pan Stanislav. "Where has the like of it happened? Save me, gentlemen, for I feel that there is confusion in my head. Two wars,—a third, the Cossack,—and in addition treason, like a plague: Radzyovski, Opalinski, Grudzinski, Radzivill! The end of the world is coming, and the day of judgment; it cannot be otherwise! May the earth open under our feet! As God is dear to me, I am losing my mind!"

And clasping his hands at the back of his head, he began to pace the length and width of the cellar, like a wild beast in a cage.

"Shall we begin to pray, or what?" asked he at last. "Merciful God, save us!"

"Be calm!" said Zagloba; "this is not the time to despair."

Pan Stanislav ground his teeth on a sudden; rage carried him away. "I wish you were killed!" cried he to Zagloba. "It was your thought to come to this traitor. May vengeance reach you and him!"

"Bethink yourself, Stanislav," said Pan Yan, sternly. "No one could foresee what has happened. Endure, for you are not the only man suffering; and know that our place is here, and not elsewhere. Merciful God! pity, not us, but the ill-fated country."

Stanislav made no answer, but wrung his hands till the joints were cracking.

They were silent. Pan Michael, however, began to whistle through his teeth, in despair, and feigned indifference to everything happening around him, though, in fact, he suffered doubly,—first, for the misfortune of the country, and secondly, because he had violated his obedience to the hetman. The latter was a terrible thing for him, a soldier to the marrow of his bones. He would have preferred to die a thousand times.

"Do not whistle, Pan Michael," said Zagloba.

"All one to me!"

"How is it? Is no one of you thinking whether there are not means of escape? It is worth while to exercise one's wits on this. Are we to rot in this cellar, when every hand is needed for the country, when one man of honor must settle ten traitors?"

"Father is right," said Pan Yan.

"You alone have not become stupid from pain. What do you suppose? What does that traitor think of doing with us? Surely he will not punish us with death?"

Pan Michael burst out in a sudden laugh of despair. "But why not? I am curious to learn! Has he not authority, has he not the sword? Do you not know Radzivill?"

"Nonsense! What right do they give him?"

"Over me, the right of a hetman; over you, force!"

"For which he must answer."

"To whom,—to the King of Sweden?"

"You give me sweet consolation; there is no denying that!"

"I have no thought of consoling you."

They were silent, and for a time there was nothing to be heard but the measured tread of Scottish infantry at the door of the cellar.

"There is no help here," said Zagloba, "but stratagem."

No one gave answer; therefore he began to talk again after a while: "I will not believe that we are to be put to death. If for every word spoken in haste and in drink, a head were cut off, not one noble in this Commonwealth would walk around with his head on his shoulders. But *neminem captivabimus?* Is that a trifle?"

"You have an example in yourself and in us," answered Stanislav.

"Well, that happened in haste; but I believe firmly that the prince will take a second thought. We are strangers; in no way do we come under his jurisdiction. He must respect opinion, and not begin with violence, so as not to offend the nobles. As true as life, our party is too large to have the heads cut from all of us. Over the officers he has authority, I cannot deny that; but, as I think, he will look to the army, which surely will not fail to remember its own. And where is your squadron, Michael?"

"In Upita."

"But tell me, are you sure that the men will be true to you?"

"Whence should I know? They like me well enough, but they know that the hetman is above me."

Zagloba meditated awhile. "Give me an order to them to obey me in everything, as they would you, if I appear among them."

"You think that you are free!"

"There is no harm in that. I have been in hotter places, and God saved me. Give an order for me and the two Skshetuskis. Whoso escapes first will go straight to the squadron, and bring it to rescue the others."

"You are raving! It is a pity to lose time in empty talk! Who will escape from this place? Besides, on what can I give an order; have you paper, ink, pen? You are losing your head."

"Desperation!" cried Zagloba; "give me even your ring."

"Here it is, and let me have peace!"

Zagloba took the ring, put it on his little finger, and began to walk and meditate.

Meanwhile the smoking candle went out, and darkness embraced them completely; only through the grating of the high window a couple of stars were visible, twinkling in the clear sky. Zagloba's eye did not leave the grating. "If heaven-dwelling Podbipienta were living and with us," muttered the old man, "he would tear out that grating, and in an hour we should see ourselves beyond Kyedani."

"But raise me to the window," said Pan Yan, suddenly.

Zagloba and Pan Stanislav placed themselves at the wall; in a moment Yan was on their shoulders.

"It cracks! As God is dear to me, it cracks!" cried Zagloba.

"What are you talking about, father? I haven't begun to pull it yet."

"Crawl up with your cousin; I'll hold you somehow. More than once I pitied Pan Michael because he was so slender; but now I regret that he is not still thinner, so as to slip through like a snake."

But Yan sprang down from their shoulders. "The Scots are standing on this side!" said he.

"May God turn them into pillars of salt, like Lot's wife!" said Zagloba. "It is so dark here that you might strike a man in the face, and he could not see you. It will soon be daybreak. I think they will bring us food of some kind, for even Lutherans do not put prisoners to a hunger death. Perhaps, too, God will send reflection to the hetman. Often in the night conscience starts up in a man, and the devils pinch sinners. Can it be there is only one entrance to this cellar? I will look in the daytime. My head is somehow heavy, and I cannot think out a stratagem. To-morrow God will strengthen my wit; but now we will say the Lord's Prayer, and commit ourselves to the Most Holy Lady, in this heretical dungeon."

In fact they began a moment later to say the Lord's Prayer and the litany to the Mother of God; then Yan, Stanislav, and

Volodyovski were silent, for their breasts were full of misfortune, but Zagloba growled in a low voice and muttered,—

"It must be beyond doubt that to-morrow he will say to us, *aut*, *aut!* (either, or). 'Join Radzivill and I will pardon everything.' But we shall see who outwits the other. Do you pack nobles into prison, have you no respect for age or services? Very good! To whom the loss, to him the weeping! The foolish will be under, and the wise on top. I will promise what you like, but what I observe would not make a patch for your boot. If you do not hold to the country, he is virtuous who holds not to you. This is certain, that final ruin is coming on the Commonwealth if its foremost dignitaries join the enemy. This has never been in the world hitherto, and surely a man may lose his senses from it. Are there in hell torments sufficient for such traitors? What was wanting to such a Radzivill? Is it little that the country has given him, that he should sell it like a Judas, and in the very time of its greatest misfortunes, in the time of three wars? Just is thy anger, O Lord! only give swiftest punishment. So be it! Amen! If I could only get out of here quickly, I would create partisans for thee, mighty hetman! Thou wilt know how the fruits of treason taste. Thou wilt look on me yet as a friend; but if thou findest no better, do not hunt a bear unless thy skin is not dear to thee."

Thus did Zagloba converse with himself. Meanwhile one hour passed, and a second; at last day began to dawn. The gray light falling through the grating dissipated slowly the darkness in the cellar, and brought out the gloomy figures sitting at the walls. Volodyovski and the Skshetuskis were slumbering from weariness; but when things were more visible, and when from the courtyard came the sounds of soldiers' footsteps, the clatter of arms, the tramp of hoofs, and the sound of trumpets at the gate, the knights sprang to their feet.

"The day begins not too favorably for us," said Yan.

"God grant it to end more favorably," answered Zagloba. "Do you know what I have thought in the night? They will surely treat us with the gift of life if we will take service with Radzivill and help him in his treason; we ought to agree to that, so as to make use of our freedom and stand up for the country."

"May God preserve me from putting my name to treason," answered Yan; "for though I should leave the traitor afterward, my name would remain among those of traitors as an infamy to my children. I will not do that, I prefer to die."

"Neither will I!" said Stanislav.

"But I tell you beforehand that I will. No one will think that I did it voluntarily or sincerely. May the devils take that dragon Radzivill! We shall see yet who gets the upper hand."

Further conversation was stopped by sounds in the yard. Among them were the ominous accents of anger and indignation. At the same time single voices of command, the echo of footsteps of whole crowds, and heavy thunder as of cannon in motion.

"What is going on?" asked Zagloba. "Maybe there is some help for us."

"There is surely an uncommon uproar," said Volodyovski. "But raise me to the window, for I shall see right away what it is."

Yan took Volodyovski and raised him as he would a boy. Pan Michael caught the grating, and looked carefully through the yard.

"There is something going on,—there is!" said he, with sudden alertness. "I see the Hungarian castle regiment of infantry which Oskyerko led—they loved him greatly, and he too is arrested; they are demanding him surely. As God lives! they are in order of battle. Lieutenant Stahovich is with them; he is a friend of Oskyerko."

At that moment the cries grew still louder.

"Ganhoff has ridden up. He is saying something to Stahovich, and what a shout! I see that Stahovich with two officers is walking away from the troops. They are going of course as a deputation to the hetman. As God is dear to me, mutiny is spreading in the army! The cannon are pointed against the Hungarians, and the Scottish regiment is also in order of battle. Men from the Polish squadrons are gathering to the Hungarians. Without them they would not be so daring, for in the infantry there is stern discipline."

"In God's name!" cried Zagloba. "In that is salvation for us. Pan Michael, are there many Polish squadrons? If they rise, it will be a rising!"

"Stankyevich's hussars and Mirski's mailed squadrons are two days' march from Kyedani," answered Volodyovski. "If they had been here, the hetman would not have dared to arrest their commanders. Wait! There are Kharlamp's dragoons, one regiment, Myeleshko's another; they are for the prince. Nyevyarovski declared also for the prince, but his regiment is far away,—two Scottish regiments."

"Then there are four with the prince?"

"And the artillery under Korf, two regiments."

"Oh, that's a strong force!"

"And Kmita's squadron, well equipped,—six hundred men."

"And on whose side is Kmita?"

"I do not know."

"Did you not see him? Did he throw down his baton?"

"We know not."

"Who are against the prince,—what squadrons?"

"First, these Hungarians evidently, two hundred men; then a number of detached men from the commands of Mirski and Stankyevich; some nobles and Kmita,—but he is uncertain."

308

"God grant him!—By God's mercy!—Too few, too few."

"These Hungarians are as good as two regiments, old soldiers and tried. But wait! They are lighting the matches at the cannon; it looks like a battle!"

Yan and Stanislav were silent; Zagloba was writhing as in a fever,—

"Slay the traitors! Slay the dog-brothers! Ai, Kmita! Kmita! All depends on him. Is he daring?"

"As the devil,—ready for anything."

"It must be that he will take our side."

"Mutiny in the army! See to what the hetman has brought things!" cried Volodyovski.

"Who is the mutineer,—the army, or the hetman who rose against his own king?" asked Zagloba.

"God will judge that. Wait! Again there is a movement! Some of Kharlamp's dragoons take the part of the Hungarians. The very best nobles serve in that regiment. Hear how they shout!"

"The colonels! the colonels!" cried threatening voices in the yard.

"Pan Michael! by the wounds of God, cry to them to send for your squadron and for the armored regiment and the hussars."

"Be silent!"

Zagloba began to shout himself: "But send for the rest of the Polish squadrons, and cut down the traitors!"

"Be silent there!"

Suddenly, not in the yard, but in the rear of the castle, rang forth a sharp salvo of muskets.

"Jesus Mary!" cried Volodyovski.

"Pan Michael, what is that?"

"Beyond doubt they have shot Stahovich and the two officers who went as a deputation," said Volodyovski, feverishly. "It cannot be otherwise!"

"By the passion of our Lord! Then there is no mercy. It is impossible to hope."

The thunder of shots drowned further discourse. Pan Michael grasped the grating convulsively and pressed his forehead to it, but for a while he could see nothing except the legs of the Scottish infantry stationed at the window. Salvos of musketry grew more and more frequent; at last the cannon were heard. The dry knocking of bullets against the wall over the cellar was heard distinctly, like hail. The castle trembled to its foundation.

"Jump down, Michael, or you will be killed!" cried Yan.

"By no means. The balls go higher; and from the cannon they are firing in the other direction. I will not jump down for anything."

And Volodyovski, seizing the grating more firmly, drew himself entirely to the window-sill, where he did not need the shoulder of Pan Yan to hold him. In the cellar it became really dark, for the window was small and Pan Michael though slender filled it completely; but as a recompense the men below had fresh news from the field of battle every minute.

"I see now!" cried Pan Michael. "The Hungarians are resting against the wall and are firing. I was afraid that they would be forced to a corner, then the cannon would destroy them in a moment. Good soldiers, as God is dear to me! Without officers, they know what is needed. There is smoke again! I see nothing—"

The firing began to slacken.

"O merciful God, delay not thy punishment!" cried Zagloba.

"And what, Michael?" asked Yan.

"The Scots are advancing to the attack!"

"Oh, brimstone thunderbolts, that we must sit here!" cried Stanislav.

"They are there already, the halberd-men! The Hungarians meet them with the sabre! Oh, my God! that you cannot look on. What soldiers!"

"Fighting with their own and not with an enemy."

"The Hungarians have the upper hand. The Scots are falling back on the left. As I love God! Myeleshko's dragoons are going over to them! The Scots are between two fires. Korf cannot use his cannon, for he would strike the Scots. I see Ganhoff uniforms among the Hungarians. They are going to attack the gate. They wish to escape. They are advancing like a storm,— breaking everything!"

"How is that? I wish they would capture this castle!" cried Zagloba.

"Never mind! They will come back to-morrow with the squadrons of Mirski and Stankyevich—Oh, Kharlamp is killed! No! He rises; he is wounded—they are already at the gate. What is that? Just as if the Scottish guard at the gate were coming over to the Hungarians, for they are opening the gate,—dust is rising on the outside; I see Kmita! Kmita is rushing through the gate with cavalry!"

"On whose side is he, on whose side?" cried Zagloba.

For a moment Pan Michael gave no answer; but very soon the clatter of weapons, shrieks, and shouts were heard with redoubled force.

"It is all over with them!" cried Pan Michael, with a shrill voice.

"All over with whom, with whom?"

"With the Hungarians. The cavalry has broken them, is trampling them, cutting them to pieces! Their flag is in Kmita's hand! The end, the end!"

When he had said this, Volodyovski dropped from the window and fell into the arms of Pan Yan.

"Kill me!" cried he, "kill me, for I had that man under my sabre and let him go with his life; I gave him his commission. Through me he assembled that squadron with which he will fight now against the country. I saw whom he got: dog-brothers, gallows-birds, robbers, ruffians, such as he is himself. God grant me to meet him once more with the sabre—God! lengthen my life to the death of that traitor, for I swear that he will not leave my hands again."

Meanwhile cries, the trample of hoofs, and salvos of musketry were thundering yet with full force; after a time, however, they began to weaken, and an hour later silence reigned in the castle of Kyedani, broken only by the measured tread of the Scottish patrols and words of command.

"Pan Michael, look out once more and see what has happened," begged Zagloba.

"What for?" asked the little knight. "Whoso is a soldier will guess what has happened. Besides, I saw them beaten,— Kmita triumphs here!"

"God give him to be torn with horses, the scoundrel, the hell-dweller! God give him to guard a harem for Tartars!"

CHAPTER XVII.

Pan Michael was right. Kmita had triumphed. The Hungarians and a part of the dragoons of Myeleshko and Kharlamp who had joined them, lay dead close together in the court of Kyedani. Barely a few tens of them had slipped out and scattered around the castle and the town, where the cavalry

312

pursued them. Many were caught; others never stopped of a certainty till they reached the camp of Sapyeha, voevoda of Vityebsk, to whom they were the first to bring the terrible tidings of the grand hetman's treason, of his desertion to the Swedes, of the imprisonment of the colonels and the resistance of the Polish squadrons.

Meanwhile Kmita, covered with blood and dust, presented himself with the banner of the Hungarians before Radzivill, who received him with open arms. But Pan Andrei was not delighted with the victory. He was as gloomy and sullen as if he had acted against his heart.

"Your highness," said he, "I do not like to hear praises, and would rather a hundred times fight the enemy than soldiers who might be of service to the country. It seems to a man as if he were spilling his own blood."

"Who is to blame, if not those insurgents?" answered the prince. "I too would prefer to send them to Vilna, and I intended to do so. But they chose to rebel against authority. What has happened will not be undone. It was and it will be needful to give an example."

"What does your highness think of doing with the prisoners?"

"A ball in the forehead of every tenth man. Dispose the rest among other regiments. You will go to-day to the squadrons of Mirski and Stankyevich, announce my order, to them to be ready for the campaign. I make you commander over those two squadrons, and over the third, that of Volodyovski. The lieutenants are to be subordinate to you and obey you in everything. I wished to send Kharlamp to that squadron at first, but he is useless. I have changed my mind."

"What shall I do in case of resistance? For with Volodyovski are Lauda men who hate me terribly."

313

"Announce that Mirski, Stankyevich, and Volodyovski will be shot immediately."

"Then they may come in arms to Kyedani to rescue these officers. All serving under Mirski are distinguished nobles."

"Take a regiment of Scottish infantry and a German regiment. First surround them, then announce the order."

"Such is the will of your highness."

Radzivill rested his hands on his knees and fell to thinking.

"I would gladly shoot Mirski and Stankyevich were they not respected in the whole country as well as in their own regiments. I fear tumult and open rebellion, an example of which we have just had before our eyes. I am glad, thanks to you, that they have received a good lesson, and each squadron will think twice before rising against us. But it is imperative to act swiftly, so that resisting men may not go to the voevoda of Vityebsk."

"Your highness has spoken only of Mirski and Stankyevich, you have not mentioned Volodyovski and Oskyerko."

"I must spare Oskyerko, too, for he is a man of note and widely related; but Volodyovski comes from Russia and has no relatives here. He is a valiant soldier, it is true. I counted on him,—so much the worse that I was deceived. If the devil had not brought hither those wanderers his friends, he might have acted differently; but after what has happened, a bullet in the forehead waits him, as well as those two Skshetuskis and that third fellow, that bull who began first to bellow, 'Traitor, traitor!'"

Pan Andrei sprang up as if burned with iron: "Your highness, the soldiers say that Volodyovski saved your life at Tsibyhova."

"He did his duty; therefore I wanted to give him Dydkyemie for life. Now he has betrayed me; hence I give command to shoot him."

Kmita's eyes flashed, and his nostrils began to quiver.

"Your highness, that cannot be!"

"How cannot be?" asked Radzivill, frowning.

"I implore your highness," said Kmita, carried away, "that not a hair fall from Volodyovski. Forgive me, I implore. Volodyovski had the power not to deliver to me the commission, for it was sent to him and left at his disposal. But he gave it. He plucked me out of the whirlpool. Through that act of his I passed into the jurisdiction of your highness. He did not hesitate to save me, though he and I were trying to win the same woman. I owe him gratitude, and I have vowed to repay him. Your highness, grant for my sake that no punishment touch him or his friends. A hair should not fall from the head of either of them, and as God is true, it will not fall while I live. I implore your highness."

Pan Andrei entreated and clasped his hands, but his words were ringing with anger, threats, and indignation. His unrestrained nature gained the upper hand, and he stood above Radzivill with flashing eyes and a visage like the head of an angry bird of prey. The hetman too had a storm in his face. Before his iron will and despotism everything hitherto in Lithuania and Russia had bent. No one had ever dared to oppose him, no one to beg mercy for those once condemned; but now Kmita's entreating was merely for show, in reality he presented demands; and the position was such that it was impossible to refuse him.

At the very beginning of his career of treason, the despot felt that he would have to yield more than once to the despotism of men and circumstances, and would be dependent on adherents of far less importance than this one; that Kmita, whom he wished to turn into a faithful dog, would be rather a captive wolf, ready when angry to bite its master's hand.

All this roused the proud blood of Radzivill. He resolved to resist, for his inborn terrible vengefulness urged him to that.

"Volodyovski and the other three must lose their heads," said he, with a loud voice.

But to speak thus was to throw powder on fire.

"If I had not dispersed the Hungarians, these are not the men who had lost their heads," shouted Kmita.

"How is this? Are you renouncing my service already?" asked the hetman, threateningly.

"Your highness," answered Pan Andrei, with passion, "I am not renouncing; I am begging, imploring. But the harm will not happen. These men are famous in all Poland. It cannot be, it cannot be! I will not be a Judas to Volodyovski. I will follow your highness into fire, but refuse not this favor."

"But if I refuse?"

"Then give command to shoot me; I will not live! May thunderbolts split me! May devils take me living to hell!"

"Remember, unfortunate, before whom you are speaking."

"Bring me not to desperation, your highness."

"To a prayer I may give ear, but a threat I will not consider."

"I beg,—I implore." Here Pan Andrei threw himself on his knees. "Permit me, your highness, to serve you not from constraint, but with my heart, or I shall go mad."

Radzivill said nothing. Kmita was kneeling; pallor and flushes chased each other like lightning gleams over his face. It was clear that a moment more and he would burst forth in terrible fashion.

"Rise!" said Radzivill.

Pan Andrei rose.

"To defend a friend you are able. I have the test that you will also be able to defend me and will never desert. But God made you of nitre, not of flesh, and have a care that you run not to fluid. I cannot refuse you anything. Listen to me: Stankyevich, Mirski, and Oskyerko I will send to the Swedes at Birji; let the two Skshetuskis and Volodyovski go with them. The Swedes will not tear off their heads there, and it is better that they sit out the war in quiet."

"I thank your highness, my father," cried Andrei.

"Wait," said the prince. "I have respected your oath already too much; now respect mine. I have recorded death in my soul to that old noble,—I have forgotten his name,—that bellowing devil who came here with Skshetuski. He is the man who first called me traitor. He mentioned a bribe; he urged on the others, and perhaps there would not have been such opposition without his insolence." Here the prince struck the table with his fist. "I should have expected death sooner, and the end of the world sooner, than that any one would dare to shout at me, Radzivill, to my face, 'Traitor!' In presence of people! There is not a death, there are not torments befitting such a crime. Do not beg me for him; it is useless."

But Pan Andrei was not easily discouraged when once he undertook a thing. He was not angry now, nor did he blaze forth. But seizing again the hand of the hetman, he began to cover it with kisses and to entreat with all the earnestness in his soul—

"With no rope or chain could your highness bind my heart as with this favor. Only do it not half-way nor in part, but completely. That noble said yesterday what all thought. I myself thought the same till you opened my eyes,—may fire consume me, if I did not! A man is not to blame for being unwise. That noble was so drunk that what he had on his heart he shouted forth.

317

He thought that he was defending the country, and it is hard to punish a man for love of country. He knew that he was exposing his life, and shouted what he had on his mind. He neither warms nor freezes me, but he is to Pan Volodyovski as a brother, or quite as a father. Volodyovski would mourn for him beyond measure, and I do not want that. Such is the nature within me, that if I wish good to a man I would give my soul for him. If any one has spared me, but killed my friend, may the devil take him for such a favor! Your highness, my father, benefactor, do a perfect kindness,—give me this noble, and I will give you all my blood, even tomorrow, this day, this moment!"

Radzivill gnawed his mustaches. "I determined death to him yesterday in my soul."

"What the hetman and voevoda of Vilna determined, that can the Grand Prince of Lithuania and, God grant in the future, the King of Poland, as a gracious monarch, efface."

Pan Andrei spoke sincerely what he felt and thought; but had he been the most adroit of courtiers he could not have found a more powerful argument in defence of his friends. The proud face of the magnate grew bright at the sound of those titles which he did not possess yet, and he said,—

"You have so understood me that I can refuse you nothing. They will all go to Birji. Let them expiate their faults with the Swedes; and when that has happened of which you have spoken, ask for them a new favor."

"As true as life, I will ask, and may God grant as quickly as possible!" said Kmita.

"Go now, and bear the good news to them."

"The news is good for me, not for them; and surely they will not receive it with gratitude, especially since they did not suspect what threatened them. I will not go, your highness, for it would seem as if I were hurrying to boast of my intercession."

"Do as you please about that, but lose no time in bringing the squadrons of Mirski and Stankyevich; immediately after there will be another expedition for you, from which surely you will not flee."

"What is that?"

"You will go to ask on my behalf Pan Billevich, the sword-bearer of Rossyeni, to come to me here at Kyedani, with his niece, and stay during the war. Do you understand?"

Kmita was confused. "He will not be ready to do that. He went from Kyedani in a great rage."

"I think that the rage has left him already. In every case take men, and if they will not come of their own will put them in a carriage, surround it with dragoons, and bring them. He was as soft as wax when I spoke with him; he blushed like a maiden and bowed to the floor, but he was as frightened at the name of the Swedes as the devil is at holy water, and went away. I want him here for myself and for you; I hope to form out of that wax a candle that I can light when I like and for whom I like. It will be all the better if it happens so; but if not, I will have a hostage. The Billeviches are very powerful in Jmud, for they are related to almost all the nobles. When I have one of them in my hands, and that one the eldest, the others will think twice before they undertake anything against me. Furthermore, behind them and your maiden are all that throng of Lauda men, who, if they were to go to the camp of the voevoda of Vityebsk, would be received by him with open arms. That is an important affair, so important that I think to begin with the Billeviches."

"In Volodyovski's squadron are Lauda men only."

"The guardians of your maiden. If that is true, begin by conveying her to Kyedani. Only listen: I will undertake to bring the sword-bearer to our side, but do you win the maiden as you can. When I bring over the sword-bearer, he will help you with

319

the girl. If she is willing, I will have the wedding for you at once. If not, take her to the altar without ceremony. When the storm is over, all will be well. That is the best method with women. She will weep, she will despair, when they drag her to the altar; but next day she will think that the devil is not so terrible as they paint him, and the third day she will be glad. How did you part from her yesterday?"

"As if she had given me a slap in the face."

"What did she say?"

"She called me a traitor. I was almost struck with paralysis."

"Is she so furious? When you are her husband, tell her that a distaff is fitter for her than public affairs, and hold her tight."

"Your highness does not know her. She must have a thing either virtue or vice; according to that she judges, and more than one man might envy her her mind. Before you can look around she has struck the point."

"She has struck you to the heart. Try to strike her in like manner."

"If God would grant that, your highness! Once I took her with armed hand, but afterward I vowed to do so no more. And something tells me that were I to take her by force to the altar it would not be to my heart, for I have promised her and myself not to use force again. If her uncle is convinced he will convince her, and then she will look on me differently. Now I will go to Billeviche and bring them both here, for I am afraid that she may take refuge in some cloister. But I tell your highness the pure truth, that though it is a great happiness for me to look on that maiden, I would rather attack the whole Swedish power than stand before her at present, for she does not know my honest intentions and holds me a traitor."

"If you wish I will send another,—Kharlamp or Myeleshko."

"No, I would rather go myself; besides, Kharlamp is wounded."

"That is better. I wanted to send Kharlamp yesterday to Volodyovski's squadron to take command, and if need be force it to obedience; but he is an awkward fellow, and it turns out that he knows not how to hold his own men. I have no service for him. Go first for the sword-bearer and the maiden, and then to those squadrons. In an extreme case do not spare blood, for we must show the Swedes that we have power and are not afraid of rebellion. I will send the colonels away at once under escort; I hope that Pontus de la Gardie will consider this a proof of my sincerity. Myeleshko will take them. The beginning is difficult. I see that half Lithuania will rise against me."

"That is nothing, your highness. Whoso has a clean conscience fears no man."

"I thought that all the Radzivills at least would be on my side, but see what Prince Michael writes from Nyesvyej."

Here the hetman gave Kmita the letter of Kazimir Michael. Pan Andrei cast his eyes over the letter.

"If I knew not the intentions of your highness I should think him right, and the most virtuous man in the world. God give him everything good! He speaks what he thinks."

"Set out now!" said the prince, with a certain impatience.

CHAPTER XVIII.

Kmita, however, did not start that day, nor the following, for threatening news began to arrive at Kyedani from every side. Toward evening a courier rushed in with tidings that Mirski's squadron and Stankyevich's also were marching to the hetman's residence, prepared to demand with armed hand their colonels;

that there was terrible agitation among them, and that the officers had sent deputations to all the squadrons posted near Kyedani, and farther on to Podlyasye and Zabludovo, with news of the hetman's treason, and with a summons to unite in defence of the country. From this it was easy to see that multitudes of nobles would fly to the insurgent squadrons and form an important force, which it would be difficult to resist in unfortified Kyedani, especially since not every regiment which Radzivill had at hand could be relied on with certainty.

This changed all the calculations and plans of the hetman; but instead of weakening, it seemed to rouse his courage still more. He determined to move at the head of his faithful Scottish regiments, cavalry and artillery, against the insurgents, and stamp out the fire at its birth. He knew that the soldiers without colonels were simply an unorganized throng, that would scatter from terror at the mere name of the hetman. He determined also not to spare blood, and to terrify with examples the whole army, all the nobles, nay, all Lithuania, so that it should not dare even to tremble beneath his iron hand. Everything that he had planned must be accomplished, and accomplished with his own forces.

That very day a number of foreign officers went to Prussia to make new enlistments, and Kyedani was swarming with armed men. The Scottish regiments, the foreign cavalry, the dragoons of Myeleshko and Kharlamp, with the "fire people" of Pan Korf, were preparing for the campaign. The prince's haiduks, his servants, and the citizens of Kyedani were obliged to increase the military forces; and it was determined to hasten the transfer of the prisoners to Birji, where it would be safer to keep them than in exposed Kyedani. The prince hoped with reason that to transport the colonels to a remote fortress, in which, according to treaty, there must be a Swedish garrison already, would destroy in the minds of the rebellious soldiers all hope of rescuing them, and deprive the rebellion itself of every basis. Pan Zagloba, the Skshetuskis, and Volodyovski were to share the lot of the others.

It was already evening when an officer with lantern in hand entered the cellar in which they were, and said,—

"Prepare, gentlemen, to follow me."

"Whither?" asked Zagloba, with a voice of alarm.

"That will be seen. Hurry, hurry!"

"We come."

They went out. In the corridor Scottish soldiers armed with muskets surrounded them. Zagloba grew more and more alarmed.

"Still they would not lead us to death without a priest, without confession," whispered he in the ear of Volodyovski. Then he turned to the officer; "What is your rank, I pray?"

"What is my rank to you?"

"I have many relatives in Lithuania, and it is pleasant to know with whom one has to do."

"No time for inquiries, but he is a fool who is ashamed of his name. I am Roh Kovalski, if you wish to know."

"That is an honorable stock! The men are good soldiers, the women are virtuous. My grandmother was a Kovalski, but she made an orphan of me before I came to the world. Are you from the Vyerush, or the Korab Kovalskis?"

"Do you want to examine me as a witness, in the night?"

"Oh, I do this because you are surely a relative of mine, for we have the same build. You have large bones and shoulders, just like mine, and I got my form from my grandmother."

"Well, we can talk about that on the road. We shall have time!"

"On the road?" said Zagloba; and a great weight fell from his breast. He breathed like a bellows, and gained courage at once.

"Pan Michael," whispered he, "did I not say that they would not cut our heads off?"

Meanwhile they had reached the courtyard. Night had fallen completely. In places red torches were burning or lanterns gleaming, throwing an uncertain light on groups of soldiers, horse and foot, of various arms. The whole court was crowded with troops. Clearly they were ready to march, for a great movement was manifest on all sides. Here and there in the darkness gleamed lances and gun-barrels; horses' hoofs clattered on the pavement; single horsemen hurried between the squadrons,—undoubtedly officers giving commands.

Kovalski stopped the convoy and the prisoners before an enormous wagon drawn by four horses, and having a box made as it were of ladders.

"Take your places, gentlemen," said he.

"Some one is sitting there already," said Zagloba, clambering up. "But our packs?"

"They are under the straw," said Kovalski; "hurry, hurry!"

"But who are sitting here?" asked Zagloba, looking at dark figures stretched on the straw.

"Mirski, Stankyevich, Oskyerko," answered voices.

"Volodyovski, Yan and Stanislav Skshetuski, and Zagloba," answered our knights.

"With the forehead, with the forehead!"

"With the forehead! We are travelling in honorable company. And whither are they taking us, do you know, gentlemen?"

"You are going to Birji," said Kovalski.

When he said this, he gave the command. A convoy of fifty dragoons surrounded the wagon and moved on. The prisoners began to converse in a low voice.

324

"They will give us to the Swedes," said Mirski; "I expected that."

"I would rather sit among enemies than traitors," answered Stankyevich.

"And I would rather have a bullet in my forehead," said Volodyovski, "than sit with folded arms during such an unfortunate war."

"Do not blaspheme, Michael," answered Zagloba, "for from the wagon, should a convenient moment come, you may give a plunge, and from Birji also; but it is hard to escape with a bullet in the forehead. I foresaw that that traitor would not dare to put bullets in our heads."

"Is there a thing which Radzivill does not dare to do?" asked Mirski. "It is clear that you have come from afar and know him not. On whomsoever he has sworn vengeance, that man is as good as in the grave; and I remember no instance of his forgiving any one the slightest offence."

"But still he did not dare to raise hands on me!" answered Zagloba. "Who knows if you have not to thank me for your lives?"

"And how?"

"Because the Khan loves me wonderfully, for I discovered a conspiracy against his life when I was a captive in the Crimea. And our gracious king, Yan Kazimir, loves me too. Radzivill, the son of a such a one, did not wish to break with two such potentates; for they might reach him, even in Lithuania."

"Ah! what are you saying? He hates the king as the devil does holy water, and would be still more envenomed against you did he know you to be a confidant of the king," observed Stankyevich.

"I think this," said Oskyerko. "To avoid odium the hetman would not stain himself with our blood, but I could swear that this officer is bearing an order to the Swedes in Birji to shoot us on the spot."

"Oi!" exclaimed Zagloba.

They were silent for a moment; meanwhile the wagon had rolled into the square of Kyedani. The town was sleeping, there were no lights in the windows, only the dogs before the houses snapped angrily at the passing party.

"Well," said Zagloba, "we have gained time anyhow, and perhaps a chance will serve us, and some stratagem may come to my head." Here he turned to the old colonels: "Gentlemen, you know me little, but ask my comrades about the hot places in which I have been, and from which I have always escaped. Tell me, what kind of officer is this who commands the convoy? Could he be persuaded not to adhere to a traitor, but take the side of his country and join us?"

"That is Roh Kovalski of the Korab Kovalskis," answered Oskyerko.

"I know him. You might as well persuade his horse as him; for as God is bountiful I know not which is more stupid."

"But why did they make him officer?"

"He carried the banner with Myeleshko's dragoons; for this no wit is needed. But he was made officer because his fist pleased the prince; for he breaks horseshoes, wrestles with tame bears, and the man has not yet been discovered whom he cannot bring to the earth."

"Has he such strength?"

"That he has such strength is true; but were his superior to order him to batter down a wall with his head he would fall to battering it without a moment's delay. He is ordered to take us to Birji, and he will take us, even if the earth had to sink."

"'Pon my word," said Zagloba, who listened to this conversation with great attention, "he is a resolute fellow."

326

"Yes, but with him resolution consists in stupidity alone. When he has time, and is not eating, he is sleeping. It is an astonishing thing, which you will not believe; but once he slept forty-eight hours in the barracks, and yawned when they dragged him from the plank bed."

"This officer pleases me greatly," said Zagloba, "for I always like to know with whom I have to do."

When he had said this he turned to Kovalski. "But come this way, please!" cried he, in a patronizing tone.

"What is it?" asked Kovalski, turning his horse.

"Have you gorailka?"

"I have."

"Give it!"

"How give it?"

"You know, gracious Kovalski, if it were not permitted you would have had an order not to give it; but since you have not an order, give it."

"Ah," said Kovalski, astonished, "as I live! but that is like forcing."

"Forcing or not forcing, it is permitted you; and it is proper to assist a blood relative and an older man, who, if he had married your mother, might have been your father as easily as wink."

"What relative are you of mine?"

"I am, for there are two stocks of Kovalskis,—they who use the seal of Vyerush and have a goat painted on their shield, with upraised hind leg; and they who have on their shield the ship in which their ancestor Kovalski sailed from England across the sea to Poland; and these are my relatives, through my grandmother, and this is why I, too, have the ship on my shield."

"As God lives! you are my relative."

"Are you a Korab (ship)?"

"A Korab."

"My own blood, as God is dear to me!" cried Zagloba. "It is lucky that we have met, for in very truth I have come here to Lithuania to see the Kovalskis; and though I am in bonds while you are on horseback and in freedom I would gladly embrace you, for what is one's own is one's own."

"How can I help you? They commanded me to take you to Birji; I will take you. Blood is blood, but service is service."

"Call me Uncle," said Zagloba.

"Here is gorailka for you, Uncle," said Kovalski; "I can do that much."

Zagloba took the flask gladly, and drank to his liking. Soon a pleasant warmth spread through his members. It began to grow clear in his brain, and his mind became bright.

"Come down from the horse," said he to Kovalski, "and sit here a short time in the wagon; let us talk, for I should like to have you say something about our family. I respect service, but this too is permitted."

Kovalski did not answer for a while.

"This was not forbidden," said he, at last.

Soon after he was sitting at the side of Zagloba, and stretched himself gladly on the straw with which the wagon was filled.

Zagloba embraced him heartily.

"How is the health of thy old father?—God help me,— I've forgotten his name."

"Roh, also."

"That's right, that's right. Roh begat Roh,—that is according to command. You must call your son Roh as well, so that every hoopoo may have his topknot. But are you married?"

"Of course! I am Kovalski, and here is Pani Kovalski; I don't want any other."

So saying, the young officer raised to the eyes of Zagloba the hilt of a heavy dragoon sabre, and repeated, "I don't want any other."

"Proper!" said Zagloba. "Roh, son of Roh, you are greatly pleasing to me. A soldier is best accommodated when he has no wife save such a one, and I will say more,—she will be a widow before you will be a widower. The only pity is that you cannot have young Rohs by her, for I see that you are a keen cavalier, and it would be a sin were such a stock to die out."

"Oh, no fear of that!" said Kovalski; "there are six brothers of us."

"And all Rohs?"

"Does Uncle know that if not the first, then the second, has to be Roh?—for Roh is our special patron."

"Let us drink again."

"Very well."

Zagloba raised the bottle; he did not drink all, however, but gave it to the officer and said, "To the bottom, to the bottom! It is a pity that I cannot see you," continued he. "The night is so dark that you might hit a man in the face, you would not know your own fingers by sight. But hear me, Roh, where was that army going from Kyedani when we drove out?"

"Against the insurgents."

"The Most High God knows who is insurgent,—you or they."

"I an insurgent? How could that be? I do what my hetman commands."

"But the hetman does not do what the king commands, for surely the king did not command him to join the Swedes. Would you not rather slay the Swedes than give me, your relative, into their hands?"

"I might; but for every command there is obedience."

"And Pani Kovalski would rather slay Swedes; I know her. Speaking between us, the hetman has rebelled against the king and the country. Don't say this to any one, but it is so; and those who serve him are rebels too."

"It is not proper for me to hear this. The hetman has his superior, and I have mine; what is his own belongs to the hetman, and God would punish me if I were to oppose him. That is an unheard of thing."

"You speak honestly; but think, Roh, if you were to happen into the hands of those insurgents, I should be free, and it would be no fault of yours, for *nec Hercules contra plures!*—I do not know where those squadrons are, but you must know, and you see we might turn toward them a little."

"How is that?"

"As if we went by chance to them? It would not be your fault if they rescued us. You would not have me on your conscience,—and to have a relative on a man's conscience, believe me, is a terrible burden."

"Oh Uncle, what are you saying! As God lives, I will leave the wagon and sit on my horse. It is not I who will have uncle on my conscience, but the hetman. While I live, nothing will come of this talk."

"Nothing is nothing!" said Zagloba; "I prefer that you speak sincerely, though I was your uncle before Radzivill was your hetman. And do you know, Roh, what an uncle is?"

"An uncle is an uncle."

"You have calculated very adroitly; but when a man has no father, the Scriptures say that he must obey his uncle. The power of an uncle is as that of a father, which it is a sin to resist. For consider even this, that whoever marries may easily become a father; but in your uncle flows the same blood as in your mother. I am not in truth the brother of your mother, but my grandmother must have been your grandmother's aunt. Know then that the authority of several generations rests in me; for like everything else in the world we are mortal, therefore authority passes from one of us to another, and neither the hetman nor the king can ignore it, nor force any one to oppose it. It is sacred! Has the full hetman or even the grand hetman the right to command not merely a noble or an officer, but any kind of camp-follower, to rise up against his father, his mother, his grandfather, or his blind old grandmother? Answer me that, Roh. Has he the right?"

"What?" asked Kovalski, with a sleepy voice.

"Against his blind old grandmother!" repeated Zagloba. "Who in that case would be willing to marry and beget children, or wait for grandchildren? Answer me that, Roh."

"I am Kovalski, and this is Pani Kovalski," said the still sleepier officer.

"If it is your wish, let it be so," answered Zagloba. "Better indeed that you have no children, there will be fewer fools to storm around in the world. Is it not true, Roh?"

Zagloba held down his ear, but heard nothing,—no answer now.

"Roh! Roh!" called he, in a low voice.

Kovalski was sleeping like a dead man.

"Are you sleeping?" muttered Zagloba. "Wait a bit—I will take this iron pot off your head, for it is of no use to you. This cloak is too tight at the throat; it might cause apoplexy. What sort of relative were I, did I not save you?"

Here Zagloba's hands began to move lightly about the head and neck of Kovalski. In the wagon all were in a deep sleep; the soldiers too nodded in the saddles; some in front were singing in a low voice, while looking out the road carefully,—for the night, though not rainy, was exceedingly dark.

After a time, however, the soldier leading Kovalski's horse behind the wagon saw in the darkness the cloak and bright helmet of his officer. Kovalski, without stopping the wagon, slipped out and nodded to give him the horse. In a moment he mounted.

"Pan Commandant, where shall we stop to feed?" asked the sergeant, approaching him.

Pan Roh gave no word in reply, but moving forward passed slowly those riding in front and vanished in the darkness. Soon there came to the ears of the dragoons the quick tramp of a horse.

"The commandant has gone at a gallop!" said they to one another. "Surely he wants to look around to see if there is some public house near by. It is time to feed the horses,—time."

A half-hour passed, an hour, two hours, and Pan Kovalski seemed to be ahead all the time, for somehow he was not visible. The horses grew very tired, especially those drawing the wagon, and began to drag on slowly. The stars were leaving the sky.

"Gallop to the commandant," said the sergeant; "tell him the horses are barely able to drag along, and the wagon horses are tired."

One of the soldiers moved ahead, but after an hour returned alone.

"There is neither trace nor ashes of the commandant," said the soldier; "he must have ridden five miles ahead."

The soldiers began to grumble.

"It is well for him he slept through the day, and just now on the wagon; but do thou, soldier, pound through the night with the last breath of thy horse and thyself!"

"There is an inn eighty rods distant," said the soldier who had ridden ahead. "I thought to find him there, but no! I listened, trying to hear the horse—Nothing to be heard. The devil knows where he is!"

"We will stop at the inn anyhow," said the sergeant. "We must let the horses rest."

In fact they halted before the inn. The soldiers dismounted. Some went to knock at the door; others untied bundles of hay, hanging at the saddles, to feed the horses even from their hands.

The prisoners woke when the movement of the wagon ceased.

"But where are we going?" asked old Stankyevich.

"I cannot tell in the night," answered Volodyovski, "especially as we are not going to Upita."

"But does not the load from Kyedani to Birji lie through Upita?" asked Pan Yan.

"It does. But in Upita is my squadron, which clearly the prince fears may resist, therefore he ordered Kovalski to take another road. Just outside Kyedani we turned to Dalnovo and Kroki; from the second place we shall go surely through Beysagoli and Shavli. It is a little out of the way, but Upita and Ponyevyej will remain at the right. On this road there are no squadrons, for all that were there were brought to Kyedani, so as to have them at hand."

"But Pan Zagloba," said Stankyevich, "instead of thinking of stratagems, as he promised, is sleeping sweetly, and snoring."

"Let him sleep. It is clear that he was wearied from talk with that stupid commandant, relationship with whom he confessed. It is evident that he wanted to capture him, but with no result. Whoso would not leave Radzivill for his country, will surely not leave him for a distant relative."

"Are they really relatives?" asked Oskyerko.

"They? They are as much relatives as you and I," answered Volodyovski. "When Zagloba spoke of their common escutcheon, I knew it was not true, for I know well that his is called wczele (in the forehead)."

"And where is Pan Kovalski?"

"He must be with the soldiers or in the inn."

"I should like to ask him to let me sit on some soldier's horse," said Mirski, "for my bones are benumbed."

"He will not grant that," said Stankyevich; "for the night is dark, you could easily put spurs to the horse, and be off. Who could overtake?"

"I will give him my word of honor not to attempt escape; besides, dawn will begin directly."

"Soldier, where is the commandant?" asked Volodyovski of a dragoon standing near.

"Who knows?"

"How, who knows? When I ask thee to call him, call him."

"We know not ourselves, Colonel, where he is," said the dragoon. "Since he crawled out of the wagon and rode ahead, he has not come back."

"Tell him when he comes that we would speak with him."

"As the Colonel wishes," answered the soldier.

The prisoners were silent. From time to time only loud yawning was heard on the wagon; the horses were chewing hay at one side. The soldiers around the wagon, resting on the saddles, were dozing; others talked in a low voice, or refreshed themselves each with what he had, for it turned out that the inn was deserted and tenantless.

The night had begun to grow pale. On its eastern side the dark background of the sky was becoming slightly gray; the stars, going out gradually, twinkled with an uncertain, failing light. Then the roof of the inn became hoary; the trees growing near it

334

were edged with silver. The horses and men seemed to rise out of the shade. After a while it was possible to distinguish faces, and the yellow color of the cloaks. The helmets began to reflect the morning gleam.

Volodyovski opened his arms and stretched himself, yawning from ear to ear; then he looked at the sleeping Zagloba. All at once he threw back his arms and shouted,—

"May the bullets strike him! In God's name! Gracious gentlemen, look here!"

"What has happened?" asked the colonels, opening their eyes.

"Look here, look here!" said Volodyovski, pointing at the sleeping form.

The prisoners turned their glances in the direction indicated, and amazement was reflected on every face. Under the burka, and in the cap of Zagloba, slept, with the sleep of the just, Pan Roh Kovalski; but Zagloba was not in the wagon.

"He has escaped, as God is dear to me!" said the astonished Mirski, looking around on every side, as if he did not yet believe his own eyes.

"Oh, he is a finished rogue! May the hangman—" cried Stankyevich.

"He took the helmet and yellow cloak of that fool, and escaped on his horse."

"Vanished as if he had dropped into water."

"He said he would get away by stratagem."

"They will never see him again!"

"Gentlemen," said Volodyovski, with delight, "you know not that man; and I swear to you to-day that he will rescue us yet,—I know not how, when, with what means,—but I swear that he will."

"God grant it! One cannot believe his eyesight," said Pan Stanislav.

The soldiers now saw what had happened. An uproar rose among them. One crowded ahead of the other to the wagon, stared at their commandant, dressed in a camel's hair burka and lynx-skin cap, and sleeping soundly.

The sergeant began to shake him without ceremony. "Commandant! commandant!"

"I am Kovalski, and this is Pani Kovalski," muttered Roh.

"Commandant, a prisoner has fled."

Kovalski sat up in the wagon and opened his eyes. "What?"

"A prisoner has fled,—that bulky noble who was talking with the commandant."

The officer came to his senses. "Impossible!" cried he, with terrified voice. "How was it? What happened? How did he escape?"

"In the helmet and cloak of the commandant; the soldiers did not know him, the night was dark."

"Where is my horse?" cried Kovalski.

"The horse is gone. The noble fled on him."

"On my horse?"

"Yes."

Kovalski seized himself by the head. "Jesus of Nazareth! King of the Jews!"

After a while he shouted, "Give here that dog-faith, that son of a such a one who gave him the horse!"

"Pan Commandant, the soldier is not to blame. The night was dark, you might have struck a man in the face, and he took your helmet and cloak; rode near me, and I did not know him. If your grace had not sat in the wagon, he could not have done it."

"Kill me, kill me!" cried the unfortunate officer.

"What is to be done?"

"Kill him, catch him!"

"That cannot be done in any way. He is on your horse,— the best horse; ours are terribly road-weary. He fled at the first cock-crow; we cannot overtake him."

"Hunt for a wind in the field!" said Stankyevich.

Kovalski, in a rage, turned to the prisoners. "You helped him to escape! I will—"

Here he balled his gigantic fist, and began to approach them. Then Mirski said threateningly, "Shout not, and remember that you are speaking to superiors."

Kovalski quivered, and straightened himself involuntarily; for really his dignity in presence of such a Mirski was nothing, and all his prisoners were a head above him in rank and significance.

Stankyevich added: "If you have been commanded to take us, take us; but raise no voice, for to-morrow you may be under the command of any one of us."

Kovalski stared and was silent.

"There is no doubt you have fooled away your head, Pan Roh," said Oskyerko. "To say, as you do, that we helped him is nonsense; for, to begin with, we were sleeping, just as you were, and secondly, each one would have helped himself rather than another. But you have fooled away your head. There is no one to blame here but you. I would be the first to order you shot, since being an officer you fell asleep like a badger, and allowed a prisoner to escape in your own helmet and cloak, nay, on your own horse,—an unheard of thing, such as has not happened since the beginning of the world."

"An old fox has fooled the young man!" said Mirski.

"Jesus, Mary! I have not even the sabre!" cried Kovalski.

"Will not the sabre be of use to him?" asked Stankyevich, laughing. "Pan Oskyerko has said well,—you have fooled away your head. You must have had pistols in the holsters too?"

"I had!" said Kovalski, as if out of his mind.

Suddenly he seized his head with both hands: "And the letter of the prince to the commandant of Birji! What shall I, unfortunate man, do now? I am lost for the ages! God give me a bullet in the head!"

"That will not miss you," said Mirski, seriously. "How will you take us to Birji now? What will happen if you say that you have brought us as prisoners, and we, superior in rank, say that you are to be thrown into the dungeon? Whom will they believe? Do you think that the Swedish commandant will detain us for the reason simply that Pan Kovalski will beg him to do so? He will rather believe us, and confine you under ground."

"I am lost!" groaned Kovalski.

"Nonsense!" said Volodyovski.

"What is to be done, Pan Commandant?" asked the sergeant.

"Go to all the devils!" roared Kovalski. "Do I know what to do, where to go? God give thunderbolts to slay thee!"

"Go on, go on to Birji; you will see!" said Mirski.

"Turn back to Kyedani," cried Kovalski.

"If they will not plant you at the wall there and shoot you, may bristles cover me!" said Oskyerko. "How will you appear before the hetman's face? Tfu! Infamy awaits you, and a bullet in the head,—nothing more."

"For I deserve nothing more!" cried the unfortunate man.

"Nonsense, Pan Roh! We alone can save you," said Oskyerko. "You know that we were ready to go to the end of the world with the hetman, and perish. We have shed our blood more than once for the country, and always shed it willingly; but the hetman betrayed the country,—he gave this land to the enemy; he joined with them against our gracious lord, to whom we swore allegiance. Do you think that it came easy to soldiers like us to refuse obedience to a superior, to act against discipline, to resist our own hetman? But whoso to-day is with the hetman is against the king. Whoso to-day is with the hetman is a traitor to the king and the Commonwealth. Therefore we cast down our batons at the feet of the hetman; for virtue, duty, faith, and honor so commanded. And who did it? Was it I alone? No! Pan Mirski, Pan Stankyevich, the best soldiers, the worthiest men. Who remained with the hetman? Disturbers. But why do you not follow men better, wiser, and older than yourself? Do you wish to bring infamy on your name, and be trumpeted forth as a traitor? Enter into yourself; ask your conscience what you should do,—remain a traitor with Radzivill, the traitor, or go with us, who wish to give our last breath for the country, shed the last drop of our blood for it. Would the ground had swallowed us before we refused obedience to the hetman; but would that our souls never escaped hell, if we were to betray the king and the country for the profit of Radzivill!"

This discourse seemed to make a great impression on Kovalski. He stared, opened his mouth, and after a while said, "What do you wish of me, gentlemen?"

"To go with us to the voevoda of Vityebsk, who will fight for the country."

"But when I have an order to take you to Birji?"

"Talk with him," said Mirski.

"We want you to disobey the command,—to leave the hetman, and go with us; do you understand?" said Oskyerko, impatiently.

"Say what you like, but nothing will come of that. I am a soldier; what would I deserve if I left the hetman? It is not my mind, but his; not my will, but his. When he sins he will answer for himself and for me, and it is my dog-duty to obey him. I am a simple man; what I do not effect with my hand, I cannot with my head. But I know this,—it is my duty to obey, and that is the end of it."

"Do what you like!" cried Mirski.

"It is my fault," continued Roh, "that I commanded to return to Kyedani, for I was ordered to go to Birji; but I became a fool through that noble, who, though a relative, did to me what a stranger would not have done. I wish he were not a relative, but he is. He had not God in his heart to take my horse, deprive me of the favor of the prince, and bring punishment on my shoulders. That is the kind of relative he is! But, gentlemen, you will go to Birji, let come what may afterward."

"A pity to lose time, Pan Oskyerko," said Volodyovski.

"Turn again toward Birji!" cried Kovalski to the dragoons.

They turned toward Birji a second time. Pan Roh ordered one of the dragoons to sit in the wagon; then he mounted that man's horse, and rode by the side of the prisoners, repeating for a time, "A relative, and to do such a thing!"

The prisoners, hearing this, though not certain of their fate and seriously troubled, could not refrain from laughter; at last Volodyovski said, "Comfort yourself, Pan Kovalski, for that man has hung on a hook persons not such as you. He surpassed Hmelnitski himself in cunning, and in stratagems no one can equal him."

Kovalski said nothing, but fell away a little from the wagon, fearing ridicule. He was shamefaced in presence of the prisoners and of his own soldiers, and was so troubled that he was pitiful to look at.

Meanwhile the colonels were talking of Zagloba, and of his marvellous escape.

"In truth, 'tis astonishing," said Volodyovski, "that there are not in the world straits, out of which that man could not save himself. When strength and bravery are of no avail, he escapes through stratagem. Other men lose courage when death is hanging over their heads, or they commit themselves to God, waiting for what will happen; but he begins straightway to work with his head, and always thinks out something. He is as brave in need as Achilles, but he prefers to follow Ulysses."

"I would not be his guard, though he were bound with chains," said Stankyevich; "for it is nothing that he will escape, but besides, he will expose a man to ridicule."

"Of course!" said Pan Michael. "Now he will laugh at Kovalski to the end of his life; and God guard a man from coming under his tongue, for there is not a sharper in the Commonwealth. And when he begins, as is his custom, to color his speech, then people are bursting from laughter."

"But you say that in need he can use his sabre?" asked Stankyevich.

"Of course! He slew Burlei at Zbaraj, in view of the whole army."

"Well, God save us!" cried Stankyevich, "I have never seen such a man."

"He has rendered us a great service by his escape," said Oskyerko, "for he took the letters of the hetman, and who knows what was written in them against us? I do not think that the Swedish commandant at Birji will give ear to us, and not to Kovalski. That will not be, for we come as prisoners, and he as commanding the convoy. But certainly they will not know what to do with us. In every case they will not cut off our heads, and that is the main thing."

"I spoke as I did merely to confuse Kovalski completely," said Mirski; "but that they will not cut off our heads, as you say, is no great consolation, God knows. Everything so combines that it would be better not to live; now another war, a civil war, will break out, that will be final ruin. What reason have I, old man, to look on these things?"

"Or I, who remember other times?" said Stankyevich.

"You should not say that, gentlemen; for the mercy of God is greater than the rage of men, and his almighty hand may snatch us from the whirlpool precisely when we least expect."

"Holy are these words," said Pan Yan. "And to us, men from under the standard of the late Prince Yeremi, it is grievous to live now, for we were accustomed to victory; and still one likes to serve the country, if the Lord God would give at last a leader who is not a traitor, but one whom a man might trust with his whole heart and soul."

"Oi! true, true!" said Pan Michael. "A man would fight night and day."

"But I tell you, gentlemen, that this is the greatest despair," said Mirski; "for every one wanders as in darkness, and asks himself what to do, and uncertainty stifles him, like a nightmare. I know not how it is with you, but mental disquiet is rending me. And when I think that I cast my baton at the feet of the hetman, that I was the cause of resistance and mutiny, the remnants of my gray hair stand on my head from terror. So it is! But what is to be done in presence of open treason? Happy are they who do not need to give themselves such questions, and seek for answers in their souls."

"A leader, a leader; may the merciful Lord give a leader!" said Stankyevich, raising his eyes toward heaven.

"Do not men say that the voevoda of Vityebsk is a wonderfully honest man?" asked Pan Stanislav.

"They do," replied Mirski; "but he has not the baton of grand or full hetman, and before the king clothes him with the office of hetman, he can act only on his own account. He will not go to the Swedes, or anywhere else; that is certain."

"Pan Gosyevski, full hetman, is a captive in Kyedani."

"Yes, for he is an honest man," said Oskyerko. "When news of that came to me, I was distressed, and had an immediate foreboding of evil."

Pan Michael fell to thinking, and said after a while: "I was in Warsaw once, and went to the king's palace. Our gracious lord, since he loves soldiers and had praised me for the Berestechko affair, knew me at once and commanded me to come to dinner. At this dinner I saw Pan Charnyetski, as the dinner was specially for him. The king grew a little merry from wine, pressed Charnyetski's head, and said at last: 'Even should the time come in which all will desert me, you will be faithful.' With my own ears I heard that said, as it were with prophetic spirit. Pan Charnyetski, from emotion, was hardly able to speak. He only repeated: 'To the last breath! to the last breath!' And then the king shed tears—"

"Who knows if those were not prophetic words, for the time of disaster had already come," said Mirski.

"Charnyetski is a great soldier," replied Stankyevich. "There are no lips in the Commonwealth which do not repeat his name."

"They say," said Pan Yan, "that the Tartars, who are aiding Revera Pototski against Hmelnitski, are so much in love with Charnyetski that they will not go where he is not with them."

"That is real truth," answered Oskyerko. "I heard that told in Kyedani before the hetman. We were all praising at that time Charnyetski wonderfully, but it was not to the taste of Radzivill, for he frowned and said, 'He is quartermaster of the king, but he might be under-starosta with me at Tykotsin.'"

"Envy, it is clear, was gnawing him."

"It is a well-known fact that an apostate cannot endure the lustre of virtue."

Thus did the captive colonels converse; then their speech was turned again to Zagloba. Volodyovski assured them that aid might be looked for from him, for he was not the man to leave his friends in misfortune.

"I am certain," said he, "that he has fled to Upita, where he will find my men, if they are not yet defeated, or taken by force to Kyedani. With them he will come to rescue us, unless they refuse to come, which I do not expect; for in the squadron are Lauda men chiefly, and they are fond of me."

"But they are old clients of Radzivill," remarked Mirski.

"True; but when they hear of the surrender of Lithuania to the Swedes, the imprisonment of the full hetman and Pan Yudytski, of you and me, it will turn their hearts away greatly from Radzivill. Those are honest nobles; Pan Zagloba will neglect nothing to paint the hetman with soot, and he can do that better than any of us."

"True," said Pan Stanislav; "but meanwhile we shall be in Birji."

"That cannot be, for we are making a circle to avoid Upita, and from Upita the road is direct as if cut with a sickle. Even were they to start a day later, or two days, they could still be in Birji before us, and block our way. We are only going to Shavli now, and from there we shall go to Birji directly; but you must know that it is nearer from Upita to Birji than to Shavli."

"As I live, it is nearer, and the road is better," said Mirski, "for it is a high-road."

"There it is! And we are not yet in Shavli."

Only in the evening did they see the hill called Saltuves-Kalnas, at the foot of which Shavli stands. On the road they saw that disquiet was reigning in all the villages and towns through which they passed. Evidently news of the hetman's desertion to the Swedes had run through all Jmud. Here and there the people asked the soldiers if it were true that the country was to be occupied by Swedes; here and there crowds of peasants were leaving the villages with their wives, children, cattle, and effects, and going to the depths of the forest, with which the whole region was thickly covered. In places the aspect of the peasants was almost threatening, for evidently the dragoons were taken for Swedes. In villages inhabited by nobles they were asked directly who they were and where they were going; and when Kovalski, instead of answering, commanded them to leave the road, it came to shouts and threats to such a degree that muskets levelled for firing were barely sufficient to open a passage.

The highway leading from Kovno through Shavli to Mitava was covered with wagons and carriages, in which were the wives and children of nobles wishing to take refuge from war in estates in Courland. In Shavli itself, which was an appanage of the king, there were no private squadrons of the hetman, or men of the quota; but here the captive colonels saw for the first time a Swedish detachment, composed of twenty-five knights, who had come on a reconnoissance from Birji. Crowds of Jews and citizens were staring at the strangers. The colonels too gazed at them with curiosity, especially Volodyovski, who had never before seen Swedes; hence he examined them eagerly with the desiring eyes with which a wolf looks at a flock of sheep.

Pan Kovalski entered into communication with the officer, declared who he was, where he was going, whom he was conveying, and requested him to join his men to the dragoons, for greater safety on the road. But the officer answered that he had an order to push as far as possible into the depth of the country, so as to be convinced of its condition, therefore he could not return to Birji; but he gave assurance that the road was safe everywhere, for small detachments, sent out from Birji, were moving in all directions,—some were sent even as far as Kyedani. After he had rested till midnight, and fed the horses, which were very tired, Pan Roh moved on his way, turning from Shavli to the east through Yohavishkyele and Posvut toward Birji, so as to reach the direct highway from Upita and Ponyevyej.

"If Zagloba comes to our rescue," said Volodyovski, about daylight, "it will be easiest to take this road, for he could start right at Upita."

"Maybe he is lurking here somewhere," said Pan Stanislav.

"I had hope till I saw the Swedes," said Stankyevich, "but now it strikes me that there is no help for us."

"Zagloba has a head to avoid them or to fool them; and he will be able to do so."

"But he does not know the country."

"The Lauda people know it; for some of them take hemp, wainscots, and pitch to Riga, and there is no lack of such men in my squadron."

"The Swedes must have occupied all the places about Birji."

"Fine soldiers, those whom we saw in Shavli, I must confess," said the little knight, "man for man splendid! Did you notice what well-fed horses they had?"

"Those are Livland horses, very powerful," said Mirski. "Our hussar and armored officers send to Livland for horses, since our beasts are small."

"Tell me of the Swedish infantry!" put in Stankyevich. "Though the cavalry makes a splendid appearance, it is inferior. Whenever one of our squadrons, and especially of the important divisions, rushed on their cavalry, the Swedes did not hold out while you could say 'Our Father' twice."

"You have tried them in old times," said the little knight, "but I have no chance of testing them. I tell you, gentlemen, when I saw them now in Shavli, with their beards yellow as flax, ants began to crawl over my fingers. Ei, the soul would to paradise; but sit thou here in the wagon, and sigh."

The colonels were silent; but evidently not Pan Michael alone was burning with such friendly feeling toward the Swedes, for soon the following conversation of the dragoons surrounding the wagon came to the ears of the prisoners.

"Did you see those pagan dog-faiths?" said one soldier; "we were to fight with them, but now we must clean their horses."

"May the bright thunderbolts crush them!" muttered another dragoon.

"He quiet, the Swede will teach thee manners with a broom over thy head!"

"Or I him."

"Thou art a fool! Not such as thou wish to rush at them; thou seest what has happened."

"We are taking the greatest knights to them, as if into the dog's mouth. They, the sons of Jew mothers, will abuse these knights."

"Without a Jew you cannot talk with such trash. The commandant in Shavli had to send for a Jew right away."

"May the plague kill them!"

Here the first soldier lowered his voice somewhat and said, "They say the best soldiers do not wish to fight against their own king."

"Of course not! Did you not see the Hungarians, or how the hetman used troops against those resisting. It is unknown yet what will happen. Some of our dragoons too took part with the Hungarians; these men very likely are shot by this time."

"That is a reward for faithful service!"

"To the devil with such work! A Jew's service!"

"Halt!" cried, on a sudden, Kovalski riding in front.

"May a bullet halt in thy snout!" muttered a voice near the wagon.

"Who is there?" asked the soldiers of one another.

"Halt!" came a second command.

The wagon stopped. The soldiers held in their horses. The day was pleasant, clear. The sun had risen, and by its rays was to be seen, on the highway ahead, clusters of dust rising as if herds or troops were coming.

Soon the dust began to shine, as if some one were scattering sparks in the bunches of it; and lights glittered each moment more clearly, like burning candles surrounded with smoke.

"Those are spears gleaming!" cried Pan Michael.

"Troops are coming."

"Surely some Swedish detachment!"

"With them only infantry have spears; but there the dust is moving quickly. That is cavalry,—our men!"

"Ours, ours!" repeated the dragoons.

"Form!" thundered Pan Roh.

The dragoons surrounded the wagon in a circle. Pan Volodyovski had flame in his eyes.

"Those are my Lauda men with Zagloba! It cannot be otherwise!"

Now only forty rods divided those approaching from the wagon, and the distance decreased every instant, for the coming detachment was moving at a trot. Finally, from out the dust pushed a strong body of troops moving in good order, as if to attack. In a moment they were nearer. In the first rank, a little from the right side, moved, under a bunchuk, some powerful man with a baton in his hand. Scarcely had Volodyovski put eye on him when he cried,—

"Pan Zagloba! As I love God, Pan Zagloba!"

A smile brightened the face of Pan Yan. "It is he, and no one else, and under a bunchuk! He has already created himself hetman. I should have known him by that whim anywhere. That man will die as he was born."

"May the Lord God give him health!" said Oskyerko.

Then he put his hands around his mouth and began to call, "Gracious Kovalski! your relative is coming to visit you!"

But Pan Roh did not hear, for he was just forming his dragoons. And it is only justice to declare that though he had a handful of men, and on the other side a whole squadron was rolling against him, he was not confused, nor did he lose courage. He placed the dragoons in two ranks in front of the wagon; but the others stretched out and approached in a half-circle, Tartar fashion, from both sides of the field. But evidently they wished to parley, for they began to wave a flag and cry,—

"Stop! stop!"

"Forward!" cried Kovalski.

"Yield!" was cried from the road.

"Fire!" commanded in answer Kovalski.

Dull silence followed,—not a single dragoon fired. Pan Roh was dumb for a moment; then he rushed as if wild on his own dragoons.

"Fire, dog-faiths!" roared he, with a terrible voice; and with one blow of his fist he knocked from his horse the nearest soldier.

Others began to draw back before the rage of the man, but no one obeyed the command. All at once they scattered, like a flock of frightened partridges, in the twinkle of an eye.

"Still I would have those soldiers shot!" muttered Mirski.

Meanwhile Kovalski, seeing that his own men had left him, turned his horse to the attacking ranks.

"For me death is there!" cried he, with a terrible voice.

And he sprang at them, like a thunderbolt. But before he had passed half the distance a shot rattled from Zagloba's ranks.

Pan Roh's horse thrust his nose into the dust and fell, throwing his rider. At the same moment a soldier of Volodyovski's squadron pushed forward like lightning, and caught by the shoulder the officer rising from the ground.

"That is Yuzva Butrym," cried Volodyovski, "Yuzva Footless!"

Pan Roh in his turn seized Yuzva by the skirt, and the skirt remained in his hand; then they struggled like two enraged falcons, for both had gigantic strength. Butrym's stirrup broke; he fell to the ground and turned over, but he did not let Pan Roh go, and both formed as it were one ball, which rolled along the road.

Others ran up. About twenty hands seized Kovalski, who tore and dragged like a bear in a net; he hurled men around, as a wild boar hurls dogs; he raised himself again and did not give up the battle. He wanted to die, but he heard tens of voices repeating the words, "Take him alive! take him alive!" At last his strength forsook him, and he fainted.

Meanwhile Zagloba was at the wagon, or rather on the wagon, and had seized in his embraces Pan Yan, the little knight, Mirski, Stankyevich, and Oskyerko, calling with panting voice,—

"Ha! Zagloba was good for something! Now we will give it to that Radzivill. We are free gentlemen, and we have men. We'll go straightway to ravage his property. Well! did the stratagem succeed? I should have got you out,—if not in one way, in another. I am so blown that I can barely draw breath. Now for Radzivill's property, gracious gentlemen, now for Radzivill's property! You do not know yet as much of Radzivill as I do!"

Further outbursts were interrupted by the Lauda men, who ran one after another to greet their colonel. The Butryms, the Smoky Gostsyeviches, the Domasheviches, the Stakyans, the Gashtovts, crowded around the wagon, and powerful throats bellowed continually,—

"Vivat! vivat!"

"Gracious gentlemen," said the little knight when it grew somewhat quieter, "most beloved comrades, I thank you for your love. It is a terrible thing that we must refuse obedience to the hetman, and raise hands against him; but since his treason is clear, we cannot do otherwise. We will not desert our country and our gracious king—Vivat Johannes Casimirus Rex!"

"Vivat Johannes Casimirus Rex!" repeated three hundred voices.

"Attack the property of Radzivill!" shouted Zagloba, "empty his larders and cellars!"

"Horses for us!" cried the little knight.

They galloped for horses.

Then Zagloba said, "Pan Michael, I was hetman over these people in place of you, and I acknowledge willingly that they acted with manfulness; but as you are now free, I yield the command into your hands."

"Let your grace take command, as superior in rank," said Pan Michael, turning to Mirski.

"I do not think of it, and why should I?" said the old colonel.

"Then perhaps Pan Stankyevich?"

"I have my own squadron, and I will not take his from a stranger. Remain in command; ceremony is chopped straw, satisfaction is oats! You know the men, they know you, and they will fight better under you."

"Do so, Michael, do so, for otherwise it would not be well," said Pan Yan.

"I will do so."

So saying, Pan Michael took the baton from Zagloba's hands, drew up the squadron for marching, and moved with his comrades to the head of it.

"And where shall we go?" asked Zagloba.

"To tell the truth, I don't know myself, for I have not thought of that," answered Pan Michael.

"It is worth while to deliberate on what we should do," said Mirski, "and we must begin at once. But may I be permitted first to give thanks to Pan Zagloba in the name of all, that he did not forget us in straits and rescued us so effectually?"

"Well," said Zagloba, with pride, raising his head and twisting his mustache. "Without me you would be in Birji! Justice commands to acknowledge that what no man can think out, Zagloba thinks out. Pan Michael, we were in straits not like these. Remember how I saved you when we were fleeing before the Tartars with Helena?"

Pan Michael might have answered that in that juncture not Zagloba saved him, but he Zagloba; still he was silent, and his mustache began to quiver. The old noble spoke on,—

"Thanks are not necessary, since what I did for you today you certainly would not fail to do for me to-morrow in case of need. I am as glad to see you free as if I had gained the greatest battle. It seems that neither my hand nor my head has grown very old yet."

"Then you went straightway to Upita?" asked Volodyovski.

"But where should I go,—to Kyedani?—crawl into the wolf's throat? Of course to Upita; and it is certain that I did not spare the horse, and a good beast he was. Yesterday early I was in

352

Upita, and at midday we started for Birji, in the direction in which I expected to meet you."

"And how did my men believe you at once? For, with the exception of two or three who saw you at my quarters, they did not know you."

"To tell the truth, I had not the least difficulty; for first of all, I had your ring, Pan Michael, and secondly, the men had just learned of your arrest and the treason of the hetman. I found a deputation to them from Pan Mirski's squadron and that of Pan Stankyevich, asking to join them against the hetman, the traitor. When I informed them that you were being taken to Birji, it was as if a man had thrust a stick into an ant-hill. Their horses were at pasture; boys were sent at once to bring them in, and at midday we started. I took the command openly, for it belonged to me."

"But, father, where did you get the bunchuk?" asked Pan Yan. "We thought from a distance that you were the hetman."

"Of course, I did not look worse than he? Where did I get the bunchuk? Well, at the same time with the deputations from the resisting squadrons, came also Pan Shchyt with a command to the Lauda men to march to Kyedani, and he brought a bunchuk to give greater weight to the command. I ordered his arrest on the spot, and had the bunchuk borne above me to deceive the Swedes if I met them."

"As God lives, he thought all out wisely!" cried Oskyerko.

"As Solomon!" added Stankyevich.

Zagloba swelled up as if he were yeast.

"Let us take counsel at once as to what should be done," said he at last. "If it is agreeable to the company to listen to me with patience, I will tell what I have thought over on the road. I do not advise you to commence war with Radzivill now, and this for two reasons: first, because he is a pike and we are perches. It is better for perches never to turn head to a pike, for he can

353

swallow them easily, but tail, for then the sharp scales protect them. May the devil fix him on a spit in all haste, and baste him with pitch lest he burn overmuch."

"Secondly?" asked Mirski.

"Secondly," answered Zagloba, "if at any time, by any fortune, we should fall into his hands, he would give us such a flaying that all the magpies in Lithuania would have something to scream about. See what was in that letter which Kovalski was taking to the Swedish commandant at Birji, and know the voevoda of Vilna, in case he was unknown to you hitherto."

So saying, he unbuttoned his vest, and taking from his bosom a letter, gave it to Mirski.

"Pshaw! it is in German or Swedish," said the old colonel. "Who can read this letter?"

It appeared that Pan Stanislav alone knew a little German, for he had gone frequently to Torun (Thorn), but he could not read writing.

"I will tell you the substance of it," said Zagloba. "When in Upita the soldiers sent to the pasture for their horses, there was a little time. I gave command to bring to me by the locks a Jew whom every one said was dreadfully wise, and he, with a sabre at his throat, read quickly all that was in the letter and shelled it out to me. Behold the hetman enjoined on the commandant at Birji, and for the good of the King of Sweden directed him, after the convoy had been sent back, to shoot every one of us, without sparing a man, but so to do it that no report might go abroad."

All the colonels began to clap their hands, except Mirski, who, shaking his head, said,—

"It was for me who knew him marvellous, and not find a place in my head, that he would let us out of Kyedani. There must surely be reasons to us unknown, for which he could not put us to death himself."

354

"Doubtless for him it was a question of public opinion."

"Maybe."

"It is wonderful how venomous he is," said the little knight; "for without mentioning services, I and Ganhof saved his life not so long ago."

"And I," said Stankyevich, "served under his father and under him thirty-five years."

"He is a terrible man!" added Pan Stanislav.

"It is better not to crawl into the hands of such a one," said Zagloba. "Let the devils take him! We will avoid fighting with him, but we will pluck bare these estates of his that lie on our way."

"Let us go to the voevoda of Vityebsk, so as to have some defence, some leader; and on the road we will take what can be had from the larders, stables, granaries, and cellars. My soul laughs at the thought, and it is sure that I will let no one surpass me in this work. What money we can take from land-bailiffs we will take. The more noisily and openly we go to the voevoda of Vityebsk, the more gladly will he receive us."

"He will receive us gladly as we are," said Oskyerko. "But it is good advice to go to him, and better can no one think out at present."

"Will all agree to that?" asked Stankyevich.

"As true as life!" said Pan Mirski. "So then to the voevoda of Vityebsk! Let him be that leader for whom we prayed to God."

"Amen!" said the others.

They rode some time in silence, till at last Pan Michael began to be uneasy in the saddle. "But could we not pluck the Swedes somewhere on the road?" asked he at last, turning his eyes to his comrades.

"My advice is: if a chance comes, why not?" answered Stankyevich. "Doubtless Radzivill assured the Swedes that he had all Lithuania in his hands, and that all were deserting Yan Kazimir willingly; let it be shown that this is not true."

"And properly!" said Mirski. "If some detachment crawls into our way, we will ride over it. I will say also: Attack not the prince himself, for we could not stand before him, he is a great warrior! But, avoiding battles, it is worth while to move about Kyedani a couple of days."

"To plunder Radzivill's property?" asked Zagloba.

"No, but to assemble more men. My squadron and that of Pan Stankyevich will join us. If they are already defeated,—and they may be,—the men will come to us singly. It will not pass either without a rally of nobles to us. We will bring Pan Sapyeha fresh forces with which he can easily undertake something."

In fact, that reckoning was good; and the dragoons of the convoy served as the first example, though Kovalski himself resisted—all his men went over without hesitation to Pan Michael. There might be found more such men in Radzivill's ranks. It might also be supposed that the first attack on the Swedes would call forth a general uprising in the country.

Pan Michael determined therefore to move that night toward Ponyevyej, assemble whom he could of the Lauda nobles in the vicinity of Upita, and thence plunge into the wilderness of Rogovsk, in which, as he expected, the remnants of the defeated resisting squadrons would be in hiding. Meanwhile he halted for rest at the river Lavecha, to refresh horses and men.

They halted there till night, looking from the density of the forest to the high-road, along which were passing continually new crowds of peasants, fleeing to the woods before the expected Swedish invasion.

The soldiers sent out on the road brought in from time to time single peasants as informants concerning the Swedes; but it was impossible to learn much from them. The peasants were frightened, and each repeated separately that the Swedes were here and there, but no one could give accurate information.

When it had become completely dark, Pan Volodyovski commanded the men to mount their horses; but before they started a rather distinct sound of bells came to their ears.

"What is that?" asked Zagloba, "it is too late for the Angelus."

Volodyovski listened carefully, for a while. "That is an alarm!" said he.

Then he went along the line. "And does any one here know what village or town there is in that direction?"

"Klavany, Colonel," answered one of the Gostsyeviches; "we go that way with potash."

"Do you hear bells?"

"We hear! That is something unusual."

Volodyovski nodded to the trumpeter, and in a low note the trumpet sounded in the dark forest. The squadron pushed forward.

The eyes of all were fixed in the direction from which the ringing came each moment more powerful; indeed they were not looking in vain, for soon a red light gleamed on the horizon and increased every moment.

"A fire!" muttered the men in the ranks.

Pan Michael bent toward Skshetuski. "The Swedes!" said he.

"We will try them!" answered Pan Yan.

"It is a wonder to me that they are setting fire."

"The nobles must have resisted, or the peasants risen if they attacked the church."

"Well, we shall see!" said Pan Michael. And he was panting with satisfaction.

Then Zagloba clattered up to him. "Pan Michael?"

"What?"

"I see that the odor of Swedish flesh has come to you. There will surely be a battle, will there not?"

"As God gives, as God gives!"

"But who will guard the prisoner?"

"What prisoner?"

"Of course, not me, but Kovalski. Pan Michael, it is a terribly important thing that he should not escape. Remember that the hetman knows nothing of what has happened, and will learn from no one, if Kovalski does not report to him. It is requisite to order some trusty men to guard him; for in time of battle he might escape easily, especially if he takes up some stratagem."

"He is as capable of stratagems as the wagon on which he is sitting. But you are right; it is necessary to station some one near. Will you have him under your eye during this time?"

"H'm! I am sorry to be away from the battle! It is true that in the night near fire I am as good as blind. If it were in the daytime you would never have persuaded me; but since the public good requires it, let this be so."

"Very well, I will leave you with five soldiers to assist; and if he tries to escape, fire at his head."

"I'll squeeze him like wax in my fingers, never fear!—But the fire is increasing every moment. Where shall I stay with Kovalski?"

"Wherever you like. I've no time now!" answered Pan Michael, and he rode on.

The flames were spreading rapidly. The wind was blowing from the fire and toward the squadron, and with the sound of bells brought the report of firearms.

"On a trot!" commanded Volodyovski.

CHAPTER XIX.

When near the village, the Lauda men slackened their speed, and saw a broad street so lighted by flames that pins might be picked from the ground; for on both sides a number of cottages were burning, and others were catching fire from these gradually, for the wind was strong and carried sparks, nay, whole clusters of them, like fiery birds, to the adjoining roofs. On the street the flames illuminated greater and smaller crowds of people moving quickly in various directions. The cries of men were mingled with the sounds of the church-bells hidden among trees, with the bellowing of cattle, the barking of dogs, and with infrequent discharges of firearms.

After they had ridden nearer, Volodyovski's soldiers saw troopers wearing round hats, not many men. Some were skirmishing with groups of peasants, armed with scythes and forks; firing at them from pistols, and pushing them beyond the cottages, into the gardens; others were driving oxen, cows, and sheep to the road with rapiers; others, whom it was barely possible to distinguish among whole clouds of feathers, had covered themselves with poultry, with wings fluttering in the agonies of death; some were holding horses, each man having two or three belonging to officers who were occupied evidently in plundering the cottages.

The road to the village descended somewhat from a hill in the midst of a birch-grove; so that the Lauda men, without being seen themselves, saw, as it were, a picture representing the enemy's attack on the village, lighted up by flames, in the glare of which could be clearly distinguished foreign soldiers, villagers, women dragged by troopers, and men defending themselves in disordered groups. All were moving violently, like puppets on springs, shouting, cursing, lamenting.

The conflagration shook a full mane of flame over the village, and roared each moment more terribly.

Volodyovski led his men to the open gate, and ordered them to slacken their pace. He might strike, and with one blow wipe out the invaders, who were expecting nothing; but the little knight had determined "to taste the Swedes" in open battle,—he had so arranged that they might see him coming.

Some horsemen, standing near the gate, saw the approaching squadron first. One of them sprang to an officer, who stood with drawn rapier in the midst of a considerable group of horsemen, in the middle of the road, and began to speak to him, pointing to where Volodyovski was descending with his men. The officer shaded his eyes with his hand and gazed for a time; then he gave a sign, and at once the sharp sound of a trumpet was heard, mingled with various cries of men and beasts.

And here our knight could admire the regularity of the Swedish soldiers; for barely were the first tones of the trumpet heard, when some of the horsemen rushed out in hot haste from the cottages, others left the plundered articles, the oxen and sheep, and ran to their horses. In the twinkle of an eye they stood in regular line; at sight of which the little knight's heart rose with wonder, so select were the men. All were large, sturdy fellows, dressed in coats, with leather straps over the shoulders, and black hats with rim raised on the left side; all had matched bay horses, and stood in line with rapiers at their shoulders, looking sharply, but calmly, at the road.

An officer stepped forth from the line with a trumpeter, wishing apparently to inquire what sort of men were approaching so slowly. Evidently they were thought to be one of Radzivill's squadrons, from which no encounter was expected. The officer began to wave his rapier and his hat; the trumpeter sounded continually, as a sign that they wished to parley.

"Let some one fire at him," said the little knight, "so that he may know what to expect from us."

The report sounded; but the shot did not reach, for the distance was too great. Evidently the officer thought that there was some misunderstanding, for he began to shout and to wave his hat.

"Let him have it a second time!" cried Volodyovski.

After the second discharge the officer turned and moved, though not too hurriedly, toward his own, who also approached him on a trot.

The first rank of Lauda men were now entering the gate.

The Swedish officer, riding up, shouted to his men; the rapiers, hitherto standing upright by the shoulders of the horsemen, dropped and hung at their belts; but all at the same instant drew pistols from the holsters, and rested them on the pommels of their saddles, holding the muzzle upward.

"Finished soldiers!" muttered Volodyovski, seeing the rapidity of their movements, which were simultaneous and almost mechanical. Then he looked at his own men to see if the ranks were in order, straightened himself in the saddle, and cried,—

"Forward!"

The Lauda men bent down to the necks of their horses, and rushed on like a whirlwind.

The Swedes let them come near, and then gave a simultaneous discharge from their pistols; but this did little harm to the Lauda men hidden behind the heads of their horses; only a few dropped the reins and fell backward, the rest rushed on and struck the horsemen, breast to breast.

The Lithuanian light squadrons used lances yet, which in the army of the kingdom the hussars alone used; but Volodyovski expecting a battle at close quarters, had ordered his men to plant their lances at the roadside, therefore it came to sabres at once.

361

The first impetus was not sufficient to break the Swedes, but it pushed them back, so that they began to retreat, cutting and thrusting with their rapiers; but the Lauda men pushed them furiously along the road. Bodies began to fall thickly. The throng grew denser each moment; the clatter of sabres frightened the peasants out of the broad road, in which the heat from the burning houses was unendurable, though the houses were separated from the road and the fences by gardens.

The Swedes, pressed with increasing vigor, retreated gradually, but still in good order. It was difficult moreover to scatter them, since strong fences closed the road on both sides. At times they tried to stop, but were unable to do so.

It was a wonderful battle, in which, by reason of the relatively narrow place of meeting, only the first ranks fought, those next in order could only push forward those standing in front of them; but just for this reason the struggle was turned into a furious encounter.

Volodyovski, having previously requested the old colonels and Pan Yan to look after the men during the attack, enjoyed himself to the full in the first rank. And every moment some Swedish hat fell before him in the throng, as if it had dived into the ground; sometimes a rapier, torn from the hand of a horseman, flew whistling above the rank, and at the same instant was heard the piercing cry of a man, and again a hat fell; a second took its place, then a third the place of the second; but Volodyovski pushed ever forward. His eyes glittered like two ill-omened sparks, but he was not carried away and did not forget himself; at moments, when he had no one at sword's length in front of him, he turned his face and blade somewhat to the right or left, and destroyed in the twinkle of an eye a horseman, with a movement apparently trifling; and he was terrible through these slight and lightning movements which were almost not human.

As a woman pulling hemp disappears in it and is hidden completely, but by the falling stalks her road is known easily, so he vanished from the eye for a time in the throng of large men; but where soldiers were falling like stalks under the sickle of the harvester who cuts near the ground, there was Pan Michael. Pan Stanislav and the gloomy Yuzva Butrym, called Footless, followed hard in his track.

At length the Swedish rear ranks began to push out from between the fences to the broad grass-plot before the church and the bell-tower, and after them came the front ranks. Now was heard the command of the officer, who wished evidently to bring all his men into action at once; and the oblong rectangular body of horsemen stretched out, deployed in the twinkle of an eye, into a long line to present its whole front.

But Pan Yan, who directed the battle and led the squadron, did not imitate the Swede; he rushed forward with a dense column which, striking the now weaker line, broke it, as if with a wedge, and turned swiftly to the right toward the church, taking with this movement the rear of one half of the Swedes, while on the other half Mirski and Stankyevich sprang with the reserve in which were a part of the Lauda men and all of Kovalski's dragoons.

Two battles now began; but they did not last long. The left wing, on which Pan Yan had struck, was unable to form, and scattered first; the right, in which was the commanding officer, resisted longer, but being too much extended, it began to break, to fall into disorder, and at last followed the example of the left wing.

The grass-plot was broad, but unfortunately was enclosed on all sides by a lofty fence; and the church-servants closed and propped the opposite gate when they saw what was taking place.

The scattered Swedes then ran around, but the Lauda men rushed after them. In some places larger groups fought, a number at a time, with sabres and rapiers; in other places the conflict was turned into a series of duels, and man met man, the rapier crossed the sabre, and at times the report of a pistol burst forth. Here and there a Swedish horseman, escaping from one sabre, ran, as if to a trap, under another. Here and there a Swede or a Lithuanian rose from under a fallen horse and fell that moment under the blow of a weapon awaiting him.

Through the grass-plot terrified horses rushed about riderless, with waving mane and nostrils distended from fear; some bit one another; others, blinded from fright, turned their tails to the groups of fighting men and kicked them.

Pan Volodyovski, hurling down Swedes as he went, searched the whole place with his eyes for the officer in command; at last he saw him defending himself against two Butryms, and he sprang toward him.

"Aside!" cried he to the Butryms, "aside!"

The obedient soldiers sprang aside, the little knight rushed on and closed with the Swede, the horses of the two stood on their haunches.

The officer wished evidently to unhorse his opponent with a thrust; but Volodyovski, interposing the hilt of his sabre, described a half-circle like lightning, and the rapier flew away. The officer bent to his holsters, but, cut through the cheek at that moment, he dropped the reins from his left hand.

"Take him alive!" shouted Volodyovski to the Butryms.

The Lauda men seized the wounded officer and held him tottering in the saddle; the little knight pushed on and rode farther against the Swedes, quenching them before him like candles.

But the Swedes began to yield everywhere before the nobles, who were more adroit in fencing and single combat. Some of the Swedes, seizing their rapier blades, extended the hilts to their opponents; others threw their weapons at their feet; the word

"Pardon!" was heard more and more frequently on the field. But no attention was paid to the word, for Pan Michael had commanded to spare but few. The Swedes, seeing this, rushed anew to the struggle, and died as became soldiers after a desperate defence, redeeming richly with blood their own death.

An hour later the last of them were cut down. The peasants ran in crowds from the village to the grass-plot to catch the horses, kill the wounded, and plunder the dead.

Such was the end of the first encounter of Lithuanians with Swedes.

Meanwhile Zagloba, stationed at a distance in the birch-grove with the wagon in which lay Pan Roh, was forced to hear the bitter reproach that, though a relative, he had treated that young man shamefully.

"Uncle, you have ruined me utterly, for not only is a bullet in the head waiting for me at Kyedani, but eternal infamy will fall on my name. Henceforth whoso wants to say, 'Fool,' may say, 'Roh Kovalski!'"

"The truth is that not many will be found to contradict him," answered Zagloba; "and the best proof of your folly is that you wonder at being hung on a hook by me who moved the Khan of the Crimea as a puppet. Well, did you think to yourself, worthless fellow, that I would let you take me and other men of importance to Birji, and throw us, the ornaments of the Commonwealth, into the jaws of the Swedes?"

"I was not taking you of my own will."

"But you were the servant of an executioner, and that for a noble is infamy from which you must purify yourself, or I will renounce you and all the Kovalskis. To be a traitor is worse than to be a crabmonger, but to be the servant of some one worse than a crabmonger is the lowest thing."

"I was serving the hetman."

"And the hetman the devil. There you have it! You are a fool, Roh: get that into your head once and forever, dispute not, but hold to my skirts, and a man will come of you yet; for know this, that advancement has met more than one personage through me."

The rattle of shots interrupted further conversation, for the battle was just beginning in the village. Then the discharges stopped, but the noise continued, and shouts reached that retreat in the birch-grove.

"Ah, Pan Michael is working," said Zagloba. "He is not big, but he bites like a viper. They are shelling out those devils from over the sea like peas. I would rather be there than here, and through you I must listen here. Is this your gratitude? Is this the act of a respectable relative?"

"What have I to be grateful for?" asked Roh.

"For this, that a traitor is not ploughing with you, as with an ox,—though you are grandly fitted for ploughing, since you are stupid and strong. Understand me? Ai! it is getting hotter and hotter there. Do you hear? That must be the Swedes who are bawling like calves in a pasture."

Here Zagloba became serious, for he was a little disturbed; on a sudden he asked, looking quickly into Pan Roh's eyes,—

"To whom do you wish victory?"

"To ours, of course."

"See that! And why not to the Swedes?"

"I would rather pound them. Who are ours, are ours!"

"Conscience is waking up in you. But how could you take your own blood to the Swedes?"

"For I had an order."

"But now you have no order?"

"True."

"Your superior is now Pan Volodyovski, no one else."

"Well, that seems to be true."

"You must do what Pan Volodyovski commands."

"I must."

"He commands you now to renounce Radzivill for the future, and not to serve him, but the country."

"How is that?" asked Pan Roh, scratching his head.

"A command!" cried Zagloba.

"I obey!" said Kovalski.

"That is right! At the first chance you will thrash the Swedes."

"If it is the order, it is the order!" answered Kovalski, and breathed deeply, as if a great burden had fallen from his breast.

Zagloba was equally well satisfied, for he had his own views concerning Kovalski. They began then to listen in harmony to the sounds of the battle which came to them, and listened about an hour longer, until all was silent.

Zagloba was more and more alarmed. "If they have not succeeded?" asked he.

"Uncle, you an old warrior and can say such things! If they were beaten they would come back to us in small groups."

"True! I see thy wit will be of service."

"Do you hear the tramp, Uncle? They are riding slowly. They must have cut the Swedes to pieces."

"Oi, if they are only ours! Shall I go forward, or not?"

Saying this, Zagloba dropped his sabre at his side, took his pistol in his hand, and moved forward. Soon he saw before him a dark mass moving slowly along the road; at the same time noise of conversation reached him.

In front rode a number of men talking with one another loudly; soon the well-known voice of Pan Michael struck the ear of Zagloba. "They are good men! I don't know what kind of infantry they have, but the cavalry is perfect."

Zagloba touched his horse with the spurs. "Ah! how is it, how is it? Oh, impatience was tearing me, I wanted to fly into the fire! But is no one wounded?"

"All are sound, praise to God; but we have lost more than twenty good soldiers."

"And the Swedes?"

"We laid them down like a pavement."

"Pan Michael, you must have enjoyed yourself as a dog in a spring. But was it a decent thing to leave me, an old man, on guard? The soul came near going out of me, so much did I want Swedish meat. Oh, I should have gnawed them!"

"You may have a roast now if you like, for a number of them are in the fire."

"Let the dogs eat them. And were prisoners taken?"

"A captain, and seven soldiers."

"What do you think to do with them?"

"I would have them hanged, for like robbers they fell on an innocent village and were killing the people. Yan says, however, that that will not do."

"Listen to me, gentlemen, hear what has come to my head just now: there is no good in hanging them; on the contrary, let them go to Birji as soon as possible."

"What for?"

"You know me as a soldier, know me now as a statesman. We will let the Swedes go, but we will not tell them who we are. We will say that we are Radzivill's men, that we have cut off this detachment at command of the hetman, and in future will cut off whom we meet, for the hetman only pretended, through strategy, to join the Swedes. They will break their heads over this, and thus we will undermine the hetman's credit terribly. Just think, this hits the Swedes and hits Radzivill too. Kyedani is far from Birji, and Radzivill is still farther from Pontus de la Gardie. Before they

368

explain to each other what has happened and how, they will be ready to fight. We will set the traitor against the invaders; and who will gain by this, if not the Commonwealth?"

"This is excellent counsel, and quite worth the victory. May the bullets strike him!" said Stankyevich.

"You have the mind of a chancellor," added Mirski, "for this will disturb their plans."

"Surely we should act thus," said Pan Michael. "I will set them free to-morrow; but to-day I do not wish to know of anything, for I am dreadfully wearied. It was as hot in the village as in an oven! Uf! my arms are paralyzed completely. The officer could not go to-day in any case, for his face is cut."

"But in what language shall we tell them all this? What is your counsel, father?" asked Pan Yan.

"I have been thinking of that too," answered Zagloba. "Kovalski told me that there are two Prussians among his dragoons who know how to jabber German, and are sharp fellows. Let them tell in German,—which the Swedes know of course, after fighting so many years in Germany. Kovalski is ours, soul and body. He is a man in a hundred, and we will have no small profit from him."

"Well done!" said Volodyovski. "Will some of you, gentlemen, be so kind as to see to this, for I have no voice in my throat from weariness? I have told the men that we shall stay in this grove till morning. The villagers will bring us food, and now to sleep! My lieutenant will see to the watch. 'Pon my word, I cannot see you, for my eyes are closing."

"Gentlemen," said Zagloba, "there is a stack of hay just outside the birches; let us go to the stack, we shall sleep like susliks, and to the road on the morrow. We shall not come back to this country, unless with Pan Sapyeha against Radzivill."

CHAPTER XX.

In Lithuania a civil war had begun, which, with two invasions of the Commonwealth and the ever more stubborn war of the Ukraine, filled the measure of misfortune.

The army of the Lithuanian quota, though so small in number that alone it could not offer effectual resistance to any of the enemies, was divided into two camps. Some regiments, and specially the foreign ones, remained with Radzivill; others, forming the majority, proclaimed the hetman a traitor, protested in arms against joining Sweden, but without unity, without a leader, without a plan. Sapyeha might be its leader, but he was too much occupied at that time with the defence of Byhovo and with the desperate struggle in the interior of the country, to be able to take his place immediately at the head of the movement against Radzivill.

Meanwhile the invaders, each considering a whole region as his own, began to send threatening messages to the other. From their misunderstandings might rise in time the salvation of the Commonwealth; but before it came to hostile steps between them there reigned the most terrible chaos in all Lithuania. Radzivill, deceived in the army, determined to bring it to obedience through force.

Volodyovski had barely reached Ponyevyej with his squadron, after the battle of Klavany, when news came to him of the destruction, by Radzivill, of Mirski's squadron, and that of Stankyevich. Some of the men were placed by force among Radzivill's troops; others were cut down or scattered to the four winds; the remainder were wandering singly or in small groups through villages and forests, seeking a place to hide their heads from vengeance and pursuit.

Fugitives came daily to Pan Michael's detachment, increasing his force and bringing news the most varied.

The most important item was news of the mutiny of Lithuanian troops stationed in Podlyasye, near Byalystok and Tykotsin. After the armies of Moscow had occupied Vilno the squadrons from that place had to cover the approach to the territories of the kingdom. But hearing of the hetman's treason, they formed a confederation, at the head of which were two colonels, Horotkyevich and Yakub Kmita, a cousin of Andrei, the most trusty assistant of Radzivill.

The name of the latter was repeated with horror by the soldiers. He mainly had caused the dispersion of Stankyevich's squadron and that of Mirski; he shot without mercy the captured officers. The hetman trusted him blindly, and just recently had sent him against Nyevyarovski's squadron, which, disregarding the example of its colonel, refused obedience.

Volodyovski heard the last account with great attention; then he turned to the officers summoned in counsel, and asked,—

"What would you say to this,—that we, instead of hurrying to the voevoda of Vityebsk, go to those squadrons which have formed a confederacy in Podlyasye?"

"You have taken that out of my mouth!" said Zagloba "It is nearer home there, and it is always pleasanter among one's own people."

"Fugitives mention too a report," added Pan Yan, "that the king has ordered some squadrons to return from the Ukraine, to oppose the Swedes on the Vistula. If this should prove true, we might be among old comrades instead of pounding from corner to corner."

"But who is going to command those squadrons? Does any one know?"

"They say that Charnyetski will," answered Volodyovski; "but people say this rather than know it, for positive intelligence could not come yet."

"However it may be," said Zagloba, "my advice is to hurry to Podlyasye. We can bring to our side those squadrons that have risen against Radzivill, and take them to the king, and that certainly will not be without a reward."

"Let it be so!" said Oskyerko and Stankyevich.

"It is not easy," said the little knight, "to get to Podlyasye, for we shall have to slip through the fingers of the hetman. If fortune meanwhile should grant us to snap up Kmita somewhere on the road, I would speak a couple of words in his ear, from which his skin would grow green."

"He deserves it," said Mirski. "That some old soldiers who have served their whole lives under the Radzivills hold to the hetman, is less to be wondered at; but that swaggerer serves only for his own profit, and the pleasure which he finds in betrayal."

"So then to Podlyasye?" asked Oskyerko.

"To Podlyasye! to Podlyasye!" cried all in one voice.

But still the affair was difficult, as Volodyovski had said; for to go to Podlyasye it was necessary to pass near Kyedani, as near a den in which a lion was lurking.

The roads and lines of forest, the towns and villages were in the hands of Radzivill; somewhat beyond Kyedani was Kmita, with cavalry, infantry, and cannon. The hetman had heard already of the escape of the colonels, the mutiny of Volodyovski's squadron, and the battle of Klavany; the last brought him to such rage that there was fear for his life, since a terrible attack of asthma had for a time almost stopped his breathing.

In truth he had cause enough for anger, and even for despair, since that battle brought on his head a whole Swedish tempest. People began at once after this battle to cut up here and there small Swedish detachments. Peasants did this, and individual nobles independently; but the Swedes laid it to the account of Radzivill, especially as the officers and men sent by

Volodyovski to Birji declared before the commandant that one of Radzivill's squadrons had fallen upon them at his command.

In a week a letter came to the prince from the commandant at Birji, and ten days later from Pontus de la Gardie himself, the commander-in-chief of the Swedish forces.

"Either your highness has no power and significance," wrote the latter,—"and in such case how could you conclude a treaty in the name of the whole country!—or it is your wish to bring about through artifice the ruin of the king's army. If that is the case, the favor of my master will turn from your highness, and punishment will come quickly, unless you show obedience and efface your faults by faithful service."

Radzivill sent couriers at once with an explanation of what had happened and how; but the dart had fastened in his haughty soul, and the burning wound began to rankle more and more. He whose word not long before terrified the country more than all Sweden; he for the half of whose property all the Swedish lords might have been bought; he who stood against his own king, thinking himself the equal of monarchs; he who had acquired fame in the whole world by his victories, and who walked in his own pride as in sunshine—must now listen to the threats of one Swedish general, must hear lectures on obedience and faithfulness. It is true that that general was brother-in-law to the king; but the king himself,—who was he? A usurper of the throne belonging by right and inheritance to Yan Kazimir.

Above all, the rage of the hetman was turned against those who were the cause of that humiliation, and he swore to himself to trample Volodyovski and those colonels who were with him and the whole squadron of Lauda. With this object he marched against them; and as hunters to clear out the wolf's nest surround a forest with shares, he surrounded them and began to pursue without rest.

Meanwhile tidings came that Kmita had crushed Nyevyarovski's squadron, cut down or scattered the officers, and joined the men to his own. Radzivill, to strike the more surely, commanded Pan Andrei to send him some of these troops.

"Those men," wrote the hetman, "for whose lives you interceded with us so persistently, and mainly Volodyovski with that other straggler, escaped on the road to Birji. We sent the stupidest officer with them on purpose, so that they might not win him over; but even he either became a traitor, or they fooled him. Now Volodyovski has the whole Lauda squadron, and fugitives are reinforcing him. They cut to pieces one hundred and twenty Swedes at Klavany, saying that they did it at our command, from which great distrust has arisen between us and Pontus. The whole cause may be ruined by those traitors, whose heads, had it not been for your interference, would have been cut off at our command, as God is in heaven. So we have to repent of our mildness, though we hope in God that vengeance will soon overtake them. Tidings have come to us, too, that in Billeviche nobles assemble at the house of the sword-bearer and conspire against us. This must be stopped! You will send all the cavalry to us, and the infantry to Kyedani to guard the castle and the town, for from those traitors anything may be expected. You will go yourself with some tens of horsemen to Billeviche, and bring the sword-bearer and his niece to Kyedani. At present it is important, not only for you, but for us; for whoso has them in hand has the whole Lauda region, in which the nobles, following the example of Volodyovski, are beginning to rise against us. We have sent Harasimovich to Zabludovo with instructions how to begin with those confederates. Of great importance among them is Yakub, your cousin, to whom you will write, if you think you can act on him through a letter. Signifying to you our continual favor, we commit you to the care of God."

When Kmita had read this letter, he was content at heart that the colonels had succeeded in escaping the Swedes, and in secret he wished them to escape Radzivill. Still he carried out all commands of the prince, sent him the cavalry, garrisoned Kyedani with infantry, and began to make trenches along the castle and the town, promising himself to go immediately after this work was done to Billeviche for the sword-bearer and the young woman.

"I will use no force, unless in the last resort," thought he, "and in no case will I urge Olenka. Finally, it is not my will, 'tis the command of the prince. She will not receive me pleasantly, I know; but God grant that in time she will know my intentions, and that I serve Radzivill not against the country, but for its salvation."

Thinking thus, he labored zealously at fortifying Kyedani, which was to be the residence of his Olenka in the future.

Meanwhile Volodyovski was slipping away before the hetman, but the hetman pursued him furiously. It was, however, too narrow for Pan Michael; for from Birji considerable detachments of Swedish troops pushed toward the south, the east of the country was occupied by the legions of the Tsar, and on the road to Kyedani the hetman was lying in wait.

Zagloba was greatly depressed by such a condition of affairs, and he turned with increasing frequency to Pan Michael with questions: "Pan Michael, by the love of God, shall we break through or shall we not break through?"

"There is not even talk of breaking through here," answered the little knight. "You know that I am not lined with cowardice, and that I attack whom I will, even the devil himself. But I cannot meet the hetman, for I am not equal to him. You have said yourself that he is a pike and we perches. I shall do what is in my power to slip out, but if it comes to a battle, I tell you plainly that he will defeat us."

"Then he will command to chop us up and throw us to the dogs. As God lives! into any man's hands save Radzivill's! But in this case why not turn to Pan Sapyeha?"

"It is too late now, for the hetman's troops and the Swedes have closed the roads."

"The devil tempted me when I persuaded Pan Yan and his cousin to go to Radzivill!" said Zagloba, in despair.

But Pan Michael did not lose hope yet, especially since the nobles, and even the peasants, brought him warning of the hetman's movements; for all hearts were turning from Radzivill. Pan Michael twisted out therefore as he knew how,—and he knew how famously, for almost from childhood he had inured himself to war with Tartars and Cossacks. He had been made renowned in the army of Yeremi by descents on Tartar chambuls, by scouting expeditions, unexpected attacks, lightning escapes, in which he surpassed other officers.

At present hemmed in between Upita and Rogova on one side and Nyevyaja on the other, he doubled around on the space of a few miles, avoiding battle continually, worrying the Radzivill squadrons, and even plucking them a little as a wolf hunted by dogs slips by often near the hunters, and when the dogs press him too closely, turns and shows his white gleaming teeth.

But when Kmita's cavalry came up, the hetman closed the narrowest gaps with them, and went himself to see that the two ends of the snare came together.

That was at Nyevyaja.

The regiments of Myeleshko and Ganhoff with two squadrons of cavalry, under the lead of the prince himself, formed as it were a bow, the string of which was the river. Volodyovski with his squadron was in the centre of the bow. He had in front of him, it is true, one ford which led through a swampy stream, but just on the other side of the ford were two Scottish regiments and two hundred of Radzivill's Cossacks, with six fieldpieces, turned in such manner that even one man could not have reached the other side under the fire of them.

Now the bow began to contract. The middle of it was led by the hetman himself.

Happily for Volodyovski, night and a storm with pouring rain stopped the advance; but for the enclosed men there remained not more than a square half-mile of meadow, grown over with willows, in the middle of the half-ring of Radzivill's army, and the river guarded on the other side by the Scots.

Next morning when the early dawn was just whitening the tops of the willows, the regiments moved forward to the river and were struck dumb with amazement.

Volodyovski had gone through the earth,—there was not a living soul in the willows.

The hetman himself was astounded, and then real thunders fell on the heads of the officers commanding at the ford. And again an attack of asthma seized the prince with such force that those present trembled for his life. But rage overcame even the asthma. Two officers, intrusted with guarding the bank, were to be shot; but Ganhoff prevailed on the prince to have inquiries made first as to how the beast had escaped from the toils.

It appeared in fact that Volodyovski, taking advantage of the darkness and rain, had led his whole squadron out of the willows into the river, and swimming or wading with the current had slipped along Radzivill's right wing, which touched the bank at that point. Some horses, sunk to their bellies in the mud, indicated the place where he had come out on the right bank. From farther tracks it was easy to see that he had moved with all horse-breath in the direction of Kyedani. The hetman guessed at once from this that he wished to make his way to Horotkyevich and Yakub Kmita in Podlyasye.

"But in passing near Kyedani would he not burn the town or try to plunder the castle?"

A terrible fear straitened the heart of the prince. The greater part of his ready money and treasures were in Kyedani. Kmita, it is true, was bound to supply it with infantry; but if he had not done so, the undefended castle would easily become plunder for the insolent colonel. Radzivill felt sure that courage would not be wanting Volodyovski to attack the residence of Kyedani itself. It might be that time would not be wanting, for escaping in the beginning of the night he had left pursuit at least six hours behind.

In every case it was imperative to hasten with all breath to the rescue. The prince left the infantry, and pushed on with the cavalry. When he arrived at Kyedani he did not find Kmita, but he found everything quiet; and the opinion which he had of the young colonel's ability increased doubly at sight of the finished trenches and field-cannon standing on them. That same day he reviewed them in company with Ganhoff, to whom he remarked in the evening,—

"He acted thus of his own mind, without my order, and finished those trenches so well that a protracted defence might be made here, even against artillery. If that man does not break his neck too early, he may rise high."

There was another man, at thought of whom the hetman could not restrain a certain kind of admiration, but mingled with rage, for the man was Pan Michael. "I could finish the mutiny soon," said he to Ganhoff, "if I had two such servants. Kmita may be still more alert, but he has not the experience, and the other was brought up in the school of Yeremi, beyond the Dnieper."

"Does your highness give command to pursue him?" asked Ganhoff.

The prince looked at Ganhoff, and said with emphasis, "He would beat you and escape from me." But after a while he frowned, and added, "Everything is quiet here now; but we must move to Podlyasye at once, and finish those there."

"Your highness," said Ganhoff, "as soon as we move a foot out of this place, all will seize arms against the Swedes."

"Which all?"

"The nobles and peasants. And not stopping with the Swedes, they will turn against the dissidents, for they put all the blame of this war on our co-religionists, saying that we sent to the enemy, and in fact brought the enemy in."

"It is a question with me of my cousin Boguslav. I know not whether he is able to hold out against the confederates in Podlyasye."

"It is a question of Lithuania to keep it in obedience to us and the King of Sweden."

The prince began to walk through the room, saying, "If I could in any way get Horotkyevich and Yakub Kmita into my hands! They will devour my property, destroy, plunder it; they will not leave a stone upon a stone."

"Unless we stipulate with General de la Gardie to send hither as many troops as possible, while we are in Podlyasye."

"With Pontus,—never!" answered Radzivill, to whose head a wave of blood rushed. "If with any one, with the king himself. I do not need to treat with servants when I can treat with their master. If the king were to command Pontus to place two thousand cavalry at my disposal, that would be another thing. But I will not ask Pontus for them. It is needful to send some one to the king; it is time to negotiate with him directly."

The lean face of Ganhoff flushed slightly, and his eyes were lighted with desire. "If your highness commanded—"

"You would go; but for you to arrive there is another thing. You are a German, and it is dangerous for a foreigner to enter an uprisen country. Who knows where the king is at this moment, and where he will be in half a month or a month? It is necessary to ride through the whole country. Besides, it cannot be! You will not go, for it is necessary to send one of my own people, a man of high family, so as to convince the king that not all the nobles have left me."

"An inexperienced man might do much harm," said Ganhoff, timidly.

"An envoy will have no work there except to deliver my letter, and bring back an answer; and any man can explain that it was not I who gave orders to beat the Swedes at Klavany."

Ganhoff was silent.

The prince began again to walk with unquiet steps through the room; on his forehead was manifest a continual struggle of thought. In truth, he had not known a moment of peace from the time of his treaty with the Swedes. Pride devoured him, his conscience gnawed him, the unexpected resistance of the country and the army gnawed him; the uncertainty of the future, and the threat of ruin terrified him. He struggled, he fought, he passed sleepless nights, he was failing in health. His eyes were sinking, he was growing thin; his face, formerly red, became blue, and almost with every hour silver threads increased in his mustaches and his forelock. In a word, he lived in torment, and bent under the burden.

Ganhoff followed him with his eyes as he walked through the room; he had still a little hope that the prince would bethink himself, and send him.

But the prince halted suddenly, and struck his forehead with his palm. "Two squadrons of cavalry, to horse at once! I will lead them myself."

Ganhoff looked on him with wonderment. "An expedition?" inquired he, involuntarily.

"Move on!" said the prince. "God grant that it be not too late!"

CHAPTER XXI.

When Kmita had finished the trenches and secured Kyedani from sudden attack, he was unable to delay further his expedition for the sword-bearer and Olenka, especially since the command of the prince to bring them to Kyedani was imperative. But still Pan Andrei loitered, and when at last he did move at the head of fifty dragoons, he was as unquiet as if going on a forlorn hope. He felt that he would not be thankfully received, and he trembled at the thought that the old man might try to resist, even with armed hand, and in such an event it would be necessary to use force. But he determined first to persuade and entreat. With the intent of stripping his visit of all semblance of armed attack, he left the dragoons at an inn a quarter of a mile from the village, and two from the house, and ordering the carriage to follow a little later, rode ahead himself, with only the sergeant and one attendant.

It was in the afternoon, and the sun was already well inclined toward the west, but after a rainy and stormy night the day was beautiful and the sky pure, only here and there was it variegated on the western side by small rosy clouds which pushed slowly beyond the horizon, like a flock of sheep leaving a field. Kmita rode through the village with throbbing heart and as uneasy as the Tartar who entering a village first, in advance of a chambul, looks around on every side to see if he can discover armed men in ambush. But the three horsemen attracted no attention. Barefooted little peasant boys merely jumped out of the road before the horses; peasants seeing the handsome officer, bowed to him, sweeping the ground with their caps. He rode on, and passing the village saw ahead a large dwelling, the old Billevich nest; behind it broad gardens ending far beyond in the flat fields.

Kmita slackened his pace still more, and began to talk with himself, evidently framing answers to questions; and meanwhile he gazed with anxious eye on the buildings rising before him. It was not at all a lordly mansion, but at the first glance it would have been guessed that a noble lived there of more than medium fortune. The house itself, with its back to the gardens and front to the highway, was enormous, but of wood. The pine of the walls had grown so dark with age that the panes in the windows seemed white in contrast. Above the walls rose a gigantic roof with four chimneys in the middle, and two dovecotes at the gables. A whole cloud of white doves were collected on the roof, now flying away with clapping of wings, now dropping, like snowy kerchiefs, on the black ridges, now flapping around the pillars supporting the entrance.

That entrance, adorned with a shield on which the Billevich arms were painted, disturbed the proportions of the house, for it was not in the middle, but toward one side of it. Evidently the house had once been smaller, but new parts were added subsequently from one side, though the added parts had grown so black with the passage of years as not to differ in anything from the old. Two wings, of enormous length, rose on both sides of the house proper, and formed as it were two arms of a horseshoe. In these wings were guest-chambers used in time of great gatherings, kitchens, store-houses, carriage-houses, stables for carriage horses which the masters wished to keep near at hand, rooms for officials, servants, and house Cossacks.

In the middle of the broad yard grew old linden-trees, on them were storks' nests. Among the trees was a bear chained to a pillar. Two well-sweeps at the sides of the yard, a cross with the

382

Passion of the Lord between two spears at the entrance, completed this picture of the residence of a powerful, noble family. At the right of the house, in the middle of frequent linden-trees, rose the straw roofs of stables, cow-houses, sheep-houses, and granaries.

Kmita entered the gate, which was open on both sides; like the arms of a noble awaiting the arrival of a guest. Then two dogs loitering through the yard announced the stranger, and from a wing two boys ran to take the horses.

At the same moment in the door of the main building stood a female figure, in which Kmita recognized Olenka at once. His heart beat more quickly, and throwing the reins to the servant, he went toward the porch with uncovered head, holding in one hand his sabre, and in the other his cap.

She stood before him like a charming vision, shading her eyes with her hand against the setting sun, and then vanished on a sudden, as if frightened by the sight of the approaching guest.

"Bad!" thought Pan Andrei; "she hides from me."

He was pained, and his pain was all the greater since just before the mild sunset, the view of that house, and the calm so spread around it filled his heart with hope, though perhaps Pan Andrei did not note that.

He cherished as it were an illusion that he was going to his betrothed, who would receive him with eyes gleaming from joy and a blush on her cheeks.

And the illusion was broken. Scarcely had she seen him when she rushed away, as if from an evil spirit; and straightway Pan Tomash came out to meet him with a face at once unquiet and cloudy.

Kmita bowed and said, "I have long wished to express duly my devotion to you, my benefactor; but I was unable to do so sooner in these times of disturbance, though surely there was no lack in me of desire."

"I am very grateful, and I beg you to enter," answered the sword-bearer, smoothing the forelock on his head,—an act usual with him when confused or uncertain of himself. And he stepped aside from the door to let the guest pass.

Kmita for a while did not wish to enter first, and they bowed to each other on the threshold; at last Pan Andrei took the step before the sword-bearer, and in a moment they were in the room.

They found there two nobles,—one, a man in the bloom of life, Pan Dovgird of Plemborg, a near neighbor of the Billeviches; the other, Pan Hudzynski, a tenant in Eyragoly. Kmita noticed that they had barely heard his name when their faces changed and they seemed to act like dogs at sight of a wolf; he looked at them first defiantly, and then feigned not to see them.

A disagreeable silence succeeded.

Pan Andrei grew impatient and gnawed his mustaches; the guests looked at him with a fixed frown, and the sword-bearer stroked his forelock.

"Will you drink a glass of poor nobles' mead with us?" asked he at last, pointing to a decanter and a glass. "I request you—"

"I will drink with a gentleman!" said Kmita, rather abruptly.

Dovgird and Hudzynski began to puff, taking the answer as an expression of contempt for them; but they would not begin a quarrel at once in a friendly house, and that with a roisterer who had a terrible reputation throughout all Jmud. Still the insult nettled them.

Meanwhile the sword-bearer clapped his hands for a servant, and ordered him to bring a fourth glass; then he filled it, raised his own to his lips, and said, "Into your hands— I am glad to see you in my house."

"I should be sincerely glad were that true."

"A guest is a guest," said the sword-bearer, sententiously.

After awhile, conscious evidently of his duty as a host to keep up the conversation, he asked, "What do you hear at Kyedani? How is the health of the hetman?"

"Not strong," answered Kmita, "and in these unquiet times it cannot be otherwise. The prince has a world of troubles and annoyances."

"I believe that!" said Pan Hudzynski.

Kmita looked at him for a while, then turned to the host and continued,—

"The prince, being promised assistance by the Swedish King, expected to move against the enemy at Vilna without delay, and take vengeance for the ashes of that place, which have not yet grown cold. And it must be known also to you that now it is necessary to search for Vilna in Vilna, for it was burning seventeen days. They say that nothing is visible among the ruins but the black holes of cellars from which smoke is still rising continually."

"Misfortune!" said the sword-bearer.

"Of course a misfortune, which if it could not have been prevented should be avenged and similar ruins made of the enemy's capital. In fact, it was coming to this when disturbers, suspecting the best intentions of an honorable man, proclaimed him a traitor, and resisted him in arms instead of aiding him against the enemy. It is not to be wondered, therefore, that the health of the prince totters, since he, whom God predestined to great things, sees that the malice of man is ever preparing new obstacles through which the entire undertaking may come to naught. The best friends of the prince have deceived him; those on whom he counted most have left him, or gone to the enemy."

"So it is," said the sword-bearer, seriously.

"That is very painful," continued Kmita, "and I myself have heard the prince say, 'I know that honorable men pass evil judgments on me; but why do they not come to Kyedani, why do they not tell me to my face what they have against me, and listen to my reasons?'"

"Whom has the prince in mind?" asked the sword-bearer.

"In the first rank you, my benefactor, for whom he has a genuine regard, and he suspects that you belong to the enemy."

The sword-bearer began to smooth his forelock quickly. At last, seeing that the conversation was taking an undesirable turn, he clapped his hands.

A servant appeared in the doorway.

"Seest not that it is growing dark? Bring lights!" cried Pan Tomash.

"God sees," continued Kmita, "that I had intended to lay before you proper assurances of my own devotion separately, but I have come here also at the order of the prince, who would have come in person to Billeviche if the time were more favoring."

"Our thresholds are too lowly," said the sword-bearer.

"Do not say that, since it is customary for neighbors to visit one another; but the prince has no time unoccupied, therefore he said to me, 'Explain in my name to Pan Billevich that I am not able to visit him, but let him come to me with his niece, and that of course without delay, for to-morrow or the day following I know not where I shall be.' So I have come with a request, and I trust that both of you are in good health; for when I drove in here I saw Panna Aleksandra in the door, but she vanished at once, like mist from the field."

"That is true," said the sword-bearer; "I sent her myself to see who had come."

"I am waiting for your reply, my benefactor," said Kmita.

At that moment the attendant brought in a light and placed it on the table; by the shining of the light it was seen that Billevich was greatly confused.

"This is no small honor for me," said he, "but—I cannot go at once. Be pleased to excuse me to the hetman—you see that I have guests."

"Oh, surely that will not hinder, for these gentlemen will yield to the prince."

"We have our own tongues in our mouths, and can answer for ourselves," said Pan Hudzynski.

"Without waiting for others to make decisions concerning us," added Dovgird.

"You see," continued Kmita, pretending to take in good part the churlish words of the nobles, "I knew that these were polite cavaliers. But to avoid slighting any one, I invite them also in the name of the prince to come to Kyedani."

"Too much favor," said both; "we have something else to do."

Kmita looked on them with a peculiar expression, and then said coldly, as if speaking to some fourth person, "When the prince invites, it is not permitted to refuse."

At that they rose from their chairs.

"But is that constraint?" asked the sword-bearer.

"Pan Billevich, my benefactor," answered Kmita, quickly, "those gentlemen will go whether they wish or not, for thus it has pleased me; but I desire not to use force with you, and I beg most sincerely that you will deign to gratify the prince. I am on service, and have an order to bring you; but as long as I do not lose hope of effecting something with entreaty, I shall not cease to entreat,—and I swear to you that not a hair will fall from your head while there. The prince wishes to talk with you, and wishes you to live in Kyedani during these troubled times, when even peasants collect in crowds and plunder. This is the whole affair! You will be treated with fitting respect in Kyedani, as a guest and a friend; I give my word of honor for that."

"As a noble, I protest," said the sword-bearer, "and the law protects me."

"And sabres!" cried Hudzynski and Dovgird.

Kmita laughed, frowned, and said, "Put away your sabres, gentlemen, or I shall give the order to place you both against the barn and put a bullet into the head of each one of you."

At this they grew timid, and began to look at each other and at Kmita; but the sword-bearer cried,—

"The most outrageous violence against the freedom of nobles, against privileges!"

"There will be no violence if you comply of your own will," said Kmita; "and the proof is in this that I left dragoons in the village, and came here alone to invite you as one neighbor another. Do not refuse, for the times are such that it is difficult to pay attention to refusals. The prince himself will excuse you therefore, and know that you will be received as a neighbor and a friend. Understand, too, that could you be received otherwise, I would a hundred times rather have a bullet in my head than come here for you. Not a hair will fall from any Billevich head while I am alive. Call to mind who I am, remember Heraclius Billevich, remember his will, and consider whether the prince would have selected me did he not intend to deal with you in sincerity."

"Why then does he use force, why have I to go under constraint? How am I to trust him, when all Lithuania talks of the oppression under which honorable citizens are groaning in Kyedani?"

Kmita drew breath; for, from his words and voice he knew that Billevich was beginning to weaken in his resistance.

"Worthy benefactor," said he, almost joyously, "constraint among neighbors often rises from affection. And when you order servants to put the carriage-wheel of a welcome guest in the storehouse, or his provision-chest in the larder, is not that constraint? And when you force him to drink, even when wine is flowing out through his nostrils, is not that constraint? And be assured that even had I to bind you and take you bound to Kyedani among dragoons, that would be for your good. Just think, insurgent soldiers are wandering about and committing lawless deeds, peasants are mustering, Swedish troops are approaching, and do you think to save yourself from accident in the uproar, or that some of these will not come to-day or tomorrow, plunder and burn your property, and attack your person? Is Billeviche a fortress? Can you defend yourself here? What does the prince wish for you? Safety; for Kyedani is the only place where you are not in danger. A detachment of the prince's troops will guard your property here, as the eyes in their heads, from all disorder of soldiers; and if one fork is lost, then take my whole fortune."

Billevich began to walk through the room. "Can I trust your word?"

At that moment Panna Aleksandra entered the room. Kmita approached her quickly, but suddenly remembered the events of Kyedani, and her cold face fixed him to the floor; he bowed therefore from a distance, in silence.

Pan Billevich stood before her. "We have to go to Kyedani," said he.

"And for what reason?" asked she.

"For the hetman invites."

"Very kindly,—as a neighbor," added Kmita.

"Yes, very kindly," said Billevich, with a certain bitterness; "but if we do not go of our own will, this cavalier has the order to surround us with dragoons and take us by force."

"God preserve us from that!" said Kmita.

"Have not I told you, Uncle," asked Panna Aleksandra, "that we ought to flee as far as possible, for they would not leave us here undisturbed? Now my words have come true."

"What's to be done, what's to be done? There is no remedy against force," cried Billevich.

"True," answered the lady: "but we ought not to go to that infamous house of our own will. Let murderers take us, bind us, and bear us. Not we alone shall suffer persecution, not us alone will the vengeance of traitors reach; but let them know that we prefer death to infamy."

Here she turned with an expression of supreme contempt to Kmita: "Bind us, sir officer, or sir executioner, and take us with horses, for in another way we will not go."

The blood rushed to Kmita's face; it seemed for a time that he would burst forth in terrible anger, but he restrained himself.

"Ah, gracious lady," said he, with a voice stifled from excitement, "I have not favor in your eyes, since you wish to make me a murderer, a traitor, and a man of violence. May God judge who is right,—whether I serving the hetman, or you insulting me as a dog. God gave you beauty, but a heart venomous and implacable. You are glad to suffer yourself, that you may inflict still greater pain on another. You exceed the measure,—as I live, you exceed it,—and nothing will come of that."

"The maiden speaks well," cried Billevich, to whom daring came suddenly; "we will not go of our own will. Take us with dragoons."

But Kmita paid no attention whatever to him, so much was he excited, and so deeply touched.

"You are in love with the sufferings of people," continued he to Olenka, "and you proclaim me a traitor without judgment, without considering a reason, without permitting me to say a word in my own defence. Let it be so. But you will go to Kyedani,—of your own will or against your will; it is all one. There my intentions will become evident; there you will know whether you have justly accused me of wrong, there conscience will tell you who of us was whose executioner. I want no other vengeance. God be with you, but I want that vengeance. And I want nothing more of you, for you have bent the bow to the breaking. There is a serpent under your beauty as under a flower."

"We will not go!" repeated Billevich, still more resolutely.

"As true as life we will not!" shouted Hudzynski and Dovgird.

Kmita turned to them; but he was very pale now, for rage was throttling him, and his teeth chattered as in a fever.

"Ei! Try now to resist! My horses are to be heard,—my dragoons are coming. Will some one say again that he will not go?"

In fact the tramp of numerous horses was heard. All saw that there was no help, and Kmita said,—

"Young lady, within the time that a man could repeat the Lord's Prayer twice you must be in the carriage, or your uncle will have a bullet in his head."

And it was evident that the wild frenzy of anger was taking possession more and more of Pan Andrei, for suddenly he shouted till the panes rattled in the windows, "To the road!"

That same instant the door of the front chamber opened quietly, and some strange voice inquired,—

"To what place, Cavalier?"

All became as stone from amazement, and every eye was turned to the door, in which stood some small man in armor, and with a naked sabre in his hand.

Kmita retreated a step, as if he had seen an apparition. "Pan Volodyovski!" cried he.

"At your service!" answered the little man. And he advanced into the middle of the chamber; after him entered in a crowd Mirski, Zagloba, Pan Yan, Pan Stanislav, Stankyevich, Oskyerko and Roh Kovalski.

"Ha!" cried Zagloba; "the Cossack caught a Tartar, and the Tartar holds him by the head!"

Billevich began to speak: "Whoever you are, gentlemen, save a citizen whom in spite of law, birth, and office they wish to arrest and confine. Save, brothers, the freedom of a noble, whoever you may be."

"Fear not!" answered Volodyovski, "the dragoons of this cavalier are already in fetters, and now he needs rescue himself more than you do."

"But a priest most of all!" added Zagloba.

"Sir Knight," said Volodyovski, turning to Kmita, "you have no luck with me; a second time I stand in your way. You did not expect me?"

"I did not! I thought you were in the hands of the prince."

"I have just slipped out of those hands,—this is the road to Podlyasye. But enough! The first time that you bore away this lady I challenged you to sabres, is it not true?"

"True," answered Kmita, reaching involuntarily to his head.

"Now it is another affair. Then you were given to fighting,—a thing usual with nobles, and not bringing the last infamy. To-day you do not deserve that an honest man should challenge you."

"Why is that?" asked Kmita; and raising his proud head, he looked Volodyovski straight in the eyes.

"You are a traitor and a renegade," answered Volodyovski, "for you have cut down, like an executioner, honest soldiers who stood by their country,—for it is through your work that this unhappy land is groaning under a new yoke. Speaking briefly, prepare for death, for as God is in heaven your last hour has come."

"By what right do you judge and execute me?" inquired Kmita.

"Gracious sir," answered Zagloba, seriously, "say your prayers instead of asking us about a right. But if you have anything to say in your defence, say it quickly, for you will not find a living soul to take your part. Once, as I have heard, this lady here present begged you from the hands of Pan Volodyovski; but after what you have done now, she will surely not take your part."

Here the eyes of all turned involuntarily to Panna Aleksandra, whose face at that moment was as if cut from stone; and she stood motionless, with downcast lids, icy-cold, but she did not advance a step or speak a word.

The voice of Kmita broke the silence—"I do not ask that lady for intercession."

Panna Aleksandra was silent.

"This way!" called Volodyovski, turning toward the door.

Heavy steps were heard, followed by the gloomy rattle of spurs; and six soldiers, with Yuzva Butrym in front, entered the room.

"Take him!" commanded Volodyovski, "lead him outside the village and put a bullet in his head."

The heavy hand of Butrym rested on the collar of Kmita, after that two other hands.

"Do not let them drag me like a dog!" said Kmita to Volodyovski. "I will go myself."

Volodyovski nodded to the soldiers, who released him at once, but surrounded him; and he walked out calmly, not speaking to any man, only whispering his prayers.

Panna Aleksandra went out also, through the opposite door, to the adjoining rooms. She passed the first and the second, stretching out her hand in the darkness before her; suddenly her head whirled, the breath failed in her bosom, and she fell, as if dead, on the floor.

Among those who were assembled in the first room a dull silence reigned for some time; at last Billevich broke it. "Is there no mercy for him?" asked he.

"I am sorry for him," answered Zagloba, "for he went manfully to death."

To which Mirski said, "He shot a number of officers out of my squadron, besides those whom he slew in attack."

"And from mine too," added Stankyevich; "and he cut up almost all of Nyevyarovski's men."

"He must have had orders from Radzivill," said Zagloba.

"Gentlemen," said Billevich, "you bring the vengeance of Radzivill on my head."

"You must flee. We are going to Podlyasye, for there the squadrons have risen against traitors; go with us. There is no other help. You can take refuge in Byalovyej, where a relative of Pan Skshetuski is the king's hunter. There no one will find you."

"But my property will be lost."

"The Commonwealth will restore it to you."

"Pan Michael," said Zagloba, suddenly, "I will gallop off and see if there are not some orders of the hetman on that unfortunate man. You remember what I found on Roh Kovalski."

"Mount a horse. There is time yet; later the papers will be bloody. I ordered them to take him beyond the village, so that the lady might not be alarmed at the rattle of muskets, for women are sensitive and given to fright."

Zagloba went out, and after a while the tramp of the horse on which he rode away was heard. Volodyovski turned to the host.

"What is the lady doing?"

"Beyond doubt she is praying for that soul which must go before God."

"May the Lord give him eternal rest!" said Pan Yan. "Were it not for his willing service with Radzivill, I should be the first to speak in his favor; but if he did not wish to stand by his country, he might at least not have sold his soul to Radzivill."

"That is true!" added Volodyovski.

"He is guilty and deserves what has come upon him," said Pan Stanislav; "but I would that Radzivill were in his place, or Opalinski—oh, Opalinski!"

"Of how far he is guilty, you have best proof here," put in Oskyerko; "this lady, who was his betrothed, did not find a word in his favor. I saw clearly that she was in torment, but she was silent; for how could she take the part of a traitor."

"She loved him once sincerely, I know that," said Billevich. "Permit me, gentlemen, to go and see what has befallen her, as this is a grievous trial for a woman."

"Make ready for the road!" cried the little knight, "for we shall merely give rest to the horses. We move farther. Kyedani is too near this place, and Radzivill must have returned already."

"Very well!" said the noble, and he left the room.

After a while his piercing cry was heard. The knights sprang toward the sound, not knowing what had happened; the servants also ran in with the lights, and they saw Billevich raising Olenka, whom he had found lying senseless on the floor.

Volodyovski sprang to help him, and together they placed her on the sofa. She gave no sign of life. They began to rub her. The old housekeeper ran in with cordials, and at last the young lady opened her eyes.

"Nothing is the matter," said the old housekeeper; "go ye to that room, we will take care of her."

Billevich conducted his guests. "Would that this had not happened!" said the anxious host. "Could you not take that unfortunate with you, and put him out of the way somewhere on the road, and not on my place? How can I travel now, how flee, when the young woman is barely alive, on the brink of serious illness?"

"The illness is all over now," answered Volodyovski. "We will put the lady in a carriage; you must both flee, for the vengeance of Radzivill spares no man."

"The lady may recover quickly," said Pan Yan.

"A comfortable carriage is ready, with horses attached, for Kmita brought it with him," said Volodyovski. "Go and tell the lady how things are, and that it is impossible to delay flight. Let her collect her strength. We must go, for before to-morrow morning Radzivill's troops may be here."

"True," answered Billevich; "I go!"

He went, and after a while returned with his niece, who had not only collected her strength, but was already dressed for the road. She had a high color on her face, and her eyes were gleaming feverishly.

"Let us go, let us go!" repeated she, entering the room.

Volodyovski went out on the porch for a moment to send men for the carriage; then he returned, and all began to make ready for the road.

Before a quarter of an hour had passed, the roll of wheels was heard outside the windows, and the stamping of horses' hoofs on the pavement with which the space before the entrance was covered.

"Let us go!" said Olenka.

"To the road!" cried the officers.

That moment the door was thrown open, and Zagloba burst into the room like a bomb.

"I have stopped the execution!" cried he.

Olenka from being ruddy became in one moment as white as chalk; she seemed ready to faint again; but no one paid attention to her, for all eyes were turned on Zagloba, who was panting like a whale, trying to catch breath.

"Have you stopped the execution?" inquired Volodyovski. "Why was that?"

"Why?—Let me catch breath. This is why,—without Kmita, without that honorable cavalier, we should all of us be hanging on trees at Kyedani. Uf! we wanted to kill our benefactor, gentlemen! Uf!"

"How can that be?" cried all, at once.

"How can it be? Read this letter; in it is the answer."

Here Zagloba gave a letter to Volodyovski. He began to read, stopping every moment and looking at his comrades; for it was in fact the letter in which Radzivill reproached Kmita bitterly because by his stubborn persistence he had freed the colonels and Zagloba from death at Kyedani.

"Well, what do you think?" repeated Zagloba, at each interval.

The letter ended, as we know, with the commission for Kmita to bring Billevich and his niece to Kyedani. Pan Andrei had the letter with him, apparently to show it to the sword-bearer in case of necessity, and it had not come to that.

Above all there remained no shadow of doubt that but for Kmita the two Skshetuskis, Volodyovski, and Zagloba would have been killed without mercy in Kyedani, immediately after the famous treaty with Pontus de la Gardie.

"Worthy gentlemen," said Zagloba, "if you wish now to shoot him, as God is dear to me, I will leave your company and know you no longer."

"There is nothing more to be said here!" replied Volodyovski.

"Ah!" said Skshetuski, seizing his head with both hands, "what a happiness that father read that letter at once, instead of bringing it to us!"

"They must have fed you with starlings from childhood!" cried Mirski.

"Ha! what do you say to that?" asked Zagloba. "Every one else would have put a bullet in his head. But the moment they brought me the paper which they found on him, something touched me, because I have by nature a universal curiosity. Two men were going ahead of me with lanterns, and they were already in the field. Said I to them, 'Give me light here; let me know what is in this!' I began to read. I tell you, gentlemen, there was darkness before me as if some man had thumped my bald head with his fist. 'In God's name!' said I, 'why did you not show this letter?' And he answered, 'Because it did not suit me!' Such a haughty fellow, even at the point of death! But didn't I seize him, embrace him? 'Benefactor,' cried I, 'without you the crows would have eaten us already!' I gave orders to bring him back and lead him here; and I almost drove the breath out of the horse to tell you what had happened as quickly as possible. Uf!"

"That is a wonderful man, in whom it is clear as much good as evil resides," said Pan Stanislav. "If such would not—"

But before he had finished, the door opened and the soldiers came in with Kmita.

"You are free," said Volodyovski, at once; "and while we are alive none of us will attack you. What a desperate man you are, not to show us that letter immediately! We would not have disturbed you."

Here he turned to the soldiers: "Withdraw, and every man to horse!"

The soldiers withdrew, and Pan Andrei remained alone in the middle of the room. He had a calm face; but it was gloomy, and he looked at the officers standing before him, not without pride.

"You are free!" repeated Volodyovski; "go whithersoever you please, even to Radzivill, though it is painful to see a man of honorable blood aiding a traitor to his country."

"Reflect well," answered Kmita, "for I say beforehand that I shall go nowhere else but to Radzivill."

"Join us; let the thunderbolt crush that tyrant of Kyedani!" cried Zagloba. "You will be to us a friend and dear comrade; the country, your mother, will forgive your offences against her."

"It is no use," said Kmita, with energy. "God will decide who serves the country better,—you who begin civil war on your own responsibility, or I, serving a lord who alone can save this ill-fated Commonwealth. Go your own way, I will go mine. It is not time to convert you, and the attempt is vain; but I tell you from the depth of my soul that you are ruining the country,—you who stand in the way of its salvation. I do not call you traitors, for I know that your intentions are honorable; but this is the position,— the country is perishing, Radzivill stretches a hand to it, and you thrust swords into that hand, and in blindness make traitors of him and all those who stand by him."

"As God is true!" said Zagloba, "if I had not seen how manfully you went to meet death, I should think that terror had disturbed your mind. To whom have you given oath,—to

Radzivill or Yan Kazimir, to Sweden or the Commonwealth? You have lost your wits!"

"I knew that it would be vain to attempt to convert you. Farewell!"

"But wait," said Zagloba; "for here is a question of importance. Tell me, did Radzivill promise that he would spare us when you interceded for us in Kyedani?"

"He did," said Kmita. "You were to remain during the war in Birji."

"Know now your Radzivill, who betrays not only the country, not only the king, but his own servants." When he had said this, Zagloba gave the hetman's letter to Kmita. He took it, and began to run over it with his eyes; and as he read, the blood came to his face, and a blush of shame for his own leader covered his forehead more and more. All at once he crushed the letter in his hand, and threw it on the floor.

"Farewell!" said he. "Better I had perished at your hands!" and he went out of the room.

"Gentlemen," said Pan Yan, after a moment's silence, "an affair with that man is difficult, for he believes in his Radzivill as a Turk in Mohammed. I thought myself, as you do, that he was serving him for profit or ambition, but that is not the case. He is not a bad man, only an erring one."

"If he has had faith in his Mohammed hitherto, I have undermined that faith infernally," said Zagloba. "Did you see how he threw down the letter as soon as he had read it? There will be no small work between them, for that cavalier is ready to spring at the eyes, not only of Radzivill, but the devil. As God is dear to me, if a man had given me a herd of Turkish horses I should not be so well pleased as I am at having saved him from death."

"It is true he owes his life to you," said Billevich; "no one will deny that."

"God be with him!" said Volodyovski; "let us take counsel what to do."

"But what? Mount and take the road; the horses have rested a little," answered Zagloba.

"True, we should go as quickly as possible! Are you going with us?" asked Mirski of the sword-bearer.

"I cannot remain here in peace, I must go. But if you wish to take the road at once, gentlemen, I say sincerely that it is not convenient to tear away now with you. Since that man has left here alive, they will not burn me up immediately, neither will they kill any one; and before such a journey it is necessary to provide one's self with this thing and that. God knows when I shall return. It is necessary to make one arrangement and another,—to secrete the most valuable articles, send my cattle to the neighbors, pack trunks. I have also a little ready money which I would take with me. I shall be ready to-morrow at daybreak; but to go now, in seize-grab fashion, I cannot."

"On our part we cannot wait, for the sword is hanging over our heads," said Volodyovski. "And where do you wish to take refuge?"

"In the wilderness, as you advised. At least, I shall leave the maiden there; for I am not yet old, and my poor sabre may be of use to the country and the king."

"Farewell! God grant us to meet in better times!"

"God reward you, gentlemen, for coming to rescue me. Doubtless we shall see one another in the field."

"Good health!"

"Happy journey!"

They began to take farewell of one another, and then each came to bow down before Panna Billevich.

"You will see my wife and little boys in the wilderness: embrace them for me, and bloom in good health," said Pan Yan.

"Remember at times the soldier, who, though he had no success in your eyes, is always glad to bend the skies for you."

After them others approached, and last Zagloba.

"Receive, charming flower, farewell from an old man too. Embrace Pani Skshetuski and my little stumps. They are boys in a hundred!"

Instead of an answer, Olenka seized his hand, and pressed it in silence to her lips.

CHAPTER XXII.

That night, at the latest two hours after the departure of Volodyovski's detachment, Radzivill himself came to Billeviche at the head of his cavalry. He came to the assistance of Kmita, fearing lest he might fall into the hands of Volodyovski. When he learned what had happened he took the sword-bearer and Olenka and returned to Kyedani, without even giving rest to the horses.

The hetman was enraged beyond measure when he heard the story from the mouth of the sword-bearer, who told everything in detail, wishing to turn from himself the attention of the terrible magnate. He dared not protest, for the same reason, against the journey to Kyedani, and was glad in his soul that the storm ended thus. Radzivill, on his part, though suspecting Billevich of "practices" (conspiracy), had in fact too many cares to remember the matter at that moment.

The escape of Volodyovski might change affairs in Podlyasye. Horotkyevich and Yakub Kmita, who were there at the head of squadrons confederated against the hetman, were good soldiers, but not important; hence the whole confederacy had no weight. But now with Volodyovski had fled such men as Mirski, Stankyevich, and Oskyerko, without counting the little knight himself,—all excellent officers, enjoying universal respect.

402

But in Podlyasye was Prince Boguslav also, who with the castle squadrons was opposing the confederates, waiting meanwhile for aid from his uncle the elector; but the elector delayed, evidently waiting for events; and the confederated forces were gaining strength, and adherents came to them every day.

For some time the hetman had been wishing to march to Podlyasye himself, and crush the insurgents with one blow, but he was restrained by the thought that let him set foot over the boundary of Jmud the whole country would rise, and the importance of the Radzivills be reduced in the eyes of the Swedes to zero. The prince was meditating whether it were not better to abandon Podlyasye altogether for the time, and bring Prince Boguslav to Jmud.

That was necessary and urgent. On the other hand threatening news came touching the deeds of the voevoda of Vityebsk. The hetman had tried to negotiate and bring him over to his plans, but Sapyeha sent back the letters unanswered; and besides, as report said, the voevoda was selling his effects at auction, disposing of what he could, melting silver into coin, selling his cattle for ready money, pawning tapestry and valuables to the Jews, renting his lands and collecting troops.

The hetman, greedy by nature and incapable of making sacrifices of money, refused to believe, at first, that any man would cast his whole fortune without hesitation on the altar of the country; but time convinced him that this was really the case, for Sapyeha's military power increased daily. Fugitives, settled nobles, patriots gathered around him,—enemies of the hetman, and still worse, his blood relatives, such as Prince Michael Radzivill, of whom news came that he had ordered all the income of his estates still unoccupied by the enemy to be given to the voevoda of Vityebsk.

In this way then did the edifice, built by the pride of Yanush Radzivill, crack from its foundations and totter. The whole Commonwealth was to find a place in that edifice, but now it appeared in advance that it could not contain even Jmud.

The condition was becoming more and more like a vicious circle; for Radzivill might summon against the voevoda of Vityebsk Swedish forces which were occupying the country by degrees, but that would be to acknowledge his own weakness. Besides, the relations of the hetman with the generalissimo of the Swedes were strained since the affair at Klavany, thanks to the plan of Zagloba; and in spite of all explanations, irritation and distrust reigned between them.

The hetman, when setting out to aid Kmita, had hope that perhaps he might yet seize Volodyovski and destroy him; therefore, when his reckoning was at fault, he returned to Kyedani angry and frowning. It astonished him too that he did not meet Kmita on the road to Billeviche; this happened because Pan Andrei, whose dragoons Volodyovski did not fail to take with him, returned alone, and therefore chose the shortest road through the forest, avoiding Plemborg and Eyragoly.

After a night spent entirely on horseback the hetman came back to Kyedani on the following day at noon with his troops, and his first question was about Kmita. He was informed that Pan Andrei had returned, but without soldiers. Of that last circumstance the prince knew already; but he was curious to hear from the lips of Kmita himself the story, therefore he gave command to call him at once.

"There was no success for you, as there was none for me," said he, when Kmita stood before him. "The sword-bearer told me that you fell into the hands of that little devil."

"That is true," answered Kmita.

"And my letter saved you?"

"Of what letter are you speaking, your highness? For when they had read themselves the one found on me, they read to me in return another letter, written to the commandant of Birji."

The gloomy face of Radzivill was covered as it were with a bloody skin. "Then do you know?"

"I know!" answered Kmita, emphatically. "Your highness, how could you act so with me? For a common noble it is a shame to break his word, but what is it for a prince and a leader?"

"Silence!" cried Radzivill.

"I will not be silent, for before the eyes of those men I had to take your place. They were urging me to join them; but I would not, and said, 'I serve Radzivill; for with him is justice, with him virtue.' Then they showed me that letter: 'See what a man your Radzivill is!' I had to shut my mouth and gulp shame."

The hetman's lips began to quiver from fury. A wild desire seized him to wring that insolent head from its shoulders, and he was already raising his hands to clap for the servants. Rage closed his eyes, stopped the breath in his breast; and surely Kmita would have paid dearly for his outburst were it not for the sudden attack of asthma which at that moment seized the prince. His face grew black, he sprang up from the chair and began to beat the air with his hands, his eyes were coming out of his head, and from his throat rose a hoarse bellow, in which Kmita barely heard the word, "Choking!"

At the alarm the servants and the castle physicians ran in. They tried to restore the prince, who had lost consciousness. They roused him in about an hour; and when he showed signs of life Kmita left the room.

In the corridor he met Kharlamp, who had recovered from the wounds and bruises received in the battle with Oskyerko's insurgent Hungarians.

"What news?" asked Great Mustache.

"He has come to himself," answered Kmita.

"H'm! But any day he may not come! Bad for us, Colonel; for when the prince dies they will grind out his deeds on us. My whole hope is in Volodyovski. I trust that he will shield his old comrades; therefore I tell you" (here Kharlamp lowered his voice) "that I am glad he escaped."

"Was he cornered so closely, then?"

"What, cornered! From that willow grove in which we surrounded him wolves could not have sprung out, and he sprang out. May the bullets strike him! Who knows, who knows that we shall not have to grasp hold of his skirts, for there is something bad about us here. The nobles are turning away terribly from our prince, and all say that they would rather have a real enemy, a Swede, even a Tartar, than a renegade. That is the position. And, besides, the prince gives more and more orders to seize and imprison citizens,—which, speaking between us, is against law and liberty. To-day they brought in the sword-bearer of Rossyeni."

"Have they indeed?"

"Yes, with his niece. The lady is a beauty. You are to be congratulated!"

"Where are they lodged?"

"In the right wing. Five rooms are assigned them; they cannot complain, unless of this,—that a guard walks before their doors. And when will the wedding be, Colonel?"

"The music is not yet engaged for it. Farewell!" added Kmita.

Pan Andrei went from Kharlamp to his own room. A sleepless night with its stormy events, and his last meeting with the prince had wearied him to such a degree that he was barely able to stand. And as every touch causes pain to a wearied, bruised body, so had he a soul full of anguish. Kharlamp's simple question

'When will the wedding be?' pierced him sorely; for before his eyes at once appeared, as if alive, the icy face of Olenka, and her fixed lips when their silence confirmed the death-sentence against him. Even a word from her would have saved him. Volodyovski would have respected it. All the sorrow and pain which Kmita felt at that moment consisted in this, that she did not say that word. Still she had not hesitated to save him twice before. Such now was the precipice between them, so utterly quenched in her heart was not merely love, but simple kind feeling, which it was possible to have even for a stranger,—simple pity, which it is incumbent to have for every one. The more Kmita thought over this, the more cruel did Olenka seem to him, the greater his complaint against her, and the deeper his wrong. "What have I done of such character," asked he of himself, "that I am scorned, like one cursed by the church? Even if it were evil to serve Radzivill, still I feel innocent, since I can answer on my conscience, that not for promotion, not for gain, nor for bread do I serve him, but because I see profit to the country from my service. Why am I condemned without trial? Well, well! Let it be so! I will not go to clear myself of uncommitted offences, nor to beg love," repeated he for the thousandth time.

Still the pain did not cease; it increased. On returning to his quarters Pan Andrei cast himself on the bed and tried to sleep; but he could not, despite all his weariness. After a while he rose and began to walk through the room. From time to time he raised his hands to his forehead and said aloud to himself,—

"Oh, the heart of that woman is hard!"

And again,—

"I did not expect that of you, young lady,—May God reward you!"

In these meditations an hour passed, and a second. At last he tired himself out and began to doze, sitting on the bed; but

407

before he fell asleep an attendant of Radzivill, Pan Skillandz, roused him and summoned him to the prince.

Radzivill felt better already, and breathed more freely, but on his leaden face could be seen a great weakening. He sat in a deep armchair, covered with leather, having before him a physician whom he sent out immediately after Kmita entered.

"I had one foot in the other world and through you," said he to Pan Andrei.

"Your highness, it was not my fault; I said what I thought."

"Let no further mention be made of this. But do not add to the weight of the burden which I bear; and know this, that what I have forgiven you I would not forgive another."

Kmita was silent.

"If I gave order," added the prince, after a while, "to execute in Birji these men whom at your request I pardoned in Kyedani, it was not because I wanted to deceive you, but to spare you pain. I yielded apparently, because I have a weakness for you. But their death was imperative. Am I an executioner, or do you think that I spill blood merely to feast my eyes on red? But when older you will know that if a man would achieve anything in this world, he is not free to sacrifice great causes to smaller. It was imperative that these men should die here in Kyedani, for see what has happened through your prayers: resistance is increased in the country, civil war begun, friendship with the Swedes is strained, an evil example given to others, from which mutiny is spreading like a plague. More than this, I had to go on a later expedition in my own person, and be filled with confusion in the presence of the whole army; you came near death at their hands, and now they will go to Podlyasye and become chiefs of an uprising. Behold and learn! If they had perished in Kyedani, nothing of all this would have happened; but when imploring for them you were thinking only of your own feelings. I sent them to die at Birji, for I am experienced, I see farther; for I know from practice that whoso in running stumbles, even against a small stone, will easily fall, and whoso falls may not rise again, and the faster he was running the less likely is he to rise. God save us, what harm these people have done!"

"They are not so important as to undo the whole work of your highness."

"Had they done no more than rouse distrust between me and Pontus, the harm would be incalculable. It has been explained that they, not my men, attacked the Swedes; but the letter with threats which Pontus wrote to me remains, and I do not forgive him that letter. Pontus is brother-in-law of the king, but it is doubtful whether he could become mine, and whether the Radzivill thresholds are not too high for him."

"Let your highness treat with the king himself, and not with his servant."

"So I intend to do; and if vexation does not kill me I will teach that little Swede modesty,—if troubles do not kill me; and would that that were all, for no one here spares me thorns or pain. It is grievous to me, grievous! Who would believe that I am the man who was at Loyovo, Jechytsa, Mozyr, Turoff, Kieff, Berestechko? The whole Commonwealth gazed at me and Vishnyevetski, as at two suns. Everything trembled before Hmelnitski, but he trembled before me. And the very men whom in time of universal disaster I led from victory to victory, forsake me to-day and raise their hands against me as against a parricide."

"But all are not thus, for there are some who believe in your highness yet," said Kmita, abruptly.

"They believe till they stop," added Radzivill, with bitterness. "Great is the love of the nobles! God grant that I be not poisoned by it! Stab after stab does each one of you give me, though it occurs not to any that—"

"Consider intentions, not words, your highness."

"I give thanks for the counsel. Henceforth I will consider carefully what face each common man shows me, and endeavor with care to please all."

"Those are bitter words, your highness."

"But is life sweet? God created me for great things, and look at me; I must wear out my powers in district struggles, which village might wage against village. I wanted to measure myself with mighty monarchs, and I have fallen so low that I must hunt some Volodyovski through my own estates. Instead of astonishing the world with my power, I astonish it with my weakness; instead of paying for the ashes of Vilna with the ashes of Moscow, I have to thank you for digging trenches around Kyedani. Oh, it is narrow for me, and I am choking,—not alone because the asthma is throttling me; helplessness is killing me, inactivity is killing me! It is narrow for me and heavy for me! Do you understand?"

"I thought myself that affairs would go differently," answered Kmita, gloomily.

Radzivill began to breathe with effort.

"Before another crown can come to me they have crowned me with thorns. I commanded the minister, Aders, to look at the stars. He made a figure and said that the conjunctions were evil, but that they would pass. Meanwhile I am suffering torments. In the night there is something which will not let me sleep; something walks in the room, faces of some kind stare at me in the bed, and at times a sudden cold comes. This means that death is walking around me. I am suffering. I must be prepared for more treason and apostasy, for I know that there are men still who waver."

"There are no longer such," answered Kmita, "for whoso was to go has gone."

"Do not deceive yourself; you see that the remnant of the Polish people are beginning to take thought."

Kmita remembered what he had heard from Kharlamp and was silent.

"Never mind!" continued Radzivill, "it is oppressive and terrible, but it is necessary to endure. Tell no one of what you have heard from me. It is well that this attack came to-day, for it will not be repeated; and especially to-day I need strength, for I wish to have a feast, and show a glad face to strengthen the courage of people. And do you brighten your face and tell nothing to any man, for what I say to you is for this purpose only, that you at least refrain from tormenting me. Anger carried me away to-day. Be careful that this happen not again, for it is a question of your head. But I have forgiven you. Of those trenches with which you surrounded Kyedani, Peterson himself would not be ashamed. Go now and send me Myeleshko. They have brought in deserters from his squadron,—common soldiers. I shall order them hanged to a man. We need to give an example. Farewell! It must be joyful to-day in Kyedani."

CHAPTER XXIII.

The sword-bearer of Rossyeni had a difficult struggle with Panna Aleksandra before she consented to go to that feast which the hetman had prepared for his people. He had to implore almost with tears the stubborn, bold girl, and swear that it was a question of his head; that all, not only the military, but citizens dwelling in the region of Kyedani, as far as Radzivill's hand reached, were obliged to appear under terror of the prince's wrath: how then could they oppose who were subject to the favor and disfavor of the terrible man? Olenka, not to endanger her uncle, gave way.

The company was really not small, for he had forced many of the surrounding nobles to come with their wives and daughters.

But the military were in the majority, and especially officers of the foreign regiments, who remained nearly all with the prince. Before he showed himself to the guests he prepared an affable countenance, as if no care had weighed on him previously; he wished with that banquet to rouse courage, not only in his adherents and the military, but to show that most of the citizens were on his side, and only turbulent people opposed the union with Sweden. He did not spare therefore trouble or outlay to make the banquet lordly, that the echo of it might spread as widely as possible through the land. Barely had darkness covered the country when hundreds of barrels were set on fire along the road leading to the castle and in the courtyard; from time to time cannons were thundering, and soldiers were ordered to give forth joyous shouts.

Carriages and covered wagons followed one another on the road, bringing personages of the neighborhood and the "cheaper" (smaller) nobility. The courtyard was filled with equipages, horses, and servants, who had either come with guests or belonged to the town. Crowds dressed in velvet, brocade, and costly furs filled the so-called "Golden Hall;" and when the prince appeared at last, all glittering from precious stones, and with a welcoming smile on his face, usually gloomy, and besides wrinkled at that time by sickness, the first officers shouted in one voice,—

"Long live the prince hetman! Long live the voevoda of Vilna!"

Radzivill cast his eyes suddenly on the assembled citizens, wishing to convince himself whether they repeated the cries of the soldiers. In fact a few tens of voices from the most timid breasts repeated the cry; the prince on his part began at once to bow, and to thank them for the sincere and "unanimous" love.

"With you, gracious gentlemen!" said he, "we will manage those who would destroy the country. God reward you! God reward you!"

And he went around through the hall, stopped before acquaintances, not sparing titles in his speech,—"Lord brother," "dear neighbor;" and more than one gloomy face grew bright under the warm rays of the magnate's favor.

"But it is not possible," said those who till recently looked on his deeds with dislike, "that such a lord, such a lofty senator should wish ill to his country; either he could not act differently from what he has acted, or there is some secret in this, which will come out for the good of the Commonwealth."

"In fact, we have more rest already from one enemy who does not wish to light about us with the Swedes."

"God grant that all turn out for the best."

Some, however, shook their heads, or said with a look to one another, "We are here because they put the knife to our throats."

But these were silent; meanwhile others, more easily brought over, said in loud voices, to be heard by the prince,—

"It is better to change the king than ruin the Commonwealth."

"Let the kingdom think of itself, but we will think of ourselves."

"Besides, who has given us an example, if not Great Poland? *Extrema necessitas, extremis nititur rationibus! Tentanda omnia!*"

"Let us put all confidence in our prince, and trust him in everything. Let him have Lithuania and the government in his hands."

"He deserves both. If he will not save us, we perish,—in him is salvation."

"He is nearer to us than Yan Kazimir, for he is our blood."

Radzivill caught with an eager ear those voices, dictated by fear or flattery, and did not consider that they came from the mouths of weak persons, who in danger would be the first to desert him,—from the mouths of persons whom every breath of wind might bend as a wave. And he was charmed with those expressions, and tempted himself, or his own conscience, repeating from the maxims he had heard that which seemed to excuse him the most: "*Extrema necessitas, extremis nititur rationibus!*"

But when passing a large group of nobles he heard from the lips of Pan Yujits, "He is nearer to us than Yan Kazimir," his face grew bright altogether. To compare him with the king, and then to prefer him, flattered his pride; he approached Pan Yujits at once and said,—

"You are right, brothers, for in Yan Kazimir, in one pot of blood there is a quart of Lithuanian, but in me there is nothing but Lithuanian. If hitherto the quart has commanded the potful, it depends on you, brothers, to change that condition."

"We are ready to drink a potful to your health," answered Pan Yujits.

"You have struck my mind. Rejoice, brothers; I would gladly invite hither all Lithuania."

"It would have to be trimmed still better," said Pan Shchanyetski of Dalnovo,—a bold man, and cutting with the tongue as with the sword.

"What do you mean by that?" asked the prince, fixing his eyes on him.

"That the heart of your highness is wider than Kyedani."

Radzivill gave a forced laugh and went farther.

At this moment the marshal of the castle approached him with the announcement that the banquet was ready. Crowds began to flow, like a river, after the prince to the same hall in which not long before the union with Sweden was declared. The marshal seated the guests according to dignity, calling each one by name and rank. But it was evident that the orders of the prince had been issued in advance on this point, for Kmita's place was between Billevich and Panna Aleksandra.

The hearts jumped in both when they heard their names called in succession, and both hesitated at the first moment; but it occurred to them that to refuse would be to draw on themselves the eyes of all present, therefore they sat side by side. They were angry and ill at ease. Pan Andrei determined to be as indifferent as if a stranger were sitting next him; but soon he understood that he could not be so indifferent, and that his neighbor was not such a stranger that they could begin an ordinary conversation. But both saw that in that throng of persons of the most varied feelings, interests, and passions, he thinks only of her and she of him. For this very reason it was awkward for them. They would not and could not tell sincerely, clearly, and openly, what lay on their hearts. They had the past, but no future. Recent feelings, confidence, even acquaintance, were all broken. There was nothing between them save the feeling of disappointment and offence. If this link should burst, they would be freer; but time only could bring forgetfulness: it was too soon for that.

For Kmita it was so disagreeable that he almost suffered torments; still he would not have yielded, for anything in the world, the place which the marshal had given him. He caught with his ear the rustle of her dress; he watched every movement of hers,—he watched while feigning not to watch; he felt the warmth beating from her, and all this caused him a certain painful delight.

At the same moment he discovered that she too was equally on the alert, though she was as if not paying attention. An unconquerable desire of looking at her drew him on; therefore he glanced sidewise, until he saw her clear forehead, her eyes covered with dark lashes, and her fair face, not touched by paint, as were those of other ladies. For him there had always been something attractive in that face, so that the heart in the poor knight was shivering from sorrow and pain. "To think that such animosity could find a place with such beauty," thought he. But the offence was too deep; hence he added soon in his soul, "I have nothing to do with you; let some other man take you."

And he felt suddenly that if that "other" were merely to try to make use of the permission, he would cut him into pieces as small as chopped straw. At the very thought terrible anger seized him; but he calmed himself when he remembered that he was still alone, that no "other" was sitting near her, and that no one, at least at that moment, was trying to win her.

"I will look at her once more and turn to the other side," thought he.

And again he cast a sidelong glance; but just at that moment she did the same, and both dropped their eyes with all quickness, terribly confused, as if they had been caught in a crime.

Panna Aleksandra too was struggling with herself. From all that had happened, from the action of Kmita at Billeviche, from the words of Zagloba and Pan Yan, she learned that Kmita erred, but that he was not so guilty and did not deserve such contempt, such unreserved condemnation, as she had thought previously. Besides, he had saved those worthy men from death, and there was so much in him of a certain grand pride that when he had fallen into their hands, having a letter on his person sufficient to vindicate him, or at least to save him from execution, he did not show that letter, he said not a word, but went to death with head erect.

Olenka, reared by an old soldier who placed contempt for death above all virtues, worshipped courage with her whole heart; therefore she could not resist an involuntary admiration for that stern knightly daring which could be driven from the body only with the soul.

She understood also that if Kmita served Radzivill he did so in perfect good faith; what a wrong therefore to condemn him for intentional treason! And still she had put that wrong on him, she had spared him neither injustice nor contempt, she would not forgive him even in the face of death.

"Right the wrong," said her heart; "all is finished between you, but it is thy duty to confess that thou hast judged him unjustly. In this is thy duty to thyself also."

But there was in this lady no little pride, and perhaps something of stubbornness; therefore it came at once to her mind that that cavalier was not worth such satisfaction, and a flush came to her face.

"If he is not worth it, let him go without it," said her mind.

But conscience said further that whether the injured one is worth satisfaction or not, it is needful to give it; but on the other side her pride brought forth continually new arguments,—

"If—which might be—he was unwilling to listen, she would have to swallow her shame for nothing. And secondly, guilty or not guilty, whether he acts purposely or through blindness, it is enough that he holds with traitors and enemies of the country, and helps them to ruin it. It is the same to the country whether he lacks reason or honesty. God may forgive him; men must and ought to condemn, and the name of traitor will remain with him. That is true! If he is not guilty, is she not right in despising a man who has not the wit to distinguish wrong from right, crime from virtue?"

Here anger began to carry the lady away, and her cheeks flushed.

"I will be silent!" said she to herself. "Let him suffer what he has deserved. Until I see penitence I have the right to condemn him."

Then she turned her glance to Kmita, as if wishing to be convinced whether penitence was yet to be seen in his face. Just then it was that the meeting of their eyes took place, at which both were so shame-stricken.

Olenka, it may be, did not see penitence in the face of the cavalier, but she saw pain and suffering; she saw that face pale as after sickness; therefore deep pity seized her, tears came perforce to her eyes, and she bent still more over the table to avoid betraying emotion.

Meanwhile the banquet was becoming animated. At first all were evidently under a disagreeable impression, but with the cups came fancy. The bustle increased. At last the prince rose,—

"Gracious gentlemen, I ask leave to speak."

"The prince wishes to speak! The prince wishes to speak!" was called from every side.

"I raise the first toast to the Most Serene King of Sweden, who gives us aid against our enemies, and ruling meanwhile this country, will not leave it till he brings peace. Arise, gentlemen, for that health is drunk standing."

The guests rose, except ladies, and filled their glasses, but without shouts, without enthusiasm. Pan Shchanyetski of Dalnovo muttered something to his neighbors, and they bit their mustaches to avoid laughter. It was evident that he was jeering at the King of Sweden.

It was only when the prince raised the other toast to his "beloved guests" kind to Kyedani, who had come even from

418

distant places to testify their confidence in the intentions of the host, that they answered him with a loud shout,—

"We thank you from our hearts!"

"The health of the prince!"

"Our Hector of Lithuania!"

"May he live! Long life to the prince hetman, our voevoda."

Now Pan Yujits, a little drunk already, cried with all the strength of his lungs, "Long life to Yanush I., Grand Prince of Lithuania!"

Radzivill blushed like a young lady at her betrothal, but remarking that those assembled were stubbornly silent and looking at him with astonishment, he said,—

"That is in your power; but your wishes are premature, Pan Yujits, premature."

"Long live Yanush I., Grand Prince of Lithuania!" repeated Pan Yujits, with the stubbornness of a drunken man.

Pan Shchanyetski rose in his turn and raised his glass. "True," said he, coolly, "Grand Prince of Lithuania, King of Poland, and Emperor of Germany!"

Again an interval of silence. Suddenly the company burst out into laughter. All were staring, their mustaches were dancing on their reddened faces, and laughter shook their bodies, echoed from the arches of the hall, and lasted long; and as suddenly as it rose so suddenly did it die on the lips of all at sight of the hetman's face, which was changing like a rainbow.

Radzivill restrained the terrible anger which had seized his breast and said, "Low jests, Pan Shchanyetski."

The noble pouted, and not at all disconcerted answered: "That also is an elective throne, and we cannot wish your highness too much. If as a noble your highness may become King of Poland, as a prince of the Gorman Empire you might be raised

419

to the dignity of Emperor. It is as far or near for you to the one as to the other; and who does not wish this to you, let him rise. I will meet him with the sabre." Here he turned to the company: "Rise, whoso does not wish the crown of the German Empire to the voevoda of Vilna!"

Of course no one rose. They did not laugh either, for in the voice of Pan Shchanyetski there was so much insolent malice that an involuntary disquiet came upon all as to what would happen.

Nothing happened, save that relish for the banquet was spoiled. In vain did the servants of the castle fill the glasses every moment. Wine could not scatter gloomy thoughts in the minds of the banqueters, nor the disquiet increasing every moment. Radzivill concealed his anger with difficulty, for he felt that, thanks to the toasts of Pan Shchanyetski, he was belittled in the eyes of the assembled nobles, and that, intentionally or not, that man had forced the conviction on those present that the voevoda of Vilna was no nearer the throne of grand prince than the crown of Germany. Everything was turned into jests, into ridicule, while the banquet was given mainly to accustom men's minds to the coming rule of the Radzivills. What is more, Radzivill was concerned lest this ridicule of his hopes should make a bad impression on the officers, admitted to the secret of his plans. In fact, deep dissatisfaction was depicted on their faces.

Ganhoff filled glass after glass, and avoided the glance of the prince. Kmita, however, did not drink, but looked at the table before him with frowning brow, as if he were thinking of something, or lighting an internal battle. Radzivill trembled at the thought that a light might flash into that mind any moment, and bring forth truth from the shadows, and then that officer, who furnished the single link binding the remnants of the Polish squadrons with the cause of Radzivill, would break the link, even if he had at the same time to drag the heart out of his own breast.

Kmita had annoyed Radzivill already over much; and without the marvellous significance given him by events, he would long since have fallen a victim to his own impetuosity and the wrath of the hetman. But the prince was mistaken in suspecting him of a hostile turn of thought, for Pan Andrei was occupied wholly with Olenka and that deep dissension which separated them.

At times it seemed to him that he loved that woman sitting at his side beyond the whole world; then again he felt such hatred that he would give death to her if he could but give it to himself as well.

Life had become so involved that for his simple nature it was too difficult, and he felt what a wild beast feels when entangled in a net from which it cannot escape.

The unquiet and gloomy humor of the whole banquet irritated him in the highest degree. It was simply unendurable.

The banquet became more gloomy every moment. It seemed to those present that they were feasting under a leaden roof resting on their heads.

At that time a new guest entered the hall. The prince, seeing him, exclaimed,—

"That is Pan Suhanyets, from Cousin Boguslav! Surely with letters!"

The newly arrived bowed profoundly. "True, Most Serene Prince, I come straight from Podlyasye."

"But give me the letters, and sit at the table yourself. The worthy guests will pardon me if I do not defer the reading, though we are sitting at a banquet, for there may be news which I shall need to impart to you. Sir Marshal, pray think of the welcome envoy there."

Speaking thus, he took from the hands of Pan Suhanyets a package of letters, and broke the seal of the first in haste.

All present fixed curious eyes on his face, and tried to divine the substance of the letter. The first letter did not seem to announce anything favorable, for the face of the prince was filled with blood, and his eyes gleamed with wild anger.

"Brothers!" said the hetman, "Prince Boguslav reports to me that those men who have chosen to form a confederation rather than march against the enemy at Vilna, are ravaging at this moment my villages in Podlyasye. It is easier of course to wage war with peasant women in villages. Worthy knights, there is no denying that!—Never mind! Their reward will not miss them."

Then he took the second letter, but had barely cast his eyes on it when his face brightened with a smile of triumph and delight,—

"The province of Syeradz has yielded to the Swedes!" cried he, "and following Great Poland, has accepted the protection of Karl Gustav."

And after a while another,—

"This is the latest dispatch. Good for us, worthy gentlemen, Yan Kazimir is beaten at Vidava and Jarnov. The army is leaving him! He is retreating on Cracow; the Swedes are pursuing. My cousin writes that Cracow too must fall."

"Let us rejoice, gracious gentlemen," said Shchanyetski, with a strange voice.

"Yes, let us rejoice!" repeated the hetman, without noticing the tone in which Shchanyetski had spoken. And delight issued from the whole person of the prince, his face became in one moment as it were younger, his eyes gained lustre; with hands trembling from happiness, he broke the seal of the last letter, looked, became all radiant as the sun, and cried,—

"Warsaw is taken! Long life to Karl Gustav!"

Here he first noticed that the impression which these tidings produced on those present was entirely different from that which he felt himself. For all sat in silence, looking forward with uncertain glance. Some frowned; others covered their faces with their hands. Even courtiers of the hetman, even men of weak spirit, did not dare to imitate the joy of the prince at the tidings that Warsaw was taken, that Cracow must fall, and that the provinces, one after the other, would leave their legal king and yield to the enemy. Besides, there was something monstrous in the satisfaction with which the supreme leader of half the armies of the Commonwealth, and one of its most exalted senators, announced its defeats. The prince saw that it was necessary to soften the impression.

"Gentlemen," said he, "I should be the first to weep with you, if harm were coming to the Commonwealth; but here the Commonwealth suffers no harm, it merely changes kings. Instead of the ill-fated Yan Kazimir we shall have a great and fortunate warrior. I see all wars now finished, and enemies vanquished."

"Your highness is right," answered Shchanyetski. "Cup for cup, the same thing that Radzeyovski and Opalinski held forth at Uistsie. Let us rejoice, gracious gentlemen! Death to Yan Kazimir!"

When he had said this, Shchanyetski pushed back his chair with a rattle, and walked out of the hall.

"The best of wines that are in the cellar!" cried the prince.

The marshal hastened to carry out the order. In the hall it was as noisy as in a hive. When the first impression had passed, the nobles began to talk of the news and discuss. They asked Pan Suhanyets for details from Podlyasye, and adjoining Mazovia, which the Swedes had already occupied.

After a while pitchy kegs were rolled into the hall and opened. Spirits began to grow brighter and improve by degrees.

More and more frequently voices were heard to repeat: "All is over! perhaps it is for the best!" "We must bend to

423

fortune!" "The prince will not let us be wronged." "It is better for us than for others. Long life to Yanush Radzivill, our voevoda, hetman, and prince!"

"Grand Prince of Lithuania!" cried again Pan Yujits.

But at this time neither silence nor laughter answered him; but a number of tens of hoarse throats roared at once,—

"That is our wish,—from heart and soul our wish! Long life to him! May he rule!"

The magnate rose with a face as red as purple. "I thank you, brothers," said he, seriously.

In the hall it had become as suffocating and hot, from lights and the breath of people, as in a bath.

Panna Aleksandra bent past Kmita to her uncle. "I am weak," said she; "let us leave here."

In truth her face was pale, and on her forehead glittered drops of perspiration; but the sword-bearer of Rossyeni cast an unquiet glance at the hetman, fearing lest it be taken ill of him to leave the table. In the field he was a gallant soldier, but he feared Radzivill with his whole soul.

At that moment, to complete the evil, the hetman said,—

"He is my enemy who will not drink all my toasts to the bottom, for I am joyful to-day."

"You have heard?" asked Billevich.

"Uncle, I cannot stay longer, I am faint," said Olenka, with a beseeching voice.

"Then go alone," answered Pan Tomash.

The lady rose, wishing to slip away unobserved; but her strength failed, and she caught the side of the chair in her weakness.

Suddenly a strong knightly arm embraced her, and supported the almost fainting maiden.

"I will conduct you," said Pan Andrei.

And without asking for permission he caught her form as if with an iron hoop. She leaned on him more and more; before they reached the door, she was hanging powerless on his arm.

Then he raised her as lightly as he would a child, and bore her out of the hall.

CHAPTER XXIV.

That evening after the banquet, Pan Andrei wished absolutely to see the prince, but he was told that the prince was occupied in a secret interview with Pan Suhanyets.

He went therefore early next morning, and was admitted at once.

"Your highness," said he "I have come with a prayer."

"What do you wish me to do for you?"

"I am not able to live here longer. Each day increases my torment. There is nothing for me here in Kyedani. Let your highness find some office for me, send me whithersoever it please you. I have heard that regiments are to move against Zolotarenko; I will go with them."

"Zolotarenko would be glad to have an uproar with us, but he cannot get at us in any way, for Swedish protection is here already, and we cannot go against him without the Swedes. Count Magnus advances with terrible dilatoriness because he does not trust me. But is it so ill for you here in Kyedani at our side?"

"Your highness is gracious to me, and still my suffering is so keen that I cannot describe it. To tell the truth, I thought everything would take another course,—I thought that we should fight, that we should live in fire and smoke, day and night in the saddle. God created me for that. But to sit here, listen to quarrels and disputes, rot in inactivity, or hunt down my own people instead of the enemy,—I cannot endure it, simply I am unable. I prefer death a hundred times. As God is dear to me, this is pure torture!"

"I know whence that despair comes. From love,—nothing more. When older, you will learn to laugh at these torments. I saw yesterday that you and that maiden were more and more angry with each other."

"I am nothing to her, nor she to me. What has been is ended."

"But what, did she fall ill yesterday?"

"She did."

The prince was silent for a while, then said: "I have advised you already, and I advise once more, if you care for her take her. I will give command to have the marriage performed. There will be a little screaming and crying,—that's nothing! After the marriage take her to your quarters; and if next day she still cries, that will be the most."

"I beg, your highness, for some office in the army, not for marriage," said Kmita, roughly.

"Then you do not want her?"

"I do not. Neither I her, nor she me. Though it were to tear the soul within me, I will not ask her for anything. I only wish to be as far away as possible, to forget everything before my mind is lost. Here there is nothing to do; and inactivity is the worst of all, for trouble gnaws a man like sickness. Remember, your highness, how grievous it was for you yesterday till good news came. So it is with me to-day, and so it will be. What have I to do? Seize my head, lest bitter thoughts split it, and sit down? What can I wait for? God knows what kind of times these are, God knows what kind of war this is, which I cannot understand nor grasp with my mind,—which causes me still more grief. Now, as God is dear to me, if your highness will not use me in some way, I will flee, collect a party, and fight."

426

"Whom?" asked the prince.

"Whom? I will go to Vilna, and attack as I did Hovanski. Let your highness permit my squadron to go with me, and war will begin."

"I need your squadron here against internal enemies."

"That is the pain, that is the torment, to watch in Kyedani with folded arms, or chase after some Volodyovski whom I would rather have as a comrade by my side."

"I have an office for you," said the prince. "I will not let you go to Vilna, nor will I give you a squadron; and if you go against my will, collect a squadron and fight, know that by this you cease to serve me."

"But I shall serve the country."

"He serves the country who serves me,—I have convinced you of that already. Remember also that you have taken an oath to me. Finally, if you go as a volunteer you will go also from under my jurisdiction, and the courts are waiting for you with sentences. In your own interest you should not do this."

"What power have courts now?"

"Beyond Kovno none; but here, where the country is still quiet, they have not ceased to act. It is true you may not appear, but decisions will be given and will weigh upon you until times of peace. Whom they have once declared they will remember even in ten years, and the nobles of Lauda will see that you are not forgotten."

"To tell the truth to your highness, when it comes to atonement I will yield. Formerly I was ready to war with the whole Commonwealth, and to win for myself as many sentences as the late Pan Lashch, who had a cloak lined with them. But now a kind of galled spot has come out on my conscience. A man fears to wade farther than he wished, and mental disquiet touching everything gnaws him."

427

"Are you so squeamish? But a truce to this! I will tell you, if 'tis your wish to go hence, I have an office for you and a very honorable one. Ganhoff is creeping into my eyes for this office, and talks of it every day. I have been thinking to give it to him. Still 'tis impossible to do so, for I must have a man of note, not with a trifling name, not a foreigner, but a Pole, who by his very person will bear witness that not all men have left me, that there are still weighty citizens on my side. You are just the man; you have so much good daring, are more willing to make others bend than to bow down yourself."

"What is the task?"

"To go on a long journey."

"I am ready to-day!"

"And at your own cost, since I am straitened for money. Some of my revenues the enemy have taken; others, our own people are ravaging, and no part comes in season; besides, all the army which I have here, has fallen to my expense. Of a certainty the treasurer, whom I have now behind a locked door, does not give me a copper,—first, because he has not the wish to do so; second; because he has not the coin. Whatever public money there is, I take without asking; but is there much? From the Swedes you will get anything sooner than money, for their hands tremble at sight of a farthing."

"Your highness need not explain. If I go, it will be at my own expense."

"But it will be necessary to appear with distinction, without sparing."

"I will spare nothing."

The hetman's face brightened; for in truth he had no ready money, though he had plundered Vilna not long before, and, besides, he was greedy by nature. It was also true that the revenues from his immense estates, extending from Livonia to

Kieff and from Smolensk to Mazovia, had really ceased to flow in, and the cost of the army increased every day.

"That suits me," said he; "Ganhoff would begin at once to knock on my coffers, but you are another kind of man. Hear, then, your instructions."

"I am listening with care."

"First, you will go to Podlyasye. The road is perilous; for the confederates, who left the camp, are there and acting against me. How you will escape them is your own affair. Yakub Kmita might spare you; but beware of Horotkyevich, Jyromski, and especially of Volodyovski with his Lauda men."

"I have been in their hands already, and no evil has happened to me."

"That is well. You will go to Zabludovo, where Pan Harasimovich lives; you will order him to collect what money he can from my revenues, the public taxes and whencesoever it is possible, and send it to me,—not to this place, however, but to Tyltsa, where there are effects of mine already. What goods or property he can pawn, let him pawn; what he can get from the Jews, let him take. Secondly, let him think how to ruin the confederates. But that is not your mission; I will send him instructions under my own hand. You will give him the letter and move straight to Tykotsin, to Prince Boguslav—"

Here the hetman stopped and began to breathe heavily, for continuous speaking tortured him greatly. Kmita looked eagerly at Radzivill, for his own soul was chafing to go, and he felt that the journey, full of expected adventures, would be balsam to his grief.

After a while the hetman continued: "I am astonished that Boguslav is loitering still in Podlyasye. As God is true, he may ruin both me and himself. Pay diligent attention to what he says; for though you will give him my letters, you should supplement

429

them with living speech, and explain that which may not be written. Now understand that yesterday's intelligence was good, but not so good as I told the nobles,—not so good, in fact, as I myself thought at first. The Swedes have the upper hand, it is true; they have occupied Great Poland, Mazovia, Warsaw; the province of Syeradz has yielded to them, they are pursuing Yan Kazimir to Cracow, and as God is in heaven, they will besiege the place. Charnyetski is to defend it. He is a newly baked senator, but, I must confess, a good soldier. Who can foresee what will happen? The Swedes, of course, know how to take fortresses, and there was no time to fortify Cracow. Still, that spotted little castellan (Charnyetski) may hold out there a month, two, three. Such wonders take place at times, as we all remember in the case of Zbaraj. If he will stand obstinately, the devil may turn everything around. Learn now political secrets. Know first that in Vienna they will not look with willing eye on the growing power of Sweden, and may give aid. The Tartars, too, I know this well, are inclined to assist Yan Kazimir, and to move against the Cossacks and Moscow with all force; and then the armies in the Crimea under Pototski would assist. Yan Kazimir is in despair, but tomorrow his fortune may be preponderant."

Here the prince was forced to give rest again to his wearied breast, and Pan Andrei experienced a wonderful feeling which he could not himself account for at once. Behold, he, an adherent of Radzivill and Sweden, felt as it were a great joy at the thought that fortune might turn from the Swedes!

"Suhanyets told me," said the prince, "how it was at Vidava and Jarnov. There in the first onset our advance guard—I mean the Polish—ground the Swedes into the dust. They were not general militia, and the Swedes lost courage greatly."

"Still victory was with the Swedes, was it not?"

"It was, for the squadrons mutinied against Yan Kazimir, and the nobles declared that they would stand in line, but would not fight. Still it was shown that the Swedes are no better in the field than the quarter soldiers. Only let there be one or two victories and their courage may change. Let money come to Yan Kazimir to pay wages, and the troops will not mutiny. Pototski has not many men, but they are sternly disciplined and as resolute as hornets. The Tartars will come with Pototski, but the elector will not move with his reinforcement."

"How is that?"

"Boguslav and I concluded that he would enter at once into a league with the Swedes and with us, for we know how to measure his love for the Commonwealth. He is too cautious, however, and thinks only of his own interest. He is waiting to see what will happen; meanwhile he is entering into a league, but with the Prussian towns, which remain faithful to Yan Kazimir. I think that in this there will be treason of some kind, unless the elector is not himself, or doubts Swedish success altogether. But until all this is explained, the league stands against Sweden; and let the Swedes stumble in Little Poland, Great Poland and Mazovia will rise, the Prussians will go with them, and it may come to pass—" Here the prince shuddered as if terrified at his supposition.

"What may come to pass?" asked Kmita.

"That not a Swedish foot will go out of the Commonwealth," answered the prince, gloomily.

Kmita frowned and was silent.

"Then," continued the hetman, in a low voice, "our fortune will have fallen as low as before it was high."

Pan Andrei, springing from his seat, cried with sparkling eyes and flushed face: "What is this? Why did your highness say not long ago that the Commonwealth was lost,—that only in league with the Swedes, through the person and future reign of your highness, could it possibly be saved? What have I to believe,—what I heard then, or what I hear now? If what your highness says to-day is true, why do we hold with the Swedes, instead of beating them?—and the soul laughs at the thought of this."

Radzivill looked sternly at Kmita. "You are over bold!" said he.

But Kmita was careering on his own enthusiasm as on a horse. "Speak later of what kind of man I am; but now answer my question, your highness."

"I will give this answer," said Radzivill, with emphasis: "if things take the turn that I mention, we will fall to beating the Swedes."

Pan Andrei ceased distending his nostrils, slapped his forehead with his palm, and cried, "I am a fool! I am a fool!"

"I do not deny that," answered the prince. "I will say more: you exceed the measure of insolence. Know then that I send you to note the turns of fortune. I desire the good of the country, nothing else. I have mentioned to you suppositions which may not, which certainly will not, come true. But there is need to be cautious. Whoso wishes that water should not bear him away must know how to swim, and whoso goes through a pathless forest must stop often to note the direction in which he should travel. Do you understand?"

"As clearly as sunshine."

"We are free to draw back, and we are bound to do so if it will be better for the country; but we shall not be able if Prince Boguslav stays longer in Podlyasye. Has he lost his head, or what? If he stays there, he must declare for one side or the other,—either for the Swedes or Yan Kazimir,—and that is just what would be worst of all."

"I am dull, your highness, for again I do not understand."

"Podlyasye is near Mazovia; and either the Swedes will occupy it or reinforcements will come from the Prussian towns against the Swedes. Then it will be necessary to choose."

"But why does not Prince Boguslav choose?"

"Until he chooses, the Swedes will seek us greatly and must win our favor; the same is true of the elector. If it comes to retreating and turning against the Swedes, he is to be the link between me and Yan Kazimir. He is to ease my return, which he could not do if previously he had taken the side of the Swedes. But since he will be forced to make a final choice if he remains in Podlyasye, let him go to Prussia, to Tyltsa, and wait there for events. The elector stays in Brandenburg. Boguslav will be of greater importance in Prussia; he may take the Prussians in hand altogether, increase his army, and stand at the head of a considerable force. And then both the Swedes and Yan Kazimir will give what we ask in order to win us both; and our house will not only not fall, but will rise higher, and that is the main thing."

"Your highness said that the good of the country was the main thing."

"But do not break in at every word, since I told you at first that the two are one; and listen farther. I know well that Prince Boguslav, though he signed the act of union with Sweden here in Kyedani, does not pass as an adherent of theirs. Though the report will be baseless, do you declare along the road that I forced him to sign it against his heart. People will believe this readily, for it happens frequently that even full brothers belong to different parties. In this way he will be able to gain the confidence of the confederates, invite the leaders to his camp as if for negotiations, and then seize and take them to Prussia. That will be a good method, and salutary for the country, which those men will ruin completely unless they are stopped."

433

"Is this all that I have to do?" asked Kmita, with a certain disillusion.

"This is merely a part, and not the most important. From Prince Boguslav you will go with my letters to Karl Gustav himself. I cannot come to harmony with Count Magnus from the time of that battle at Klavany. He looks at me askance, and does not cease from supposing that if the Swedes were to stumble, if the Tartars were to rush at the other enemy, I would turn against the Swedes."

"By what your highness has said just now, his supposition is correct."

"Correct or not, I do not wish it held, or wish him to see what trumps I have in my hand. Besides, he is ill-disposed toward me personally. Surely he has written more than once against me to the king, and beyond a doubt one of two things,—either that I am weak, or that I am not reliable. This must be remedied. You will give my letter to the king. If he asks about the Klavany affair, tell the truth, neither adding nor taking away. You may confess that I condemned those officers to death, and you obtained their pardon. That will cost you nothing, but the sincerity may please him. You will not complain against Count Magnus directly in presence of the king, for he is his brother-in-law. But if the king should ask, so, in passing, what people here think, say that they are sorry because Count Magnus does not repay the hetman sufficiently, in view of his sincere friendship for the Swedes; that the prince himself (that is I) grieves greatly over this. If he asks if it is true that all the quota troops have left me, say that 'tis not true; and as proof offer yourself. Tell him that you are colonel; for you are. Say that the partisans of Pan Gosyevski brought the troops to mutiny, but add that there is a mortal enmity between us. Say that if Count Magnus had sent me cannon and cavalry I should have crushed the confederates long ago,—that this is the

434

general opinion. Finally, take note of everything, give ear to what they are saying near the person of the king, and report, not to me, but, if occasion offers, to Prince Boguslav in Prussia. You may do so even through the elector's men, should you meet them. Perhaps you know German?"

"I had an officer, a noble of Courland, a certain Zend, whom the Lauda men slew; from him I learned German not badly. I have also been often in Livonia."

"That is well."

"But, your highness, where shall I find the King of Sweden?"

"You will find him where he will be. In time of war he may be here to-day and there to-morrow. Should you find him at Cracow, it would be better, for you will take letters to other persons who live in those parts."

"Then I am to go to others?"

"Yes. You must make your way to the marshal of the kingdom, Pan Lyubomirski. It is of great moment to me that he come to our views. He is a powerful man, and in Little Poland much depends on him. Should he declare sincerely for the Swedes, Yan Kazimir would have no place in the Commonwealth. Conceal not from the King of Sweden that you are going from me to Lyubomirski to win him for the Swedes. Do not boast of this directly, but speak as it were inadvertently. That will influence him greatly in my favor. God grant that Lyubomirski declare for us. He will hesitate, that I know; still I hope that my letters will turn the scale, for there is a reason why he must care greatly for my good will. I will tell you the whole affair, that you may know how to act. You see Pan Lyubomirski has been coming around me for a long time, as men go around a bear in a thicket, and trying from afar to see if I would give my only daughter to his son Heraclius. They are children yet, but the contract might be made,—which is very important for the marshal, more than for me, since there is not another such heiress in the Commonwealth, and if the two fortunes were united, there would not be another such in the world. That is a well-buttered toast! But if the marshal were to conceive the hope that his son might receive the crown of the Grand Principality as the dower of my daughter! Rouse that hope in him and he will be tempted, as God is in heaven, for he thinks more of his house than he does of the Commonwealth."

"What have I to tell him?"

"That which I cannot write. But it must be placed before him with skill. God preserve you from disclosing that you have heard from me how I desire the crown,—it is too early for that yet,—but say, 'All the nobles in Lauda and Lithuania talk of crowning Radzivill, and rejoice over it; the Swedes themselves mention it, I have heard it near the person of the king.' You will observe who of his courtiers is the marshal's confidant, and suggest to that courtier the following thought: 'Let Lyubomirski join the Swedes and ask in return the marriage of Heraclius and Radzivill's daughter, then let him support Radzivill as Grand Prince. Heraclius will be Radzivill's heir.' That is not enough; suggest also that once Heraclius has the Lithuanian crown he will be elected in time to the throne of Poland, and so the two crowns may be united again in these two families. If they do not grasp at this idea with both hands, they will show themselves petty people. Whoso does not aim high and fears great plans, should be content with a little baton, with a small castellanship; let him serve, bend his neck, gain favor through chamber attendants, for he deserves nothing better! God has created me for something else, and therefore I dare to stretch my hands to everything which it is in the power of man to reach, and to go to those limits which God alone has placed to human effort."

Here the prince stretched his hands, as if wishing to seize some unseen crown, and gleamed up altogether, like a torch; from emotion the breath failed in his throat again.

After a while he calmed himself and said with a broken voice,—

"Behold—where my soul flies—as if to the sun—Disease utters its warning—let it work its will—I would rather death found me on the throne—than in the antechamber of a king."

"Shall the physician be called?" asked Kmita.

Radzivill waved his hand.

"No need of him—I feel better now—That is all I had to say—In addition keep your eyes open, your ears open—See also what the Pototskis will do. They hold together, are true to the Vazas (that is, to Yan Kazimir)—and they are powerful—It is not known either how the Konyetspolskis and Sobyeskis will turn— Observe and learn—Now the suffocation is gone. Have you understood everything clearly?"

"Yes. If I err, it will be my own fault."

"I have letters written already; only a few remain. When do you wish to start?"

"To-day! As soon as possible."

"Have you no request to make?"

"Your highness," began Kmita, and stopped suddenly. The words came from his mouth with difficulty, and on his face constraint and confusion were depicted.

"Speak boldly," said the hetman.

"I pray," said Kmita, "that Billevich and she—suffer no harm while here."

"Be certain of that. But I see that you love the girl yet."

"Impossible," answered Kmita. "Do I know! An hour I love her, an hour I hate her. The devil alone knows! All is over, as I have said,—suffering only is left. I do not want her, but I do not want another to take her. Your highness, pardon me, I know not myself what I say. I must go,—go with all haste! Pay no heed to my words, God will give back my mind the moment I have gone through the gate."

"I understand that, because till love has grown cold with time, though not wanting her yourself, the thought that another might take her burns you. But be at rest on that point, for I will let no man come here, and as to going away they will not go. Soon it will be full of foreign soldiers all around, and unsafe. Better, I will send her to Tanrogi, near Tyltsa, where my daughter is. Be at rest, Yendrek. Go, prepare for the road, and come to me to dine."

Kmita bowed and withdrew, and Radzivill began to draw deep breaths. He was glad of the departure of Kmita. He left him his squadron and his name as an adherent; for his person the prince cared less.

But Kmita in going might render him notable services; in Kyedani he had long since grown irksome to the hetman, who was surer of him at a distance than near at hand. The wild courage and temper of Kmita might at any instant bring an outburst in Kyedani and a rupture very dangerous for both. The departure put danger aside.

"Go, incarnate devil, and serve!" muttered the prince, looking at the door through which the banneret of Orsha had passed. Then he called a page and summoned Ganhoff.

"You will take Kmita's squadron," said the prince to him, "and command over all the cavalry. Kmita is going on a journey."

Over the cold face of Ganhoff there passed as it were a ray of joy. The mission had missed him, but a higher military office had come. He bowed in silence, and said,—

"I will pay for the favor of your highness with faithful service." Then he stood erect and waited.

"And what will you say further?" asked the prince.

438

"Your highness, a noble from Vilkomir came this morning with news that Pan Sapyeha is marching with troops against your highness."

Radzivill quivered, but in the twinkle of an eye he mastered his expression.

"You may go," said he to Ganhoff.

Then he fell into deep thought.

CHAPTER XXV.

Kmita was very busily occupied in preparations for the road, and in choosing the men of his escort; for he determined not to go without a certain-sized party, first for his own safety, and second for the dignity of his person as an envoy. He was in a hurry, since he wished to start during the evening of that day, or if the rain did not cease, early next morning. He found men at last,—six trusty fellows who had long served under him in those better days when before his journey to Lyubich he had stormed around Hovanski,—old fighters of Orsha, ready to follow him even to the end of the earth. They were themselves nobles and attendant boyars, the last remnant of that once powerful band cut down by the Butryms. At the head of them was the sergeant Soroka, a trusty servant of the Kmitas,—an old soldier and very reliable, though numerous sentences were hanging over him for still more numerous deeds of violence.

After dinner the prince gave Pan Andrei the letters and a pass to the Swedish commanders whom the young envoy might meet in the more considerable places; he took farewell of him and sent him away with much feeling, really like a father, recommending wariness and deliberation.

Meanwhile the sky began to grow clear; toward evening the weak sun of autumn shone over Kyedani and went down behind red clouds, stretched out in long lines on the west.

There was nothing to hinder the journey. Kmita was just drinking a stirrup cup with Ganhoff, Kharlamp, and some other officers when about dusk Soroka came in and asked,—

"Are you going, Commander?"

"In an hour," answered Kmita.

"The horses and men are ready now in the yard."

The sergeant went out, and the officers began to strike glasses still more; but Kmita rather pretended to drink than to drink in reality. The wine had no taste for him, did not go to his head, did not cheer his spirit, while the others were already merry.

"Worthy Colonel," said Ganhoff, "commend me to the favor of Prince Boguslav. That is a great cavalier; such another there is not in the Commonwealth. With him you will be as in France. A different speech, other customs, every politeness may be learned there more easily than even in the palace of the king."

"I remember Prince Boguslav at Berestechko," said Kharlamp; "he had one regiment of dragoons drilled in French fashion completely,—they rendered both infantry and cavalry service. The officers were French, except a few Hollanders; of the soldiers the greater part were French, all dandies. There was an odor of various perfumes from them as from a drug-shop. In battle they thrust fiercely with rapiers, and it was said that when one of them thrust a man through he said, 'Pardonnez-moi!' (pardon me); so they mingled politeness with uproarious life. But Prince Boguslav rode among them with a handkerchief on his sword, always smiling, even in the greatest din of battle, for it is the French fashion to smile amid bloodshed. He had his face touched with paint, and his eyebrows blackened with coal, at which the old soldiers were angry and called him a bawd. Immediately after battle he had new ruffs brought him, so as to be always dressed as if for a banquet, and they curled his hair with irons, making marvellous ringlets out of it. But he is a manful fellow, and goes first into the thickest fire. He challenged Pan Kalinovski because he said something to him, and the king had to make peace."

"There is no use in denying," said Ganhoff. "You will see curious things, and you will see the King of Sweden himself, who next to our prince is the best warrior in the world."

"And Pan Charnyetski," said Kharlamp; "they are speaking more and more of him."

"Pan Charnyetski is on the side of Yan Kazimir, and therefore is our enemy," remarked Ganhoff, severely.

"Wonderful things are passing in this world," said Kharlamp, musingly. "If any man had said a year or two ago that the Swedes would come hither, we should all have thought, 'We shall be fighting with the Swedes;' but see now."

"We are not alone; the whole Commonwealth has received them with open arms," said Ganhoff.

"True as life," put in Kmita, also musingly.

"Except Sapyeha, Gosyevski, Charnyetski, and the hetmans of the crown," answered Kharlamp.

"Better not speak of that," said Ganhoff. "But, worthy Colonel, come back to us in good health; promotion awaits you."

"And Panna Billevich?" added Kharlamp.

"Panna Billevich is nothing to you," answered Kmita, brusquely.

"Of course nothing, I am too old. The last time— Wait, gentlemen, when was that? Ah, the last time during the election of the present mercifully reigning Yan Kazimir."

"Cease the use of that name from your tongue," interrupted Ganhoff. "To-day rules over us graciously Karl Gustav."

"True! *Consuetudo altera natura* (custom is a second nature). Well, the last time, during the election of Yan Kazimir, our ex-king and Grand Duke of Lithuania, I fell terribly in love with one lady, an attendant of the Princess Vishnyevetski. Oh, she was an attractive little beast! But when I wanted to look more nearly into her eyes, Pan Volodyovski thrust up his sabre. I was to fight with him; then Bogun came between us,—Bogun, whom Volodyovski cut up like a hare. If it had not been for that, you would not see me alive. But at that time I was ready to fight, even with the devil. Volodyovski stood up for her only through friendship, for she was betrothed to another, a still greater swordsman. Oh, I tell you, gentlemen, that I thought I should wither away—I could not think of eating or drinking. When our prince sent me from Warsaw to Smolensk, only then did I shake off my love on the road. There is nothing like a journey for such griefs. At the first mile I was easier, before I had reached Vilna my head was clear, and to this day I remain single. That is the whole story. There is nothing for unhappy love like a journey."

"Is that your opinion?" asked Kmita.

"As I live, it is! Let the black ones take all the pretty girls in Lithuania and the kingdom, I do not need them."

"But did you go away without farewell?"

"Without farewell; but I threw a red ribbon behind me, which one old woman, very deeply versed in love matters, advised me to do."

"Good health!" interrupted Ganhoff, turning again to Pan Andrei.

"Good health!" answered Kmita, "I give thanks from my heart."

"To the bottom, to the bottom! It is time for you to mount, and service calls us. May God lead you forth and bring you home."

"Farewell!"

"Throw the red ribbon behind," said Kharlamp, "or at the first resting-place put out the fire yourself with a bucket of water; that is, if you wish to forget."

"Be with God!"

"We shall not soon see one another."

"Perhaps somewhere on the battlefield," added Ganhoff. "God grant side by side, not opposed."

"Of course not opposed," said Kmita.

And the officers went out.

The clock on the tower struck seven. In the yard the horses were pawing the stone pavement with their hoofs, and through the window were to be seen the men waiting. A wonderful disquiet seized Pan Andrei. He was repeating to himself, "I go, I go!" Imagination placed before his eyes unknown regions, and a throng of strange faces which he was to see, and at the same time wonder seized him at the thought of the journey, as if hitherto it had never been in his mind.

He must mount and move on. "What happens, will happen. What will be, will be!" thought he to himself.

When, however, the horses were snorting right there at the window, and the hour of starting had struck, he felt that the new life would be strange, and all with which he had lived, to which he had grown accustomed, to which he had become attached heart and soul, would stay in that region, in that neighborhood, in that place. The former Kmita would stay there as well. Another man as it were would go hence,—a stranger to all outside, as all outside were strangers to him. He would have to begin there an entirely new life. God alone knew whether there would be a desire for it.

Pan Andrei was mortally wearied in soul, and therefore at that moment he felt powerless in view of those new scenes and new people. He thought that it was bad for him here, that it would be bad for him there, at least it would be burdensome.

But it is time, time. He must put his cap on his head and ride off.

But will he go without a last word? Is it possible to be so near and later to be so far, to say not one word and go forth? See to what it has come! But what can he say to her? Shall he go and say, "Everything is ruined; my lady, go thy way, I will go mine"? Why, why say even that, when without saying it is so? He is not her betrothed, as she is not and will not be his wife. What has been is lost, is rent, and will not return, will not be bound up afresh. Loss of time, loss of words, and new torture.

"I will not go!" thought Pan Kmita.

But, on the other hand, the will of a dead man binds them yet. It is needful to speak clearly and without anger of final separation, and to say to her, "My lady, you wish me not; I return you your word. Therefore we shall both act as though there had been no will, and let each seek happiness where each can find it?"

But she may answer: "I have said that long since; why tell it to me now?"

"I will not go, happen what may!" repeated Kmita to himself.

And pressing the cap on his head, he went out of the room into the corridor. He wished to mount straightway and be outside the gate quickly.

All at once, in the corridor, something caught him as it were by the hair. Such a desire to see her, to speak to her, possessed him, that he ceased to think whether to go or not to go, he ceased to reason, and rather pushed on with closed eyes, as if wishing to spring into water.

Before the very door whence the guard had just been removed, he came upon a youth, a servant of the sword-bearer.

"Is Pan Billevich in the room?" asked he.

"The sword-bearer is among the officers in the barracks."

"And the lady?"

"The lady is at home."

"Tell her that Pan Kmita is going on a long journey and wishes to see the lady."

The youth obeyed the command; but before he returned with an answer Kmita raised the latch and went in without question.

"I have come to take farewell," said he, "for I do not know whether we shall meet again in life."

Suddenly he turned to the youth: "Why stand here yet?"

"My gracious lady," continued Kmita, when the door had closed after the servant, "I intended to go without parting, but had not the power. God knows when I shall return, or whether I shall return, for misfortunes come lightly. Better that we part without anger and offence in our hearts, so that the punishment of God fall not on either of us. There is much to say, much to say, and now the tongue cannot say it all. Well, there was no happiness, clearly by the will of God there was not; and now, O man, even if thou batter thy head against the wall, there is no cure! Blame me not, and I will not blame you. We need not regard that testament now, for as I have said, the will of man is nothing against the will of God. God grant you happiness and peace. The main thing is that we forgive each other. I know not what will meet me outside, whither I am going. But I cannot sit longer in torture, in trouble, in sorrow. A man breaks himself on the four walls of a room without result, gracious lady, without result! One has no labor here,—only to take grief on the shoulders, only think for whole days of unhappy events till the head aches, and in the end think out nothing. This journey is as needful to me, as water to a fish, as air to a bird, for without it I should go wild."

445

"God grant you happiness," said Panna Aleksandra.

She stood before him as if stunned by the departure, the appearance, and the words of Pan Kmita. On her face were confusion and astonishment, and it was clear that she was struggling to recover herself; meanwhile she gazed on the young man with eyes widely open.

"I do not cherish ill will against you," said she after a time.

"Would that all this had not been!" said Kmita. "Some evil spirit came between us and separated us as if with a sea, and that water is neither to be swum across nor waded through. The man did not do what he wanted, he went not where he wished, but something as it were pushed him till we both entered pathless regions. But since we are to vanish the one from the eyes of the other, it is better to cry out even from remoteness, 'God guide!' It is needful also for you to know that offence and anger are one thing, and sorrow another. From anger I have freed myself, but sorrow sits in me—maybe not for you. Do I know myself for whom and for what? Thinking, I have thought out nothing; but still it seems to me that it will be easier both to you and to me if we talk. You hold me a traitor, and that pricks me most bitterly of all, for as I wish my soul's salvation, I have not been and shall not be a traitor."

"I hold you that no longer," said Olenka.

"Oi, how could you have held me that even one hour? You know of me, that once I was ready for violence, ready to slay, burn, shoot; that is one thing, but to betray for gain, for advancement, never! God guard me, God judge me! You are a woman, and cannot see in what lies the country's salvation; hence it beseems you not to condemn, to give sentence. And why did you utter the sentence? God be with you! Know this, that salvation is in Prince Radzivill and the Swedes; and who thinks otherwise, and especially acts, is just ruining the country. But it is no time to discuss, it is time to go. Know that I am not a traitor, not one who sells. May I perish if I ever be that! Know that unjustly you scorned me, unjustly consigned me to death—I tell you this under oath and at parting, and I say it that I may say with it, I forgive you from my heart; but do you forgive me as well."

Panna Aleksandra had recovered completely. "You say that I have judged you unjustly; that is true. It is my fault; I confess it and beg your forgiveness."

Here her voice trembled, her blue eyes filled with tears, and he cried with transport,—

"I forgive! I forgive! I would forgive you even my death!"

"May God guide you and bring you to the right road. May you leave that on which you are erring."

"But give peace, give peace!" cried Kmita, excitedly; "let no misunderstanding rise between us again. Whether I err or err not, be silent on that point. Let each man follow the way of his conscience; God will judge every intention. Better that I have come hither, than to go without farewell. Give me your hand for the road. Only that much is mine; for to-morrow I shall not see you, nor after tomorrow, nor in a month, perhaps never—Oi, Olenka! and in my head it is dim—Olenka! And shall we never meet again?"

Abundant tears like pearls were falling from Panna Aleksandra's lashes to her cheeks.

"Pan Andrei, leave traitors, and all may be."

"Quiet, oh, quiet!" said Kmita, with a broken voice. "It may not be—I cannot—better say nothing— Would I were slain! less should I suffer— For God's sake, why does this meet us? Farewell for the last time. And then let death close my eyes somewhere outside— Why are you weeping? Weep not, or I shall go wild!"

And in supreme excitement he seized her half by constraint, and though she resisted, he kissed her eyes and her mouth, then fell at her feet. At last he sprang up, and grasping his hair like a madman, rushed forth from the chamber.

"The devil could do nothing here, much less a red ribbon."

Olenka saw him through the window as he was mounting in haste; the seven horsemen then moved forward. The Scots on guard at the gate made a clatter with their weapons, presenting arms; then the gate closed after the horsemen, and they were not to be seen on the dark road among the trees.

Night too had fallen completely.

CHAPTER XXVI.

Kovno, and the whole region on the left bank of the Vilia, with all the roads, were occupied by the enemy (the Russians); therefore Kmita, not being able to go to Podlyasye by the high-road leading from Kovno to Grodno and thence to Byalystok, went by side-roads from Kyedani straight down the course of the Nyevyaja to the Nyemen, which he crossed near Vilkovo, and found himself in the province of Trotsk.

All that part of the road, which was not over great, he passed in quiet, for that region lay as it were under the hand of Radzivill.

Towns, and here and there even villages, were occupied by castle squadrons of the hetman, or by small detachments of Swedish cavalry which the hetman pushed forward thus far of purpose against the legions of Zolotarenko, which stood there beyond the Vilia, so that occasions for collisions and war might be more easily found.

Zolotarenko would have been glad too to have an "uproar" with the Swedes, according to the words of the hetman; but those whose ally he was did not wish war with them, or in every case wished to put it off as long as possible. Zolotarenko therefore received the strictest orders not to cross the river, and in case that Radzivill himself, together with the Swedes, moved on him, to retreat with all haste.

For these reasons the country on the right side of the Vilia was quiet; but since from one side Cossack pickets, from the other those of the Swedes and Radzivill were looking at one another, one musket-shot might at any moment let loose a terrible war.

In prevision of this, people took timely refuge in safe places. Therefore the whole country was quiet, but empty. Pan Andrei saw deserted towns, everywhere the windows of houses held up by sticks, and whole villages depopulated. The fields were also empty, for there was no crop that year. Common people secreted themselves in fathomless forests, to which they drove all their cattle; but the nobles fled to neighboring Electoral Prussia, at that time altogether safe from war. For this reason there was an uncommon movement over the roads and trails of the wilderness, and the number of fugitives was still more increased by those who from the left bank of the Vilia were able to escape the oppression of Zolotarenko.

The number of these was enormous, and especially of peasants; for the nobles who had not been able hitherto to flee from the left bank went into captivity or yielded their lives on their thresholds.

Pan Andrei, therefore, met every moment whole crowds of peasants with their wives and children, and driving before them flocks of sheep with horses and cattle. That part of the province of Trotsk touching upon Electoral Prussia was wealthy and productive; therefore the well-to-do people had something to save and guard. The approaching winter did not alarm fugitives, who preferred to await better days amid mosses of the forest, in snow covered huts, than to await death in their native villages at the hands of the enemy.

Kmita often approached the fleeing crowds, or fires gleaming at night in dense forest places. Wherever he met people from the left bank of the Vilia, from near Kovno, or from still remoter neighborhoods, he heard terrible tales of the cruelties of Zolotarenko and his allies, who exterminated people without regard to age or sex; they burned villages, cut down even trees in the gardens, leaving only land and water. Never had Tartar raids left such desolation behind.

Not death alone was inflicted on the inhabitants, but before death they were put to the most ingenious tortures. Many of those people fled with bewildered minds. These filled the forest depths at night with awful shrieks; others were ever in a species of continual fear and expectation of attack, though they had crossed the Nyemen and Vilia, though forests and morasses separated them from Zolotarenko's bands. Many of these stretched their hands to Kmita and his horsemen of Orsha, imploring rescue and pity, as if the enemy were standing there over them.

Carriages belonging to nobles were moving toward Prussia; in them old men, women, and children; behind them, dragged on wagons with servants, effects, supplies of provisions, and other things. All these fleeing people were panic-stricken, terrified and grieved because they were going into exile.

Pan Andrei comforted these unfortunates at times by telling them that the Swedes would soon pass over and drive that enemy far away. Then the fugitives stretched their hands to heaven and said,—

"God give health, God give fortune to the prince voevoda! When the Swedes come we will return to our homes, to our burned dwellings."

And they blessed the prince everywhere. From mouth to mouth news was given that at any moment he might cross the Vilia at the head of his own and Swedish troops. Besides, they praised the "modesty" of the Swedes, their discipline, and good treatment of the inhabitants. Radzivill was called the Gideon of Lithuania, a Samson, a savior. These people from districts steaming with fresh blood and fire were looking for him as for deliverance.

And Kmita, hearing those blessings, those wishes, those almost prayers, was strengthened in his faith concerning Radzivill, and repeated in his soul,—

"I serve such a lord! I will shut my eyes and follow blindly his fortune. At times he is terrible and beyond knowing; but he has a greater mind than others, he knows better what is needed, and in him alone is salvation."

It became lighter and calmer in his breast at this thought; he advanced therefore with greater solace in his heart, dividing his soul between sorrow for Kyedani and thoughts on the unhappy condition of the country.

His sorrow increased continually. He did not throw the red ribbon behind him, he did not put out the fire with water; for he felt, first, that it was useless, and then he did not wish to do so.

"Oh that she were present, that she could hear the wailing and groans of people, she would not beg God to turn me away, she would not tell me that I err, like those heretics who have left the true faith. But never mind! Earlier or later she will be convinced, she will see that her own judgment was at fault. And then what God will give will be. Maybe we shall meet again in life."

And yearning increased in the young cavalier; but the conviction that he was marching by the right, not by the wrong road, gave him a peace long since unknown. The conflict of thought, the gnawing, the doubts left him by degrees, and he rode forward; he sank in the shoreless forest almost with gladness. From the time that he had come to Lyubich, after his famous raids on Hovanski, he had not felt so vivacious.

Kharlamp was right in this, that there is no cure like the road for cares and troubles. Pan Andrei had iron health; his daring and love of adventures were coming back every hour. He saw these adventures before him, smiled at them, and urged on his convoy unceasingly, barely stopping for short night-rests.

Olenka stood ever before the eyes of his spirit, tearful, trembling in his arms like a bird, and he said to himself, "I shall return."

At times the form of the hetman passed before him, gloomy, immense, terrible. But it may be just because he was moving away more and more, that that form became almost dear to him. Hitherto he had bent before Radzivill; now he began to love him. Hitherto Radzivill had borne him along as a mighty whirlpool of water seizes and attracts everything that comes within its circle; now Kmita felt that he wished with his whole soul to go with him.

And in the distance that gigantic voevoda increased continually in the eyes of the young knight, and assumed almost superhuman proportions. More than once, at his night halt, when Pan Andrei had closed his eyes in sleep, he saw the hetman sitting on a throne loftier than the tops of the pine-trees. There was a crown on his head; his face was the same, gloomy, enormous; in his hand a sword and a sceptre, at his feet the whole Commonwealth. And in his soul Kmita did homage to greatness.

On the third day of the journey they left the Nyemen far behind, and entered a country of still greater forests. They met whole crowds of fugitives on the roads; but nobles unable to bear arms were going almost without exception to Prussia before the bands of the enemy, who, not held in curb there, as on the banks of the Vilia, by the regiments of Sweden and Radzivill, pushed at times far into the heart of the country, even to the boundary of Electoral Prussia. Their main object was plunder.

Frequently these were detachments as if from the army of Zolotarenko, but really recognizing no authority,—simply robber companies, so called "parties" commanded at times even by local bandits. Avoiding engagements in the field with troops and even with townspeople, they attacked small villages, single houses, and travellers.

The nobles on their own account attacked these parties with their household servants, and ornamented with them the pine-trees along the roads; still it was easy in the forest to stumble upon their frequent bands, and therefore Pan Andrei was forced to exercise uncommon care.

But somewhat beyond Pilvishki on the Sheshupa, Kmita found the population living quietly in their homes. The townspeople told him, however, that not longer than a couple of days before, a strong band of Zolotarenko's men, numbering as many as five hundred, had made an attack, and would, according to their custom, have cut down all the people, and let the place rise in smoke, were it not for unexpected aid which fell as it were from heaven.

"We had already committed ourselves to God," said the master of the inn in which Pan Andrei had taken lodgings, "when the saints of the Lord sent some squadrons. We thought at first that a new enemy had come, but they were ours. They sprang at once on Zolotarenko's ruffians, and in an hour they laid them out like a pavement, all the more easily as we helped them."

"What kind of a squadron was it?" asked Kmita.

"God give them health! They did not say who they were, and we did not dare to ask. They fed their horses, took what hay and bread there was, and rode away."

"But whence did they come, and whither did they go?"

"They came from Kozlova Ruda, and they went to the south. We, who before that wished to flee to the woods, thought the matter over and stayed here, for the under-starosta said that after such a lesson the enemy would not look in on us again soon."

The news of the battle interested Kmita greatly, therefore he asked further: "And do you not know who commanded that squadron?"

"We do not know; but we saw the colonel, for he talked with us on the square, he is young, and sharp as a needle. He does not look like the warrior that he is."

"Volodyovski!" cried Kmita.

"Whether he is Volodyovski, or not, may his hands be holy, may God make him hetman!"

Pan Andrei fell into deep thought. Evidently he was going by the same road over which a few days before Volodyovski had marched with the Lauda men. In fact, that was natural, for both were going to Podlyasye. But it occurred to Pan Andrei that if he hastened he might easily meet the little knight and be captured; in that case, all the letters of Radzivill would fall with him into possession of the confederates. Such an event might destroy his mission, and bring God knows what harm to the cause of Radzivill. For this reason Pan Andrei determined to stay a couple of days in Pilvishki, so that the squadron of Lauda might have time to advance as far as possible.

The men, as well as the horses, travelling almost with one sweep from Kyedani (for only short halts had been given on the road hitherto), needed rest; therefore Kmita ordered the soldiers to remove the packs from the horses and settle themselves comfortably in the inn.

Next day he was convinced that he had acted not only cleverly but wisely, for scarcely had he dressed in the morning, when his host stood before him.

"I bring news to your grace," said he.

"It is good?"

"Neither good nor bad, but that we have guests. An enormous court arrived here to-day, and stopped at the starosta's house. There is a regiment of infantry, and what crowds of cavalry and carriages with servants!—The people thought that the king himself had come."

"What king?"

The innkeeper began to turn his cap in his hand. "It is true that we have two kings now, but neither one came,—only the prince marshal."

Kmita sprang to his feet. "What prince marshal? Prince Boguslav?"

"Yes, your grace; the cousin of the prince voevoda of Vilna."

Pan Andrei clapped his hands from astonishment. "And so we have met."

The innkeeper, understanding that his guest was an acquaintance of Prince Boguslav, made a lower bow than the day before, and went out of the room; but Kmita began to dress in haste, and an hour later was before the house of the starosta.

The whole place was swarming with soldiers. The infantry were stacking their muskets on the square; the cavalry had dismounted and occupied the houses at the side. The soldiers and attendants in the most varied costumes had halted before the houses, or were walking along the streets. From the mouths of the officers were to be heard French and German. Nowhere a Polish soldier, nowhere a Polish uniform; the musketeers and dragoons were dressed in strange fashion, different, indeed, from the foreign squadrons which Pan Andrei had seen in Kyedani, for they were not in German but in French style. The soldiers, handsome men and so showy that each one in the ranks might be taken for an officer, delighted the eyes of Pan Andrei. The officers looked on him also with curiosity, for he had arrayed himself richly in velvet and brocade, and six men, dressed in new uniforms, followed him as a suite.

Attendants, all dressed in French fashion, were hurrying about in front of the starosta's house; there were pages in caps and feathers, armor-bearers in velvet kaftans, and equerries in Swedish, high, wide-legged boots.

Evidently the prince did not intend to tarry long in Pilvishki, and had stopped only for refreshment, for the carriages were not taken to the shed; and the equerries, in waiting, were feeding horses out of tin sieves which they held in their hands.

Kmita announced to an officer on guard before the house who he was and what was his mission; the officer went to inform the prince. After a while he returned hastily, to say that the prince was anxious to see a man sent from the hetman; and showing Kmita the way, he entered the house with him.

After they had passed the antechamber, they found in the dining-hall a number of attendants, with legs stretched out, slumbering sweetly in arm-chairs; it was evident that they must have started early in the morning from the last halting-place: The officer stopped before the door of the next room, and bowing to Pan Andrei, said,—

"The prince is there."

Pan Andrei entered and stopped at the threshold. The prince was sitting before a mirror fixed in the corner of the room, and was looking so intently at his own face, apparently just touched with rouge and white, that he did not turn attention to the incomer. Two chamber servants, kneeling before him, were fastening buckles at the ankles on his high travelling-boots, while he was arranging slowly with his fingers the luxuriant, evenly cut forelock of his bright gold-colored wig, or it might be of his own abundant hair.

He was still a young man, of thirty-five years, but seemed not more than five and twenty. Kmita knew the prince, but looked on him always with curiosity: first, because of the great knightly fame which surrounded him, and which was won mainly through duels fought with various foreign magnates; second, by reason of his peculiar figure,—whoso saw his form once was forced to remember it ever after. The prince was tall and powerfully built, but on his broad shoulders stood a head as diminutive as if taken from another body. His face, also, was uncommonly small, almost childlike; but in it, too, there was no proportion, for he had a great Roman nose and enormous eyes of unspeakable beauty and brightness, with a real eagle boldness of glance. In presence of those eyes and the nose, the rest of his face, surrounded, moreover, with plentiful tresses of hair, disappeared almost completely; his mouth was almost that of a child; above it was a slight mustache barely covering his upper lip. The delicacy of his complexion, heightened by rouge and white paint, made him almost like a young lady; and at the same time the insolence, pride, and self-confidence depicted in that face permitted no one to forget that he was that *chercheur de noises* (seeker of quarrels), as he was nicknamed at the French court,—a man out of whose mouth a sharp word came with ease, but whose sword came from its scabbard with still greater ease.

In Germany, in Holland, in France, they related marvels of his military deeds, of his disputes, quarrels, adventures, and duels. He was the man who in Holland rushed into the thickest

457

whirl of battle, among the incomparable regiments of Spanish infantry, and with his own princely hand captured a flag and a cannon; he, at the head of the regiments of the Prince of Orange, captured batteries declared by old leaders to be beyond capture; he, on the Rhine, at the head of French musketeers, shattered the heavy squadrons of Germany, trained in the Thirty Years' War; he wounded, in a duel in France, the most celebrated fencer among French knights, Prince de Fremouille; another famous fighter, Baron Von Goetz, begged of him life, on his knees; he wounded Baron Grot, for which he had to hear bitter reproaches from his cousin Yanush, because he was lowering his dignity as prince by fighting with men beneath him in rank; finally, in presence of the whole French court, at a ball in the Louvre, he slapped Marquis de Rieux on the face, because he had spoken to him "unbecomingly." The duels that he had fought incognito in smaller towns, in taverns and inns, did not enter into reckoning.

He was a mixture of effeminacy and unbounded daring. During rare and short visits to his native land he amused himself by quarrels with the Sapyehas, and with hunting; but on those occasions the hunters had to find for him she-bears with their young, as being dangerous and enraged; against these he went armed only with a spear.

But it was tedious for him in his own country, to which he came, as was said, unwillingly, most frequently in time of war; he distinguished himself by great victories at Berestechko, Mogilyoff, and Smolensk. War was his element, though he had a mind quick and subtle, equally fitted for intrigues and diplomatic exploits. In these he knew how to be patient and enduring, far more enduring than in the "loves," of which a whole series completed the history of his life. The prince, at the courts where he had resided, was the terror of husbands who had beautiful wives. For that reason, doubtless, he was not yet married, though his high birth and almost inexhaustible fortune made him one of the most desirable matches in Europe. The King and Queen of France, Marya Ludvika of Poland, the Prince of Orange, and his uncle, the Elector of Brandenburg, tried to make matches for him; but so far he preferred his freedom.

"I do not want a dower," said he, cynically; "and of the other pleasures I have no lack as I am."

In this fashion he reached the thirty-fifth year of his age.

Kmita, standing on the threshold, examined with curiosity Boguslav's face, which the mirror reflected, while he was arranging with seriousness the hair of his forelock; at last, when Pan Andrei coughed once and a second time, he said, without turning his head,—

"But who is present? Is it a messenger from the prince voevoda?"

"Not a messenger, but from the prince voevoda," replied Pan Andrei.

Then the prince turned his head, and seeing a brilliant young man, recognized that he had not to do with an ordinary servant.

"Pardon, Cavalier," said he, affably, "for I see that I was mistaken in the office of the person. But your face is known to me, though I am not able to recall your name. You are an attendant of the prince hetman?"

"My name is Kmita," answered Pan Andrei, "and I am not an attendant; I am a colonel from the time that I brought my own squadron to the prince hetman."

"Kmita!" cried the prince, "that same Kmita, famous in the last war, who harried Hovanski, and later on managed not worse on his own account? I have heard much about you."

Having said this, the prince began to look more carefully and with a certain pleasure at Pan Andrei, for from what he had heard he thought him a man of his own cut.

"Sit down," said he, "I am glad to know you more intimately. And what is to be heard in Kyedani?"

"Here is a letter from the prince hetman," answered Kmita.

The servants, having finished buckling the prince's boots, went out. The prince broke the seal and began to read. After a while there was an expression of weariness and dissatisfaction on his face. He threw the letter under the mirror and said,—

"Nothing new! The prince voevoda advises me to go to Prussia, to Tyltsa or to Taurogi, which, as you see, I am just doing. *Ma foi*, I do not understand my cousin. He reports to me that the elector is in Brandenburg, and that he cannot make his way to Prussia through the Swedes, and he writes at the same time that the hairs are standing on his head because I do not communicate with him, either for health or prescription; and how can I? If the elector cannot make his way through the Swedes, how can my messenger do so? I am in Podlyasye, for I have nothing else to do. I tell you, my cavalier, that I am as much bored as the devil doing penance. I have speared all the bears near Tykotsin; the fair heads of that region have the odor of sheepskin, which my nostrils cannot endure. But— Do you understand French or German?"

"I understand German," answered Kmita.

"Praise be to God for that! I will speak German, for my lips fly off from your language."

When he had said this the prince put out his lower lip and touched it with his fingers, as if wishing to be sure that it had not gone off: then he looked at the mirror and continued,—

"Report has come to me that in the neighborhood of Lukovo one Skshetuski, a noble, has a wife of wonderful beauty. It is far from here; but I sent men to carry her off and bring her. Now, if you will believe it, Pan Kmita, they did not find her at home."

"That was good luck," said Pan Andrei, "for she is the wife of an honorable cavalier, a celebrated man, who made his way out of Zbaraj through the whole power of Hmelnitski."

"The husband was besieged in Zbaraj, and I would have besieged the wife in Tykotsin. Do you think she would have held out as stubbornly as her husband?"

"Your highness, for such a siege a counsel of war is not needed, let it pass without my opinion," answered Pan Andrei, brusquely.

"True, loss of time!" said the prince. "Let us return to business. Have you any letters yet?"

"What I had to your highness I have delivered; besides those I have one to the King of Sweden. Is it known to your highness where I must seek him?"

"I know nothing. What can I know? He is not in Tykotsin; I can assure you of that, for if he had once seen that place he would have resigned his dominion over the whole Commonwealth. Warsaw is now in Swedish hands, but you will not find the king there. He must be before Cracow, or in Cracow itself, if he has not gone to Royal Prussia by this time. To my thinking Karl Gustav must keep the Prussian towns in mind, for he cannot leave them in his rear. Who would have expected, when the whole Commonwealth abandons its king, when all the nobles join the Swedes, when the provinces yield one after the other, that just then towns, German and Protestant, would not hear of the Swedes but prepare for resistance? They wish to save the Commonwealth and adhere to Yan Kazimir. In beginning our

461

work we thought that it would be otherwise: that before all they would help us and the Swedes to cut that loaf which you call your Commonwealth; but now they won't move! The luck is that the elector has his eye on them. He has offered them forces already against the Swedes; but the Dantzig people do not trust him, and say that they have forces enough of their own."

"We knew that already in Kyedani," said Kmita.

"If they have not forces enough, in every case they have a good sniff," continued the prince, laughing; "for the elector cares as much, I think, about the Commonwealth as I do, or as the prince voevoda of Vilna does."

"Your highness, permit me to deny that," said Kmita, abruptly. "The prince cares that much about the Commonwealth that he is ready at every moment to give his last breath and spill his last blood for it."

Prince Boguslav began to laugh.

"You are young, Cavalier, young! But enough! My uncle the elector wants to grab Royal Prussia, and for that reason only, he offers his aid. If he has the towns once in hand, if he has his garrisons in them, he will be ready to agree with the Swedes next day, nay, even with the Turks or with devils. Let the Swedes add a bit of Great Poland, he will be ready to help them with all his power to take the rest. The only trouble is in this, that the Swedes are sharpening their teeth against Prussia, and hence the distrust between them and the elector."

"I hear with astonishment the words of your highness," said Kmita.

"The devils were taking me in Podlyasye," answered the prince,—"I had to stay there so long in idleness. But what was I to do? An agreement was made between me and the prince voevoda, that until affairs were cleared up in Prussia, I was not to take the Swedish side publicly. And that was right, for thus a gate remains open. I sent even secret couriers to Yan Kazimir, announcing that I was ready to summon the general militia in Podlyasye if a manifesto were sent me. The king, as king, might have let himself be tricked; but the queen it is clear does not trust me, and must have advised against it. If it were not for that woman, I should be to-day at the head of all the nobles of Podlyasye; and what is more, those confederates who are now ravaging the property of Prince Yanush would have no choice but to come under my orders. I should have declared myself a partisan of Yan Kazimir, but, in fact, having power in my hand, would treat with the Swedes. But that woman knows how grass grows, and guesses the most secret thought. She is the real king, not queen! She has more wit in one finger than Yan Kazimir in his whole body."

"The prince voevoda—" began Kmita.

"The prince voevoda," interrupted Boguslav, with impatience, "is eternally late with his counsel; he writes to me in every letter, 'Do this and do that,' while I have in fact done it long before. Besides, the prince voevoda loses his head. For listen what he asks of me."

Here the prince took up the letter and began to read aloud,—

"Be cautious yourself on the road; and those rascals, the confederates, who have mutinied against me and are ravaging Podlyasye, for God's sake think how to disperse them, lest they go to the king. They are preparing to visit Zabludovo, and beer in that place is strong; when they get drunk, let them be cut off,— each host may finish his guest. Nothing better is needed; for when the heads are removed, the rest will scatter—"

Boguslav threw the letter with vexation on the table.

"Listen, Pan Kmita," said he, "you see I have to go to Prussia and at the same time arrange a slaughter in Zabludovo. I must feign myself a partisan of Yan Kazimir and a patriot, and at the same time cut off those people who are unwilling to betray the king and the country. Is that sense? Does one hang to the other? *Ma foi*, the prince is losing his head. I have met now, while coming to Pilvishki, a whole insurgent squadron travelling along through Podlyasye. I should have galloped over their stomachs with gladness, even to gain some amusement; but before I am an open partisan of the Swedes, while my uncle the elector holds formally with the Prussian towns, and with Yan Kazimir too, I cannot permit myself such pleasure, God knows I cannot. What could I do more than to be polite to those insurgents, as they are polite to me, suspecting me of an understanding with the hetman, but not having black on white?"

Here the prince lay back comfortably in the armchair, stretched out his legs, and putting his hands behind his head carelessly, began to repeat,—

"Ah, there is nonsense in this Commonwealth, nonsense! In the world there is nothing like it!"

Then he was silent for a moment; evidently some idea came to his head, for he struck his wig and inquired,—

"But will you not be in Podlyasye?"

"Yes," said Kmita, "I must be there, for I have a letter with instructions to Harasimovich, the under-starosta in Zabludovo."

"In God's name!" exclaimed the prince, "Harasimovich is here with me. He is going with the hetman's effects to Prussia, for we were afraid that they might fall into the hands of the confederates. Wait, I will have him summoned."

Here the prince summoned a servant and ordered him to call the under-starosta.

"This has happened well," said the prince, "You will save yourself a journey,—though it may be too bad that you will not visit Podlyasye, for among the heads of the confederacy there is a namesake of yours whom you might secure."

"I have no time for that," said Kmita, "since I am in a hurry to go to the king and Pan Lyubomirski."

"Ah, you have a letter to the marshal of the kingdom? Well, I can divine the reason of it. Once the marshal thought of marrying his son to Yanush's daughter. Did not the hetman wish this time to renew negotiations delicately?"

"That is just the mission."

"Both are quite children. H'm! that's a delicate mission, for it does not become the hetman to speak first. Besides—"

Here the prince frowned.

"Nothing will come of it. The daughter of the hetman is not for Heraclius, I tell you that! The prince hetman must understand that his fortune is to remain in possession of the Radzivills."

Kmita looked with astonishment on the prince, who was walking with quicker and quicker pace through the room.

All at once he stopped before Pan Andrei, and said, "Give me the word of a cavalier that you will answer truly my question."

"Gracious prince," said Kmita, "only those lie who are afraid, and I fear no man."

"Did the prince voevoda give orders to keep secret from me the negotiations with Lyubomirski?"

"Had I such a command, I should not have mentioned Lyubomirski."

"It might have slipped you. Give me your word."

"I give it," said Kmita, frowning.

"You have taken a weight from my heart, for I thought that the voevoda was playing a double game with me."

"I do not understand, your highness."

"I would not marry, in France, Rohan, not counting half threescore other princesses whom they were giving me. Do you know why?"

"I do not."

"There is an agreement between me and the prince voevoda that his daughter and his fortune are growing up for me. As a faithful servant of the Radzivills, you may know everything."

"Thank you for the confidence. But your highness is mistaken. I am not a servant of the Radzivills."

Boguslav opened his eyes widely. "What are you?"

"I am a colonel of the hetman, not of the castle; and besides I am the hetman's relative."

"A relative?"

"I am related to the Kishkis, and the hetman is born of a Kishki."

Prince Boguslav looked for a while at Kmita, on whose face a light flush appeared. All at once he stretched forth his hands and said,—

"I beg your pardon, cousin, and I am glad of the relationship."

The last words were uttered with a certain inattentive though showy politeness, in which there was something directly painful to Pan Andrei. His face flushed still more, and he was opening his mouth to say something hasty, when the door opened and Harasimovich appeared on the threshold.

"There is a letter for you," said Boguslav.

Harasimovich bowed to the prince, and then to Pan Andrei, who gave him the letter.

"Read it!" said Prince Boguslav.

Harasimovich began to read,—

"Pan Harasimovich! Now is the time to show the good will of a faithful servant to his lord. As whatever money you are able to collect, you in Zabludovo and Pan Pjinski in Orel—"

"The confederates have slain Pan Pjinski in Orel, for which reason Pan Harasimovich has taken to his heels," interrupted the prince.

The under-starosta bowed and read further,—

"—and Pan Pjinski in Orel, even the public revenue, even the excise, rent—"

"The confederates have already taken them," interrupted Boguslav again.

"—send me at once," continued Harasimovich. "If you can mortgage some villages to neighbors or townspeople, obtaining as much money on them as possible, do so, and whatever means there may be of obtaining money, do your best in the matter, and send the money to me. Send horses and whatever effects there are in Orel. There is a great candlestick too, and other things,—pictures, ornaments, and especially the cannons on the porch at my cousins; for robbers may be feared—"

"Again counsel too late, for these cannons are going with me," said the prince.

"If they are heavy with the stocks, then take them without the stocks and cover them, so it may not be known that you are bringing them. And take these things to Prussia with all speed, avoiding with utmost care those traitors who have caused mutiny in my army and are ravaging my estates—"

"As to ravaging, they are ravaging! They are pounding them into dough," interrupted the prince anew.

"—ravaging my estates, and are preparing to move against Zabludovo on their way perhaps to the king. With them it is difficult to fight, for they are many; but if they are admitted, and given plenty to drink, and killed in the night while asleep (every host can do that), or poisoned in strong beer, or (which is not difficult in that place) a wild crowd let in to plunder them—"

"Well, that is nothing new!" said Prince Boguslav. "You may journey with me, Pan Harasimovich."

"There is still a supplement," said the under-starosta. And he read on,

"The wines, if you cannot bring them away (for with us such can be had nowhere), sell them quickly—"

Here Harasimovich stopped and seized himself by the head,—

"For God's sake! those wines are coming half a day's road behind us, and surely have fallen into the hands of that insurgent squadron which was hovering around us. There will be a loss of some thousands of gold pieces. Let your highness give witness with me that you commanded me to wait till the barrels were packed in the wagons."

Harasimovich's terror would have been still greater had he known Pan Zagloba, and had he known that he was in that very squadron. Meanwhile Prince Boguslav smiled and said,—

"Oh, let the wines be to their health! Read on!"

"—if a merchant cannot be found—"

Prince Boguslav now held his sides from laughter. "He has been found," said he, "but you must sell to him on credit."

"—but if a merchant cannot be found," read Harasimovich, in a complaining voice, "bury it in the ground secretly, so that more than two should not know where it is; but leave a keg in Orel and one in Zabludovo, and those of the best and sweetest, so that the officers may take a liking to it; and put in plenty of poison, so that the officers at least may be killed, then the squadron will break up. For God's sake, serve me faithfully in this, and secretly, for the mercy of God. Burn what I write, and whoso finds out anything send him to me. Either the confederates will find and drink the wine, or it may be given as a present to make them friendly."

The under-starosta finished reading, and looked at Prince Boguslav, as if waiting for instructions; and the prince said,—

"I see that my cousin pays much attention to the confederates; it is only a pity that, as usual, he is too late. If he had come upon this plan two weeks ago, or even one week, it might have been tried. But now go with God, Pan Harasimovich; I do not need you."

Harasimovich bowed and went out.

Prince Boguslav stood before the mirror, and began to examine his own figure carefully; he moved his head slightly from right to left, then stepped back from the mirror, then approached it, then shook his curls, then looked askance, not paying any attention to Kmita, who sat in the shade with his back turned to the window.

But if he had cast even one look at Pan Andrei's face he would have seen that in the young envoy something wonderful was taking place; for Kmita's face was pale, on his forehead stood thick drops of sweat, and his hands shook convulsively. After a while he rose from the chair, but sat down again immediately, like a man struggling with himself and suppressing an outburst of anger or despair. Finally his features settled and became fixed; evidently he had with his whole strong force of will and energy enjoined calm on himself and gained complete self-control.

"Your highness," said he, "from the confidence which the prince hetman bestows on me you see that he does not wish to make a secret of anything. I belong soul and substance to his work; with him and your highness my fortune may increase; therefore, whither you both go, thither go I also. I am ready for everything. But though I serve in those affairs and am occupied

469

in them, still I do not of course understand everything perfectly, nor can I penetrate all the secrets of them with my weak wit."

"What do you wish then, Sir Cavalier, or rather, fair cousin?"

"I ask instruction, your highness; it would be a shame indeed were I unable to learn at the side of such statesmen. I know not whether your highness will be pleased to answer me without reserve—"

"That will depend on your question and on my humor," answered Boguslav, not ceasing to look at the mirror.

Kmita's eyes glittered for a moment, but he continued calmly,—

"This is my question: The prince voevoda of Vilna shields all his acts with the good and salvation of the Commonwealth, so that in fact the Commonwealth is never absent from his lips; be pleased to tell me sincerely, are these mere pretexts, or has the hetman in truth nothing but the good of the Commonwealth in view?"

Boguslav cast a quick glance on Pan Andrei. "If I should say that they are pretexts, would you give further service?"

Kmita shrugged his shoulders carelessly. "Of course! As I have said, my fortune will increase with the fortune of your highness and that of the hetman. If that increase comes, the rest is all one to me."

"You will be a man! Remember that I foretell this. But why has my cousin not spoken openly with you?"

"Maybe because he is squeamish, or just because it did not happen to be the topic."

"You have quick wit, Cousin Cavalier, for it is the real truth that he is squeamish and shows his true skin unwillingly. As God is dear to me, true! Such is his nature. So, even in talking with me, the moment he forgets himself he begins to adorn his speech with love for the country. When I laugh at him to his eyes, he comes to his senses. True! true!"

"Then it is merely a pretext?" asked Kmita.

The prince turned the chair around and sat astride of it, as on a horse, and resting his arms on the back of it was silent awhile, as if in thought; then he said,—

"Hear me, Pan Kmita. If we Radzivills lived in Spain, France, or Sweden, where the son inherits after the father, and where the right of the king comes from God himself, then, leaving aside civil war, extinction of the royal stock, or some uncommon event, we should serve the king and the country firmly, being content with the highest offices which belong to us by family and fortune. But here, in the land where the king has not divine right at his back, but the nobles create him, where everything is in free suffrage, we ask ourselves with reason,—Why should a Vaza rule, and not a Radzivill? There is no objection so far as the Vazas are concerned, for they take their origin from hereditary kings; but who will assure us, who will guarantee that after the Vazas the nobles will not have the whim of seating on the throne of the kingdom and on the throne of the Grand Principality even Pan Harasimovich, or some Pan Myeleshko, or some Pan Pyeglasyevich from Psivolki? Tfu! can I guess whom they may fancy? And must we, Radzivills, and princes of the German Empire, come to kiss the hand of King Pyeglasyevich? Tfu! to all the horned devils, Cavalier, it is time to finish with this! Look meanwhile at Germany,—how many provincial princes there, who in importance and fortune are fitted to be under-starostas for us. Still they have their principalities, they rule, wear crowns on their heads, and take precedence of us, though it would be fitter for them to bear the trains of our mantles. It is time to put an end to this, and accomplish that which was already planned by my father."

471

Here the prince grew vivacious, rose from the chair, and began to walk through the room.

"This will not take place without difficulty and obstacles," continued he, "for the Radzivills of Olyta and Nyesvyej are not willing to aid us. I know that Prince Michael wrote to my cousin that he would better think of a hair-shirt than of a royal mantle. Let him think of a hair-shirt himself, let him do penance, let him sit on ashes, let the Jesuits lash his skin with disciplines; if he is content with being a royal carver, let him carve capons virtuously all his virtuous life, till his virtuous death! We shall get on without him and not drop our hands, for just now is the time. The devils are taking the Commonwealth; for now it is so weak, has gone to such dogs, that it cannot drive them away. Every one is crawling in over its boundaries, as into an unfenced garden. What has happened here with the Swedes has happened nowhere on earth to this day. We, Sir Cavalier, may sing in truth 'Te Deum laudamus.' In its way the event is unheard of, unparalleled. Just think: an invader attacks a country, an invader famous for rapacity; and not only does he not find resistance, but every living man deserts his old king and hurries to a new one,—magnates, nobles, the army, castles, towns, all,—without honor, without fame, without feeling, without shame! History gives not another such example. Tfu! tfu! trash inhabit this country,—men without conscience or ambition. And is such a country not to perish? They are looking for our favor! Ye will have favor! In Great Poland already the Swedes are thumb-screwing nobles; and so will it be everywhere,—it cannot be otherwise."

Kmita grew paler and paler, but with the remnant of his strength he held in curb an outburst of fury; the prince, absorbed in his own speech, delighted with his own words, with his own wisdom, paid no attention to his listener, and continued,—

"There is a custom in this land that when a man is dying his relatives at the last moment pull the pillow from under his head, so that he may not suffer longer. I and the prince voevoda of Vilna have determined to render this special service to the Commonwealth. But because many plunderers are watching for the inheritance and we cannot get it all, we wish that a part, and that no small one, should come to us. As relatives, we have that right. If with this comparison I have not spoken on a level with your understanding, and have not been able to hit the point, I will tell you in other words: Suppose the Commonwealth a red cloth at which are pulling the Swedes, Hmelnitski, the Hyperboreans, the Tartars, the elector, and whosoever lives around. But I and the prince voevoda of Vilna have agreed that enough of that cloth must remain in our hands to make a robe for us; therefore we do not prevent the dragging, but we drag ourselves. Let Hmelnitski stay in the Ukraine; let the Swedes and the elector settle about Prussia and Great Poland; let Rakotsy, or whoever is nearer, take Little Poland,—Lithuania must be for Prince Yanush, and, together with his daughter, for me."

Kmita rose quickly. "I give thanks, your highness; that is all I wanted to know."

"You are going out, Sir Cavalier?"

"I am."

The prince looked carefully at Kmita, and at that moment first noted his pallor and excitement.

"What is the matter, Pan Kmita?" asked he. "You look like a ghost."

"Weariness has knocked me off my feet, and my head is dizzy. Farewell, your highness; I will come before starting, to bow to you again."

"Make haste, then, for I start after midday myself."

"I shall return in an hour at furthest."

473

When he had said this, Kmita bent his head and went out. In the other room the servants rose at sight of him, but he passed like a drunken man, seeing no one. At the threshold of the room he caught his head with both hands, and began to repeat, almost with a groan,—

"Jesus of Nazareth, King of the Jews! Jesus, Mary, Joseph!"

With tottering steps he passed through the guard, composed of six men with halberds. Outside the gate were his own men, the sergeant Soroka at the head of them.

"After me!" called Kmita. And he moved through the town toward the inn.

Soroka, an old soldier of Kmita's, knowing him perfectly, noticed at once that something uncommon had happened to the colonel.

"Let your soul be on guard," said he quietly to the men; "woe to him on whom his anger falls now!"

The soldiers hastened their steps in silence, but Kmita did not go at a walk; he almost ran, waving his hand and repeating words well-nigh incoherent.

To the ears of Soroka came only broken phrases,—

"Poisoners, faith-breakers, traitors! Crime and treason,— the two are the same—"

Then he began to mention his old comrades. The names Kokosinski, Kulvyets, Ranitski, Rekuts, and others fell from his lips one after another; a number of times he mentioned Volodyovski. Soroka heard this with wonder, and grew more and more alarmed; but in his mind he thought,—

"Some one's blood will flow; it cannot be otherwise."

Meanwhile they had come to the inn. Kmita shut himself in his room at once, and for about an hour he gave no sign of life.

The soldiers meanwhile had tied on the packs and saddled the horses without order.

"That is no harm," said Soroka; "it is necessary to be ready for everything."

"We too are ready!" answered the old fighters, moving their mustaches.

In fact, it came out soon that Soroka knew his colonel well; for Kmita appeared suddenly in the front room, without a cap, in his trousers and shirt only.

"Saddle the horses!" cried he.

"They are saddled."

"Fasten on the packs!"

"They are fastened."

"A ducat a man!" cried the young colonel, who in spite of all his fever and excitement saw that those soldiers had guessed his thought quickly.

"We give thanks, Commander!" cried all in chorus.

"Two men will take the pack-horses and go out of the place immediately toward Dembova. Go slowly through the town; outside the town put the horses on a gallop, and stop not till the forest is reached."

"According to command!"

"Four others load their pistols. For me saddle two horses, and let another be ready."

"I knew there would be something!" muttered Soroka.

"Now, Sergeant, after me!" cried Kmita.

And undressed as he was, in trousers only, and open shirt, he went out of the front room. Soroka followed him, opening his eyes widely with wonder; they went in this fashion to the well in the yard of the inn. Here Kmita stopped, and pointing to the bucket hanging from the sweep, said,—

"Pour water on my head!"

Soroka knew from experience how dangerous it was to ask twice about an order; he seized the rope, let the bucket down into the water, drew up quickly, and taking the bucket in his hands, threw the water on Pan Andrei, who, puffing and blowing like a whale, rubbed his wet hair with his hands, and cried,—

"More!"

Soroka repeated the act, and threw water with all his force, just as if he were putting out a fire.

"Enough!" said Kmita, at length. "Follow me, help me to dress."

Both went to the inn. At the gate they met the two men going out with two pack-horses.

"Slowly through the town; outside the town on a gallop!" commanded Kmita; and he went in.

Half an hour later he appeared dressed completely, as if for the road, with high boots and an elkskin coat, girded with a leather belt into which was thrust a pistol.

The soldiers noticed, too, that from under his kaftan gleamed the edge of chain mail, as if he were going to battle. He had his sabre also girt high, so as to seize the hilt more easily. His face was calm enough, but stern and threatening. Casting a glance at the soldiers to see if they were ready and armed properly, he mounted his horse, and throwing a ducat at the innkeeper, rode out of the place.

Soroka rode at his side; three others behind, leading a horse. Soon they found themselves on the square filled by Boguslav's troops. There was movement among them already; evidently the command had come to prepare for the road. The horsemen were tightening the girths of the saddle and bridling the horses; the infantry were taking their muskets, stacked before the houses; others were attaching horses to wagons.

Kmita started as it were from meditation.

476

"Hear me, old man," said he to Soroka; "from the starosta's house does the road go on,—it will not be necessary to come back through the square?"

"But where are we going, Colonel?"

"To Dembova."

"Then we must go from the square past the house. The square will be behind us."

"It is well," said Kmita.

"Oh, if only those men were alive now! Few are fitted for work like this,—few!"

Meanwhile they passed the square, and began to turn toward the starosta's house, which lay about one furlong and a half farther on, near the roadside.

"Stop!" cried Kmita, suddenly.

The soldiers halted, and he turned to them. "Are you ready for death?" asked he, abruptly.

"Ready!" answered in chorus these dare-devils of Orsha.

"We crawled up to Hovanski's throat, and he did not devour us,—do you remember?"

"We remember!"

"There is need to dare great things to-day. If success comes, our gracious king will make lords of you,—I guarantee that! If failure, you will go to the stake!"

"Why not success?" asked Soroka, whose eyes began to gleam like those of an old wolf.

"There will be success!" said three others,—Biloüs, Zavratynski, and Lubyenyets.

"We must carry off the prince marshal!" said Kmita. Then he was silent, wishing to see the impression which the mad thought would make on the soldiers. But they were silent too, and looked on him as on a rainbow; only, their mustaches quivered, and their faces became terrible and murderous.

"The stake is near, the reward far away," added Kmita.

"There are few of us," muttered Zavratynski.

"It is worse than against Hovanski," said Lubyenyets.

"The troops are all in the market-square, and at the house are only the sentries and about twenty attendants," said Kmita, "who are off their guard, and have not even swords at their sides."

"You risk your head; why should we not risk ours?" said Soroka.

"Hear me," continued Kmita. "If we do not take him by cunning, we shall not take him at all. Listen! I will go into the room, and after a time come out with the prince. If the prince will sit on my horse, I will sit on the other, and we will ride on. When we have ridden about a hundred or a hundred and fifty yards, then seize him from both sides by the shoulders, and gallop the horses with all breath."

"According to order!" answered Soroka.

"If I do not come out," continued Kmita, "and you hear a shot in the room, then open on the guards with pistols, and give me the horse as I rush from the door."

"That will be done," answered Soroka.

"Forward!" commanded Kmita.

They moved on, and a quarter of an hour later halted at the gate of the starosta's house. At the gate were six guards with halberds; at the door of the anteroom four men were standing. Around a carriage in the front yard were occupied equerries and outriders, whom an attendant of consequence was overseeing,— a foreigner, as might be known from his dress and wig.

Farther on, near the carriage-house, horses were being attached to two other carriages, to which gigantic Turkish grooms were carrying packs. Over these watched a man dressed in black, with a face like that of a doctor or an astrologer.

Kmita announced himself as he had previously, through the officer of the day, who returned soon and asked him to the prince.

"How are you, Cavalier?" asked the prince, joyfully. "You left me so suddenly that I thought scruples had risen in you from my words, and I did not expect to see you again."

"Of course I could not go without making my obeisance."

"Well, I thought: the prince voevoda has known whom to send on a confidential mission. I make use of you also, for I give you letters to a number of important persons, and to the King of Sweden himself. But why armed as if for battle?"

"I am going among confederates; I have heard right here in this place, and your highness has confirmed the report, that a confederate squadron passed. Even here in Pilvishki they brought a terrible panic on Zolotarenko's men, for a famed soldier is leading that squadron."

"Who is he?"

"Pan Volodyovski; and with him are Mirski, Oskyerko, and the two Skshetuskis,—one that man of Zbaraj, whose wife your highness wanted to besiege in Tykotsin. All rebelled against the prince voevoda; and it is a pity, for they were good soldiers. What is to be done? There are still fools in the Commonwealth who are unwilling to pull the red cloth with Cossacks and Swedes."

"There is never a lack of fools in the world, and especially in this country," said the prince. "Here are the letters; and besides, when you see his Swedish grace, say as if in confidence that in heart I am as much his adherent as my cousin, but for the time I must dissemble."

"Who is not forced to that?" answered Kmita. "Every man dissembles, especially if he thinks to do something great."

"That is surely the case. Acquit yourself well, Sir Cavalier, I will be thankful to you, and will not let the hetman surpass me in rewarding."

"If the favor of your highness is such, I ask reward in advance."

"You have it! Surely my cousin has not furnished you over abundantly for the road. There is a serpent in his money-box."

"May God guard me from asking money! I did not ask it of the hetman, and I will not take it from your highness. I am at my own expense, and I will remain so."

Prince Boguslav looked at the young knight with wonder. "I see that in truth the Kmitas are not of those who look at men's hands. What is your wish then, Sir Cavalier?"

"The matter is as follows: without thinking carefully in Kyedani, I took a horse of high blood, so as to show myself before the Swedes. I do not exaggerate when I say there is not a better in the stables of Kyedani. Now I am sorry for him, and I am afraid to injure him on the road, in the stables of inns, or for want of rest. And as accidents are not hard to meet, he may fall into enemies' hands, even those of that Volodyovski, who personally is terribly hostile to me. I have thought, therefore, to beg your highness to take him to keep and use until I ask for him at a more convenient time."

"Better sell him to me."

"Impossible,—it would be like selling a friend. At a small estimate that horse has taken me a hundred times out of the greatest danger; for he has this virtue too, that in battle he bites the enemy savagely."

"Is he such a good horse?" asked Prince Boguslav, with lively interest.

"Is he good? If I were sure your highness would not be offended, I would bet a hundred gold florins without looking, that your highness has not such a one in your stables."

"Maybe I would bet, if it were not that to-day is not the time for a trial. I will keep him willingly, though; if possible, I would buy. But where is this wonder kept?"

"My men are holding him just here in front of the gate. As to his being a wonder, he is a wonder; for it is no exaggeration to say that the Sultan might covet such a horse. He is not of this country, but from Anatolia; and in Anatolia, as I think, only one such was found."

"Then let us look at him."

"I serve your highness."

Before the gate Kmita's men were holding two horses completely equipped: one was indeed of high breed, black as a raven, with a star on his forehead, and a white fetlock to a leg like a lance; he neighed slightly at sight of his master.

"I guess that to be the one," said Boguslav. "I do not know whether he is such a wonder as you say, but in truth he is a fine horse."

"Try him!" cried Kmita; "or no, I will mount him myself!"

The soldiers gave Kmita the horse; he mounted, and began to ride around near the gate. Under the skilled rider the horse seemed doubly beautiful. His prominent eyes gained brightness as he moved at a trot; he seemed to blow forth inner fire through his nostrils, while the wind unfolded his mane. Pan Kmita described a circle, changed his gait; at last he rode straight on the prince, so that the nostrils of the horse were not a yard from his face, and cried,—

"Halt!"

The horse stopped with his four feet resisting, and stood as if fixed to the ground.

"What do you say?" asked Kmita.

"The eyes and legs of a deer, the gait of a wolf, the nostrils of an elk, and the breast of a woman!" said Boguslav. "Here is all that is needed. Does he understand German command?"

"Yes; for my horse-trainer Zend, who was a Courlander, taught him."

"And the beast is swift?"

"The wind cannot come up with him; a Tartar cannot escape him."

"Your trainer must have been a good one, for I see that the horse is highly taught."

"Is he taught? Your highness will not believe. He goes so in the rank that when the line is moving at a trot, you may let the reins drop and he will not push one half of his nose beyond the line. If your highness will be pleased to try, and if in two furlongs he will push beyond the others half a head, then I will give him as a gift."

"That would be the greatest wonder, not to advance with dropped reins."

"It is wonderful and convenient, for both hands of the rider are free. More than once have I had a sabre in one hand and a pistol in the other, and the horse went alone."

"But if the rank turns?"

"Then he will turn too without breaking the line."

"Impossible!" exclaimed the prince; "no horse will do that. I have seen in France horses of the king's musketeers, greatly trained, of purpose not to spoil the court ceremonies, but still it was necessary to guide them with reins."

"The wit of man is in this horse. Let your highness try him yourself."

"Give him here!" said the prince, after a moment's thought.

Kmita held the horse till Boguslav mounted. He sprang lightly into the saddle, and began to pat the steed on his shining neck.

"A wonderful thing," said he; "the best horses shed their hair in the autumn, but this one is as if he had come out of water. In what direction shall we go?"

"Let us move in a line, and if your highness permits, toward the forest. The road is even and broad, but in the direction of the town some wagon might come in the way."

"Let us ride toward the forest."

"Just two furlongs. Let your highness drop the reins and start on a gallop. Two men on each side, and I will ride a little behind."

"Take your places!" said the prince.

The line was formed; they turned the horses' heads from the town. The prince was in the middle.

"Forward!" said he. "On a gallop from the start,—march!"

The line shot on, and after a certain time was moving like a whirlwind. A cloud of dust hid them from the eyes of the attendants and equerries, who, collecting in a crowd at the gate, looked with curiosity at the racing. The trained horses going at the highest speed, snorting from effort, had run already a furlong or more; and the prince's steed, though not held by the reins, did not push forward an inch. They ran another furlong. Kmita turned, and seeing behind only a cloud of dust, through which the starosta's house could barely be seen, and the people standing before it not at all, cried with a terrible voice,—

"Take him!"

At this moment Biloüs and the gigantic Zavratynski seized both arms of the prince, and squeezed them till the bones cracked in their joints, and holding him in their iron fists, put spurs to their own horses.

483

The prince's horse in the middle held the line, neither pushing ahead nor holding back an inch. Astonishment, fright, the whirlwind beating in his face, deprived Prince Boguslav of speech for the first moment. He struggled once and a second time,—without result, however, for pain from his twisted arms pierced him through.

"What is this, ruffians? Know ye not who I am?" cried he at last.

Thereupon Kmita pushed him with the barrel of the pistol between the shoulders. "Resistance is useless; it will only bring a bullet in your body!" cried he.

"Traitor!" said the prince.

"But who are you?" asked Kmita.

And they galloped on farther.

CHAPTER XXVII.

They ran long through the pine-forest with such speed that the trees by the roadside seemed to flee backward in panic; inns, huts of forest guards, pitch-clearings, flashed by, and at times wagons singly or a few together, going to Pilvishki. From time to time Boguslav bent forward in the saddle as if to struggle; but his arms were only wrenched the more painfully in the iron hands of the soldiers, while Pan Andrei held the pistol-barrel between the princess shoulders again, and they rushed on till the white foam was falling in flakes from the horses.

At last they were forced to slacken the speed, for breath failed both men and beasts, and Pilvishki was so far behind that all possibility of pursuit had ceased. They rode on then a certain time at a walk and in silence, surrounded by a cloud of steam, which was issuing from the horses.

For a long time the prince said nothing; he was evidently trying to calm himself and cool his blood. When he had done this he asked,—

"Whither are you taking me?"

"Your highness will know that at the end of the road," answered Kmita.

Boguslav was silent, but after a while said, "Cavalier, command these trash to let me go, for they are pulling out my arms. If you command them to do so, they will only hang; if not, they will go to the stake."

"They are nobles, not trash," answered Kmita; "and as to the punishment which your highness threatens, it is not known whom death will strike first."

"Know ye on whom ye have raised hands?" asked the prince, turning to the soldiers.

"We know," answered they.

"By a million horned devils!" cried Boguslav, with an outburst. "Will you command these people to let me go, or not?"

"Your highness, I will order them to bind your arms behind your back; then you will be quieter."

"Impossible! You will put my arms quite out of joint."

"I would give orders to let another off on his word that he would not try to escape, but you know how to break your word," said Kmita.

"I will give another word," answered the prince,—"that not only will I escape at the first opportunity, but I will have you torn apart with horses, when you fall into my hands."

"What God wants to give, he gives!" said Kmita. "But I prefer a sincere threat to a lying promise. Let go his hands, only hold his horse by the bridle; but, your highness, look here! I have but to touch the trigger to put a bullet into your body, and I shall not miss, for I never miss. Sit quietly; do not try to escape."

"I do not care, Cavalier, for you or your pistol."

When he had said this, the prince stretched his aching arms, to straighten them and shake off the numbness. The soldiers caught the horse's bridle on both sides, and led him on.

After a while Boguslav said, "You dare not look me in the eyes, Pan Kmita; you hide in the rear."

"Indeed!" answered Kmita; and urging forward his horse, he pushed Zavratynski away, and seizing the reins of the prince's horse, he looked Boguslav straight in the face. "And how is my horse? Have I added even one virtue?"

"A good horse!" answered the prince. "If you wish, I will buy him."

"This horse deserves a better fate than to carry a traitor till his death."

"You are a fool, Pan Kmita."

"Yes, for I believed the Radzivills."

Again came a moment of silence, which was broken by the prince.

"Tell me, Pan Kmita, are you sure that you are in your right mind, that your reason has not left you? Have you asked yourself what you have done, madman? Has it not come to your head that as things are now it would have been better for you if your mother had not given you birth, and that no one, not only in Poland, but in all Europe, would have ventured on such a dare-devil deed?"

"Then it is clear that there is no great courage in that Europe, for I have carried off your highness, hold you, and will not let you go."

"It can only be an affair with a madman," said the prince, as if to himself.

"My gracious prince," answered Pan Andrei, "you are in my hands; be reconciled to that, and waste not words in vain.

Pursuit will not come up, for your men think to this moment that you have come off with me voluntarily. When my men took you by the arms no one saw it, for the dust covered us; and even if there were no dust, neither the equerries nor the guards could have seen, it was so far. They will wait for you two hours; the third hour they will be impatient, the fourth and fifth uneasy, and the sixth will send out men in search; but we meanwhile shall be beyond Maryapole."

"What of that?"

"This, that they will not pursue; and even if they should start immediately in pursuit, your horses are just from the road, while ours are fresh. Even if by some miracle they should come up, that would not save you, for, as truly as you see me here, I should open your head,—which I shall do if nothing else is possible. This is the position! Radzivill has a court, an army, cannon, dragoons; Kmita has six men, and Kmita holds Radzivill by the neck."

"What further?" asked the prince.

"Nothing further! We will go where it pleases me. Thank God, your highness, that you are alive; for were it not that I gave orders to throw many gallons of water on my head to-day, you would be in the other world already, that is, in hell, for two reasons,—as a traitor and as a Calvinist."

"And would you have dared to do that?"

"Without praising myself I say that your highness would not easily find an undertaking on which I would not venture; you have the best proof of that in yourself."

The prince looked carefully at the young man and said, "Cavalier, the devil has written on your face that you are ready for anything, and that is the reason why I have a proof in myself. I tell you, indeed, that you have been able to astonish me with your boldness, and that is no easy thing."

487

"That's all one to me. Give thanks to God, your highness, that you are alive yet, and quits."

"No, Cavalier. First of all, do you thank God; for if one hair had fallen from my head, then know that the Radzivills would find you even under the earth. If you think that because there is disunion between us and those of Nyesvyej and Olyta, and that they will not pursue you, you are mistaken. Radzivill blood must be avenged, an awful example must be given, otherwise there would be no life for us in this Commonwealth. You cannot hide abroad, either: the Emperor of Germany will give you up, for I am a prince of the German Empire; the Elector of Brandenburg is my uncle; the Prince of Orange is his brother-in-law; the King and Queen of France and their ministers are my friends. Where will you hide? The Turks and Tartars will sell you, though we had to give them half our fortune. You will not find on earth a corner, nor such deserts, nor such people—"

"It is a wonder to me," replied Kmita, "that your highness takes such thought in advance for my safety. A great person a Radzivill! Still I have only to touch a trigger."

"I do not deny that. More than once it has happened in the world that a great man died at the hands of a common one. A camp-follower killed Pompey; French kings perished at the hands of low people. Without going farther, the same thing happened to my great father. But I ask you what will come next?"

"What is that to me? I have never taken much thought of what will be to-morrow. If it comes to close quarters with all the Radzivills, God knows who will be warmed up best. The sword has been long hanging over my head, but the moment I close my eyes I sleep as sweetly as a suslik. And if one Radzivill is not enough for me, I will carry off a second, and a third."

"As God is dear to me, Cavalier, you please me much; for I repeat that you alone in Europe could dare a deed like this. The beast does not care, nor mind what will come to-morrow. I love daring people, and there are fewer and fewer of them in the world. Just think! he has carried off a Radzivill and holds him as his own. Where were you reared in this fashion, Cavalier? Whence do you come?"

"I am banneret of Orsha."

"Pan Banneret of Orsha, I grieve that the Radzivills are losing a man like you, for with such men much might be done. If it were not a question of myself—h'm! I would spare nothing to win you."

"Too late!" said Kmita.

"That is to be understood," answered the prince. "Much too late! But I tell you beforehand that I will order you only to be shot, for you are worthy to die a soldier's death. What an incarnate devil to carry me off from the midst of my men!"

Kmita made no answer; the prince meditated awhile, then cried,—

"If you free me at once, I will not take vengeance. Only give me your word that you will tell no one of this, and command your men to be silent."

"Impossible!" replied Kmita.

"Do you want a ransom?"

"I do not."

"What the devil, then, did you carry me off for? I cannot understand it."

"It would take a long time to tell. I will tell your highness later."

"But what have we to do on the road unless to talk? Acknowledge, Cavalier, one thing: you carried me off in a moment of anger and desperation, and now you don't know well what to do with me."

"That is my affair!" answered Kmita; "and if I do not know what to do, it will soon be seen."

Impatience was depicted on Prince Boguslav's face.

"You are not over-communicative, Pan Banneret of Orsha; but answer me one question at least sincerely: Did you come to me, to Podlyasye, with a plan already formed of attacking my person, or did it enter your head in the last moment?"

"To that I can answer your highness sincerely, for my lips are burning to tell you why I left your cause; and while I am alive, while there is breath in my body, I shall not return to it. The prince voevoda of Vilna deceived me, and in advance brought me to swear on the crucifix that I would not leave him till death."

"And you are keeping the oath well. There is nothing to be said on that point."

"True!" cried Kmita, violently. "If I have lost my soul, if I must be damned, it is through the Radzivills. But I give myself to the mercy of God, and I would rather lose my soul, I would rather burn eternally, than to sin longer with knowledge and willingly,—than to serve longer, knowing that I serve sin and treason. May God have mercy on me! I prefer to burn, I prefer a hundred times to burn; I should burn surely, if I remained with you. I have nothing to lose; but at least I shall say at the judgment of God: 'I knew not what I was swearing, and had I discovered that I had sworn treason to the country, destruction to the Polish name, I should have broken the oath right there.' Now let the Lord God be my judge."

"To the question, to the question!" said Boguslav, calmly.

But Pan Andrei breathed heavily, and rode on some time in silence, with frowning brow and eyes fixed on the earth, like a man bowed down by misfortune.

"To the question!" repeated the prince.

Kmita roused himself as if from a dream, shook his head, and said,—

"I believed the prince hetman as I would not have believed my own father. I remember that banquet at which he announced his union with the Swedes. What I suffered then, what I passed through, God will account to me. Others, honorable men, threw their batons at his feet and remained with their country; but I stood like a stump with the baton, with shame, with submission, with infamy, in torture, for I was called traitor to my eyes. And who called me traitor? Oi, better not say, lest I forget myself, go mad, and put a bullet right here in the head of your highness. You are the men, you the traitors, the Judases, who brought me to that."

Here Kmita gazed with a terrible expression on the prince, and hatred came out on his face from the bottom of his soul, like a dragon which had crawled out of a cave to the light of day; but Boguslav looked at the young man with a calm, fearless eye. At last he said,—

"But that interests me, Pan Kmita; speak on."

Kmita dropped the bridle of the prince's horse, and removed his cap as if wishing to cool his burning head.

"That same night," continued he, "I went to the hetman, for he gave command to call me. I thought to myself, 'I will renounce his service, break my oath, suffocate him, choke him with these hands, blow up Kyedani with powder, and then let happen what may.' He knew too that was ready for anything, knew what I was; I saw well that he was fingering a box in which there were pistols. 'That is nothing,' thought I to myself; 'either he will miss me or he will kill me.' But he began to reason, to speak, to show such a prospect to me, simpleton, and put himself forward as such a savior, that your highness knows what happened."

491

"He convinced the young man," said Boguslav.

"So that I fell at his feet," cried Kmita, "and saw in him the father, the one savior, of the country; so that I gave myself to him soul and body as to a devil. For him, for his honesty I was ready to hurl myself headlong from the tower of Kyedani."

"I thought such would be the end," said Boguslav.

"What I lost in his cause I will not say, but I rendered him important services. I held in obedience my squadron, which is in Kyedani now,—God grant to his ruin! Others, who mutinied, I cut up badly. I stained my hands in brothers' blood, believing that a stern necessity for the country. Often my soul was pained at giving command to shoot honest soldiers; often the nature of a noble rebelled against him, when one time and another he promised something and did not keep his word. But I thought: 'I am simple, he is wise!—it must be done so.' But to-day, when I learned for the first time from those letters of the poisons, the marrow stiffened in my bones. How? Is this the kind of war? You wish to poison soldiers? And that is to be in hetman fashion? That is to be the Radzivill method, and am I to carry such letters?"

"You know nothing of politics, Cavalier," interrupted Boguslav.

"May the thunders crush it! Let the criminal Italians practise it, not a noble whom God has adorned with more honorable blood than others, but at the same time obliged him to war with a sabre and not with a drug-shop."

"These letters, then, so astonished you that you determined to leave the Radzivills?"

"It was not the letters,—I might have thrown them to the hangman, or tossed them into the fire, for they refer not to my duties; it was not the letters. I might have refused the mission without leaving the cause. Do I know what I might have done? I might have joined the dragoons, or collected a party again, and

492

harried Hovanski as before. But straightway a suspicion came to me: 'But do they not wish to poison the country as well as those soldiers?' God granted me not to break out, though my head was burning like a grenade, to remember myself, to have the power to think: 'Draw him by the tongue, and discover the whole truth; betray not what you have at heart, give yourself out as worse than the Radzivills themselves, and draw him by the tongue.'"

"Whom,—me?"

"Yes! God aided me, so that I, simple man, deceived a politician,—so that your highness, holding me the last of ruffians, hid nothing of your own ruffianism, confessed everything, told everything, as if it had been written on the hand. The hair stood on my head, but I listened and listened to the end. O traitors! arch hell-dwellers! O parricides! How is it, that a thunderbolt has not stricken you down before now? How is it that the earth has not swallowed you? So you are treating with Hmelnitski, with the Swedes, with the elector, with Rakotsy, and with the devil himself to the destruction of this Commonwealth? Now you want to cut a mantle out of it for yourself, to sell it to divide it, to tear your own mother like wolves? Such is your gratitude for all the benefits heaped on you,—for the offices, the honors, the dignities, the wealth, the authority, the estates which foreign kings envy you? And you were ready without regard to those tears, torments, oppression. Where is your conscience, where your faith, where your honesty? What monster brought you into the world?"

"Cavalier," interrupted Boguslav, coldly, "you have me in your hand, you can kill me; but I beg one thing, do not bore me."

Both were silent.

However, it appeared plainly, from the words of Kmita, that the soldier had been able to draw out the naked truth from the diplomat, and that the prince was guilty of great incautiousness, of a great error in betraying his most secret plans and those of the hetman. This pricked his vanity; therefore, not caring to hide his ill-humor, he said,—

"Do not ascribe it to your own wit merely, Pan Kmita, that you got the truth from me. I spoke openly, for I thought the prince voevoda knew people better, and had sent a man worthy of confidence."

"The prince voevoda sent a man worthy of confidence," answered Kmita, "but you have lost him. Henceforth only scoundrels will serve you."

"If the way in which you seized me was not scoundrelly, then may the sword grow to my hand in the first battle."

"It was a stratagem! I learned it in a hard school. You wish, your highness, to know Kmita. Here he is! I shall not go with empty hands to our gracious lord."

"And you think that a hair of my head will fall from the hand of Yan Kazimir?"

"That is a question for the judges, not for me."

Suddenly Kmita reined in his horse: "But the letter of the prince voevoda,—have you that letter on your person?"

"If I had, I would not give it. The letter remained in Pilvishki."

"Search him!" cried Kmita.

The soldiers seized the prince again by the arms. Soroka began to search his pockets. After a while he found the letter.

"Here is one document against you and your works," said Pan Andrei, taking the letter. "The King of Poland will know from it what you have in view; the Swedish King will know too, that although now you are serving him, the prince voevoda reserves to himself freedom to withdraw if the Swedish foot stumbles. All your treasons will come out, all your machinations. But I have, besides, other letters,—to the King of Sweden, to Wittemberg, to Radzeyovski. You are great and powerful; still I am not sure that it will not be too narrow for you in this Commonwealth, when both kings will prepare a recompense worthy of your treasons."

Prince Boguslav's eyes gleamed with ill-omened light, but after a while he mastered his anger and said,—

"Well, Cavalier! For life or death between us! We have met! You may cause us trouble and much evil, but I say this: No man has dared hitherto to do in this country what you have done. Woe be to you and to yours!"

"I have a sabre to defend myself, and I have something to redeem my own with," answered Kmita.

"You have me as a hostage," said the prince.

And in spite of all his anger he breathed calmly; he understood one thing at this moment, that in no case was his life threatened,—that his person was too much needed by Kmita.

Then they went again at a trot, and after an hour's ride they saw two horsemen, each of whom led a pair of packhorses. They were Kmita's men sent in advance from Pilvishki.

"What is the matter?" asked Kmita.

"The horses are terribly tired, for we have not rested yet."

"We shall rest right away!"

"There is a cabin at the turn, maybe 'tis a public house."

"Let the sergeant push on to prepare oats. Public house or not, we must halt."

"According to order, Commander."

Soroka gave reins to the horses, and they followed him slowly. Kmita rode at one side of the prince, Lubyenyets at the other. Boguslav had become completely calm and quiet; he did not draw Pan Andrei into further conversation. He seemed to be exhausted by the journey, or by the position in which he found himself, and dropping his head somewhat on his breast, closed his eyes. Still from time to time he cast a side look now at Kmita, now at Lubyenyets, who held the reins of the horse, as if studying to discover who would be the easier to overturn so as to wrest himself free.

They approached the building situated on the roadside at a bulge of the forest. It was not a public house, but a forge and a wheelwright-shop, in which those going by the road stopped to shoe their horses and mend their wagons. Between the forge and the road there was a small open area, sparsely covered with trampled grass; fragments of wagons and broken wheels lay thrown here and there on that place, but there were no travellers. Soroka's horses stood tied to a post. Soroka himself was talking before the forge to the blacksmith, a Tartar, and two of his assistants.

"We shall not have an over-abundant repast," said the prince; "there is nothing to be had here."

"We have food and spirits with us," answered Kmita.

"That is well! We shall need strength."

They halted. Kmita thrust his pistol behind his belt, sprang from the saddle, and giving his horse to Soroka, seized again the reins of the prince's horse, which however Lubyenyets had not let go from his hand on the other side.

"Your highness will dismount!" said Kmita.

"Why is that? I will eat and drink in the saddle," said the prince, bending down.

"I beg you to come to the ground!" said Kmita, threateningly.

"But into the ground with you!" cried the prince, with a terrible voice; and drawing with the quickness of lightning the pistol from Kmita's belt, he thundered into his very face.

"Jesus, Mary!" cried Kmita.

At this moment the horse under the prince struck with spurs reared so that he stood almost erect; the prince turned like a snake in the saddle toward Lubyenyets, and with all the strength of his powerful arm struck him with the pistol between the eyes.

Lubyenyets roared terribly and fell from the horse.

Before the others could understand what had happened, before they had drawn breath, before the cry of fright had died on their lips, Boguslav scattered them as a storm would have done, rushed from the square to the road, and shot on like a whirlwind toward Pilvishki.

"Seize him! Hold him! Kill him!" cried wild voices.

Three soldiers who were sitting yet on the horses rushed after him; but Soroka seized a musket standing at the wall, and aimed at the fleeing man, or rather at his horse.

The horse stretched out like a deer, and moved forward like an arrow urged from the string. The shot thundered. Soroka rushed through the smoke for a better view of what he had done; he shaded his eyes with his hand, gazed awhile, and cried at last,—

"Missed!"

At this moment Boguslav disappeared beyond the bend, and after him vanished the pursuers.

Then Soroka turned to the blacksmith and his assistants, who were looking up to that moment with dumb astonishment at what had happened, and cried,—

"Water!"

The blacksmith ran to draw water, and Soroka knelt near Pan Andrei, who was lying motionless. Kmita's face was covered with powder from the discharge, and with drops of blood; his eyes were closed, his left brow and left temple were blackened. The sergeant began first to feel lightly with his fingers the head of his colonel.

"His head is sound."

But Kmita gave no signs of life, and blood came abundantly from his face. The blacksmith's assistants brought a bucket of water and a cloth. Soroka, with equal deliberation and care, began to wipe Kmita's face.

Finally the wound appeared from under the blood and blackness. The ball had opened Kmita's left cheek deeply, and had carried away the end of his ear. Soroka examined to see if his cheek-bone were broken.

After a while he convinced himself that it was not, and drew a long breath. Kmita, under the influence of cold water and pain, began to give signs of life. His face quivered, his breast heaved with breath.

"He is alive!—nothing! he will be unharmed," cried Soroka, joyfully; and a tear rolled down the murderous face of the sergeant.

Meanwhile at the turn of the road appeared Biloüs, one of the three soldiers who had followed the prince.

"Well, what?" called Soroka.

The soldier shook his head. "Nothing!"

"Will the others return soon?"

"The others will not return."

With trembling hands the sergeant laid Kmita's head on the threshold of the forge, and sprang to his feet. "How is that?"

"Sergeant, that prince is a wizard! Zavratynski caught up first, for he had the best horse, and because the prince let him catch up. Before our eyes Boguslav snatched the sabre from his hand and thrust him through. We had barely to cry out. Vitkovski was next, and sprang to help; and him this Radzivill cut down before my eyes, as if a thunderbolt had struck him. He did not give a sound. I did not wait my turn. Sergeant, the prince is ready to come back here."

498

"There is nothing in this place for us," said Soroka. "To horse!"

That moment they began to make a stretcher between the horses for Kmita. Two of the soldiers, at the command of Soroka, stood with muskets on the road, fearing the return of the terrible man.

But Prince Boguslav, convinced that Kmita was not alive, rode quietly to Pilvishki. About dark he was met by a whole detachment of horsemen sent out by Patterson, whom the absence of the prince had disturbed for some time. The officer, on seeing the prince, galloped to him,—

"Your highness, we did not know—"

"That is nothing!" interrupted Prince Boguslav. "I was riding this horse in the company of that cavalier, of whom I bought him."

And after a while he added: "I paid him well."

CHAPTER XXVIII.

The trusty Soroka carried his colonel through the deep forest, not knowing himself what to begin, whither to go or to turn.

Kmita was not only wounded, but stunned by the shot. Soroka from time to time moistened the piece of cloth in a bucket hanging by the horse, and washed his face; at times he halted to take fresh water from the streams and forest ponds; but neither halts nor the movement of the horse could restore at once consciousness to Pan Andrei, and he lay as if dead, till the soldiers going with him, and less experienced in the matter of wounds than Soroka, began to be alarmed for the life of their colonel.

"He is alive," answered Soroka; "in three days he will be on horseback like any of us."

In fact, an hour later, Kmita opened his eyes; but from his mouth came forth one word only,—

"Drink!"

Soroka held a cup of pure water to his lips; but it seemed that to open his mouth caused Pan Andrei unendurable pain, and he was unable to drink. But he did not lose consciousness: he asked for nothing, apparently remembered nothing; his eyes were wide open, and he gazed, without attention, toward the depth of the forest, on the streaks of blue sky visible through the dense branches above their heads, and at his comrades, like a man roused from sleep, or like one recovered from drunkenness, and permitted Soroka to take care of him without saying a word,— nay, the cold water with which the sergeant washed the wound seemed to give him pleasure, for at times his eyes smiled. But Soroka comforted him,—

"To-morrow the dizziness will pass, Colonel; God grant recovery."

In fact, dizziness began to disappear toward evening; for just before the setting of the sun Kmita seemed more self-possessed and asked on a sudden, "What noise is that?"

"What noise? There is none," answered Soroka.

Apparently the noise was only in the head of Pan Andrei, for the evening was calm. The setting sun, piercing the gloom with its slanting rays, filled with golden glitter the forest darkness, and lighted the red trunks of the pine-trees. There was no wind, and only here and there, from hazel, birch, and hornbeam trees leaves dropped to the ground, or timid beasts made slight rustle in fleeing to the depths of the forest in front of the horsemen.

The evening was cool; but evidently fever had begun to attack Pan Andrei, for he repeated,—

"Your highness, it is life or death between us!"

At last it became dark altogether, and Soroka was thinking of a night camp; but because they had entered a damp forest and the ground began to yield under the hoofs of their horses, they continued to ride in order to reach high and dry places.

They rode one hour and a second without being able to pass the swamp. Meanwhile it was growing lighter, for the moon had risen. Suddenly Soroka, who was in advance, sprang from the saddle and began to look carefully at the ground.

"Horses have passed this way," said he, at sight of tracks in the soft earth.

"Who could have passed, when there is no road?" asked one of the soldiers supporting Pan Kmita.

"But there are tracks, and a whole crowd of them! Look here between the pines,—as evident as on the palm of the hand!"

"Perhaps cattle have passed."

"Impossible. It is not the time of forest pastures; horse-hoofs are clearly to be seen, somebody must have passed. It would be well to find even a forester's cabin."

"Let us follow the trail."

"Let us ride forward!"

Soroka mounted again and rode on. Horses' tracks in the turfy ground were more distinct; and some of them, as far as could be seen in the light of the moon, seemed quite fresh. Still the horses sank to their knees, and beyond. The soldiers were afraid that they could not wade through, or would come to some deeper quagmire; when, at the end of half an hour, the odor of smoke and rosin came to their nostrils.

"There must be a pitch-clearing here," said Soroka.

"Yes, sparks are to be seen," said a soldier.

And really in the distance appeared a line of reddish smoke, filled with flame, around which were dancing the sparks of a fire burning under the ground.

When they had approached, the soldiers saw a cabin, a well, and a strong shed built of pine logs. The horses, wearied from the road, began to neigh; frequent neighing answered them from under the shed, and at the same time there stood before the riders some kind of a figure, dressed in sheepskin, wool outward.

"Are there many horses?" asked the man in the sheepskin.

"Is this a pitch-factory?" inquired Soroka.

"What kind of people are ye? Where do ye come from?" asked the pitch-maker, in a voice in which astonishment and alarm were evident.

"Never fear!" answered Soroka; "we are not robbers."

"Go your own way; there is nothing for you here."

"Shut thy mouth, and guide us to the house since we ask. Seest not, scoundrel, that we are taking a wounded man?"

"What kind of people are ye?"

"Be quick, or we answer from guns. It will be better for thee to hurry. Take us to the house; if not, we will cook thee in thy own pitch."

"I cannot defend myself alone, but there will be more of us. Ye will lay down your lives here."

"There will be more of us too; lead on!"

"Go on yourselves; it is not my affair."

"What thou hast to eat, give us, and gorailka. We are carrying a man who will pay."

"If he leaves here alive."

Thus conversing, they entered the cabin; a fire was burning in the chimney, and from pots, hanging by the handles, came the odor of boiling meat. The cabin was quite large. Soroka saw at the walls six wooden beds, covered thickly with sheepskins.

"This is the resort of some company," muttered he to his comrades. "Prime your guns and watch well. Take care of this scoundrel, let him not slip away. The owners sleep outside to-night, for we shall not leave the house."

"The men will not come to-day," said the pitch-maker.

"That is better, for we shall not quarrel about room, and to-morrow we will go on," replied Soroka; "but now dish the meat, for we are hungry, and spare no oats on the horses."

"Where can oats be found here, great mighty soldiers?"

"We heard horses under the shed, so there must be oats; thou dost not feed them with pitch."

"They are not my horses."

"Whether they are yours or not, they must eat as well as ours. Hurry, man, hurry! if thy skin is dear to thee!"

The pitch-maker said nothing. The soldiers entered the house, placed the sleeping Kmita on a bed, and sat down to supper. They ate eagerly the boiled meat and cabbage, a large kettle of which was in the chimney. There was millet also, and in a room at the side of the cabin Soroka found a large decanter of spirits.

He merely strengthened himself with it slightly, and gave none to the soldiers, for he had determined to hold it in reserve for the night. This empty house with six beds for men, and a shed in which a band of horses were neighing, seemed to him strange and suspicious. He judged simply that this was a robbers' retreat, especially since in the room from which he brought the decanter he found many weapons hanging on the wall, and a keg of powder, with various furniture, evidently plundered from noble houses. In case the absent occupants of the cabin returned, it was impossible to expect from them not merely hospitality, but even mercy. Soroka therefore resolved to hold the house with armed hand, and maintain himself in it by superior force or negotiations.

This was imperative also in view of the health of Pan Kmita, for whom a journey might be fatal, and in view of the safety of all.

Soroka was a trained and seasoned soldier, to whom one feeling was foreign,—the feeling of fear. Still in that moment, at thought of Prince Boguslav, fear seized him. Having been for long years in the service of Kmita, he had blind faith, not only in the valor, but the fortune of the man; he had seen more than once deeds of his which in daring surpassed every measure, and touched almost on madness, but which still succeeded and passed without harm. With Kmita he had gone through the "raids" on Hovanski; had taken part in all the surprises, attacks, fights, and onsets, and had come to the conviction that Pan Andrei could do all things, succeed in all things, come out of every chaos, and destroy whomsoever he wished. Kmita therefore was for him the highest impersonation of power and fortune,—but this time he had met his match seemingly, nay, he had met his superior. How was this? One man carried away, without weapons, and in Kmita's hands, had freed himself from those hands; not only that, he had overthrown Kmita, conquered his soldiers, and terrified them so that they ran away in fear of his return. That was a wonder of wonders, and Soroka lost his head pondering over it. To his thinking, anything might come to pass in the world rather than this, that a man might be found who could ride over Kmita.

"Has our fortune then ended?" muttered he to himself, gazing around in wonder.

It was not long since with eyes shut he followed Pan Kmita to Hovanski's quarters surrounded by eighty thousand men; now at the thought of that long-haired prince with lady's eyes and a painted face, superstitious terror seized him, and he knew not what to do. The thought alarmed him, that to-morrow or the next day he would have to travel on highways where the

504

terrible prince himself or his pursuers might meet him. This was the reason why he had gone from the road to the dense forest, and at present wished to stay in that cabin until pursuers were deluded and wearied.

But since even that hiding-place did not seem to him safe for other reasons, he wished to discover what course to take; therefore he ordered the soldiers to stand guard at the door and the windows, and said to the pitch-maker,—

"Here, man, take a lantern and come with me."

"I can light the great mighty lord only with a pitch-torch, for we have no lantern."

"Then light the torch; if thou burn the shed and the horses, it is all one to me."

After such words a lantern was found right away. Soroka commanded the fellow to go ahead, and followed himself with a pistol in his hand.

"Who live in this cabin?" asked he on the road.

"Men live here."

"What are their names?"

"That is not free for me to say."

"It seems to me, fellow, that thou'lt get a bullet in thy head."

"My master," answered the pitch-maker, "if I had told in a lie any kind of name, you would have to be satisfied."

"True! But are there many of those men?"

"There is an old one, two sons, and two servants."

"Are they nobles?"

"Surely nobles."

"Do they live here?"

"Sometimes here, and sometimes God knows where."

"But the horses, whence are they?"

"God knows whence they bring them."

"Tell the truth; do thy masters not rob on the highway?"

"Do I know? It seems to me they take horses, but whose,—that's not on my head."

"What do they do with the horses?"

"Sometimes they take ten or twelve of them, as many as there are, and drive them away, but whither I know not."

Thus conversing, they reached the shed, from which was heard the snorting of horses.

"Hold the light," said Soroka.

The fellow raised the lantern, and threw light on the horses standing in a row at the wall. Soroka examined them one after another with the eye of a specialist, shook his head, smacked his lips, and said,—

"The late Pan Zend would have rejoiced. There are Polish and Muscovite horses here,—there is a Wallachian, a German,—a mare. Fine horses! What dost thou give them to eat?"

"Not to lie, my master, I sowed two fields with oats in springtime."

"Then thy masters have been handling horses since spring?"

"No, but they sent a servant to me with a command."

"Then art thou theirs?"

"I was till they went to the war."

"What war?"

"Do I know? They went far away last year, and came back in the summer."

"Whose art thou now?"

"These are the king's forests."

"Who put thee here to make pitch?"

"The royal forester, a relative of these men, who also brought horses with them; but since he went away once with them, he has not come back."

"And do guests come to these men?"

"Nobody comes here, for there are swamps around, and only one road. It is a wonder to me that ye could come, my master; for whoso does not strike the road, will be drawn in by the swamp."

Soroka wanted to answer that he knew these woods and the road very well; but after a moment's thought he determined that silence was better, and inquired,—

"Are these woods very great?"

The fellow did not understand the question. "How is that?"

"Do they go far?"

"Oh! who has gone through them? Where one ends another begins, and God knows where they are not; I have never been in that place."

"Very well!" said Soroka.

Then he ordered the man to go back to the cabin, and followed himself.

On the way he was pondering over what he should do, and hesitated. On one hand the wish came to him to take the horses while the cabin-dwellers were gone, and flee with this plunder. The booty was precious, and the horses pleased the old soldier's heart greatly; but after a while he overcame the temptation. To take them was easy, but what to do further. Swamps all around, one egress,—how hit upon that? Chance had served him once, but perhaps it would not a second time. To follow the trail of hoofs was useless, for the cabin-dwellers had surely wit enough to make by design false and treacherous trails leading straight into quagmires. Soroka knew clearly the methods of men who steal horses, and of those who take booty.

He thought awhile, therefore, and meditated; all at once he struck his head with his fist,—

"I am a fool!" muttered he. "I'll take the fellow on a rope, and make him lead me to the highway."

Barely had he uttered the last word when he shuddered, "To the highway? But that prince will be there, and pursuit. To lose fifteen horses!" said the old fox to himself, with as much sorrow as if he had cared for the beasts from their colthood. "It must be that our fortune is ended. We must stay in the cabin till Pan Kmita recovers,—stay with consent of the owners or without their consent; and what will come later, that is work for the colonel's head."

Thus meditating, he returned to the cabin. The watchful soldiers were standing at the door, and though they saw a lantern shining in the dark from a distance,—the same lantern with which Soroka and the pitch-maker had gone out,—still they forced them to tell who they were before they let them enter the cabin. Soroka ordered his soldiers to change the watch about midnight, and threw himself down on the plank bed beside Kmita.

It had become quiet in the cabin; only the crickets raised their usual music in the adjoining closet, and the mice gnawed from moment to moment among the rubbish piled up there. The sick man woke at intervals and seemed to have dreams in his fever, for to Soroka's ears came the disconnected words,—

"Gracious king, pardon—Those men are traitors—I will tell all their secrets—The Commonwealth is a red cloth—Well, I have you, worthy prince—Hold him!—Gracious king, this way, for there is treason!"

Soroka rose on the bed and listened; but the sick man, when he had screamed once and a second time, fell asleep, and then woke and cried,—

"Olenka, Olenka, be not angry!"

About midnight he grew perfectly calm and slept soundly. Soroka also began to slumber; but soon a gentle knocking at the door of the cabin roused him.

The watchful soldier opened his eyes at once, and springing to his feet went out.

"But what is the matter?" asked he.

"Sergeant, the pitch-maker has escaped."

"A hundred devils! he'll bring robbers to us right away."

"Who was watching him?"

"Biloüs."

"I went with him to water our horses," said Biloüs, explaining. "I ordered him to draw the water, and held the horses myself."

"And what? Did he jump into the well?"

"No, Sergeant, but between the logs, of which there are many near the well, and into the stump-holes. I let the horses go; for though they scattered there are others here, and sprang after him, but I fell into the first hole. It was night,—dark; the scoundrel knows the place, and ran away. May the pest strike him!"

"He will bring those devils here to us,—he'll bring them. May the thunderbolts split him!"

The sergeant stopped, but after a while said,—

"We will not lie down; we must watch till morning. Any moment a crowd may come."

And giving an example to the others, he took his place on the threshold of the cabin with a musket in his hand. The soldiers sat near him talking in an undertone, listening sometimes to learn if in the night sounds of the pine-woods the tramp and snort of coming horses could reach them.

It was a moonlight night, and calm, but noisy. In the forest depths life was seething. It was the season of mating; therefore the wilderness thundered with terrible bellowing of stags. These sounds, short, hoarse, full of anger and rage, were heard round about in all parts of the forest, distant and near,—sometimes right there, as if a hundred yards from the cabin.

"If men come, they will bellow too, to mislead us," said Biloüs.

"Eh! they will not come to-night. Before the pitch-maker finds them 'twill be day," said the other soldiers.

"In the daytime, Sergeant, it would be well to examine the cabin and dig under the walls; for if robbers dwell here there must be treasures."

"The best treasures are in that stable," said Soroka, pointing with his finger to the shed.

"But we'll take them?"

"Ye are fools! there is no way out,—nothing but swamps all around."

"But we came in."

"God guided us. A living soul cannot come here or leave here without knowing the road."

"We will find it in the daytime."

"We shall not find it, for tracks are made everywhere purposely, and the trails are misleading. It was not right to let the man go."

"It is known that the highroad is a day's journey distant, and in that direction," said Biloüs.

Here he pointed with his finger to the eastern part of the forest.

"We will ride on till we pass through,—that's what we'll do! You think that you will be a lord when you touch the highway? Better the bullet of a robber here than a rope there."

"How is that, father?" asked Biloüs.

"They are surely looking for us there."

"Who, father?"

"The prince."

Soroka was suddenly silent; and after him were silent the others, as if seized with fear.

"Oi!" said Biloüs, at last. "It is bad here and bad there; though you twist, you can't turn."

"They have driven us poor devils into a net; here robbers, and there the prince," said another soldier.

"May the thunderbolts burn them there! I would rather have to do with a robber than with a wizard," added Biloüs; "for that prince is possessed, yes, possessed. Zavratynski could wrestle with a bear, and the prince took the sword from his hands as from a child. It can only be that he enchanted him, for I saw, too, that when he rushed at Vitkovski Boguslav grew up before the eyes to the size of a pine-tree. If he had not, I shouldn't have let him go alive."

"But you were a fool not to jump at him."

"What had I to do, Sergeant? I thought this way: he is sitting on the best horse; if he wishes, he will run away, but if he attacks me I shall not be able to defend myself, for with a wizard is a power not human! He becomes invisible to the eye or surrounds himself with dust—"

"That is truth," answered Soroka; "for when I fired at him he was surrounded as it were by a fog, and I missed. Any man mounted may miss when the horse is moving, but on the ground that has not happened to me for ten years."

"What's the use in talking?" said Biloüs, "better count: Lyubyenyets, Vitkovski, Zavratynski, our colonel; and one man brought them all down, and he without arms,—such men that each of them has many a time stood against four. Without the help of the devil he could not have done this."

"Let us commend our souls to God; for if he is possessed, the devil will show him the road to this place."

"But without that he has long arms for such a lord."

"Quiet!" exclaimed Soroka, quickly; "something is making the leaves rustle."

The soldiers were quiet and bent their ears. Near by, indeed, were heard some kind of heavy steps, under which the fallen leaves rustled very clearly.

"I hear horses," whispered Soroka.

But the steps began to retreat from the cabin, and soon after was heard the threatening and hoarse bellowing of a stag.

"That is a stag! He is making himself known to a doe, or fighting off another horned fellow."

"Throughout the whole forest are entertainments as if at the wedding of Satan."

They were silent again and began to doze. The sergeant raised his head at times and listened for a while, then dropped it toward his breast. Thus passed an hour, and a second; at last the nearest pine-trees from being black became gray, and the tops grew whiter each moment, as if some one had burnished them with molten silver. The bellowing of stags ceased, and complete stillness reigned in the forest depths. Dawn passed gradually into day; the white and pale light began to absorb rosy and golden gleams; at last perfect morning had come, and lighted the tired faces of the soldiers sleeping a firm sleep at the cabin.

Then the door opened, Kmita appeared on the threshold, and called,—

"Soroka! come here!"

The soldiers sprang up.

"For God's sake, is your grace on foot?" asked Soroka.

"But you have slept like oxen; it would have been possible to cut off your heads and throw them out before any one would have been roused."

"We watched till morning, Colonel; we fell asleep only in the broad day."

Kmita looked around. "Where are we?"

"In the forest, Colonel."

"I see that myself. But what sort of a cabin is this?"

"We know not ourselves."

"Follow me," said Kmita. And he turned to the inside of the cabin. Soroka followed.

"Listen," said Kmita, sitting on the bed. "Did the prince fire at me?"

"He did."

"And what happened to him?"

"He escaped."

A moment of silence followed.

"That is bad," said Kmita, "very bad! Better to lay him down than to let him go alive."

"We wanted to do that, but—"

"But what?"

Soroka told briefly all that had happened. Kmita listened with wonderful calmness; but his eyes began to glitter, and at last he said,—

"Then he is victor; but we'll meet again. Why did you leave the highroad?"

"I was afraid of pursuit."

"That was right, for surely there was pursuit. There are too few of us now to fight against Boguslav's power,—too few. Besides, he has gone to Prussia; we cannot reach him there, we must wait—"

Soroka was relieved. Pan Kmita evidently did not fear Boguslav greatly, since he talked of overtaking him. This confidence was communicated at once to the old soldier accustomed to think with the head of his colonel and to feel with his heart.

Meanwhile Pan Andrei, who had fallen into deep thought, came to himself on a sudden, and began to seek something about his person with both his hands.

"Where are my letters?" asked he.

"What letters?"

"Letters that I had on my body. They were fastened to my belt; where is the belt?" asked Pan Andrei, in haste.

"I unbuckled the belt myself, that your grace might breathe more easily; there it is."

"Bring it."

Soroka gave him a belt lined with white leather, to which a bag was attached by cords. Kmita untied it and took out papers hastily.

"These are passes to the Swedish commandants; but where are the letters?" asked he, in a voice full of disquiet.

"What letters?" asked Soroka.

"Hundreds of thunders! the letters of the hetman to the Swedish King, to Pan Lyubomirski, and all those that I had."

"If they are not on the belt, they are nowhere. They must have been lost in the time of the riding."

"To horse and look for them!" cried Kmita, in a terrible voice.

But before the astonished Soroka could leave the room Pan Andrei sank to the bed as if strength had failed him, and seizing his head with his hands, began to repeat in a groaning voice,—

"Ai! my letters, my letters!"

Meanwhile the soldiers rode off, except one, whom Soroka commanded to guard the cabin. Kmita remained alone in the room, and began to meditate over his position, which was not deserving of envy. Boguslav had escaped. Over Pan Andrei was hanging the terrible and inevitable vengeance of the powerful Radzivills. And not only over him, but over all whom he loved, and speaking briefly, over Olenka. Kmita knew that Prince Yanush would not hesitate to strike where he could wound him most painfully,—that is, to pour out his vengeance on the person of Panna Billevich. And Olenka was still in Kyedani at the mercy of the terrible magnate, whose heart knew no pity. The more Kmita meditated over his position, the more clearly was he convinced that it was simply dreadful. After the seizure of Boguslav, the Radzivills will hold him a traitor; the adherents of Yan Kazimir, the partisans of Sapyeha, and the confederates who had risen up in Podlyasye look on him as a traitor now, and a damned soul of the Radzivills. Among the many camps, parties, and foreign troops occupying at that moment the fields of the Commonwealth, there is not a camp, a party, a body of troops which would not count him as the greatest and most malignant enemy. Indeed, the reward offered for his head by Hovanski is still in force, and now Radzivill and the Swedes will offer rewards,—and who knows if the adherents of the unfortunate Yan Kazimir have not already proclaimed one?

"I have brewed beer and must drink it," thought Kmita. When he bore away Prince Boguslav, he did so to throw him at the feet of the confederate's, to convince them beyond question that he had broken with the Radzivills, to purchase a place with them, to win the right of fighting for the king and the country. Besides, Boguslav in his hands was a hostage for the safety of Olenka. But since Boguslav has crushed Kmita and escaped, not only is Olenka's safety gone, but also the proof that Kmita has really left the service of the Radzivills. But the road to the confederates is open to him; and if he meets Volodyovski's division and his friends the colonels, they may grant him his life, but will they take him as a comrade, will they believe him, will they not think that he has appeared as a spy, or has come to tamper with their courage and bring over people to Radzivill? Here he remembered that the blood of confederates was weighing on him; that to begin with, he had struck down the Hungarians and dragoons in Kyedani, that he had scattered the mutinous squadrons or forced them to yield, that he had shot stubborn officers and exterminated soldiers, that he had surrounded Kyedani with trenches and fortified it, and thus assured the triumph of Radzivill in Jmud. "How could I go?" thought he; "the plague would in fact be a more welcome guest there than I! With Boguslav on a lariat at the saddle it would be possible; but with only my mouth and empty hands!"

If he had those letters he might join the confederates, he would have had Prince Yanush in hand, for those letters might undermine the credit of the hetman, even with the Swedes,—even with the price of them he might save Olenka; but some evil spirit had so arranged that the letters were lost.

When Kmita comprehended all this, he seized his own head a second time.

"For the Radzivills a traitor, for Olenka a traitor, for the confederate's a traitor, for the king a traitor! I have ruined my fame, my honor, myself, and Olenka!"

The wound in his face was burning, but in his soul hot pain, a hundred-fold greater, was burning him. In addition to all, his self-love as a knight was suffering. For he was shamefully beaten by Boguslav. Those slashes which Volodyovski had given him in Lyubich were nothing. There he was finished by an armed man whom he had called out in a duel, here by a defenceless prisoner whom he had in his hand.

With every moment increased in Kmita the consciousness of how terrible and shameful was the plight into which he had fallen. The longer he examined it the more clearly he saw its horror; and every moment he saw new black corners from which were peering forth infamy and shame, destruction to himself, to Olenka, wrong against the country,—till at last terror and amazement seized him.

"Have I done all this?" asked he of himself; and the hair stood on his head.

"Impossible! It must be that fever is shaking me yet," cried he. "Mother of God, this is not possible!"

"Blind, foolish quarreller," said his conscience, "this would not have come to thee in fighting for the king and the country, nor if thou hadst listened to Olenka."

And sorrow tore him like a whirlwind. Hei! if only he could say to himself: "The Swedes against the country, I against them! Radzivill against the king, I against him!" Then it would be clear and transparent in his soul. Then he might collect a body of cut-throats from under a dark star and, frolic with them as a gypsy at a fair, fall upon the Swedes, and ride over their breasts with pure heart and conscience; then he might stand in glory as in sunlight before Olenka, and say,—

"I am no longer infamous, but *defensor patriæ* (a defender of the country); love me, as I love thee."

But what was he now? That insolent spirit, accustomed to self-indulgence, would not confess to a fault altogether at first. It was the Radzivills who (according to him) had pushed him down in this fashion; it was the Radzivills who had brought him to ruin, covered him with evil repute, bound his hands, despoiled him of honor and love.

517

Here Pan Kmita gnashed his teeth, stretched out his hands toward Jmud, on which Yanush, the hetman, was sitting like a wolf on a corpse, and began to call out in a voice choking with rage,—

"Vengeance! Vengeance!"

Suddenly he threw himself in despair on his knees in the middle of the room, and began to cry,—

"I vow to thee, O Lord Christ, to bend those traitors and gallop over them with justice, with fire, and with sword, to cut them, while there is breath in my throat, steam in my mouth, and life for me in this world! So help me, O Nazarene King! Amen!"

Some kind of internal voice told him in that moment, "Serve the country, vengeance afterward."

Pan Andrei's eyes were flaming, his lips were baked, and he trembled as in a fever; he waved his hands, and talking with himself aloud, walked, or rather ran, through the room, kicked the bed with his feet; at last he threw himself once more on his knees.

"Inspire me, O Christ, what to do, lest I fall into frenzy."

At that moment came the report of a gun, which the forest echo threw from pine-tree to pine-tree till it brought it like thunder to the cabin.

Kmita sprang up, and seizing his sabre ran out.

"What is that?" asked he of the soldier standing at the threshold.

"A shot, Colonel."

"Where is Soroka?"

"He went to look for the letters."

"In what direction was the shot?"

The soldier pointed to the eastern part of the forest, which was overgrown with dense underwood.

"There!"

At that moment was heard the tramp of horses not yet visible.

"Be on your guard!" cried Kmita.

But from out the thicket appeared Soroka, hurrying as fast as his horse could gallop, and after him the other soldier. They rushed up to the cabin, sprang from the horses, and from behind them, as from behind breastworks, took aim at the thicket.

"What is there?" asked Kmita.

"A party is coming," answered Soroka.

CHAPTER XXIX.

Silence succeeded; but soon something began to rustle in the near thicket, as if wild beasts were passing. The movement, however, grew slower the nearer it came. Then there was silence a second time.

"How many of them are there?" asked Kmita.

"About six, and perhaps eight; for to tell the truth I could not count them surely," said Soroka.

"That is our luck! They cannot stand against us."

"They cannot. Colonel; but we must take one of them alive, and scorch him so that he will show the road."

"There will be time for that. Be watchful!"

Kmita had barely said, "Be watchful," when a streak of white smoke bloomed forth from the thicket, and you would have said that birds had fluttered in the near grass, about thirty yards from the cabin.

"They shot from old guns, with hob-nails!" said Kmita; "if they have not muskets, they will do nothing to us, for old guns will not carry from the thicket."

Soroka, holding with one hand the musket resting on the saddle of the horse standing in front of him, placed the other hand in the form of a trumpet before his mouth, and shouted,—

"Let any man come out of the bushes, he will cover himself with his legs right away."

A moment of silence followed; then a threatening voice was heard in the thicket,—

"What kind of men are you?"

"Better than those who rob on the highroad."

"By what right have you found out our dwelling?"

"A robber asks about right! The hangman will show you right! Come to the cabin."

"We will smoke you out just as if you were badgers."

"But come on; only see that the smoke does not stifle you too."

The voice in the thicket was silent; the invaders, it seemed, had begun to take counsel. Meanwhile Soroka whispered to Kmita,—

"We must decoy some one hither, and bind him; we shall then have a guide and a hostage."

"Pshaw!" answered Kmita, "if any one comes it will be on parole."

"With robbers parole may be broken."

"It is better not to give it!" said Kmita.

With that questions sounded again from the thicket.

"What do you want?"

Now Kmita began to speak. "We should have gone as we came if you had known politeness and not fired from a gun."

"You will not stay there,—there will be a hundred horse of us in the evening."

"Before evening two hundred dragoons will come, and your swamps will not save you, for they will pass as we passed."

"Are you soldiers?"

"We are not robbers, you may be sure."

"From what squadron?"

"But are you hetman? We will not report to you."

"The wolves will devour you, in old fashion."

"And the crows will pick you!"

"Tell what you want, a hundred devils! Why did you come to our cabin?"

"Come yourselves, and you will not split your throat crying from the thicket. Nearer, nearer!"

"On your word."

"A word is for knights, not for robbers. If it please you, believe; if not, believe not."

"May two come?"

"They may."

After a while from out the thicket a hundred yards distant appeared two men, tall and broad-shouldered. One somewhat bent seemed to be a man of years; the other went upright, but stretched his neck with curiosity toward the cabin. Both wore short sheepskin coats covered with gray cloth of the kind used by petty nobles, high cowhide boots, and fur caps drawn down to their ears.

"What the devil!" said Kmita, examining the two men with care.

"Colonel!" cried Soroka, "a miracle indeed, but those are our people."

Meanwhile they approached within a few steps, but could not see the men standing near the cabin, for the horses concealed them.

All at once Kmita stepped forward. Those approaching did not recognize him, however, for his face was bound up; they halted, and began to measure him with curious and unquiet eyes.

"And where is the other son, Pan Kyemlich?" asked Kmita; "he has not fallen, I hope."

"Who is that—how is that—what—who is talking?" asked the old man, in a voice of amazement and as it were terrified.

And he stood motionless, with mouth and eyes widely open; then the son, who since he was younger had quicker vision, took the cap from his head.

"For God's sake, father! that's the colonel!" cried he.

"O Jesus! sweet Jesus!" cried the old man, "that is Pan Kmita!"

And both took the fixed posture of subordinates saluting their commanders, and on their faces were depicted both shame and wonder.

"Ah! such sons," said Pan Andrei, laughing, "and greeted me from a gun?"

Here the old man began to shout,—

"Come this way, all of you! Come!"

From the thicket appeared a number of men, among whom were the second son of the old man and the pitch-maker; all ran up at breakneck speed with weapons ready, for they knew not what had happened. But the old man shouted again,—

"To your knees, rogues, to your knees! This is Pan Kmita! What fool was it who fired? Give him this way!"

"It was you, father," said young Kyemlich.

"You lie,—you lie like a dog! Pan Colonel, who could know that it was your grace who had come to our cabin? As God is true, I do not believe my own eyes yet."

"I am here in person," answered Kmita, stretching his hand toward him.

"O Jesus!" said the old man, "such a guest in the pine-woods. I cannot believe my own eyes. With what can we receive your grace here? If we expected, if we knew!"

Here he turned to his sons: "Run, some blockhead, to the cellar, bring mead!"

"Give the key to the padlock, father."

The old man began to feel in his belt, and at the same time looked suspiciously at his son.

"The key of the padlock? But I know thee, gypsy; thou wilt drink more thyself than thou'lt bring. What's to be done? I'll go myself; he wants the key of the padlock! But go roll off the logs, and I'll open and bring it myself."

"I see that you have spoons hidden under the logs, Pan Kyemlich," said Kmita.

"But can anything be kept from such robbers!" asked the old man, pointing to the sons. "They would eat up their father. Ye are still here? Go roll away the logs. Is this the way ye obey him who begat you?"

The young men went quickly behind the cabin to the pile of logs.

"You are in disagreement with your sons in old fashion, it seems?" said Kmita.

"Who could be in agreement with them? They know how to fight, they know how to take booty; but when it comes to divide with their father, I must tear my part from them at risk of my life. Such is the pleasure I have; but they are like wild bulls. I beg your grace to the cabin, for the cold bites out here. For God's sake! such a guest, such a guest! And under the command of your grace we took more booty than during this whole year. We are in poverty now, wretchedness! Evil times, and always worse; and old age, too, is no joy. I beg you to the cabin, over our lowly threshold. For God's sake! who could have looked for your grace here!"

Old Kyemlich spoke with a marvellously rapid and complaining utterance, and while speaking cast quick, restless

523

glances on every side. He was a bony old man, enormous in stature, with a face ever twisted and sullen! He, as well as his two sons, had crooked eyes. His brows were bushy, and also his mustaches, from beneath which protruded beyond measure an underlip, which when he spoke came to his nose, as happens with men who are toothless. The agedness of his face was in wonderful contrast to the quickness of his movements, which displayed unusual strength and alertness. His movements were as rapid as if a spring stirred him; he turned his head continually, trying to take in with his eyes everything around,—men as well as things. Toward Kmita he became every minute more humble, in proportion as subservience to his former leader, fear, and perhaps admiration or attachment were roused in him.

Kmita knew the Kyemliches well, for the father and two sons had served under him when single-handed he had carried on war in White Russia with Hovanski. They were valiant soldiers, and as cruel as valiant. One son, Kosma, was standard-bearer for a time in Kmita's legion; but he soon resigned that honorable office, since it prevented him from taking booty. Among the gamblers and unbridled souls who formed Kmita's legion, and who drank away and lost in the day what they won with blood in the night from the enemy, the Kyemliches were distinguished for mighty greed. They accumulated booty carefully, and hid it in the woods. They took with special eagerness horses, which they sold afterward at country houses and in towns. The father fought no worse than the twin sons, but after each battle he dragged away from them the most considerable part of the booty, scattering at the same time complaints and regrets that they were wronging him, threatening a father's curse, groaning and lamenting. The sons grumbled at him, but being sufficiently stupid by nature they let themselves be tyrannized over. In spite of their endless squabbles and scoldings, they stood up, one for the other, in battle venomously without sparing blood. They were not liked by their comrades, but were feared universally, for in quarrels they were terrible; even officers avoided provoking them. Kmita was the one man who had roused indescribable fear in them, and after Kmita, Pan Ranitski, before whom they trembled when from anger his face was covered with spots. They revered also in both lofty birth; for the Kmitas, from old times, had high rank in Orsha, and in Ranitski flowed senatorial blood.

It was said in the legion that they had collected great treasures, but no one knew surely that there was truth in this statement. On a certain day Kmita sent them away with attendants and a herd of captured horses; from that time they vanished. Kmita thought that they had fallen; his soldiers said that they had escaped with the horses, the temptation in this case being too great for their hearts. Now, as Pan Andrei saw them in health, and as in a shed near the cabin horses were neighing, and the rejoicing and subservience of the old man were mingled with disquiet, he thought that his soldiers were right in their judgment. Therefore, when they had entered the cabin he sat on a plank bed, and putting his hands on his sides, looked straight into the old man's eyes and asked,—

"Kyemlich, where are my horses?"

"Jesus! sweet Jesus!" groaned the old man. "Zolotarenko's men took the horses; they beat us and wounded us, drove us ninety miles; we hardly escaped with our lives. Oh, Most Holy Mother! we could not find either your grace or your men. They drove us thus far into these pine-woods, into misery and hunger, to this cabin and these swamps. God is kind that your grace is living and in health, though, I see, wounded. Maybe we can nurse you, and put on herbs; and those sons of mine went to roll off the logs, and they have disappeared. What are the rogues doing? They are ready to take out the door and get at the mead.

Hunger here and misery; nothing more! We live on mushrooms; but for your grace there will be something to drink and a bite to eat. Those men took the horses from us, robbed us,—there is no denying that! And they deprived us of service with your grace. We shall not have a bit of bread for old age, unless your grace takes us back into service."

"That may happen too," answered Kmita.

Now the two sons of the old man came in,—Kosma and Damian, twins, big fellows, awkward, with enormous heads completely overgrown with an immensely thick bush of hair, stiff as a brush, sticking out unevenly around the ears, forming hair-screws and fantastic tufts on their skulls. When they came in they stood near the door, for in presence of Kmita they dared not sit down; and Damian said,—

"The cellar is cleared."

"'Tis well," answered old Kyemlich, "I will go to bring mead."

Here he looked significantly at his sons.

"And Zolotarenko's men took the horses," said he, with emphasis; and went out of the cabin.

Kmita glanced at the two who stood by the door, and who looked as if they had been hewn out of logs roughly with an axe.

"What are you doing now?"

"We take horses!" answered the twins at the same time.

"From whom?"

"From whomsoever comes along."

"But mostly?"

"From Zolotarenko's men."

"That is well, you are free to take from the enemy; but if you take from your own you are robbers, not nobles. What do you do with those horses?"

"Father sells them in Prussia."

"Has it happened to you to take from the Swedes? Swedish companies are not far from here. Have you attacked the Swedes?"

"We have."

"Then you fall on single men or small companies; but when they defend themselves, what then?"

"We pound them."

"Ah, ha, you pound them! Then you have a reckoning with Zolotarenko's men and with the Swedes, and surely you could not have got away dry had you fallen into their hands."

Kosma and Damian were silent.

"You are carrying on a dangerous business, more becoming to robbers than nobles. It must be, also, that some sentences are hanging over you from old times?"

"Of course there are!" answered Kosma and Damian.

"So I thought. From what parts are you?"

"We are from these parts."

"Where did your father live before?"

"In Borovichko."

"Was that his village?"

"Yes, together with Pan Kopystynski."

"And what became of him?"

"We killed him."

"And you had to flee before the law. It will be short work with you Kyemliches, and you'll finish on trees. The hangman will light you, it cannot be otherwise!"

Just then the door of the room creaked, and the old man came in bringing a decanter of mead and two glasses. He looked unquietly at his sons and at Kmita, and then said,—

"Go and cover the cellar."

The twins went out at once. The old man poured mead into one glass; the other he left empty, waiting to see if Kmita would let him drink with him.

But Kmita was not able to drink himself, for he even spoke with difficulty, such pain did the wound cause him. Seeing this, the old man said,—

"Mead is not good for the wound, unless poured in, to clear it out more quickly. Your grace, let me look at the wound and dress it, for I understand this matter as well as a barber."

Kmita consented. Kyemlich removed the bandage, and began to examine the wound carefully.

"The skin is taken off, that's nothing! The ball passed along the outside; but still it is swollen."

"That is why it pains me."

"But it is not two days old. Most Holy Mother! some one who must have been very near shot at your grace."

"How do you know that?"

"Because all the powder was not burned, and grains like cockle are under the skin. They will stay with your grace. Now we need only bread and spider-web. Terribly near was the man who fired. It is well that he did not kill your grace."

"It was not fated me. Mix the bread and the spider-web and put them on as quickly as possible, for I must talk with you, and my jaws pain me."

The old man looked suspiciously at the colonel, for in his heart there was fear that the talk might touch again on the horses said to have been taken by the Cossacks; but he busied himself at once, kneaded the moistened bread first, and since it was not hard to find spider-webs in the cabin he attended promptly to Kmita.

"I am easy now," said Pan Andrei; "sit down, worthy Kyemlich."

"According to command of the colonel," answered the old man, sitting on the edge of a bench and stretching out his iron-gray bristly head uneasily toward Kmita.

But Kmita, instead of conversing, took his own head in his hands and fell into deep thought. Then he rose and began to walk in the room; at moments he halted before Kyemlich and gazed at him with distraught look; apparently he was weighing something, wrestling with thoughts. Meanwhile about half an hour passed; the old man squirmed more and more uneasily. All at once Kmita stopped before him.

"Worthy Kyemlich," said he, "where are the nearest of those squadrons which rose up against the prince voevoda of Vilna?"

The old man began to wink his eyes suspiciously. "Does your grace wish to go to them?"

"I do not request you to ask, but to answer."

"They say that one squadron is quartered in Shchuchyn,— that one which came here last from Jmud."

"Who said so?"

"The men of the squadron themselves."

"Who led it?"

"Pan Volodyovski."

"That's well. Call Soroka!"

The old man went out, and returned soon with the sergeant.

"Have the letters been found?" asked Kmita.

"They have not, Colonel," answered Soroka.

Kmita shook his hands. "Oh, misery, misery! You may go, Soroka. For those letters which you have lost you deserve to hang. You may go. Worthy Kyemlich, have you anything on which to write?"

"I hope to find something," answered the old man.

"Even two leaves of paper and a pen."

The old man vanished through the door of a closet which was evidently a storeroom for all kinds of things, but he searched long. Kmita was walking the while through the room, and talking to himself,—

"Whether I have the letters or not," said he, "the hetman does not know that they are lost, and he will fear lest I publish them. I have him in hand. Cunning against cunning! I will threaten to send them to the voevoda of Vityebsk. That is what I will do. In God is my hope, that the hetman will fear this."

Further thought was interrupted by old Kyemlich, who, coming out of the closet, said,—

"Here are three leaves of paper, but no pens or ink."

"No pens? But are there no birds in the woods here? They may be shot with a gun."

"There is a falcon nailed over the shed."

"Bring his wing hither quickly!"

Kyemlich shot off with all speed, for in the voice of Kmita was impatience, and as it were a fever. He returned in a moment with the falcon's wing. Kmita seized it, plucked out a quill, and began to make a pen of it with his dagger.

"It will do!" said he, looking at it before the light; "but it is easier to cut men's heads than quills. Now we need ink."

So saying, he rolled up his sleeve, cut himself deeply in the arm, and moistened the quill in blood.

"Worthy Kyemlich," said he, "leave me."

The old man left the room, and Pan Andrei began to write at once:—

I renounce the service of your highness, for I will not serve traitors and deceivers. And if I swore on the crucifix not to leave your highness, God will forgive me; and even if he were to damn me, I would rather burn for my error than for open and purposed treason to my country and king. Your highness deceived me, so that I was like a blind sword in your hand, ready to spill the blood of my brethren. Therefore I summon your highness to the judgment of God, so that it may be known on whose side was treason, and on whose honest intention. Should we ever meet, though you are powerful and able to strike unto death, not only a private man, but the whole Commonwealth, and I have only a sabre in my hand, still I will vindicate my own, and will strike your highness, for which my regret and compunction will give me power. And your highness knows that I am of those who without attendant squadrons, without castles and cannon, can injure. While in me there is breath, over you there is vengeance, so that you can be sure neither of the day nor the hour. And this is as certain to be as that this is my own blood with which I write. I have your letters, letters to ruin you, not only with the King of Poland, but the King of Sweden, for in them treason to the Commonwealth is made manifest, as well as this too, that you are ready to desert the Swedes if only a leg totters under them. Even had you twice your present power, your ruin is in my hands, for all men must believe signatures and seals. Therefore I say this to your highness: If a hair falls from the heads which I love and which are left in Kyedani, I will send those letters and documents to Pan Sapyeha, and I will have copies printed and scattered through the land. Your highness can go by land or water (you have your choice); but after the war, when peace comes to the Commonwealth, you will give me the Billeviches, and I will give you the letters, or if I hear evil tidings Pan Sapyeha will show them straightway to Pontus de la Gardie. Your highness wants a crown, but where will you put it when your head falls either from the Polish or the Swedish axe? It is better, I think, to have this understanding now; though I shall not forget revenge hereafter, I shall take it only in private, excepting this case. I would commend

531

you to God were it not that you put the help of the devil above that of God.   Kmita.

P. S. Your highness will not poison the confederates, for there will be those who, going from the service of the devil to that of God, will forewarn them to drink beer neither in Orel nor Zabludovo.

Here Kmita sprang up and began to walk across the room. His face was burning, for his own letter had heated him like fire. This letter was a declaration of war against the Radzivills; but still Kmita felt in himself some extraordinary power, and was ready, even at that moment, to stand eye to eye before that powerful family who shook the whole country. He, a simple noble, a simple knight, an outlaw pursued by justice, who expected assistance from no place, who had offended all so that everywhere he was accounted an enemy,—he, recently overthrown, felt in himself now such power that he saw, as if with the eyes of a prophet, the humiliation of Prince Yanush and Boguslav, and his own victory. How he would wage war, where he would find allies, in what way he would conquer, he knew not,—what is more, he had not thought of this. But he had profound faith that he would do what he ought to do,—that is, what is right and just, in return for which God would be with him. He was filled with confidence beyond measure and bounds. It had become sensibly easier in his soul. Certain new regions were opened as it were entirely before him. Let him but sit on his horse and ride thither to honor, to glory, to Olenka.

"But a hair will not fall from her head," repeated he to himself, with a certain feverish joy; "the letters will defend her. The hetman will guard her as the eye in his head,—as I myself would. Oh, I have settled this! I am a poor worm, but they will be afraid of my sting."

Then this thought came to him: "And shall I write to her too? The messenger who will take the letter to the hetman can give a slip of paper to her secretly. Why not inform her that I have broken with the Radzivills, and that I am going to seek other service?"

This thought struck his heart greatly. Cutting his arm again, he moistened the pen and began to write,—

Olenka,—I am no longer on the Radzivill side, for I have seen through them at last—

But suddenly he stopped, thought awhile, and said to himself, "Let deeds, not words, bear witness for me henceforth; I will not write." And he tore the paper. But he wrote on a third sheet a short letter to Volodyovski in the following words,—

Gracious Colonel,—The undersigned friend warns you and the other colonels to be on your guard. There were letters from the hetman to Prince Boguslav and Pan Harasimovich to poison you, or to have men under you in your own quarters. Harasimovich is absent, for he has gone with Prince Boguslav to Tyltsa in Prussia; but there may be similar commands to other managers. Be careful of those managers, receive nothing from them, and at night do not sleep without guards. I know also to a certainty that the hetman will march against you soon with an army; he is waiting only for cavalry which General de la Gardie is to send, fifteen hundred in number. See to it, therefore, that he does not fall upon you and destroy you singly. But better send reliable men to the voevoda of Vityebsk to come, with all haste and take chief command. A well-wisher counsels this,—believe him. Meanwhile keep together, choosing quarters for the squadrons one not far from the other, so that you may be able to give mutual assistance. The hetman has few cavalry, only a small number of dragoons, and Kmita's men, but they are not reliable. Kmita himself is absent. The hetman found some other office for him; it being likely that he does not trust him. Kmita too is not such a traitor as men say; he is merely led astray. I commit you to God.

Babinich.

Pan Andrei did not wish to put his own name to the letter, for he judged that it would rouse in each one aversion and especially distrust. "In case they understand," thought he, "that it would be better for them to retreat before the hetman than to meet him in a body, they will suspect at once, if they see my name, that I wish to collect them, so that the hetman may finish them at a blow; they will think this a new trick, but from some Babinich they will receive warning more readily."

Pan Andrei called himself Babinich from the village Babiniche, near Orsha, which from remote times belonged to the Kmitas.

When he had written the letter, at the end of which he placed a few timid words in his own defence, he felt new solace in his heart at the thought that with that letter he had rendered the first service, not only to Volodyovski and his friends, but to all the colonels who would not desert their country for Radzivill. He felt also that that thread would go farther. The plight into which he had fallen was difficult, indeed, almost desperate; but still there was some help, some issue, some narrow path which would lead to the highroad.

But now when Olenka in all probability was safe from the vengeance of Radzivill, and the confederates from an unexpected attack. Pan Andrei put the question, What was he to do himself?

He had broken with traitors, he had burned the bridges in the rear, he wished now to serve his country, to devote to it his strength, his health, his life; but how was he to do this, how begin, to what could he put his hand?

Again it came to his head to join the confederates; but if they will not receive him, if they will proclaim him a traitor and cut him down, or what is worse, expel him in disgrace?

"I would rather they killed me!" cried Pan Andrei; and he flushed from shame and the feeling of his own disgrace. Perhaps it is easier to save Olenka or the confederates than his own fame.

Now the position was really desperate, and again the young hero's soul began to seethe.

"But can I not act as I did against Hovanski?" asked he of himself. "I will gather a party, will attack the Swedes, burn, pursue. That is nothing new for me! No one has resisted them; I will resist until the time comes when the whole Commonwealth will ask, as did Lithuania, who is that hero who all alone dares to creep into the mouth of the lion? Then I will remove my cap and say, 'See, it is I, it is Kmita!'"

And such a burning desire drew him on to that bloody work that he wished to rush out of the room and order the Kyemliches, their attendants, and his own men to mount and move on. But before he reached the door he felt as if some one had suddenly punched him in the breast and pushed him back from the threshold. He stood in the middle of the room, and looked forward in amazement.

"How is this? Shall I not efface my offences in this way?"

And at once he began to reckon with his own conscience.

"Where is atonement for guilt?" asked his conscience. "Here something else is required!"

"What?" asked Kmita.

"With what can thy guilt be effaced, if not with service of some kind, difficult and immense, honorable and pure as a tear? Is it service to collect a band of ruffians and rage like a whirlwind with them through the fields and the wilderness? Dost thou not desire this because fighting has for thee a sweet odor, as has roast

535

meat for a dog? That is amusement, not service; a carnival, not war; robbery, not defence of the country! And didst thou not do the same against Hovanski, but what didst thou gain? Ruffians infesting the forests are ready also to attack the Swedish commands, and whence canst thou get other men? Thou wilt attack the Swedes, but also the inhabitants; thou wilt bring vengeance on these inhabitants, and what wilt thou effect? Thou art trying to escape, thou fool, from toil and atonement."

So conscience spoke in Kmita; and Kmita saw that it was right, and vexation seized him, and a species of grief over his own conscience because it spoke such bitter truth.

"What shall I begin?" asked he, at last; "who will help me, who will save me?"

Here somehow his knees began to bend till at last he knelt down at the plank bed and began to pray aloud, and implore from his whole soul and heart,—

"O Jesus Christ, dear Lord," said he, "as on the cross thou hadst pity for the thief, so now have pity for me. Behold I desire to cleanse myself from sins, to begin a new life, and to serve my country honestly; but I know not how, for I am foolish. I served those traitors, O Lord, also not so much from malice, but especially as it were through folly; enlighten me, inspire me, comfort me in my despair, and rescue me in thy mercy, or I perish."

Here Pan Andrei's voice quivered; he beat his broad breast till it thundered in the room, and repeated, "Be merciful to me, a sinner! be merciful to me, a sinner! Be merciful to me, a sinner!" Then placing his hands together and stretching them upward, he said, "And thou, Most Holy Lady, insulted by heretics in this land, take my part with thy Son, intercede for my rescue, desert me not in my suffering and misery, so that I may be able to serve thee, to

536

avenge the insults against thee, and at the hour of my death have thee as a patroness for my unhappy soul."

When Pan Andrei was imploring thus, tears began to fall from his eyes; at last he dropped his head on the plank bed and sank into silence, as if waiting for the effect of his ardent prayer. Silence followed in the room, and only the deep sound of the neighboring pine-trees entered from outside. Then chips crackled under heavy steps beyond the window, and two men began to speak,—

"What do you think, Sergeant? Where shall we go from here?"

"Do I know?" answered Soroka. "We shall go somewhere, maybe far off, to the king who is groaning under the Swedish hand."

"Is it true that all have left him?"

"But the Lord God has not left him."

Kmita rose suddenly from the bed, but his face was clear and calm; he went straight to the door, and opening it said to the soldier,—

"Have the horses ready! it is time for the road!"

CHAPTER XXX.

A movement rose quickly among the soldiers, who were glad to go out of the forest to the distant world, all the more since they feared pursuit on the part of Boguslav Radzivill; and old Kyemlich went to the cabin, understanding that Kmita would need him.

"Does your grace wish to go?" asked he.

"I do. Will you guide me out of the forest? Do you know all the roads?"

"I know all the roads in these parts. But whither does your grace wish to go?"

"To our gracious king."

The old man started back in astonishment. "O Wise Lady!" cried he. "To what king."

"Not to the Swedish, you may be sure."

Kyemlich not only failed to recover, but began to make the sign of the cross.

"Then surely your grace does not know that people say our lord the king has taken refuge in Silesia, for all have deserted him. Cracow is besieged."

"We will go to Silesia."

"Well, but how are we to pass through the Swedes?"

"Whether we pass through as nobles or peasants, on horseback or on foot, is all one to me, if only we pass."

"Then too a tremendous lot of time is needed."

"We have time enough, but I should be glad to go as quickly as possible."

Kyemlich ceased to wonder. The old man was too cunning not to surmise that there was some particular and secret cause for this undertaking of Pan Kmita's, and that moment a thousand suppositions began to crowd into his head. But as the soldiers, on whom Pan Andrei had enjoined silence, said nothing to the old man or his sons about the seizure of Prince Boguslav, the supposition seemed to him most likely that the prince voevoda of Vilna had sent the young colonel on some mission to the king. He was confirmed in this opinion specially because he counted Kmita a zealous adherent of Prince Yanush, and knew of his services to the hetman; for the confederate squadrons had spread tidings of him throughout the whole province of Podlyasye, creating the opinion that Kmita was a tyrant and a traitor.

"The hetman is sending a confidant to the king," thought the old man; "that means that surely he wishes to agree with him and leave the Swedes. Their rule must be bitter to him already, else why send?"

Old Kyemlich did not struggle long over this question, for his interest in the matter was altogether different; and namely, what profit could he draw from such circumstances? If he served Kmita he would serve at the same time the hetman and the king, which would not be without a notable reward. The favor of such lords would be of service, too, should he be summoned to account for old sins. Besides, there will surely be war, the country will flame up, and then plunder will crawl of itself into his hands. All this smiled at the old man, who besides was accustomed to obey Kmita, and had not ceased to fear him like fire, cherishing toward him also a certain kind of love, which Kmita knew how to rouse in all his subordinates.

"Your grace," said he, "must go through the whole Commonwealth to reach the king. Swedish troops are nothing, for we may avoid the towns and go through the woods; but the worst is that the woods, as is usual in unquiet times, are full of parties of freebooters, who fall upon travellers; and your grace has few men."

"You will go with me, Pan Kyemlich, and your sons and the men whom you have; there will be more of us."

"If your grace commands I will go, but I am a poor man. Only misery with us; nothing more. How can I leave even this poverty and the roof over my head?"

"Whatever you do will be paid for; and for you it is better to take your head out of this place while it is yet on your shoulders."

"All the Saints of the Lord! What does your grace say? How is that? What threatens me, innocent man, in this place? Whom do we hinder?"

"I know you robbers!" answered Pan Andrei. "You had partnership with Kopystynski, and killed him; then you ran away from the courts, you served with me, you took away my captured horses.

"As true as life! O Mighty Lady!" cried the old man.

"Wait and be silent! Then you returned to your old lair, and began to ravage in the neighborhood like robbers, taking horses and booty everywhere. Do not deny it, for I am not your judge, and you know best whether I tell the truth. If you take the horses of Zolotarenko, that is well; if the horses of the Swedes, that is well. If they catch you they will flay you; but that is their affair."

"True, true; but we take only from the enemy," said the old man.

"Untrue; for you attack your own people, as your sons have confessed to me, and that is simple robbery, and a stain on the name of a noble. Shame on you, robbers! you should be peasants, not nobles."

"Your grace wrongs us," said old fox, growing red, "for we, remembering our station, do no peasant deed. We do not take horses at night from any man's stable. It is something different to drive a herd from the fields, or to capture horses. This is permitted, and there is no prejudice to a noble therefrom in time of war. But a horse in a stable is sacred; and only a gypsy, a Jew, or a peasant would steal from a stable,—not a noble. We, your grace, do not do that. But war is war!"

"Though there were ten wars, only in battle can plunder be taken; if you seek it on the road, you are robbers."

"God is witness to our innocence."

"But you have brewed beer here. In few words, it is better for you to leave this place, for sooner or later the halter will take you. Come with me; you will wash away your sins with faithful service and win honor. I will receive you to my service, in which there will be more profit than in those horses."

"We will go with your grace everywhere; we will guide you through the Swedes and through the robbers,—for true is the speech of your grace, that evil people persecute us here terribly, and for what? For our poverty,—for nothing but our poverty. Perhaps God will take pity on us, and save us from suffering."

Here old Kyemlich rubbed his hands mechanically, and his eyes glittered. "From these works," thought he, "it will boil in the country as in a kettle, and foolish the man who takes no advantage."

Kmita looked at him quickly. "Only don't try to betray me!" said he, threateningly, "for you will not be able, and the hand of God only could save you."

"We have never betrayed," answered Kyemlich, gloomily, "and may God condemn me if such a thought entered my head."

"I believe you," said Kmita, after a short silence, "for treason is something different from robbery; no robber will betray."

"What does your grace command now?" asked Kyemlich.

"First, here are two letters, requiring quick delivery. Have you sharp men?"

"Where must they go?"

"Let one go to the prince voevoda, but without seeing Radzivill himself. Let him deliver the letter in the first squadron of the prince, and come back without awaiting an answer."

"The pitch-maker will go; he is a sharp man and experienced."

"He will do. The second letter must be taken to Podlyasye; inquire for Pan Volodyovski's Lauda squadron, and give it into the hands of the colonel himself."

The old man began to mutter cunningly, and thought, "I see work on every side; since he is sniffing with the confederates there will be boiling water,—there will be, there will be!"

"Your grace," said he, aloud, "if there is not such a hurry with this letter, when we leave the forest it perhaps might be given to some man on the road. There are many nobles here friendly to the confederates; any one would take it willingly, and one man more would remain to us."

"You have calculated shrewdly," answered Kmita, "for it is better that he who delivers the letter should not know from whom he takes it. Shall we go out of the forest soon?"

"As your grace wishes. We can go out in two weeks, or to-morrow."

"Of that later; but now listen to me carefully, Kyemlich."

"I am attending with all my mind, your grace."

"They have denounced me in the whole Commonwealth as a tyrant, as devoted to the hetman, or altogether to Sweden. If the king knew who I am, he might not trust me, and might despise my intention, which, if it is not sincere, God sees! Are you attending, Kyemlich?"

"I am, your grace."

"Therefore I do not call myself Kmita, but Babinich, do you understand? No one must know my real name. Open not your lips; let not a breath out. If men ask whence I come, say that you joined me on the road and do not know, but say, 'Whoso is curious, let him ask the man himself.'"

"I understand, your grace."

"Warn your sons, and also your men. Even if straps were cut out of them, they must say my name is Babinich. You will answer for this with your life."

"It will be so, your grace. I will go and tell my sons, for it is necessary to put everything into the heads of those rogues with a shovel. Such is the joy I have with them. God has punished me for the sins of my youth; that is the trouble. Let me say another word, your grace."

"Speak boldly."

"It seems to me better not to tell soldiers or men where we are going."

"That is true."

"It is enough for them to know that Babinich, not Pan Kmita, is travelling. And on such a journey it is better to conceal your grace's rank."

"Why?"

"Because the Swedes give passes to the more considerable people; and whoso has not a pass, him they take to the commandant."

"I have passes to the Swedish troops."

Astonishment gleamed in the cunning eyes of Kyemlich; but after a while he asked, "Will your grace let me say once more what I think?"

"If you give good counsel and delay not, speak; for I see that you are a clever man."

"If you have passes, it is better, for in need they may be shown; but if your grace is travelling on an errand that should remain secret, it is safer not to show the passes. I know not whether they are given in the name of Babinich or Kmita; but if you show them, the trace will remain and pursuit will be easier."

"You have struck the point!" cried Kmita. "I prefer to reserve the passes for another time, if it is possible to go through without them."

"It is possible, your grace; and that disguised either as a peasant or a petty noble,—which will be easier, for I have some clean clothes, a cap and gray coat, for example, just such as petty nobles wear. We may travel with a band of horses, as if we were going to the fairs, and drive farther till we come to Lovich and Warsaw, as I have done more than once during peace, and I know the roads. About this time there is a fair in Sobota, to which people come from afar. In Sobota we shall learn of other places where there are fairs, and so on. The Swedes too take less note of small nobles, for crowds of them stroll about at all the fairs. If some commandant inquires we will explain ourselves, but if a small party asks we will gallop over their bellies, God and the Most Holy Lady permitting."

"But if they take our horses? Requisitions in time of war are of daily occurrence."

"Either they will buy or they will take them. If they buy we will go to Sobota, not to sell, but to buy horses; and if they take them, we will raise a lament and go with our complaint to Warsaw and to Cracow."

"You have a cunning mind," said Kmita, "and I see that you will serve me. Even if the Swedes take these horses, some man will be found to pay for them."

"I was going to Elko in Prussia with them; this turns out well, for just in that direction does our road lie. From Elko we will go along the boundary, then turn to Ostrolenko, thence through the wilderness to Pultusk and to Warsaw."

"Where is that Sobota?"

"Not far from Pyantek."

"Are you jesting, Kyemlich?"

"How should I dare," answered the old man, crossing his arms on his breast and bending his head; "but they have such wonderful names for towns in this region. It is a good bit of road beyond Lovich, your grace."

"Are there large fairs in that Sobota?"

"Not such as in Lovich; but there is one at this time of year, to which horses are driven from Prussia, and crowds of people assemble. Surely it will not be worse this year, for it is quiet about there. The Swedes are in power everywhere, and have garrisons in the towns. Even if a man wanted to rise against them, he could not."

"Then I will take your plan. We will go with horses, and that you suffer no loss I will pay for them in advance."

"I thank your grace for the rescue."

"Only get sheepskin coats ready and common saddles and sabres, for we will start at once. Tell your sons and men who I am, what my name is, that I am travelling with horses, that you and they are hired assistants. Hurry!"

When the old man turned to the door, Pan Andrei said further, "No one will call me grace nor commandant nor colonel, only *you* and *Babinich*."

Kyemlich went out, and an hour later all were sitting on their horses ready to start on the long journey. Kmita dressed in the gray coat of a poor noble, a cap of worn sheepskin, and with a bandaged face, as if after a duel in some inn, was difficult of recognition, and looked really like some poor devil of a noble, strolling from one fair to another. He was surrounded by people dressed in like fashion, armed with common poor sabres, with long whips to drive the horses, and lariats to catch those that might try to escape.

The soldiers looked with astonishment at their colonel, making various remarks, in low tones, concerning him. It was a wonder to them that he was Babinich instead of Pan Kmita, that they were to say *you* to him; and most of all shrugged his shoulders old Soroka, who, looking at the terrible colonel as at a rainbow, muttered to Biloüs,—

"That *you* will not pass my throat. Let him kill me, but I will give him, as of old, what belongs to him."

The soldiers knew not that the soul in Pan Andrei had changed as well as his external form.

"Move on!" cried Babinich, on a sudden.

The whips cracked; the riders surrounded the horses, which were huddled together, and they moved on.

CHAPTER XXXI.

Passing along the very boundary between the province of Trotsk and Prussia, they travelled through broad and pathless forests known only to Kyemlich, until they entered Prussia and reached Leng, or, as old Kyemlich, called it, Elko, where they got news of public affairs from nobles stopping there, who, taking their wives, children, and effects, had fled from the Swedes and sought refuge under the power of the elector.

Leng had the look of a camp, or rather it might be thought that some petty diet was in session there. The nobles drank Prussian beer in the public houses, and talked, while every now and then some one brought news. Without making inquiries and merely by listening with care, Babinich learned that Royal Prussia and the chief towns in it had taken decisively the side of Yan Kazimir, and had made a treaty of mutual defence with the elector against every enemy. It was said, however, that in spite of the treaty the most considerable towns were unwilling to admit the elector's garrisons, fearing lest that adroit prince, when he had once entered with armed hand, might hold them for good, or might in the decisive moment join himself treacherously to the Swedes,—a deed which his inborn cunning made him capable of doing.

The nobles murmured against this distrust entertained by townspeople; but Pan Andrei, knowing the Radzivill intrigues with the elector, had to gnaw his tongue to refrain from telling what was known to him. He was held back by the thought that it was dangerous in Electoral Prussia to speak openly against the elector; and secondly, because it did not beseem a small gray-coated noble who was going to a fair with horses, to enter into the intricate subject of politics, over which the ablest statesmen were racking their brains to no purpose.

He sold a pair of horses, bought new ones, and journeyed farther, along the Prussian boundary, but by the road leading from Leng to Shchuchyn, situated in the very corner of the province of Mazovia, between Prussia on the one side and the province of Podlyasye on the other. To Shchuchyn Pan Andrei had no wish to go, for he learned that in that town were the quarters of the confederate squadron commanded by Volodyovski.

Volodyovski must have passed over almost the same road on which Kmita was travelling, and stopped before the very boundary of Podlyasye, either for a short rest or for temporary quarters, in Shchuchyn, where it must have been easier to find food for men and horses than in greatly plundered Podlyasye.

Kmita did not wish to meet the famous colonel, for he judged that having no proofs, except words, he would not be able to persuade Volodyovski of his conversion and sincerity. He gave command, therefore, to turn to the west toward Vansosh, ten miles from Shchuchyn. As to the letter he determined to send it to Pan Michael at the first opportunity.

But before arriving at Vansosh, they stopped at a wayside inn called "The Mandrake," and disposed themselves for a night's rest, which promised to be comfortable, for there was no one at the inn save the host, a Prussian.

But barely had Kmita with the three Kyemliches and Soroka sat down to supper when the rattling of wheels and the tramp of horses were heard. As the sun had not gone down yet, Kmita went out in front of the inn to see who was coming, for he was curious to know if it was some Swedish party; but instead of

Swedes he saw a carriage, and following it two pack-wagons, surrounded by armed men.

At the first glance it was easy to see that some personage was coming. The carriage was drawn by four good Prussian horses, with large bones and rather short backs; a jockey sat on one of the front horses, holding two beautiful dogs in a leash; on the seat was a driver, and at his side a haiduk dressed in Hungarian fashion; in the carriage was the lord himself, in a cloak lined with wolfskin and fastened with numerous gilded buttons.

In the rear followed two wagons, well filled, and at each of them four servants armed with sabres and guns.

The lord, though a personage, was still quite young, a little beyond twenty. He had a plump, red face, and in his whole person there was evidence that he did not stint himself in eating.

When the carriage stopped, the haiduk sprang to give his hand to help down the lord; but the lord, seeing Kmita standing on the threshold, beckoned with his glove, and called,—

"Come this way, my good friend!"

Kmita instead of going to him withdrew to the interior, for anger seized him at once. He had not become accustomed yet to the gray coat, or to being beckoned at with a glove. He went back therefore, sat at the table, and began to eat. The unknown lord came in after him. When he had entered he half closed his eyes, for it was dark in the room, since there was merely a small fire burning in the chimney.

"But why did no one come out as I was driving up?" asked the unknown lord.

"The host has gone to another room," answered Kmita, "and we are travellers, like your grace."

"Thank you for the confidence. And what manner of travellers?"

"Oh, a noble travelling with horses."

"And your company are nobles too?"

"Poor men, but nobles."

"With the forehead, then, with the forehead. Whither is God guiding you?"

"From fair to fair, to sell horses."

"If you stay here all night, I'll see, perhaps I'll pick out something. Meanwhile will you permit me to join you at the table?"

The unknown lord asked, it is true, if they would let him sit with them, but in such a tone as if he were perfectly sure that they would; and he was not mistaken. The young horse-dealer said,—

"We beg your grace very kindly, though we have nothing to offer but sausage and peas."

"There are better dainties in my bags," answered the lordling, not without a certain pride; "but I have a soldier's palate, and sausage with peas, if well cooked, I prefer to everything." When he had said this,—and he spoke very slowly, though he looked quickly and sharply,—he took his seat on the bench on which Kmita pushed aside to give convenient room.

"Oh, I beg, I beg, do not incommode yourself. On the road rank is not regarded; and though you were to punch me with your elbow, the crown would not fall from my head."

Kmita, who was pushing a plate of peas to the unknown, and who, as has been said, was not used to such treatment, would certainly have broken the plate on the head of the puffed up young man if there had not been something in that pride of his which amused Pan Andrei; therefore not only did he restrain his internal impulse at once, but laughed and said,—

"Such times are the present, your grace, that crowns fall from the loftiest heads; for example, our king Yan Kazimir, who by right should wear two crowns, has none, unless it be one of thorns."

The unknown looked quickly at Kmita, then sighed and said, "Times are such now that it is better not to speak of this unless with confidants." Then after a moment he added: "But you have brought that out well. You must have served with polished people, for your speech shows more training than your rank."

"Rubbing against people, I have heard this and that, but I have never been a servant."

"Whence are you by birth, I beg to ask?"

"From a village in the province of Trotsk."

"Birth in a village is no drawback, if you are only noble; that's the main thing. What is to be heard in Lithuania?"

"The old story,—no lack of traitors."

"Traitors, do you say? What kind of traitors?"

"Those who have deserted the king and the Commonwealth."

"How is the prince voevoda of Vilna?"

"Sick, it is said; his breath fails him."

"God give him health, he is a worthy lord!"

"For the Swedes he is, since he opened the gates to them."

"I see that you are not a partisan of his."

Kmita noticed that the stranger, while asking him questions as it were good-naturedly, was observing him.

"What do I care!" said he; "let others think of him. My fear is that the Swedes may take my horses in requisition."

"You should have sold them on the spot, then. In Podlyasye are stationed, very likely, the squadrons which rebelled against the hetman, and surely they have not too many horses."

"I do not know that, for I have not been among them, though some man in passing gave me a letter to one of their colonels, to be delivered when possible."

"How could that passing man give you a letter when you are not going to Podlyasye?"

"Because in Shchuchyn one confederate squadron is stationed, therefore the man said to me, 'Either give it yourself or find an opportunity in passing Shchuchyn.'"

"That comes out well, for I am going to Shchuchyn."

"Your grace is fleeing also before the Swedes?"

The unknown, instead of an answer, looked at Kmita and asked phlegmatically, "Why do you say *also*, since you not only are not fleeing from the Swedes, but are going among them and will sell them horses, if they do not take your beasts by force?"

At this Kmita shrugged his shoulders. "I said *also*, because in Leng I saw many nobles who escaped before the Swedes; and as to me, if all were to serve them as much as I wish to serve them, I think they would not warm the places here long."

"Are you not afraid to say this?"

"I am not afraid, for I am not a coward, and in the second place your grace is going to Shchuchyn, and there every one says aloud what he thinks. God grant a quick passage from talking to action."

"I see that you are a man of wit beyond your station," repeated the unknown. "But if you love not the Swedes, why leave these squadrons, which have mutinied against the hetman? Have they mutinied because their wages were kept back, or from caprice? No! but because they would not serve the hetman and the Swedes. It would have been better for those soldiers, poor fellows, to remain under the hetman, but they preferred to give themselves the name of rebels, to expose themselves to hunger, hardships, and many destructive things, rather than act against the king. That it will come to war between them and the Swedes is certain, and it would have come already were it not that the

Swedes have not advanced to that corner as yet. Wait, they will come, they will meet here, and then you will see!"

"I think, too, that war will begin here very soon," said Kmita.

"Well, if you have such an opinion, and a sincere hatred for the Swedes,—which looks out of your eyes, for you speak truth, I am a judge of that,—then why not join these worthy soldiers? Is it not time, do they not need hands and sabres? Not a few honorable men are serving among them, who prefer their own king to a foreign one, and soon there will be more of these. You come from places in which men know not the Swedes as yet, but those who have made their acquaintance are shedding hot tears. In Great Poland, though it surrendered to them of its own will, they thumbscrew nobles, plunder, make requisitions, seize everything they can. At present in this province their manner is no better. General Stenbok gave forth a manifesto that each man remain quietly at home, and his property would be respected. But what good was in that! The General has his will, and the smallest commandants have theirs, so that no man is sure of to-morrow, nor of what property he holds. Every man wishes to get good of what he has, to use it in peace, wants it to bring him pleasure. But now the first best adventurer will come and say, 'Give.' If you do not give, he will find reason to strip you of your property, or without reason will have your head cut off. Many shed bitter tears, when they think of their former king. All are oppressed and look to those confederates unceasingly, to see if some rescue for the country and the people will not come from them."

"Your grace, as I see, has no better wish for the Swedes than I have," said Kmita.

The unknown looked around as it were with a certain alarm, but soon calmed himself and spoke on,—

"I would that pestilence crushed them, and I hide that not from you, for it seems to me that you are honest; and though you were not honest, you would not bind me and take me to the Swedes, for I should not yield, having armed men, and a sabre at my side."

"Your grace may be sure that I will not harm you; your courage is to my heart. And it pleases me that your grace did not hesitate to leave property behind, in which the enemy will not fail to punish you. Such good-will to the country is highly deserving of praise."

Kmita began unwittingly to speak in a patronizing tone, as a superior to a subordinate, without thinking that such words might seem strange in the mouth of a small horse-dealing noble; but apparently the young lord did not pay attention to that, for he merely winked cunningly and said,—

"But am I a fool? With me the first rule is that my own shall not leave me, for what the Lord God has given must be respected. I stayed at home quietly with my produce and grain, and when I had sold in Prussia all my crops, cattle, and utensils, I thought to myself: 'It is time for the road. Let them take vengeance on me now, let them take whatever pleases their taste.'"

"Your grace has left the hind and the buildings for good?"

"Yes, for I hired the starostaship of Vansosh from the voevoda of Mazovia, and just now the term has expired. I have not paid the last rent, and I will not, for I hear the voevoda of Mazovia is an adherent of the Swedes. Let the rent be lost to him for that, and it will add to my ready money."

"'Pon my word," said Kmita, smiling, "I see that your grace is not only a brave cavalier, but an adroit one."

"Of course," replied the unknown. "Adroitness is the main thing! But I was not speaking of that. Why is it that, feeling the

553

wrongs of our country and of our gracious king, you do not go to those honorable soldiers in Podlyasye and join their banner? You would serve both God and yourself; luck might come, for to more than one has it happened to come out of war a great man, from being a small noble. It is evident that you are bold and resolute, and since your birth is no hindrance, you might advance quickly to some fortune, if God favors you with booty. If you do not squander that which here and there will fall into your hands, the purse will grow heavy. I do not know whether you have land or not, but you may have it; with a purse it is not hard to rent an estate, and from renting an estate to owning one, with the help of the Lord, is not far. And so, beginning as an attendant, you may die an officer, or in some dignity in the country, in case you are not lazy in labor; for whoso rises early, to him God gives treasure."

Kmita gnawed his mustache, for laughter seized him; then his face quivered, and he squirmed, for from time to time pain came from the healing wound. The unknown continued,—

"As to receiving you there, they will receive you, for they need men; besides, you have pleased me, and I take you under my protection, with which you may be certain of promotion."

Here the young man raised his plump face with pride, and began to smooth his mustaches; at last he said,—

"Will you be my attendant, carry my sabre, and manage my men?"

Kmita did not restrain himself, but burst out in sincere, joyous laughter, so that all his teeth gleamed.

"Why laugh?" asked the unknown, frowning.

"From delight at the service."

But the youthful personage was offended in earnest, and said,—

"He was a fool who taught you such manners, and be careful with whom you are speaking, lest you exceed measure in familiarity."

"Forgive me, your grace," answered Kmita, joyously, "for really I do not know before whom I am standing."

The young lord put his hands on his hips: "I am Pan Jendzian of Vansosh," said he, with importance.

Kmita had opened his mouth to tell his assumed name, when Biloüs came hurriedly into the room.

"Pan Com—"

Here the soldier, stopped by the threatening look of Kmita, was confused, stammered, and finally coughed out with effort,—

"I beg to tell you some people are coming."

"Where from?"

"From Shchuchyn."

Kmita was embarrassed, but hiding his confusion quickly, he answered, "Be on your guard. Are there many?"

"About ten men on horseback."

"Have the pistols ready. Go!"

When the soldier had gone out, Kmita turned to Pan Jendzian of Vansosh and asked,—

"Are they not Swedes?"

"Since you are going to them," answered Pan Jendzian, who for some time had looked with astonishment on the young noble, "you must meet them sooner or later."

"I should prefer the Swedes to robbers, of whom there are many everywhere. Whoso goes with horses must go armed and keep on the watch, for horses are very tempting."

"If it is true that Pan Volodyovski is in Shchuchyn," said Pan Jendzian, "this is surely a party of his. Before they take up their quarters there they wish to know if the country is safe, for with Swedes at the border it would be difficult to remain in quiet."

When he heard this, Pan Andrei walked around in the room and sat down in its darkest corner, where the sides of the chimney cast a deep shadow on the corner of the table; but meanwhile the sound of the tramp and snorting of horses came in from outside, and after a time a number of men entered the room.

Walking in advance, a gigantic fellow struck with wooden foot the loose planks in the floor of the room. Kmita looked at him, and the heart died within his bosom. It was Yuzva Butrym, called Footless.

"But where is the host?" inquired he, halting in the middle of the room.

"I am here!" answered the innkeeper, "at your service."

"Oats for the horses!"

"I have no oats, except what these men are using." Saying this, he pointed at Jendzian and the horse-dealer's men.

"Whose men are you?" asked Jendzian.

"And who are you yourself?"

"The starosta of Vansosh."

His own people usually called Jendzian starosta, as he was the tenant of a starostaship, and he thus named himself on the most important occasions.

Yuzva Butrym was confused, seeing with what a high personage he had to do; therefore he removed his cap, and said,—

"With the forehead, great mighty lord. It was not possible to recognize dignity in the dark."

"Whose men are these?" repeated Jendzian, placing his hands on his hips.

"The Lauda men from the former Billevich squadron, and now of Pan Volodyovski's."

"For God's sake! Then Pan Volodyovski is in the town of Shchuchyn?"

"In his own person, and with other colonels who have come from Jmud."

"Praise be to God, praise be to God!" repeated the delighted starosta. "And what colonels are with Pan Volodyovski?"

"Pan Mirski was," answered Butrym, "till apoplexy struck him on the road; but Pan Oskyerko is there, and Pan Kovalski, and the two Skshetuskis."

"What Skshetuskis?" cried Jendzian. "Is not one of them Skshetuski from Bujets?"

"I do not know where he lives," said Butrym, "but I know that he was at Zbaraj."

"Save us! that is my lord!"

Here Jendzian saw how strangely such a word would sound in the mouth of a starosta, and added,—

"My lord godson's father, I wanted to say."

The starosta said this without forethought, for in fact he had been the second godfather to Skshetuski's first son, Yaremka.

Meanwhile thoughts one after another were crowding to the head of Pan Kmita, sitting in the dark corner of the room. First the soul within him was roused at sight of the terrible graycoat, and his hand grasped the sabre involuntarily. For he knew that Yuzva, mainly, had caused the death of his comrades, and was his most inveterate enemy. The old-time Pan Kmita would have commanded to take him and tear him with horses, but the Pan Babinich of that day controlled himself. Alarm, however, seized him at the thought that if the man were to recognize him various dangers might come to his farther journey and the whole undertaking. He determined, therefore, not to let himself be known, and he pushed ever deeper into the shade; at last he put his elbow on the table, and placing his head in his palms began to feign sleep; but at the same time he whispered to Soroka, who was sitting at the table,—

"Go to the stable, let the horses be ready. We will go in the night."

Soroka rose and went out; Kmita still feigned sleep. Various memories came to his head. These people reminded him of Lauda, Vodokty, and that brief past which had vanished as a dream. When a short time before Yuzva Butrym said that he belonged to the former Billevich squadron, the heart trembled in Pan Andrei at the mere name. And it came to his mind that it was also evening, that the fire was burning in the chimney in the same way, when he dropped unexpectedly into Vodokty, as if with the snow, and for the first time saw in the servants' hall Olenka among the spinners.

He saw now with closed lids, as if with eyesight, that bright, calm lady; he remembered everything that had taken place,—how she wished to be his guardian angel, to strengthen him in good, to guard him from evil, to show him the straight road of worthiness. If he had listened to her, if he had listened to her! She knew also what ought to be done, on what side to stand; knew where was virtue, honesty, duty, and simply would have taken him by the hand and led him, if he had listened to her.

Here love, roused by remembrance, rose so much in Pan Andrei's heart that he was ready to pour out all his blood, if he could fall at the feet of that lady; and at that moment he was ready to fall on the neck of that bear of Lauda, that slayer of his comrades, simply because he was from that region, had named the Billeviches, had seen Olenka.

His own name repeated a number of times by Yuzva Butrym roused him first from his musing. The tenant of Vansosh inquired about acquaintances, and Yuzva told him what had happened in Kyedani from the time of the memorable treaty of the hetman with the Swedes; he spoke of the oppression of the army, the imprisonment of the colonels, of sending them to Birji, and their fortunate escape. The name of Kmita, covered with all the horror of treason and cruelty, was repeated prominently in those narratives. Yuzva did not know that Pan Volodyovski, the Skshetuskis, and Zagloba owed their lives to Kmita; but he told of what had happened in Billeviche,—

"Our colonel seized that traitor in Billeviche, as a fox in his den, and straightway commanded to lead him to death; I took him with great delight, for the hand of God had reached him, and from moment to moment I held the lantern to his eyes, to see if he showed any sorrow. But no! He went boldly, not considering that he would stand before the judgment of God,—such is his reprobate nature. And when I advised him to make even the sign of the cross, he answered, 'Shut thy mouth, fellow; 'tis no affair of thine!' We posted him under a pear-tree outside the village, and I was already giving the word, when Pan Zagloba, who went with us, gave the order to search him, to see if he had papers on his person. A letter was found. Pan Zagloba said, 'Hold the light!' and he read. He had barely begun reading when he caught his head: 'Jesus, Mary! bring him back to the house!' Pan Zagloba mounted his horse and rode off, and we brought Kmita back, thinking they would burn him before death, to get information from him. But nothing of the kind! They let the traitor go free. It was not for my head to judge what they found in the letter, but I would not have let him go."

"What was in that letter?" asked the tenant of Vansosh.

"I know not; I only think that there must have been still other officers in the hands of the prince voevoda, who would have had them shot right away if we had shot Kmita. Besides, our colonel may have taken pity on the tears of Panna Billevich, for she fell in a faint so that hardly were they able to bring her to her senses. I do not make bold to complain; still evil has happened, for the harm which that man has done, Lucifer himself would not be ashamed of. All Lithuania weeps through him; and how many widows and orphans and how many poor people complain against him is known to God only. Whoso destroys him will have merit in heaven and before men."

Here conversation turned again to Pan Volodyovski, the Skshetuskis, and the squadrons in Podlyasye.

"It is hard to find provisions," said Butrym, "for the lands of the hetman are plundered completely,—nothing can be found in them for the tooth of a man or a horse; and the nobles are poor in the villages, as with us in Jmud. The colonels have determined therefore to divide the horses into hundreds, and post them five or ten miles apart. But when winter comes, I cannot tell what will happen."

Kmita, who had listened patiently while the conversation touched him, moved now, and had opened his mouth to say from his dark corner, "The hetman will take you, when thus divided, one by one, like lobsters from a net." But at that moment the door opened, and in it stood Soroka, whom Kmita had sent to get the horses ready for the road. The light from the chimney fell straight on the stern face of the sergeant. Yuzva Butrym glanced at him, looked a long time, then turned to Jendzian and asked,—

"Is that a servant of your great mightiness? I know him from some place or another."

"No," replied Jendzian; "those are nobles going with horses to fairs."

"But whither?" asked Yuzva.

"To Sobota," said old Kyemlich.

"Where is that?"

"Not far from Pyantek."

Yuzva accounted this answer an untimely jest, as Kmita had previously, and said with a frown, "Answer when people ask!"

"By what right do you ask?"

"I can make that clear to you, for I am sent out to see if there are not suspicious men in the neighborhood. Indeed it seems to me there are some, who do not wish to tell where they are going."

Kmita, fearing that a fight might rise out of this conversation, said, without moving from the dark corner,—

"Be not angry, worthy soldier, for Pyantek and Sobota are towns, like others, in which horse-fairs are held in the fall. If you do not believe, ask the lord starosta, who must know of them."

"They are regular places," said Jendzian.

"In that case it is all right. But why go to those places? You can sell horses in Shchuchyn, where there is a great lack of them, and those which we took in Pilvishki are good for nothing; they are galled."

"Every man goes where it is better for him, and we know our own road," answered Kmita.

"I know not whether it is better for you; but it is not better for us that horses are driven to the Swedes and informants go to them."

"It is a wonder to me," said the tenant of Vansosh. "These people talk against the Swedes, and somehow they are in a hurry to go to them." Here he turned to Kmita: "And you do not seem to me greatly like a horse-dealer, for I saw a fine ring on your finger, of which no lord would be ashamed."

"If it has pleased your grace, buy it of me; I gave two quarters for it in Leng."

"Two quarters? Then it is not genuine, but a splendid counterfeit. Show it."

"Take it, your grace."

"Can you not move yourself? Must I go?"

"I am terribly tired."

"Ah, brother, a man would say that you are trying to hide your face."

Hearing this, Yuzva said not a word, but approached the chimney, took out a burning brand, and holding it high above his head, went straight toward Kmita and held the light before his eyes.

Kmita rose in an instant to his whole height, and during one wink of an eyelid they looked at each other eye to eye. Suddenly the brand fell from the hand of Yuzva, scattering a thousand sparks on the way.

"Jesus, Mary!" screamed Butrym, "this is Kmita!"

"I am he!" said Pan Andrei, seeing that there were no further means of concealment.

"This way, this way! Seize him!" shouted Yuzva to the soldiers who had remained outside. Then turning to Pan Andrei, he said,—

"Thou art he, O hell-dweller, traitor! Thou art that Satan in person! Once thou didst slip from my hands, and now thou art hurrying in disguise to the Swedes. Thou art that Judas, that torturer of women and men! I have thee!"

So saying, he seized Pan Andrei by the shoulder; but Pan Andrei seized him. First, however, the two young Kyemliches, Kosma and Damian, had risen from the bench, almost touching the ceiling with their bushy heads, and Kosma asked,—

"Shall we pound, father?"

"Pound!" answered old Kyemlich, unsheathing his sabre.

The doors burst open, and Yuzva's soldiers rushed in; but behind them, almost on their necks, came Kyemlich's men.

Yuzva caught Pan Andrei by the shoulder, and in his right hand held a naked rapier, making a whirlwind and lightning with it around himself. But Pan Andrei, though he had not the gigantic strength of his enemy, seized Butrym's throat as if in a vice. Yuzva's eyes were coming out; he tried to stun Kmita with the hilt of his rapier, but did not succeed, for Kmita thundered first on his forehead with the hilt of his sabre. Yuzva's fingers, holding the shoulder of his opponent, opened at once; he tottered and bent backward under the blow. To make room for a second blow, Kmita pushed him again, and slashed him with full sweep on the face with his sabre. Yuzva fell on his back like an oak-tree, striking the floor with his skull.

"Strike!" cried Kmita, in whom was roused, in one moment, the old fighting spirit.

But he had no need to urge, for it was boiling in the room, as in a pot. The two young Kyemliches slashed with their sabres, and at times butted with their heads, like a pair of bullocks, putting down a man with each blow; after them advanced their old father, bending every moment to the floor, half closing his eyes, and thrusting quickly the point of his weapon under the arms of his sons.

But Soroka, accustomed to fighting in inns and close quarters, spread the greatest destruction. He pressed his opponents so sorely that they could not reach him with a blade; and when he had discharged his pistols in the crowd, he smashed heads with the butts of the pistols, crushing noses, knocking out teeth and eyes. Kyemlich's servants and Kmita's two soldiers aided their masters.

The fight moved from the table to the upper end of the room. The Lauda men defended themselves with rage; but from the moment that Kmita, having finished Yuzva, sprang into the fight and stretched out another Butrym, the victory began to incline to his side.

Jendzian's servants also sprang into the room with sabres and guns; but though their master cried, "Strike!" they were at a loss what to do, for they could not distinguish one side from the other, since the Lauda men wore no uniforms, and in the disturbance the starosta's young men were punished by both sides.

Jendzian held himself carefully outside the battle, wishing to recognize Kmita, and point him out for a shot; but by the faint light of the fire Kmita vanished time after time from his eye,—at one instant springing to view as red as a devil, then again lost in darkness.

Resistance on the part of the Lauda men grew weaker and weaker, for the fall of Yuzva and the terrible name of Kmita had lessened their courage; still they fought on with rage. Meanwhile the innkeeper went past the strugglers quietly with a bucket of water in his hand and dashed it on the fire. In the room followed black darkness; the strugglers gathered into such a dense crowd that they could strike with fists only; after a while cries ceased; only panting breaths could be heard, and the orderless stamp of boots. Through the door, then flung open, sprang first Jendzian's people, after them the Lauda men, then Kmita's attendants.

Pursuit began in the first room, in the bins before the house, and in the shed. Some shots were heard; then uproar and the noise of horses. A battle began at Jendzian's wagons, under which his people hid themselves; the Lauda men too sought refuge there, and Jendzian's people, taking them for the other party, fired at them a number of times.

"Surrender!" cried old Kyemlich, thrusting the point of his sabre between the spokes of the wagon and stabbing at random the men crouched beneath.

564

"Stop! we surrender!" answered a number of voices.

Then the people from Vansosh threw from under the wagon their sabres and guns; after that the young Kyemliches began to drag them out by the hair, till the old man cried,—

"To the wagons! take what comes under your hands! Quick! quick! to the wagons!"

The young men did not let the command be given thrice, but rushed to untie the coverings, from beneath which the swollen sides of Jendzian's sacks appeared. They had begun to throw out the sacks, when suddenly Kmita's voice thundered,—

"Stop!"

And Kmita, supporting his command by his hand, fell to slashing them with the flat of his bloody sabre.

Kosma and Damian sprang quickly aside.

"Cannot we take them, your grace?" asked the old man, submissively.

"Stand back!" cried Kmita. "Find the starosta for me."

Kosma and Damian rushed to the search in a moment, and behind them their father; in a quarter of an hour they came bringing Jendzian, who, when he saw Kmita, bowed low and said,—

"With the permission of your grace, I will say that wrong is done me here, for I did not attack any man, and to visit acquaintances, as I am going to do, is free to all."

Kmita, resting on his sabre, breathed heavily and was silent; Jendzian continued,—

"I did no harm here either to the Swedes or the prince hetman. I was only going to Pan Volodyovski, my old acquaintance; we campaigned together in Russia. Why should I seek a quarrel? I have not been in Kyedani, and what took place there is nothing to me. I am trying to carry off a sound skin; and what God has given me should not be lost, for I did not steal it, but earned it in the sweat of my brow. I have nothing to do with this whole question! Let me go free, your great mightiness—"

Kmita breathed heavily, looking absently at Jendzian all the time.

"I beg humbly, your great mightiness," began the starosta again. "Your great mightiness saw that I did not know those people, and was not a friend of theirs. They fell upon your grace, and now they have their pay; but why should I be made to suffer? Why should my property be lost? How am I to blame? If it cannot be otherwise, I will pay a ransom to the soldiers of your great mightiness, though there is not much remaining to me, poor man. I will give them a thaler apiece, so that their labor be not lost,—I will give them two; and your great mightiness will receive from me also—"

"Cover the wagons!" cried Kmita, suddenly. "But do you take the wounded men and go to the devil!"

"I thank your grace humbly," said the lord tenant of Vansosh.

Then old Kyemlich approached, pushing out his underlip with the remnants of his teeth, and groaning,—

"Your grace, that is ours. Mirror of justice, that is ours."

But Kmita gave him such a look that the old man cowered, and dared not utter another word.

Jendzian's people rushed, with what breath they had, to put the horses to the wagons. Kmita turned again to the lord starosta,—

"Take all the wounded and killed, carry them to Pan Volodyovski, and tell him from me that I am not his enemy, but may be a better friend than he thinks. I wish to avoid him, for it is not yet time for us to meet. Perhaps that time will come later; but to-day he would neither believe me, nor have I that wherewith to convince him,—perhaps later—Do you understand? Tell him that those people fell upon me and I had to defend myself."

"In truth it was so," responded Jendzian.

"Wait; tell Pan Volodyovski, besides, to keep the troops together, for Radzivill, the moment he receives cavalry from Pontus de la Gardie, will move on them. Perhaps now he is on the road. Yanush and Boguslav Radzivill are intriguing with the Elector of Brandenburg, and it is dangerous to be near the boundary. But above all, let them keep together, or they will perish for nothing. The voevoda of Vityebsk wishes to come to Podlyasye; let them go to meet him, so as to give aid in case of obstruction."

"I will tell everything, as if I were paid for it."

"Though Kmita says this, though Kmita gives warning, let them believe him, take counsel with other colonels, and consider that they will be stronger together. I repeat that the hetman is already on the road, and I am not an enemy of Pan Volodyovski."

"If I had some sign from your grace, that would be still better," said Jendzian.

"What good is a sign?"

"Pan Volodyovski would straightway have greater belief in your grace's sincerity; would think, 'There must be something in what he says if he has sent a sign.'"

"Then here is the ring; though there is no lack of signs of me on the heads of those men whom you are taking to Pan Volodyovski."

Kmita drew the ring from his finger. Jendzian on his part took it hastily, and said,—

"I thank your grace humbly."

An hour later, Jendzian with his wagons and his people, a little shaken up however, rode forward quietly toward Shchuchyn, taking three killed and the rest wounded, among whom were

567

Yuzva Butrym, with a cut face and a broken head. As he rode along Jendzian looked at the ring, in which the stone glittered wonderfully in the moonlight, and he thought of that strange and terrible man, who having caused so much harm to the confederates and so much good to the Swedes and Radzivill, still wished apparently to save the confederates from final ruin.

"For he gives sincere advice," said Jendzian to himself. "It is always better to hold together. But why does he forewarn? Is it from love of Volodyovski, because the latter gave him his life in Billeviche? It must be from love! Yes, but that love may come out with evil result for the hetman. Kmita is a strange man; he serves Radzivill, wishes well to our people, and is going to the Swedes; I do not understand this." After a while he added: "He is a bountiful lord; but it is evil to come in his way."

As earnestly and vainly as Jendzian, did old Kyemlich rack his brain in effort to find an answer to the query, "Whom does Pan Kmita serve?"

"He is going to the king, and kills the confederates, who are fighting specially on the king's side. What is this? And he does not trust the Swedes, for he hides from them. What will happen to us?"

Not being able to arrive at any conclusion, he turned in rage to his sons: "Rascals! You will perish without blessing! And you could not even pull away a little from the slain?"

"We were afraid!" answered Kosma and Damian.

Soroka alone was satisfied, and he clattered joyously after his colonel.

"Evil fate has missed us," thought he, "for we killed those fellows. I'm curious to know whom we shall kill next time."

And it was all one to him, as was also this,—whither he was faring.

No one dared approach Kmita or ask him anything, for the young colonel was as gloomy as night. He grieved terribly that he had to kill those men, at the side of whom he would have been glad to stand as quickly as possible in the ranks. But if he had yielded and let himself be taken to Volodyovski, what would Volodyovski have thought on learning that he was seized making his way in disguise to the Swedes, and with passes to the Swedish commandants?

"My old sins are pursuing and following me," said Kmita to himself. "I will flee to the farthest place; and guide me, O God!"

He began to pray earnestly and to appease his conscience, which repeated, "Again corpses against thee, and not corpses of Swedes."

"O God, be merciful!" answered Kmita. "I am going to my king; there my service will begin."

CHAPTER XXXII.

Jendzian had no intention of passing a night at "The Mandrake," for from Vansosh to Shchuchyn was not far,—he wanted merely to give rest to his horses, especially to those drawing the loaded wagons. Therefore, when Kmita let him travel farther, Jendzian lost no time, and entered Shchuchyn late in the evening. Having announced himself to the sentries, he took his place on the square; for the houses were occupied by soldiers, who even then were not all able to find lodgings. Shchuchyn passed for a town, but was not one in reality; for it had not yet even walls, a town hall, courts of justice, or the college of monks, founded in the time of King Yan III. It had a few houses, but a greater number of cabins than houses, and was called a town, because it was built in a quadrangular form with a market-place in the centre, slightly less swampy than the pond at which the paltry little place was situated.

Jendzian slept under his warm wolfskin till morning, and then went straight to Pan Volodyovski, who, as he had not seen him for an age, received him with gladness and took him at once to Pan Yan and Zagloba. Jendzian shed tears at sight of his former master, whom he had served faithfully so many years; and with whom he had passed through so many adventures and worked himself finally to fortune. Without shame of his former service, Jendzian began to kiss the hands of Pan Yan and repeat with emotion,—

"My master, my master, in what times do we meet again!"

Then all began in a chorus to complain of the times; at last Zagloba said,—

"But you, Jendzian, are always in the bosom of fortune, and as I see have come out a lord. Did I not prophesy that if you were not hanged you would have fortune? What is going on with you now?"

"My master, why hang me, when I have done nothing against God, nothing against the law? I have served faithfully; and if I have betrayed any man, he was an enemy,—which I consider a special service. And if I destroyed a scoundrel here and there by stratagem, as some one of the rebels, or that witch,—do you remember, my master?—that is not a sin; but even if it were a sin, it is my master's, not mine, for it was from you that I learned stratagems."

"Oh, that cannot be! See what he wants!" said Zagloba. "If you wish me to howl for your sins after death, give me their fruit during life. You are using alone all that wealth which you gained with the Cossacks, and alone you will be turned to roast bacon in hell."

"God is merciful, my master, though it is untrue that I use wealth for myself alone; for first I beggared our wicked neighbors with lawsuits, and took care of my parents, who are living now quietly in Jendziane, without any disputes,—for the Yavorskis have gone off with packs to beg, and I, at a distance, am earning my living as I can."

"Then you are not living in Jendziane?" asked Pan Yan.

"In Jendziane my parents live as of old, but I am living in Vansosh, and I cannot complain, for God has blessed me. But when I heard that all you gentlemen were in Shchuchyn, I could not sit still, for I thought to myself, 'Surely it is time to move again!' There is going to be war, let it come!"

"Own up," said Zagloba, "the Swedes frightened you out of Vansosh?"

"There are no Swedes yet in Vidzka, though small parties appear, and cautiously, for the peasants are terribly hostile."

"That is good news for me," said Volodyovski, "for yesterday I sent a party purposely to get an informant concerning the Swedes, for I did not know whether it was possible to stay in Shchuchyn with safety; surely that party conducted you hither?"

"That party? Me? I have conducted it, or rather I have brought it, for there is not even one man of that party who can sit on a horse alone."

"What do you say? What has happened?" inquired Volodyovski.

"They are terribly beaten!" explained Jendzian.

"Who beat them?"

"Pan Kmita."

The Skshetuskis and Zagloba sprang up from the benches, one interrupting the other in questioning,—

"Pan Kmita? But what was he doing here? Has the prince himself come already? Well! Tell right away what has happened."

Pan Volodyovski rushed out of the room to see with his eyes, to verify the extent of the misfortune, and to look at the men; therefore Jendzian said,—

"Why should I tell? Better wait till Pan Volodyovski comes back; for it is more his affair, and it is a pity to move the mouth twice to repeat the same story."

"Did you see Kmita with your own eyes?" asked Zagloba.

"As I see you, my master!"

"And spoke with him?"

"Why should I not speak with him, when we met at 'The Mandrake' not far from here? I was resting my horses, and he had stopped for the night. An hour would have been short for our talk. I complained of the Swedes, and he complained also of the Swedes—"

"Of the Swedes? He complained also?" asked Pan Yan.

"As of devils, though he was going among them."

"Had he many troops?"

"He had no troops, only a few attendants; true, they were armed, and had such snouts that even those men who slaughtered the Holy Innocents at Herod's command had not rougher or viler. He gave himself out as a small noble in pigskin boots, and said that he went with horses to the fairs. But though he had a number of horses, his story did not seem clear to me, for neither his person nor his bearing belonged to a horse-dealer, and I saw a fine ring on his finger,—this one." Here Jendzian held a glittering stone before the listeners.

Zagloba struck himself on the side and cried: "Ah, you gypsied that out of him! By that alone might I know you, Jendzian, at the end of the world!"

"With permission of my master, I did not gypsy it; for I am a noble, not a gypsy, and feel myself the equal of any man, though I live on rented lands till I settle on my own. This ring Pan

572

Kmita gave as a token that what he said was true; and very soon I will repeat his words faithfully to your graces, for it seems to me that in this case our skins are in question."

"How is that?" asked Zagloba.

At this moment Volodyovski came in, roused to the utmost, and pale from anger; he threw his cap on the table and cried,—

"It passes imagination! Three men killed; Yuzva Butrym cut up, barely breathing!"

"Yuzva Butrym? He is a man with the strength of a bear!" said the astonished Zagloba.

"Before my eyes Pan Kmita stretched him out," put in Jendzian.

"I've had enough of that Kmita!" cried Volodyovski, beside himself; "wherever that man shows himself he leaves corpses behind, like the plague. Enough of this! Balance for balance, life for life; but now a new reckoning! He has killed my men, fallen upon good soldiers; that will be set to his account before our next meeting."

"He did not attack them, but they him; for he hid himself in the darkest corner, so they should not recognize him," explained Jendzian.

"And you, instead of giving aid to my men, testify in his favor!" said Volodyovski, in anger.

"I speak according to justice. As to aid, my men tried to give aid; but it was hard for them, for in the tumult they did not know whom to beat and whom to spare, and therefore they suffered. That I came away with my life and my sacks is due to the sense of Pan Kmita alone, for hear how it happened."

Jendzian began a detailed account of the battle in "The Mandrake," omitting nothing; and when at length he told what

Kmita had commanded him to tell, they were all wonder fully astonished.

"Did he say that himself?" asked Zagloba.

"He himself," replied Jendzian. "'I,' said he, 'am not an enemy to Pan Volodyovski or the confederates, though they think differently. Later this will appear; but meanwhile let them come together, in God's name, or the voevoda of Vilna will take them one by one like lobsters from a net.'"

"And did he say that the voevoda was already on the march?" asked Tan Yan.

"He said that the voevoda was only waiting for Swedish reinforcements, and that he would move at once on Podlyasye."

"What do you think of all this, gentlemen?" asked Volodyovski, looking at his comrades.

"Either that man is betraying Radzivill, or he is preparing some ambush for us. But of what kind? He advises us to keep in a body. What harm to us may rise out of that?"

"To perish of hunger," answered Volodyovski. "I have just received news that Jyromski, Kotovski, and Lipnitski must dispose their cavalry in parties of some tens each over the whole province, for they cannot get forage together."

"But if Radzivill really does come," asked Pan Stanislav, "who can oppose him?"

No one could answer that question, for really it was as clear as the sun that if the grand hetman of Lithuania should come and find the confederates scattered, he could destroy them with the greatest ease.

"An astonishing thing!" repeated Zagloba; and after a moment's silence he continued: "Still I should think that he had abandoned Radzivill. But in such a case he would not be slipping past in disguise, and to whom,—to the Swedes." Here he turned to Jendzian: "Did he tell you that he was going to Warsaw?"

574

"He did."

"But the Swedish forces are there already."

"About this hour he must have met the Swedes, if he travelled all night," answered Jendzian.

"Have you ever seen such a man?" asked Zagloba, looking at his comrades.

"That there is in him evil with good, as tares with wheat, is certain," said Pan Yan; "but that there is any treason in this counsel that he gives us at present, I simply deny. I do not know whither he is going, why he is slipping past in disguise; and it would be idle to break my head over this, for it is some mystery. But he gives good advice, warns us sincerely: I will swear to that, as well as to this,—that the only salvation for us is to listen to his advice. Who knows if we are not indebted to him again, for safety and life?"

"For God's sake," cried Volodyovski, "how is Radzivill to come here when Zolotarenko's men and Hovanski's infantry are in his way? It is different in our case! One squadron may slip through, and even with one we had to open a way through Pilvishki with sabres. It is another thing with Kmita, who is slipping by with a few men; but when the prince hetman passes with a whole army? Either he will destroy those first—"

Volodyovski had not finished speaking when the door opened and an attendant came in.

"A messenger with a letter to the Colonel," said he.

"Bring it."

The attendant went out and returned in a moment with the letter. Pan Michael broke the seal quickly and read,—

That which I did not finish telling the tenant of Vansosh yesterday, I add to-day in writing. The hetman of himself has troops enough against you, but he is waiting for Swedish reinforcements, so as to go with the authority of the King of

575

Sweden; for then if the Northerners attack him they will have to strike the Swedes too, and that would mean war with the King of Sweden. They will not venture to make war without orders, for they fear the Swedes, and will not take on themselves the responsibility of beginning a war. They have discovered that it is Radzivill's purpose to put the Swedes forward against them everywhere; let them shoot or cut down even one man, there would be war at once. The Northerners themselves know not what to do now, for Lithuania is given up to the Swedes; they stay therefore in one place, only waiting for what will be, and warring no further. For these reasons they do not restrain Radzivill, nor oppose him. He will go directly against you, and will destroy you one after the other, unless you collect in one body. For God's sake, do this, and beg the voevoda of Vityebsk to come quickly, since it is easier for him to reach you now through the Northerners while they stand as if stupefied. I wanted to warn you under another name, so that you might more easily believe, but because tidings are given you already from another, I write my own name. It is destruction if you do not believe. I am not now what I was, and God grant that you will hear something altogether different about me.

Kmita.

"You wished to know how Radzivill would come to us; here is your answer!" said Pan Yan.

"That is true, he gives good reasons," answered Volodyovski.

"What good reasons! holy reasons!" cried Zagloba. "There can be no doubt here. I was the first to know that man; and though there are no curses that have not been showered on his head, I tell you we shall bless him yet. With me it is enough to look at a man to know his value. You remember how he dropped into my heart at Kyedani? He loves us, too, as knightly people.

When he heard my name the first time, he came near suffocating me with admiration, and for my sake saved you all."

"You have not changed," remarked Jendzian; "why should Pan Kmita admire you more than my master or Pan Volodyovski?"

"You are a fool!" answered Zagloba. "He knew you at once; and if he called you the tenant, and not the fool of Vansosh, it was through politeness."

"Then maybe he admired you through politeness!" retorted Jendzian.

"See how the bread swells; get married, lord tenant, and surely you will swell better—I guarantee that."

"That is all well," said Volodyovski; "but if he is so friendly, why did he not come to us himself instead of slipping around us like a wolf and biting our men?"

"Not your head, Pan Michael. What we counsel do you carry out, and no evil will come of it. If your wit were as good as your sabre, you would be grand hetman already, in place of Revera Pototski. And why should Kmita come here? Is it not because you would not believe him, just as you do not now believe his letter, from which it might come to great trouble, for he is a stubborn cavalier. But suppose that you did believe him, what would the other colonels do, such as Kotovski, Jyromski, or Lipnitski? What would your Lauda men say? Would not they cut him down the moment you turned your head away?"

"Father is right!" said Pan Yan; "he could not come here."

"Then why was he going to the Swedes?" insisted the stubborn Pan Michael.

"The devil knows, whether he is going to the Swedes; the devil knows what may flash into Kmita's wild noddle. That is nothing to us, but let us take advantage of the warning, if we wish to carry away our heads."

"There is nothing to meditate on here," said Pan Stanislav.

"It is needful to inform with all speed Kotovski, Jyromski, Lipnitski, and that other Kmita," said Pan Yan. "Send to them, Michael, news at once; but do not write who gave the warning, for surely they would not believe."

"We alone shall know whose the service, and in due time we shall not fail to publish it!" cried Zagloba, "Onward, lively, Michael!"

"And we will move to Byalystok ourselves, appointing a muster there for all. God give us the voevoda of Vityebsk at the earliest," said Yan.

"From Byalystok we must send a deputation from the army to him. God grant that we shall stand before the eyes of the hetman of Lithuania," said Zagloba, "with equal force or greater than his own. It is not for us to rush at him, but it is different with the voevoda. He is a worthy man, and honest; there is not another such in the Commonwealth."

"Do you know Pan Sapyeha?" asked Stanislav.

"Do I know him! I knew him as a little boy, not higher than my sabre. But he was then like an angel."

"And now he has turned into money, not only his property, not only his silver and jewels, but most likely he has melted into coin the metal of his horse-trappings, so as to collect as many troops as possible against the enemy," said Volodyovski.

"Thank God that there is even one such man," answered Pan Stanislav, "for remember how we trusted in Radzivill."

"Oh that is blasphemous!" cried Zagloba. "Voevoda of Vityebsk, ba! ba! Long life to the voevoda of Vityebsk! And you, Michael, to the road with all speed, to the road! Let the mudfish remain in these swamps of Shchuchyn, but we will go to Byalystok, where perhaps we shall find other fish. The Jews there, on Sabbath, bake very excellent bread. Well, at least war will begin; I am yearning for it. And if we break through Radzivill we will begin at the Swedes. We have shown them already what we can do. To the road, Michael, for *periculum in mora* (there is danger in delay)!"

"I will go to put the squadrons in line!" said Pan Yan.

An hour later, messengers, between ten and twenty in number, were flying as a horse gallops toward Podlyasye, and soon after them moved the whole squadron of Lauda. The officers went in advance, arranging and discussing; and Roh Kovalski, the lieutenant, led the soldiers. They went through Osovyets and Gonyandz, shortening for themselves the road to Byalystok, where they hoped to find other confederate squadrons.

CHAPTER XXXIII.

Pan Volodyovski's letters, announcing the expedition of Radzivill, found hearing with all the colonels, scattered throughout the whole province of Podlyasye. Some had divided their squadrons already into smaller detachments, so as to winter them more easily; others permitted officers to lodge in private houses, so that there remained at each flag merely a few officers and some tens of soldiers. The colonels permitted this partly in view of hunger, and partly through the difficulty of retaining in just discipline squadrons which after they had refused obedience to their own proper authority were inclined to oppose officers on the slightest pretext. If a chief of sufficient weight had been found, and had led them at once to battle against either of the two enemies, or even against Radzivill, discipline would have remained surely intact; but it had become weakened by idleness in Podlyasye, where the time passed in shooting at Radzivill's castles, in plundering the goods of the voevoda, and in parleying with Prince Boguslav. In these circumstances the soldier grew accustomed only to violence and oppression of peaceful people in the province. Some of the soldiers, especially attendants and camp-followers, deserted, and forming unruly bands, worked at robbery on the highway. And so that army, which had not joined any enemy and was the one hope of the king and the patriots, was dwindling day by day. The division of squadrons into small detachments had dissolved them completely. It is true that it was difficult to subsist in a body, but still it may be that the fear of want was exaggerated purposely. It was autumn, and the harvest had been good; no enemy had up to that time ravaged the province with fire and sword. Just then the robberies of the confederate soldiers were destroying this province precisely as inactivity was destroying the soldiers themselves; for things had combined so wonderfully that the enemy left those squadrons in peace.

The Swedes, flooding the country from the west and extending to the south, had not yet come to that corner which between the province of Mazovia and Lithuania formed Podlyasye; from the other side the legions of Hovanski, Trubetskoi, and Serebryani, stood in inactivity in the district occupied by them, hesitating, or rather not knowing what to lay hold on. In the Russian provinces Buturlin and Hmelnitski sent parties out in old fashion, and just then they had defeated at Grodek a handful of troops led by Pototski, grand hetman of the kingdom. But Lithuania was under Swedish protection. To ravage and to occupy it further meant, as was stated justly by Kmita in his letter, to declare war against the Swedes, who were terrible and roused universal alarm in the world. "There was therefore a moment of relief from the Northerners;" and some experienced men declared that they would soon be allies of Yan Kazimir and the Commonwealth against the King of Sweden, whose power, were he to become lord of the whole Commonwealth, would not have an equal in Europe.

Hovanski therefore attacked neither Podlyasye nor the confederate squadrons, while these squadrons, scattered and without a leader, attacked no one, and were unable to attack or to undertake anything more important than plundering the property of Radzivill; and withal they were dwindling away. But Volodyovski's letters, touching the impending attack by the hetman, roused the colonels from their inactivity and slumber. They assembled the squadrons, called in scattered soldiers, threatening with penalties those who would not come. Jyromski, the most important of the colonels, and whose squadron was in the best condition, moved first, and without delay, to Byalystok; after him came in one week Yakub Kmita,—true, with only one hundred and twenty men; then the soldiers of Kotovski and Lipnitski began to assemble, now singly, now in crowds; petty nobles from the surrounding villages also came in as volunteers, such as the Zyentsinkis, the Sviderskis, the Yavorskis, the Jendzians, the Mazovyetskis; volunteers came even from the province of Lyubelsk, such as the Karvovskis and the Turs; and from time to time appeared a more wealthy noble with a few servants, well armed. Deputies were sent from the squadrons to levy contributions, to collect money and provisions for receipts; in a word, activity reigned everywhere, and military preparations sprang up. When Volodyovski with his Lauda squadron arrived, there were already some thousands of people under arms, to whom only a leader was wanting.

These men were unorganized and unruly, though not so unorganized nor so unruly as those nobles of Great Poland, who a few months before had the task of defending the passage of Uistsie against the Swedes; for these men from Podlyasye, Lublin, and Lithuania were accustomed to war, and there were none among them, unless youths, who had not smelled powder, and who "had not used the snuff-box of Gradivus." Each in his time had fought,—now against the Cossacks, now against the Turks, now against Tartars; there were some who still held in remembrance the Swedish wars. But above all towered in military experience and eloquence Pan Zagloba; and he was glad to be in that assemblage of soldiers, in which there were no deliberations with a dry throat.

Zagloba extinguished the importance of colonels the most important. The Lauda men declared that had it not been for him, Volodyovski, the Skshetuskis, Mirski, and Oskyerko would have died at the hands of Radzivill, for they were being taken to Birji to execution. Zagloba did not hide his own services, but rendered complete justice to himself, so that all might know whom they had before them.

"I do not like to praise myself," said he, "nor to speak of what has not been; for with me truth is the basis, as my sister's son also can testify."

Here he turned to Roh Kovalski, who straightway stepped forth from behind Pan Zagloba, and said, with a ringing, stentorian voice,—

"Uncle never lies!"

And, puffing, Pan Roh rolled his eyes over the audience, as if seeking the insolent man who would dare to gainsay him.

But no one ever gainsaid him. Then Zagloba began to tell of his old-time victories,—how during the life of Konyetspolski he had caused victory twice over Gustavus Adolphus, how in later times he staggered Hmelnitski, how he acted at Zbaraj, how Prince Yeremi relied on his counsels in everything, how he confided to him the leadership in sorties.

"And after each sortie," said ho, "when we had spoiled five or ten thousand of the ruffians, Hmelnitski in despair used to butt his head against the wall, and repeat, 'No one has done this but that devil of a Zagloba!' and when it came to the treaty of

Zborovo, the Khan himself looked at me as a wonder, and begged for my portrait, since he wished to send it as a gift to the Sultan."

"Such men do we need now more than ever," said the hearers.

And since many had heard besides of the marvellous deeds of Zagloba, accounts of which were travelling over the whole Commonwealth, and since recent events in Kyedani, such as the liberation of the colonels, and the battle with the Swedes at Klavany, confirmed the old opinion concerning the man,—his glory increased still more; and Zagloba walked in it, as in the sunlight, before the eyes of all men, bright and radiant beyond others.

"If there were a thousand such men in the Commonwealth, it would not have come to what it has!" said the soldiers.

"Let us thank God that we have even one among us."

"He was the first to proclaim Radzivill a traitor."

"And he snatched honorable men from his grasp, and on the road he so pommelled the Swedes at Klavany that a witness of their defeat could not escape."

"He won the first victory!"

"God grant, not the last!"

Colonels like Jyromski, Kotovski, Yakub Kmita, and Lipnitski looked also on Zagloba with great respect. They urged him to their quarters, seizing him from one another by force; and his counsel was sought in everything, while they wondered at his prudence, which was quite equal to his bravery.

And just then they were considering an important affair. They had sent, it is true, deputies to the voevoda of Vityebsk, asking him to come and take command; but since no one knew clearly where the voevoda was at that moment, the deputies went away, and as it were fell into water. There were reports that they had been taken by Zolotarenko's parties, which came as far as Volkovysk, plundering on their own account.

The colonels at Byalystok therefore decided to choose a temporary leader who should have management of all till the arrival of Sapyeha. It is not needful to say that, with the exception of Volodyovski, each colonel was thinking of himself.

Then began persuading and soliciting. The army gave notice that it wished to take part in the election, not through deputies, but in the general circle which was formed for that purpose.

Volodyovski, after advising with his comrades, gave strong support to Jyromski, who was a virtuous man and important; besides, he impressed the troops by his looks, and a senatorial beard to his girdle. He was also a ready and experienced soldier. He, through gratitude, recommended Volodyovski; but Kotovski, Lipnitski, and Yakub Kmita opposed this, insisting that it was not possible to select the youngest, for the chief must represent before the country the greatest dignity.

"But who is the oldest here?" asked many voices.

"Uncle is the oldest," cried suddenly Roh Kovalski, with such a thundering voice that all turned toward him.

"It is a pity that he has no squadron!" said Yahovich, Jyromski's lieutenant.

But others began to cry: "Well, what of that? Are we bound to choose only a colonel? Is not the election in our power? Is this not free suffrage? Any noble may be elected king, not merely commander."

Then Pan Lipnitski, as he did not favor Jyromski, and wished by all means to prevent his election, raised his voice,—

"As true as life! You are free, gracious gentlemen, to vote as may please you. If you do not choose a colonel, it will be better;

for there will be no offence to any man, nor will there be jealousy."

Then came a terrible uproar. Many voices cried, "To the vote! to the vote!" but others, "Who here is more famous than Pan Zagloba? Who is a greater knight? Who is a more experienced soldier? We want Pan Zagloba! Long life to him! Long life to our commander!"

"Long life to Pan Zagloba! long life to him!" roared more and more throats.

"To the sabres with the stubborn!" cried the more quarrelsome.

"There is no opposition! By acclamation!" answered crowds.

"Long life to him! He conquered Gustavus Adolphus! He staggered Hmelnitski!"

"He saved the colonels themselves!"

"He conquered the Swedes at Klavany!"

"Vivat! vivat! Zagloba dux! Vivat! vivat!"

And throngs began to hurl their caps in the air, while running through the camp in search of Zagloba.

He was astonished, and at the first moment confused, for he had not sought the office. He wanted it for Pan Yan, and did not expect such a turn of affairs. So when a throng of some thousands began to shout his name, his breath failed him, and he became as red as a beet. Then his comrades rushed around him; but in their enthusiasm they interpreted everything in a good sense, for seeing his confusion they fell to shouting,—

"Look at him! he blushes like a maiden! His modesty is equal to his manhood! Long life to him, and may he lead us to victory!"

Meanwhile the colonels also came up,—glad, not glad; they congratulated him on his office, and perhaps some were even glad that it had missed their rivals. Pan Volodyovski merely moved his mustaches somewhat, he was not less astonished than Zagloba; and Jendzian, with open eyes and mouth, stared with unbelief, but already with respect, at Zagloba, who came to himself by degrees, and after a while put his hands on his hips, and rearing his head, received with fitting dignity the congratulations.

Jyromski congratulated first on behalf of the colonels, and then of the army. Pan Jymirski, an officer of Kotovski's squadron, spoke very eloquently, quoting the maxims of various sages.

Zagloba listened, nodded; finally, when the speaker had finished, the commander gave utterance to the following words,—

"Gracious gentlemen! Even if a man should endeavor to drown honest merit in the unfordable ocean, or cover it with the heaven-touching Carpathians, still, having like oil the property of floating to the surface, it would work itself out, so as to say to the eyes of men, 'I am that which trembles not before light, which has no fear of judgment, which waits for reward.' But as a precious stone is set in gold, so should that virtue be set in modesty; therefore, gracious gentlemen, standing here in your presence, I ask: Have I not hidden myself and my services? Have I praised myself in your presence? Have I asked for this office, with which you have adorned me? You yourselves have discovered my merits, for I am this moment ready to deny them, and to say to you: There are better than I, such as Pan Jyromski, Pan Kotovski, Pan Lipnitski, Pan Kmita, Pan Oskyerko, Pan Skshetuski, Pan Volodyovski,—such great cavaliers that antiquity itself might be proud of them. Why choose me leader, and not some one of them? It is still time. Take from my shoulders this office, and clothe in this mantle a worthier man!"

"Impossible! impossible!" bellowed hundreds and thousands of voices.

"Impossible!" repeated the colonels, delighted with the public praise, and wishing at the same time to show their modesty before the army.

"I see myself that it is impossible now," said Zagloba; "then, gracious gentlemen, let your will be done. I thank you from my heart, lords brothers, and I have faith that God will grant that you be not deceived in the trust which you have placed in me. As you are to stand with me to death, so I promise to stand with you; and if an inscrutable fate brings us either victory or destruction, death itself will not part us, for even after death we shall share a common renown."

Tremendous enthusiasm reigned in the assembly. Some grasped their sabres, others shed tears; sweat stood in drops on the bald head of Zagloba, but the ardor within him grew greater.

"We will stand by our lawful king, by our elected, and by our country," shouted he; "live for them, die for them! Gracious gentlemen, since this fatherland is a fatherland never have such misfortunes fallen on it. Traitors have opened the gates, and there is not a foot of land, save this province, where an enemy is not raging. In you is the hope of the country, and in me your hope; on you and on me the whole Commonwealth has its eyes fixed! Let us show that it holds not its hands forth in vain. As you ask from me manhood and faith, so I ask of you discipline and obedience; and if we be worthy, if we open, by our example, the eyes of those whom the enemy has deceived, then half the Commonwealth will fly to us! Whoso has God and faith in his heart will join us, the forces of heaven will support us, and who in that hour can oppose us?"

"It will be so! As God lives, it will be so! Solomon is speaking! Strike! strike!" shouted thundering voices.

But Zagloba stretched forth his hands to the north, and shouted,—

"Come now, Radzivill! Come now, lord hetman, lord heretic, voevoda of Lucifer! We are waiting for you,—not scattered, but standing together; not in discord, but in harmony; not with papers and compacts, but with swords in our hands! An army of virtue is waiting for you, and I am its leader. Take the field! Meet Zagloba! Call the devils to your side; let us make the trial! Take the field!"

Here he turned again to the army, and roared till his voice was heard throughout the whole camp,—

"As God is true, gracious gentlemen, prophecies support me! Only harmony, and we shall conquer those scoundrels, those wide-breeches and stocking fellows, fish-eaters and lousy rogues, sheepskin tanners who sleigh-ride in summer! We'll give them pepper, till they wear off their heels racing home. Let every living man slay them, the dog brothers! Slay, whoso believes in God, to whom virtue and the country are dear!"

Several thousand sabres were gleaming at once. Throngs surrounded Zagloba, crowding, trampling, pushing, and roaring,—

"Lead us on! lead us on!"

"I will lead you to-morrow! Make ready!" shouted Zagloba, with ardor.

This election took place in the morning, and in the afternoon there was a review of the army. The squadrons were disposed on the plain of Horoshchan, one by the other in great order, with the colonels and banners in front; and before the regiments rode the commander, under a horse-tail standard, with a gilded baton in his hand, and a heron feather in his cap,—you would have said, a born hetman! And so he reviewed in turn the squadrons, as a shepherd examines his flock, and courage was added to the soldiers at sight of that lordly figure. Each colonel came out to him in turn, and he spoke with each,—praised something, blamed something; and in truth those of the new-comers who in the beginning were not pleased with the choice were forced to admit in their souls that the new commander was a soldier very well conversant with military affairs, and for whom leadership was nothing new.

Volodyovski alone moved his mustaches somewhat strangely when the new commander clapped him on the shoulder at the review, in presence of the other colonels, and said,—

"Pan Michael, I am satisfied with you, for your squadron is in such order as no other. Hold on in this fashion, and you may be sure that I'll not forget you."

"'Pon my word!" whispered Volodyovski to Pan Yan on the way home from the review, "what else could a real hetman have told me?"

That same day Zagloba sent detachments in directions in which it was needful to go, and in direction in which there was no need of going. When they returned in the morning, he listened with care to every report; then he betook himself to the quarters of Volodyovski, who lived with Pan Yan and Pan Stanislav.

"Before the army I must uphold dignity," said he, kindly; "when we are alone we can have our old intimacy,—here I am a friend, not a chief. Besides, I do not despise your counsel, though I have my own reason; for I know you as men of experience such as few in the Commonwealth have."

They greeted him therefore in old fashion, and "intimacy" soon reigned completely. Jendzian alone dared not be with him as formerly, and sat on the very edge of his bench.

"What does father think to do?" asked Pan Yan.

"First of all to uphold order and discipline, and keep the soldiers at work, that they may not grow mangy from laziness. I

589

said well, Pan Michael, that you mumbled like a suckling when I sent those parties toward the four points of the world; but I had to do so to inure men to service, for they have been idle a long time. That first, second, what do we need? Not men, for enough of them come, and more will come yet. Those nobles who fled from Mazovia to Prussia before the Swedes, will come too. Men and sabres will not be wanting; but there are not provisions enough, and without supplies no army on earth can remain in the field. I had the idea to order parties to bring in whatever falls into their hands,—cattle, sheep, pigs, grain, hay; and in this province and the district of Vidzko in Mazovia, which also has not seen an enemy yet, there is abundance of everything."

"But those nobles will raise heaven-climbing shouts," said Pan Yan, "if their crops and cattle are taken."

"The army means more for me than the nobles. Let them cry! Supplies will not be taken for nothing. I shall command to give receipts, of which I have prepared so many during the night, that half the Commonwealth might be taken under requisition with them. I have no money; but when the war is over and the Swedes driven out, the Commonwealth will pay. What is the use in talking! It would be worse for the nobles if the army were to grow hungry, go around and rob. I have a plan too of scouring the forests, for I hear that very many peasants have taken refuge there with their cattle. Let the army people return thanks to the Holy Ghost, who inspired them to choose me, for no other man would have managed in such fashion."

"On your great mightiness is a senator's head, that is certain!" exclaimed Jendzian.

"Hei!" retorted Zagloba, rejoiced at the flattery, "and you are not to be imposed on, you rogue! Soon it will be seen how I'll make you lieutenant, only let there be a vacancy."

"I thank your great mightiness humbly," replied Jendzian.

"This is my plan," continued Zagloba: "first to collect such supplies that we could stand a siege, then to make a fortified camp, and let Radzivill come with Swedes or with devils. I'm a rascal if I do not make a second Zbaraj here!"

"As God is dear to me, a noble idea!" cried Volodyovski; "but where can we get cannon?"

"Pan Kotovski has two howitzers, and Yakub Kmita has one gun for firing salutes; in Byalystok are four eight-pounders which were to be sent to the castle of Tykotsin; for you do not know, gentlemen, that Byalystok was left by Pan Vyesyolovski for the support of Tykotsin Castle, and those cannon were bought the past year with the rent, as Pan Stempalski, the manager here, told me. He said also that there were a hundred charges of powder for each cannon. We'll help ourselves, gracious gentlemen; only support me from your souls, and do not forget the body either, which would be glad to drink something, for it is time now for that."

Volodyovski gave orders to bring drink, and they talked on at the cups.

"You thought that you would have the picture of a commander," continued Zagloba, sipping lightly the old mead. "Never, never! I did not ask for the favor; but since they adorn me with it, there must be obedience and order. I know what each office means, and see if I am not equal to every one. I'll make a second Zbaraj in this place, nothing but a second Zbaraj! Radzivill will choke himself well; and the Swedes will choke themselves before they swallow me. I hope that Hovanski will try us too; I would bury him in such style that he would not be found at the last judgment. They are not far away, let them try!—Mead, Pan Michael!"

Volodyovski poured out mead. Zagloba drank it at a draught, wrinkled his forehead, and as if thinking of something said,—

"Of what was I talking? What did I want?—Ah! mead, Pan Michael!"

Volodyovski poured out mead again.

"They say," continued Zagloba, "that Pan Sapyeha likes a drink in good company. No wonder! every honorable man does. Only traitors, who have false thoughts for their country, abstain, lest they tell their intrigues. Radzivill drinks birch sap, and after death will drink pitch. I think that Sapyeha and I shall be fond of each other; but I shall have everything here so arranged that when he comes all will be ready. There is many a thing on my head; but what is to be done? If there is no one in the country to think, then think thou, old Zagloba, while breath is in thy nostrils. The worst is that I have no chancellery."

"And what does father want of a chancellery?" asked Pan Yan.

"Why has the king a chancellery? And why must there be a military secretary with an army? It will be necessary to send to some town to have a seal made for me."

"A seal?" repeated Jendzian, with delight, looking with growing respect at Zagloba.

"And on what will your lordship put the seal?" asked Volodyovski.

"In such a confidential company you may address me as in old times. The seal will not be used by me, but by my chancellor,—keep that in mind, to begin with!"

Here Zagloba looked with pride and importance at those present, till Jendzian sprang up from the bench, and Pan Stanislav muttered,—

"*Honores mutant mores* (honors change manners)!"

"What do I want of a chancellery? But listen to me!" said Zagloba. "Know this, to begin with, that those misfortunes which have fallen upon our country, according to my understanding, have come from no other causes than from license, unruliness, and excesses—Mead, Pan Michael!—and excesses, I say, which like a plague are destroying us; but first of all, from heretics blaspheming with ever-growing boldness the true faith, to the damage of our Most Holy Patroness, who may fall into just anger because of these insults."

"He speaks truly," said the knights, in chorus; "the dissidents were the first to join the enemy, and who knows if they did not bring the enemy hither?"

"For example, the grand hetman of Lithuania!"

"But in this province, where I am commander, there is also no lack of heretics, as in Tykotsin and other towns; therefore to obtain the blessing of God on our undertaking at its inception, a manifesto will be issued, that whoso is living in error must turn from it in three days, and those who will not do that will have their property confiscated to the army."

The knights looked at one another with astonishment. They knew that there was no lack of adroit reason and stratagem in Zagloba, but they did not suppose him to be such a statesman and judge of public questions.

"And you ask," continued Zagloba, with triumph, "where we shall get money for the army? But the confiscations, and all the wealth of the Radzivills, which by confiscation will become army property?"

"Will there be right on our side?" asked Volodyovski.

"There are such times at present that whoever has a sword is right. And what right have the Swedes and all those enemies who are raging within the boundaries of the Commonwealth?"

"It is true!" answered Pan Michael, with conviction.

"That is not enough!" cried Zagloba, growing warmer, "another manifesto will be issued to the nobles of Podlyasye, and those lands in the neighboring provinces which are not yet in the hands of the enemy, to assemble a general militia. These nobles must arm their servants, so that we may not lack infantry. I know that many would be glad to appear, if only they could see some government. They will have a government and manifestoes."

"You have, in truth, as much sense as the grand chancellor of the kingdom," cried Volodyovski.

"Mead, Pan Michael!—A third letter will be sent to Hovanski, telling him to go to destruction; if not, we will smoke him out of every town and castle. They (the Northerners) are quiet now in Lithuania, it is true, and do not capture castles; but Zolotarenko's men rob, going along in parties of one or two thousand. Let him restrain them, or we will destroy them."

"We might do that, indeed," said Pan Yan, "and the troops would not be lying idle."

"I am thinking of this, and I will send new parties today, precisely to Volkovysk; but some things are to be done, and others are not to be omitted. I wish to send a fourth letter to our elected, our good king, to console him in his sorrow; saying that there are still men who have not deserted him, that there are sabres and hearts ready at his nod. Let our father have at least this comfort in a strange land; our beloved lord, our Yagellon blood, which must wander in exile,—think of it, think of it!"

Here Zagloba fell to sobbing, for he had much mead in his head, and at last he roared from pity over the fate of the king, and Pan Michael at once seconded him in a thinner voice. Jendzian sobbed too, or pretended to sob; but Pan Yan and Pan Stanislav rested their heads on their hands, and sat in silence.

The silence continued for a while; suddenly Zagloba fell into a rage.

"What is the elector doing?" cried he. "If he has made a pact with the Prussian towns, let him take the field against the Swedes, let him not intrigue on both sides, let him do what a loyal vassal is bound to do, and take the field in defence of his lord and benefactor."

"Who can tell that he will not declare for the Swedes?" asked Pan Stanislav.

"Declare for the Swedes? Then I will declare to him! The Prussian boundary is not far, and I have some thousands of sabres within call! You will not deceive Zagloba! As true as you see me here, the commander of this noble army, I will visit him with fire and sword. We have not provisions; well, we shall find all we need in Prussian storehouses."

"Mother of God!" cried Jendzian, in ecstasy. "Your great mightiness will conquer crowned heads!"

"I will write to him at once: 'Worthy Pan Elector, there is enough of turning the cat away by the tail, enough of evasion and delay! Come out against the Swedes, or I will come on a visit to Prussia. It cannot be otherwise.'—Ink, pen, and paper!— Jendzian, will you go with the letter?"

"I will go!" answered the tenant of Vansosh, delighted with his new dignity.

But before pen, ink, and paper were brought to Zagloba, shouts were raised in front of the house, and throngs of soldiers darkened the windows. Some shouted "Vivat!" others cried, "Allah," in Tartar. Zagloba and his comrades went out to see what was taking place.

It appeared that they were bringing those eight pounders which Zagloba had remembered, and the sight of which was now delighting the hearts of the soldiers.

Pan Stempalski, the manager of Byalystok, approached Zagloba, and said,—

"Serene, great mighty Commander! From the time that he of immortal memory, the lord marshal of the Grand Principality of Lithuania, left by will his property at Byalystok to support the castle of Tykotsin, I, being manager of that property, have applied faithfully and honestly all its income to the benefit of that castle, as I can show to the whole Commonwealth by registers. So that working more than twenty years I have provided that castle with powder and guns and brass; holding it as a sacred duty that every copper should go to that object to which the serene great mighty marshal of the Grand Principality of Lithuania commanded that it should go. But when by the changing wheel of fate the castle of Tykotsin became the greatest support in this province of the enemies of the country, I asked God and my own conscience whether I ought to strengthen it more, or whether I was not bound to give into the hands of your great mightiness this wealth and these military supplies obtained from the income of the present year."

"You should give them to me!" interrupted Zagloba, with importance.

"I ask but one thing,—that your great mightiness be pleased, in presence of the whole army and in writing, to give me a receipt, that I applied nothing from that property to my own use, and that I delivered everything into the hands of the Commonwealth, worthily represented here by you, the great mighty commander."

Zagloba motioned with his head as a sign of assent, and began at once to look over the register.

It appeared that besides the eight-pounders there were put away in the storehouses three hundred German muskets, very good ones; besides two hundred Moscow halberts, for infantry in the defence of walls and breastworks; and six thousand ducats in ready money.

"The money will be divided among the army," said Zagloba; "and as to the muskets and halberts,"—here he looked around,—"Pan Oskyerko, you will take them and form a body of infantry; there are a few foot-soldiers here from the Radzivill fugitives, and as many as are lacking may be taken from the millers."

Then he turned to all present: "Gracious gentlemen, there is money, there are cannons, there will be infantry and provisions,—these are my orders, to begin with."

"Vivat!" shouted the army.

"And now, gracious gentlemen, let all the young men go on a jump to the villages for spades, shovels, and pickaxes. We will make a fortified camp, a second Zbaraj! But whether a man belongs to cavalry or infantry, let none be ashamed of the shovel, and to work!"

Then the commander withdrew to his quarters, attended by the shouts of the army.

"As God is true, that man has a head on his shoulders," said Volodyovski to Pan Yan, "and things begin to go in better order."

"If only Radzivill does not come soon," put in Pan Stanislav, "for he is such a leader that there is not another like him in the Commonwealth. Our Pan Zagloba is good for provisioning the camp; but it is not for him to measure strength with such a warrior as Radzivill."

"That is true!" answered Pan Yan. "When it comes to action we will help him with counsel, for he does not understand war. Besides, his rule will come to an end the moment Sapyeha arrives."

"He can do much good before that time," said Volodyovski.

In truth, the army needed some leader, even Zagloba; for from the day of his election better order reigned in the camp. On the following day they began to make breastworks near the Byalystok ponds. Pan Oskyerko, who had served in foreign armies and understood fortification, directed the whole labor. In three days there had arisen a very strong entrenchment, really something like Zbaraj, for the sides and the rear of it were defended by swampy ponds. The sight of this work raised the hearts of the soldiers; the whole army felt that it had some ground under its feet. But courage was strengthened still more at sight of the supplies of food brought by strong parties. Every day they drove in oxen, sheep, pigs; every day came wagons bringing all kinds of grain and hay. Some things came from Lukovo, others from Vidzko. There came also, in continually greater numbers, nobles, small and great, for when the tidings went around that there was a government, an army, and a commander, there was more confidence among people. It was burdensome for the inhabitants to support a "whole division:" but to begin with, Zagloba did not inquire about that; in the second place, it was better to give half to the army and enjoy the rest in peace, than to be exposed every moment to losing all through the unruly bands, which had increased considerably and raged like Tartars, and which, at command of Zagloba, were pursued and destroyed.

"If the commander turns out to be such a leader as he is a manager," said the soldiers in camp, "the Commonwealth does not know yet how great a man it has."

Zagloba himself was thinking, with definite alarm, of the coming of Yanush Radzivill. He called to mind all the victories of Radzivill; then the form of the hetman took on monstrous shapes in the imagination of the new commander, and in his soul he said,—

"Oh, who can oppose that dragon? I said that he would choke himself with me, but he will swallow me as a sheat-fish a duck."

And he promised himself, under oath, not to give a general battle to Radzivill.

"There will be a siege," thought he, "and that always lasts long. Negotiations can be tried too, and by that time Sapyeha will come up."

In case he should not come up, Zagloba determined to listen to Pan Yan in everything, for he remembered how highly Prince Yeremi prized this officer and his military endowments.

"You, Pan Michael," said Zagloba to Volodyovski, "are just created for attack, and you may be sent scouting, even with a large party, for you know how to manage, and fall on the enemy, like a wolf on sheep; but if you were commanded to be hetman of a whole army,—I pass, I pass! You will not fill a vault with your mind, since you have no wit for sale; but Yan, he has the head of a commander, and if I were to die he is the only man who could fill my place."

Meanwhile contradictory tidings came. First it was reported that Radzivill was marching through Electoral Prussia; second, that having defeated Hovanski's troops, he had taken Grodno and was marching thence with great force; further, there were men who insisted that not Prince Yanush, but Sapyeha, with the aid of Prince Michael Radzivill, had defeated Hovanski. Scouting-parties brought no reliable news, saving this, that a body of Zolotarenko's men, about two thousand in number, were at Volkovysk, and threatened the town. The neighborhood was in flames.

One day later fugitives began to come in who confirmed the news, reporting besides that the townspeople had sent envoys to Hovanski and Zolotarenko with a prayer to spare the place, to which they received answer from Hovanski that that band was a separate one, having nothing to do with his army. Zolotarenko advised the people to ransom themselves; but they, as poor men after the recent fire and a number of plunderings, had no ransom to give. They implored the commander in God's name to hasten to their rescue, while they were conducting negotiations to ransom the town, for afterward there would not be time. Zagloba selected fifteen hundred good troops, among them the Lauda men, and calling Volodyovski, said,—

"Now, Pan Michael, it is time to show what you can do. Go to Volkovysk and destroy those ruffians who are threatening an undefended town. Such an expedition is not a novelty for you; I think you will take it as a favor that I give such functions." Here he turned to the other colonels: "I must remain in camp myself, for all the responsibility is on me, that is, first; and second, it does not beseem my office to go on an expedition against ruffians. But let Radzivill come, then in a great battle it will be shown who is superior,—the hetman or the commander."

Volodyovski set out with alacrity, for he was weary of camp life and yearned for battle. The squadrons selected marched out willingly and with singing; the commander appeared on the rampart on horseback, and blessed the departing, making over them the sign of the cross for the road. There were some who wondered that Zagloba sent off that party with such solemnity, but he remembered that Jolkyevski and other hetmans had the habit of making the sign of the cross over squadrons when going to battle; besides, he loved to do everything with ceremony, for that raised his dignity in the eyes of the soldiers.

Barely had the squadrons vanished in the haze of the distance, when he began to be alarmed about them.

"Yan!" said he, "another handful of men might be sent to Volodyovski."

"Be at rest, father," answered Pan Yan. "For Volodyovski to go on such an expedition is the same as to eat a plate of fried eggs. Dear God, he has done nothing else all his life!"

"That is true; but if an overwhelming force should attack him? *Nec Hercules contra plures* (Neither Hercules against [too] many)."

"What is the use in talking about such a soldier? He will test everything carefully before he strikes; and if the forces against him are too great, he will pluck off what he can and return, or will send for reinforcements. You may sleep quietly, father."

"Ah, I also knew whom I was sending, but I tell you that Pan Michael must have given me some herb; I have such a weakness for him. I have never loved any one so, except Podbipienta and you. It cannot be but that little fellow has given me something."

Three days passed. Provisions were brought continually, volunteers also marched in, but of Pan Michael not a sound. Zagloba's fears increased, and in spite of Pan Yan's remonstrance that in no way could Volodyovski return yet from Volkovysk, Zagloba sent one hundred of Yakub Kmita's light horse for intelligence.

The scouts marched out, and two days more passed without news.

On the seventh day, during a gray misty nightfall, the camp-attendants sent for food to Bobrovniki returned in great haste, with the report that they had seen some army coming out of the forest beyond Bobrovniki.

"Pan Michael!" exclaimed Zagloba, joyfully.

But the men contradicted that. They had not gone to meet it for the special reason that they saw strange flags, not belonging to Volodyovski's troops. And besides, this force was greater. The attendants, being attendants, could not fix the number exactly;

601

some said there were three thousand; others five thousand, or still more.

"I will take twenty horsemen and go to meet them," said Captain Lipnitski.

He went.

An hour passed, and a second; at last it was stated that not a party was approaching, but a whole army.

It is unknown why, but on a sudden it was thundered through the camp,—

"Radzivill is coming!"

This report, like an electric shock, moved and shook the whole camp; the soldiers rushed to the bulwarks. On some faces terror was evident; the men did not stand in proper order; Oskyerko's infantry only occupied the places indicated. Among the volunteers there was a panic at the first moment. From mouth to mouth flew various reports: "Radzivill has cut to pieces Volodyovski and the second party formed of Yakub Kmita's men," repeated some. "Not a witness of the defeat has escaped!" said others. "And now Lipnitski has gone, as it were, under the earth." "Where is the commander? Where is the commander?"

The colonels rushed to establish order; and since all in the camp, save a few volunteers, were old soldiers, they soon stood in order, waiting for what would appear.

When the cry came, "Radzivill is coming!" Zagloba was greatly confused; but in the first moment he would not believe it.

"What has happened to Volodyovski? Has he let himself be surrounded, so that not a man has come back with a warning? And the second party? And Pan Lipnitski? Impossible!" repeated Zagloba to himself, wiping his forehead, which was sweating profusely. "Has this dragon, this man-killer, this Lucifer, been able to come from Kyedani already? Is the last hour approaching?"

Meanwhile from every side voices more and more numerous cried, "Radzivill! Radzivill!"

Zagloba ceased to doubt. He sprang up and rushed to Pan Yan's quarters. "Oh, Yan, save! It is time now!"

"What has happened?" asked Pan Yan.

"Radzivill is coming! To your head I give everything, for Prince Yeremi said that you are a born leader. I will superintend myself, but do you give counsel and lead."

"That cannot be Radzivill!" said Pan Yan. "From what direction are the troops marching?"

"From Volkovysk. It is said that they have taken Volodyovski and the second party which I sent not long ago."

"Volodyovski let himself be taken! Oh, father, you do not know him. He is coming back himself,—no one else!"

"But it is said that there is an enormous army!"

"Praise be to God! it is clear then that Sapyeha is coming."

"For God's sake! what do you tell me? Why then was it said that Lipnitski went against them?"

"That is just the proof that it is not Radzivill who is coming. Lipnitski discovered who it was, joined, and all are coming together. Let us go out, let us go out!"

"I said that the first moment!" cried Zagloba. "All were frightened, but I thought, 'That cannot be!' I saw the position at once. Come! hurry, Yan, hurry! Those men out there are confused. Aha!"

Zagloba and Pan Yan hastened to the ramparts, occupied already by the troops, and began to pass along. Zagloba's face was radiant; he stopped every little while, and cried so that all heard him,—

"Gracious gentlemen, we have guests! I have no reason to lose heart! If that is Radzivill, I'll show him the road back to Kyedani!"

"We'll show him!" cried the army.

"Kindle fires on the ramparts! We will not hide ourselves; let them see us, we are ready! Kindle fires!"

Straightway they brought wood, and a quarter of an hour later the whole camp was flaming, till the heavens grew red as if from daybreak. The soldiers, turning away from the light, looked into the darkness in the direction of Bobrovniki. Some of them cried that they heard a clatter and the stamp of horses.

Just then in the darkness musket-shots were heard from afar. Zagloba pulled Pan Yan by the skirts.

"They are beginning to fire!" said he, disquieted.

"Salutes!" answered Pan Yan.

After the shots shouts of joy were heard. There was no reason for further doubt; a moment later a number of riders rushed in on foaming horses, crying,—

"Pan Sapyeha! the voevoda of Vityebsk!"

Barely had the soldiers heard this, when they rushed forth from the walls, like an overflowed river, and ran forward, roaring so that any one hearing their voices from afar might think them cries from a town in which victors were putting all to the sword.

Zagloba, wearing all the insignia of his office, with a baton in his hand and a heron's feather in his cap, rode out under his horse-tail standard, at the head of the colonels, to the front of the fortifications.

After a while the voevoda of Vityebsk at the head of his officers, and with Volodyovski at his side, rode into the lighted circle. He was a man already in respectable years, of medium weight, with a face not beautiful, but wise and kindly. His mustaches, cut evenly over his upper lip, were iron-gray, as was also a small beard, which made him resemble a foreigner, though he dressed in Polish fashion. Though famous for many military exploits he looked more like a civilian than a soldier; those who knew him more intimately said that in the countenance of the voevoda Minerva was greater than Mars. But, besides Minerva and Mars, there was in that face a gem rarer in those times; that is honesty, which flowing forth from his soul was reflected in his eyes as the light of the sun is in water. At the first glance people recognized that he was a just and honorable man.

"We waited as for a father!" cried the soldiers.

"And so our leader has come!" repeated others, with emotion.

"Vivat, vivat!"

Pan Zagloba, at the head of his colonels, hurried toward Sapyeha, who reined in his horse and began to bow with his lynx-skin cap.

"Serene great mighty voevoda!" began Zagloba, "though I possessed the eloquence of the ancient Romans, nay, of Cicero himself, or, going to remoter times, of that famous Athenian, Demosthenes, I should not be able to express the delight which has seized our hearts at sight of the worthy person of the serene great mighty lord. The whole Commonwealth is rejoicing in our hearts, greeting the wisest senator and the best son, with a delight all the greater because unexpected. Behold, we were drawn out here on these bulwarks under arms, not ready for greeting, but for battle,—not to hear shouts of delight, but the thunder of cannon,—not to shed tears, but our blood! When however hundred-tongued Fame bore around the news that the defender of the fatherland was coming, not the heretic,—the voevoda of Vityebsk, not the grand hetman of Lithuania,—Sapyeha, not Radzivill—"

But Pan Sapyeha was in an evident hurry to enter; for he waved his hand quickly, with a kindly though lordly inattention, and said,—

"Radzivill also is coming. In two days he will be here!"

Zagloba was confused; first, because the thread of his speech was broken, and second, because the news of Radzivill made a great impression on him. He stood therefore a moment before Sapyeha, not knowing what further to say; but he came quickly to his mind, and drawing hurriedly the baton from his belt, said with solemnity, calling to mind what had taken place at Zbaraj,—

"The army has chosen me for its leader, but I yield this into worthier hands, so as to give an example to the younger how we must resign the highest honors for the public good."

The soldiers began to shout; but Pan Sapyeha only smiled and said,—

"Lord brother, I would gladly receive it, but Radzivill might think that you gave it through fear of him."

"Oh, he knows me already," answered Zagloba, "and will not ascribe fear to me. I was the first to stagger him in Kyedani; and I drew others after me by my example."

"If that is the case, then lead on to the camp," said Sapyeha. "Volodyovski told me on the road that you are an excellent manager and have something on which to subsist; and we are wearied and hungry."

So saying, he spurred on his horse, and after him moved the others; and all entered the camp amid measureless rejoicing. Zagloba, remembering what was said of Sapyeha,—that he liked feasts and the goblet,—determined to give fitting honor to the day of his coming; hence he appeared with a feast of such splendor as had not been yet in the camp. All ate and drank. At the cups Volodyovski told what had happened at Volkovysk,—how forces, considerably greater than his own, had been sent out by Zolotarenko, how the traitor had surrounded him, how straitened he was when the sudden arrival of Sapyeha turned a desperate defence into a brilliant victory.

"We gave them something to think of," said he, "so that they will not stick an ear out of their camp."

Then the conversation turned to Radzivill. The voevoda of Vityebsk had very recent tidings, and knew through reliable people of everything that took place in Kyedani. He said therefore that the hetman had sent a certain Kmita with a letter to the King of Sweden, and with a request to strike Podlyasye from two sides at once.

"This is a wonder of wonders to me!" exclaimed Zagloba; "for had it not been for that Kmita, we should not have concentrated our forces to this moment, and if Radzivill had come he might have eaten us up, one after the other, like puddings of Syedlets."

"Volodyovski told me all that," said Sapyeha, "from which I infer that Kmita has a personal affection for you. It is too bad that he hasn't it for the country. But people who see nothing above themselves, serve no cause well and are ready to betray any one, as in this case Kmita Radzivill."

"But among us there are no traitors, and we are ready to stand up with the serene great mighty voevoda to the death!" said Jyromski.

"I believe that here are most honorable soldiers," answered Sapyeha, "and I had no expectation of finding such order and abundance, for which I must give thanks to his grace Pan Zagloba."

Zagloba blushed with pleasure, for somehow it had seemed to him hitherto that though the voevoda of Vityebsk had treated him graciously, still he had not given him the recognition and respect which he, the ex-commander, desired. He began therefore to relate how he had made regulations, what he had done, what supplies he had collected, how he had brought cannon, and formed infantry, finally what an extensive correspondence he had carried on; and not without boasting did he make mention of the letters sent to the banished king, to Hovanski, and to the elector.

"After my letter, his grace the elector must declare for us openly or against us," said he, with pride.

The voevoda of Vityebsk was a humorous man, and perhaps also he was a little joyous from drink; therefore he smoothed his mustache, laughed maliciously, and said,—

"Lord brother, but have you not written to the Emperor of Germany?"

"No!" answered Zagloba, astonished.

"That is a pity," said the voevoda; "for there an equal would have talked with an equal."

The colonels burst into a thundering laugh; but Zagloba showed at once that if the voevoda wished to be a scythe, he had struck a stone.

"Serene great mighty lord," said he, "I can write to the elector, for as a noble I am an elector myself, and I exercised my rights not so long ago when I gave my voice for Yan Kazimir."

"You have brought that out well," answered Sapyeha.

"But with such a potentate as the Emperor I do not correspond," continued Zagloba, "lest he might apply to me a certain proverb which I heard in Lithuania."

"What was the proverb?"

"Such a fool's head as that must have come out of Vityebsk!" answered Zagloba, without confusion.

Hearing this, the colonels were frightened; but the voevoda leaned back and held his sides from laughter.

"Ah, but you have settled me this time! Let me embrace you! Whenever I want to shave my beard I'll borrow your tongue!"

The feast continued till late in the night; it was broken up by the arrival of nobles from Tykotsin, who brought news that Radzivill's scouts had already reached that place.

CHAPTER XXXIV.

Radzivill would have fallen on Podlyasye long before, had not various reasons held him back in Kyedani. First, he was waiting for the Swedish reinforcements, which Pontus de la Gardie delayed by design. Although bonds of relationship connected the Swedish general with the king himself, he could not compare in greatness of family, in importance, in extensive connections by blood, with that Lithuanian magnate; and as to fortune, though at that time there was no ready money in Radzivill's treasury, all the Swedish generals might have been portioned with one half of the prince's estates and consider themselves wealthy. Now, when by the turn of fortune Radzivill was dependent on Pontus, the general could not deny himself the pleasure of making that lord feel his dependence and the superiority of De la Gardie.

Radzivill did not need reinforcements to defeat the confederates, since for that he had forces enough of his own; but the Swedes were necessary to him for the reasons mentioned by Kmita in his letter to Volodyovski. He was shut off from Podlyasye by the legions of Hovanski, who might block the road to him; but if Radzivill marched together with Swedish troops, and under the ægis of the King of Sweden, every hostile step on the part of Hovanski would be considered a challenge to Karl Gustav. Radzivill wished this in his soul, and therefore he waited impatiently for the arrival of even one Swedish squadron, and while urging Pontus he said more than once to his attendants,—

609

"A couple of years ago he would have thought it a favor to receive a letter from me, and would have left the letter by will to his descendants; but to-day he takes on the airs of a superior."

To which a certain noble, loud-mouthed and truth-telling, known in the whole neighborhood, allowed himself to answer at once,—

"According to the proverb, mighty prince, 'As a man makes his bed, so must he sleep on it.'"

Radzivill burst out in anger, and gave orders to cast the noble into the tower; but on the following day he let him out and presented him with a gold button; for of this noble it was said that he had ready money, and the prince wanted to borrow money of him on his note. The noble accepted the button, but gave not the money.

Swedish reinforcements came at last, to the number of eight hundred horse, of the heavy cavalry. Pontus sent directly to the castle of Tykotsin three hundred infantry and one hundred light cavalry, wishing to have his own garrison there in every event.

Hovanski's troops withdrew before them, making no opposition; they arrived therefore safely at Tykotsin, for this took place when the confederate squadrons were still scattered over all Podlyasye, and were occupied only in plundering the estates of Radzivill.

It was hoped that the prince, after he had received the desired reinforcements, would take the field at once; but he loitered yet. The cause of this was news from Podlyasye of disagreement in that province; of lack of union among the confederates, and misunderstandings between Kotovski, Lipnitski, and Yakub Kmita.

"It is necessary to give them time," said the prince, "to seize one another by the heads. They will gnaw one another to

610

pieces; their power will disappear without war; and then we will strike on Hovanski."

But on a sudden contradictory news began to come; the colonels not only did not fight with one another, but had assembled in one body at Byalystok. The prince searched his brain for the cause of this change. At last the name of Zagloba, as commander, came to his ears. He was informed also of the making of a fortified camp, the provisioning of the army, and the cannon dug out at Byalystok by Zagloba, of the increase of confederate strength, of volunteers coming from the interior. Prince Yanush fell into such wrath that Ganhoff, a fearless soldier, dared not approach him for some time.

At last the command was issued to the squadrons to prepare for the road. In one day a whole division was ready,—one regiment of German infantry, two of Scottish, one of Lithuanian. Pan Korf led the artillery; Ganhoff took command of the cavalry. Besides, Kharlamp's dragoons, the Swedish cavalry, and the light regiment of Nyevyarovski, there was the princess own heavy squadron, in which Slizyen was lieutenant. It was a considerable force, and composed of veterans. With a force no greater the prince, during the first wars with Hmelnitski, had won those victories which had adorned his name with immortal glory; with a power no greater he had beaten Nebaba at Loyovo, crushed a number of tens of thousands led by the famous Krechovski, destroyed Mozyr and Turoff, had taken Kieff by storm, and so pushed Hmelnitski in the steppes that he was forced to seek safety in negotiations.

But the star of that powerful warrior was evidently setting, and he had no good forebodings himself. He cast his eyes into the future, and saw nothing clearly. He would go to Podlyasye, tear apart with horses the insurgents, give orders to pull out of his skin the hated Zagloba,—and what would come of that? What further?

611

What change of fate would come? Would he then strike Hovanski, would he avenge the defeat at Tsibyhova, and adorn his own head with new laurels? The prince said that he would, but he doubted, for just then reports began to circulate widely that the Northerners, fearing the growth of Swedish power, would cease to wage war, and might even form an alliance with Yan Kazimir. Sapyeha continued to pluck them still, and defeated them where he could; but at the same time he negotiated with them. Pan Gosyevski had the same plans.

Then in case of Hovanski's retreat that field of action would be closed, and the last chance of showing his power would vanish from Radzivill; or if Yan Kazimir could make a treaty with those who till then had been his enemies, and urge them against the Swedes, fortune might incline to his side against Sweden, and thereby against Radzivill.

From Poland there came, it is true, the most favorable news. The success of the Swedes surpassed all expectation. Provinces yielded one after another; in Great Poland Swedes ruled as in Sweden; in Warsaw, Radzeyovski governed; Little Poland offered no resistance; Cracow might fall at any moment; the king, deserted by the army and the nobles, with confidence in his people broken to the core, went to Silesia; and Karl Gustav himself was astonished at the ease with which he had crushed that power, always victorious hitherto in war with the Swedes.

But just in that ease had Radzivill a foreboding of danger to himself; for the Swedes, blinded by triumph, would not count with him, would not consider him, especially because he had not shown himself so powerful and so commanding as all, not excepting himself, had thought him.

Will the Swedish King give him then Lithuania, or even White Russia? Will he not prefer to pacify an eternally hungry neighbor with some eastern slice of the Commonwealth, so as to have his own hands free in the remnants of Poland?

These were the questions which tormented continually the soul of Prince Yanush. Days and nights did he pass in disquiet. He conceived that Pontus de la Gardie would not have dared to treat him so haughtily, almost insultingly, had he not thought that the king would confirm such a manner of action, or what is worse, had not his instructions been previously prepared.

"As long as I am at the head of some thousands of men," thought Radzivill, "they will consider me; but when money fails, when my hired regiments scatter, what then?"

And the revenues from his enormous estates did not come in. An immense part of them, scattered throughout Lithuania and far away to Polesie or Kieff, lay in ruins; those in Podlyasye the confederates had plundered completely. At times it seemed to the prince that he would topple over the precipice; that from all his labor and plotting only the name traitor would remain to him,— nothing more.

Another phantom terrified him—the phantom of death, which appeared almost every night before the curtain of his bed, and beckoned with its hand, as if wishing to say to him, "Come into darkness, cross the unknown river."

Had he been able to stand on the summit of glory, had he been able to place on his head, even for one day, for one hour, that crown desired with such passion, he might meet that awful and silent phantom with unterrified eye. But to die and leave behind evil fame and the scorn of men, seemed to that lord, who was as proud as Satan himself, a hell during life.

More than once then, when he was alone or with his astrologer, in whom he placed the greatest trust, did he seize his temples and repeat with stifled voice,—

"I am burning, burning, burning!"

Under these conditions he was preparing for the campaign against Podlyasye, when the day before the march it was announced that Prince Boguslav had left Taurogi.

At the mere news of this, Prince Yanush, even before he saw his cousin, revived as it were; for that Boguslav brought with him his youth and a blind faith in the future. In him the line of Birji was to be renewed, for him alone was Prince Yanush toiling.

When he heard that Boguslav was coming, the hetman wished to go out to meet him, but etiquette did not permit him to go forth to meet a younger cousin; he sent therefore a gilded carriage, and a whole squadron as escort, and from the breastworks raised by Kmita and from the castle itself mortars were fired at his command, just as at the coming of a king.

When the cousins, after a ceremonial greeting, were left alone at last, Yanush seized Boguslav in his embrace and began to repeat, with a voice of emotion,—

"My youth has returned! My health has returned in a moment!"

But Boguslav looked at him carefully and asked,—

"What troubles your highness?"

"Let us not give ourselves titles if no one obeys us. What troubles me? Sickness irritates me so that I am falling like a rotten tree. But a truce to this! How is my wife and Maryska?"

"They have gone from Taurogi to Tyltsa. They are both well, and Marie is like a rosebud; that will be a wonderful rose when it blooms. *Ma foi!* more beautiful feet there are not in the world, and her tresses flow to the very ground."

"Did she seem so beautiful to you? That is well. God inspired you to come; I feel better in spirit when I see you. But what do you bring touching public affairs? What is the elector doing?"

"You know that he has made a league with the Prussian towns?"

"I know."

"But they do not trust him greatly. Dantzig will not receive his garrisons. The Germans have a good sniff."

"I know that too. But have you not written to him? What are his plans touching us?"

"Touching us?" repeated Boguslav, inattentively.

He cast his eyes around the room, then rose. Prince Yanush thought that he was looking for something; but he hurried to a mirror in the corner, and withdrawing a proper distance, rubbed his whole face with a finger of his right hand; at last he said,—

"My skin is chapped a little from the journey, but before morning it will be healed. What are the elector's plans touching us? Nothing; he wrote to me that he will not forget us."

"What does that mean?"

"I have the letter with me; I will show it to you. He writes that whatever may happen he will not forget us; and I believe him, for his interests enjoin that. The elector cares as much for the Commonwealth as I do for an old wig, and would be glad to give it to Sweden if he could seize Prussia; but the power of Sweden begins to alarm him, therefore he would be glad to have an ally ready for the future; and he will have one if you mount the throne of Lithuania."

"Would that had happened! Not for myself do I wish that throne!"

"All Lithuania cannot be had, perhaps, at first, but even if we get a good piece with White Russia and Jmud—"

"But what of the Swedes?"

"The Swedes will be glad also to use us as a guard against the East."

615

"You pour balsam on me."

"Balsam! Aha! A certain necromancer in Taurogi wanted to sell me balsam, saying that whoever would anoint himself with it would be safe from spears, swords, and sabres. I ordered a soldier to rub him with it at once and thrust a spear into him. Can you imagine, the spear went right through his body."

Here Prince Boguslav laughed, showing teeth as white as ivory. But this conversation was not to the taste of Yanush; he began again therefore on public affairs.

"I sent letters to the King of Sweden, and to many others of our dignitaries. You must have received a letter through Kmita."

"But wait! I was coming to that matter. What is your idea of Kmita?"

"He is hot-headed, wild, dangerous, and cannot endure restraint; but he is one of those rare men who serve us in good faith."

"Surely," answered Boguslav; "and he came near earning the kingdom of heaven for me."

"How is that?" asked Yanush, with alarm.

"They say, lord brother, that if your bile is stirred suffocation results. Promise me to listen with patience and quietly, and I will tell something of your Kmita, from which you will know him better than you have up to this moment."

"Well, I will be patient, only begin."

"A miracle of God saved me from the hands of that incarnate devil," said Boguslav; and he began to relate all that had happened in Pilvishki.

It was no smaller miracle that Prince Yanush did not have an attack of asthma, but it might be thought that apoplexy would strike him. He trembled all over, he gnashed his teeth, he covered his eyes with his hand; at last he cried with a hoarse voice,—

616

"Is that true? Very well! He has forgotten that his little wench is in my hands—"

"Restrain yourself, for God's sake! Hear on. I acquitted myself with him as beseems a cavalier, and if I have not noted this adventure in my diary, and do not boast of it, I refrain because 'tis a shame that I let myself be tricked by that clown, as if I were a child,—I, of whom Mazarin said that in intrigue and adroitness there was not my equal in the whole court of France. But no more of this! I thought at first that I had killed your Kmita; now I have proof in my hands that he has slipped away."

"That is nothing! We will find him! We will dig him out! We will get him, even from under the earth! Meanwhile I will give him a sorer blow than if I were to flay him alive."

"You will give him no blow, but only injure your own health. Listen! in coming hither I noticed some low fellow on a pied horse, who held himself at no great distance from my carriage. I noticed him specially because his horse was pied, and I gave the order at last to summon him. 'Where art thou going?' 'To Kyedani.' 'What art thou taking?' 'A letter to the prince voevoda.' I ordered him to give the letter, and as there are no secrets between us I read it. Here it is!"

Then he gave Prince Yanush Kmita's letter, written from the forest at the time when he was setting out with the Kyemliches.

The prince glanced over the letter, and crushing it with rage, cried,—

"True! in God's name, true! He has my letters, and in them are things which may make the King of Sweden himself suspicious, nay more, give him mortal offence."

Here choking seized him, and the expected attack came on. His mouth opened widely, and he gasped quickly after air; his hands tore the clothing near his throat. Prince Boguslav, seeing this, clapped his hands, and when the servants ran in, he said,—

"Save the prince your lord, and when he recovers breath beg him to come to my chamber; meanwhile I will rest a little." And he went out.

Two hours later, Yanush, with bloodshot eyes, hanging lids, and a blue face, knocked at Prince Boguslav's chamber. Boguslav received him lying in bed, his face rubbed with milk of almonds, which was to enhance the softness and freshness of his skin. Without a wig on his head, without the colors on his face, and with unblackened brows, he seemed much older than in full dress; but Prince Yanush paid no heed to that.

"I have come to the conclusion," said he, "that Kmita will not publish those letters, for if he should he would by that act write the sentence of death for the maiden. He understands well that only by keeping them does he hold me; but I cannot pour out my vengeance, and that gnaws me, as if I were carrying about a mad dog in my breast."

"Still, it will be necessary to get those letters," said Boguslav.

"But *quo modo* (in what way)?"

"Some adroit man must be sent after him, to enter into friendship and at a given opportunity seize the letters and punch Kmita with a knife. It is necessary to offer a great reward."

"Who here would undertake that deed?"

"If it were only in Paris, or even in Germany, I could find a hundred volunteers in one day, but in this country such wares are not found."

"And one of our own people is needed, for he would be on his guard against a stranger."

"It seems to me that I can find some one in Prussia."

"Oh, if he could be taken alive and brought to my hands, I would pay him once for all. I say that the insolence of that man passes every measure. I sent him away because he enraged me, for he would spring at my throat for any reason, just like a cat; he hurled at me his own wishes in everything. A hundred times lacking little had I the order just—just in my mouth to shoot him; but I could not, I could not."

"Tell me, is he really a relative of ours?"

"He is a relative of the Kishkis, and through the Kishkis of us."

"In his fashion he is a devil, and an opponent dangerous in the highest degree."

"He? You might command him to go to Tsargrad and pull the Sultan from his throne, or tear out the beard of the King of Sweden and bring it to Kyedani. But what did he not do here in time of war?"

"He has that look, but he has promised us vengeance to the last breath. Luckily he has a lesson from me that 'tis not easy to encounter us. Acknowledge that I treated him in Radzivill fashion; if a French cavalier had done a deed like mine, he would boast of it whole days, excepting the hours of sleeping, eating, and kissing; for they, when they meet, emulate one another in lying, so that the sun is ashamed to shine."

"It is true that you squeezed him, but I would that it had not happened."

"And I would that you had chosen better confidants, with more respect for the Radzivill bones."

"Those letters! those letters!"

The cousins were silent for a while. Boguslav spoke first.

"But what sort of a maiden is she?"

"Panna Billevich?"

"Billevich or Myeleshko, one is the equal of the other. I do not ask for her name, but if she is beautiful."

"I do not look on those things; but this is certain,—the Queen of Poland need not be ashamed of such beauty."

"The Queen of Poland? Marya Ludvika? In the time of Cinq-Mars maybe the Queen of Poland was beautiful, but now the dogs howl when they see her. If your Panna Billevich is such as she, then I'll hide myself; but if she is really a wonder, let me take her to Tanrogi, and there she and I will think out a vengeance for Kmita."

Yanush meditated a moment.

"I will not give her to you," said he at last, "for you will constrain her with violence, and then Kmita will publish the letters."

"I use force against one of your tufted larks! Without boasting I may say that I have had affairs with not such as she, and I have constrained no one. Once only, but that was in Flanders,—she was a fool,—the daughter of a jeweller. After me came the infantry of Spain, and the affair was accounted to them."

"You do not know this girl; she is from an honorable house, walking virtue, you would say a nun."

"Oh, we know the nuns too!"

"And besides she hates us, for she is a patriot. She has tried to influence Kmita. There are not many such among our women. Her mind is purely that of a man; and she is the most ardent adherent of Yan Kazimir."

"Then we will increase his adherents."

"Impossible, for Kmita will publish the letters. I must guard her like the eyes in my head—for a time. Afterward I will give her to you or to your dragoons, all one to me!"

"I give my word of a cavalier that I will not constrain her; and a word given in private I always keep. In politics it is another thing. It would be a shame for me indeed if I could gain nothing by her."

"You will not."

"In the worst case I'll get a slap in the face, and from a woman that is no shame. You are going to Podlyasye, what will you do with her? You will not take her with you, you cannot leave her here; for the Swedes will come to this place, and the girl should remain always in our hands as a hostage. Is it not better that I take her to Tanrogi and send Kmita, not an assassin, but a messenger with a letter in which I shall write, 'Give the letters and I'll give you the maiden.'"

"True," answered Prince Yanush; "that's a good method."

"But if," continued Boguslav, "not altogether as I took her, that will be the first step in vengeance."

"But you have given your word not to use violence."

"I have, and I say again that it would be a shame for me—"

"Then you must take also her uncle, the sword-bearer of Rossyeni, who is staying here with her."

"I do not wish to take him. The noble in the fashion of this region wears, of course, straw in his boots, and I cannot bear that."

"She will not go alone."

"That's to be seen. Ask them to supper this evening, so that I may see and know whether she is worth putting between the teeth, and immediately I'll think out methods against her. Only, for God's sake, mention not Kmita's act, for that would confirm her in devotion to him. But during supper, no matter what I say, contradict not. You will see my methods, and they will remind you of your own years of youth."

Prince Yanush waved his hands and went out; and Boguslav put his hands under his head, and began to meditate over means.

CHAPTER XXXV.

To the supper, besides the sword-bearer of Rossyeni and Olenka, were invited the most distinguished officers of Kyedani and some attendants of Prince Boguslav. He came himself in such array and so lordly that he attracted all eyes. His wig was dressed in beautiful waving curls; his face in delicacy of color called to mind milk and roses; his small mustache seemed to be of silken hair, and his eyes stars. He was dressed in black, in a kaftan made of stripes of silk and velvet, the sleeves of which were slashed and fastened together the length of the arm. Around his neck he had a broad collar, of the most marvellous Brabant lace, of inestimable value, and at the wrists ruffles of the same material. A gold chain fell on his breast, and over the right shoulder along the whole kaftan went to his left hip a sword-strap of Dutch leather, so set with diamonds that it looked like a strip of changing light. The hilt of his sword glittered in like manner, and in his shoe-buckles gleamed the two largest diamonds, as large as hazel-nuts. The whole figure seemed imposing, and as noble as it was beautiful.

In one hand he held a lace handkerchief; in the other he carried, according to the fashion of the time, on his sword-hilt, a hat adorned with curling black ostrich feathers of uncommon length.

All, not excepting Prince Yanush, looked at him with wonder and admiration. His youthful years came to the memory of the prince voevoda, when he in the same way surpassed all at the French court with his beauty and his wealth. Those years were now far away, but it seemed at that moment to the hetman that he was living again in that brilliant cavalier who bore the same name.

Prince Yanush grew vivacious, and in passing he touched with his index finger the breast of his cousin.

"Light strikes from you as from the moon," said he. "Is it not for Panna Billevich that you are so arrayed?"

"The moon enters easily everywhere," answered Boguslav, boastingly.

And then he began to talk with Ganhoff, near whom he halted, perhaps of purpose to exhibit himself the better, for Ganhoff was a man marvellously ugly; he had a face dark and pitted with small-pox, a nose like the beak of a hawk, and mustaches curled upward. He looked like the spirit of darkness, but Boguslav near him like the spirit of light.

The ladies entered,—Pani Korf and Olenka. Boguslav cast a swift glance at Olenka, and bowed promptly to Pani Korf; he was just putting his fingers to his mouth, to send in cavalier fashion a kiss to Panna Billevich, when he saw her exquisite beauty, both proud and dignified. He changed his tactics in an instant, caught his hat in his right hand, and advancing toward the lady bowed so low that he almost bent in two; the curls of his wig fell on both sides of his shoulders, his sword took a position parallel with the floor, and he remained thus, moving purposely his cap and sweeping the floor in front of Olenka with the ostrich feather, in sign of respect. A more courtly homage he could not have given to the Queen of France. Panna Billevich, who had learned of his coming, divined at once who stood before her; therefore seizing her robe with the tips of her fingers, she gave him in return a courtesy equally profound.

All wondered at the beauty and grace of manners of the two, which was evident from the greeting itself,—grace not over usual in Kyedani, for, as a Wallachian, Yanush's princess was more in love with eastern splendor than with courtliness, and Yanush's daughter was still a little girl.

Boguslav now raised his head, shook the curls of his wig over his shoulders, and striking his heels together with force, moved quickly toward Olenka; at the same time he threw his hat to a page and gave her his hand.

"I do not believe my eyes, and see as it were in a dream what I see," said he, conducting her to the table; "but tell me, beautiful goddess, by what miracle you have descended from Olympus to Kyedani?"

"Though simply a noble woman, not a goddess," answered Olenka, "I am not so simple-minded as to take the words of your highness as anything beyond courtesy."

"Though I tried to be politest of all, your glass would tell more than I."

"It would not tell more, but more truly," answered Olenka, pursing her mouth according to the fashion of the time.

"Were there a mirror in the room, I would conduct you to it straightway; meanwhile look into my eyes, and you will see if their admiration is not sincere."

Here Boguslav bent his head before Olenka; his eyes gleamed large, black as velvet, sweet, piercing, and at the same time burning. Under the influence of their fire the maiden's face was covered with a purple blush. She dropped her glance and pushed away somewhat, for she felt that with his arm Boguslav pressed lightly her arm to his side.

So he came to the table. He sat near her, and it was evident that in truth her beauty had made an uncommon impression on him. He expected to find a woman of the nobles, shapely as a deer, laughing and playful as a nutcracker, ruddy as a poppy-flower; but he found a proud lady, in whose black brows unbending will was revealed, in whose eyes were reason and

624

dignity, in whose whole face was the transparent repose of a child; and at the same time she was so noble in bearing, so charming and wonderful, that at any king's castle she might be the object of homage and courtship from the first cavaliers of the realm.

Her beauty aroused admiration and desire; but at the same time there was in it a majesty which curbed these, so that despite himself Boguslav thought, "I pressed her arm too early; with such a one subtlety is needed, not haste!"

Nevertheless he determined to possess her heart, and he felt a wild delight at the thought that the moment would come when the majesty of the maiden and that purest beauty would yield to his love or his hatred. The threatening face of Kmita stood athwart these imaginings; but to that insolent man this was but an incentive the more. Under the influence of these feelings he grew radiant; blood began to play in him, as in an Oriental steed; all his faculties flashed up uncommonly, and light gleamed from his whole form as from his diamonds.

Conversation at the table became general, or rather it was turned into a universal chorus of praise and flattery of Boguslav, which the brilliant cavalier heard with a smile, but without overweening delight, since it was common and of daily occurrence. They spoke first of his military deeds and duels. The names of the conquered princes, margraves, barons, streamed as if out of a sleeve. He threw in carelessly from time to time one more. The listeners were astonished; Prince Yanush stroked his long mustaches with delight, and at last Ganhoff said,—

"Even if fortune and birth did not stand in my way, I should not like to stand in the way of your highness, and the only wonder to me is that men of such daring have been found."

"What is to be done, Ganhoff? There are men of iron visage and wild-cat glance, whose appearance alone causes terror;

but God has denied me that power,—even a young lady would not be frightened at my face."

"Just as darkness is not afraid of a torch," said Pani Korf, simpering and posing, "until the torch burns in it."

Boguslav laughed, and Pani Korf talked on without ceasing to pose,—

"Duels concern soldiers more, but we ladies would be glad to hear of your love affairs, tidings of which have come to us."

"Untrue ones, my lady benefactress, untrue,—they have all merely grown on the road. Proposals were made for me, of course. Her Grace, the Queen of France was so kind—"

"With the Princess de Rohan," added Yanush.

"With another too,—De la Forse," added Boguslav; "but even a king cannot command his own heart to love, and we do not need, praise be to God, to seek wealth in France, hence there could be no bread out of that flour. Graceful ladies they were, 'tis true, and beautiful beyond imagination; but we have still more beautiful, and I need not go out of this hall to find such."

Here he looked long at Olenka, who, feigning not to hear, began to say something to the sword-bearer; and Pani Korf raised her voice again,—

"There is no lack here of beauties; still there are none who in fortune and birth could be the equal of your highness."

"Permit me, my benefactress, to differ," responded Boguslav, with animation; "for first I do not think that a Polish noble lady is inferior in any way to a Rohan or De la Forse; second, it is not a novelty for the Radzivills to marry a noble woman, since history gives many examples of that. I assure you, my benefactress, that that noble lady who should become Radzivill would have the step and precedence of princesses in France."

"An affable lord!" whispered the sword-bearer to Olenka.

626

"That is how I have always understood," continued Boguslav, "though more than once have I been ashamed of Polish nobles, when I compare them with those abroad; for never would that have happened there which has happened in this Commonwealth,—that all should desert their king, nay, even men are ready to lay in wait for his life. A French noble may permit the worst action, but he will not betray his king—"

Those present began to look at one another and at the prince with astonishment. Prince Yanush frowned and grew stern; but Olenka fixed her blue eyes on Boguslav's face with an expression of admiration and thankfulness.

"Pardon, your highness," said Boguslav, turning to Yanush, who was not able yet to recover himself, "I know that you could not act otherwise, for all Lithuania would have perished if you had followed my advice; but respecting you as older, and loving you as a brother, I shall not cease to dispute with you touching Yan Kazimir. We are among ourselves, I speak therefore what I think. Our insufficiently lamented king, good, kind, pious, and doubly dear to me,—I was the first of Poles to attend him when he was freed from durance in France. I was almost a child at the time, but all the more I shall never forget him; and gladly would I give my blood to protect him, at least from those who plot against his sacred person."

Though Yanush understood Boguslav's game now, still it seemed to him too bold and too hazardous for such a trifling object; therefore without hiding his displeasure he said,—

"In God's name, of what designs against the safety of our ex-king are you speaking? Who cherishes them, where could such a monster be found among the Polish people? True as life, such a thing has not happened in the Commonwealth since the beginning of the world."

Boguslav hung his head.

627

"Not longer than a month ago," said he, with sadness in his voice, "on the road between Podlyasye and Electoral Prussia, when I was going to Tanrogi, there came to me a noble of respectable family. That noble, not being aware of my real love for our gracious king, and thinking that I, like others, was an enemy of his, promised for a considerable reward to go to Silesia, carry off Yan Kazimir and deliver him to the Swedes, either living or dead."

All were dumb with amazement.

"And when with anger and disgust I rejected such an offer," said Boguslav, in conclusion, "that man with brazen forehead said, 'I will go to Radzeyovski; he will buy and pay me gold by the pound.'"

"I am not a friend of the ex-king," said Yanush; "but if the noble had made me a proposal like that, I should have placed him by a wall, and in front of him six musketeers."

"At the first moment I wanted to do so, but did not," answered Boguslav, "as the conversation was with four eyes, and people might cry out against the violence and tyranny of the Radzivills. I frightened him, however, by saying that Radzeyovski and the King of Sweden, even Hmelnitski, would put him to death for such a proposal; in one word, I brought that criminal so far that he abandoned his plan."

"That was not right; it was not proper to let him go living, he deserved at least the impaling-stake," cried Korf.

Boguslav turned suddenly to Yanush.

"I cherish also the hope that punishment will not miss him, and first I propose that he perish not by an ordinary death; but your highness alone is able to punish him, for he is your attendant and your colonel."

"In God's name! my colonel? Who is he,—who? Speak!

"His name is Kmita," said Boguslav.

"Kmita!" repeated all, with astonishment.

"That is not true!" cried Panna Billevich at once, rising from her chair, with flashing eyes and heaving breast.

Deep silence followed. Some had not recovered yet from the fearful news given by Boguslav; others were astonished at the boldness of that lady who had dared to throw a lie in the eyes of Prince Boguslav; the sword-bearer began to stutter, "Olenka! Olenka!" But Boguslav veiled his face in sorrow, and said without anger,—

"If he is your relative or betrothed, I am grieved that I mentioned this fact; but cast him out of your heart, for he is not worthy of you, O lady."

She remained yet a moment in pain, flushed, and astonished; but by degrees her face became cool, until it was cold and pale. She sank down in the chair, and said,—

"Forgive me, your highness, I made an unseemly contradiction. All is possible for that man."

"May God punish me if I feel aught save pity!" answered Boguslav, mildly.

"He was the betrothed of this lady," said Prince Yanush, "and I myself made the match. He was a young man, hot-headed; he caused a world of turmoil. I saved him from justice, for he was a good soldier. I saw that he was lawless, and would be; but that he, a noble, could think of such infamy, I did not expect."

"He is an evil man; that I knew long since," said Ganhoff.

"And why did you not forewarn me?" inquired Yanush, in a tone of reproach.

"I was afraid that your highness might suspect me of envy, for he had everywhere the first step before me."

"*Horribile dictu et auditu* (horrible in the speaking and the hearing)," said Korf.

"Gracious gentlemen," exclaimed Boguslav, "let us give peace to him. If it is grievous for you to hear of this, what must it be for Panna Billevich?"

"Your highness, be pleased not to consider me," said Olenka; "I can listen to everything now."

The evening was drawing toward its close. Water was given for the washing of fingers; then Prince Yanush rose first and gave his arm to Pani Korf, and Prince Boguslav to Olenka.

"God has punished the traitor already," said he to her; "for whoso has lost you has lost heaven. It is less than two hours since I first saw you, charming lady, and I should be glad to see you forever, not in pain and in tears, but in joy and in happiness."

"I thank your highness," answered Olenka.

After the departure of the ladies the men returned to the table to seek consolation in cups, which went around frequently. Prince Boguslav drank deeply, for he was satisfied with himself. Prince Yanush conversed with the sword-bearer of Rossyeni.

"I march to-morrow with the army for Podlyasye," said he. "A Swedish garrison will come to Kyedani. God knows when I shall return. You cannot stay here with the maiden; it would not be a fit place for her among soldiers. You will both go with Prince Boguslav to Taurogi, where she may stay with my wife among her ladies in waiting."

"Your highness," answered the sword-bearer, "God has given us a corner of our own; why should we go to strange places? It is a great kindness of your highness to think of us: but not wishing to abuse favor, we prefer to return to our own roof."

The prince was unable to explain to the sword-bearer all the reasons for which he would not let Olenka out of his hands at any price; but some of them he told with all the rough outspokenness of a magnate.

"If you wish to accept it as a favor, all the better, but I will tell you that it is precaution as well. You will be a hostage there; you will be responsible to me for all the Billeviches, who I know well do not rank themselves among my friends, and are ready to raise Jmud in rebellion when I am gone. Advise them to sit in peace, and do nothing against the Swedes, for your head and that of your niece will answer for their acts."

At this juncture patience was evidently lacking to the sword-bearer, for he answered quickly,—

"It would be idle for me to appeal to my rights as a noble. Power is on the side of your highness, and it is all one to me where I must sit in prison; I prefer even that place to this."

"Enough!" said the prince, threateningly.

"What is enough, is enough!" answered the sword-bearer. "God grant to this violence an end, and to justice new power. Speaking briefly, do not threaten, your highness, for I fear not."

Evidently Boguslav saw lightnings of anger gleaming on the face of Yanush, for he approached quickly.

"What is the question?" asked he, standing between them.

"I was telling the hetman," said the sword-bearer, with irritation, "that I choose imprisonment in Taurogi rather than in Kyedani."

"In Taurogi there is for you not a prison, but my house, in which you will be as if at home. I know that the hetman chooses to see in you a hostage; I see only a dear guest."

"I thank your highness," answered the sword-bearer.

"And I thank you. Let us strike glasses and drink together, for they say that a libation must be made to friendship, or it will wither at its birth."

So saying, Boguslav conducted the sword-bearer to the table, and they fell to touching glasses and drinking to each other often and frequently. An hour later the sword-bearer turned with somewhat uncertain step toward his room, repeating in an undertone,—

"An amiable lord! A worthy lord! A more honest one could not be found with a lantern,—gold, pure gold! I would gladly shed my blood for him!"

Meanwhile the cousins found themselves alone. They had something yet to talk over, and besides, certain letters came; a page was sent to bring these from Ganhoff.

"Evidently," said Yanush, "there is not a word of truth in what you reported of Kmita?"

"Evidently. You know best yourself. But, well? Acknowledge, was not Mazarin right? With one move to take terrible vengeance on an enemy, and to make a breach in that beautiful fortress,—well, who could do that? This is called intrigue worthy of the first court in the world! But that Panna Billevich is a pearl, and charming too, lordly and distinguished as if of princely blood. I thought I should spring from my skin."

"Remember that you have given your word,—remember that he will ruin us if he publishes those letters."

"What brows! What a queenly look, so that respect seizes one! Whence is there such a girl, such well-nigh royal majesty? I saw once in Antwerp, splendidly embroidered on Gobelin tapestry Diana hunting the curious Actæon with dogs. She was like this one as cup is like cup."

"Look out that Kmita does not publish the letters, for then the dogs would gnaw us to death."

"Not true! I will turn Kmita into an Actæon, and hunt him to death. I have struck him down on two fields, and it will come to battle between us yet."

Further conversation was interrupted by the entrance of a page with a letter. The voevoda of Vilna took the letter in his hand and made the sign of the cross. He did that always to guard against evil tidings; then, instead of opening, he began to examine it carefully. All at once his countenance changed.

"Sapyeha's arms are on the seal!" exclaimed he; "it is from the voevoda of Vityebsk."

"Open quickly!" said Boguslav.

The hetman opened and began to read, interrupting himself from time to time with exclamations.

"He is marching on Podlyasye! He asks if I have no messages for Tykotsin! An insult to me! Still worse; for listen to what he writes further,—

"'Do you wish civil war, your highness? do you wish to sink one more sword in the bosom of the mother? If you do, come to Podlyasye. I am waiting for you, and I trust that God will punish your pride with my hands. But if you have pity on the country, if conscience stirs within you, if you value your deeds of past times and you wish to make reparation, the field is open before you. Instead of beginning a civil war, summon the general militia, raise the peasants, and strike the Swedes while Pontus, feeling secure, suspects nothing and is exercising no vigilance. From Hovanski you will have no hindrance, for reports come to me from Moscow that they are thinking there of an expedition against Livonia, though they keep that a secret. Besides, if Hovanski wished to undertake anything I hold him in check, and if I could have sincere trust I would certainly help you with all my forces to save the country. All depends on you, for there is time yet to turn from the road and efface your faults. Then it will appear clearly that you did not accept Swedish protection for personal purposes, but to avert final defeat from Lithuania. May God thus inspire you; for this I implore him daily, though your highness is pleased to accuse me of envy.

"'P. S. I have heard that the siege of Nyesvyej is raised, and that Prince Michael will join us as soon as he repairs his

633

losses. See, your highness, how nobly your family act, and consider their example; in every case remember that you have now a boat and a carriage.'

"Have you heard?" asked Prince Yanush, when he had finished reading.

"I have heard—and what?" answered Boguslav, looking quickly at his cousin.

"It would be necessary to abjure all, leave all, tear down our work with our own hands."

"Break with the powerful Karl Gustav, and seize the exiled Yan Kazimir by the feet, that he might deign to forgive and receive us back to his service, and also implore Sapyeha's intercession."

Yanush's face was filled with blood.

"Have you considered how he writes to me: 'Correct yourself, and I will forgive you,' as a lord to an underling."

"He would write differently if six thousand sabres were hanging over his neck."

"Still—" Here Prince Yanush fell to thinking gloomily.

"Still, what?"

"Perhaps for the country it would be salvation to do as Sapyeha advises."

"But for you,—for me, for the Radzivills?"

Yanush made no answer; he dropped his head on his fists and thought.

"Let it be so!" said he, at last; "let it be accomplished!"

"What have you decided?"

"To-morrow I march on Podlyasye, and in a week I shall strike on Sapyeha."

"You are a Radzivill!" cried Boguslav. And they grasped each other's hands.

After a while Boguslav went to rest. Yanush remained alone. Once, and a second time he passed through the room with heavy steps. At last he clapped his hands. A page entered the room.

"Let the astrologer come in an hour to me with a ready figure," said he.

The page went out, and the prince began again to walk and repeat his Calvinistic prayers. After that he sang a psalm in an undertone, stopping frequently, for his breath failed him, and looking from time to time through the window at the stars twinkling in the sky.

By degrees the lights were quenched in the castle; but besides the astrologer and the prince one other person was watching in a room, and that was Olenka Billevich.

Kneeling before her bed, she clasped both hands over her head, and whispered with closed eyes,—

"Have mercy on us! Have mercy on us!"

The first time since Kmita's departure she would not, she could not pray for him.

CHAPTER XXXVI.

Kmita had, it is true, Radzivill's passes to all the Swedish captains, commandants, and governors, to give him a free road everywhere, and make no opposition, but he did not dare to use those passes; for he expected that Prince Boguslav, immediately after Pilvishki, had hurried off messengers in every direction with information to the Swedes of what had happened, and with an order to seize him. For this reason Pan Andrei had assumed a strange name, and also changed his rank. Avoiding therefore Lomja and Ostrolenko, to which the first warning might have come, he directed his horses and his company to Pjasnysh, whence he wished to go through Pultusk to Warsaw.

635

But before he reached Pjasnysh he made a bend on the Prussian boundary through Vansosh, Kolno, and Myshynyets, because the Kyemliches, knowing those wildernesses well, were acquainted with the forest trails, and besides had their "cronies" among the Bark-shoes, from whom they might expect aid in case of emergency.

The country at the boundary was occupied for the most part by the Swedes, who limited themselves, however, to occupying the most considerable towns, going not too boldly into the slumbering and fathomless forests inhabited by armed men,—hunters who never left the wilderness, and were still so wild that just a year before, the Queen, Marya Ludvika, had given a command to build a chapel in Myshynyets and settle there Jesuits, who were to teach religion and soften the manners of those men of the wilderness.

"The longer we do not meet the Swedes," said old Kyemlich, "the better for us."

"We must meet them at last," answered Pan Andrei.

"If a man meets them in a large town they are often afraid to do him injustice; for in a town there is always some government and some higher commandant to whom it is possible to make complaint. I have always asked people about this, and I know that there are commands from the King of Sweden forbidding violence and extortion. But the smaller parties sent far away from the eyes of commandants have no regard for orders, and plunder peaceful people."

They passed on then through the forests, meeting Swedes nowhere, spending the nights with pitch-makers in forest settlements. The greatest variety of tales concerning the invasion were current among the Bark-shoes, though almost none of them had known the Swedes hitherto. It was said that a people had come from over the sea who did not understand human speech, who did not believe in Christ the Lord, the Most Holy Lady, or the Saints, and that they were wonderfully greedy. Some told of the uncommon desire of those enemies for cattle, skins, nuts, mead, and dried mushrooms, which if refused, they burned the woods straightway. Others insisted that, on the contrary, they were a people of were-wolves, living on human flesh, and feeding specially on the flesh of young girls.

Under the influence of those terrible tidings, which flew into the remotest depths of the wilderness, the Bark-shoes began to watch and to search through the forests. Those who were making potash and pitch; those who worked at gathering hops; wood-cutters and fishermen, who had their wicker nets fixed in the reedy banks, of the Rosoga; trappers and snarers, bee-keepers and beaver-hunters, assembled at the most considerable settlements, listening to tales, communicating news, and counselling how to drive out the enemy in case they appeared in the wilderness.

Kmita, going with his party, met more than once greater or smaller bands of these men, dressed in hemp shirts, and skins of wolves, foxes, or bears. More than once he was stopped at narrow places, and by inquiries,—

"Who art thou? A Swede?"

"No!" answered Pan Andrei.

"God guard thee!"

Kmita looked with curiosity at those men who lived always in the gloom of forests, and whose faces the open sun had never burned; he wondered at their stature, their boldness of look, the sincerity of their speech, and their daring, not at all peasant-like.

The Kyemliches, who knew them, assured Pan Andrei that there were no better shots than these men in the whole Commonwealth. When he discovered that they all had good

German muskets bought in Prussia for skins, he asked them to show their skill in shooting, was astonished at sight of it, and thought, "Should I need to collect a party, I will come here."

At Myshynyets itself he found a great assembly. More than a hundred marksmen held constant watch at the mission, for it was feared that the Swedes would show themselves there first, especially because the starosta of Ostrolenko had commanded them to cut out a road in the forest so that the priests settled at the mission might have "access to the world."

The hop-raisers, who took their produce to Pjasnysh to the celebrated breweries there, and hence passed for men of experience, related that Lomja, Ostrolenko, and Pjasnysh were swarming with Swedes, who were managing and collecting taxes there as if at home.

Kmita tried to persuade the Bark-shoes not to wait for the Swedes in the wilderness, but to strike on them at Ostrolenko, and begin war; he offered to command them himself. He found a great willingness among them; but two priests led them away from this mad enterprise, telling them to wait till the whole country moved, and not draw on themselves the terrible vengeance of the enemy by premature attack.

Pan Andrei departed, but regretted his lost opportunity. The only consolation remaining was this,—he had convinced himself that if powder were to explode anywhere, neither the Commonwealth nor the king would lack defenders in those parts.

"This being the case," thought he, "it is possible to begin in another place."

His fiery nature was restive for quick action, but judgment said: "The Bark-shoes alone cannot conquer the Swedes. You will go through a part of the country; you will look around, examine, and then obey the king's order."

He travelled on therefore. He went out of the deep wilderness to the forest borders, to a neighborhood more thickly settled; he saw an uncommon movement in all the villages. The roads were crowded with nobles going in wagons, carriages, and carts, of various kinds, or on horseback. All were hastening to the nearest towns and villages to give Swedish commanders an oath of loyalty to the new king. In return they received certificates which were to preserve their persons and property. In the capitals of provinces and districts "capitulations" were published securing freedom of confession and privileges pertaining to the order of nobles.

The nobles went with the requisite oath, not only willingly, but in haste; for various punishments threatened the stubborn, and especially confiscation and robbery. It was said that here and there the Swedes had already begun, as in Great Poland, to thumb-screw suspected men. It was repeated also, with alarm, that they were casting suspicion on the wealthiest on purpose to rob them.

In view of all this, it was unsafe to remain in the country; the wealthier therefore hurried to the towns to live under the immediate eye of Swedish commandants, so as to avoid suspicion of intrigue against the King of Sweden.

Pan Andrei bent his ear carefully to what nobles were saying, and though they did not wish greatly to speak with him, since he was a poor fellow, he discovered this much, that near neighbors, acquaintances, even friends, did not speak among themselves with sincerity touching the Swedes or the new government. It is true they complained loudly of the "requisitions;" and in fact there was reason, for to each village, each hamlet, came letters from commandants with orders to furnish great quantities of grain, bread, salt, cattle, money; and frequently these orders exceeded the possible, especially because when supplies of one kind were exhausted, others were demanded; whoso did not pay, to him was sent an execution in thrice the amount.

But the old days had gone! Each man extricated himself as best he was able, took out of his own mouth, gave, paid; complaining, groaning, and thinking in his soul that long ago it was different. But they comforted themselves for the time, saying that when the war was over the requisitions would cease. The Swedes promised the same, saying, "Only let the king gain the whole country, he will begin to govern at once like a father."

For the nobles who had given up their own king and country; who before, and not long before, had called the kindly Yan Kazimir a tyrant, suspecting him of striving for absolute power; who opposed him in everything, protesting in provincial and national diets, and in their hunger for novelty and change went so far that they recognized, almost without opposition, an invader as lord, so as to have some change,—it would be a shame then even to complain. Karl Gustav had freed them from the tyrant, they had abandoned of their own will their lawful king; but they had the change so greatly desired.

Therefore the most intimate did not speak sincerely among themselves touching what they thought of that change, inclining their ears willingly to those who asserted that the attacks, requisitions, robberies, and confiscations were, of course burdens, but only temporary ones, which would cease as soon as Karl Gustav was firm on the throne.

"This is grievous, brother, grievous," said one noble to another at times, "but still we must be thankful for the new ruler. He is a great potentate and warrior; he will conquer the Tartars, restrain the Turks, drive the Northerners away from the boundaries; and we together with Sweden will flourish."

"Even if we were not glad," answered another, "what is to be done against such power? We cannot fly to the sun on a spade."

At times, too, they referred to the fresh oath. Kmita was enraged listening to such talks and discussions; and once when a certain noble said in his presence in an inn that a man must be faithful to him to whom he had taken oath. Pan Andrei shouted out to him,—

"You must have two mouths,—one for true and the other for false oaths, for you have sworn to Yan Kazimir!"

There were many other nobles present, for this happened not far from Pjasnysh. Hearing these words, all started. On some faces wonder was visible at the boldness of Kmita; others flushed. At last the most important man said,—

"No one here has broken his oath to the former king. He broke it himself; for he left the country, not watching over its defence."

"Would you were killed!" cried Kmita. "But King Lokyetek,—how many times was he forced to leave the country, and still he returned, for the fear of God was yet in men's hearts. It was not Yan Kazimir who deserted, but those who sold him and who now calumniate him, so as to palliate their own sins before God and the world!"

"You speak too boldly, young man! Whence come you who wish to teach us people of this place the fear of God? See to it that the Swedes do not overhear you."

"If you are curious, I will tell you whence I am. I am from Electoral Prussia, and belong to the elector. But being of Sarmatian blood, I feel a good will toward the country, and am ashamed of the indifference of this people."

Here the nobles, forgetting their anger, surrounded him and began to inquire hurriedly and with curiosity,—

"You are from Electoral Prussia? But tell what you know! What is the elector doing there? Does he think of rescuing us from oppression?"

"From what oppression? You are glad of the new ruler, so do not talk of oppression. As you have made your bed, so you must sleep on it."

"We are glad, for we cannot help it. They stand with swords over our necks. But speak out, as if we were not glad."

"Give him something to drink, let his tongue be loosened! Speak boldly, there are no traitors here among us."

"You are all traitors!" roared Pan Andrei, "and I don't wish to drink with you; you are servants of the Swedes."

Then he went out of the room, slamming the door, and they remained in shame and amazement; no man seized his sabre, no man moved after Kmita to avenge the insult.

But he went directly to Pryasnysh. A few furlongs before the place Swedish patrols took him and led him before the commandant. There were only six men in the patrol, and an under-officer was the seventh; therefore Soroka and the two Kyemliches began to look at them hungrily, like wolves at sheep, and asked Kmita with their eyes, if he would not give order to surround them.

Pan Andrei also felt no small temptation, especially since the Vengyerka flowed near, between banks overgrown with reeds; but he restrained himself, and let the party be taken quietly to the commandant.

There he told the commandant who he was,—that he had come from the elector's country, and that he went every year with horses to Sobota. The Kyemliches too had certificates with which they provided themselves in Leng, for the place was well known to them; therefore the commandant, who was himself a Prussian

German, made no difficulty, only inquired carefully what kind of horses they were driving and wished to see them.

When Kmita's attendants drove the beasts up, in accordance with the commandant's wish, he looked at them carefully and said,—

"I will buy these. From another I would have taken them without pay; but since you are from Prussia, I will not harm you."

Kmita seemed somewhat confused when it came to selling, for by this the reason for going farther was lost, and he would have to go back to Prussia. He asked therefore a price so high that it was almost twice the real value of the horses. Beyond expectation the officer was neither angry, nor did he haggle about the price.

"Agreed!" said he. "Drive the horses into the shed, and I will bring you the pay at once."

The Kyemliches were glad in their hearts, but Pan Andrei fell into anger and began to curse. Still there was no way but to drive in the horses. If they refused, they would be suspected at once of trading only in appearance.

Meanwhile the officer came back, and gave Kmita a piece of paper with writing.

"What is this?" asked Pan Andrei.

"Money or the same as money,—an order."

"And where will they pay me?"

"At headquarters!"

"Where are headquarters?"

"In Warsaw," said the officer, laughing maliciously.

"We sell only for ready money."

"How's that, what's that, oh, gates of heaven?" began old Kyemlich, groaning.

Kmita turned, and looking at him threateningly, said,—

"For me the word of the commandant is the same as ready money. I will go willingly to Warsaw, for there I can buy honest goods from the Armenians, for which I shall be well paid in Prussia."

Then, when the officer walked away, Pan Andrei said, to comfort Kyemlich,—

"Quiet, you rogue! These orders are the best passes; we can go to Cracow with our complaints, for they will not pay us. It is easier to press cheese out of a stone than money out of the Swedes. But this is just playing into my hand. This breeches fellow thinks that he has tricked me, but he knows not what service he has rendered. I'll pay you out of my own pocket for the horses; you will be at no loss."

The old man recovered himself, and it was only from habit that he did not cease yet for a while to complain,—

"They have plundered us, brought us to poverty!"

But Pan Andrei was glad to find the road open before him, for he foresaw that the Swedes would not pay for the horses in Warsaw, and in all likelihood they would pay nowhere,—hence he would be able to go on continually as it were seeking for justice, even to the Swedish king, who was at Cracow occupied with the siege of the ancient capital.

Meanwhile Kmita resolved to pass the night in Pjasnysh to give his horses rest, and without changing his assumed name to throw aside his exterior of a poor noble. He saw that all despised a poor horse-dealer, that any one might attack him more readily and have less fear to answer for injustice to an insignificant man. It was more difficult in that dress to have approach to important nobles, and therefore more difficult to discover what each one was thinking.

He procured therefore clothing answering to his station and his birth, and went to an inn so as to talk with his brother nobles. But he was not rejoiced at what he heard. In the taverns and public houses the nobles drank to the health of the King of Sweden, and to the success of the protector, struck glasses with the Swedish officers, laughed at the jokes which these officers permitted themselves to make at the expense of Yan Kazimir and Charnyetski.

Fear for their own lives and property had debased people to such a degree that they were affable to the invaders, and hurried to keep up their good humor. Still even that debasement had its limits. The nobles allowed themselves, their king, the hetmans, and Pan Charnyetski to be ridiculed, but not their religion; and when a certain Swedish captain declared that the Lutheran faith was as good as the Catholic, Pan Grabkovski, sitting near him, not being able to endure that blasphemy, struck him on the temple with a hatchet, and taking advantage of the uproar, slipped out of the public house and vanished in the crowd.

They fell to pursuing him, but news came which turned attention in another direction. Couriers arrived with news that Cracow had surrendered, that Pan Charnyetski was in captivity, and that the last barrier to Swedish dominion was swept away.

The nobles were dumb at the first moment, but the Swedes began to rejoice and cry "Vivat." In the church of the Holy Ghost, in the church of the Bernardines, and in the cloister of Bernardine nuns, recently erected by Pani Muskovski, it was ordered to ring the bells. The infantry and cavalry came out on the square, from the breweries and cloth-shearing mills, in battle-array, and began to fire from cannons and muskets. Then they rolled out barrels of gorailka, mead, and beer for the army and the citizens; they burned pitch-barrels and feasted till late at night. The Swedes dragged out the inhabitants from the houses to dance with them, to rejoice and frolic; and together with throngs of soldiers straggled along nobles who drank with the cavalry, and were

645

forced to feign joy at the fall of Cracow and the defeat of Charnyetski.

Disgust carried away Kmita, and he took refuge early in his quarters outside the town, but he could not sleep. A fever tormented him, and doubts besieged his soul. Had he not turned from the road too late, when the whole country was in the hands of the Swedes? It came into his head that all was lost now, and the Commonwealth would never rise from its fall.

"This is not a mere unlucky war," thought he, "which may end with the loss of some province; this is accomplished ruin! This means that the whole Commonwealth becomes a Swedish province. We have caused this ourselves, and I more than others."

This thought burned him, and conscience gnawed. Sleep fled from him. He knew not what to do,—to travel farther, remain in the place, or return. Even if he collected a party and harried the Swedes, they would hunt him as a bandit, and not treat him as a soldier. Besides, he is in a strange region, where no one knows who he is. Who will join him? Fearless men rallied to him in Lithuania, where he, the most famous, called them together; but here, even if some had heard of Kmita, they held him a traitor and a friend of the Swedes, but surely no one had ever heard of Babinich.

All is useless! It is useless to go to the king, for it is too late; it is useless to go to Podlyasye, for the Confederates think him a traitor; it is useless to go to Lithuania, for there the Radzivills own all; it is useless to stay where he is, for there he has nothing to do. The best would be to drive out the soul, and not look on this world, but flee from remorse.

But will it be better in that world for those who having sinned their fill in this life, have not effaced their sins in any way, and will stand before judgment beneath the whole weight of these sins? Kmita struggled in his bed, as if lying on a bed of torture.

Such unendurable torments he had not passed through, even in the forest cabin of the Kyemliches.

He felt strong, healthy, enterprising,—the soul in him was rushing out to begin something, to do something,—and here every road was blocked; even knock the head against a wall,—there is no issue, no salvation, no hope.

After he had tossed during the night on his bed, he sprang up before daybreak, roused his men, and rode on. They went toward Warsaw, but he knew not himself wherefore or why. He would have escaped to the Saitch in despair, if times had not changed, and if Hmelnitski, together with Buturlin, had not just overborne the grand hetman of the kingdom, at Grodek, carrying at the same time fire and sword through the southwestern regions of the Commonwealth, and sending predatory bands as far as Lublin.

Along the roads to Pultusk, Pan Andrei met at all points Swedish parties, escorting wagons with provisions, grain, bread, beer, and herds of every kind of cattle. With the herds and wagons went crowds of peasants, small nobles, weeping and groaning, for they were dragged away numbers of miles with the wagons. Happy the man who was allowed to return home with his wagon; and this did not happen in every case, for after they had brought the supplies peasants and petty nobles were forced to labor at repairing castles, building sheds and magazines.

Kmita saw also that in the neighborhood of Pultusk the Swedes acted more harshly with the people than in Pjasnysh; and not being able to understand the cause, he inquired about it of the nobles whom he met on the road.

"The nearer you go to Warsaw," answered one of the travellers, "the harsher you will find the oppressors. Where they have just come and are not secure, they are more kindly, publish the commands of the king against oppression, and promulgate the capitulations; but where they feel safe, and have occupied castles in the neighborhood, they break all promises, have no consideration, commit injustice, plunder, rob, raise their hands against churches, the clergy, and sacred nuns. It is nothing here yet, but to describe what is going on in Great Poland words fail in the mouths of men."

Here the noble began to describe what was taking place in Great Poland,—what extortions, violence, and murders the savage enemy committed; how men were thumbscrewed and tortured to discover money; how the Provincial, Father Branetski, was killed in Poznan itself; and peasants were tortured so fearfully that the hair stood on one's head at the mere thought of it.

"It will come to this everywhere," said the noble; "it is the punishment of God. The last judgment is near. Worse and worse every day,—and salvation from no point."

"It is a marvel to me," said Kmita, "for I am not of these parts and know not how people feel here, that you, gracious gentlemen, being nobles and knightly persons, endure these oppressions in patience."

"With what can we rise up?" answered the noble. "In their hands are the castles, fortresses, cannon, powder, muskets; they have taken from us even fowling-pieces. There was still some hope in Charnyetski; but since he is in prison, and the king in Silesia, who will think of resistance? There are hands, but nothing in them, and there is no head."

"And there is no hope," added Kmita, in a hollow voice.

Here they dropped the conversation, for a Swedish division came up convoying wagons, small nobles, and a "requisition." It was a wonderful spectacle. Sitting on horses as fat as bullocks, mustached and bearded troopers rode on in a cloud of dust, with their right hands on their hips, with their hats on the sides of their heads, with tens of geese and hens hanging at their saddles. Looking at their warlike and insolent faces, it was easy to see that they felt like lords, gladsome and safe. But the brotherhood of petty nobles walked at the side of the wagons, not only barefooted, but with heads drooping on their bosoms, abused, troubled, frequently urged forward with whips.

On seeing this, Kmita's lips quivered as in a fever, and he fell to repeating to the noble near whom he was riding,—

"Oh, my hands are itching, my hands are itching, my hands are itching!"

"Quiet, in the name of the Merciful God! you will ruin yourself, me, and my little children."

More than once, however, Pan Andrei had before him sights still more marvellous. Behold at times, among parties of horsemen, he saw marching groups, larger or smaller, of Polish nobles, with armed attendants; these nobles were joyous, singing songs, drunk, and with Swedes and Germans on the footing of "lord brother."

"How is this?" asked Kmita. "They are persecuting some nobles and crushing them, while with others they enter into friendship. It must be that those citizens whom I see among the soldiers are fanatical traitors?"

"Not merely fanatical traitors, but worse, for they are heretics," answered the noble. "They are more grievous to us Catholics than the Swedes; they are the men who plunder most, burn houses, carry off maidens, commit private offences. The whole country is in alarm from them, for everything drops from these men altogether without punishment, and it is easier to get justice from Swedish commanders against a Swede, than against one of our own heretics. Every commandant, if you utter a word, will answer at once, 'I have no right to touch him, for he is not my man; go to your own tribunals.' And what tribunals are there

here now, and what execution of law when everything is in Swedish hands? Where the Swede cannot go the heretics will take him, and they are the men chiefly who incite the Swedes against churches and clergy. This is the way in which they punish the country, our mother, for having given them refuge here and freedom for their blasphemous faith when they were persecuted in other Christian lands justly, for their intrigues and abominations."

The noble stopped and looked with alarm at Kmita,—

"But you say that you are from Electoral Prussia, so you may be a Lutheran?"

"God save me from that," answered Pan Andrei. "I am from Prussia, but of a family Catholic for ages, for we went from Lithuania to Prussia."

"Then praise to the Most High, for I was frightened. My dear sir, as to Lithuania there is no lack of dissidents there; and they have a powerful chief in Radzivill, who has turned out so great a traitor that he can come into comparison with Radzeyovski alone."

"May God grant the devils to pull the soul out through his throat before the New Year!" exclaimed Kmita, with venom.

"Amen!" answered the noble, "and also the souls of his servants, his assistants, his executioners, of whom tidings have come even to us, and without whom he would not have dared to bring destruction on this country."

Kmita grew pale and said not a word. He did not ask even—he did not dare to ask—of what assistants, servants, and executioners that noble was speaking.

Travelling slowly, they came to Pultusk late in the evening; there they called Kmita to the bishop's palace or castle to give answer to the commandant.

"I am furnishing horses to the army of his Swedish Grace," said Pan Andrei, "and I have orders with which I am going to Warsaw for money."

Colonel Israel (such was the name of the commandant) smiled under his mustaches and said,—

"Oh, make haste, make haste, and take a wagon for the return, so as to have something to carry that money in!"

"I thank you for the counsel," answered Pan Andrei. "I understand that you are jeering at me; but I will go for my own, even if I have to go to his grace the king!"

"Go! don't give away your own; a very nice sum belongs to you."

"The hour will come when you'll pay me," retorted Kmita, going out.

In the town itself he came on celebrations again, for rejoicing over the capture of Cracow was to last three days. He learned, however, that in Pjasnysh the Swedish triumph was exaggerated, perhaps by design. Charnyetski, the castellan of Kieff, had not fallen into captivity, but had obtained the right of marching from the city with his troops, with arms and lighted matches at the cannon. It was said that he was to retire to Silesia. This was not a great consolation, but still a consolation.

In Pultusk there were considerable forces which were to go thence to the Prussian boundary, under command of Colonel Israel, to alarm the elector; therefore neither the town nor the castle, though very spacious, could furnish lodging for the soldiers. Here too, for the first time, Kmita saw soldiers encamped in a church,—in a splendid Gothic structure, founded almost two hundred years before by Bishop Gijytski, were quartered hireling German infantry. Inside the sanctuary it was flaming with light as on Easter, for on the stone floor were burning fires kindled in various places. Kettles were steaming over the fires. Around kegs

651

of beer were groups of common soldiers,—hardened robbers, who had plundered all Catholic Germany, and of a certainty were not spending their first night in a church. In the church were heard talking and shouting. Hoarse voices were singing camp songs; there sounded also the outcry and merriment of women, who in those days straggled usually in the wake of an army.

Kmita stood in the open door; through the smoke in the midst of ruddy flames he saw the red, mustached faces of soldiers who, inflamed with drink, were sitting on kegs and quaffing beer; some throwing dice or playing cards, some selling church vestments, others embracing low women dressed in bright garments. Uproar, laughter, the clatter of tankards, the sound of muskets, the echoes thundering in the vaults deafened him. His head whirled; he could not believe what his eyes saw; the breath died in his breast; hell would not have more greatly amazed him. At last he clutched his hair and ran out repeating as if in bewilderment,—

"O God, aid us! O God, correct us! O God, deliver us!"

CHAPTER XXXVII.

In Warsaw the Swedes had been managing for a long time. Wittemberg, the real governor of the city and the commander of the garrison, was at that moment in Cracow; Radzeyovski carried on the government in his place. Not less than two thousand soldiers were in the city proper surrounded by walls, and in the jurisdictions beyond the walls built up with splendid edifices belonging to the church and the world. The castle and the city were not destroyed; for Pan Vessel, starosta of Makovo, had yielded them up without battle, and he with the garrison disappeared hurriedly, fearing the personal vengeance of Radzeyovski, his enemy.

But when Pan Kmita examined more closely and carefully, he saw on many houses the traces of plundering hands. These were the houses of those citizens who had fled from the city, not wishing to endure foreign rule, or who had offered resistance when the Swedes were breaking over the walls.

Of the lordly structures in the jurisdictions those only retained their former splendor the owners of which stood soul and body with the Swedes. Therefore the Kazanovski Palace remained in all its magnificence, for Radzeyovski had saved that, his own, and the palace of Konyetspolski, the standard-bearer, as well as the edifice reared by Vladislav IV., and which was afterward known as the Kazimirovski Palace. But edifices of the clergy were injured considerably; the Denhof Palace was half wrecked; the chancellor's or the so-called Ossolinski Palace, on Reformatski Street, was plundered to its foundations. German hirelings looked out through its windows; and that costly furniture which the late chancellor had brought from Italy at such outlay,— those Florentine leathers, Dutch tapestry, beautiful cabinets inlaid with mother-of-pearl, pictures, bronze and marble statues, clocks from Venice and Dantzig, and magnificent glasses were either lying in disordered heaps in the yard, or, already packed, were waiting to be taken, when the time came, by the Vistula to Sweden. Guards watched over these precious things, but meanwhile they were being ruined under the wind and rain.

In other cities the same thing might be seen; and though the capital had yielded without battle, still thirty gigantic flat-boats were ready on the Vistula to bear away the plunder.

The city looked like a foreign place. On the streets foreign languages were heard more than Polish; everywhere were met Swedish soldiers, German, French, English, and Scottish mercenaries, in the greatest variety of uniforms,—in hats, in lofty helmets, in kaftans, in breastplates, half breastplates, in stockings, or Swedish boots, with legs as wide as water-buckets. Everywhere a foreign medley, foreign garments, foreign faces, foreign songs. Even the horses had forms different from those to which the eye was accustomed. There had also rushed in a multitude of Armenians with dark faces, and black hair covered with bright skull-caps; they had come to buy plundered articles.

But most astonishing of all was the incalculable number of gypsies, who, it is unknown for what purpose, had gathered after the Swedes from all parts of the country. Their tents stood at the side of the Uyazdovski Palace, and along the monastery jurisdiction, forming as it were a special town of linen houses within a town of walled structures.

In the midst of these various-tongued throngs the inhabitants of the city almost vanished; for their own safety they sat gladly enclosed in their houses, showing themselves rarely, and then passing swiftly along the streets. Only occasionally the carriage of some magnate, hurrying from the Cracow suburbs to the castle, and surrounded by haiduks, Turkish grooms, or troops in Polish dress, gave reminder that the city was Polish.

Only on Sundays and holidays, when the bells announced services, did crowds come forth from the houses, and the capital put on its former appearance,—though even then lines of foreign soldiers stood hedgelike in front of the churches, to look at the women or pull at their dresses when, with downcast eyes, they walked past them. These soldiers laughed, and sometimes sang vile songs just when the priests were singing Mass in the churches.

All this flashed past the astonished eyes of Pan Kmita like jugglery; but he did not warm his place long in Warsaw, for not knowing any man he had no one before whom to open his soul. Even with those Polish nobles who were stopping in the city and living in public houses built during the reign of King Sigismund

III. on Dluga Street, Pan Andrei did not associate closely. He conversed, it is true, with this one and that, to learn the news; but all were fanatical adherents of the Swedes, and waiting for the return of Karl Gustav, clung to Radzeyovski and the Swedish officers with the hope of receiving starostaships, confiscated private estates, and profits from church and other recoupments. Each man of them would have been served rightly had some one spat in his eyes, and from this Kmita did not make great effort to restrain himself.

From the townspeople Kmita only heard that they regretted past times, and the good king of the fallen country. The Swedes persecuted them savagely, seized their houses, exacted contributions, imprisoned them. They said also that the guilds had arms secreted, especially the linen-weavers, the butchers, the furriers, and the powerful guild of tailors; that they were looking continually for the return of Yan Kazimir, did not lose hope, and with assistance from outside were ready to attack the Swedes.

Hearing this, Kmita did not believe his own ears. It could not find place in his head that men of mean station and rank should exhibit more love for the country and loyalty to their lawful king than nobles, who ought to bring those sentiments into the world with their birth.

But it was just the nobles and magnates who stood by the Swedes, and the common people who for the greater part wished to resist; and more than once it happened that when the Swedes were driving common people to work at fortifying Warsaw, these common people chose to endure flogging, imprisonment, even death itself, rather than aid in confirming Swedish power.

Beyond Warsaw the country was as noisy as in a beehive. All the roads, the towns, and the hamlets were occupied by soldiers, by attendants of great lords and nobles, and by lords and nobles serving the Swedes. All was captured, gathered in, subdued; everything was as Swedish as if the country had been always in their hands.

Pan Andrei met no people save Swedes, adherents of the Swedes, or people in despair, indifferent, who were convinced to the depth of their souls that all was lost. No one thought of resistance; commands were carried out quietly and promptly one half or a tenth part of which would have been met in times not long past with opposition and protest. Fear had reached that degree that even those who were injured praised loudly the kind protector of the Commonwealth.

Formerly it happened often enough that a noble received his own civil and military deputies of exaction with gun in hand, and at the head of armed servants; now such tributes were imposed as it pleased the Swedes to impose, and the nobles gave them as obediently as sheep give their wool to the shearer. It happened more than once that the same tribute was taken twice. It was vain to use a receipt as defence; it was well if the executing officer did not moisten it in wine and make the man who showed it swallow the paper. That was nothing! "Vivat protector!" cried the noble; and when the officer had departed he ordered his servant to crawl out on the roof and see if another were not coming. And well if only all were ended with Swedish contributions; but worse than the enemy were, in that as in every other land, the traitors. Old private grievances, old offences were brought up; ditches were filled, meadows and forests were seized, and for the friend of the Swedes everything went unpunished. Worst, however, were the dissidents; and they were not all. Armed bands were formed of unfortunates, desperadoes, ruffians, and gamblers. Assisted by Swedish marauders, Germans, and disturbers of all kinds, these bands fell upon peasants and nobles. The country was filled with fires; the armed hand of the soldier was heavy on the towns; in the forest the robber attacked. No one thought of curing the Commonwealth; no one dreamed of rescue, of casting off the yoke; no one had hope.

It happened that Swedish and German plunderers near Sohachev besieged Pan Lushchevski, the starosta of that place, falling upon him at Strugi, his private estate. He, being of a military turn, defended himself vigorously, though an old man. Kmita came just then; and since his patience had on it a sore ready to break at any cause, it broke at Strugi. He permitted the Kyemliches, therefore, "to pound," and fell upon the invaders himself with such vigor that he scattered them, struck them down; no one escaped, even prisoners were drowned at his command. The starosta, to whom the aid was as if it had fallen from heaven, received his deliverer with thanks and honored him at once. Pan Andrei, seeing before him a personage, a statesman, and besides a man of old date, confessed his hatred of the Swedes, and inquired of the starosta what he thought of the future of the Commonwealth, in the hope that he would pour balsam on his soul.

But the starosta viewed the past differently, and said: "My gracious sir, I know not what I should have answered had this question been put when I had ruddy mustaches and a mind clouded by physical humor; but to-day I have gray mustaches, and the experience of seventy years on my shoulders, and I see future things, for I am near the grave; therefore I say that not only we, even if we should correct our errors, but all Europe, cannot break the Swedish power."

"How can that be? Where did it come from?" cried Kmita. "When was Sweden such a power? Are there not more of the Polish people on earth, can we not have a larger army? Has that army yielded at any time to Sweden in bravery?"

"There are ten times as many of our people. God has increased our produce so that in my starostaship of Sohachev more wheat is grown than in all Sweden; and as to bravery, I was at Kirchholm when three thousand hussars of us scattered in the dust eighteen thousand of the best troops of Sweden."

"If that is true," said Kmita, whose eyes flashed at remembrance of Kirchholm, "what earthly causes are there why we should not put an end to them now?"

"First, this," answered the old man, with a deliberate voice, "that we have become small and they have grown great; that they have conquered us with our own hands, as before now they conquered the Germans with Germans. Such is the will of God; and there is no power, I repeat, that can oppose them to-day."

"But if the nobles should come to their senses and rally around their ruler,—if all should seize arms, what would you advise to do then, and what would you do yourself?"

"I should go with others and fall, and I should advise every man to fall; but after that would come times on which it is better not to look."

"Worse times cannot come! As true as life, they cannot! It is impossible!" cried Kmita.

"You see," continued the starosta, "before the end of the world and before the last judgment Antichrist will come, and it is said that evil men will get the upper hand of the good. Satans will go through the world, will preach a faith opposed to the true one, and will turn men to it. With the permission of God, evil will conquer everywhere until the moment in which trumpeting angels shall sound for the end of the world."

Here the starosta leaned against the back of the chair on which he was sitting, closed his eyes, and spoke on in a low, mysterious voice,—

"It was said, 'There will be signs.' There have been signs on the sun in the form of a hand and a sword. God be merciful to us, sinners! The evil gain victory over the just, for the Swedes and their adherents are conquering. The true faith is failing, for behold the Lutheran is rising. Men! do ye not see that *dies iræ, dies illa* (the day of wrath, that day) is approaching? I am seventy years old; I stand on the brink of the Styx,—I am waiting for the ferryman and the boat,—I see—"

Here the starosta became silent, and Kmita looked at him with terror; for the reasons seemed to him just, the conclusions fitting, therefore he was frightened at his decisions and reflected deeply. But the starosta did not look at him; he only looked in front of himself, and said at last,—

"And of course the Swedes conquer here when that is the permission of God, the express will mentioned and spoken of in the Prophecies—Oi, people, to Chenstohova, to Chenstohova!" And again the starosta was silent.

The sun was just setting, and looking only aslant into the room, its light broke into colors on the glass fitted in lead, and made seven colored stripes on the floor; the rest of the room was in darkness. It became more and more awe-inspiring for Kmita; at moments it seemed to him that if the light were to vanish, that instant the trumpeting angel would summon to judgment.

"Of what prophecies is your grace speaking?" asked Kmita, at last; for the silence seemed to him still more solemn.

The starosta instead of an answer turned to the door of an adjoining room, and called,—

"Olenka! Olenka!"

"In God's name!" cried Kmita, "whom are you calling?"

At that moment he believed everything,—believed that his Olenka by a miracle was brought from Kyedani and would appear before his eyes. He forgot everything, fastened his gaze on the door, and waited without breath in his breast.

"Olenka! Olenka!"

The door opened, and there entered not Panna Billevich, but a young woman, shapely, slender, tall, a little like Olenka, with dignity and calm spread over her face. She was pale, perhaps ill, and maybe frightened at the recent attack; she walked with downcast eyes as lightly and quietly as if some breath were moving her forward.

"This is my daughter," said the starosta. "I have no sons at home; they are with Pan Pototski, and with him near our unfortunate king."

Then he turned to his daughter: "Thank first this manful cavalier for rescuing us, and then read to him the prophecy of Saint Bridget."

The maiden bowed down before Pan Andrei, then went out, and after a while returned with a printed roll in her hand, and standing in that many-colored light, began to read in a resonant and sweet voice,—

"The prophecy of Saint Bridget, I will declare to you first of the five kings and their rule: Gustav the son of Erick, the lazy ass, because neglecting the right worship he went over to the false. Rejecting the faith of the Apostles, he brought to the kingdom the Augsburg Confession, putting a stain on his reputation. Look at Ecclesiastes, where it is stated of Solomon that lie defiled his glory with idolatry—"

"Are you listening?" asked the starosta, pointing toward Kmita with the index finger of his left hand and holding the others, ready for counting.

"Yes," answered Kmita.

"Erick, the son of Gustavus, a wolf of unsatiable greed," read the lady, "with which he drew on himself the hatred of all men and of his brother Yan. First, suspecting Yan of intrigues with Denmark and Poland, he tormented him with war, and taking him with his wife he held them four years in a dungeon. Yan, at last

660

brought out of imprisonment and aided by change of fortune, conquered Erick, expelled him from the kingdom, and put him into prison forevermore. There is an unforeseen event!"

"Consider," said the old man. "Here is another."

The lady read further:—

"Yan, the brother of Erick, a lofty eagle, thrice conqueror over Erick, the Danes, and the Northerners. His son Sigismund, in whom dwells nobility of blood, chosen to the Polish throne. Praise to his offshoots!"

"Do you understand?" asked the starosta.

"May God prosper the years of Yan Kazimir!" answered Kmita.

"Karl, the prince of Sudermanii, the ram, who as rams lead the flock, so he led the Swedes to injustice; and he attacked justice."

"That is the fourth!" interrupted the starosta.

"The fifth, Gustavus Adolphus," read the lady, "is the lamb slain, but not spotless, whose blood was the cause of suffering and misfortune—"

"Yes; that is Gustavus Adolphus!" said the starosta. "Of Christiana there is no mention, for only men are counted. Read now the end, which refers accurately to the present time."

She read as follows:—

"I will show to thee the sixth, who distracts land and sea and brings trouble on the simple; whose hour of punishment I will place in my own hand. Though he attained his end quickly, my judgment draws near him; he will leave the kingdom in suffering and it will be written: They sowed rebellion and reap suffering and pain. Not only will I visit that kingdom, but rich cities and powerful; for the hungry are called, who will devour their sufficiency. Internal evils will not be lacking, and misfortune will abound. The foolish will rule, and the wise and the old men will not raise their heads. Honor and truth will fall, till that man shall come who will implore away my anger and who will not spare his own soul in love of truth."

"There you have it!" said the starosta.

"All is verified, so that only a blind man could doubt!" answered Kmita.

"Therefore the Swedes cannot be conquered," said the starosta.

"Till that man shall come who will not spare his soul for the love of truth!" exclaimed Kmita. "The prophecy leaves hope! Not judgment, but salvation awaits us."

"Sodom was to be spared if ten just men could be found in it," said the starosta; "but that many were not found. In the same manner will not be found the man who will not spare his soul for love of truth; and the hour of judgment will strike."

"It cannot be but that he will be found," called out Kmita.

Before the starosta answered the door opened, and into the room walked a man no longer young, in armor and with a musket in his hand.

"Pan Shchebjytski?" said the starosta.

"Yes," answered the newly arrived. "I heard that ruffians had besieged you, and I hastened with my servants to the rescue."

"Without the will of God a hair will not fall from the head of a man," answered the starosta. "This cavalier has already freed me from oppression. But whence do you come?"

"From Sohachev."

"Have you heard anything new?"

"Every news is worse. New misfortune—"

"What has happened?"

"The provinces of Cracow, Sandomir, Rus, Lubelsk, Belzk, Volynia, and Kieff have surrendered to Karl Gustav. The act is already signed by envoys and by Karl."

The starosta shook his head, and turned to Kmita,—

"See," said he, "do you still think that the man will be found who will not spare his soul for the love of truth?"

Kmita began to tear the hair from his forelock; "Despair! despair!" repeated he, in distraction.

And Pan Shchebjytski continued: "They say also that the remnants of the army, which are with Pototski, the hetman, have already refused obedience and wish to go to the Swedes. The hetman probably is not sure of safety or life among them, and must do what they want."

"They sow rebellion and reap suffering and pain," said the starosta. "Whoso wishes to do penance for his sins, now is his time!"

Kmita could not hear further either prophecies or news; he wanted to sit with all speed on his horse and cool his head in the wind. He sprang up therefore, and began to take farewell of the starosta.

"But whither so hastily?" asked the latter.

"To Chenstohova, for I too am a sinner!"

"Though glad to entertain, I will not delay you, since your work is more urgent, for the day of judgment is at hand."

Kmita went out; and after him went the young lady, wishing instead of her father to do honor to the guest, for the old man was weak on his feet.

"Be in good health, young lady," said Kmita; "you do not know how thankful I am to you."

"If you are thankful to me," answered the young lady, "do me one service. You are going to Chenstohova; here is a ruddy ducat,—take it, I beg, and give it for a Mass in the chapel."

"For whose intention?" asked Kmita.

The prophetess dropped her eyes, trouble spread over her face; at the same time a slight flush came to her cheeks, and she said with a low voice, like the rustle of leaves,—

"For the intention of Andrei, that God may turn him from sinful ways."

Kmita pushed back two steps, stared, and from astonishment could not speak for a time.

"By the wounds of Christ!" cried he, at last, "what manner of house is this? Where am I? The prophecy itself, the soothsaying, and the indications—Your name is Olenka, and you give me for a Mass for the intentions of a sinful Andrei. This cannot be chance; it is the finger of God,—it is, it is. I shall go wild!—As God lives, I shall!"

"What is the matter?"

He caught her hands violently and began to shake them. "Prophesy further, speak to the end! If that Andrei will return and efface his faults, will Olenka keep faith with him? Speak, answer, for I shall not go away without that!"

"What is your trouble?"

"Will Olenka keep faith with him?" repeated Kmita.

Tears came suddenly into the eyes of the maiden: "To the last breath, to the hour of death!" said she, with sobbing.

She had not finished speaking when Kmita fell his whole length at her feet. She wanted to flee; he would not let her, and kissing her feet, he said,—

"I too am a sinful Andrei, who wants to return. I too have my loved one, Olenka. May yours return, and may mine keep faith. May your words be prophetic. You have poured balsam and hope into my suffering soul,—God reward you, God reward you!"

Then he sprang up, sat on his horse, and rode away.

CHAPTER XXXVIII.

The words of the young daughter of the starosta of Sohachev filled Kmita with great consolation, and for three days they did not leave his head. In the daytime on horseback, in the night on the bed, he was thinking of what had happened to him, and he came always to the conclusion that this could not be simple chance, but an indication from God, and a presage that if he would hold out, if he would not leave the good road, that same road which Olenka had shown him, she would keep faith and give him her former affection.

"If the starosta's daughter," thought Kmita, "keeps faith with her Andrei, who has not begun to grow better, there is still hope for me, with my honest intention of serving virtue, the country, and the king."

But, on the other hand, suffering was not absent from Pan Andrei. He had an honest intention, but had it not come too late? Was there yet any road, were there yet any means? The Commonwealth seemed to sink deeper each day, and it was difficult to close one's eyes to the terrible truth that for it there was no salvation. Kmita wished nothing more intently than to begin some kind of work, but he saw no willing people. Every moment new figures, every moment new faces, passed before him in the time of his journey; but the sight of them, their talk and discussions, merely took from him the remnant of his hopes.

Some had gone body and soul to the Swedish camp, seeking in it their own profit; these people drank and caroused as at a wake, drowning, in cups and in riot, shame and the honor of nobles; others told, with blindness beyond understanding, of that power which the Commonwealth would form in union with Sweden, under the sceptre of the first warrior on earth; and these were the most dangerous, for they were sincerely convinced that the whole earth must bow before such an alliance. A third party, like the starosta of Sohachev, honorable people and wishing well to the country, sought signs on the earth and in the heavens, repeated prophecies, and seeing the will of God and unbending predestination in all things that happened, came to the conclusion that there was no hope, no salvation; that the end of the world was drawing nigh; therefore it would be madness to think of earthly instead of heavenly salvation. Others hid in the forest, or escaped with their lives beyond the boundaries of the Commonwealth. Kmita met only unrestrained, corrupted, mad, timid, or desperate people. He met no man who had hope.

Meanwhile the fortune of the Swedes was increasing. News that the rest of the army had revolted, were conspiring, threatening the hetmans, and wishing to go over to the Swedes, gained certainty every day. The report that Konyetspolski with his division had joined Karl Gustav reverberated like thunder through every corner of the Commonwealth, and drove out the remnant of faith from men's hearts, for Konyetspolski was a knight of Zbaraj. He was followed by the starosta of Yavor and Prince Dymitr Vishnyevetski, who was not restrained by a name covered with immortal glory.

Men had begun now to doubt Lyubomirski, the marshal. Those who knew him well asserted that ambition surpassed in him both reason and love of country; that for the time being he was on the king's side because he was flattered, because all eyes were turned to him, because one side and the other tried to win him, to persuade him, because he was told that he had the fate of the country in his hands. But in view of Swedish success he began to hesitate, to delay; and each moment he gave the unfortunate Yan Kazimir to understand more clearly that he could save him, or sink him completely.

The refugee king was living in Glogov with a handful of trusted persons, who shared his fate. Each day some one deserted him, and went over to the Swedes. Thus do the weak bend in days of misfortune, even men to whom the first impulse of the heart points out the thorny path of honor. Karl Gustav received the deserters with open arms, rewarded them, covered them with promises, tempted and attracted the remnant of the faithful, extended more widely his rule; fortune itself pushed from before his feet every obstacle; he conquered Poland with Polish forces; he was a victor without a battle.

Crowds of voevodas, castellans, officials of Poland and Lithuania, throngs of armed nobles, complete squadrons of incomparable Polish cavalry, stood in his camp, watching the eyes of their newly made lord and ready at his beck.

The last of the armies of the kingdom was calling more and more emphatically to its hetman: "Go, incline thy gray head before the majesty of Karl,—go, for we wish to belong to the Swedes."

"To the Swedes! to the Swedes!"

And in support of these words thousands of sabres flashed forth.

At the same time war was flaming continually on the east. The terrible Hmelnitski was besieging Lvoff again; and legions of his allies, rolling on past the unconquered walls of Zamost, spread over the whole province of Lubelsk, reaching even to Lublin.

Lithuania was in the hands of the Swedes and Hovanski. Radzivill had begun war in Podlyasye, the elector was loitering, and any moment he might give the last blow to the expiring Commonwealth; meanwhile he was growing strong in Royal Prussia.

Embassies from every side were hastening to the King of Sweden, wishing him a happy conquest.

Winter was coming; leaves were falling from the trees; flocks of ravens, crows, and jackdaws had deserted the forests, and were flying over the villages and towns of the Commonwealth.

Beyond Pyotrkoff Kmita came again upon Swedish parties, who occupied all the roads and highways. Some of them, after the capture of Cracow, were marching to Warsaw, for it was said that Karl Gustav, having received homage from the northern and eastern provinces and signed the "capitulations," was only waiting for the submission of those remnants of the army under Pototski and Lantskoronski; that given, he would go straightway to Prussia, and therefore he was sending the army ahead. The road was closed in no place to Pan Andrei, for in general nobles roused no suspicion. A multitude of armed attendants were going with the Swedes; others were going to Cracow,—one to bow down before the new king, another to obtain something from him. No one was asked for a pass or a letter, especially since in the neighborhood of Karl, who was counterfeiting kindness, no man dared trouble another.

The last night before Chenstohova met Pan Andrei in Krushyn; but barely had he settled down when guests arrived. First a Swedish detachment of about one hundred horse, under the lead of a number of officers and some important captain. This captain was a man of middle age, of a form rather imposing, large, powerful, broad-shouldered, quick-eyed; and though he wore a foreign dress and looked altogether like a foreigner, still when he entered the room he spoke to Pan Andrei in purest Polish, asking who he was and whither he was going.

Pan Andrei answered at once that he was a noble from Sohachev, for it might have seemed strange to the officer that a subject of the elector had come to that remote place. Learning that Pan Andrei was going to the King of Sweden with complaint that payment of money due him by the Swedes was refused, the officer said,—

"Prayer at the high altar is best, and wisely you go to the king; for though he has a thousand affairs on his head, he refuses hearing to no one, and he is so kind to Polish nobles that you are envied by the Swedes."

"If only there is money in the treasury?"

"Karl Gustav is not the same as your recent Yan Kazimir, who was forced to borrow even of Jews, for whatever he had he gave straightway to him who first asked for it. But if a certain enterprise succeeds, there will be no lack of coin in the treasury."

"Of what enterprise is your grace speaking?"

"I know you too little to speak confidentially, but be assured that in a week or two the treasury of the King of Sweden will be as weighty as that of the Sultan."

"Then some alchemist must make money for him, since there is no place from which to get it in this country."

"In this country? It is enough to stretch forth daring hands. And of daring there is no lack among us, as is shown by the fact that we are now rulers here."

"True, true," answered Kmita; "we are very glad of that rule, especially if you teach us how to get money like chips."

"The means are in your power, but you would rather die of hunger than take one copper."

Kmita looked quickly at the officer, and said,—

"For there are places against which it is terrible, even for Tartars, to raise hands."

"You are too mysterious. Sir Cavalier," answered the officer, "and remember that you are going, not to Tartars, but to Swedes for money."

Further conversation was interrupted by the arrival of a new party of men, whom the officer was evidently expecting, for he hurried out of the inn. Kmita followed and stood in the door to see who were coming.

In front was a closed carriage drawn by four horses, and surrounded by a party of Swedish horsemen; it stopped before the inn. The officer who had just been talking to Kmita went up to the carriage quickly, and opening the door made a low bow to the person sitting inside.

"He must be some distinguished man," thought Kmita.

That moment they brought from the inn a flaming torch. Out of the carriage stepped an important personage dressed in black, in foreign fashion, with a cloak to his knees, lined with fox-skin, and a hat with feathers. The officer seized the torch from the hands of a horseman, and bowing once more, said,—

"This way, your excellency!"

Kmita pushed back as quickly as possible, and they entered after him. In the room the officer bowed a third time and said,—

"Your excellency, I am Count Veyhard Vjeshchovich, ordinarius proviantmagister, of his Royal Grace Karl Gustav, and am sent with an escort to meet your excellency."

"It is pleasant for me to meet such an honorable cavalier," said the personage in black, giving bow for bow.

"Does your excellency wish to stop here some time or to go on at once? His Royal Grace wishes to see your excellency soon."

"I had intended to halt at Chenstohova for prayers," answered the newly arrived, "but in Vyelunie I received news that his Royal Grace commands me to hurry; therefore, after I have rested, we will go on. Meanwhile dismiss the escort, and thank the captain who led it."

The officer went to give the requisite order. Pan Andrei stopped him on the way.

"Who is that?" asked he.

"Baron Lisola, the Imperial Envoy, now on his way from the court of Brandenburg to our lord," answered the officer. Then he went out, and after a while returned.

"Your excellency's orders are carried out," said he to the baron.

"I thank you," said Lisola; and with great though very lofty affability he indicated to Count Veyhard a place opposite himself. "Some kind of storm is beginning to whistle outside," said he, "and rain is falling. It may continue long; meanwhile let us talk before supper. What is to be heard here? I have been told that the voevodas of Little Poland have submitted to his Grace of Sweden."

"True, your excellency; his Grace is only waiting for the submission of the rest of the troops, then he will go at once to Warsaw and to Prussia."

"Is it certain that they will surrender?"

"Deputies from the army are already in Cracow. They have no choice, for if they do not come to us Hmelnitski will destroy them utterly."

Lisola inclined his reasoning head upon his breast. "Terrible, unheard of things!" said he.

The conversation was carried on in the German language. Kmita did not lose a single word of it.

"Your excellency," said Count Veyhard, "that has happened which had to happen."

"Perhaps so; but it is difficult not to feel compassion for a power which has fallen before our eyes, and for which a man who is not a Swede must feel sorrow."

"I am not a Swede; but if Poles themselves do not feel sorrow, neither do I," answered the count.

Lisola looked at him seriously. "It is true that your name is not Swedish. From what people are you, I pray?"

"I am a Cheh" (Bohemian).

"Indeed? Then you are a subject of the German emperor? We are under the same rule."

"I am in the service of the Most Serene King of Sweden," said Veyhard, with a bow.

"I wish not to derogate from that service in the least," answered Lisola, "but such employments are temporary; being then a subject of our gracious sovereign, whoever you may be, whomsoever you may serve, you cannot consider any one else as your natural sovereign."

"I do not deny that."

"Then I will tell you sincerely, that our lord mourns over this illustrious Commonwealth, over the fate of its noble monarch, and he cannot look with a kindly or willing eye on those of his subjects who are aiding in the final ruin of a friendly power. What have the Poles done to you, that you show them such ill will?"

"Your excellency, I might answer many things, but I fear to abuse your patience."

"You seem to me not only a famous soldier, but a wise man. My office obliges me to observe, to listen, to seek causes; speak then, even in the most minute way, and fear not to annoy my patience. If you incline at any time to the service of the emperor, which I wish most strongly, you will find in me a friend who will explain and repeat your reasons, should any man wish to consider your present service as wrong."

"Then I will tell you all that I have on my mind. Like many nobles, younger sons, I had to seek my fortune outside my native land. I came to this country where the people are related to my own, and take foreigners into service readily."

"Were you badly received?"

"Salt mines were given to my management. I found means of livelihood, of approach to the people and the king himself; I serve the Swedes at present, but should any one wish to consider me unthankful, I could contradict him directly."

"How?"

"Can more be asked of me than of the Poles themselves? Where are the Poles to-day? Where are the senators of this kingdom, the princes, the magnates, the nobles, if not in the Swedish camp? And still they should be the first to know what they ought to do, where the salvation of their country is, and where its destruction. I follow their example; who of them then has the right to call me unthankful? Why should I, a foreigner, be more faithful to the King of Poland and the Commonwealth than they themselves are? Why should I despise that service for which they themselves are begging?"

Lisola made no answer. He rested his head on his hand and fell into thought. It would seem that he was listening to the whistle of the wind and the sound of the autumn rain, which had begun to strike the windows of the inn.

"Speak on," said he, at last; "in truth you tell me strange things."

"I seek fortune where I can find it," continued Count Veyhard; "and because this people are perishing, I do not need to care for them more than they do for themselves, besides, even if I were to care, it would avail nothing, for they must perish."

"But why is that?"

"First, because they wish it themselves; second, because they deserve it. Your excellency, is there another country in the world where so many disorders and such violence may be seen? What manner of government is there here? The king does not rule, because they will not let him; the diets do not rule, because the

673

members break them; there is no army, because the Poles will not pay taxes; there is no obedience, for obedience is opposed to freedom; there is no justice, for there is no one to execute decisions, and each strong man tramples on decisions; there is no loyalty in this people, for all have deserted their king; there is no love for the country, for they have given it to the Swede, for the promise that he will not prevent them from living in old fashion according to their ancient violence. Where could anything similar be found? What people in the world would aid an enemy in conquering their own country? Who would desert a king, not for his tyranny, not for his evil deeds, but because a stronger one came? Where is there a people who love private profits more, or trample more on public affairs? What have they, your excellency? Let any one mention to me even one virtue,—prudence, reason, cleverness, endurance, abstinence. What have they? Good cavalry? that and nothing more. But the Numidians were famous for cavalry, and the Gauls, as may be read in Roman history, had celebrated soldiers; but where are they? They have perished as they were bound to perish. Whoso wishes to save the Poles is merely losing time, for they will not save themselves. Only the mad, the violent, the malicious, and the venal inhabit this land."

Count Veyhard pronounced the last words with a genuine outburst of hatred marvellous in a foreigner who had found bread among that people; but Lisola was not astonished. A veteran diplomat, he knew the world and men. He knew that whoso does not know how to pay his benefactor with his heart, seeks in him faults, so as to shield with them his own unthankfulness. Besides, it may be that he recognized that Count Veyhard was right. He did not protest, but asked quickly, "Are you a Catholic?"

The count was confused. "Yes, your excellency," answered he.

"I have heard in Vyelunie that there are persons who persuade the king, Karl Gustav, to occupy the monastery of Yasna Gora. Is it true?"

"Your excellency, the monastery lies near the Silesian boundary, and Yan Kazimir can easily receive messages therefrom. We must occupy it to prevent that. I was the first to direct attention to this matter, and therefore his Royal Grace has confided these functions to me."

Here Count Veyhard stopped suddenly, remembered Kmita, sitting in the other corner of the room, and coming up to him, asked,—

"Do you understand German?"

"Not a word, even if a man were to pull my teeth," answered Pan Andrei.

"That is too bad, for we wished to ask you to join our conversation." Then he turned to Lisola.

"There is a strange noble here, but he does not understand German; we can speak freely."

"I have no secret to tell," said Lisola; "but as I am a Catholic too, I should not like to see such injustice done to a sacred place. And because I am certain that the most serene emperor has the same feeling, I shall beg his Grace the King of Sweden to spare the monks. And do not hurry with the occupation until there is a new decision."

"I have express, though secret, instructions; but I shall not withhold them from your excellency, for I wish to serve faithfully my lord the emperor. I can assure your excellency that no profanation will come to the sacred place. I am a Catholic."

Lisola laughed, and wishing to extort the truth from a man less experienced than himself, asked jokingly,—

"But you will shake up their treasury for the monks? It will not pass without that, will it?"

675

"That may happen," answered Count Veyhard. "The Most Holy Lady will not ask for thalers from the priors' caskets. When all others pay, let the monks pay too."

"But if the monks defend themselves?"

The count laughed. "In this country no man will defend himself, and to-day no man is able. There was a time for defence,—now it is too late."

"Too late," repeated Lisola.

The conversation ended there. After supper they went away. Kmita remained alone. This was for him the bitterest night that he had spent since leaving Kyedani. While listening to the words of Count Veyhard, Kmita had to restrain himself with all his power to keep from shouting at him, "Thou liest, thou cur!" and from falling on him with his sabre. But if he did not do so, it was unhappily because he felt and recognized truth in the words of the foreigner,—awful truth burning like fire, but genuine.

"What could I say to him?" thought he; "with what could I offer denial except with my fist? What reasons could I bring? He snarled out the truth. Would to God he were slain! And that statesman of the emperor acknowledged to him that in all things and for all defence it was too late."

Kmita suffered in great part perhaps because that "too late" was the sentence not only of the country, but of his own personal happiness. And he had had his fill of suffering; there was no strength left in him, for during all those weeks he had heard nothing save, "All is lost, there is no time left, it is too late." No ray of hope anywhere fell into his soul.

Ever riding farther, he had hastened greatly, night and day, to escape from those prophecies, to find at last some place of rest, some man who would pour into his spirit even one drop of consolation. But he found every moment greater fall, every moment greater despair. At last the words of Count Veyhard filled that cup of bitterness and gall; they showed to him clearly this, which hitherto was an undefined feeling, that not so much the Swedes, the Northerners, and the Cossacks had killed the country, as the whole people.

"The mad, the violent, the malicious, the venal, inhabit this land," repeated Kmita after Count Veyhard, "and there are no others! They obey not the king, they break the diets, they pay not the taxes, they help the enemy to the conquest of this land. They must perish.

"In God's name, if I could only give him the lie! Is there nothing good in us save cavalry; no virtue, nothing but evil itself?"

Kmita sought an answer in his soul. He was so wearied from the road, from sorrows, and from everything that had passed before him, that it grew cloudy in his head. He felt that he was ill and a deathly sickness seized possession of him. In his brain an ever-growing chaos was working. Faces known and unknown pushed past him,—those whom he had known long before and those whom he had met on this journey. Those figures spoke, as if at a diet, they quoted sentences, prophecies; and all was concerning Olenka. She was awaiting deliverance from Kmita; but Count Veyhard held him by the arms, and looking into his eyes repeated: "Too late! what is Swedish is Swedish!" and Boguslav Radzivill sneered and supported Count Veyhard. Then all of them began to scream: "Too late, too late, too late!" and seizing Olenka they vanished with her somewhere in darkness.

It seemed to Pan Andrei that Olenka and the country were the same, that he had ruined both and had given them to the Swedes of his own will. Then such measureless sorrow grasped hold of him that he woke, looked around in amazement and listening to the wind which in the chimney, in the walls, in the roof, whistled in various voices and played through each cranny, as if on an organ.

But the visions returned, Olenka and the country were blended again in his thoughts in one person whom Count Veyhard was conducting away saying: "Too late, too late!"

So Pan Andrei spent the night in a fever. In moments of consciousness he thought that it would come to him to be seriously ill, and at last he wanted to call Soroka to bleed him. But just then dawn began; Kmita sprang up and went out in front of the inn.

The first dawn had barely begun to dissipate the darkness; the day promised to be mild; the clouds were breaking into long stripes and streaks on the west, but the east was pure; on the heavens, which were growing pale gradually, stars, unobscured by mist, were twinkling. Kmita roused his men, arrayed himself in holiday dress, for Sunday had come and they moved to the road.

After a bad sleepless night, Kmita was wearied in body and spirit. Neither could that autumn morning, pale but refreshing, frosty and clear, scatter the sorrow crushing the heart of the knight. Hope in him had burned to the last spark, and was dying like a lamp in which the oil is exhausted. What would that day bring? Nothing!—the same grief, the same suffering, rather it will add to the weight on his soul; of a surety it will not decrease it.

He rode forward in silence, fixing his eyes on some point which was then greatly gleaming upon the horizon. The horses were snorting; the men fell to singing with drowsy voices their matins.

Meanwhile it became clearer each moment, the heavens from pale became green and golden and that point on the horizon began so to shine that Kmita's eyes were dazzled by its glitter.

The men ceased their singing and all gazed in that direction, at last Soroka said,—

"A miracle or what?—That is the west, and it is as if the sun were rising."

In fact, that light, increased in the eyes: from a point it became a ball, from a ball a globe; from afar you would have said that some one had hung above the earth a giant star, which was scattering rays immeasurable.

Kmita and his men looked with amazement on that bright, trembling, radiant vision, not knowing what was before their sight. Then a peasant came along from Krushyn in a wagon with a rack. Kmita turning to him saw that the peasant, holding his cap in his hand and looking at the light, was praying.

"Man," asked Pan Andrei, "what is that which shines so?"

"The church on Yasna Gora."

"Glory to the Most Holy Lady!" cried Kmita. He took his cap from his head, and his men removed theirs.

After so many days of suffering, of doubts, and of struggles, Pan Andrei felt suddenly that something wonderful was happening in him, Barely had the words, "the church on Yasna Gora," sounded in his ears when the confusion fell from him as if some hand had removed it.

A certain inexplicable awe seized hold of Pan Andrei, full of reverence, but at the same time a joy unknown to experience, great and blissful. From that church shining on the height in the first rays of the sun, hope, such as for a long time Pan Andrei had not known, was beating,—a strength invincible on which he wished to lean. A new life, as it were, entered him and began to course through his veins with the blood. He breathed as deeply as a sick man coming to himself out of fever and unconsciousness.

But the church glittered more and more brightly, as if it were taking to itself all the light of the sun. The whole region lay at its feet, and the church gazed at it from the height; you would have said, "'Tis the sentry and guardian of the land."

For a long time Kmita could not take his eyes from that light; he satisfied and comforted himself with the sight of it. The faces of his men had grown serious, and were penetrated with awe. Then the sound of a bell was heard in the silent morning air.

"From your horses!" cried Pan Andrei.

All sprang from their saddles, and kneeling on the road began the litany. Kmita repeated it, and the soldiers responded together.

Other wagons came up. Peasants seeing the praying men on the road joined them, and the crowd grew greater continually. When at length the prayers were finished Pan Andrei rose, and after him his men; but they advanced on foot, leading their horses and singing: "Hail, ye bright gates!"

Kmita went on with alertness as if he had wings on his shoulders. At the turns of the road the church vanished, then came out again. When a height or a mist concealed it, it seemed to Kmita that light had been captured by darkness; but when it gleamed forth again all faces were radiant.

So they went on for a long time. The cloister and the walls surrounding it came out more distinctly, became more imposing, more immense. At last they saw the town in the distance, and under the mountain whole lines of houses and cottages, which, compared with the size of the church, seemed as small as birds' nests.

It was Sunday; therefore when the sun had risen well the road was swarming with wagons, and people on foot going to church. From the lofty towers the bells great and small began to peal, filling the air with noble sounds. There was in that sight and in those metal voices a strength, a majesty immeasurable, and at the same time a calm. That bit of land at the foot of Yasna Gora resembled in no wise the rest of the country.

Throngs of people stood black around the walls of the church. Under the hill were hundreds of wagons, carriages, and equipages; the talk of men was blended with the neighing of horses tied to posts. Farther on, at the right, along the chief road leading to the mountain, were to be seen whole rows of stands, at which were sold metal offerings, wax candles, pictures, and scapulars. A river of people flowed everywhere freely.

The gates were wide open; whoso wished entered, whoso wished went forth; on the walls, at the guns, were no soldiers. Evidently the very sacredness of the place guarded the church and the cloister, and perhaps men trusted in the letters of Karl Gustav in which he guaranteed safety.

CHAPTER XXXIX.

From the gates of the fortress peasants and nobles, villagers from various neighborhoods, people of every age, of both sexes, of all ranks, pressed forward to the church on their knees, singing prayerful hymns. That river flowed slowly, and its course was stopped whenever the bodies of people crowded against one another too densely. At times the songs ceased and the crowds began to repeat a litany, and then the thunder of words was heard from one end of the place to the other. Between hymn and litany, between litany and hymn, the people were silent, struck the ground with their foreheads, or cast themselves down in the form of a cross. At these moments were heard only the imploring and shrill voices of beggars, who sitting at both banks of the human river exposed their deformed limbs to public gaze. Their howling was mingled with the clinking of coppers thrown into tin and wooden dishes. Then again the river of heads flowed onward, and again the hymns thundered.

681

As the river flowed nearer to the church door, excitement grew greater, and was turned into ecstasy. You could see hands stretched toward heaven, eyes turned upward, faces pale from emotion or glowing with prayer. Differences of rank disappeared: the coat of the peasant touched the robe of the noble, the jacket of the soldier the yellow coat of the artisan.

In the church door the crush was still greater. The bodies of men had become not a river, but a bridge, so firm that you might travel on their heads and their shoulders without touching the ground with a foot. Breath failed their breasts, space failed their bodies; but the spirit which inspired gave them iron endurance. Each man was praying; no one thought of aught else. Each one bore on himself the pressure and weight of the whole of that mass, but no man fell; and pressed by those thousands he felt in himself power against thousands, and with that power he pushed forward, lost in prayer, in ecstasy, in exaltation.

Kmita, creeping forward in the first ranks with his men, reached the church with the earliest; then the current carried him too to the chapel of miracles, where the multitude fell on their faces, weeping, embracing the floor with their hands, and kissing it with emotion. So also did Pan Andrei; and when at last he had the boldness to raise his head, delight, happiness, and at the same time mortal awe, almost took from him consciousness.

In the chapel there was a ruddy gloom not entirely dispersed by the rays of candles burning on the altar. Colored rays fell also through the window-panes; and all those gleams, red, violet, golden, fiery, quivered on the walls, slipped along the carvings and windings, made their way into dark depths bringing forth to sight indistinct forms buried as it were in a dream. Mysterious glimmers ran along and united with darkness, so undistinguishable that all difference between light and darkness was lost. The candles on the altar had golden halos; the smoke from the censers formed purple mist; the white robes of the monks serving Mass played with the darkened colors of the rainbow. All things there were half visible, half veiled, unearthly; the gleams were unearthly, the darkness unearthly, mysterious, majestic, blessed, filled with prayer, adoration, and holiness.

From the main nave of the church came the deep sound of human voices, like the mighty sound of the sea; but in the chapel deep silence reigned, broken only by the voice of the priest chanting Mass.

The image was still covered; expectation therefore held the breath in all breasts. There were only to be seen, looking in one direction, faces as motionless as if they had parted with earthly life, hands palm to palm and placed before mouths, like the hands of angels in pictures.

The organ accompanied the singing of the priest, and gave out tones mild and sweet, flowing as it were from flutes beyond the earth. At moments they seemed to distil like water from its source; then again they fell softly but quickly like dense rain showers in May.

All at once the thunder of trumpets and drums roared, and a quiver passed through all hearts. The covering before the picture was pushed apart from the centre to the sides, and a flood of diamond light flashed from above on the faithful.

Groans, weeping, and cries were heard throughout the chapel.

"*Salve, Regina!*" (Hail, O Queen!) cried the nobles, "*Monstra te esse matrem!*" (Show thyself a mother); but the peasants cried, "O Most Holy Lady! Golden Lady! Queen of the Angels! save us, assist us, console us, pity us!"

Long did those cries sound, together with sobs of women and complaints of the hapless, with prayers for a miracle on the sick or the maimed.

683

The soul lacked little of leaving Kmita; he felt only that he had before him infinity, which he could not grasp, could not comprehend, and before which all things were effaced. What were doubts in presence of that faith which all existence could not exhaust? what was misfortune in presence of that solace? what was the power of the Swedes in presence of that defence? what was the malice of men before the eyes of such protection?

Here his thoughts became settled, and turned into faculties; he forgot himself, ceased to distinguish who he was, where he was. It seemed to him that he had died, that his soul was now flying with the voices of organs, mingled in the smoke of the censers; his hands, used to the sword and to bloodshed, were stretched upward, and he was kneeling in ecstasy, in rapture.

The Mass ended. Pan Andrei knew not himself how he reached again the main nave of the church. The priest gave instruction from the pulpit; but Kmita for a long time heard not, understood not, like a man roused from sleep, who does not at once note where his sleeping ended and his waking moments began.

The first words which he heard were: "In this place hearts change and souls are corrected, for neither can the Swedes overcome this power, nor those wandering in darkness overcome the true light!"

"Amen!" said Kmita in his soul, and he began to strike his breast; for it seemed to him then that he had sinned deeply through thinking that all was lost, and that from no source was there hope.

After the sermon Kmita stopped the first monk he met, and told him that he wished to see the prior on business of the church and the cloister.

He got hearing at once from the prior, who was a man in ripe age, inclining then toward its evening. He had a face of unequalled calm. A thick black beard added to the dignity of his face; he had mild azure eyes with a penetrating look. In his white habit he seemed simply a saint Kmita kissed his sleeve; he pressed Kmita's head, and inquired who he was and whence he had come.

"I have come from Jmud," answered Kmita, "to serve the Most Holy Lady, the suffering country, and my deserted king, against all of whom I have hitherto sinned, and in sacred confession I beg to make a minute explanation. I ask that to-day or to-morrow my confession be heard, since sorrow for my sins draws me to this. I will tell you also, revered father, my real name,—under the seal of confession, not otherwise, for men ill inclined to me prevent and bar me from reform. Before men I wish to be called Babinich, from one of my estates, taken now by the enemy. Meanwhile I bring important information to which do you, revered father, give ear with patience, for it is a question of this sacred retreat and this cloister."

"I praise your intentions and the change of life which you have undertaken," said the prior, Father Kordetski; "as to confession, I will yield to your urgent wish and hear it now."

"I have travelled long," added Kmita, "I have seen much and I have suffered not a little. Everywhere the enemy has grown strong, every where heretics are raising their heads, nay, even Catholics themselves are going over to the camp of the enemy; who, emboldened by this, as well as by the capture of two capitals, intend to raise now sacrilegious hands against Yasna Gora."

"From whom have you this news?" asked the prior.

"I spent last night at Krushyn, where I saw Count Veyhard Vjeshchovich and Baron Lisola, envoy of the Emperor of Germany, who was returning from the Brandenburg court, and is going to the King of Sweden."

"The King of Sweden is no longer in Cracow," said the prior, looking searchingly into the eyes of Pan Andrei.

But Pan Andrei did not drop his lids and talked on,—

"I do not know whether he is there or not. I know that Lisola is going to him, and Count Veyhard was sent to relieve the escort and conduct him farther. Both talked before me in German, taking no thought of my presence; for they did not suppose that I understood their speech. I knowing German, was able to learn that Count Veyhard has proposed the occupation of this cloister and the taking of its treasure, for which he has received permission from the king."

"And you have heard this with your own ears?"

"Just as I am standing here."

"The will of God be done!" said the priest, calmly.

Kmita was alarmed. He thought that the priest called the command of the King of Sweden the will of God and was not thinking of resistance; therefore he said,—

"I saw in Pultusk a church in Swedish hands, the soldiers were playing cards in the sanctuary of God, kegs of beer were on the altars, and shameless women were there with the soldiers."

The prior looked steadily, directly in the eyes of the soldier. "A wonderful thing!" said he; "sincerity and truth are looking out of your eyes."

Kmita flushed. "May I fall a corpse here if what I say is not true."

"In every case these tidings over which we must deliberate are important."

"You will permit me to ask the older fathers and some of the more important nobles who are now dwelling with us. You will permit,—"

"I will repeat gladly the same thing before them."

Father Kordetski went out, and in quarter of an hour returned with four older fathers. Soon after Pan Rujyts-Zamoyski, the sword-bearer of Syeradz, entered,—a dignified man; Pan Okyelnitski, banneret of Vyelunie; Pan Pyotr Charnyetski, a young cavalier with a fierce war-like face, like an oak in stature and strength; and other nobles of various ages. The prior presented to them Pan Babinich from Jmud, and repeated in the presence of all the tidings which he had brought. They wondered greatly and began to measure Pan Andrei with their eyes inquiringly and incredulously, and when no one raised his voice the prior said,—

"May God preserve me from attributing to this cavalier evil intention or calumny; but the tidings which he brings seem to me so unlikely that I thought it proper for us to ask about them in company. With the sincerest intention this cavalier may be mistaken; he may have heard incorrectly, understood incorrectly, or have been led into error through heretics. To fill our hearts with fear, to cause panic in a holy place, to harm piety, is for them an immense delight, which surely no one of them in his wickedness would like to deny himself."

"That seems to me very much like truth," said Father Nyeshkovski, the oldest in the assembly.

"It would be needful to know in advance if this cavalier is not a heretic himself?" said Pyotr Charnyetski.

"I am a Catholic, as you are!" answered Kmita.

"It behooves us to consider first the circumstances," put in Zamoyski.

"The circumstances are such," said the prior, Kordetski, "that surely God and His Most Holy Mother have sent blindness of purpose on these enemies, so that they might exceed the measure in their iniquities; otherwise they never would have dared to raise the sword against this sacred retreat. Not with their own power have they conquered this Commonwealth, whose own sons have helped them. But though our people have fallen low, though they are wading in sin, still in sin itself there is a certain limit which they would not dare to pass. They have deserted their king, they have fallen away from the Commonwealth; but they have not ceased to revere their Mother, their Patroness and Queen. The enemy jeer at us and ask with contempt what has remained to us of our ancient virtues. I answer they have all perished; still something remains, for faith in the Most Holy Lady and reverence for Her have remained to them, and on this foundation the rest may be built. I see clearly that, let one Swedish ball make a dint in these sacred walls, the most callous men will turn from the conqueror,—from being friends will become enemies of the Swedes and draw swords against them. But the Swedes have their eyes open to their own danger, and understand this well. Therefore, if God, as I have said, has not sent upon them blindness intentionally, they will never dare to strike Yasna Gora; for that day would be the day of their change of fortune and of our revival."

Kmita heard the words of the prior with astonishment, words which were at the same time an answer to what had come from the mouth of Count Veyhard against the Polish people. But recovering from astonishment, he said,—

"Why should we not believe, revered father, that God has in fact visited the enemy with blindness? Let us look at their pride, their greed of earthly goods, let us consider their unendurable oppression and the tribute which they levy even on the clergy, and we may understand with ease that they will not hesitate at sacrilege of any kind."

The prior did not answer Kmita directly, but turning to the whole assembly, continued,—

"This cavalier says that he saw Lisola, the envoy, going to the King of Sweden. How can that be since I have undoubted news from the Paulists in Cracow that the king is not in Cracow, nor in Little Poland, since he went to Warsaw immediately after the surrender of Cracow."

"He cannot have gone to Warsaw," answered Kmita, "and the best proof is that he is waiting for the surrender and homage of the quarter soldiers, who are with Pototski."

"General Douglas is to receive homage in the name of the king, so they write me from Cracow."

Kmita was silent; he knew not what to answer.

"But I will suppose," continued the prior, "that the King of Sweden does not wish to see the envoy of the emperor and has chosen purposely to avoid him. Carolus likes to act thus,—to come on a sudden, to go on a sudden; besides the mediation of the emperor displeases him. I believe then readily that he went away pretending not to know of the coming of the envoy. I am less astonished that Count Veyhard, a person of such note, was sent out to meet Lisola with an escort, for it may be they wished to show politeness and sugar over the disappointment for the envoy; but how are we to believe that Count Veyhard would inform Baron Lisola at once of his plans."

"Unlikely!" said Father Nyeshkovski, "since the baron is a Catholic and friendly both to us and the Commonwealth."

"In my head too that does not find place," added Zamoyski.

"Count Veyhard is a Catholic himself and a well-wisher of ours," said another father.

"Does this cavalier say that he has heard this with his own ears?" asked Charnyetski, abruptly.

"Think, gentlemen, over this too," added the prior, "I have a safeguard from Carolus Gustavus that the cloister and the church are to be free forever from occupation and quartering."

"It must be confessed," said Zamoyski, with seriousness, "that in these tidings no one thing holds to another. It would be a loss for the Swedes, not a gain, to strike Yasna Gora; the king is not present, therefore Lisola could not go to him; Count Veyhard would not make a confidant of him; farther, Count Veyhard is not a heretic, but a Catholic,—not an enemy of the cloister, but its benefactor; finally, though Satan tempted him to make the attack, he would not dare to make it against the order and safeguard of the king." Here he turned to Kmita,—

"What then will you say, Cavalier, and why, with what purpose, do you wish to alarm the reverend fathers and us in this place?"

Kmita was as a criminal before a court. On one hand, despair seized him, because if they would not believe, the cloister would become the prey of the enemy; on the other, shame burned him, for he saw that all appearances argued against his information, and that he might easily be accounted a calumniator. At thought of this, anger tore him, his innate impulsiveness was roused, his offended ambition was active; the old-time half-wild Kmita was awakened. But he struggled until he conquered himself, summoned all his endurance, and repeated in his soul: "For my sins, for my sins!" and said, with a changing face,—

"What I have heard, I repeat once more: Count Veyhard is going to attack this cloister. The time I know not, but I think it will be soon,—I give warning and on you will fall the responsibility if you do not listen."

"Calmly, Cavalier, calmly," answered Pyotr Charnyetski, with emphasis. "Do not raise your voice." Then he spoke to the assembly,—"Permit me, worthy fathers, to put a few questions to the newly arrived."

"You have no right to offend me," cried Kmita.

"I have not even the wish to do so," answered Pan Pyotr, coldly; "but it is a question here of the cloister and the Holy Lady and Her capital. Therefore you must set aside offence; or if you do not set it aside, do so at least for the time, for be assured that I will meet you anywhere. You bring news which we want to verify—that is proper and should not cause wonder; but if you do not wish to answer, we shall think that you are afraid of self-contradiction."

"Well, put your questions!" said Babinich, through his teeth.

"You say that you are from Jmud?"

"True."

"And you have come here so as not to serve the Swedes and Radzivill the traitor?"

"True."

"But there are persons there who do not serve him, and oppose him on the side of the country; there are squadrons which have refused him obedience; Sapyeha is there. Why did you not join them?"

"That is my affair."

"Ah, ha! your affair," said Charnyetski. "You may give me that answer to other questions."

Pan Andrei's hands quivered, he fixed his eyes on the heavy brass bell standing before him on the table, and from that bell they were turned to the head of the questioner. A wild desire seized him to grasp that bell and bring it down on the skull of Charnyetski. The old Kmita was gaining the upper hand over the pious and penitent Babinich; but he broke himself once more and said,—

691

"Inquire."

"If you are from Jmud, then you must know what is happening at the court of the traitor. Name to me those who have aided in the ruin of the country, name to me those colonels who remain with him."

Kmita grew pale as a handkerchief, but still mentioned some names. Charnyetski listened and said, "I have a friend, an attendant of the king, Pan Tyzenhauz, who told me of one, the most noted. Do you know nothing of this arch criminal?"

"I do not know."

"How is this? Have you not heard of him who spilled his brother's blood, like Cain? Have you not heard, being from Jmud, of Kmita?"

"Revered fathers!" screamed Pan Andrei, on a sudden, shaking as in a fever, "let a clerical person question me, I will tell all. But by the living God do not let this noble torment me longer!"

"Give him peace," said the prior, turning to Pan Pyotr. "It is not a question here of this cavalier."

"Only one more question," said Zamoyski; and turning to Babinich, he asked,—"You did not expect that we would doubt your truth?"

"As God is in heaven I did not!"

"What reward did you expect?"

Pan Andrei, instead of giving an answer, plunged both hands into a small leather sack which hung at his waist from a belt, and taking out two handfuls of pearls, emeralds, turquoises, and other precious stones, scattered them on the table. "There!" said he, with a broken voice, "I have not come here for money! Not for your rewards! These are pearls and other small stones; all taken from the caps of boyars. You see what I am. Do I want a reward? I wish to offer these to the Most Holy Lady; but only

692

after confession, with a clean heart. Here they are—That's the reward which I ask. I have more, God grant you—"

All were silent in astonishment, and the sight of jewels thrown out as easily as grits from a sack made no small impression; for involuntarily every one asked himself what reason could that man have, if he had no thought of rewards?

Pan Pyotr was confused; for such is the nature of man that the sight of another's power and wealth dazzles him. Finally his suspicions fell away, for how could it be supposed that that great lord, scattering jewels, wanted to frighten monks for profit.

Those present looked at one another and Kmita stood over his jewels with head upraised like the head of a roused eagle, with fire in his eyes and a flush on his face. The fresh wound passing through his cheek and his temple was blue; and terrible was Pan Babinich threatening with his predatory glance Charnyetski, on whom his anger was specially turned.

"Through your anger truth itself bursts forth," said Kordetski; "but put away those jewels, for the Most Holy Lady cannot receive that which is offered in anger, even though the anger be just; besides, as I have said, it is not a question here of you, but of the news which has filled us with terror and fear. God knows whether there is not some misunderstanding or mistake in it, for, as you see yourself, what you say does not fit with reality. How are we to drive out the faithful, diminish the honor of the Most Holy Lady, and keep the gates shut night and day?"

"Keep the gates shut, for God's mercy, keep the gates shut!" cried Pan Andrei, wringing his hands till his fingers cracked in their joints.

There was so much truth and unfeigned despair in his voice that those present trembled in spite of themselves, as if danger was really there at hand, and Zamoyski said,—

"As it is, we give careful attention to the environs, and repairs are going on in the walls. In the day-time we can admit people for worship; but it is well to observe caution even for this reason, that the king has gone, and Wittemberg rules in Cracow with iron hand, and oppresses the clergy no less than the laity."

"Though I do not believe in an attack, I have nothing to say against caution," answered Charnyetski.

"And I," said the prior, "will send monks to Count Veyhard to enquire if the safeguard of the king has validity."

Kmita breathed freely and cried,—

"Praise be to God, praise be to God!"

"Cavalier," said the prior, "God reward you for the good intention. If you have warned us with reason, you will have a memorable merit before the Holy Lady and the country; but wonder not if we have received your information with incredulity; more than once have we been alarmed. Some frightened us out of hatred to our faith, to destroy the honor shown the Most Holy Lady; others, out of greed, so as to gain something; still others, so as to bring news and gain consideration in the eyes of people; and maybe there were even those who were deceived. Satan hates this place most stubbornly, and uses every endeavor to hinder piety here and to permit the faithful to take as little part in it as possible, for nothing brings the court of hell to such despair as reverence for Her who crushed the head of the serpent. But now it is time for vespers. Let us implore Her love, let us confide ourselves to her guardianship, and let each man go to sleep quietly; for where should there be peace and safety, if not under Her wings?"

All separated. When vespers were finished Father Kordetski himself heard the confession of Pan Andrei, and listened to him long in the empty church; after that, Pan Andrei lay in the form of a cross before the closed doors of the chapel till midnight. At midnight he returned to his room, roused Soroka, and commanded the old man to flog him before he went to sleep, so that his shoulders and back were covered with blood.

CHAPTER XL.

Next morning, a wonderful and unusual movement reigned in the cloister. The gate was open, and entrance was not refused to the pious. Services were celebrated in the usual course; but after services all strangers were directed to leave the circuit of the cloister. Kordetski himself, in company with Zamoyski and Pan Pyotr, examined carefully the embrasures, and the escarpments supporting the walls from the inside and outside. Directions were given for repairing places here and there; blacksmiths in the town received orders to make hooks and spears, scythes fixed on long handles, clubs and heavy sticks of wood filled with strong spikes. And since it was known that they had already a considerable supply of such implements in the cloister, people in the town began at once to say that the cloister expected a sudden attack. New orders in quick succession seemed to confirm these reports. Toward night two hundred men were working at the side of the walls. Twelve heavy guns sent at the time of the siege of Cracow by Pan Varshytski, castellan of Cracow, were placed on new carriages and properly planted.

From the cloister storehouses monks and attendants brought out balls, which were placed in piles near the guns; carts with powder were rolled out; bundles of muskets were untied, and distributed to the garrison. On the towers and bastions watchmen were posted to look carefully, night and day, on the region about; men were sent also to make investigation through the neighborhood,—to Pjystaini, Klobuchek, Kjepitsi, Krushyn, and Mstov.

To the cloister storehouses, which were already well filled, came supplies from the town, from Chenstohovka and other villages belonging to the cloister.

The report went like thunder through the whole neighborhood. Townspeople and peasants began to assemble and take counsel. Many were unwilling to believe that any enemy would dare to attack Yasna Gora.

It was said that only Chenstohova itself was to be occupied; but even that excited the minds of men, especially when some of them remembered that the Swedes were heretics, whom nothing restrained, and who were ready to offer a purposed affront to the Most Holy Lady.

Therefore men hesitated, doubted, and believed in turn. Some wrung their hands, waiting for terrible signs on earth and in heaven,—visible signs of God's anger; others were sunk in helpless and dumb despair; an anger more than human seized a third party, whose heads were filled as it were with flame. And when once the fancy of men had spread its wings for flight, straightway there was a whirl of news, ever changing, ever more feverish, ever more monstrous.

And as when a man thrusts a stick or throws fire into an ant-hill, unquiet swarms rush forth at once, assemble, separate, reassemble; so was the town, so were the neighboring hamlets, in an uproar.

In the afternoon crowds of townspeople and peasants, with women and children, surrounded the walls of the cloister, and held them as it were in siege, weeping and groaning. At sunset Kordetski went out to them, and pushing himself into the throng, asked,—

"People, what do you want?"

"We want to go as a garrison to the cloister to defend the Mother of God," cried men, shaking their flails, forks, and other rustic weapons.

"We wish to look for the last time on the Most Holy Lady," groaned women.

The prior went on a high rock and said,—

"The gates of hell will not prevail against the might of heaven. Calm yourselves, and receive consolation into your hearts. The foot of a heretic will not enter these holy walls. Neither Lutherans nor Calvinists will celebrate their superstitious incantations in this retreat of worship and faith. I know not in truth whether the insolent enemy will come hither; but I know this, that if he does come, he will be forced to retreat in shame and disgrace, for a superior power will crush him, his malice will be broken, his power rubbed out, and his fortune will fail. Take consolation to your hearts. You are not looking for the last time on our Patroness: you will see her in still greater glory, and you will see new miracles. Take consolation, dry your tears, and strengthen yourselves in faith; for I tell you—and it is not I who speak, but the Spirit of God speaks through me—that the Swede will not enter these walls; grace will flow hence, and darkness will not put out the light, just as the night which is now coming will not hinder God's sun from rising to-morrow."

It was just sunset. Dark shade had covered already the region about; but the church was gleaming red in the last rays of the sun. Seeing this, the people knelt around the walls, and consolation flowed into their hearts at once. Meanwhile the Angelus was sounded on the towers, and Kordetski began to sing, "The Angel of the Lord;" and after him whole crowds sang. The nobles and the soldiers standing on the walls joined their voices, the bells greater and smaller pealed in accompaniment, and it seemed that the whole mountain was singing and sounding like a gigantic organ to the four points of the earth.

They sang till late; the prior blessed the departing on their way, and said,—

"Those men who have served in war, who know how to wield weapons and who feel courage in their hearts, may come in the morning to the cloister."

"I have served, I was in the infantry, I will come!" cried numerous voices.

And the throngs separated slowly. The night fell calmly. All woke next morning with a joyous cry: "The Swede is not here!" Still, all day workmen were bringing supplies which had been called for. An order went out also to those who had shops at the eastern walls of the cloister to bring their goods to the cloister; and in the cloister itself work did not cease on the walls. Secured especially were the so-called "passages;" that is, small openings in the walls, which were not gates, but which might serve in making sallies. Pan Zamoyski gave orders to bring beams, bricks, and dung, so at a given moment they could be easily closed from within.

All day, too, wagons were coming in with supplies and provisions; there came also some noble families who were alarmed by the news of the impending attack of the enemy. About midday the men who had been sent out the preceding day to gather tidings came back; but no one had seen the Swedes nor even heard of them, except those who were stationed near Kjepitsi.

Still, preparations were not abandoned in the cloister. By order of the prior, those of the townspeople and peasantry came who had formerly served in the infantry and who were accustomed to service. They were assigned to the command of Pan Mosinski, who was defending the northeastern bastion. Pan

Zamoyski was occupied during the day either in disposing the men in their places, instructing each one what to do, or holding counsel with the fathers in the refectory.

Kmita with joy in his heart looked at the military preparations, at the soldiers as they were mustered, at the cannon, at the stacks of muskets, spears, and hooks. That was his special element. In the midst of those terrible implements, in the midst of the urgent preparations and military feverishness, it was light, pleasant, and joyous for him. It was the easier and more joyous because he had made a general confession of his whole life, and beyond his own expectations had received absolution, for the prior took into account his intention, his sincere desire to reform, and this too, that he had already entered on the road.

So Pan Andrei had freed himself from the burdens under which he was almost falling. Heavy penances had been imposed on him, and every day his back was bleeding under Soroka's braided lash; he was enjoined to practice obedience, and that was a penance still more difficult, for he had not obedience in his heart; on the contrary, he had pride and boastfulness. Finally, he was commanded to strengthen his reformation by virtuous deeds; but that was the easiest, he desired and asked for nothing more; his whole soul was tearing forth toward exploits, for by exploits he understood war and killing the Swedes from morning till evening without rest and without mercy. And just then, what a noble road was opening to him! To kill Swedes, not only in defence of the country, not only in defence of the king to whom he had sworn loyalty, but in defence of the Queen of the Angels,—that was a happiness beyond his merit.

Whither had those times gone when he was standing as it were on the parting of the roads, asking himself whither he should go? where are those times in which he knew not what to begin, in which he was always meeting doubt, and in which he had begun to lose hope? And those men, those white monks, and that handful of peasants and nobles were preparing for serious defence, for a life-and-death struggle. That was the one spot of such character in the Commonwealth, and Pan Andrei had come just to that spot, as if led by some fortunate star. And he believed sacredly in victory, though the whole power of Sweden were to encircle those walls; hence in his heart he had prayer, joy, and gratitude.

In this frame of mind he walked along the walls, and with a bright face examined, inspected, and saw that good was taking place. With the eye of experience, he saw at once from the preparations that they were made by men of experience, who would be able to show themselves when it came to the test. He wondered at the calmness of the prior, for whom he had conceived a deep reverence; he was astonished at the prudence of Zamoyski, and even of Pan Charnyetski; though he was displeased at him, he did not show a wry face. But that knight looked on Pan Andrei harshly, and meeting him on the wall the day after the return of the messengers, he said,—

"No Swedes are to be seen; and if they do not come, the dogs will eat your reputation."

"If any harm should result from their coming to this holy place, then let the dogs eat my reputation."

"You would rather not smell their powder. We know knights who have boots lined with hare's skin."

Kmita dropped his eyes like a young girl. "You might rather let disputes rest," said he. "In what have I offended you? I have forgotten your offences against me, do you forget mine against you."

"You called me a whipper-snapper," said Charnyetski, sharply. "I should like to know who you are. In what are the Babiniches better than the Charnyetskis? Are they a senatorial family too?"

"My worthy sir," said Kmita, with a pleasant face, "if it were not for the obedience which was imposed on me in confession, if it were not for those blows which are given me every day on my back for my follies of past time, I would speak to you differently; but I am afraid of relapsing into previous offences. As to whether the Babiniches or the Charnyetskis are better, that will appear when the Swedes come."

"And what kind of office do you think of getting? Do you suppose that they will make you one of the commanders?"

Kmita grew serious. "You accused me of seeking profit; now you speak of office. Know that I have not come here for honor. I might have received higher honor elsewhere. I will remain a simple soldier, even under your command."

"Why, for what reason?"

"Because you do me injustice, and are ready to torment me."

"H'm! There is no reason for that. It is very beautiful of you to be willing to remain a simple soldier when it is clear that you have wonderful daring, and obedience does not come easy. Would you like to fight?"

"That will appear with the Swedes, as I have said."

"But if the Swedes do not come?"

"Then do you know what? we will go to look for them," said Kmita.

"That pleases me!" cried Charnyetski. "We could assemble a nice party. Silesia is not far from this place, and at once soldiers could be collected. Officers, like my uncle, have promised, but nothing has been said about soldiers; a great number of them might be had at the first call."

"And this would give a saving example to others!" cried Kmita, with warmth. "I have a handful of men too,—you ought to see them at work."

"Good, good!" said Charnyetski, "as God is dear to me! let me have your face!"

"And give yours," said Kmita.

And without long thinking they rushed into each other's arms. Just then the prior was passing, and seeing what had happened he began to bless both. They told at once of what they had been talking. The prior merely smiled quietly, and went on saying to himself,—

"Health is returning to the sick."

Toward evening preparations were finished, and the fortress was entirely ready for defence. Nothing was wanting,— neither supplies, nor powder, nor guns; only walls sufficiently strong and a more numerous garrison.

Chenstohova, or rather Yasna Gora, though strengthened by nature and art, was counted among the smallest and weakest fortresses of the Commonwealth. But as to the garrison, as many people might have been had for the summoning as any one wished; but the prior purposely did not overburden the walls with men, so that supplies might hold out for a long time. Still there were those, especially among the German gunners, who were convinced that Chenstohova could not defend itself.

Fools! they thought that it had no defence but its walls and its weapons; they knew not what hearts filled with faith are. The prior then fearing lest they might spread doubt among the people, dismissed them, save one who was esteemed a master in his art.

That same day old Kyemlich and his sons came to Kmita with a request to be freed from service. Anger carried away Pan Andrei. "Dogs!" cried he, "you are ready to resign such a service and will not defend the Most Holy Lady.—Well, let it be so! You have had pay for your horses, you will receive the rest for your services soon."

Here he took a purse from a casket, and threw it on the floor to them. "Here are your wages! You choose to seek plunder on that side of the walls,—to be robbers instead of defenders of Mary! Out of my sight! you are not worthy to be here! you are not worthy of Christian society! you are not worthy to die such a death as awaits you in this place! Out, out!"

"We are not worthy," answered the old man, spreading his hands and bending his head, "we are not worthy to have our dull eyes look on the splendors of Yasna Gora, Fortress of heaven! Morning Star! Refuge of sinners! We are not worthy, not worthy." Here he bent so low that he bent double, and at the same time with his thin greedy hands, grown lean, seized the purse lying on the floor. "But outside the walls," said he, "we shall not cease to serve your grace. In sudden need, we will let you know everything; we will go where 'tis needful; we will do what is needful. Your grace will have ready servants outside the walls."

"Be off!" repeated Pan Andrei.

They went out bowing; for fear was choking them, and they were happy that the affair had ended thus. Toward evening they were no longer in the fortress.

A dark and rainy night followed. It was November 8; an early winter was approaching, and together with waves of rain the first flakes of wet snow were flying to the ground. Silence was broken only by the prolonged voices of guards calling from bastion to bastion, "Hold watch!" and in the darkness slipped past here and there the white habit of the prior, Kordetski. Kmita slept not; he was on the walls with Charnyetski, with whom he spoke of his past campaigns. Kmita narrated the course of the war with Hovanski, evidently not mentioning the part which he had taken in it himself; and Charnyetski talked of the skirmishes with the Swedes at Pjedbor, at Jarnovtsi, and in the environs of Cracow, of which he boasted somewhat and said,—

"What was possible was done. You see, for every Swede whom I stretched out I made a knot on my sword-sash. I have six knots, and God grant me more! For this reason I wear the sword higher toward my shoulder. Soon the sash will be useless; but I'll not take out the knots, in every knot I will have a turquoise set; after the war I will hang up the sash as a votive offering. And have you one Swede on your conscience?"

"No!" answered Kmita, with shame. "Not far from Sohachev I scattered a band, but they were robbers."

"But you might make a great score of Northerners?"

"I might do that."

"With the Swedes it is harder, for rarely is there one of them who is not a wizard. They learned from the Finns how to use the black ones, and each Swede has two or three devils in his service, and there are some who have seven. These guard them terribly in time of battle; but if they come hither, the devils will help them in no way, for the power of devils can do nothing in a circle where the tower on Yasna Gora is visible. Have you heard of this?"

Kmita made no answer; he turned his head to listen attentively.

"They are coming!" said he, suddenly.

"Who, in God's name? What do you say?"

"I hear cavalry."

"That is only wind and the beating of rain."

"By the wounds of Christ! that is not the wind, but horses! I have a wonderfully sharp ear. A multitude of cavalry are marching, and are near already; but the wind drowns the noise. The time has come! The time has come!"

The voice of Kmita roused the stiffened guards, dozing near at hand; but it had not yet ceased when below in the darkness was heard the piercing blare of trumpets, and they began to sound, prolonged, complaining, terrible. All sprang up from slumber in amazement, in fright, and asked one another,—

"Are not those the trumpets sounding to judgment in this gloomy night?"

Then the monks, the soldiers, the nobles, began to come out on the square.

The bell-ringers rushed to the bells; and soon they were all heard, the great, the smaller, and the small bells, as if for a fire, mingling their groans with the sounds of the trumpets, which had not ceased to play.

Lighted matches were thrown into pitch-barrels, prepared of purpose and tied with chains; then they were drawn upward with cranks. Red light streamed over the base of the cliff, and then the people on Yasna Gora saw before them a party of mounted trumpeters,—those standing nearest with trumpets at their mouths, behind them long and deep ranks of mounted men with unfurled flags.

The trumpeters played some time yet, as if they wished with those brazen sounds to express the whole power of the Swedes, and to terrify the monks altogether. At last they were silent; one of them separated from the rank, and waving a white kerchief, approached the gate.

"In the name of his Royal Grace," cried the trumpeter, "the Most Serene King of the Swedes, Goths, and Vandals, Grand Prince of Finland, Esthonia, Karelia, Stettin, Pomerania, and the Kashubes, Prince of Rugen, Lord of Ingria, Wismark, and Bavaria, Count of the Rhenish Palatinate, open the gates."

"Admit him," said Kordetski.

They opened, but only a door in the gate.

The horseman hesitated for a time; at last he came down from his horse, entered within the circle of the walls, and seeing a crowd of white habits, he asked,—

"Who among you is the superior?"

"I am," answered Kordetski.

The horseman gave him a letter with seals, and said: "Count Veyhard will wait for an answer at Saint Barbara's."

The prior summoned at once the monks and nobles to the council-chamber to deliberate.

On the way, Pan Charnyetski said to Kmita: "Come you also."

"I will go, but only through curiosity," answered Pan Andrei; "for I have no work there. Henceforward I will not serve the Most Holy Lady with my mouth."

When they had entered the council-chamber, the prior broke the seal and read as follows:—

"It is not a secret to you, worthy fathers, with what favorable mind and with what heart I have always looked on this holy place and your Congregation; also, how constantly I have surrounded you with my care and heaped benefits on you. Therefore I desire that you remain in the conviction that neither my inclination nor good wishes toward you have ceased in the present juncture. Not as an enemy, but as a friend, do I come this day. Put your cloister under my protection without fear, as the time and present circumstances demand. In this way you will find the calm which you desire, as well as safety. I promise you solemnly that the sacredness of the place will be inviolate; your property will not be destroyed. I will bear all expenses myself, and in fact add to your means. Consider also carefully how much you will profit if, satisfying me, you confide to me your cloister. Remember my advice, lest a greater misfortune reach you from the terrible General Miller, whose orders will be the more severe because he is a heretic and an enemy of the true faith. When he comes, you must yield to necessity and carry out his commands;

and you will raise useless complaints with pain in your souls and your bodies, because you disregarded my mild counsel."

The memory of recent benefactions of Count Veybard touched the monks greatly. There were some who had confidence in his good-will, and wished to see in his counsel the avoidance of future defeats and misfortunes. But no one raised a voice, waiting for what Kordetski would say. He was silent for a while, but his lips were moving in prayer; then he said,—

"Would a true friend draw near in the night-time and terrify with such a dreadful voice of trumpets and crooked horns the sleeping servants of God? Would he come at the head of those armed thousands who are now standing under these walls? Why did he not come with four or nine others, if he hoped for the reception given a welcome benefactor? What do those stern legions mean, if not a threat in case we refuse to yield up this cloister? Listen; remember, too, dearest brothers, that this enemy has never kept word nor oath nor safeguard. We too have that of the King of Sweden sent us spontaneously, in which is an express promise that the cloister shall remain free of occupation. And why are they standing now under its walls, trumpeting their own lie with fearful brazen sound? My dear brothers, let each man raise his heart to heaven, so that the Holy Ghost may enlighten it, and then let us consider what conscience dictates to each one touching the good of this holy retreat."

Silence followed. Then Kmita's voice rose: "I heard in Krushyn Lisola ask him, 'Will you shake up their treasury for the monks?' to which the count, who now stands under these walls, answered, 'The Mother of God will not ask for the thalers in the priors' chests.' To-day this same Count Veyhard writes to you, reverend fathers, that he will bear all expenses himself, and besides add to your means. Consider his sincerity!"

707

To this Father Myelko, one of the oldest in the assembly, and besides a former soldier, answered: "We live in poverty, and burn these torches before the altar of the Most Holy Lady in Her praise. But though we were to take them from the altar so as to purchase immunity for this holy place, where is our guarantee that the Swedes will respect the immunity, that they with sacrilegious hands will not remove offerings, sacred vestments, church furniture? Is it possible to trust liars?"

"Without the Provincial to whom we owe obedience, we can do nothing," said Father Dobrosh.

"War is not our affair," added Father Tomitski; "let us listen to what these knights will say who have taken refuge under the wings of the Mother of God in this cloister."

All eyes were now turned to Pan Zamoyski, the oldest in years, the highest in dignity and office. He rose and spoke in the following words:—

"It is a question here of your fate, reverend fathers. Compare then the strength of the enemy with the resistance which you can place against him according to your force and will. What counsel can we, guests here, impart to you? But, reverend fathers, since you ask us what is to be done, I will answer: Until the inevitable forces us, let the thought of surrender be far away; for it is a shameful and an unworthy act to purchase with vile submission an uncertain peace from a faithless enemy. We have taken refuge here of our own will, with our wives and children; surrendering ourselves to the guardianship of the Most Holy Lady, we have determined with unswerving faith to live with you, and, if God shall so desire, to die with you. It is indeed better for us thus than to accept a shameful captivity or behold an affront to a holy place; of a certainty, that Mother of the Most High God who has inspired our breasts with a desire of defending Her against godless and sacrilegious heretics will second the pious endeavors of Her servants and support the cause of Her own defence."

At this point Pan Zamoyski ceased speaking; all paid attention to his words, strengthening themselves with the meaning of them; and Kmita, without forethought, as was his wont, sprang forward and pressed the hand of the old man to his lips. The spectators were edified by this sight, and each one saw a good presage in that youthful ardor, and a desire to defend the cloister increased and seized all hearts.

Meanwhile a new presage was given: outside the window of the refectory was heard unexpectedly the trembling and aged voice of Constantsia, the old beggar woman of the church, singing a pious hymn:—

"In vain dost thou threaten me, O savage Hussite, In vain dost thou summon devils' horns to thy aid, In vain dost thou burn, sparing no blood,

For thou'lt not subdue me;

Though thousands of pagans were now rushing hither, Though armies were flying against me on dragons, Neither sword, flame, nor men will avail thee,

For I shall be victor!"

"Here," said Kordetski, "is the presage which God sends through the lips of that old beggar woman. Let us defend ourselves, brothers; for in truth besieged people have never yet had such aids as will come to us."

"We will give our lives willingly," said Charnyetski.

"We will not trust faith-breakers! We will not trust heretics, nor those among Catholics who have accepted the service of the evil spirit!" shouted others, who did not wish to let those speak who opposed.

It was decided to send two priests to Count Veyhard with information that the gates would remain closed and the besieged

709

would defend themselves, to which action the safeguard of the king gave them a right.

But in their own way the envoys were to beg the Count humbly to desist from his design, or at least to defer it for a time until the monks could ask permission of Father Teofil Bronyevski, Provincial of the order, who was then in Silesia.

The envoys, Fathers Benedykt Yarachevski and Martseli Tomitski, passed out through the gate; the others awaited, in the refectory, their return with throbbing hearts, for terror had seized those monks, unused to war, when the hour had struck and the moment had come in which they were forced to choose between duty and the anger and vengeance of the enemy.

But half an hour had barely elapsed when the two fathers appeared before the council. Their heads were hanging over their breasts, on their faces were pallor and grief. In silence they gave Kordetski a letter from Count Veyhard, which he took from their hands and read aloud. There were eight points of capitulation under which the count summoned the monks to surrender the cloister.

When he had finished reading, the prior looked long in the faces of those assembled; at last he said with a solemn voice,—

"In the name of the Father, Son, and Holy Ghost! in the name of the Most Pure and Most Holy Mother of God! to the walls, beloved brethren!"

"To the walls, to the walls!" was the answer of all.

A little later a bright flame lighted the base of the cloister. Count Veyhard had given orders to burn the buildings connected with the church of Saint Barbara. The fire seizing the old houses grew with each moment. Soon pillars of red smoke reared themselves toward the sky; in the midst of these, fiery sparkling tongues were gleaming. Finally one conflagration was spreading in clouds.

By the gleam of the fire, divisions of mounted soldiers could be seen passing quickly from place to place. The usual license of soldiers had begun. The horsemen drove out from the stables cattle, which running with fright, filled the air with plaintive bellowing; sheep, gathered in groups, pushed at random toward the fire. Many of the defenders saw for the first time the bloody face of war, and their hearts grew benumbed with terror at sight of people driven by soldiers and slashed with sabres, at sight of women dragged by the hair through the market-place. And by the bloody gleams of the fire all this was as visible as on the palm of the hand. Shouts, and even words, reached the ears of the besieged perfectly.

Since the cannon of the cloister had not answered yet, horsemen sprang from their horses and approached the foot of the mountain itself, shaking their swords and muskets. Every moment some sturdy fellow, dressed in a yellow cavalry jacket, putting his hands around his mouth, jeered and threatened the besieged, who listened patiently, standing at their guns with lighted matches.

Kmita was at the side of Charnyetski, just in front of the church, and saw everything clearly. On his cheeks a deep flush came out, his eyes were like two torches, and in his hand he held an excellent bow, which he had received as an inheritance from his father, who had captured it from a celebrated Agá at Hotsin. He heard the threats and invectives, and finally when a gigantic horseman had come under the cliff and was making an uproar he turned to Charnyetski,—

"As God is true, he is blaspheming against the Most Holy Lady. I understand German; he blasphemes dreadfully! I cannot endure it!" And he lowered the bow; but Charnyetski touched him with his hand,—

"God will punish him for his blasphemy," said he; "but Kordetski has not permitted us to shoot first, let them begin."

711

He had barely spoken when the horseman raised his musket to his face; a shot thundered, and the ball, without reaching the walls, was lost somewhere among the crannies of the place.

"We are free now!" cried Kmita.

"Yes," answered Charnyetski.

Kmita, as a true man of war, became calm in a moment. The horseman, shading his eyes with his hands, looked after the ball; Kmita drew the bow, ran his finger along the string till it twittered like a swallow, then he bent carefully and cried,—

"A corpse, a corpse!"

At the same moment was hoard the whirring whistle of the terrible arrow; the horseman dropped his musket, raised both hands on high, threw up his head, and fell on his back. He struggled for a while like a fish snatched from water, and dug the earth with his feet; but soon he stretched himself and remained without motion.

"That is one!" said Kmita.

"Tie it in your sword-sash," answered Charnyetski.

"A bell-rope would not be long enough, if God will permit!" cried Pan Andrei.

A second horseman rushed to the dead man, wishing to see what had happened to him, or perhaps to take his purse, but the arrow whistled again, and the second fell on the breast of the first. Meanwhile the field-pieces which Count Veyhard had brought with him opened fire. He could not storm the fortress with them, neither could he think of capturing it, having only cavalry, but he gave command to open fire to terrify the priests. Still a beginning was made.

Kordetski appeared at the side of Charnyetski, and with him came Father Dobrosh, who managed the cloister artillery in time of peace, and on holidays fired salutes; therefore he passed as an excellent gunner among the monks.

The prior blessed the cannon and pointed them out to the priest, who rolled up his sleeves and began to aim at a point in a half circle between two buildings where a number of horsemen were raging, and among them an officer with a rapier in his hand. The priest aimed long, for his reputation was at stake. At last he took the match and touched the priming.

Thunder shook the air and smoke covered the view; but after a while the wind bore it aside. In the space between the buildings there was not a single horseman left. A number were lying with their horses on the ground; the others had fled.

The monks on the walls began to sing. The crash of buildings falling around Saint Barbara's church accompanied the songs. It grew darker, but vast swarms of sparks sent upward by the fall of timbers pierced the air.

Trumpets were sounded again in the ranks of Count Veyhard's horsemen; but the sound from them receded. The fire was burning to the end. Darkness enveloped the foot of Yasna Gora. Here and there was heard the neighing of horses; but ever farther, ever weaker, the Count was withdrawing to Kjepitsi.

Kordetski knelt on the walls.

"Mary! Mother of the one God," said he, with a powerful voice, "bring it to pass that he whose attack comes after this man will retreat in like manner,—with shame and vain anger in his soul."

While he prayed thus the clouds broke suddenly above his head, and the bright light of the moon whitened the towers, the walls, the kneeling prior and the burned ruins of buildings at Saint Barbara.

CHAPTER XLI.

The following day peace reigned at the foot of Yasna Gora; taking advantage of which, the monks were occupied the more earnestly in preparations for defence. The last repairs were made in the walls and the curtains, and still more appliances were prepared to serve in resisting assault.

From Zdebov, Krovodja, Lgota, and Grabuvka a number of tens of peasants volunteered, who had served before in the land-infantry. These were accepted and placed among the defenders. Kordetski doubled and trebled himself. He performed divine service, sat in council, neglected the sick neither day nor night, and in the interval visited the walls, talked with nobles and villagers. Meanwhile he had in his face and whole person a calm of such character that one might almost say it belonged to stone statues only. Looking at his face, grown pale from watching, it might be thought that that man slept an easy and sweet sleep; but the calm resignation and almost joy burning in his eyes, his lips moving in prayer, announced that he watched, thought, prayed, and made offerings for all. From his spirit, with all its powers intent upon God, faith flowed in a calm and deep stream; all drank of this faith with full lips, and whoso had a sick soul was made well. Wherever his white habit was seen, there calm appeared on the faces of men, their eyes smiled, and their lips repeated: "Our kind father, our comforter, our defender, our good hope." They kissed his hands and his habit; he smiled like the dawn, and went farther, while around him, above and before him, went confidence and serenity.

Still he did not neglect earthly means of salvation; the fathers who entered his cell found him, if not on his knees, over letters which he sent in every direction. He wrote to Wittemberg, the commander-in-chief at Cracow, imploring him to spare a sacred place; and to Yan Kazimir, who in Opola had made the last effort to save a thankless people; to Stefan Charnyetski, held by his own word as on a chain at Syevyej; to Count Veyhard; and to Colonel Sadovski, a Lutheran Cheh, who served under Miller, but who, having a noble soul, had endeavored to dissuade the fierce general from this attack on the cloister.

Two conflicting councils were held before Miller. Count Veyhard, irritated by the stubbornness which he had met on November 8, used all efforts to incline the general to a campaign; he promised him untold treasures and profit, he asserted that in the whole world there were scarcely churches which could be compared with Chenstohova or Yasna Gora. Sadovski opposed in the following manner:—

"General," said he to Miller, "you who have taken so many famed fortresses that you have been justly named Poliorcetes by cities in Germany, know how much blood and time it may cost to take even the weakest fortress, if the assaulted are willing to resist unto death.

"But the monks will not resist?" asked Miller.

"I think just the contrary. The richer they are, the more stubborn a defence will they make; they are confident not only in the might of arms, but in the sacredness of the place, which the Catholic superstition of this whole country considers inviolable. It is enough to recall the German war; how often have monks given an example of daring and stubbornness, even in cases where soldiers themselves despaired of defence! It will take place this time too, all the more since the fortress is not so insignificant as Count Veyhard would like to consider it. It is situated on a rocky eminence difficult for the miner, the walls which, if they were not indeed in good condition, have been repaired before this time; and as to supplies of arms, powder, and provisions, a cloister so rich has inexhaustible supplies; fanaticism will animate their hearts and,—"

"And do you think, gracious colonel, that they will force me to retreat?"

"I do not think that, but I believe that we shall be forced to remain long under the walls, we shall have to send for larger guns than those we have here, and you must go to Prussia. It is necessary to calculate how much time we can devote to Chenstohova; for if his Grace the King of Sweden summons you from the siege for the more important affairs of Prussia, the monks will report without fail that you were forced to retreat. And then think, your grace, what a loss your fame as Poliorcetes will sustain, not to speak of the encouragement which the resisting will find in the whole country. Only [here Sadovski lowered his voice] let the mere intention of attacking this cloister be noised about, and it will make the worst impression. You do not know—for no foreigner, not a papist, can know—what Chenstohova is to this people. Very important for us are those nobles, who yielded so readily; those magnates; the quarter troops, who together with the hetmans, have come over to our side. Without them we could not have done what we have done. With their hands we have occupied half the country,—nay, more than half; but let one shot fall at Chenstohova,—who knows? perhaps not a Pole will remain with us. So great is the strength of superstition! A new most terrible war may flame up!"

Miller recognized in his soul the justice of Sadovski's reasoning, all the more since he considered monks in general, and the Chenstohova monks in particular, wizards,—that Swedish general feared enchantments more than guns; still wishing to irritate, and maybe prolong the dispute, he said,—

"You speak as though you were prior of Chenstohova, or as if they had begun to pay you a ransom."

Sadovski was a daring soldier and impulsive, and because he knew his value he was easily offended.

"I will not say another word," answered he, haughtily.

Miller in his turn was angry at the tone in which the above words were spoken.

"I will make no further request of you," said he; "Count Veyhard is enough for me, he knows this country better."

"We shall see!" responded Sadovski, and went out of the room.

Count Veyhard in fact took his place. He brought a letter, which he had received from Varshytski with a request to leave the cloister in peace; but from this letter the obstinate man drew counsel directly opposed.

"They beg," said he to Miller; "therefore they know that there will be no defence."

A day later the expedition against Chenstohova was decided upon at Vyelunie.

It was not kept a secret; therefore Father Yatsek Rudnitski, provost of the monastery at Vyelunie, was able to go in time to Chenstohova with the news. The poor monk did not admit for one moment that the people of Yasna Gora would defend themselves. He only wanted to forewarn them so that they might know what course to take and seek favorable conditions. In fact, the news bowed down the minds of the monks. In some souls courage weakened at once. But Kordetski strengthened it; he warmed the cold with the heat of his own heart, he promised days of miracle, he made the very presence of death agreeable, and changed them so much through the inspiration of his own soul that unwittingly they began to prepare for the attack as they were accustomed to prepare for great church festivals,—hence with joy and solemnity.

The chiefs of the lay garrison, Zamoyski and Charnyetski, also made their final preparations. They burned all the shops which were nestled around the walls of the fortress and which might lighten an assault for the enemy; the buildings near the

717

mountain were not spared either, so that for a whole day a ring of flame surrounded the fortress; but when there remained of the shops merely the ashes of timbers and planks, the guns of the cloister had before them empty space, unhedged by any obstacles. Their black jaws gaped freely into the distance, as if searching for the enemy impatiently and wishing to greet them at the earliest moment with ominous thunder.

Meanwhile winter was drawing near with swift step. A sharp north wind was blowing, swamps were turned into lumps of earth; and in the mornings, water in shallow places was congealed into frail icy shells. The prior, Kordetski, making the rounds of the walls, rubbed his hands blue from cold, and said,—

"God will send frost to assist us. It will be hard to intrench batteries and dig mines; meanwhile you will take rest in warm rooms, and the north wind will soon disgust them with the siege."

But for this very reason Miller was anxious to finish quickly. He had nine thousand troops, mostly infantry, and nineteen guns. He had also two squadrons of Polish cavalry, but he could not count on them; first, because he could not employ the cavalry in taking the lofty fortress; and second, because the men went unwillingly, and gave notice beforehand that they would take no part in the struggles. They went rather to protect the fortress, in case of capture, against the greed of the conquerors,—so at least the colonels declared to the soldiers; they went finally because the Swedes commanded, for the whole army of the country was in their camp and had to obey.

From Vyelunie to Chenstohova the road is short. On November 18 the siege was to begin. But the Swedish general calculated that it would not last above a couple of days, and that he would take the precious fortress by negotiation.

Meanwhile Kordetski, the prior, prepared the souls of men. They went to divine services as on a great and joyous festival; and had it not been for the unquiet and pallor of some faces, it might have been supposed that that was a joyous and solemn thanksgiving. The prior himself celebrated Mass; all the bells were ringing. The services did not end with Mass, for a grand procession went out on the walls.

The prior, bearing the Most Holy Sacrament, was supported under the arms by Zamoyski and Pan Pyotr Charnyetski. In front walked young boys in robes, they carried censers with myrrh and incense; before and after the baldachin marched ranks of white-habited monks, with eyes and heads raised toward heaven,—men of various years, from decrepit old men to tender youths who had just begun their novitiate. The yellow flames of the candles quivered in the air; but the monks moved onward and sang, buried altogether in God, as if mindful of naught else in the world. Behind them appeared the shaven temples of nobles, the tearful faces of women, but calm beneath their tears, inspired with faith and trust; peasants marched also, long-haired, wearing coarse coats, resembling the primitive Christians; little children, maidens, and boys mingled with the throng, joining their thin voices with the general chorus. And God heard that pouring forth of hearts, that fleeing from earthly oppression to the single defence of His wings. The wind went down, the air grew calm, the heavens became azure, and the autumnal sun poured a mild pale golden, but still warm, light on the earth. The procession passed once around the walls, but did not return, did not disperse,—went farther. Rays from the monstrance fell on the face of the prior, and that face seemed golden and radiant from their light. Kordetski kept his eyes closed, and on his lips was a smile not of earth,—a smile of happiness, of sweetness, of exaltation; his soul was in heaven, in brightness, in endless delight, in unbroken calm. But as if taking orders from above, and forgetting not this earthly church, the

719

men, the fortress, and that hour then impending, he halted at moments, opened his eyes, elevated the monstrance, and gave blessing.

He blessed the people, the army, the squadrons, blooming like flowers and gleaming like a rainbow; he blessed the walls, and that eminence which looked down and around upon the land; he blessed the cannon, the guns, smaller and greater, the balls, iron and lead, the vessels with powder, the planking at the cannon, the piles of harsh implements used to repel the assaults of the enemy; he blessed the armies lying at a distance; he blessed the north, the south, the east, and the west, as if to cover that whole region, that whole land, with the power of God.

It had struck two in the afternoon, the procession was still on the walls; but meanwhile on those edges, where the sky and the earth seemed to touch, a bluish haze was spread out, and just in that haze something began to shimmer, to move,—forms of some kind were creeping. At first dim, unfolding gradually, these forms became every moment more distinct. A cry was heard suddenly at the end of the procession,—

"The Swedes are coming; the Swedes are coming!"

Then silence fell, as if hearts and tongues had grown numb; bells only continued to sound. But in the stillness the voice of the prior thundered, far reaching though calm,—

"Brothers, let us rejoice! the hour of victories and miracles is drawing near!"

And a moment later he exclaimed: "Under Thy protection we take refuge, Our Mother, Our Lady, Our Queen!"

Meanwhile the Swedish cloud had changed into an immeasurable serpent, which was crawling forward ever nearer. Its terrible curves were visible. It twisted, uncoiled; at one time it glittered under the light with its gleaming steel scales, fit another it grew dark, crawled, crawled on, emerged from the distance.

720

Soon eyes looking from the walls could distinguish everything in detail. In advance came the cavalry, after it infantry in quadrangles; each regiment formed a long rectangular body, over which rose a smaller one formed of erect spears; farther on, behind, after the infantry, came cannon with jaws turned rearward and inclined to the earth.

Their slowly moving barrels, black or yellowish, shone with evil omen in the sun; behind them clattered over the uneven road the powder-boxes and the endless row of wagons with tents and every manner of military appliance.

Dreadful but beautiful was that advance of a regular army, which moved before the eyes of the people on Yasna Gora, as if to terrify them. A little later the cavalry separated from the rest of the army and approached at a trot, trembling like waves moved by wind. They broke soon into a number of greater and smaller parties. Some pushed toward the fortress; some in the twinkle of an eye scattered through the neighboring villages in pursuit of plunder; others began to ride around the fortress, to examine the walls, study the locality, occupy the buildings which were nearest. Single horsemen flew back continually as fast as a horse could gallop from the larger parties to the deep divisions of infantry to inform the officers where they might dispose themselves.

The tramp and neighing of horses, the shouts, the exclamations, the murmur of thousands of voices, and the dull thump of cannon, came distinctly to the ears of the besieged, who till that moment were standing quietly on the wall, as if for a spectacle, looking with astonished eyes at that great movement and deploying of the enemy's troops.

At last the infantry regiments arrived and began to wander around the fortress, seeking places best fitted for fortification. Now they struck, on Chenstohovka, an estate near the cloister, in which there were no troops, only peasants living in huts.

A regiment of Finns, who had come first, fell savagely on the defenceless peasants. They pulled them out of the huts by the hair, and simply cut down those who resisted; the rest of the people driven from the manor-house were pursued by cavalry and scattered to the four winds.

A messenger was sent with Miller's summons to surrender; he had already sounded his trumpet before the gates of the church; but the defenders, at sight of the slaughter and cruelty of the soldiers in Chenstohova, answered with cannon fire.

Now, when the people of the town had been driven out of all the nearer buildings, and the Swedes had disposed themselves therein, it behooved to destroy them with all haste, so that the enemy might not injure the cloister under cover of those buildings. Therefore the walls of the cloister began to smoke all around like the sides of a ship surrounded by a storm and by robbers. The roar of cannon shook the air till the walls of the cloister were trembling, and glass in the windows of the church and other buildings was rattling. Fiery balls in the form of whitish cloudlets describing ill-omened arcs fell on the Swedish places of refuge, they broke rafters, roofs, walls; and columns of smoke were soon rising from the places into which balls had descended.

Conflagration had enwrapped the buildings. Barely had the Swedish regiments taken possession when they fled from the new quarters with all breath, and, uncertain of their positions, hurried about in various directions. Disorder began to creep among them; they removed the cannon not yet mounted, so as to save them from being struck. Miller was amazed; he had not expected such a reception, nor such gunners on Yasna Gora.

Meanwhile night came, and since he needed to bring the army into order, he sent a trumpeter with a request for a cessation. The fathers agreed to that readily.

In the morning, however, they burned another enormous storehouse with great supplies of provisions, in which building the Westland regiment had taken its quarters. The fire caught the building so quickly, the shots fell, one after another, with such precision that the Westlanders were unable to carry off their muskets or ammunition, which exploded, hurling far around burning brands.

The Swedes did not sleep that night; they made preparations, entrenchments for the guns, filled baskets with earth, formed a camp. The soldiers, though trained during so many years in so many battles, and by nature valiant and enduring, did not wait for the following day with joy. The first day had brought defeat.

The cannon of the cloister caused such loss among the Swedes that the oldest warriors were confounded, attributing this to careless approach to the fortress, and to going too near the walls.

But the next day, even should it bring victory, did not promise glory; for what was the capture of an inconsiderable fortress and a cloister to the conquerors of so many famed cities, a hundred times better fortified? The greed of rich plunder alone upheld their willingness, but that oppressive alarm with which the allied Polish squadrons had approached this greatly renowned Yasna Gora was imparted in a mysterious way to the Swedes. Some of them trembled at the thought of sacrilege, while others feared something indefinite, which they could not explain, and which was known under the general name of enchantment. Miller himself believed in it; why should not the soldiers believe?

It was noticed that when Miller was approaching the church of Saint Barbara, the horse under him slipped suddenly, started back, distended his nostrils, pricked up his ears, snorted with fright, and refused to advance. The old general showed no personal alarm; still the next day he assigned that place to the Prince of Hesse, and marched himself with the heavier guns to the northern side of the cloister, toward the village of Chenstohova; there he made intrenchments during the night, so as to attack in the morning.

Barely had light begun to gleam in the sky when heavy artillery firing began; but this time the Swedish guns opened first. The enemy did not think of making a breach in the walls at once, so as to rush through it to storm; he wanted only to terrify, to cover the church and the cloister with balls, to set fire, to dismount cannon, to kill people, to spread alarm.

A procession went out again on the walls of the fortress, for nothing strengthened the combatants like a view of the Holy Sacrament, and the monks marching forward with it calmly. The guns of the cloister answered,—thunder for thunder, lightning for lightning, so far as the defenders were able, so far as breath held out in the breast. The very earth seemed to tremble in its foundations. A sea of smoke stretched over the cloister and the church.

What moments, what sights for men who had never in their lives beheld the bloody face of war! and there were many such in the fortress. That unbroken roar, lightnings, smoke, the howling of balls tearing the air, the terrible hiss of bombs, the clatter of shot on the pavement, the dull blows against the wall, the sound of breaking windows, the explosions of bursting bombs, the whistling of fragments of them, the breaking and cracking of timbers; chaos, annihilation, hell!

In those hours there was not a moment of rest nor cessation; breasts half-suffocated with smoke, every moment new flocks of cannon-balls; and amid the confusion shrill voices in various parts of the fortress, the church, and the cloister, were crying,—

"It is on fire! water, water!"

"To the roof with barefooted men! more cloth!"

"Aim the cannon higher!—higher!—aim at the centre of the buildings—fire!"

About noon the work of death increased still more. It might seem that, if the smoke were to roll away, the Swedes would see only a pile of balls and bombs in place of the cloister. A cloud of lime, struck from the walls by the cannon, rose up, and mingling with the smoke, hid the light. Priests went out with relics to exorcise these clouds, lest they might hinder defence. The thunders of cannon were interrupted, but were as frequent as the breath gulps of a panting dragon.

Suddenly on a tower, newly built after a fire of the previous year, trumpets began to sound forth the glorious music of a church hymn. That music flowed down through the air and was heard round about, was heard everywhere, as far as the batteries of the Swedes. The sound of the trumpets was accompanied by the voices of people, and amidst the bellowing and whistling, amidst the shouts, the rattle and thunder of muskets, were heard the words,—

"Mother   of   God,   Virgin, Glorified by God Mary!"

Here a number of bombs burst; the cracking of rafters and beams, and then the shout: "Water!" struck the ear, and again the song flowed on in calmness.

"From Thy Son the Lord
Send down to us, win for us,
A time of bread, a time of plenty."

Kmita, who was standing on the wall at the cannon, opposite the village of Chenstohova, in which Miller's quarters were, and whence the greatest fire came, pushed away a less accurate cannoneer to begin work himself; and worked so well that soon, though it was in November and the day cold, he threw off his fox-skin coat, threw off his vest, and toiled in his trousers and shirt.

The hearts grew in people unacquainted with war, at sight of this soldier blood and bone, to whom all that was passing—that bellowing of cannon, those flocks of balls, that destruction and death—seemed as ordinary an element as fire to a salamander.

His brow was wrinkled, there was fire in his eyes, a flush on his cheeks, and a species of wild joy in his face. Every moment he bent to the cannon, altogether occupied with the aiming, altogether given to the battle, thinking of naught else; he aimed, lowered, raised, at last cried, "Fire!" and when Soroka touched the match, he ran to the opening and called out from time to time,—

"One by the side of the other!"

His eagle eyes penetrated through smoke and dust, and when among the buildings he saw somewhere a dense mass of caps or helmets, straightway he crushed it with an accurate shot, as if with a thunderbolt. At times he burst out into laughter when he had caused greater or less destruction. The balls flew over him and at his side,—he did not look at anything; suddenly, after a shot he sprang to the opening, fixed his eyes in the distance, and cried,—

"The gun is dismounted! Only three pieces are playing there now!"

He did not rest until midday. Sweat was pouring from him, his shirt was steaming; his face was blackened with soot, and his eyes glittering. Pyotr Charnyetski himself wondered at his aim, and said to him repeatedly,—

"War is nothing new to you; that is clear at a glance. Where have you learned it so well?"

At three o'clock in the afternoon a second Swedish gun was silent, dismounted by Kmita's accurate aim. They drew out the remaining guns from the intrenchments about an hour later. Evidently the Swedes saw that the position was untenable.

Kmita drew a deep breath.

"Rest!" said Charnyetski to him.

"Well! I wish to eat something. Soroka, give me what you have at hand."

The old sergeant bestirred himself quickly. He brought some gorailka in a tin cup and some dried fish. Kmita began to eat eagerly, raising his eyes from time to time and looking at the bombs flying over at no great distance, just as if he were looking at crows. But still they flew in considerable number, not from Chenstohova, but from the opposite side; namely, all those which passed over the cloister and the church.

"They have poor gunners, they point too high," said Pan Andrei, without ceasing to eat; "see, they all go over us, and they are aimed at us."

A young monk heard these words,—a boy of seventeen years, who had just entered his novitiate. He was the first always to bring balls for loading, and he did not leave his place though every vein in him was trembling from fear, for he saw war for the first time. Kmita made an indescribable impression on him by his calmness, and hearing his words he took refuge near him with an involuntary movement as if wishing to seek protection and safety under the wings of that strength.

"Can they reach us from that side?" asked he.

"Why not?" answered Kmita. "And why, my dear brother, are you afraid?"

"I thought," answered the trembling youth, "that war was terrible; but I did not think it was so terrible."

"Not every bullet kills, or there would not be men in the world, there would not be mothers enough to give birth to them."

"I have the greatest fear of those fiery balls, those bombs. Why do they burst with such noise? Mother of God, save us! and they wound people so terribly."

"I will explain to you, and you will discover by experience, young father. That ball is iron, and inside it is loaded with powder. In one place there is an opening rather small, in which is a fuse of paper or sometimes of wood."

"Jesus of Nazareth! is there a fuse in it?"

"There is; and in the fuse some tow steeped in sulphur, which catches fire when the gun is discharged. Then the ball should fall with the fuse toward the ground, so as to drive it into the middle; then the fire reaches the powder and the ball bursts. But many balls do not fall on the fuse; that does not matter, however, for when the fire burns to the end, the explosion comes."

On a sudden Kmita stretched out his hand and cried, "See, see! you have an experiment."

"Jesus! Mary! Joseph!" cried the young brother, at sight of the coming bomb.

The bomb fell on the square that moment, and snarling and rushing along began to bound on the pavement, dragging behind a small blue smoke, turned once more, and rolling to the foot of the wall on which they were sitting, fell into a pile of wet sand, which it scattered high to the battlement, and losing its power altogether, remained without motion.

Luckily it had fallen with the fuse up; but the sulphur was not quenched, for the smoke rose at once.

"To the ground! on your faces!" frightened voices began to shout. "To the ground, to the ground!"

But Kmita at the same moment sprang to the pile of sand, with a lightning movement of his hand caught the fuse, plucked it, pulled it out, and raising his hand with the burning sulphur cried,—

"Rise up! It is just as if you had pulled the teeth out of a dog! It could not kill a fly now."

When he had said this, he kicked the bomb, those present grew numb at sight of this deed, which surpassed human daring, and for a certain time no one made bold to speak; at last Charnyetski exclaimed,—

"You are a madman! If that had burst, it would have turned you into powder!"

Pan Andrei laughed so heartily that his teeth glittered.

"But do we not need powder? You could have loaded a gun with me, and after my death I could have done harm to the Swedes."

"May the bullets strike you! Where is your fear?"

The young monk placed his hands together and looked with mute homage on Kmita. But the deed was also seen by Kordotski, who was approaching on that side. He came up, took Pan Andrei with his hands by the head, and then made the sign of the cross on him.

"Such men as you will not surrender Yasna Gora; but I forbid exposing a needful life to danger. When the firing is over and the enemy leave the field, take that bomb, pour the powder out of it, and bear it to the Most Holy Lady. That gift will be dearer to Her than those pearls and bright stones which you offered Her."

"Father," answered Kmita, deeply moved, "what is there great in that? For the Most Holy Lady I would—Oh! words do not rise in my mouth—I would go to torments, to death. I know not what I would not do to serve Her."

Tears glistened in the eyes of Pan Andrei, and the prior said,—

"Go to Her with those tears before they dry. Her favor will flow to thee, calm thee, comfort thee, adorn thee with glory and honor."

When he had said this he took him by the arm and led him to the church. Pan Charnyetski looked after them for a time. At last he said,—

"I have seen many daring men in my life, who counted no danger to themselves; but this Lithuanian is either the D——"

Here Charnyetski closed his mouth with his hand, so not to speak a foul name in the holy place.

Made in the USA
Columbia, SC
20 June 2025